CHINA'S DOMESTIC
TRANSFORMATION
IN A GLOBAL CONTEXT

Other titles in the China Update Book Series include:

The titles are available online at http://press.anu.edu.au/titles/china-update-series/

CHINA'S DOMESTIC
TRANSFORMATION
IN A GLOBAL CONTEXT

LIGANG SONG, ROSS GARNAUT
CAI FANG & LAUREN JOHNSTON (eds)

Australian
National
University

PRESS

社会科学文献出版社
SOCIAL SCIENCES ACADEMIC PRESS(CHINA)

ANU PRESS

Published by ANU Press
The Australian National University
Acton ACT 2601, Australia
Email: anupress@anu.edu.au
This title is also available online at http://press.anu.edu.au

National Library of Australia Cataloguing-in-Publication entry

Title: China's domestic transformation in a global context /
                  editors: Ligang Song, Ross Garnaut, Cai
                  Fang, Lauren Johnston.

ISBN: 9781925022681 (paperback) 9781925022698 (ebook)

Series: China update series ; 2015.

Subjects: Economic development--China.
                  China--Economic conditions--2000-
                  China--Economic policy--2000-
                  China--Commercial policy--2000-
                  China--Social conditions--2000-

Other Creators/Contributors:
                  Song, Ligang, editor.
                  Garnaut, Ross, editor.
                  Cai, Fang, editor.
                  Johnston, Lauren, editor.

Dewey Number: 330.95106

Cover design and layout by ANU Press

Contents

Part I: Domestic transformation and structural change

Part II: China's participation in global integration

Tables

Figures

Contributors

Ligang Song
Associate Professor and Director,
China Economy Program,
Crawford School of Public Policy,
The Australian National University.

Ross Garnaut
Professorial Research Fellow
in Economics, the University
of Melbourne.

Cai Fang
Vice President, The Chinese Academy
of Social Sciences.

Lauren Johnston
Research Fellow, Melbourne
Institute of Applied Economic and
Social Research, the University
of Melbourne.

Ran Li
PhD Candidate, National School
of Development, Peking University.

Guonan Ma
Senior Fellow, Fung Global Institute,
Hong Kong.

Liqing Zhang
Professor and Dean of School
of Finance, Central University
of Finance and Economics, Beijing.

Qin Gou
Assistant Professor of Economics,
School of Finance, Central University
of Finance and Economics, Beijing.

Xunpeng Shi
Senior Fellow, Energy Studies
Institute, National University
of Singapore.

Fan He
Senior Fellow, Institute of World
Economics and Politics, Chinese
Academy of Social Sciences.

Meiyan Wang
Institute of Population and Labour
Economics, the Chinese Academy
of Social Sciences.

Xiang Li
PhD Candidate, National School
of Development, Peking University.

Wen Lei
PhD Candidate, National School
of Development, Peking University.

Yiping Huang
Professor, National School of
Development, Peking University.

Qing King Guo
Division of Business and
Management, United International
College (UIC), Beijing Normal
University-Hong Kong Baptist
University.

Chi Keung Marco Lau
Newcastle Business School,
University of Northumbria, United
Kingdom.

Kunwang Li
Professor, Department of
International Economics and Trade,
Nankai University.

Hari Malamakkavu Padinjare Variam
Research Associate, Energy Studies
Institute, National University
of Singapore.

Stephen Wilson
Director, Cape Otway Associates.

Yufeng Yang
Tsinghua University.

Jane Kuang
Rio Tinto Energy, Rio Tinto, Brisbane.

Rod Tyers
Professor, School of Business and
Economics, University of Western
Australia.

Eden Hatzvi
International Department,
Reserve Bank of Australia.

Michelle Wright
International Department,
Reserve Bank of Australia.

Will Nixon
International Department,
Reserve Bank of Australia.

Kevin H. Zhang
Professor, Department of Economics,
Illinois State University.

Mei Lisa Wang
Deputy Director, National Economy
Research Institute.

Zhen Qi
PhD Candidate, the Chinese Academy
of Social Sciences.

Chunlai Chen
Associate Professor, Crawford School
of Public Policy, The Australian
National University.

Xiaoming Pan
Research Fellow, Shanghai Institute
for International Studies.

Gao Xiang
Dean, College of Comparative Law,
China University of Political Science
and Law.

Huiqin Jiang
College of Comparative Law,
China University of Political Science
and Law.

Jijing Zhang
Vice President, CITIC Group
Corporation.

Acknowledgements

The China Economy Program gratefully acknowledges the financial support for the *China Update 2015* provided by Rio Tinto through the Rio Tinto–ANU China Partnership, as well as the coordination provided by Program Manager Elizabeth Buchanan, editorial assistance from Luke Meehan and our colleagues at the East Asia Forum at The Australian National University. The 2015 *China Update* book is the 15th edition in the *China Update* book series and we wish to thank Tim Lane for his unwavering support for the research unit. We sincerely thank our contributors from around the world for their valuable contributions to the book series and the *Update* events throughout these years. Thanks also go to the ANU Press team, notably Lorena Kanellopoulos, Emily Tinker and Jan Borrie, for the expeditious publication of the book series, and to Social Science Academic Press (China) in Beijing for translating and publishing the Chinese versions of the *Update* book series to make the research work available to the readers in China.

Abbreviations

AC	alternating current
ACQ	annual contract quantity
ADF	augmented Dickey–Fuller test
AGTM	Asian Gas Trade Model
AIIB	Asian Infrastructure Investment Bank
AP	advanced-passive reactor
APEC	Asia-Pacific Economic Cooperation
AREAER	*Annual Report on Exchange Arrangements and Exchange Restrictions*
ASEAN	Association of South-East Asian Nations
AU	African Union
BEA	British Electricity Authority
BIS	Bank for International Settlements
BIT	bilateral investment treaty
BOCHK	Bank of China, Hong Kong
BoE	Bank of England
BoJ	Bank of Japan
BOT	build-operate-transfer
CAD	China–Africa Development
CBM	coalbed methane
CBRC	China Banking Regulatory Commission
CCCME	China Chamber of Commerce for the Import and Export of Machinery and Electronic Products
CDB	China Development Bank
CEA	Central Electricity Authority
CEGB	Central Electricity Generating Board
CES	constant elasticity of substitution
CFIUS	Committee on Foreign Investment in the United States
CGE	computable general equilibrium
CGN	China General Nuclear Corporation
China EXIM	Export–Import Bank of China
CIF	cost, insurance and freight
CIPS	China International Payments System

CLSA	Credit Lyonnais Securities Asia
CMM	coalmine methane
CNNC	China National Nuclear Corporation
CNOOC	China National Offshore Oil Corporation
CNPC	China National Petroleum Corporation
CNY	yuan
COE	collectively owned enterprise
COFCO	China National Cereals, Oils and Foodstuffs Corporation
CPC	Communist Party of China
CPI	consumer price index
CPI Corp	China Power Investment Corporation
CRP	coastal and resource-poor
CULS	China Urban Labour Survey
DC	direct current
DID	difference in differences
DR Congo	Democratic Republic of the Congo
ECB	European Central Bank
EdF	Electricité de France
EIA	Energy Information Administration (US)
EKS	Elteto-Köves-Szulc procedure
EPZ	export processing zone
EU	European Union
FCI	financial conditions index
FDI	foreign direct investment
FIE	foreign-invested enterprise
FOB	free-on-board
FOCAC	Forum on China and Africa Cooperation
FTA	free trade agreement
FTAAP	Free Trade Agreement for the Asia-Pacific
FTZ	free trade zone
FX	foreign exchange
GAC	General Administration of Customs
GDP	gross domestic product
GFC	Global Financial Crisis
GNI	gross national income
GNP	gross national product

GVC	global value chain
HF	Heritage Foundation
HH	'Henry Hub'
HKEx	Hong Kong Stock Exchange
HKIMR	Hong Kong Institute for Monetary Research
HKMA	Hong Kong Monetary Authority
IC	industrial competiveness
ICBC	Industrial and Commercial Bank of China
ICSID	International Centre for Settlement of Investment Disputes
IEA	International Energy Agency
IMF	International Monetary Fund
IPP	independent power producer
ISO	independent system operator
JCC	Japan Customs-cleared Crude
JV	joint venture
LDC	least-developed country
LNG	liquefied natural gas
LOP	law of one price
M&A	merger and acquisition
MAS	Monetary Authority of Singapore
MEP	Ministry of Environment Protection
MFN	most-favoured nation
MNE	multinational enterprise
MoC	Ministry of Construction
MoF	Ministry of Finance
MOFCOM	Ministry of Commerce
MoU	memorandum of understanding
MP	manufacturing performance
Mt	megatonne
NBS	National Bureau of Statistics of China
NDRC	National Development and Reform Commission
NEA	National Energy Administration
NEM	National Electricity Market
NERI	National Economic Research Institute
NIM	net interest margins
NNSS	series-specific nonlinear panel unit root test model

NOC	national oil company
NOI	net outward investment
NPC	National People's Congress
NPCSC	National People's Congress Standing Committee
NPL	non-performing loan
OBM	original brand manufacturer
ODI	overseas/outbound direct investment
ODM	original design manufacturer
OECD	Organisation for Economic Cooperation and Development
OEM	original equipment manufacturer
OFDI	outward foreign direct investment
OLS	ordinary least squares
OOC	other official flows
PBC	People's Bank of China
PLPs	primary liquidity providers
PM	particulate matter
PNV	Power Networks Victoria
POE	privately owned enterprise
PPA	power purchase agreement
PPG	pipeline gas
PPI	producer price index
PPP	purchasing power parity
PRC	People's Republic of China
PWR	pressurised water reactor
QDII	qualified domestic institutional investor
QFII	qualified foreign institutional investor
R&D	research and development
RBA	Reserve Bank of Australia
RCEP	Regional Comprehensive Economic Partnership
REC	regional electricity company
repo	repurchase agreement
RMB	renminbi
ROE	return of equity
RQFII	renminbi qualified foreign institutional investor
RRR	reserve requirement ratio
SAR	special administrative region

SASAC	State-Owned Assets Supervision and Administration Commission
SCSA	special customs supervision area
SDRs	special drawing rights
SEC	State Electricity Company
SECV	State Electricity Commission of Victoria
SERC	State Electricity Regulatory Commission
SEZ	special economic zone
SHIAC	Shanghai International Arbitration Centre
Sinopec	China Petroleum & Chemical Corporation
SITC	Standard International Trade Classification
SNPTC	State Nuclear Power Technology Corporation
SOB	state-owned bank
SOE	state-owned enterprise
SPC	State Power Corporation
SPFTZ	China (Shanghai) Pilot Free Trade Zone
SSA	sub-Saharan Africa
SSE	Shanghai Stock Exchange
SUR	seemingly unrelated regression
tcm	trillion cubic metres
TFP	total factor productivity
TICAD	Tokyo International Conference on African Development
TISA	Trade in Services Agreement
TNC	transnational corporation
TOP	take-or-pay
TPA	third-party access
TPP	Trans-Pacific Partnership
TTIP	Transatlantic Trade and Investment Partnership
UAE	United Arab Emirates
UHV	ultra-high voltage
UK	United Kingdom
UMP	unconventional monetary policy
UNCTAD	United Nations Conference on Trade and Development
UNIDO	United Nations Industrial Development Organization
US	United States
VoLL	value of lost load

VPX	Victoria Power Exchange
WDI	World Development Indicators
WGM	World Gas Model
WIPO	World Intellectual Property Organization
WTO	World Trade Organization
yoy	year-on-year

1. Domestic Transformation in the Global Context

Ross Garnaut, Ligang Song, Cai Fang and Lauren Johnston

Introduction

China is experiencing its most persistent substantial slowdown in economic growth since the early years of reform. Annual growth has sagged from an average of 10 per cent per annum in the first decade of the century to just more than 7 per cent in 2014. As we discussed in the *China Updates* for 2006 and 2013, some slowing was inevitable and welcome to authorities. The slowdown anticipated in 2006 and 2013 is auspicious—driven by structural factors and necessary to sustain economic growth. The question now is whether we are observing the slowdown that is anticipated, and necessary to establish a foundation for a drive towards the productivity frontiers of the world economy, or a slowdown that has other causes.

There are two candidates for something else. One is a cyclical slump from withdrawal of the extraordinary fiscal and monetary stimulus to maintain growth after the global financial crisis (GFC). This prospect is rendered more severe by associated weaknesses in the financial system revealed by the withdrawal of stimulus, and from continuing weakness in the developed world's economy and therefore in demand for Chinese exports. The second is a less auspicious structural slowdown, deriving not from productive structural change within a new model of economic growth, but from the accumulation of uncorrected structural weaknesses from the old model of growth that become more and more damaging as China moves closer to the world's productivity frontiers.

The main focus of this year's *China Update* is on the detail of structural change within the new model of growth. Many chapters take a close look at one or other area of the economy in which change is required to sustain growth. The authors generally record nascent progress and grounds for hope, but rarely evidence that China is well on its way to the structural change that would see its emergence in the next decade as a high-income modern economy.

There has nonetheless been productive structural change in two areas. One is the structural change driven by the labour market transformation associated with the shift from abundance to scarcity of unskilled labour. The other is the substantial and continuing change in the relationship between growth and pressure on the natural environment that is being driven by policy.

The past two growth slowdowns in China occurred in response to the Asian Financial Crisis (1998–99) and the GFC (2008–09). Now, as then, there have been suggestions that the deceleration of the actual economy is greater than has been recorded in the official statistics. It was common during the two previous slowdowns to point to much slower growth in partial indicators, such as electricity demand or freight volumes, as evidence that the actual economy had slowed more than the official statistical economy. Premier Li Keqiang, in an earlier provincial role, once suggested that the partial indicators were more reliable than the statistical aggregates. Significance has therefore been attached to the recent absolute declines in electricity use (1.1 per cent in April 2015 compared with the previous April) and rail freight volume (down 9 per cent in the first quarter of 2015 compared with the corresponding period of 2014). Huang (2015) has suggested that the real growth in output could have been something like 5 per cent rather than the official statistical 7 per cent in the year to early 2015.

Analysis at the time of the two preceding growth slowdowns suggested some basis for downgrading the official statistical aggregates at times of slower growth. These related to difficulties of calculating price deflators in conditions of weak demand and tendencies to deflation. There could be some overestimation in the recent data. Structural change, especially related to use of energy, has, however, been large enough for us to expect fundamental shifts in the old relationships between the favourite partial indicators and actual growth. The 5.6 per cent decline in energy intensity of economic activity, to which the decline in electricity consumption is related, is only a small extension of the rate of decline in 2014. This in turn is only moderately above the 4 per cent per annum decline envisaged in the Twelfth Five-Year Plan. In these circumstances, a small decline in electricity consumption, while unlikely to continue for long, is not hopelessly inconsistent with a 7 per cent increase in total output. Similarly, coal accounts for a high proportion of rail freight in China, so the large movement away from coal as a source of energy associated with the new environmental objectives—leading to coal use in the first quarter of 2015 being well below the corresponding quarter of the previous year—accounts for much of the slump in freight volumes.

The slowdown could be a bit larger than measured by official data, and in any case is substantial. More importantly, the weakness so far of structural change associated with the new model of growth means that some powerful headwinds will be felt more strongly in future than now. In the best of circumstances, a period of lower growth has still to be experienced before a foundation has been laid for China's drive towards high-income status.

Chapters 2, 3 and 9 discuss how some of the slowing of growth has been driven by demographic and labour market change, and how much of the remainder has cyclical or inauspicious structural causes. The inauspicious structural causes are mostly related to imbalances that emerged in the fiscal and monetary response to the GFC.

Our 2006 *Update* highlighted the consequences of the demographic and labour market changes summed up as 'the turning period in economic growth'. Unskilled labour in the countryside ceased to be abundant and available in large amounts at fairly steady wages from the middle of the first decade of the new century, soon causing wages to grow more rapidly than output. Other changes were driven by the turning period in the labour market: increased wages led to the reversal of the longstanding increase in the investment share of output, and the slow beginnings of a rise in the consumption share. The rise in the wages share of income led to reversal of the longstanding tendency for inequality in income distribution to increase over time. This could be expected to incrementally reduce the investment share of domestic expenditure, so that slower growth in the capital stock would join the decline in the labour force to place downward pressure on the rate of growth (Garnaut and Song 2006). How far that decline went would depend on policies to make the economy more flexible and better able to allocate resources to their most productive uses—that is, productivity-raising economic reform.

The 2013 volume introduced the idea that China was working within a new model of economic growth, driven by policy change to promote new objectives as well as by the economic pressures from the labour market (Garnaut et al. 2013). The new objectives include more equitable income distribution; higher household consumption, especially of services and especially in rural areas; acceptance of a moderately lower rate of growth; and a reduction in the pressure applied by each increment in economic activity on the natural environment. The new model of economic growth was judged to be necessary to sustain growth so that China could join the minority of countries so far that, having attained upper middle-income status, as China has now done, go on to join the high-income countries. A further doubling of output per person after 2010 was required for China to achieve this outcome. Reform of many institutions and policies was necessary for this to be possible. These new priorities and model of growth were embodied in the reform decisions of the Third Plenary meeting of the Chinese Communist Party's Eighteenth Central Committee late in 2013.

The view that recent declines in economic growth reflect stronger influence from cyclical than structural policies is supported in Chapters 2 and 3. The slowdown so far has clear footprints from the turning point in the labour market. However, beyond important changes in the relationship between growth and pressure on the environment, there is so far little evident influence of new policies designed to bring economic outcomes more closely in line with community objectives and to lay the foundations for transition to an advanced modern economy.

The continuation of the deceleration in growth that has been evident for several years into the first quarter of 2015 is more than a 'regression to the mean' (Pritchett and Summers 2014). It reflects the overlapping of three tendencies: the changing of gears associated with the new model of growth, which is necessary to keep growth going; the painful adjustment associated with the removal of external and internal imbalances from the old growth model; and the absorption of the excesses hanging over from the extraordinary fiscal and monetary stimulus that powered China through the aftermath of the GFC. The third, cyclical set of influences includes high debt levels, especially at the local government level, and overcapacity in many industrial sectors, both of which increase risks in China's financial sector.

What we called 'China's new model of economic growth' has since been described by the government and others in China as the 'new normal'. New normal growth requires extensive institutional reform, including changes in the *hukou* system to remove artificial impediments to efficient use of rural labour in urban areas; in the financial system, to allow capital to be allocated to its most productive use; in land management, to ensure that the opportunity cost of scarce land is reflected in its use and that peasants are adequately compensated for transfer of land to more economically valuable uses; in increased investment and better use of resources in education, especially in rural areas, to increase opportunities for all citizens in an expanding modern economy; in removal of barriers to innovation and effective use of intellectual capital by strengthening property rights and facilitating the exchange of knowledge; and in removal or economically efficient regulation of state monopolies to raise efficiency in goods and services markets. Reforms in these areas can increase productivity, generating a 'reform dividend' partially to compensate for the loss of the 'demographic dividend' and for lower contributions to growth from increase in the capital stock (Lu and Cai 2014). Stronger impetus to growth from productivity-raising reform could be augmented in the longer term by relaxation of population policy, although the actual effect of changing the one-child policy at this stage of Chinese development is uncertain.

China's drive towards high-income status needs mutually reinforcing contributions from reform in many areas. Productivity has to be raised in all activities, and resources must be encouraged to move from less to more productive uses. The structural change from less to more productive uses of resources has many dimensions: from less to more profitable firms; from low-value to high-value goods and services; from rural to urban locations; and from less to more productive regions. As Kuznets (1961) noted more than half a century ago, resources need to continue to shift from low-productivity areas such as agriculture to high-productivity areas such as industry—just as they did under the old model of growth, within which more than 250 million rural workers migrated into cities. China has to accept 'creative destruction' wherever it increases economic value, and needs to reform institutions and policies to allow creative destruction to do its work.

There are several risks to China right now continuing to shift resources from relatively low to high-productivity activities (Cai 2015). First, there may not be enough new migrant workers moving from rural areas to towns to replace migrant workers returning to rural areas from now on. This risk arises from demographic change as well as from institutional barriers that prevent migrant workers from settling permanently in cities. The annual growth rate of migrant workers flowing into cities has fallen from 4 per cent in the period 2005–10 to about 1.3 per cent in 2014. The continuation of this trend would undermine an important source of productivity growth, since rural–urban migration is estimated to have contributed about half of China's total factor productivity (TFP) improvement over considerable periods in the reform era.

Second, the rate of urban growth is bound to fall, and unless there is timely downward adjustment in rates of urban infrastructure investment, capital will be wasted in overcapacity.

Third, upgrading of the industrial structure associated with the new model of growth requires increasingly educated and experienced labour. Current rural education standards and incentives for migrants to accumulate and apply skills in urban employment may not make this more sophisticated labour available to expanding urban industries. In these circumstances, rural migrant workers are particularly vulnerable to structural unemployment when they are not covered by urban insurance for unemployment and other social security provisions. At the same time, they cannot easily be re-employed in the agricultural sector because of changes in their own preferences and in technology applied in increasingly productive agriculture. The resulting structural unemployment could be a potential source of social instability.

Fourth, China's rebalancing towards a rising share of services and falling share of secondary industry could lower the overall rate of productivity improvement. Secondary industry in general has higher labour productivity than tertiary industry. For example, average labour productivity (defined as the ratio of industrial value added over total employment) in China was 1.45 for secondary industry and 1.22 for tertiary industry in 2013. However, the impact on productivity depends on whether secondary industry is progressing towards producing higher value-added products and the service industries, including research and development (R&D), design, marketing and post-sales services, which support them. In that case, overall productivity could be enhanced by the development of the service sector. However, industrial restructuring that mainly involves shifting workers from low-end manufacturing production to low-end services could have a negative impact on productivity growth.

These risks highlight the importance of reform to direct resources continually into more productive areas. An important requirement for continuous structural economic upgrading is creative destruction (Schumpeter 1934). This allows inefficient or unproductive activities to depart from the market, so saving resources for use in more efficient, innovative and productive activities. For creative destruction to succeed, governments, especially local governments, should desist from seeking to save industries making losses and losing comparative advantage. Instead, they should nurture market competition and minimise the social costs of structural transition.

The arrival of the Lewis turning period has weakened the competitiveness of China's traditional labour-intensive industries. China's revealed comparative advantage (RCA) index for labour-intensive goods (the ratio of China's labour-intensive exports to total exports, relative to the same ratio for the world as a whole) fell from 4.4 in 2003 to 3.4 in 2013. The downward trend continues.

China's integration into the global economy has forced a worldwide reallocation of economic activities. China's massive labour-intensive industries have started moving from the coastal regions to inland regions and at the same time to other countries, especially in South-East and South Asia but also in Africa. This 'flying geese' or 'flying dragon' pattern is potentially positive for global as well as Chinese development, alongside the upgrading of China's industrial production towards high value-added manufacturing products.

China's State Council unveiled a national plan recently, which is called 'Made in China 2025'. It is a 10-year action plan designed to transform China from a low-end to a high-end manufacturing giant. It covers 10 sectors (*People's Daily online*, 22 May 2015): new information technology; numerical control tools and robotics; aerospace equipment; ocean engineering equipment and high-tech ships; railway equipment; energy-saving and new energy equipment and vehicles; power equipment; new materials; biological medicine and medical devices; and agricultural machinery. This new strategy, coupled with the international strategy of 'one belt and one road', supported by the formation of the Asian Infrastructure Investment Bank (AIIB), reflects a comprehensive approach to a new growth model. If successfully implemented, China's exports of manufactured goods at a higher level will dominate a changing global division of labour, supporting productive structural change in China itself.

Comprehensive success requires a favourable international environment. This is increasingly problematic. There is increasing concern about the sustainability of the export-oriented growth model in China and other East Asian economies, against a weakening of the multilateral trading system and the proliferation of preferential arrangements. These are likely soon to be joined by the formation of a large preferential trading area that excludes the large Asian countries: China, India and Indonesia. Optimists see this as being a stepping stone to comprehensive free trade in the Asia-Pacific. Realists see risks in the immense gains from free multilateral trade that have underpinned Asia-Pacific development in the past half-century.

Outside Asia, the capacity and willingness of developed countries to accept the structural change required for absorption of large quantities of exports from newly competitive suppliers of high-value products are diminished by slow economic growth and the increase in protectionist instincts that this inspires. Continued deepening of international integration would help all countries to meet the economic challenges they face; a reversal of the globalisation process would make life harder for everyone. China's circumstances provide an opportunity for gains from global leadership (Garnaut and Song 2006). China's leadership role in championing a new wave of globalisation is present in some areas but not in others. The establishment of the AIIB is a good sign: new mechanisms to support capital outflow alongside increased export of capital goods from the higher-income countries to support infrastructure for development in lower-income countries are needed now to restore momentum for economic growth in developed and developing countries alike. China would do global development as well as its own development a good turn by demonstrating similar leadership in unilateral trade liberalisation, which is the most likely way out of the increasingly dense maze of preferential trading arrangements in the Asia-Pacific.

The rebalancing from exports to consumption as a source of growth within China's new economic model also reduces adjustment pressures in the rest of the world. This creates a different set of opportunities for export expansion in the rest of the world than the old model of growth, which favoured exports of minerals and energy commodities, with all of the challenges of resource-led growth in the exporting countries (Collier 2007; Sachs and Warner 1997).

The next five years of transition are crucial to the success of the new model of growth. Success would deliver the targeted doubling of per capita income by 2020 from the 2010 level. That would lift China across the income threshold of a developed country. There is a good chance but no certainty of success. Reforms must be deepened to lift productivity and to make growth more inclusive and environmentally sustainable.

This year's *China Update* offers both domestic insight and global context into this challenging new phase of China's economic transformation. The following chapters shine a light on policy reform, institutional change and economic performance in a number of specialised areas of the Chinese economy. Many are important in themselves, and all provide insights into the complex process of transition through which China is seeking to make its way from middle income into the ranks of the developed countries.

A complex set of institutional changes covering political rather than narrowly economic transition will help to determine the fate of China's advance into the ranks of developed economies. Inductive logic would draw from the experience of the countries that are now developed: the conclusion that all high-income countries have (more or less) competitive political systems in which the votes of citizens can change the political party of government. It would draw the conclusion that all high-income countries provide freedom of exchange of information among citizens and between citizens and other people that extends well beyond common practice in China.

It is in the nature of inductive logic that a new set of observations can transform our knowledge. Nassim Taleb (2007) in his classic book about financial irrationality notes that the swan was synonymous with whiteness until Willem de Vlamingh sailed through the heads of what is now Fremantle Harbour in 1696. He then observed the black swans that were of sufficient note for him to give the name Swan to the river that opened before him. If China achieves advanced-economy status without fundamental political change, a majority of people living in high-income countries will live under authoritarian and not democratic governments. The world will see another black swan.

Inductive logic raises some questions about whether China can reach the status of a high-income country without large changes in political institutions. This book does not cover these important matters. They have been discussed by economists elsewhere (Dollar 2015; Huang 2015), and will be part of the agenda of the *China Update* on future occasions.

Structure of the book

Chapters 2, 3 and 9 take a closer look at the macroeconomic story, focusing on the influences on the growth slowdown and the policies proposed to remedy it.

In Chapter 2, Ross Garnaut examines structural change within China's economic growth. Change is being driven by pressures endogenous to economic development, and by new objectives and policy. The former include rising wages and changes in the relative priorities of increases in income and the quality of health, longevity and the natural environment that come with higher incomes. The new model of growth that accepts the growing scarcity and value of labour, and the higher priority of equity in income distribution and environmental amenity are necessary to sustain growth so that China can enter the ranks of high-income countries. The transition to a new model of growth, and, if that transition is successful, to an advanced economy, could be smooth or rough. Smooth adjustment would see investment falling and consumption rising by a commensurate amount—and productivity growth rising so as partially to balance the declining contribution to growth of increase in the amount of labour and capital deployed in the economy.

There are some positive signs suggesting progress in applying the new model of growth. Real wages are rising at a faster rate than gross domestic product (GDP). Inequality as measured by the Gini coefficient is falling after many years of moving in the opposite direction. Trends in the share of investment and household consumption of GDP are in the right direction, but almost imperceptible in size. There is so far only a weak footprint of the new growth model in the economic indicators.

The slowdown in growth is larger than the limited progress in implementing the new model of growth would lead us to expect. That suggests large cyclical and unproductive structural causes of the slowdown in growth since 2011. Growth in TFP is falling markedly—although the experience of other countries suggests that the causes may not all be specific to China. This suggests little progress in the qualitative reforms that are at the heart of the new model of growth—and of the decisions of the Third Plenum in 2013.

One area in which the new model does have bite is in changes in the relationship between economic growth and pressure on the environment. Use of low-emissions energy is rising rapidly, and the early twenty-first-century explosion in the use of coal and other fossil fuels has come to an abrupt end. Changes in the intensity and composition of energy use are being driven by domestic concerns for health and longevity as well as international concerns about climate change and desires to limit insecurity derived from dependence on imported fossil fuels. Implementation of the more narrowly economic dimensions of the new model of growth—for example, through the decline in the investment share of expenditure—would accelerate progress on environmental objectives, and can be expected in future with success in China's transition to a developed country.

In Chapter 9, Rod Tyers explains how the GFC forced China to confront the economic imbalances that are the legacy of three decades of rapid growth. For one-quarter of a century into the reform era, until about 2005, China's abundant and cheap labour kept labour costs low and increased consumer choice and welfare in high-income economies. The gains within China and in its trading partners favoured the owners of capital, and in some industries had adverse consequences for workers. What will be the consequences of China's new growth model for high-income economies?

Tyers explores that question using a global macroeconomic model that allows for rebalancing of national asset portfolios and endogenous representation of unconventional monetary policy. Modelling results suggest that high-income countries could see modest increases in inflation, but the associated adverse fall in the terms of trade could help to restore employment levels. Those results also suggest that successful Chinese transition towards higher consumption and lower savings should reverse the impact on high-income economies of China's old model of growth.

In Chapter 3, Guonan Ma makes the case for monetary easing in China—a policy shift that began in late 2014. The international context of Chinese monetary easing is the post–financial crisis monetary easing by the central banks of Japan, the United States, the European Union and the United Kingdom. One consequence of the developed countries' monetary policies was an unintended tightening of Chinese policy. Ma argues that this is a cause of Chinese growth in recent years being slower than would be optimal. This carries risks and increases the difficulties of reform.

Ma's chapter makes a compelling case for monetary reform around three perspectives: the Taylor rule for the domestic monetary expansion; China's tight monetary conditions in the face of unconventional monetary policy operations by the central banks of the big four economies; and the relationship between Chinese and fiscal policies in determining the exchange rate. Ma sees monetary easing as being important for short-term stability as well as to provide a congenial context for economic reform to the new model of growth.

In Chapter 4, Meiyan Wang and Cai Fang explore one area of untapped consumer potential: China's vast pool of migrant workers. The *hukou* residency registration system—which limits cross-provincial and urban–rural cross-worker access to social security, health and education—forces higher levels of precautionary savings than are considered acceptable by local peers.

Meiyan Wang and Cai Fang use data from the China Urban Labour Survey to analyse consumption patterns among migrant and local households in six cities in China. Finding the difference between migrant and local consumption to be statistically significant, the authors extrapolate the consumption potential were migrant workers to enjoy the same benefits and rights as locals. The chapter concludes that reform that empowers China's migrant workers to consume at the level of their local peers would support China's new economic strategy by unlocking massive untapped consumer potential.

In Chapter 5, Ran Li, Xiang Li, Wen Lei and Yiping Huang debate the options for accelerating reform and opening of China's banking sector. Since shortly after China joined the World Trade Organization (WTO), foreign banks have dramatically expanded their absolute presence in China, with their assets growing at an average annual rate of 20 per cent. Contrary to earlier fears, they have failed to crowd out Chinese banks and have encountered many difficulties in operating in China. Their shares of total banking assets have fallen. Chinese banks seem to have benefited from the learning and competition spillovers generated by foreign banks in China without losing business to them.

The authors seek to quantify the impact of foreign banks on competition in China's banking sector. Exploring a subset of China's banking sector—the non-state banking sector at the provincial level—the authors find that foreign banks are associated with positive competition effects in China. Net interest margins and non-interest expenses as a share of total earnings are both lower where foreign banks are active.

Reform is delivering efficiency advantages without obviously damaging established Chinese interests.

In Chapter 6, Qing King Guo, Chi Keung Marco Lau, Kunwang Li and Ligang Song explore whether the efficiency of coal, gasoline and gas markets is increasing in China. They do this by focusing on changes in price differentials across regions. Recent advances in the collection of spot-price data allow the 'law of one price' to be tested. The chapter also assesses progress in the integration of markets across China's regions. The massive increase in demand for energy in the past few decades makes this an interesting area for testing changes in the efficiency of markets.

There is little support for the law of one price in China in the analysis of energy price changes across the regions and years that were studied. An average convergence rate of 40 per cent is calculated. Diesel prices converged most, with 60 per cent of the diesel sample suggesting convergence in price across regions over time. Electricity prices remained most divergent. There were also indications of the extent of convergence varying within category groupings, especially with respect to coal products. The results were attributed to price protection, geographic barriers and other government policies.

In Chapter 7, Xunpeng Shi and Hari Malamakkavu Padinjare Variam explore the case of liberalisation of China's gas market, which began a decade ago. Those reforms include the creation of gas trading hubs and gas benchmark pricing—intended to improve the infrastructure and liquidity of the gas market. Since China is now a net gas importer, the world's third-largest consumer of gas and intends to increase the role of gas in its energy mix, understanding gas market liberalisation in China is important to the global gas industry. The first part of the chapter provides a qualitative summary of these trends and changes, and of the powerful role of China's three large state-owned gas companies.

The chapter then applies an empirical model to examine the impact of China's gas liberalisation on trade flows and gas prices. An Asian gas trade model utilises a dataset covering 2006 and projections forward to 2035. China would lose if it was alone among East Asia's major gas importers in deregulating its gas market. A unique study of China–Australia gas ties finds that Australia is likely to do best under the continuation of a long-term contract system. For China, the optimal scenario is one of a mixed-economy model: a combination of long-term contracts and spot-price purchasing.

In Chapter 8, Stephen Wilson, Yufeng Yang and Jane Kuang outline the complex challenges facing China's electricity producers. After suffering persistent blackouts in the 1980s, by the first decade of the new century, the electricity sector instead had a 'golden decade', characterised by rising growth in demand and generation capacity. China now has the world's largest hydropower sector, the world's largest and most rapid nuclear plant construction program and the largest installed capacity for wind and solar power. Managing this sector against demand for power, environmental concerns, industrial competitiveness and, finally, equality and livelihood concerns necessitates continuous reforms.

The main focus of the chapter is on models of price deregulation and their relevance to China. The authors extract lessons from the experiences of major electricity-consuming countries for China's own electricity reforms. Early this century, China's electricity reforms were most influenced by the UK example of separation of power generation and the grid, parallel with establishing an electricity supervision council. Benchmarking against different international experience continues. The period 2020–50 is cited as expected to produce major milestones in energy, the economy and the environment for China, and thus future trends in China's electricity market could be future trends in the global electricity market. Most of the data end in 2010, so the insights from the chapter are of historical relevance.

In Chapter 10, Liqing Zhang and Qin Gou lay out alternative approaches for China's prospective opening of the capital account. An extreme choice is to open with a 'big bang'. This could be efficient in terms of capital allocation and risk diversification but is subject to large financial volatility risks. The choice of opening model is complicated by the need for synchronisation with decisions on reform of the banking sector, liberalisation of finance and floating the national currency. Consequences of reform are affected by the international business cycle.

Zhang and Gou review the theoretical and empirical literature, which explores both the mode and the sequencing of capital account opening. They add a random effects probit model to that literature, and utilise a sample of 50 countries to explore how different scenarios of reform sequencing and opening mode affect the likelihood of a financial crisis in China. Under no scenario does the risk exceed 15 per cent. The risk is lowest in the case of China incrementally opening its capital account in tandem with undertaking broader financial reforms.

In Chapter 11, Will Nixon, Eden Hatzvi and Michelle Wright unravel and explain China's cautious and policy-driven approach to internationalising the renminbi (RMB). They describe the prevailing view that RMB internationalisation can only move in tandem with broader capital account liberalisation. The latter, however, is being served by the gradual rise of offshore RMB trading, for it is increasing the international flow of China's currency. This experience provides insight for Chinese central bankers seeking to understand how greater openness to currency trade might work.

Nixon, Hatzvi and Wright explain the motivations for China proceeding with these sensitive monetary reforms, and the important role of the Bank of China and the Bank of Hong Kong to that process. By early 2015 the local branches of Chinese banks in 15 cities outside mainland China had been granted official RMB clearing bank status. Some 28 central banks have signed bilateral currency swap agreements with China, while 40 invest a proportion of their foreign-exchange reserves in renminbi. The experience of the central banks and investors utilising the increasing number of RMB-denominated stock investor programs is increasing understanding of influences on the RMB exchange rate.

In Chapter 12, Kevin Zhang ponders differences in industrial goods production and industrial competitiveness, in a comparative study of China's changing industrial strength. A UN Industrial Development Organization (UNIDO) dataset of industrial competitiveness indicators provides the basis for assessing China's relative total and per capita international strength in production and exports of manufacturing value added over time.

Zhang finds that China has come a long way in terms of capacity and intensity. China's industrial intensity now exceeds that of some industrialised economies, but it has a long way to go in quality. Similarly, since much of the progress in industrial capacity and intensity was driven by foreign-invested firms and processing trade, China has a long way to go to reach its goal of more indigenous industrial strength.

In Chapter 13, Mei (Lisa) Wang, Zhen Qi and Jijing Zhang draw our attention to the massive rise in China's outbound investment activity. Of the four phases of China's outbound investment development, the first two cover the years 1980–2000, and were of modest dimension. Since 2002, however, official statistics suggest that China's outbound investment has increased 45 times, reaching US$116 billion in 2014. Since the GFC, average annual outbound foreign direct investment (FDI) has reached US$74 billion.

Unlike China's slowing 'new normal' domestic growth rate, the new normal for outbound investment carries annual growth projections in the range of 20 per cent to 2020. Growth could be volatile. The scale of China's investment is daunting. The unique and complicated institutional structure of China's state-owned enterprises present new and challenging territory for investor recipient countries.

Chunlai Chen in Chapter 14 uses a provincial-level panel dataset and employs the fixed-effects model to investigate empirically the inter-regional spillovers from coastal FDI on inland provinces. The study finds that FDI in the northern and eastern coastal provinces (which are moderately engaged in processing trade) has positive spillovers on the economic growth of inland provinces, while FDI in southern coastal provinces (those heavily engaged in processing trade) has had a negative effect on the economic growth of inland provinces. The explanation for this could be that processing trade has no industrial linkages with inland regions and cannot generate backward and forward knowledge spillovers to firms in inland provinces. China should redesign processing trade policies to focus on increasing local sourcing and enhancing industrial linkages through economic structural reform and industrial upgrading.

In Chapter 15, Fan He and Xiaoming Pan shed light on the emerging complexities of fragmenting world trade negotiations. Ostensibly in direct response to the decade-long stalemate in the multilateral Doha negotiations of the WTO, selective country groupings have now initiated more exclusive mega-regional negotiations. The fragmenting of global trade with the rise of trade-in-parts makes old trade rules less relevant. China has joined the race to update international trade rules. The chapter reveals an absence of clarity in the goals of the race. Some of the proposed new arrangements, especially the US-led Trans-Pacific Partnership (TPP), appear designed to exclude China.

In Chapter 16, Lauren Johnston writes of the evolution of China–Africa economic ties over time. Explaining the interdependent trends in flows of trade, investment and aid, Johnston notes that while today China is Africa's largest trading partner, China's investment plans offer most insight into the direction of these ties.

As a result of China's slower growth within its new model, there has been a dramatic decline in the price of many energy and metals commodities. For commodities exporters in Africa, this means a painful readjustment. In contrast, for net commodities importers, China's new model of growth is good news for the terms of trade. The chapter outlines how China plans to greatly increase investment in infrastructure, labour-intensive manufacturing and steelmaking in Africa. The precedents for sustainable growth across time and countries suggest that the prospects for growth of China's outbound investment to facilitate industrialisation in Africa are especially important in coastal economies experiencing an improvement in terms of trade, such as Kenya and Tanzania.

In Chapter 17, Gao Xiang and Huiqin Jiang explore China's new foreign investment legal regime, which took effect in September 2013. Changes to that regime centre on the China (Shanghai) Pilot Free Trade Zone (SPFTZ), and are part of China's efforts to modernise the financial sector and to move closer to the industrial frontier.

Innovations within the new investment law regime include the adoption of pre-establishment national treatment, and a negative list. The latter has attracted significant attention, and includes gambling industries and a list of national products such as types of tea. The reporting and filing system for foreign investors has also been simplified. The new systems adopted in the SPFTZ for foreign investment differ greatly from those applied previously in China, demonstrating the Chinese Government's efforts to integrate into the international economic market and adopt generally accepted international rules.

References

Cai, F. (2015), Looking at sources of economic growth under the 'new normal' from an international perspective, Unpublished, Chinese Academy of Social Sciences, Beijing.

Collier, P. (2007), *The bottom billion: Why the poorest countries are failing and what can be done about it*, Oxford: Oxford University Press.

Dollar, D. (2015), Institutional quality and growth trends, PAFTAD37 Conference, Institute of Southeast Asian Studies, Singapore, June.

Garnaut, R. and Song, L. (2006), Truncated globalisation: The fate of the Asia Pacific economies?, in Soesastro, H. and Findlay, C. (eds), *Reshaping the Asia Pacific economic order*, London: Routledge, pp. 46–81.

Garnaut, R., Cai, F. and Song, L. (2013), China's new strategy for long-term growth and development, in Garnaut, R., Cai, F. and Song, L. (eds), *China: A new model for growth and development*, Canberra: ANU E Press, pp. 1–16.

Huang, Y. (2015), Can China rise to high income, PAFTAD37 Conference, Institute of Southeast Asian Studies, Singapore, June.

Kuznets, S. (1961), Economic growth and the contribution of agriculture: Notes on measurement, *International Journal of Agrarian Affairs*, 3(April): 56–75.

Lu, Y. and Cai, F. (2014), China's shift from the demographic dividend to the reform dividend, in Song, L., Garnaut, R. and Cai, F. (eds), *Deepening reform for China's long-term growth and development*, Canberra: ANU Press, pp. 27–50.

Pritchett, L. and Summers, L.H. (2014), Asiaphoria meets regression to the mean, NBER Working Paper No. 20573, Cambridge, Mass.: National Bureau of Economic Research.

Sachs, J.D. and Warner, A.M. (1997), *Natural resource abundance and economic growth*, Cambridge, Mass.: Harvard University Press.

Schumpeter, J.A. (1934), *The theory of economic development*, Cambridge, Mass.: Harvard University Press.

Taleb, N. (2007), *The black swan: The impact of the highly improbable*, New York: Random House.

Part I: Domestic transformation and structural change

2. The New Model of Growth and the Global Resources Economy

Ross Garnaut[1]

We said in the introductory chapter to the 2013 China Update book that contemporary changes in economic policy and structure were so comprehensive and profound that they represented a new model of Chinese economic growth (Garnaut et al. 2013a). We called the volume *China: A New Model of Growth and Development*.

The new model had conventional economic and more subtle institutional dimensions. Cai Fang, Ligang Song and I (Garnaut et al. 2013b) and Huang et al. (2013) explored the former, and Dwight Perkins (2013) explored the institutional changes.

We noted in 2013 that these changes in China would have large international consequences. The changes were particularly important for trade in resource-based commodities. The old model of growth produced, in the world's most populous country, the strongest, most resource-intensive economic growth the world has ever seen. This gave rise to the extraordinary resources boom of the early twenty-first century. This was of immense importance to development in Australia and many other resource-rich countries.

How is the new model going and how is its progress affecting the global resources economy? This chapter briefly explores the more straightforward economic dimensions of progress so far, and the impact of those changes on some aspects of global resources trade of importance to Australia.

From old to new: The changing character of growth

The old model of economic development was built on high and rapidly increasing levels of investment, especially in industrial activity and urban infrastructure. It was supported by the movement of huge numbers of workers from the countryside to the towns and cities, allowing strong growth in urban

---

1 I am grateful for research support from Ligang Song, Ran Li, Derek Cheng and Veronica Webster.

employment with modest increases in real wages. With wages growing less rapidly than the value of output, the profit share of income rose continually, in turn supporting increases in savings. Much of the massive increase in savings was committed to investment, reinforcing the process of investment-led growth.

Investment-led growth was accompanied by relatively high total factor productivity (TFP) growth, encouraged by deep and deepening integration into the global economy. The internationally oriented growth saw China contributing the majority of the increase in world trade in the early twenty-first century, and a majority of the increase in the surplus of domestic savings over investment that was available for international investment.

Chinese growth in the early twenty-first century was the most rapid over a sustained period in any country since modern economic growth emerged in the United Kingdom a quarter of a millennium ago. It was also the most investment intensive and therefore the most metals intensive and energy intensive the world has ever seen.

The high investment share of expenditure in the reform era was reinforced by the Chinese policy response to massive recessionary shocks from abroad. The first of these was the Asian Financial Crisis of 1997–99 (McLeod and Garnaut 1998). The Chinese Government chose to maintain the exchange value of the renminbi (RMB) against the US dollar despite massive currency depreciation in all of its Western Pacific trading partners. To maintain a reasonable if diminished rate of growth in economic output, employment and incomes through a huge deceleration of export growth and fall in net exports, the authorities engaged in a large Keynesian monetary and fiscal expansion. The second shock was from the global financial crisis (GFC) of 2008. The immediate effects on China were even larger and potentially more destabilising than those of the Asian Financial Crisis. Again, the response was to maintain a fixed exchange rate against the US dollar despite large currency depreciation in other Western Pacific economies, and massive monetary and fiscal expansion to maintain growth in output and employment. Fiscal and monetary expansions were applied on a much larger scale in 2008–09 than during and after the Asian Financial Crisis.

The Keynesian expansions of 1998–99 and 2008–09 were brilliantly successful in supporting the continuation of strong economic growth. They were implemented principally through expansion in the resources made available through state-connected entities—through local, provincial and national governments as suppliers of infrastructure, and through state-owned enterprises (SOEs), which were disproportionately active in heavy industry—all drawing large amounts of finance from the state-owned banks.

The outcome was an intensification of the role of investment in the growth process. Investment is much more metals intensive and energy intensive than consumption, so development in the early twenty-first century and especially after the GFC further increased the extraordinary pressure that Chinese growth was placing on world energy and metals markets.

The extraordinary rates, investment intensity, energy intensity and metals intensity of growth in the world's most populous country generated the largest, longest and most broadly based increase in commodity demand that the world economy has ever experienced. Figures 2.1 and 2.2 illustrate how China contributed most of the strong increase in global demand from the beginning of the new century to 2011 for the energy source (thermal coal, Figure 2.1) and metal (steel, Figure 2.2) that were most important in Chinese growth. The central role of China was especially pronounced after the GFC, when growth in demand for energy and metals accelerated in China and decelerated in the rest of the world.

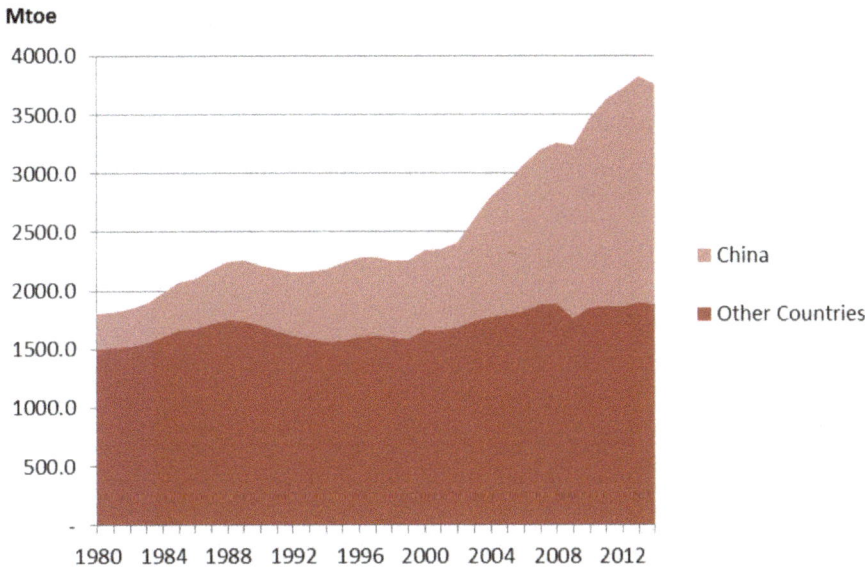

Figure 2.1 Coal consumption of China compared with other countries

Source: BP (2015); and author's estimation.

Thousand Mt

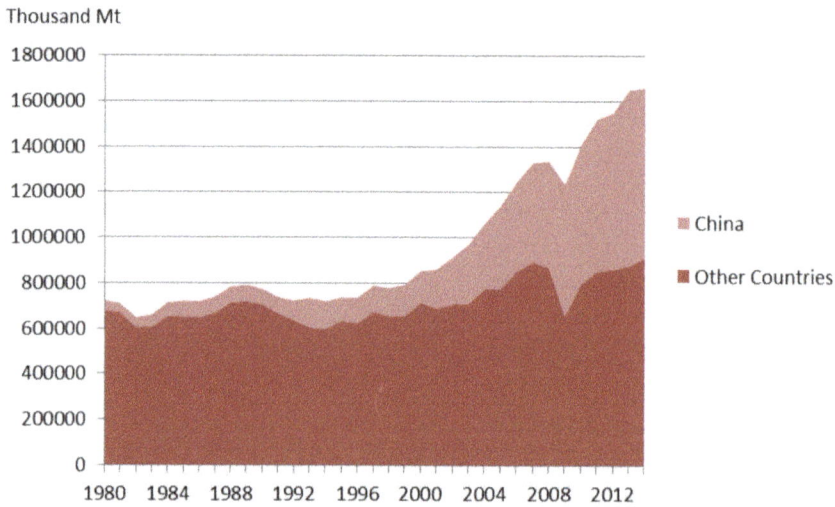

Figure 2.2 Steel consumption of China compared with other countries

Source: World Steel Association (2015); and author's estimation.

The increase in China's demand took suppliers of metals and energy by surprise. Investment in expanding mining capacity lagged a long way behind demand for all metals and major energy sources. Prices rose to or close to their highest levels ever in real terms (see Figures 2.3, 2.4 and 2.5 for thermal coal, oil and copper, respectively).

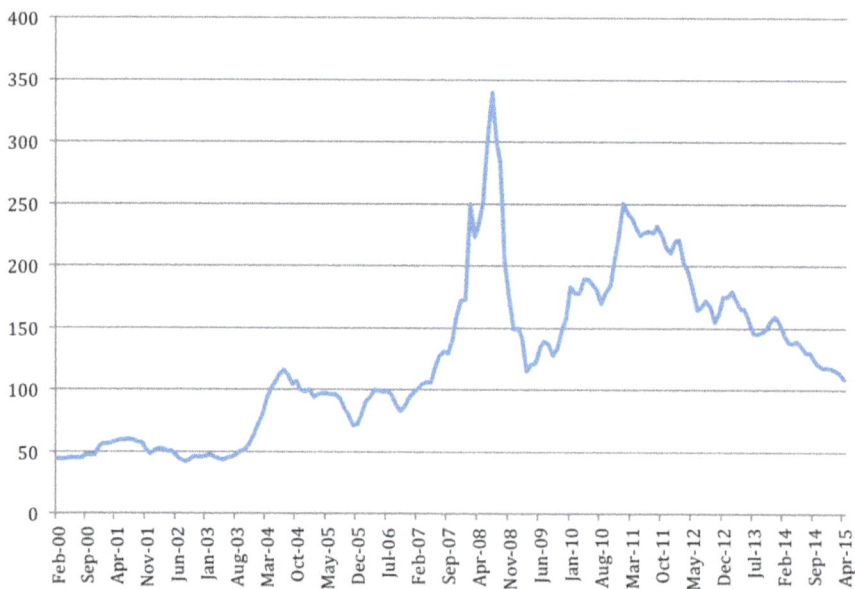

Figure 2.3 Thermal coal price index (US$/Mt; 2007 prices, 2007=100)

Note: FOB Newcastle/Port Kembla.

Source: Index Mundi (2014). Reproduced from Garnaut (forthcoming 2015).

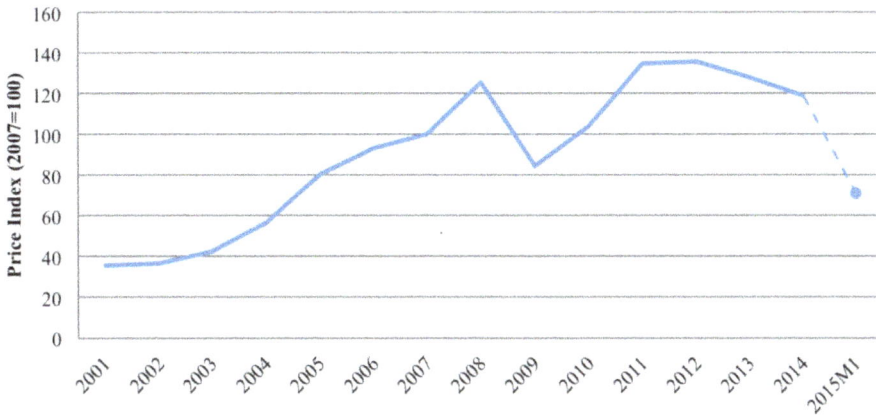

Figure 2.4 Crude oil price index (US$/bbl; 2007 prices, 2007=100)

Source: Price data from World Bank and EIA; US goods deflator from IMF International Financial Statistics (2007$). Reproduced from Garnaut (forthcoming 2015).

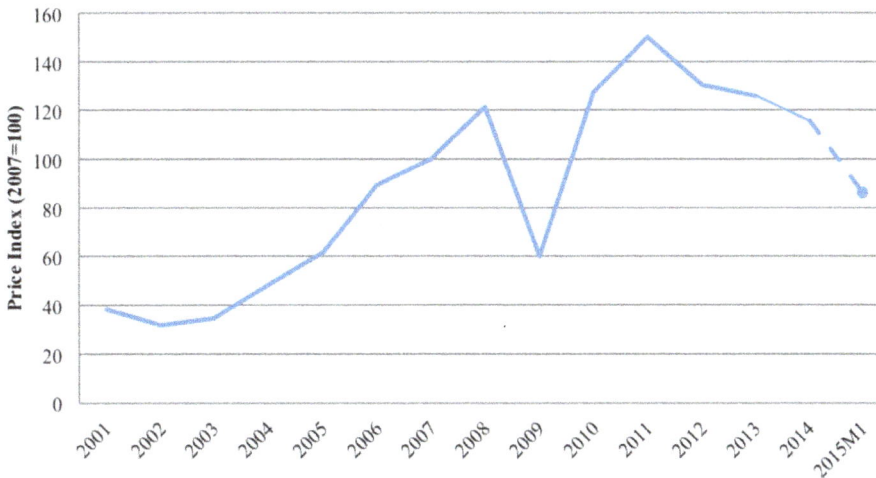

Figure 2.5 Copper price index (US$/Mt; 2007 prices, 2007=100)

Source: Price data from London Metal Exchange via Datastream; US Goods Deflator from IMF International Financial Statistics (2007$). Reproduced from Garnaut (forthcoming 2015).

Two separate forces are driving the transition to the new model of economic growth. One is straightforwardly economic: pressures that emerge naturally from successful economic development. The other is the change in national objectives and policy, towards more equitable distribution of income and less damaging impacts on the domestic and international natural environment. The changes in objectives and policy are themselves partly a response to rising incomes, which reduce the priority of higher material living standards relative to other dimensions of the quality of life.

The economic pressures from successful development come from the raising of the wage at which people are prepared to leave the countryside for work in urban areas (Cai 2010; Garnaut 2010; Garnaut and Song 2006; Huang and Cai 2013; Huang and Jiang 2010). The movement of people from the countryside to urban employment reduces pressures on agricultural resources and raises rural material standards of living. The people who remain in rural villages after the early decades of rapid economic growth tend to have better opportunities at home and require greater inducements to migrate to the towns than those who went before them. To the extent that some of the fruits of economic development are allocated by government as transfers to rural residents and to rural services such as health, education, telecommunications and transport, the urban wage required to induce migration increases. A long history of fertility well below replacement levels eventually causes the number of new entrants into the labour force each year to fall. And the increase in urban demand for labour with sustained rapid growth increases demand for labour at a steady wage (Huang et al. 2013).

Scarcity of low-skilled labour and a tendency for wages to rise more rapidly than the value of output were evident in the major coastal cities from about 2005 and became more widespread with each passing year until the disruption of the GFC. The tendency was broken briefly by the GFC, but returned late in 2009 as the powerful monetary and fiscal expansion became effective. It has continued since then, despite the slowing of economic growth.

These pressures from the labour market began to force profound change in the composition and rate of growth. Sooner or later, they were bound to be associated with a rise in the consumption and fall in the savings and investment shares of national income. The reduction in the investment share of expenditure, in turn, could be expected to reduce the rate of growth of the capital stock and therefore the aggregate rate of growth. The rate of growth of the labour contribution fell to near zero with the stagnation and then decline of the working-age population from about 2012. The decline in the rate of growth in the capital and labour contributions might be expected to reduce over time the overall rate of growth by several percentage points, from about 10 per cent per annum to about 7 per cent, and eventually lower still.

The changes in objectives and policy emerged gradually, but had taken full shape by 2012. Implementation of policy took longer but now has considerable momentum.

The widening of the dispersion of income distribution was a source of comment and growing concern among economists and parts of the population and leadership from the early years of the century. Policies to increase rural incomes and services and to expand consumption especially of services were defined and gradually strengthened throughout the Hu–Wen period of government. They were eclipsed during the slowdown after the GFC, but were back on the agenda by 2010 and were central in the Twelfth Five-Year Plan 2011–15.

The energy-intensive pattern of growth of the early twenty-first century placed immense pressure on the global environment through growing greenhouse gas emissions. It was also causally important in the deterioration of air and water quality to an extent that was seriously damaging to human health and life expectancy. Both global and local environmental costs were especially high because of the exceptionally large role of coal as an energy source in power generation and industry.

China contributed a majority of the global increase in greenhouse gas emissions through the first decade of the century. This attracted increasing disquiet within the Chinese scientific community, which had access to the premier and other leading policymakers. It also attracted critical comment from the governments of developed countries as the international community geared up for stronger action to mitigate human-induced climate change in the lead-up to and after the Copenhagen conference of the United Nations in December 2009. China made commitments on reductions in the emissions intensity of economic activity to the international community at Cancun in 2010 that required a substantial change in the structure of economic growth.

Concern over local environmental effects has risen in a number of steps since the GFC. The focus on dangerously high concentrations of small carbon particulates in the air in cities of eastern and northern China has intensified with scientific study of their effects on health and increasing attention in popular media (Chen et al. 2013). This has been a major focus of popular concern at least since early 2013 (Chai 2015). It has become a separate and powerful driver of policy to diminish the energy intensity of economic activity and the dominant position of coal in energy use.

Official policy continues to elevate the priority of reductions in energy intensity and the substitution of all of the low-emission alternatives for coal.

Smooth and rough adjustment

The new model of economic growth embodies structural change at an immense scale and pace.

One can define a possible path of smooth adjustment that would see rapid but gradual offsetting changes in the main growth parameters that together ensure the continuation of reasonably strong growth in output, employment and incomes of most people. But one can also identify the possibility of investment falling more than consumption is rising and productivity failing to rise to compensate for lower contributions from other sources of growth in output and incomes. The latter possibility would involve disruption of growth in output and incomes. Disruption would introduce risks of financial or political dislocation, compounding the initial loss of growth momentum.

Smooth adjustment would see the maintenance or even some acceleration of TFP growth as the contributions of growth in the capital stock and labour force declined. Rising real wages introduce pressure to raise productivity. There is an opportunity to lift productivity growth to an extent that moderates considerably the decline in the rate of output growth within the new development model. The focus on improvement of the institutions for market regulation and exchange can raise productivity. The focus on increased investment in education within the new model of growth combines with the large decline in the school-age population to introduce prospects for greatly improved labour quality, which shows up as increased TFP. Success in raising productivity growth depends especially on the institutional reforms discussed by Perkins (2013) in his contribution to this series two years ago. It depends on maintenance of openness to the international economy in all of its dimensions. It requires far-reaching financial system reform to allow capital to move quickly and in large quantities to its most productive uses. Strong growth in TFP requires acceptance of rapid changes in the composition of economic activity in line with rapidly changing comparative advantage. It requires improvement of market institutions, including through increased transparency and reliability of state mechanisms for regulating legal relations between the state and private entities and among private businesses. These improvements require strengthening of rights to intellectual and real property. Success in maintaining and lifting productivity growth requires heavy investment in education and training. It requires easy and low-cost transfers of economic information within China and between Chinese and overseas individuals and enterprises.

Adjustment to the new model of growth requires an absolute reduction in total investment and not just a fall in the investment share of expenditure. Changes in the required level of investment—and therefore demand for inputs into investment—depend not on the rate of growth in the economy, but on changes in the rate of growth. Here we have the old-fashioned Keynesian accelerator at work. The rate of growth of output is expected to fall by about one-third within the new model of growth—from about 10 per cent per annum to about 7 per cent (and eventually to lower levels). In the absence of changes in the productivity-related influences that determine the capital–output ratio, the level of investment can be expected to fall by a similar proportion. Consumption has to rise quickly and by a large amount to maintain domestic demand that is consistent with maintenance of the new, lower potential rate of growth.

Smooth adjustment would see consumption rising as investment falls. Rising consumption shares of a more slowly growing national output and income—reversing many years of falling consumption shares—could see the rate of growth in consumption remaining as strong or stronger than in earlier years under the old growth model. But the absence of timely and large increases in consumption introduces the risk of disturbingly large slumps in the growth of incomes, expenditure and output.

The decline in the share and level of investment has massive effects on the inter-industrial structure of demand. In particular, investment uses metals and energy far more intensively than consumption, so that sharply lower investment means a slump in demand for the products of heavy industry that had central roles in the old model of growth. Coal and steel are the most prominent of the industries subject to lower demand growth—with coal being affected as well by the shift to low-emission sources of power generation that follows the elevation of environmental amenity among national objectives. The slowing rate of urbanisation after the turning period of Chinese economic development induces deceleration in growth in demand for all of the infrastructure required by a growing urban population, including housing and transport infrastructure. As with demand for investment goods, this induces an absolute fall in demand for many goods that occupied a large place within the old model of growth. This is an important part of the current anxiety about oversupply of housing in many Chinese cities—an oversupply that is transmitted with acceleration into supplying industries.

The massive structural adjustment required by the new model of growth compounds risks of disruption that emerged in the mature stage of the old model of growth. The unprecedentedly high investment shares of gross domestic product (GDP) channelled disproportionately through state agencies led to overinvestment in some areas of heavy industry and infrastructure. Provincial and local government sponsorship of real estate developments in particular was associated with strong growth in revenue during the later years of the old model of growth. Financial institutions that had provided funds for infrastructure and heavy industry are vulnerable to the deterioration in the fortunes of these mainstays of the old growth model—as are provincial and local governments, whose revenues came to depend excessively on new urban development during the period of rapid, investment-led growth. The pullback in investment in urban development and heavy industry under the new model has led to severe imbalances in local government finances and vulnerability in the balance sheets of many financial institutions (Wong 2015; Yu 2009). Financial reform is necessary for success in transition to the new model of economic growth, but is inhibited by the fragility of financial institutions deriving from the lending patterns of the era of investment-led growth.

The materialisation of severe macroeconomic or financial sector imbalances would affect the state's capacity to implement in a timely way policies to secure transition to the new model of growth. The possibility of smooth adjustment is surrounded by risks of a much rougher ride. The large fall in real estate activity and therefore demand for steel and cement in early 2015 contain elements of temporary disruption on top of the tendencies to secular decline.

Changes in growth so far

These are early years in the change of policy in a great state and the change of the trajectory of economic development in an immense economy—now the world's largest in purchasing power terms. The natural economic pressures driving the new model of growth have been working consistently since the recovery from the GFC in 2010. The policy changes have been applied in more and more areas since 2011. Anticipated changes in economic structure are apparent in the statistical record, but mostly weakly.

Here I focus on the conventional economic dimensions of change. The qualitative, institutional changes required by the new model were emphasised in the elaborate decisions of the Third Plenum of the Eighteenth Central Committee in 2013. They are being taken seriously, without so far being applied consistently and effectively. Institutional change takes time in the best of circumstances and it will be some years before sound judgments can be made about reform achievements in these areas.

The rate of growth has slowed decisively—consistent with the requirements of the new model (Figure 2.6). Recent expressions of goals for the rate of growth by leading members of the government have gathered around 7 per cent with acknowledgement that outcomes may turn out to be weaker. Major easing of monetary policy so far in 2015 is directed at supporting growth near these levels, modest as they are by the standards of the reform era.

Real wages rose well above output growth for the first time in 2009. Since then, wage growth has remained much stronger than output as the latter has eased in recent years.

The standard measure of inequality, the Gini coefficient, rose to a peak in 2008 and has eased steadily, if slowly, since then (Figure 2.7). The change in trajectory of the Gini coefficient reflects the acceleration of increases in wages relative to output as well as the introduction of policies designed to reduce inequality.

%

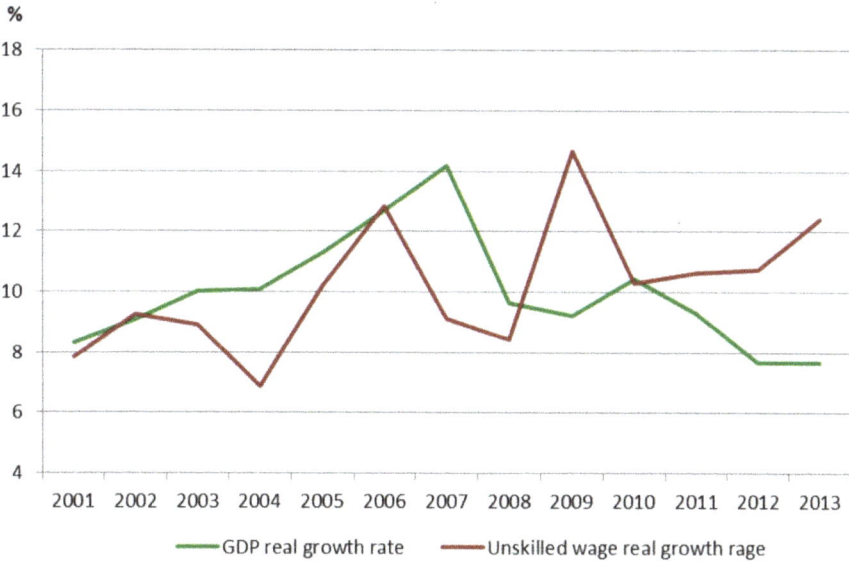

Figure 2.6 Real growth rate of GDP and wage of low-skilled workers

Note: Average wage in the construction industry is used as a proxy for that in low-skilled industries.
Sources: IMF-IFS; National Bureau of Statistics.

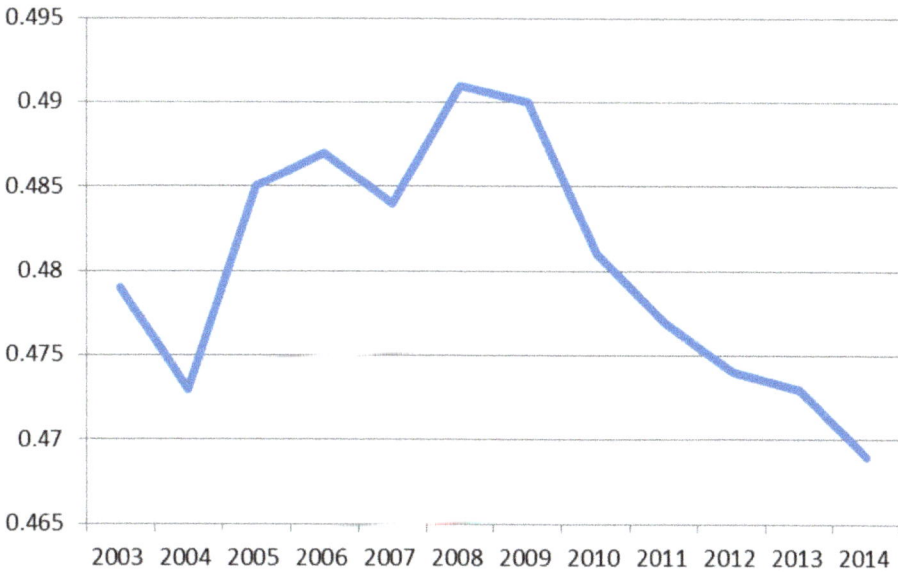

Figure 2.7 Gini coefficient of China

Source: National Bureau of Statistics.

The investment share of output continued to rise, to a peak of nearly 50 per cent in 2011, as the fiscal and monetary expansion in response to the GFC worked its way through the economy (Figure 2.8). This is extraordinarily high compared with the experience of China in earlier times and of other economies at any time. The consumption share fell to its lowest point a year or so before that (2009 for government and 2010 for household consumption) and has slowly lifted itself from the floor since then. The fall in the investment share and rise in consumption are in the directions suggested by the new model but so far are weak to the point of imperceptibility.

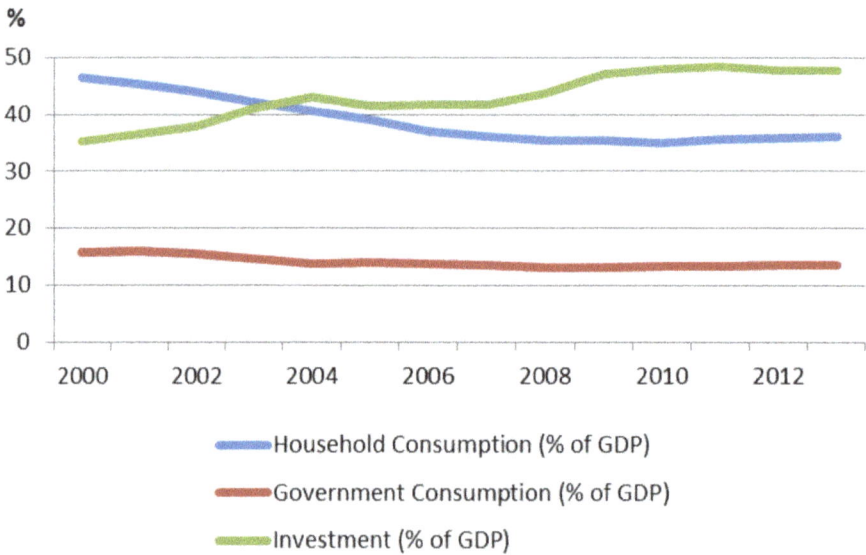

Figure 2.8 Consumption and investment share of GDP

Source: National Bureau of Statistics.

The rapid increase in domestic expenditure in the recovery from the crisis was driven much more by investment than by consumption. This was the major influence behind the rapid reduction of China's trade and current account surpluses through the post-2008 expansion (Figure 2.9).

So far, we have seen only a weak structural footprint from the new model of economic growth. This becomes clearer in Figure 2.10, which sets out The Conference Board's Beijing estimates of the contributions of growth in the labour stock, capital stock and TFP so far this century.

%

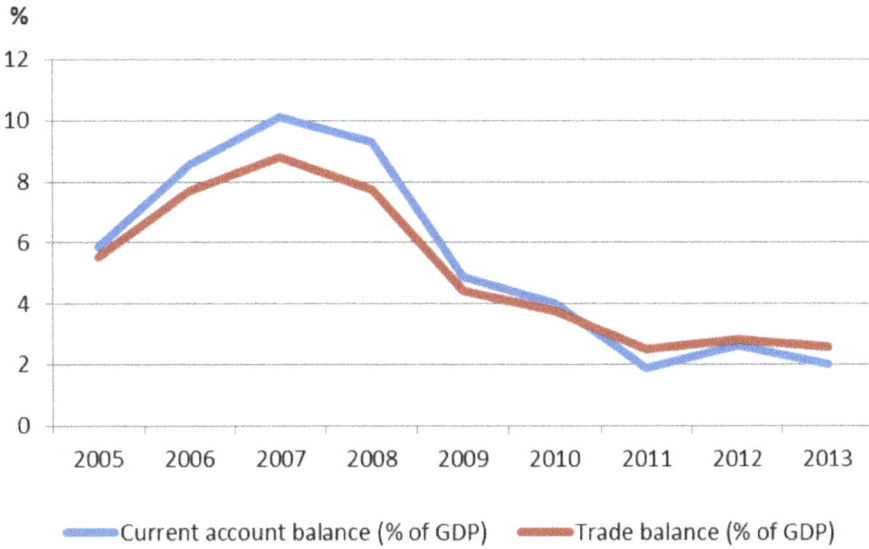

Current account balance (% of GDP) ———— Trade balance (% of GDP)

Figure 2.9 Trade balance and current account balance

Source: World Bank (various years).

%

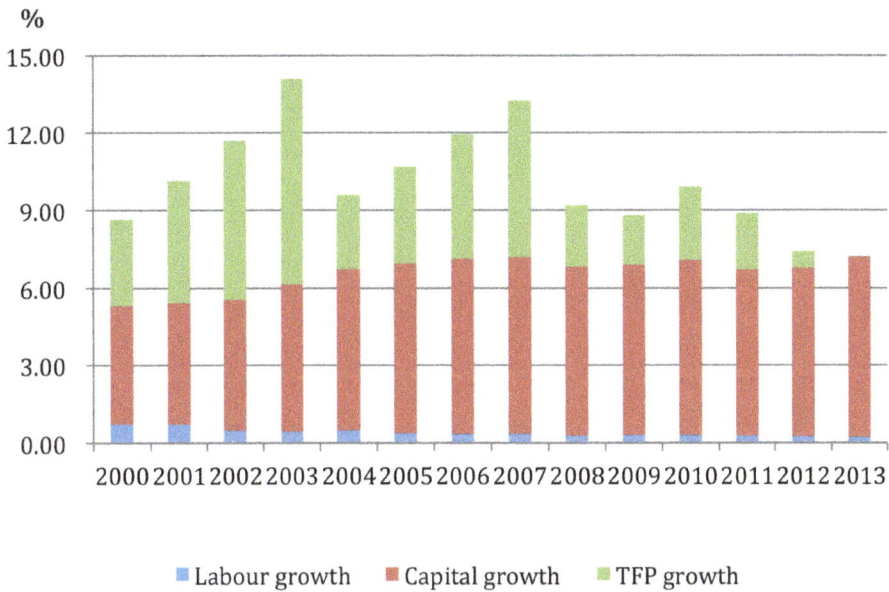

■ Labour growth ■ Capital growth ■ TFP growth

Figure 2.10 Contributions of components of GDP growth

Notes: All growth rates are calculated as the difference in the log of the levels of each variable. GDP is measured in constant 2012 US dollars. It is updated from 2005 Elteto-Köves-Szulc (EKS) procedure purchasing power parity (PPP) with GDP deflator changes. These 2005 EKS PPPs are from Penn World, which are benchmarked on 2005 PPPs from the International Comparisons Project (ICP) at the World Bank (2005).
Source: The Conference Board (2014).

The labour supply contribution to growth was small but positive early in the century and has since shrunk to negligible levels. That it remains slightly positive in the face of a declining population in the age cohorts that are conventionally considered to be the years of employment reflects some increase in labour force participation rates.

The growth in the capital stock has been the major contributor to growth in output through this century so far, except in 2003. It reached a high plateau of about 7 percentage points' contribution in 2006 and has remained there ever since.

While quantitatively less important than the capital contribution to growth in all but one year, the increase in TFP has made contributions to growth that are exceptionally large by the standards of other countries. Or, more accurately, it has made exceptionally large contributions until recently. The contribution fell markedly after the GFC in 2008 to almost negligibly low levels in 2012, and disappeared in 2013. There has been no sign of a decisive lift since then.

So, economic development since 2011 has been characterised by greater reliance on increases in the capital stock than at any time in the reform period from 1978.

This is such a striking and important piece of information that it is worth being cautious about its use. The April 2015 *World economic outlook* of the International Monetary Fund (IMF 2015) examines on a global scale the powerful tendency for TFP growth to proceed at historically low rates in many countries and regions in the twenty-first century so far, and especially in the aftermath of the GFC (Figure 2.11). It calculates 'growth potential' for many countries and sets of countries, and analyses the respective contributions to that growth potential in the labour and capital stocks and TFP. It therefore undertakes a different but similar exercise to that of The Conference Board for China.

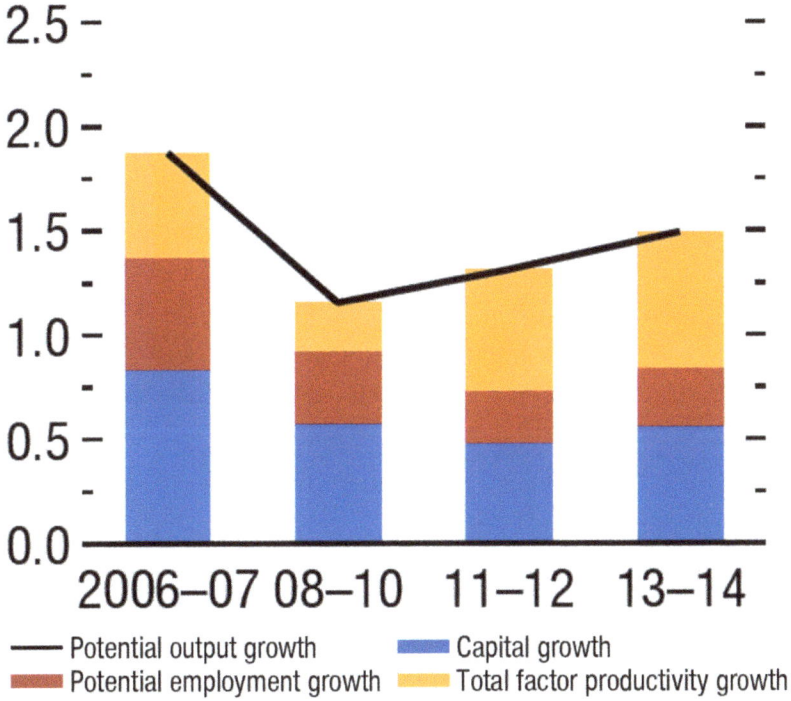

Figure 2.11 Contributions of components of potential output growth, 2006–14: Developed countries (per cent)

Source: IMF (2015).

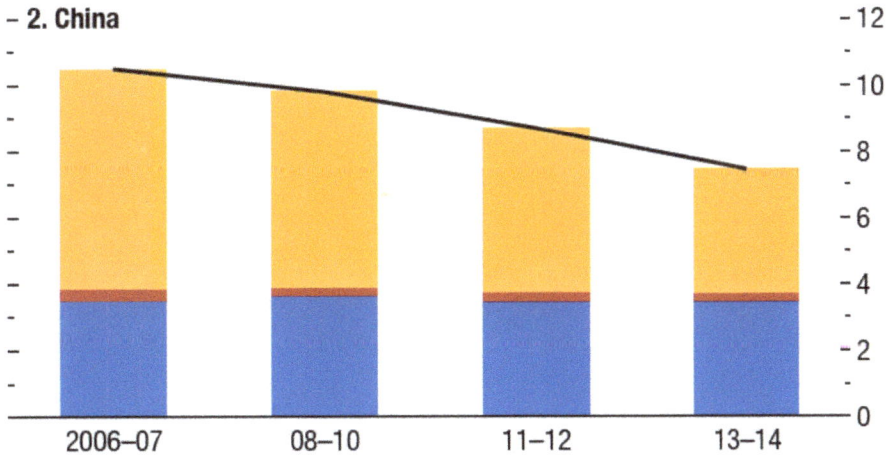

Figure 2.12 Contributions of components of potential output growth, 2006–14: China (per cent)

Source: IMF (2015).

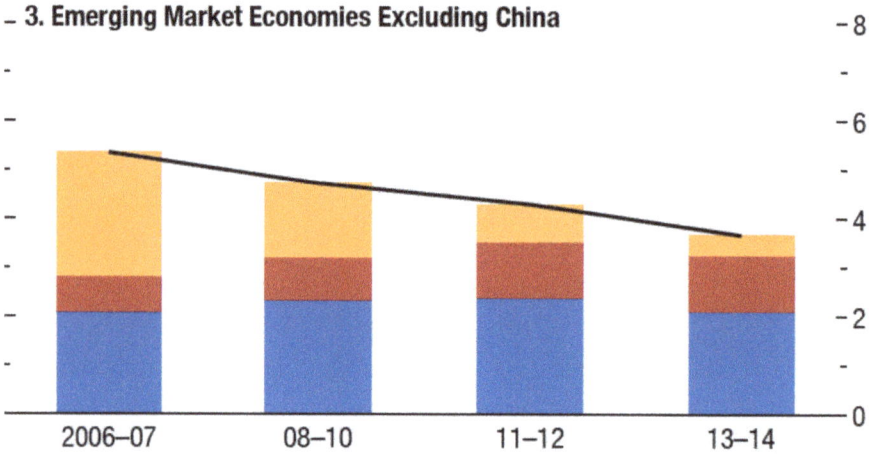

Figure 2.13 Contributions of components of potential output growth, 2006–14: Other emerging market economies (per cent)

Source: IMF (2015).

The IMF's conclusions for China are set out in Figure 2.12. They are similar to The Conference Board's results in two respects and different in two. Like The Conference Board, the IMF attributes to capital a large and steady contribution to growth potential. Like The Conference Board, it attributes a large contribution to TFP growth early in the century, and sees that contribution declining sharply during and since the GFC. However, the IMF sees TFP continuing to make a substantial if falling contribution to growth of factor productivity. And the IMF sees the capital stock continuing to make the main contribution to growth potential, but not an overwhelming one.

Part of the difference between the IMF and The Conference Board calculations derives from one looking at potential growth and the other at actual growth. If actual growth falls below potential growth, the difference will come out in the calculations as a smaller contribution from productivity growth in the former but not in the latter. In addition, there are large measurement challenges in the calculation of growth in the capital stock and therefore in calculating TFP as a residual. Differences in assumptions about rates of depreciation of the capital stock can lead to large differences in measurement of the capital stock and inversely in large differences in productivity.

We should not concern ourselves with details in the calculations. It is more useful to focus on the main general conclusions. The proportionate contribution of increase in the capital stock to growth was expected to decline over time within the new model of growth. To date, there is little sign of it having done so.

In a scenario of smooth adjustment to China's new model of growth, steady or rising contributions from increased productivity could have offset a decline in the capital contribution. Here the evidence points to the reverse: since the GFC in 2008, productivity growth has declined markedly and economic growth is now more reliant than ever on growth in the capital stock.

We cannot avoid the conclusion that China so far has made little progress towards the macroeconomic structural changes that are necessary for success. Most of the structural change required within the new model of growth lies ahead.

The recent IMF report provides some global perspective on the recent decline in total productivity growth in China. The productivity growth decline since the GFC is also significant in the developed countries (Figure 2.12; but the decline is larger when we go back to earlier years in the current century) and other 'emerging market' economies (Figure 2.13)—larger than it is in China. This adds another note of caution about the outlook for economic growth in China. Productivity growth everywhere faces stronger headwinds in the early twenty-first century, and especially since the GFC. Growth strategies that rely on return to rates of productivity growth of earlier years could turn out to be impractical. China may have to make the structural changes required for the new model of development with lower overall rates of growth than would once have been expected and that would be helpful to smooth adjustment.

Effects on the global resource sector so far

The period in which China's growth dominated world demand for energy and metals and lifted global commodities prices to unprecedented levels has come to an end. The end of the era is most decisive for commodities for which production or use has large negative effects on local and global environmental amenity.

The end of the era is illustrated in Figures 2.1 (coal) and 2.2 (steel). China accounted for most of the global increase in demand for coal and steel from early in the century and more than the whole from the GFC of 2008 until 2011. By 2011, China accounted for close to half of global use of each of these commodities. Chinese demand growth for both commodities decelerated sharply in 2012 and 2013, and became negative in 2014. This caused growth in global demand for both commodities to turn negative in 2014.

The reduction of the local and global environmental impact of Chinese economic growth has been assisted by the structural changes associated with the new model of growth. The greater immediate effects, however, have come from the focus on environmental priorities in the new model of growth, and from transitional adjustment challenges left over from the old growth model. The main contributions from the new model of growth lie ahead, as the diminution of the investment share of expenditure gathers pace.

Many elements of Chinese policy aimed at directly changing the relationship between economic growth and pressure on the natural environment have been introduced since 2011. Many policy interventions have had multiple objectives: to reduce Chinese dependence on potentially unreliable external sources of resource supply; to moderate the huge deterioration in Chinese terms of trade between 2003 and 2011; to reduce and then reverse the deterioration of local air and water quality and so to diminish detrimental impacts on health and longevity; to reduce greenhouse gas emissions and therefore to contribute to the global effort to mitigate climate change; and, in a world in which 'green' outcomes are going to be increasingly important in future, to establish China as a competitive supplier of the capital goods and services that will become important in the emerging global economy.

All of these causal influences have been at work for coal and several of them for steel.

The moderation in growth and then decline in demand for coal began with commitments to reduce the intensity of economic activity from 2006. This goal was strengthened as a commitment to reduce energy intensity of economic activity by an average of 4 per cent per annum in the Twelfth Five-Year Plan. The energy intensity of economic output fell at an increasing rate in each year from 2011, reaching nearly 5 percentage points in 2014. Chinese developments within the old growth model used energy with unusual profligacy. The improvements in energy efficiency since the GFC are part of a global tendency but go well beyond developments elsewhere because they are correcting earlier excesses. The reduction in energy intensity in China in recent years has proceeded more rapidly than in any other economy.

The developments in the electricity sector are particularly important. Electricity demand grew more rapidly than economic output through the first decade of the century. Growth in economic activity has run ahead of demand for electricity since then. In 2014, when economic output increased by 7.4 per cent, demand for electricity grew by only 3.8 per cent. The whole of the diminished demand growth plus several percentage points of total electricity supply came from zero-emissions sources: in diminishing quantitative order, hydro-electricity, wind, nuclear and solar (Table 2.1). Growth in solar electricity supply has been most rapid from a base near zero four years ago. The absolute contribution of solar to the increase in electricity supply was similar to wind and nuclear in 2014, and is set to exceed them in the years immediately ahead.

Table 2.1 Electricity generation by source, 2010–14

Quantity (million Mwh)						
Year	Total	Thermal	Hydro	Nuclear	Wind	Solar
2010	4,228	3,416	687	75	49	0
2011	4,731	3,900	668	87	74	1
2012	4,986	3,925	856	98	103	4
2013	5,372	4,222	892	112	138	9
2014	5,550	4,205	1,070	126	156	23
Rise over previous year (%)						
Year	Total	Thermal	Hydro	Nuclear	Wind	Solar
2010	14.9	13.4	20.1	6.7	78.9	74
2011	11.9	14.2	−2.7	16.7	49.9	459
2012	5.4	0.6	28.1	12.7	39.1	412
2013	7.7	7.6	4.2	14.3	34	125
2014	3.3	−0.4	20	12.5	13	156

Source: National Bureau of Statistics of China and China's National Energy Administration.

Thermal electricity output fell in 2014. Within the diminishing total, the share of zero-emission (biomass) and low-emission (gas) sources of thermal electricity rose rapidly from a low base. Thermal coal consumption fell by 2.9 per cent.

The early months of 2015 have seen an accelerated decline in thermal power generation from coal. Thermal coal use was 10 per cent lower in the March quarter than in the corresponding period of the previous year. Chinese imports of coal, which became the largest in the world through the period of strong, energy-intensive growth, fell by 42 per cent in the first quarter of 2015 compared with the previous year.

Many and varied policy interventions have been applied to moderate demand for electricity and to shift supply away from use of coal. The most powerful early interventions were regulatory: the forced closure or transformation of facilities that failed to meet increasingly high emissions standards. Propaganda played an important role in changing behaviour. Many subsidies for production and use of low-emission technologies were influential. Increased taxes and reduced subsidies on fossil fuels had large effects.

For the future, the government has heralded a shift towards greater reliance on market-based mechanisms. It has announced that the pilot emissions trading schemes in five cities and two provinces will be merged into a national emissions trading scheme from 2016. Regulatory interventions, taxes and subsidies are likely to remain important in maintaining momentum in the transformation of the local and global environmental impact of the Chinese energy sector.

Steel demand also decelerated markedly from 2012. It fell absolutely in 2014, and again in the first quarter of 2015. Production has also fallen but by smaller amounts as part of the Chinese supply has been exported with losses by the steelmaking enterprises.

For steel, the long-term structural effects of the new model of growth are large, but have been eclipsed for the time being by more immediate challenges. Steel demand has been affected powerfully by the cutback in infrastructure and real estate investment in response to oversupply and the associated fragility of financial institutions. The focus on environmental amenity, especially near the great urban regions of coastal China—Beijing–Hebei–Tianjin, Shanghai–Jiangsu–Zhejiang and the Pearl River Delta—has led to early closure of many steelmaking facilities. The effects of reduced investment shares of output lie ahead.

The deceleration of growth in Chinese steel demand after 2011, and the absolute decline in 2014 and early 2015, has been the main factor behind the absolute fall in global steel demand since 2012 (Figure 2.2). Chinese steel demand can be expected to continue to fall with the investment share of expenditure within the new model of growth. Production of new steel and demand for primary steelmaking raw materials can be expected to fall more rapidly than steel demand, as the proportion of scrap available as an input into steel production rises towards the normal levels of the developed countries with the maturation of Chinese development.

Global supply of energy and metals was slow to recognise and then respond to the acceleration of Chinese demand growth from the beginning of the century. That contributed to the extraordinary increase in global prices for almost all metals and energy. Global supply eventually responded to higher prices and prospects for increased demand; but the largest expansion in supply, from 2011, coincided with the deceleration of and then decline in Chinese demand.

The global price profiles for coal, oil and copper in Figures 2.3, 2.4 and 2.5 are similar to those for nickel, iron ore, gas and most other commodities: sharp increases from 2003 to the eve of the GFC in 2008; large falls in late 2008 and 2009; a rise to near or beyond pre-GFC heights in 2010 and 2011; and declines from 2011 with the coincidence of deceleration of demand growth in China and increased global supply. The global resources industries are left with a problem of oversupply and the challenge of adjustment of historic dimension.

China, like other resource-importing countries, has benefited from oversupply of metals and energy through a large improvement in its terms of trade. Continued gains from this source will ease the costs of adjustment to the new model of growth. Low and declining prices can be expected to continue until enough old or new supply capacity has been removed to establish a global balance between supply and demand at a lower level of Chinese demand.

The improvement of Chinese terms of trade since 2011 has already been of large dimension and has further to go. It is the other side of the coin to the large fall in the terms of trade, adjustment challenges and setbacks to economic growth in resource-exporting countries. Australia has been experiencing slow growth in incomes and employment since Chinese demand and global prices for metals and energy began to fall in 2011, and will be grappling with the consequences of the end of the resources boom for many years (Garnaut 2013). Indonesian policy dampened the supply response to the higher metals and energy prices for all commodities except coal, but the supply response in coal was strong enough to leave the country with a major adjustment problem in the aftermath of the boom (Garnaut forthcoming 2015). Johnston has drawn attention to the sharp deceleration of growth in West African countries with the fall in export prices for metals and energy (Johnston this volume).

China's increased prominence in the global economy in the twenty-first century has made adjustment to its new model of growth a major challenge for the rest of the world.

The prospects for Chinese growth and the global resources sector

The lower rates of growth in China since 2011 seem to reflect the effects of structural problems inherent in the old model of growth as much or more than the effects of transition to the new model of growth. While the long, upward movement in the investment share of output and the fall in the consumption share have been brought to an end, the reversal of the old trends has barely begun. While the upward adjustment in domestic expenditure relative to income has secured the necessary moderation of the immense pre-crisis trade and current account surpluses, it did this through increasing investment more than consumption. There has been considerable moderation in investment in industries excessively favoured by the old model of growth so far without significant moderation of overall rates of investment. And the large decline in productivity growth is reducing the prospects for the eventual decline in the capital contribution to growth being substantially offset from this source, at least in the early stages of transition.

China has made a start on the transition to its new model of growth. It has made a big start in reduction of the environmental impact of economic growth; but all elements of transition have a long way to go.

References

BP (2015), *Energy charting tool*, London: BP. Available from: www.bp.com/en/global/corporate/about-bp/energy-economics/energy-charting-tool.html.

Cai, F. (2010), Demographic transition, demographic dividend and Lewis turning point in China, *China Economic Journal*, 3(2): 107–19.

Chai, J. (2015), *Under the dome*, [Documentary]. Available from: www.youtube.com/watch?v=MhIZ50HKIp0. Retrieved May 2015.

Chen, Y.Y., Ebenstein, A., Greenstone, M. and Li, H.B. (2013), Evidence on the impact of sustained exposure to air pollution on life expectancy from China's Huai River policy, *Proceedings of National Academy of Sciences of the US*, 8 July, Beijing.

Datastream, a standing online commercial data service provider.

EIA U.S. Energy Information Administration providing Official Energy Statistics from the U.S. Government

Garnaut, R. (2010), Macro-economic implications of the turning point, *China Economic Journal*, 3(2): 181–90.

Garnaut, R. (2013), *Dog days: Australia after the boom*, Melbourne: Black Inc.

Garnaut, R. (forthcoming 2015), Indonesia's resources boom in international perspective: Policy dilemmas and options for continued strong growth (the Ninth Sadli Lecture), *Bulletin of Indonesian Economic Studies*.

Garnaut, R. and Song, L.G. (eds) (2006), *The turning point in China's economic development*, Canberra: ANU E Press.

Garnaut, R., Cai, F. and Song, L.G. (eds) (2013a), *China: A new model for growth and development*, Canberra: ANU E Press.

Garnaut, R., Cai, F. and Song, L.G. (2013b), China's new strategy for long-term growth and development: Imperatives and implications, in Garnaut, R., Cai, F. and Song, L.G. (eds), *China: A new model for growth and development*, Canberra: ANU E Press, pp. 1–16.

Huang, Y. and Cai, F. (eds) (2013), *Debating the Lewis turning point in China*, London: Routledge.

Huang, Y. and Jiang, T. (2010), What does the Lewis turning point mean for China? A computable general equilibrium analysis, *China Economic Journal*, 3(2): 191–207.

Huang, Y., Fang, F., Xu, P. and Xin, G. (2013), The new normal of Chinese development, in Garnaut, R., Cai, F. and Song, L.G. (eds), *China: A new model for growth and development*, Canberra: ANU E Press, pp. 35–54.

Index Mundi (2014), *Coal, Australian thermal coal monthly price: US dollars per metric ton*, Index Mundi. Available from: www.indexmundi.com/commodities/?commodity=coal-australian.

International Monetary Fund (IMF) (2015), *World economic outlook: Uneven growth—Short- and long-term factors April 2015*, Washington, DC: IMF. Available from: www.imf.org/external/pubs/ft/weo/2015/01/. Retrieved May 2015.

IMF—IFS International Financial Statistics of the IMF, an international organization publishing a range of time series data on IMF lending, exchange rates and other economic and financial indicators.

McLeod, R.H. and Garnaut, R. (eds) (1998), *East Asia in crisis: From being a miracle to needing one?*, London and New York: Routledge.

National Bureau of Statistics of China, a government agency directly under the State Council, in charge of statistics and economic accounting in China.

National Energy Administration of China, responsible for formulating and implementing energy development plans and industrial policies, and also provides related data series.

Penn World Table from Center for International Comparisons at the University of Pennsylvania, provides purchasing power parity and national income accounts converted to international prices for 189 countries/territories for some or all of the years 1950–2010.

Perkins, D.H. (2013), New institutions for a new development model, in Garnaut, R., Cai, F. and Song, L.G. (eds), *China: A new model for growth and development*, Canberra: ANU E Press, pp. 17–34.

The Conference Board (2014), *Total economy database*, January, New York: The Conference Board. Available from: www.conference-board.org/data/economydatabase/.

Wong, C. (2015), Can Xi Jinping's reforms be implemented? Let's look at China's fiscal architecture, Centre for Contemporary Chinese Studies academic seminar, 5 March 2015, University of Melbourne.

World Bank (various years), *World development indicators*, Washington, DC: The World Bank. Available from: data.worldbank.org/data-catalog/world-development-indicators.

World Steel Association (2015), *Crude steel production 2014–2015*, Brussels: World Steel Association. Available from: www.worldsteel.org/statistics/crude-steel-production.html.

Yu, Y. (2009), China's policy responses to the global financial crisis, The 2009 Snape Lecture, Australian Productivity Commission, Melbourne. Available from: www.pc.gov.au/news-media/snape-lectures/yongding. Retrieved May 2015.

3. A Compelling Case for Chinese Monetary Easing

Guonan Ma[1]

Introduction

This chapter makes a strong case for Chinese monetary policy easing, contributing to the debate over whether China's latest monetary policy shift is warranted and desirable. Chinese monetary policy was excessively tight in 2014 but started loosening more meaningfully from late 2014, in an attempt to cushion growth, facilitate rebalancing, support reform and mitigate financial risk.

There are three main reasons justifying this shift in monetary policy stance. First, there is evidence that the Chinese economy has been operating below its potential capacity. Second, among the big-five (G5) economies, both China's monetary policy stance and its broader financial condition tightened the most in the wake of the global financial crisis (GFC). This weighed on Chinese domestic demand. Third, a mix of accommodative monetary policy and neutral fiscal policy would serve China the best now, as the country opens up its capital account and moves away from its dollar peg, while restructuring its local government finance.

However, such a warranted shift in monetary policy faces challenges of uncertain potential growth, a more liberal financial system, an evolving monetary policy framework, a legacy of excess leverage and a politicised policy debate.

The rest of the chapter is organised as follows. Section two highlights the two competing schools of thought in the heated debate over Chinese monetary policy that took place in mid-2014. Sections three to five lay out the three arguments for monetary policy easing: a Taylor rule perspective, a global perspective and an optimal monetary policy mix perspective. Section six concludes, suggesting that a timely and sensible monetary accommodation could be the best course of policy action for China in terms of growth, reform, rebalancing and financial stability.

---

1   The views expressed in this chapter are those of the author only and not of the affiliated institutions. The author wishes to acknowledge Warren Lu for his excellent research assistance. Any errors are mine.

The Chinese monetary policy debate

Monetary policymaking can be tough and controversial, as illustrated by discussions about whether and how the European Central Bank (ECB) ought to pursue quantitative easing (Claeys et al. 2014), and whether and when the US Federal Reserve (US Fed) should start normalising.

Similar discussions started heating up in mid-2014 about China's monetary policy stance (Ma 2014a). They centred on whether Chinese monetary policy was excessively tight at that time and thus ought to ease in a timely and meaningful way. From late 2014, the People's Bank of China (PBC) started to act more decisively to ease its monetary policy—most notably, its three rate cuts and another broad reserve requirement ratio (RRR) cut during late 2014 and early 2015. Did the PBC make a big policy mistake, perhaps by succumbing to political pressure from vested interests? The short answer is no, and the rest of this chapter will make a case for Chinese monetary accommodation.

This policy debate also broadened, sometimes in a confusing manner, to encompass the related question of whether China should persist with painful but eventually rewarding economic reform or ease monetary policy to stabilise growth.

There are two views on this (Sina Finance 2014). One camp believes that monetary accommodation hampers economic reform, worsens structural imbalances in the Chinese economy and promotes unsustainable short-term pseudo-growth at the expense of sustainable long-term development. This camp's main arguments appear to be that reforms and structural adjustments are necessarily painful and that the recent economic slowdown is simply structural and healthy. According to this view, demand-side factors matter little in the recent Chinese growth slowdown. Thus, an accommodative monetary policy is unwarranted and at odds with reform and restructuring. Instead, monetary easing is not only a show of no confidence in reform but also an attempt to sabotage reform. In short, no pain, no gain.

The less ideologically driven argument points to a still buoyant Chinese labour market in spite of weaker growth as evidence of an economy near its lower growth potential. A shrinking Chinese labour force, a possible Lewis turning point, a bigger job-intense service sector and the attendant slower total productivity growth might all combine to trim underlying growth potential consistent with non-inflationary full employment (Ma et al. 2012). Therefore, slower headline gross domestic product (GDP) growth can still be compatible with an economy operating at or near full capacity, questioning any need for monetary accommodation. Such concerns are valid and will be addressed in this chapter.

The opposite, pro-easing camp thinks that sensible, nimble monetary easing complements economic reform, cushions growth, facilitates structural adjustment and mitigates financial risk. Reform, while imperative, is not a sacred cow but a means to improve living standards for the majority of the Chinese population. And economic reform calls for a sensible shift in the monetary policy stance in response to business cycles. The Chinese economy is unbalanced, but one does not need to strangle it in order to rebalance it. On the contrary, an excessively tight monetary policy could aggravate structural imbalances.

According to the easing camp, the Taylor rule, the global beauty contest of monetary easing among the G5 central banks—the US Fed, the PBC, Bank of Japan (BoJ), ECB and Bank of England (BoE)—and the Mundell–Fleming model all suggest an excessively tight monetary policy stance for most of 2014, and thus a need for a meaningful Chinese monetary relaxation. Both cyclically and structurally, the case for timely and measured monetary accommodation is compelling.

This controversy in China looks odd, especially when viewed through the lens of the United States, the euro area and Japan, where the consensus view among policymakers is that aggressive demand-support policy measures and strong structural reforms on the supply side should go hand-in-hand. And why not? The puzzling question is why one should have to make a stark choice between them instead of sensibly combining the two. A healthy Chinese economy needs both structural reforms on the supply side to enhance potential growth and a nimble monetary policy to exploit potential and mitigate possible cyclical headwinds on the demand side.

It is important to note that this debate takes place in a wider domestic and international context that includes issues such as diverging global monetary policies, volatile cross-border capital flows, slower domestic economic growth, falling domestic inflation, painful economic rebalancing, a gathering pace of financial liberalisation, signs of increased financial stress and an evolving monetary policy framework. So we first briefly sketch this background before discussing the debate itself.

After three decades of double-digit growth from 1980 to 2010, the Chinese economy embarked on a transition to a new phase of its development in the wake of the GFC (Ma et al. 2012). This transition features a slower pace of growth, a shrinking current account surplus and a service sector in the process of catching-up. GDP growth slowed from 10 per cent averaged during 2000–10 to 8 per cent during 2011–14, and is expected to decelerate further, to 7 per cent in 2015, while the current account surplus fell from 10 per cent of GDP in 2007 to 2 per cent in 2014. Such external rebalancing is attained mostly through an even more lopsided internal imbalance of a higher investment ratio and rising leverage.

In the midst of the heated monetary policy debate, the PBC, since mid-2014, has started loosening its monetary policy, initially tentatively and then more forcefully. Is such a policy shift warranted and desirable? I will make a strong case for meaningful Chinese monetary easing based on the following three arguments.

First, the standard Taylor rule suggests an excessively tight Chinese monetary policy stance for most of 2014. Second, after the GFC, the PBC's monetary policy stance tightened the most among the G5 central banks, and Chinese financial conditions also became most restrictive among these economies. Third, the classical Mundell–Fleming model suggests a sensible mix of accommodative monetary policy and neutral fiscal policy, as China is moving towards greater currency flexibility, incremental capital opening and tighter local fiscal conditions.

A Taylor rule perspective

First, we look at the case for monetary easing in terms of inflation, output and financial stability objectives within the standard Taylor rule framework. There is broad consensus among economists that Chinese growth has been losing momentum in recent years (Figure 3.1). There have been clear signs of rising inventories, slumping property sales, falling consumer price index (CPI) inflation, deepening producer price deflation, weakening corporate earnings, slowing investment and anaemic industrial production. Fortunately, private consumption is still holding up—but just barely—and could show early signs of weakening. If anything, some market commentators even suspect that the Chinese official headline GDP numbers overstate the underlying growth momentum (Nakamura et al. 2015).

An immediate question therefore is if Chinese monetary policy was too tight for most of 2014, relative to what was it too tight?

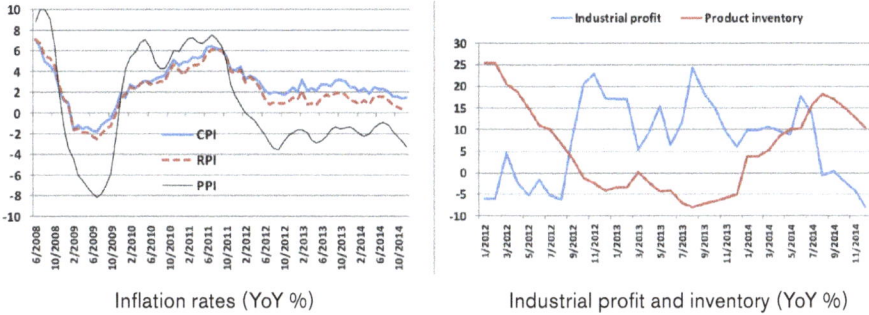

Figure 3.1 Chinese inflation, industrial profit and inventory

Source: CIEC.

As a starting point, most economists and central bankers use the well-known Taylor rule to assess the central bank's policy stance (Taylor 1993). A standard Taylor rule essentially links a short-term nominal policy rate to two gaps for a given inflation target and real long-run equilibrium interest rate consistent with trend growth: the gap between actual and targeted inflation ('the inflation gap') and the gap between actual and potential output ('the output gap'). A positive output or inflation gap, or both, suggests a need to tighten by hiking the policy rate. If the actual policy rate is below that implied by the Taylor rule, the policy stance is considered too accommodating. If the actual policy rate is above that implied by the Taylor rule, the policy stance is considered too restrictive.

In reality, many factors help to shape this 'Taylor rate'—hence the controversy in China over how tight the PBC's monetary policy was before the latest monetary relaxation. In light of this, three useful questions can be highlighted. What weight does the PBC attach to inflation? Has the Chinese economy been operating near full capacity? How should one gauge the PBC's monetary policy stance?

First, how important is inflation relative to other policy objectives? The PBC is officially not of inflation targeting type, flexible or otherwise. The 1994 Chinese central bank law explicitly stipulates four policy objectives for the PBC: price stability, employment, economic growth and balance of payments. In practice, financial stability and credit allocation are also high on the PBC's agenda. However, Girardin et al. (2014) estimate the PBC's monetary policy reaction function and conclude that inflation has been given greater weight relative to output from the 2000s. This was more so after the start of Zhou Xiaochuan's governorship of the PBC in 2001.

Chinese CPI inflation fell noticeably—from an average 2.5 per cent in 2013 to 2.2 per cent in the first half of 2014, and to 1.8 per cent in the second half of 2014, below the official 2014 target of 3.5 per cent. It even sank to about 1 per cent in the first quarter of 2015—the lowest level in five years. Retail prices also paint a broadly disinflationary picture. Producer prices have even registered outright and persistent deflation for more than two years (Figure 3.1). The pronounced disinflationary pressure emerged well before the collapse of international oil prices starting from the third quarter of 2014. Inflation in China is probably now too low for comfort. According to the Taylor rule, therefore, the PBC ought to ease monetary policy, all other things being equal.

Indeed, the intensified disinflation or even outright deflation pressure since early 2014 helped push up real interest rates even as the nominal policy rate stood still at a time of weakening growth. The first half of 2014 even witnessed rising nominal Chinese government bond yields. One can debate whether the deflation pressure is good or bad, but by doing nothing the PBC would imply a de facto tightening of its monetary policy, which might have contributed to slower economic growth on the demand side beyond what is justified by the structural trends on the supply side.

Second, is the Chinese economy operating near full employment or potential? This is a tricky question. The recent economic slowdown might simply reflect lower potential growth, which could arise from rebalancing pains, demographic headwinds, less low-hanging fruit in market liberalisation and a less accommodating global economy (Ma et al. 2012). Unfortunately, Chinese growth potential, while likely trending lower, is not directly observable, and estimates of it can be elusive and have big margins of error (Blagrave et al. 2015; Ma and Hong 2015; Morley 2014). Some Chinese labour statistics seem to suggest that employment has held up well, as wages are still rising. Thus, weaker growth might not necessarily imply a widening negative output gap and rising unemployment, and hence there would be no case for policy easing.

In the absence of more consistent, reliable and accurate estimates of the underlying Chinese potential growth rate, what can help inform us about the likely output gap? The persistent and intensifying disinflationary and even deflationary pressures at a time of marked deceleration of economic growth are the most telling signs that the Chinese economy is operating well below its potential capacity. It adds to the already high real corporate debt burden, especially for Chinese manufacturing borrowers.

Nevertheless, rapid wage hikes and an apparent lack of corporate pricing power could also combine to hurt corporate earnings, resulting in declining returns on capital and thus weaker private investment spending. Rising real interest rates will tend to punish the most productive and interest rate-sensitive sector in the Chinese economy—small, private firms—as well as consumers. Thus, lower rather than higher nominal and real interest rates are warranted.

Moreover, it is not clear whether the reported buoyancy of the headline Chinese job market is mainly in the unskilled segment or the broader labour market. Labour market data are known to be the weakest link in Chinese statistics (Amstad et al. 2014; Ma et al. 2012). In addition, the starting salary for Chinese university graduates has been stagnant in recent years. Further, the latest Chinese Purchasing Manager Index (PMI) employment subindex shows early cooling signs in the labour market. In fact, the first quarter of 2015 saw a sharp slowdown in new non-farm jobs. One might reasonably expect a much softer Chinese labour market for the rest of 2015. Therefore, monetary policymakers ought to anticipate rather than wait, as it takes a few quarters for monetary policy actions to affect the labour market.

Whichever way one argues, slower potential economic growth should ultimately point to a lower real equilibrium or natural rate of interest, as assumed by the Taylor rule. Yet, oddly, what we witnessed was rapidly rising real borrowing costs for Chinese firms and home buyers amid slowing growth, until the PBC acted more decisively to ease its policy stance from late 2014 (Figure 3.2). This rise in the 'risk-free' interest rate was the combined result of falling inflation and rising government bond yields: between 2012 and mid-2014, the 10-year Chinese government bond yield rose from 2.5 per cent to 4.5 per cent, as CPI fell from 4 per cent to 2.5 per cent. Therefore, a less stringent monetary policy stance is called for, whether the recent growth slowdown is structural or cyclical.

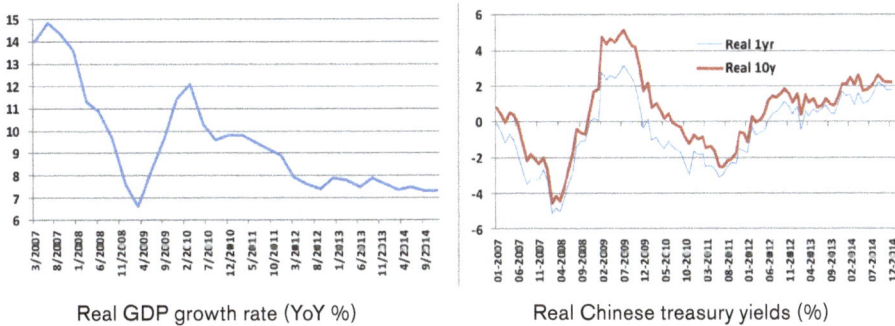

Real GDP growth rate (YoY %)   Real Chinese treasury yields (%)

Figure 3.2 Real Chinese GDP growth and government bond yields

Sources: Bloomberg and CEIC.

In short, on the grounds of both the inflation gap and the output gap, the Taylor rule recommends a shift towards a less restrictive monetary policy stance.

This case would have closed, unless financial stability concerns rank higher on the PBC's agenda. An interest rate that is too low could fuel unsustainable shadow banking expansion, excess leverage and asset price booms. China has experienced a massive credit binge since 2007, with total credit to the non-financial private sector, including the rapidly expanding shadow banking sector, rising from 120 per cent of GDP in 2007 to 180 per cent in 2014 (Figure 3.3). If central and local government debts are included, the overall leverage in China could approach 250 per cent of GDP. Thus, an excessively loose monetary policy could potentially add to the already growing financial imbalances.

Nevertheless, excessively tight monetary conditions could also run the risk of disorderly deleveraging. First, our knowledge about the effects of monetary policy on financial stability is still limited, which may involve complex dynamics of intertemporal cost–benefit trade-offs (Ajello et al. 2015; Svensson 2015). Second, macro-prudential measures rather than monetary policy might be a better instrument to deal with financial stability issues in most cases (Claeys and Darvas 2015). Third, as nominal GDP slowed from the 15–20 per cent range in the 2000s to some 10 per cent this decade and below 8 per cent lately (Figure 3.3), an excessively restrictive monetary policy could aggravate the already rising debt-service pressures rather than mitigating them and indeed could instigate a dangerous debt deflation spiral.

In any case, while the standard Taylor rule is silent on the weight placed on financial stability relative to that on both output and inflation, the increased financial stress, as witnessed by rising non-performing loans, more credit events and increased last-minute bailouts of troubled borrowers, intuitively calls for a more accommodative monetary policy to assist the tricky deleveraging process. Sticking to a tight policy in the face of increased financial fragility makes little sense.

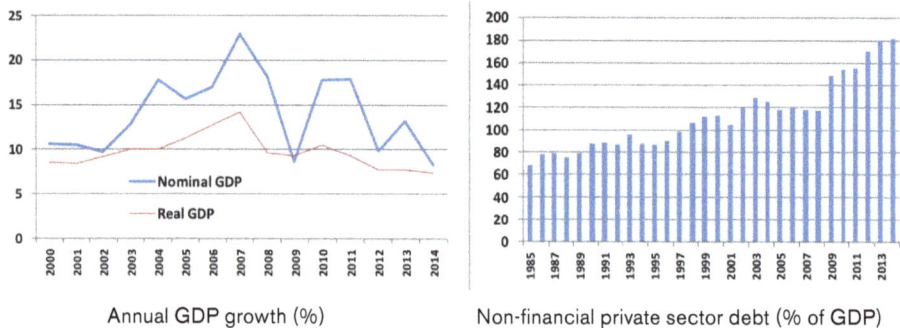

Annual GDP growth (%)   Non-financial private sector debt (% of GDP)

Figure 3.3 Nominal and real GDP growth and private-sector debt in China

Sources: BIS and CEIC.

Third, how can one tell whether the PBC has in fact loosened its stance or not? Gauging the Chinese monetary policy stance is far from straightforward (Girardin et al. 2014; Ma et al. 2012). Essentially, the PBC has pursued a three-pronged target of money supply, interest rate and exchange rate, defying any simple interpretation of its policy stance. Also, in contrast with most central banks in advanced economies, its policy rate is but one of many instruments in the PBC's toolkit. The PBC traditionally deployed multiple tools, including window guidance, soft loan quotas, regulatory rules, reserve requirements, issuance of PBC bills, open market operations, relending and interest rates, both market and administered—the interactions of which could reinforce or offset the policy effect (Ma et al. 2012).

Moreover, for most of 2014, the PBC shunned most of its traditionally favoured instruments and instead experimented with new policy tools. It suspended new issuance of PBC bills altogether from the end of 2013, stopped conducting regular open market operations for more than a year, and tested a few new weapons in its arsenal—probably in an attempt to influence market-based interest rates in an environment of volatile two-way capital flows and more liberalised interest rates.[2] The pros and cons of these new instruments aside, most PBC watchers find it harder than before to read its underlying monetary policy stance.

Further, the PBC often communicates its policy stance in a confusing manner. Its policy statements are opaque and difficult to decode even for seasoned PBC watchers. The PBC has a history of intentionally surprising and sometimes even misleading the market, which should be taken as a sign of low confidence on the part of the Chinese central bank. While many Organisation for Economic Cooperation and Development (OECD) central banks now provide 'forward guidance' to reinforce and amplify the impact of monetary policy on the full market yield curve, by communicating to the public about the expected future path of the policy rate, the PBC often appears to dilute what it has just done, by issuing puzzling 'backward guidance', cautioning the market not to interpret its latest rate and RRR cuts as monetary easing (Ma 2015).

Nevertheless, the signs of monetary easing since mid-2014 have been numerous and beyond doubt. Initially, the PBC selectively lowered its RRR and extended loans to small banks and policy banks via its refinancing facilities. It has even leaned on commercial banks to lend more to first-time homebuyers at official mortgage rates. Liquidity has also been injected via its new facilities in an apparent attempt to keep a lid on interbank interest rates. From late 2014, the PBC finally acted more decisively, by cutting outright benchmark bank deposit and lending interest rates as well as the RRR. Some of these belated moves aimed to offset the tighter domestic liquidity arising from increased dollar outflows and thus may not be as expansionary as they look. Nevertheless, in combination, these moves must be interpreted as meaningful monetary relaxation.

---

2   The PBC has in less than two years introduced and tested a number of new policy instruments, such as 'short-term liquidity operations', the 'standing lending facility', 'medium-term lending facility', 'pledged supplementary lending' and 'pledged relending'. A detailed discussion of the pros and cons of these new tools is beyond the scope of this chapter.

The PBC can be more forthright in communicating its desire to hit lower and steadier short-term or even mid-term rates, paving the way for the transition to a new monetary policy regime. A clear and firm PBC policy signal could also help flatten and stabilise the Chinese yield curve, which matters more for investment and consumption decisions. As a minimum, the PBC should avoid diluting the signalling effect of its own new policy moves.

Also, lowering the benchmark 18.5 per cent RRR would help nudge down long yields by adding permanent liquidity into the system and offsetting the tightening effect of the capital outflows seen in the fourth quarter of 2014 and the first quarter of 2015, and would also go some way towards mitigating distortions and containing shadow banking by bringing some off-balance-sheet lending back onto the books. Failures to sterilise capital outflows would result in de facto monetary tightening at a time of weakening growth and falling inflation.

More importantly, by acting swiftly and decisively, the PBC can be in a stronger position to tighten again when the cycle turns.

Monetary policy measures need to be taken early in order to counter the headwinds that the Chinese economy faces, because it typically takes two to four quarters for a change in policy stance to take effect. Indeed, timely policy response is the best way to avoid excessive monetary stimulus. Some academics and investors tend to underappreciate the fact that the mind-boggling credit binge in late 2008—mostly related to local government borrowing—was in part a poor response to the already emerging panic partially triggered by the late monetary policy actions at that time (Tanaka 2010). Much of this belated, massive monetary expansion funded quasi-fiscal spending rather than helping cushion the Chinese economy via standard channels, so this time, China ought to ease in a timely way.

To sum up, in light of growth, inflation and financial stability, the standard Taylor rule suggests that China ought to ease its monetary policy in a timely and confident manner.

A global perspective

So far, this chapter has made a domestic case for monetary relaxation, as the discussion has been framed mostly within a closed-economy version of the Taylor rule. Can a similar case be made for Chinese monetary relaxation from a global perspective? While China's capital control still binds (Ma and McCauley 2008, 2013) and central banks set monetary policy mainly to cater for domestic needs in most economies, the question is still meaningful, because China is the top trader, second-largest economy and third-largest creditor nation globally. Of course, China, known for its export-led growth model, hardly qualifies as a closed economy.

Reserve Bank of India Governor Raghuram Rajan recently raised concerns about the international spillovers from 'competitive monetary easing' among major central banks (Rajan 2014). Rajan's concerns make sense. By definition, the world is a closed economy and is often dominated by a few major central banks that behave more like price setters than price takers. 'Price' in this context used to be some benchmark short rate only, but in the wake of the GFC it also included the fuller yield curve. Thus, strong policy measures taken by major central banks ought to produce global repercussions.

This, in turn, poses the interesting question of how loose or tight China's monetary policy might be relative to its major international peers. In particular, how did the PBC fare in the global race towards monetary accommodation after the GFC? Has the PBC outdone its global peers in the monetary loosening game? This is a question of global perspective, and there is no better benchmark than the club of the central banks that issue the four constituent currencies of the International Monetary Fund (IMF) Special Drawing Rights (SDRs): the Fed, the ECB, BoJ and BoE.

We know that most of these major central banks have substantially expanded their balance sheets in recent years (Iwata and Takenaka 2012). We also know that China has experienced a massive credit binge since 2007. However, to assess the relative monetary policy stances of these four major central banks and the PBC, we need to compare apples with apples more directly.

One way to do so is to look at two key price indicators—the real policy rate and the real effective exchange rate—taking into account three considerations. First, the Taylor rule suggests that the real policy rate should relate to the deviation of actual from target inflation, the output gap and the short-term rate consistent with non-inflationary full employment. Second, the best measure of the global strength of a currency is the real effective exchange rate. Third, these two price indicators interrelate and define the two core aspects of a central bank's monetary policy operations and stance.

Both the real policy rate and the real effective exchange rate used here are ex post. I define the real policy rate as the policy rate less concurrent CPI inflation. I also use the CPI-based real effective exchange rate compiled by the Bank for International Settlements (BIS). To examine the relative monetary policy tightness of the G5 central banks since the GFC, I focus on the period between January 2007 and March 2014 before the PBC finally started easing and the US Fed hinted at normalising.

The left-hand panel of Figure 3.4 shows that all G5 central banks except the PBC have negative real policy rates. Indeed, the US Fed, the ECB and the BoE persistently maintained negative real policy rates during the period, financial repression or otherwise. Even the BoJ managed to push its real policy rate into negative territory after 2013, as inflation rose in the wake of its 'quantitative and qualitative easing'. Some other central banks—the National Bank of Denmark, ECB and Swiss National Bank—even imposed outright negative nominal policy rates. In any case, China no doubt had the highest real policy rates among the five major central banks during this period.

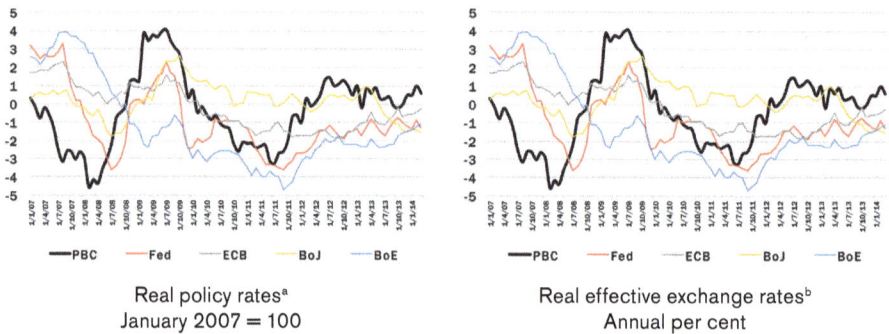

Real policy rates[a]
January 2007 = 100

Real effective exchange rates[b]
Annual per cent

Figure 3.4 Real policy rates and real effective exchange rates for G5 central banks

[a] Policy rate less actual CPI inflation. The official ceiling for the one-year deposit rate is taken as the policy rate of the PBC.
[b] CNY = Chinese renminbi; USD = US dollar; EUR = euro; JPY = Japanese yen; and GBP = British pound.
Sources: Datastream and BIS.

Of course, unconventional monetary policy went one step further to influence the long end of the yield curve. The exchange rates of the big four SDR currencies were thus indirectly influenced. In China's case, the PBC directly manages both its interest rate and its exchange rate, to some extent, given the still binding capital controls frustrating cross-border arbitrage (Ma and McCauley 2008, 2013). Either way, the real effective exchange rate serves to highlight another important aspect of monetary policy; and sustained and large movements in currencies redistribute growth across the globe.

The BIS real effective exchange rate data reveal that among the G5 currencies, only the Chinese renminbi (RMB) showed sizeable appreciation (35 per cent) from 2007 to mid-2014 (the right-hand panel of Figure 3.4). Meanwhile, the other four SDR member currencies (the dollar, euro, yen and sterling) had registered 5 per cent to 15 per cent real effective depreciation. Note that the yen appreciated noticeably between 2007 and 2012 until the start of the so-called 'Abenomics', but by March 2014 had weakened by 30 per cent from its peak in 2011. Since mid-2014, the divergent monetary policies of major central banks have led to broad and marked US dollar strength, pushing a still loosely dollar-anchored RMB even stronger in broad real effective terms (not shown in Figure 3.4). A much stronger and potentially overvalued RMB likely further redistributed growth away from China to the rest of the world.

Therefore, both the real policy rate and the real effective exchange rate suggest that the PBC maintained the most restrictive policy stance among the G5 central banks after the GFC. Among them, the BoE appears to have pursued the most aggressive monetary easing to date, and the PBC was by far the most restrained, until it more decisively embarked on a cycle of monetary relaxation from mid-2014 and the US Fed stopped its asset purchases.

What are the implications of a marked monetary tightening by the PBC relative to the four SDR central banks before its latest monetary policy shift? There are at least three as far as China is concerned.

First, China bore the brunt of the global demand and current account rebalancing from 2007 to 2014. Both rising domestic real interest rates and a strengthening real effective exchange rate have produced considerable pressures on the twin external and internal rebalancing. This tighter Chinese monetary policy stance has no doubt added significant deflationary headwinds to a slowing Chinese economy already experiencing a rapidly shrinking current-account surplus (Ma et al. 2012) and a marked weakening in domestic demand. Indeed, such a rapid adjustment in the Chinese current account balance itself could have been one important factor behind China's leveraging up in the past decade.

Second, this deflationary headwind was only partially countered by a massive credit binge that can be best viewed more as a quasi-fiscal stimulus than a proper monetary accommodation. China's relative monetary tightening thus could have aggravated its domestic imbalance, because much of this de facto fiscal stimulus funded hasty investment projects often undertaken by local governments and state firms. A timely and measured shift towards monetary relaxation would better cushion growth through those more market-based, though sometimes not very smooth, transmission channels.

Third, China's relatively tight monetary policy has probably absorbed much of the international spillover from the competitive monetary easing implemented by other major central banks, by not adding to the massive global monetary stimulus. This should in turn help dampen the volatility of those highly pro-cyclical capital flows to emerging markets and ease the competitive devaluation pressure globally. China has so far endured external deflationary shocks, acting as a source of global financial stability.

The bottom line is that in the wake of the GFC, the PBC's stance was the most restrictive among the G5 central banks. In other words, the PBC was quite restrained, while the other big four central banks pursued more aggressive monetary accommodation. There is little doubt that the relatively tight Chinese monetary policy both redistributed global demand away from domestic to foreign products and weighed on Chinese domestic demand. Therefore, China ought to loosen its relatively tight monetary policy.

This global comparative framework can be taken one step further through the construction of a broader financial conditions index (FCI) for the same G5 economies and by asking whether China's financial conditions will be another suspect contributing to its marked growth slowdown on the demand side. The rationale is that whether a given monetary policy stance will have a similarly meaningful effect on economic agents depends in part on the transmission channels. An expansionary monetary policy might or might not help deliver a more relaxed financial environment for business and consumers.

Given a particular monetary policy stance, the functioning of a financial system itself matters for growth performance. Europe's half-asleep banking sector is a case in point. If the recent Chinese economic slowdown was primarily structural, more lax financial conditions would not help and might even worsen the structural problems that dragged down economic growth in the first place. Indeed, China in the past few years has witnessed weaker growth and rising credit as a ratio to GDP, in contrast with a 'credit-less recovery' in the euro area (Darvas 2013).

To this end, my proposed crude and simple FCI aims to capture the broader financial environment that could influence the behaviour of agents in the Chinese and big-four SDR economies, by focusing on the price aspect of the financial environment. It is a weighted sum of five key financial asset prices: policy rate, one-year treasury yield, 10-year treasury yield, effective exchange rate and benchmark stock market index. Higher readings denote tightness owing to the first three rates and the effective exchange rate, so I use the inverse of the stock market index to capture changes in equity prices.

I place an equal weight of 20 per cent on each of the z-scores of these five financial prices. Thus, increases in interest rates, the effective exchange rate and the inverse stock market index all result in a rise in the FCI, indicating a tightening of financial conditions. As in the discussion of G5 central bank monetary policy, I will focus on the post-crisis period from January 2007 to March 2014 before the latest Chinese monetary easing. A positive FCI reading thus suggests tighter financial conditions than the period average, while a negative reading indicates loosening. I consider two versions of the FCI: one based on nominal interest rates and the effective exchange rate, and the other on their real (ex post) counterparts. In this way, the Chinese FCI can be compared directly both over time and with its international peers, in real and nominal terms.

The central message from these G5 FCIs is that China's financial conditions tightened the most of the major economies from the start of the GFC (Figure 3.5). Also, China started with relatively lax financial conditions on the eve of the GFC, but post-2011 tightened considerably, at least until about mid-2014 when the PBC started loosening. In contrast, the financial conditions in the G4 generally became less stringent in the same period, as shown by both their nominal and their real FCIs.

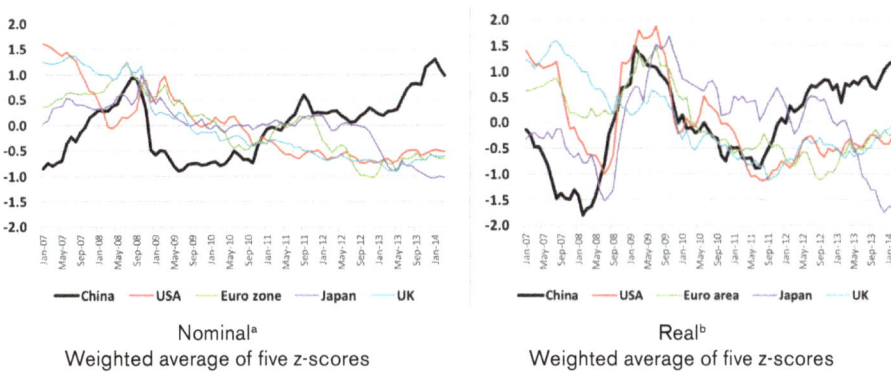

| Nominal[a] | Real[b] |
| Weighted average of five z-scores | Weighted average of five z-scores |

Figure 3.5 Financial condition indices (FCI) for G5 economies

[a] A rise suggests tightening. A positive number indicates tighter than the sample average. The official ceiling for the one-year deposit rate is taken as the policy rate of the PBC. The benchmark stock market indices are Shanghai Stock Exchange Composite Index for China, S&P 500 for the United States, Nikkei 225 for Japan, FTSE 100 for the United Kingdom, and a market cap weighted average of CAC 40, DAX 30, IBEX 35, FTSE Mid and AEX (January 2007=100) for the euro area.
[b] The real interest rate and exchange rate are nominal rates adjusted for current CPI inflation.
Sources: Datastream; BIS and author's calculation.

Moreover, all of the five asset prices underlying the Chinese FCI indicate an unmistakable financial tightening in this period: rising short and long-term interest rates, a strengthening RMB, and a languishing Shanghai stock market that lost 27 per cent of its value during this episode before its latest strong resurgence and stabilising government bond yields from the second half of 2014.

Finally, the paths of the nominal and real FCIs have differed somewhat among these big-five economies in the post-2007 period, but all indicate tighter financial conditions in China over time and relative to its international peers between 2007 and mid-2014. While the real FCIs of the five major economies have shown noticeable swings, their nominal counterparts, except China, display steady, large and synchronised declines, indicating considerable easing of the financial conditions outside China.

In sum, China's financial conditions were clearly the most restrictive during 2007–14 among the G5 economies. Intuitively, this revealed financial tightening—over time and relative to its international peers—could have meaningfully weighed on China's economy. Interestingly, our price-based FCI contrasts sharply with the observed Chinese credit surge in the wake of the GFC.

The tighter Chinese financial conditions could in part be policy-induced and in part relate to other institutional and fundamental changes in the Chinese economy, potentially contributing to slower economic growth. In any case, Chinese policymakers ought to take notice of such marked, sustained and broad-based tightness of the financial conditions. It would be very brave for anyone to claim that the tighter broad Chinese financial conditions had little to do with the recent Chinese economic slowdown. Suffice to say that a tighter broad financial environment tends to hurt private firms more and add to the financial woes of heavily indebted local governments in China. Therefore, as an insurance policy, China ought to ease its monetary policy.

Much more needs to be learned about the underlying causes of the more restrictive Chinese financial conditions against a background of falling growth and more liberal market environments. This task is beyond the scope of this chapter. For instance, a rigid 75 per cent regulatory cap on the bank loan-to-deposit ratio and a punitive 20 per cent reserve requirement ratio might have added to financial tightness in the Chinese economy, prompting policymakers in Beijing to tweak these rules in an attempt to loosen the domestic financial conditions (Ma 2014b). Another, complementary possibility is that the PBC's easing remained behind the curve, as indicated by the Chinese business cycle.

All said, in the wake of the GFC, not only did the Chinese monetary policy stance tighten the most among the big-five central banks, but also the broader Chinese financial conditions became the most restrictive among the G5 economies. Thus, the case for Chinese monetary easing is also compelling in the global context.

A perspective of optimal policy mix

Finally, I will make a case for Chinese monetary easing within the framework of optimal monetary and fiscal policy. Two arguments are put forward—one from the perspective of an open macroeconomic model and the other from the perspective of domestic fiscal and monetary policy interaction.

First, a standard Fleming–Mundell model (Dornbusch 1976) postulates that under the assumptions of open capital account and exchange-rate flexibility, a combination of loose monetary policy and neutral fiscal policy would be the best way for China to contain external deflationary shocks, cushioning growth while introducing two-way market expectations and volatility of the RMB exchange rate and incremental capital opening.

Since mid-2014, the PBC has considerably scaled down its routine foreign exchange interventions and widened the onshore daily trading band of the RMB. Moreover, the Chinese capital account has become more open over time (Ma and McCauley 2008, 2013). The recent gathering pace of the RMB internationalisation can be viewed as capital opening by stealth (Cheung et al. 2011). Increased financial openness implies greater sensitivity of cross-border financial flows to price signals, which in turn will be influenced by the mix of monetary and fiscal policies.

So, what would be a sensible mix of fiscal and monetary policies in the context of a more open capital account, effectively appreciating and more flexible currency, weakening domestic demand and broad strength of the US dollar? As discussed below, China's overall central and local government fiscal policy stance is unlikely to be meaningfully expansionary in the next few years (Zhu 2015), therefore, a key policy choice is whether one should pursue relatively tight or loose monetary policy.

According to the classical Fleming–Mundell model, given a neutral fiscal policy, an expansionary monetary policy would discourage capital inflows and slow the broad-based appreciation of the RMB in today's global environment. A less appreciated RMB would therefore discourage swings in capital flows and support the ongoing difficult domestic rebalancing, while monetary easing directly cushions domestic demand. Thus, to facilitate growth, rebalancing and currency flexibility at the same time, China ought to ease monetary policy.

Therefore, an accommodative monetary policy and neutral fiscal policy can combine to best promote both economic growth and fuller exchange rate flexibility of the RMB, especially against a global backdrop of near-zero interest rates at major central banks.

What about the global environment of broad dollar strength that could trigger capital outflows from China, putting depreciation pressure on the RMB vis-a-vis an almighty US dollar? At the time of writing, the RMB has repeatedly been testing the weak side of the daily trading band, despite serious efforts by the PBC to signal a steadier RMB–US dollar rate via its daily fixing (Figure 3.6). If managed properly, this is a healthy adjustment in a substantially appreciated RMB for three reasons.

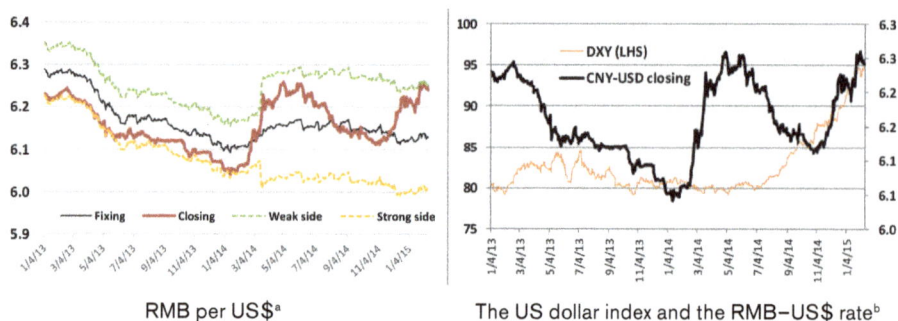

RMB per US$[a] | The US dollar index and the RMB–US$ rate[b]

Figure 3.6 The RMB daily trading band and the US dollar index

[a] The daily trading band was ±1 per cent before March 2014 and ±2 per cent afterwards.
[b] The US dollar index is the US Fed narrow basket index. The RMB–US dollar is the number of RMB per US dollar.
Source: Bloomberg.

First, a very strong RMB should loosen its link to the US dollar. The RMB will probably continue strengthening on a broad real effective basis, despite the prospect of some near-term weakness vis-a-vis a strong US dollar. In 2014, the RMB depreciated 2.5 per cent against the dollar but gained 7 per cent in trade-weighted terms, according to BIS statistics. But the Chinese currency is likely to again outperform most advanced and emerging market currencies in 2015, remaining a source of global financial stability. More importantly, China should move further away from its loose dollar peg to gain policy autonomy under an increasingly open capital account.

Second, greater two-way volatility vis-a-vis the US dollar is a crucial step to move further away from the already loose dollar peg, which has historically served China well as a credible nominal anchor. Indeed, the Chinese inflation record has fared better under the dollar peg since 1994 than during 1978–93 (Amstad et al. 2014). But its time is up, as the Chinese economy has simply become too big to be anchored to the US dollar or any single currency alone, even in a loose fashion. Effective stability of the RMB better serves China's long-term interests (Ma and McCauley 2011).

Third, some dollar outflows would facilitate orderly currency movements, allowing Chinese corporations to hedge and extinguish their dollar liabilities and the official sector to trim its dollar assets. McCauley et al. (2015) estimate that the dollar debts of Chinese corporations could exceed US$1.1 trillion. Shifting currency expectations owing to a mighty US dollar, a narrower than expected policy interest rate differential because of monetary policy divergence between China and the United States and possibly higher currency volatility given a less interventionist PBC have combined to result in a lower Sharpe ratio—an indicator of risk-adjusted returns. This in turn could prompt some unwinding of Chinese corporate carry trade to be funded in part by an orderly drawdown of the official reserves.

The next argument concerns the role fiscal policy can play in sharing the burden of cushioning economic growth and mitigating financial risk. My take is that a neutral fiscal policy stance might be the best course of action for policymakers in Beijing in the next few years, thus necessitating reasonable monetary accommodation.

With a slowing economy and weaker property market, the official fiscal policy should aim to avoid excessive tightening. First, the fiscal automatic stabilisers have already kicked in, as witnessed by a marked slowdown in overall Chinese tax revenues. Second, the Chinese Government has also undertaken selective tax and capital expenditure measures to fund infrastructure and affordable housing projects. Third, the Chinese official 2015 budget targets a deficit of 2.3 per cent of GDP compared with a 2014 out-turn of 1.8 per cent, and could actually reach a budget deficit of 2.6 per cent of GDP if the 2014 leftover budgetary funds are all to be spent in 2015.

However, despite a low level of central government debt, of 15 per cent of GDP, the combined overall fiscal position of central and local governments has been much more challenging, with their combined debt level tripling to 45 per cent. There is a real moral hazard risk associated with China's high and unsustainable level of local government debt. Local government officials have strong incentives to borrow, from both banks and the shadow banking sector, to fund their pet investment projects, but then leave messy debts to their successors. With rising local government debts since the GFC, the pressure to restructure local government finance has also been mounting.

This trend has been aggravated by a structural mismatch between fiscal revenues and expenditure obligations between the central and local governments. The financing needs of local government have been an important driver of the expansion of shadow banking in recent years, partially offsetting the potential benefits promised by the ongoing interest rate deregulation. In the longer run, China needs to rebalance the fiscal revenue sharing and outlay obligations between the central and local governments (Ma and Wang 2010). In the short term, some practical ways must be found to balance ongoing financing needs and moral hazard concerns.

Since late 2013, most local governments in China have come under mounting cash-flow pressures, which are in part market-driven and in part policy-induced. First, a cooler Chinese property sector since 2013 has significantly slowed proceeds from land sales, which mostly accrue to local governments. Indeed, some localities might face the stark new reality of diminished availability of land for sale. Nationwide, the growth of government land sale proceeds has plunged since mid-2014.[3]

Second, the policy of the central government has been to gradually tighten local government budget constraints, by curtailing their borrowing via various financing vehicles, demanding greater transparency and disclosure of local fiscal conditions, and enhancing regulation of shadow banking.

These two factors have nevertheless combined and translated into a de facto sizeable but necessary fiscal contraction in the short term, which may not be fully offset by a slightly more expansionary 2015 official budget. This fiscal tightening most likely shows up as weaker local investment expenditure, whatever the official 'proactive' fiscal policy means. Thus, the overall de facto Chinese fiscal policy stance might still be somewhat contractionary and at best neutral in 2015, calling for reasonable monetary relaxation to partially offset the possible contractionary effects of reduced local government borrowing on the Chinese economy. This picture is unlikely to become brighter in the next two to three years.

Although concerns over fiscal dominance remain real, tighter monetary policy is neither a credible nor a helpful response to the risks of moral hazard and soft budget constraints related to Chinese local governments. On the contrary, monetary accommodation should help mitigate the contractionary impact of the tighter local government budgetary constraints in the short term and facilitate gradual restoration of fiscal discipline and rebalancing of central and local fiscal resources and responsibility in the longer term.

In sum, both the insights from the Fleming–Mundell model and the need to mitigate contractionary impacts of tighter local government financing call for a sensible policy mix of monetary relaxation and a neutral fiscal stance. Therefore, the latest monetary easing by the PBC is well justified—and more can be done.

Conclusions

Since mid-2014, the PBC has embarked on a cycle of monetary easing in an attempt to mitigate slowing growth, emerging deflationary pressure, tight domestic financial conditions, waning net capital inflows and the contractionary consequences of local fiscal restructuring. This chapter makes a strong case

---

3 Proceeds from land sales accrue mostly to local governments and have plummeted from 40 per cent year-on-year in the first quarter of 2014 to 26 per cent in the second quarter, 17 per cent in the third and just 3 per cent in the final quarter. The first quarter of 2015 witnessed a plunge of 43 per cent (Zhu 2015).

that this shift in the Chinese *monetary policy stance* is warranted and desirable. Of course, whether Chinese monetary policy achieves its intended effects will depend on many factors outside the scope of this chapter, such as functioning transmission mechanisms.

Nevertheless, contrary to the view that monetary easing is a show of no confidence in reform, an act of sabotaging reform and/or a policy move that could worsen structural imbalances, a timely, measured but serious monetary policy accommodation is the best course of policy action that will serve the Chinese economy well in both the short term and the long term. Specifically, meaningful monetary easing helps cushion growth, support reform, facilitate rebalancing and mitigate financial stress.

First, prompt monetary relaxation, not tightening, supports domestic demand, reduces the headwinds from de facto fiscal contraction emanating from local government deleveraging, eases the relatively tight Chinese financial conditions and deflects global deflationary shocks. It helps mitigate adverse demand shocks, which have been non-trivial, and as a minimum, avoids rubbing salt into the wound.

Second, China's monetary policy accommodation can help accelerate liberalisation, by winning both broader political support and gaining greater headroom for implementing difficult reforms. While monetary policy is neither a magic bullet nor a substitute for the necessary institutional and structural reforms, monetary easing could provide the reform-minded PBC a window of opportunity to accelerate financial liberalisation. In contrast, maintaining tight monetary and fiscal policies as an ill-advised tactic to force through tough reform programs could be counterproductive, if not reckless.

Third, a timely monetary relaxation should help cushion an orderly slowdown of the Chinese economy, in turn facilitating the structural rebalancing task. The credit binge witnessed during the GFC was partially the consequence of the unmistakably late monetary policy response to collapsing domestic and external demand at that time. And this rapid credit expansion mostly funded local government investment, likely worsening domestic imbalances. Moreover, most of the credit allocation and industrial policy responsibilities burdening the PBC should be decommissioned, because monetary policy is not an apt instrument with which to address such structural issues.

Fourth, financial stability concerns have likely come to figure more prominently on the PBC's agenda because a key challenge is how to manage the legacy of excess leverage and increased financial imbalances in China. One sensible response is measured monetary accommodation to maintain steady nominal growth. This would help pre-empt a potentially vicious debt deflation cycle and dampen excess volatility in the financial system, while facilitating the tricky deleveraging process, not vice versa.

References

Ajello, A., Laubach, T., L'opez-Salido, D. and Nakata, T. (2015), Financial stability and optimal interest-rate policy, Federal Reserve Board paper presented at the Federal Reserve Bank of San Francisco conference 'The New Normal for Monetary Policy', San Francisco.

Amstad, M., Huan, Y. and Ma, G. (2014), *Developing an underlying inflation gauge for China*, BIS Working Paper No. 465, September, Basel: Bank for International Settlements.

Bank for International Settlement (BIS), an international organisation that also provides regular data and statistics.

Blagrave, P., Garcia-Saltos, R., Laxton, D. and Zhang, F. (2015), *A simple multivariate filter for estimating potential output*, IMF Working Paper No. 15/79, Washington, DC: International Monetary Fund.

Bloomberg, a standing online commercial data and news service provider.

CEIC, a standing online commercial data service provider.

Cheung, Y.W., Ma, G. and McCauley, R. (2011), Renminbising China's foreign assets, *Pacific Economic Review*, 16(1): 1–17.

Claeys, G. and Darvas, Z. (2015), *The financial stability risks of ultra-loose monetary policy*, Bruegel Policy Contribution No. 2015/03, March, Brussels: Bruegel.

Claeys, G., Darvas, Z., Merler, S. and Wolff, G. (2014), *Addressing weak inflation: The European Central Bank shopping list*, Bruegel Policy Contribution No. 2014/05, May, Brussels: Bruegel. Available from: www.bruegel.org/publications/publication-detail/publication/826-addressing-weak-inflation-the-european-central-banks-shopping-list/.

Darvas, Z. (2013), *Can Europe recover without credit?*, Bruegel Policy Paper No. 2013/03, Brussels: Bruegel.

Datastream, a standing online commercial data service provider.

Dornbusch, R. (1976), Exchange rate expectations and monetary policy, *Journal of International Economics*, 6(3): 231–44.

Girardin, E., Lunven, S. and Ma, G. (2014), Understanding the monetary policy rule in China: What is the role of inflation?, in *Globalisation, inflation and monetary policy in Asia and the Pacific*, BIS Papers No. 77, March, Basel: Bank for International Settlements, pp. 159–70.

Iwata, K. and Takenaka, S. (2012), *Central bank balance sheets expansion: Japan's experience*, JCER Discussion Paper No. 134, Tokyo: Japan Centre for Economic Research.

Ma, G. (2014a), Guest post: Should China cut interest rates?, *Financial Times*, 9 July. Available from: blogs.ft.com/beyond-brics/2014/07/09/guest-post-should-china-cut-interest-rates/.

Ma, G. (2014b), Tweaking China's loan-deposit ratio rule, *Bruegel Blog*, Brussels: Bruegel. Available from: www.bruegel.org/nc/blog/detail/article/1425-tweaking-chinas-loan-deposit-ratio-rule/.

Ma, G. (2015), Backward guidance, Chinese style, *Bruegel Blog*, Brussels: Bruegel. Available from: www.bruegel.org/nc/blog/detail/article/1541-backward-guidance-chinese-style/.

Ma, G. and McCauley, R. (2008), The efficacy of China's capital controls: Evidence from price and flow data, *Pacific Economic Review*, 13(1): 104–23.

Ma, G. and McCauley, R. (2011), The evolving renminbi regime and implications for Asian currency stability, *Journal of the Japanese and International Economies*, (25)(March): 23–38.

Ma, G. and McCauley, R. (2013), Is China or India more financially open?, *Journal of International Money and Finance*, (39): 6–27.

Ma, G. and Wang, Y. (2010), China's high saving rate: Myth and reality, *International Economics*, (122): 5–40.

Ma, G., McCauley, R. and Lam, L. (2012), Narrowing China's current account surplus: The roles of saving, investment and the renminbi, in McKay, H. and Song, L. (eds), *Rebalancing and sustaining growth in China*, Canberra: ANU E Press, pp. 65–91.

Ma, G., Yan, X. and Xi, L. (2012), China's reserve requirements: Practices, effects and implications, *China Economic Policy Review*, 1(2): 1–34. Ma, J. and Hong, H. (2015), The impacts of the structural factors on the long term growth potential of the Chinese economy: A DSGE model analysis, Draft.

McCauley, R., McGuire, P. and Sushko, V. (2015), *Global dollar credit: Links to US monetary policy and leverage*, BIS Working Papers No. 483, January, Basel: Bank for International Settlements.

Morley, J. (2014), *Measuring economic slack: A forecast-based approach with applications to economies in Asia and the Pacific*, BIS Working Paper No. 451, Basel: Bank for International Settlements.

Nakamura, E., Steinsson, J. and Liu, M. (2015), *Are Chinese growth and inflation too smooth? Evidence from Engel curves*, Discussion Paper, New York: Columbia University.

Rajan, R. (2014), Competitive monetary easing: Is it yesterday once more?, Speech by Governor of Reserve Bank of India at the Brookings Institution, 10 April, Washington, DC.

Sina Finance (2014), China Xinhau News and People's Daily debate over the controversial relationships between interest rate cuts and economic reform, *Sina Finance* [in Chinese], 17 September. Available from: finance.sina.com.cn/china/hgjj/20140917/165620320384.shtml.

Svensson, L. (2015), Discussion, Federal Reserve Bank of San Francisco conference 'The New Normal for Monetary Policy', San Francisco.

Tanaka, O. (2010), China's macroeconomic policy shift in 2008: Political process from tightening to easing, *Public Policy Review*, 6(3), Tokyo: Policy Research Institute, Ministry of Finance.

Taylor, J. (1993), Discretion versus policy rules in practice, *Carnegie-Rochester Conference Series on Public Policy*, 39: 195–214.

Zhu, H. (2015), *China: Will fiscal policy be expansionary in 2015?*, JP Morgan Economic Research Note, New York: JP Morgan.

4. Consequences of China's Opening to Foreign Banks

Ran Li, Xiang Li, Wen Lei and Yiping Huang

Introduction

China's government has recently implemented additional reforms to relax the regulatory environment for foreign banks. Specifically, State Council Order No. 657, signed by Premier Li Keqiang, announced a decision to revise the Regulations of the People's Republic of China on the Administration of Foreign-Funded Banks, effective from 1 January 2015. Implications of the revised regulations include removal of the requirement that a minimum of RMB100 million operating capital be transferred unconditionally from the overseas parent bank to the newly opened Chinese branch. In addition, in terms of the conditions attached to the right to carry out RMB-denominated activity, foreign banks are now eligible to apply to undertake local currency business after operating in China for one year—down from the previous three years. The requirement for two consecutive years of profit will be scrapped as well.

The opening-up of the Chinese banking sector dates back to 1980, when the first international branch of a foreign bank, from Japan, was established in Beijing. World Trade Organization (WTO) accession in late 2001 instigated a 'great leap forward', with China agreeing to undertake a series of financial liberalisation policies.

Among the points of agreement was that, on accession, earlier geographic and client restrictions on foreign currency business as applied to foreign financial institutions would be removed. For local currency business, geographic restrictions would be phased out within five years of accession. Any existing non-prudential measures restricting the ownership, operation and juridical form of foreign financial institutions (including internal branching and licences) were to be eliminated by the end of 2006. Subsectors including insurance, securities and investment fund management were also opened up, in a limited fashion, to foreign financial service providers.

Those commitments and associated incentives saw a range of seemingly panicked responses from Chinese financial market participants. Before accession to the WTO, there was a pervasive lack of confidence in Chinese financial markets, owing especially to a weak banking sector. During the Asian Financial

Crisis of the late 1990s, the ratio of non-performing loans (NPLs) of Chinese banks reached as high as 30–40 per cent. Although a series of reforms was implemented, including cleaning up NPLs and public capital injections, banks' corporate governance capacity remained low.

In this environment, commentators had two major concerns about foreign banks entering China's financial market. The first was that foreign banks possessed advantages over domestic banks, including greater product variety, broader international networks and more advanced risk-management skills. It was not implausible to think that domestic banks would be crowded out of the market, or even collapse once foreign banks enjoyed 'national treatment'. In addition, unlike domestic banks, foreign banks in China were under the control of their parent corporations, which some feared could ultimately become a source of financial instability for China.

Amid these fears, Bonin and Huang (2001) conducted research on the Chinese financial market, which suggested that these fears were unlikely to materialise in most cases. In particular, their research suggested that foreign banks should not be considered a destabilisation risk, mainly because establishing the branch of a foreign bank was no different from foreign direct investment (FDI) in other sectors. Both, for example, aim for long-term returns and not short-term profits—a contrast with speculative capital movement. Moreover, financial stability in China would be a point of common interest. Furthermore, the operations of foreign bank branches would be subject to the supervision of Chinese authorities. As for the competitiveness of the domestic banking system, this was less a concern than the possibility that foreign banks would encounter various policy restrictions, including of the scale of foreign ownership of major domestic banks.

Almost 15 years later, foreign banks have not contributed to financial risk and neither has their market share advanced greatly. In fact, the contrary is true, as Bonin and Huang (2001) expected. Foreign banks have found it very difficult to operate in the domestic Chinese market. Despite newly adopted opening-up policies—especially after China's accession to the WTO—little material improvement has been made in banking sector liberalisation. In some areas, we can even observe retrogression.

Total assets of foreign banks have expanded dramatically since 2003 (Figure 4.1). In the decade to 2013, the average annual rate of growth of foreign bank total assets was 19.9 per cent. Closer investigation shows that the relative size of foreign banks in China is negligible—less than 2 per cent of total banking assets in 2013. And that asset share has been declining in the past five years. Indeed, by 2013, the total asset share of foreign bank assets in total banking assets was just 1.5 per cent. This level is only slightly higher than the level of 10 years ago.

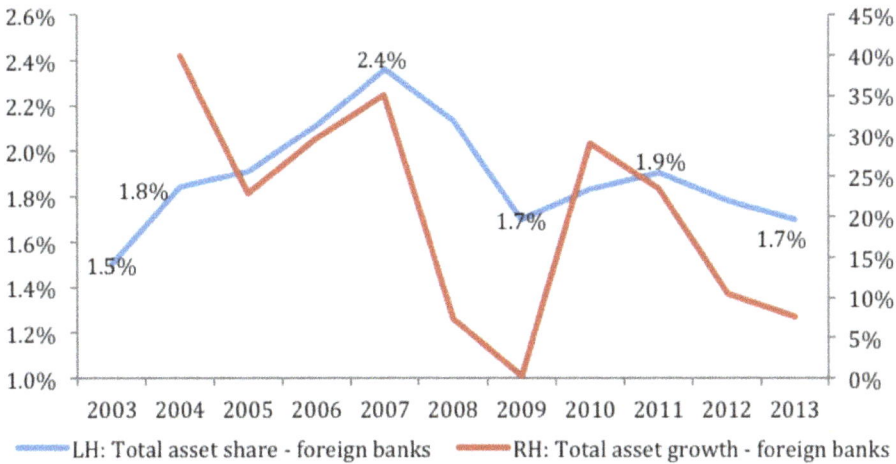

Figure 4.1 Development of foreign banks in China

Sources: CEIC China Premium Database; and authors' estimations.

Despite the fact the nightmare of a foreign bank invasion did not come to pass, discussions in China about banking sector liberalisation remain heated, and concerns persist. In this context, this chapter explores the impacts of banking sector liberalisation: what will and should happen in the future? To explore possible liberalisation scenarios, we first investigate the background of banking sector opening-up and related literature in the second and third sections. In the following two sections, we then explore two specific aspects of foreign bank entry—one for the domestic banking sector and another for domestic enterprises—so as to facilitate understanding of banking sector liberalisation, before concluding.

Foreign banks: Theory and reality

Foreign banks affect the local environment both directly and indirectly, and influence domestic economies and financial markets by interacting with domestic enterprises, including domestic banks. Direct impacts include lending, interbank trading and the influence of foreign investment considerations on local decision-making. As in the case of FDI more generally, foreign banks can also generate indirect spillovers through channels such as demonstration, personnel training and competition. Considering the small relative size of foreign banking in China, any interaction effects with local firms must be analysed carefully, as is the case for our study in section four.

In contrast with firms in other sectors, domestic banks, and in particular state-owned banks (SOBs), have more bargaining power when dealing with foreign competitors, because of the less competitive banking market. To that end, despite revisions to regulations to allow foreign banks national treatment, invisible barriers to China's banking sector mean that foreign banks are disadvantaged. For example, language and cultural barriers in reality often force foreign banks to focus on elite clients—the 'cream-skimming' effect. Another example is that when a foreign bank applies for a new business licence, they often find a domestic bank will be granted that licence.

In the early years of the century, foreign strategic investment played an important role in listings of state banks. Recently, however, most such investors have sold down those investments. There is a variety of explanations for this visible exit of foreign investors from China's banking sector. Financial difficulty in the aftermath of the 2008 global financial crisis (GFC) pressed some foreign banks to sell overseas assets. Declining returns on investments and rising risks for Chinese banks also drove foreign exits. Further, since foreign banks are only permitted to own minority shares in established domestic banks, they often find themselves unable to materially affect the decision-making process of that bank. Moreover, since all listed banks operate as SOBs, the board must include at least one official representative of the ruling Communist Party.

For China, a well-acknowledged benefit of banking sector liberalisation is that it could force domestic financial reforms. Despite that potential, and the scale of reforms already undertaken, China's financial sector remains relatively impenetrable, according to a financial liberalisation index designed by Abiad et al. (2008). For the index of 'financial institution entry barriers', China scores 35, against an average for middle-income countries of 85 and 100 for high-income countries (Figure 4.2).

Analysis of a more recent dataset reveals a similar result. According to The Heritage Foundation's '2015 Index of Economic Freedom', China's financial freedom index ranking is far behind that of other emerging markets, let alone high-income countries. Surprisingly, the index ranking for China fell in 2001 and the gap has widened since then.

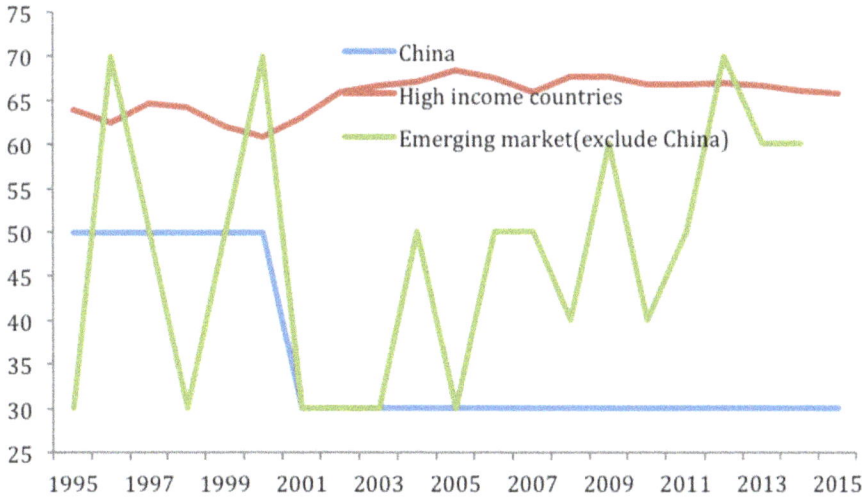

Figure 4.2 Financial freedom index, 2005

Note: The classifications of high-income countries and emerging markets are according to the World Bank and International Monetary Fund, respectively.
Source: Miller et al. (2015); and authors' estimation.

These data suggest that, despite China's progress in opening up its banking sector, little progress has been made in levelling the playing field for foreign banks. To understand the cause of this, it is important to further analyse what theory says about what should happen and compare this with the literature for the case of China.

Survey of the literature

The research question of this chapter is related to at least three branches of the literature. The first examines the spillover effects of foreign direct investment (FDI) (for example, Caves 1974; Dunning 1980, 1983; Hymer 1960). Blomström and Kokko (1998) found that in order to overcome disadvantages of operating overseas, such as cultural and language barriers, multinational corporations must possess some firm-specific advantages, including superior production technologies and advanced management skills. They argued that operation of such multinational corporations can generate productivity spillovers for the local industry through channels such as demonstration, personnel training and competition.

Some studies applied this spillover argument to the financial sector. For instance, Levine (1996) suggested two possible channels by which FDI can positively affect the domestic banking sector: the first is by directly bringing new and better skills, management techniques, training procedures, technology and products to the domestic market; and the second is through indirectly stimulating competition in domestic financial markets, which, in turn, puts pressure on profit and overhead expenses and enhances domestic banking efficiency.

The second branch of the literature concerns foreign bank entry as a special case of FDI, which can influence domestic firms through both direct and indirect channels. Foreign banks may directly provide services to local firms, and they may also indirectly affect firms by changing the domestic banking sector. The latter includes increasing competition in the banking sector and improving local banks' operating efficiency.

Some empirical studies focus on the interest rate spread, cost base and competition in the banking sector. By analysing bank-level data from 80 countries, Claessens et al. (2001) found that foreign bank entry narrowed interest rate spread and lowered management costs of local banks. Several other studies arrived at very similar conclusions: Unite and Sullivan (2003) for the Philippine case; Clarke et al. (1999) for the Argentine case; and Barajas et al. (2000) for the Colombian case. In the meantime, Petersen and Rajan (1995) argued that banking development is critical for alleviating financing constraints. Shen et al. (2009) pointed out that competition among banks is important for private firms obtaining loans.

Several papers dealt with the direct effect of foreign bank entry on firms. Some confirmed the cream-skimming effect, where foreign banks compete mainly with domestic banks for profitable and wealthy clients. Giannetti and Ongena (2009) found that foreign bank entry was beneficial for capital allocation in Eastern Europe, particularly for younger and larger firms. Sarma and Prashad (2013) provide evidence of the cream-skimming effect in India, arguing that foreign banks actually reduced the possibility of smaller firms obtaining bank loans.

The third branch of the literature analyses foreign bank entry in the People's Republic of China (PRC) as a critical component of financial liberalisation. Leung and Chan (2006) found that local banks actually improved efficiency in response to foreign bank entry. Berger et al. (2009) concluded that foreign capital significantly helped four big SOBs improve efficiency. Xu (2011) confirmed the positive effect of the existence of foreign banks on domestic bank competition and efficiency. And Mao et al. (2010) estimated the quadratic relationship between credit provided by foreign banks and total credit in the PRC.

China's banking sector liberalisation: Financial market effects

The Chinese banking sector has undergone significant changes in recent decades, especially since joining the WTO at the end of 2001. The China Banking Regulatory Commission (CBRC) once outlined four important principles for opening up the Chinese banking sector: 1) meeting the ongoing needs of domestic economic development; 2) improving competitiveness of the Chinese banking sector; 3) honouring commitments made to the WTO and creating an environment for fair competition between Chinese and foreign banks; and 4) maintaining financial stability (CBRC 2006).

Foreign banks were first allowed to open representative offices in China in 1979 and to set up branches in special economic zones (SEZs) from 1982. This geographical restriction was relaxed in 1994, after which foreign banks were allowed to operate in 23 cities after being selectively granted a licence to do so by central authorities. Foreign banks granted that licence were, however, limited in the scope of business they were allowed to conduct—to foreign currency loans and deposits for foreign-invested firms and foreign individuals in China. Four years later, in 1998, the People's Bank of China (PBC) granted eight foreign banks the right to use local currency funding; but even those foreign banks remained prohibited from conducting any consumer banking transactions in RMB with mainland residents for the duration of the 1990s.

China's joining of the WTO in late 2001 marked the beginning of a new set of rules concerning the operation of foreign banks in China. From 2002, foreign banks were allowed to conduct business with Chinese residents and enterprises in foreign currency. In addition, local currency services were also allowed in designated cities. By 2006, five years after China joined the WTO, geographic and customer restrictions on RMB businesses of foreign banks were lifted comprehensively, in accordance with the WTO accession commitments. The government also then encouraged foreign banks to incorporate locally, and those that were granted that licence did enjoy national treatment in terms of registered capital, branch opening rights, required operating capital and regulatory standards.

In 2006, most foreign banks granted national treatment banking terms in China were from Asia (Figure 4.3). Specifically, 186 foreign banks from 41 countries and regions had opened 242 representative offices in China. Of that total, the 56 per cent from Asia included 99 from Hong Kong, 19 from Japan and 17 from Singapore. From Europe, the top two countries are the United Kingdom (21) and France (15). From the United States, the number is 26.

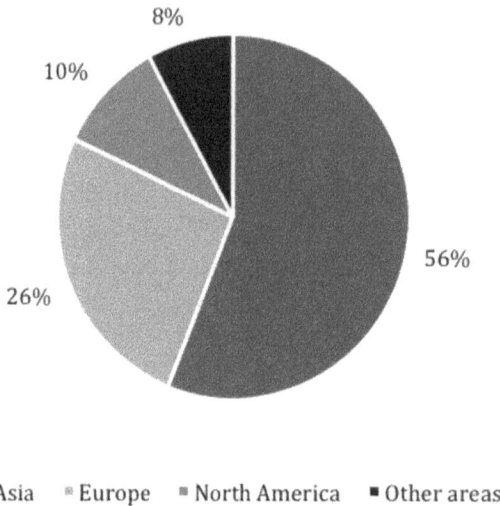

■ Asia   ▪ Europe   ▪ North America   ▪ Other areas

Figure 4.3 Distribution of host countries of foreign banks in 2006

Source: CBRC (2006).

In response to this gradual opening of the financial sector after China's WTO accession, the number of locally incorporated foreign banks with a presence in China increased significantly—from a low base. In parallel, the number of cities where locally incorporated foreign banks were present also increased rapidly. From the outbreak of the GFC in 2008 to the end of 2011, more than 40 foreign banks made additional capital (or working capital) replenishment equivalent to RMB27.1 billion in their Chinese operations (CBRC 2011), which shows strong confidence in the Chinese banking market.

By the end of 2013, banks from 51 countries and regions had established 42 locally incorporated entities, 92 foreign bank branches and 187 representative offices in China (CBRC 2013). Of the above listings, 36 locally incorporated foreign banks and 57 foreign bank branches were also approved to conduct RMB business. Six locally incorporated foreign banks—Bank of Tokyo-Mitsubishi, Mizuho Corporate Bank, Bank of East Asia, Development Bank of Singapore, Standard Chartered Bank and HSBC—had even been granted permission to issue RMB-denominated bonds, and the Bank of East Asia, Citibank, Nanyang Commercial Bank and Standard Chartered Bank obtained approval in 2014 to issue credit cards. Geographically, locally incorporated foreign banks had a presence in 69 cities and 27 provinces.

The response of foreign banks to the incremental liberalisation of China's banking sector after its WTO accession in 2001 can be understood by inspection of four trends: 1) the rise in the number of foreign banks operating in China; 2) the one-off transition of foreign banks in China from net providers of capital to non-financial institutions and residents to net receivers of capital, in 2010; 3) source funding coming from the host country and thus the limited role of the interbank market to financial banks; and 4) under government policy and for risk-management purposes, foreign banks were mostly engaged in low-risk banking activities.

On the first point, the number of foreign bank operating entities in China rose from 192 in 2003 to 419 in 2013 (Figure 4.4). The total China-based assets of those foreign banks almost doubled every four years, rising to RMB2.563 trillion in 2013 (Figure 4.5). Despite that increase in total assets, the foreign share in total banking assets in China remained low. Specifically, that share climbed between 2003 and 2007, but has fallen since the GFC—from 2.4 per cent in 2007 to 1.7 per cent in 2013.

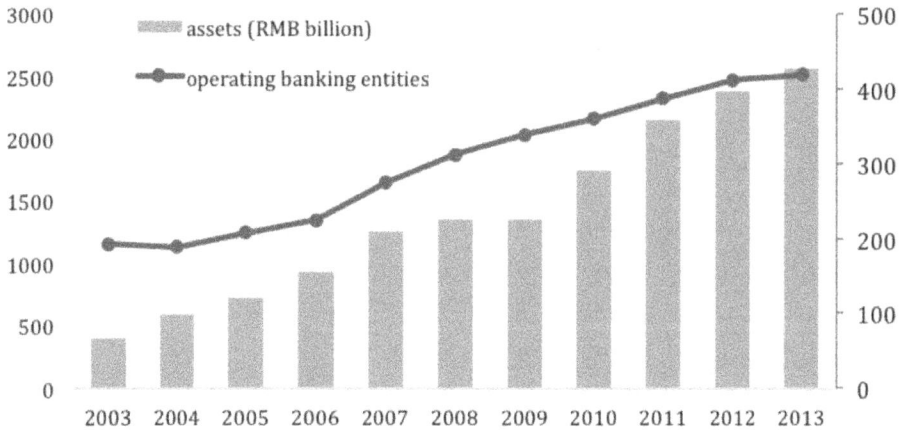

Figure 4.4 Development of foreign banks in China

Note: Operating banking entities include head offices, branches and subsidiaries of locally incorporated foreign banks and foreign bank branches.
Source: CBRC (2013).

The transition of foreign banks from net providers of capital to non-financial institutions and residents in China to net receivers of capital is demonstrated in Figure 4.5, where the net asset indicates the assets to non-financial institutions and residents less the liability to them, and foreign liability indicates the foreign liabilities of foreign banks (national level for both). Before 2010, foreign banks extended more loans than deposits collected. The situation that arose in 2010 has since reverted to the norm, possibly because RMB business with local residents was largely constrained by government regulation in the early years and the main business of foreign banks was foreign currency loans for enterprises.

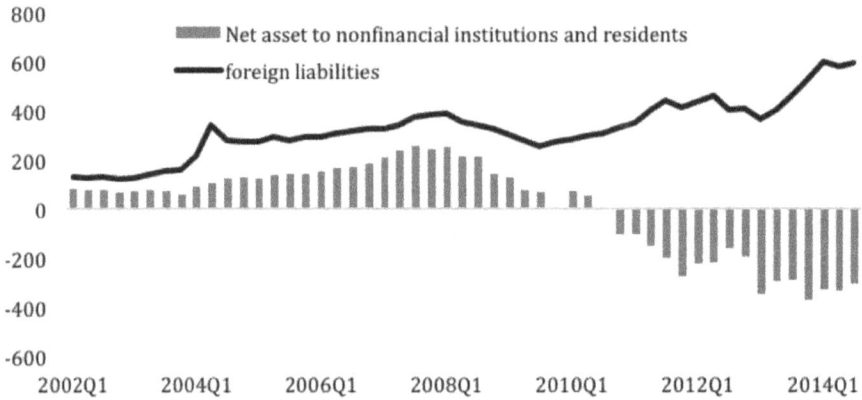

Figure 4.5 Foreign banks turning into net takers of capital

Source: CEIC.

On the third point, the main source of funding for locally incorporated foreign banks in China has come from their headquarters and subsidiaries in other host countries, and the role played in the local interbank market by foreign banks has been limited. Technically the government has made the local funding market available to foreign banks since 1998, but the conditions of that access, such as constrained lending amounts and limited loan period horizons, have limited the freedom of access to local funding pools that such banks can utilise.

The final point characterising foreign bank activity in China since it joined the WTO is that foreign banks have tended to engage in operations that are characterised by relatively low risk. For example, the share of foreign bank exposure to China's NPL portfolio is estimated to be below 1 per cent, and is consistently lower than the average ratio of the whole commercial banking system in China (Figure 4.6). Researchers have pointed out that, apart from traditional banking business, such as following existing customers in trade and investment, the main focus of foreign banks was on the niche markets and fee-based banking business where their comparative advantages lay (Xu 2011), and where they have also enjoyed consistent regulatory permission to operate.

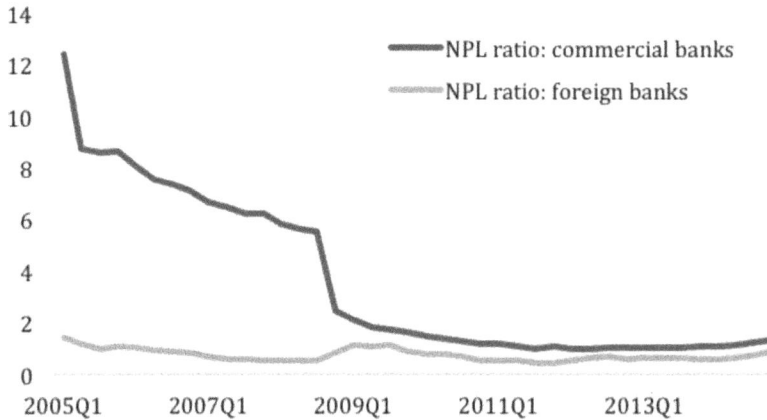

Figure 4.6 NPL ratio of commercial banks and foreign banks

Source: WIND.

In summary, the opening up and liberalisation process helped foreign banks penetrate the Chinese market and provide more sophisticated banking services to local customers. That said, the asset share of foreign banks remains low, and the main funding source of foreign banks is still from overseas. The business range of services provided by foreign banks has also not developed extensively, in part thanks to the incremental progress in areas of the banking sector that have been liberalised.

In this context, further investigation could shed light on how theoretical views of the benefits associated with foreign bank entry hold in the applied case of a transitional economy. This could include the potential of a foreign banking presence to increase competition within the domestic banking system, thus increasing the efficiency of local banks, and helping to more efficiently allocate capital through improved evaluation and pricing of credit risks. Our empirical analysis focuses, first, on the impact of foreign bank penetration on efficiency and competition in the domestic banking system, and second, on its influence on credit allocation.

There are several methods used to estimate the degree of competition in a banking system. First, bank-level indicators of net interest margins and costs, which will be affected if competition levels change. For example, when competition is strengthened, domestic banks are forced to lower lending rates or to increase deposit rates to retain market share. This in turn narrows net interest margins. Similarly, in the first instance, domestic banks often incur costs when competing with large international banks with better reputations. Without considering the increased efficiency benefits, these banks' operational costs will increase. Second, we also use provincial data on the share of deposits in non-state-owned financial institutions, to measure the effect of foreign bank entry on provincial deposit competition. The logic here is that if the presence of locally incorporated foreign banks in a province is accompanied by a larger share of deposits in the non-SOB sector, we can interpret this to mean that foreign bank entry could be associated with competition in the domestic banking system.

Net interest margins (NIM) are interest incomes minus interest expenses divided by total earnings, where expenses refer to non-interest expenses divided by total earnings ($COST$). We explore the effects of foreign bank entry (FEI), representing the asset share of foreign banks in the whole banking system, on net interest margins and cost by running two regressions in which the dependent variables are NIM (Equation 4.1) and $COST$ (Equation 4.2), respectively. We control for a bank's book value of equity over total earning assets (EQT) and national economic conditions including annual GDP growth rate (gdp), inflation (inf) and lending rate ($lendrate$). Bank-level data come from *Bankscope* and national economic data from the World Development Indicators (WDI) (World Bank various years). There are 303 bank-year observations in our unbalanced panel dataset, covering 75 commercial banks from 1999 to 2013. Like Xu (2011), we run the following two regressions with fixed effect (Equations 4.1 and 4.2).

Equation 4.1

$$NIM_{it} = \beta_0 + \beta_1 FEI_{it} + \beta_2 EQT_{it} + \beta_3 COST_{it} + \beta_4 gdp_{it} + \beta_5 \inf_{it} + \beta_6 lendrate_{it} + \varepsilon_{it}$$

Equation 4.2

$$COST_{it} = \beta_0 + \beta_1 FEI_{it} + \beta_2 EQT_{it} + \beta_3 NIM_{it} + \beta_4 gdp_{it} + \beta_5 \inf_{it} + \beta_6 lendrate_{it} + \varepsilon_{it}$$

Results from Equations 4.1 and 4.2 are shown in Table 4.1. The results suggest a statistically significant negative effect on net interest margins and a positive effect on non-interest costs are associated with foreign bank entry. These results are in line with most existing theoretical literature that supports the hypothesis that the increased competition associated with foreign bank penetration comes from domestic banks facing a narrowed interest margin, and also that their costs rise by having to spend proportionately more on operations and services against their market share. It also suggests, at least as far as the sample applies—for 1999–2013 and to the impact of foreign banks on the local provincial privately owned banking sector (which is tiny within the scheme of China's banking system)—that foreign banks appear to be associated with increased competition.

Table 4.1 Net interest margin, operational cost and foreign bank entry

	NIM	COST
FEI	−2.519	2.937
	(2.97)***	(3.75)***
EQT	0.529	−0.431
	(1.01)	(0.88)
gdp	−0.028	0.025
	(1.14)	(1.10)
inf	−0.060	0.049
	(2.62)***	(2.28)**
lendrate	0.149	−0.131
	(1.74)*	(1.64)
NIM		0.881
		(43.04)***
COST	1.013	
	(43.04)***	
_cons	−0.493	0.437
	(1.04)	(0.99)
Fixed effect	Yes	Yes
R^2	0.90	0.90
N	303	303

*** $p < 0.01$
** $p < 0.05$
* $p < 0.1$
Note: Robust standard errors in parentheses.

In a recent study, Li and Huang (forthcoming) use provincial data to run regressions of the bank competition index (*BankCompt*) on foreign bank entry (*Foreign*) (Equation 4.3). Following Fan et al. (2003, 2004, 2007, 2010), they compute the NERI Index of Marketisation for provinces in China to proxy bank competition. The index is the share of deposits in non-state-owned financial institutions. Since almost all financial institutions in China are banks, they use this index to reflect the competiveness of the banking sector.

Equation 4.3

$$BankCompt_{pt} = c + \alpha_p + \mu_t + \gamma_0 Foreign_{pt} + \epsilon_{pt}$$

The datasets used in this study were constructed by the National Bureau of Statistics (NBS) and collected through annual surveys of all large-scale industrial firms in the PRC. On average, they cover close to 190,000 enterprises, from

37 two-digit manufacturing industries and 31 provinces every year. Given that China's WTO accession took place at the end of 2001, we employ post-accession data for the period 2002–07.

Table 4.2 summarises the estimation results. Foreign bank entry actually intensifies banking competition based on the significantly positive coefficient estimates, which implies that the share of deposits in SOBs declines because the entry of foreign banks increases competition and weakens their dominance. To check if the conclusion is model-dependent, Li and Huang also include provincial GDP and provincial population (both in log form) as control variables and add a time trend to the equation. In all these exercises, the main finding remains unchanged.

Table 4.2 Foreign bank entry and bank competition

	Level		Linear trend	
Foreign	0.857**	0.887**	0.509*	0.508**
	(0.359)	(0.331)	(0.271)	(0.249)
Trend			0.365*	0.399*
			(0.214)	(0.219)
Log(provincial GDP)		4.515*		4.792**
		(2.37)		(2.168)
Log(provincial population)		0.48		−0.269
		(2.923)		(2.921)
Constant	3.253***	−34.23	3.259***	−30.29
	(0.384)	(25.25)	(0.377)	(24.05)
Observations	400	400	400	400
R-squared	0.557	0.584	0.57	0.599
Number of provinces	31	31	31	31
Year dummy	Yes	Yes	Yes	Yes

*** $p < 0.01$
** $p < 0.05$
* $p < 0.1$
Notes: The dependent variable is the bank competition index (*BankCompt*). Robust standard errors in parentheses.

More than 35 years since China's great reform and opening-up policy, and more than a decade since China became a formal member of the WTO, the achievements of that opening-up are unquestionable, and have led to China becoming a leading member of the global economic community. The degree of reform and liberalisation observed in its financial systems is remarkable compared with the early years. Based on the WTO's agenda, China has implemented its promised policy changes. The real progress since that accession has, however, been slow and conservative, especially from the perspective of foreign bank entry. Although the number of active foreign banks has expanded, many fields (such as the local funding market and business expansion) are still under regulation, explicitly or implicitly. There are even signs of reversal in market entry, judging from the asset share of foreign banks (Figure 4.1). Despite this, the entry of foreign banks has had an important influence on the domestic banking system. The presence of more experienced (in terms of customer management) and more knowledgeable (in terms of organisation efficiency) foreign banks, who furthermore have easier access to international funding, has increased the degree of competition in the domestic banking industry—an assertion supported by our empirical evidence, from both the bank level and the provincial level. For a full picture of the effects of banking sector liberalisation, the next section will focus on the impact of foreign bank entry on the allocation of firm credit.

China's banking sector liberalisation: Real economy effects

As mentioned, although the total asset share of foreign banks in the Chinese banking industry dropped to 1.9 per cent in 2013 (compared with 2 per cent in 2001), the scale of foreign bank assets has been rapidly increasing, with the average annual growth rate once reaching as high as almost 20 per cent during the decade since 2001. Their business lines, coverage of target customers, as well as business area have also been expanding. In addition, it has become a prevalent phenomenon in China for foreign banks to hold stakes in state-owned and joint stock banks, or even city commercial banks. Now that foreign bank entry has evolved, what substantive change will it bring to the Chinese economy? This section intends to analyse the impact on domestic enterprises, which are vital components of the real economy.

It is widely acknowledged that despite more than 30 years of successful reform, the Chinese economy still exhibits typical features of repressive financial policies, which protect the state sector but discriminate against private enterprises. Could the entry of foreign banks—taken as an important step in financial liberalisation—work on the efficiency of domestic enterprises and exert some effects on discriminatory policies? The existing literature on this issue has controversial conclusions. On the one hand, conventional theory suggests that foreign bank entry can enhance competition in and improve the efficiency of the domestic banking system, thus increasing credit supply to enterprises; on the other hand, banking theory incorporating information asymmetry argues that some firms' access to credit could be reduced due to the high information cost and greater competition (Petersen and Rajan 1995). High information costs can also induce foreign banks to do business with the most profitable local firms (Dell'Ariccia and Marquez 2004; Sengupta 2007). Combining these various predictions with the situation in China, we expect foreign banks will work on domestic firms through indirect channels rather than directly providing loans, as their share in China remains quite low so far.

In fact, China's gradual opening up to foreign banks since 2001 has created an excellent laboratory in which to study the effects of foreign bank entry. Li and Huang (forthcoming) have conducted a case study based on this unique policy experiment. Since the policy plan is exogenous, they construct a counterfactual using the 'difference in differences' (DID) approach, in which the control group consists of firms located in regions where foreign bank credit is unavailable and which are therefore plausibly unaffected by foreign bank entry, and the treatment group comprises firms with access to foreign bank lending. They then apply a basic DID fixed-effect model, with the log of total factor productivity (*TFP*)[1] as the dependent variable, employing a panel dataset constructed by the NBS that covers close to 190,000 enterprises in 31 provinces. They choose data from 2002 to 2007 given that the PRC's accession to the WTO took place at the end of 2001. A dummy variable (*Foreign*) is introduced to represent whether foreign bank loans are available in the region in which the firm is located. In addition, they use the age of the firm (*Age*), and, in log form, total assets (*Log(Assets)*), GDP (*Log(GDP)*) and the population of the city in which the firm is located (*Log(Population)*) as independent variables to explain productivity.

The model is estimated using both the full sample and subsamples, which are classified by different ownership types as defined by the largest shareholder[2] (Table 4.3). The results reveal several important findings. First, financial opening does exert an overall positive impact on TFP since the coefficient for foreign bank entry is significantly positive in the full sample estimation; however, as the coefficients of *Foreign* in subsample estimations indicate, the effects on TFP vary across ownership groups: negative for state-owned enterprises (SOEs) and collectively owned enterprises (COEs), positive for privately owned enterprises (POEs) and insignificant for foreign-invested firms (FIEs). These findings seem to be at odds with the information asymmetry and cream-skimming effect mentioned in previous sections. The strong policy implication behind these is that foreign bank entry does play an essential role in reversing the financial repression that favours SOEs and COEs but discriminates against POEs. Due to

---

1   They estimated TFP by the consistent semi-parametric method developed by Olley and Pakes (1996), and also provided robustness checks by calculating TFP using the Solow residual.
2   An alternative definition of ownership is also used to check the robustness of the estimation results in Li and Huang (forthcoming).

such a vital component of financial liberalisation, SOEs and COEs, which previously enjoyed more policy support from the Chinese Government, are now worse off; while POEs, previously discriminated against, now become better off.

Table 4.3 The basic model (TFP)

	Full sample	SOEs	COEs	POEs	FIEs
Foreign	0.0251**	−0.0339***	−0.0366***	0.0464***	−0.000450
	(0.0116)	(0.0130)	(0.0137)	(0.0132)	(0.0228)
Age	−0.00128***	−0.000398	−0.000855	6.10e-05	0.00312**
	(0.000347)	(0.000681)	(0.000700)	(0.000412)	(0.00140)
Log(Assets)	0.0430***	0.0282*	0.0659***	0.0256**	0.187***
	(0.0115)	(0.0156)	(0.0188)	(0.0114)	(0.0229)
Log(GDP)	−0.0109	0.0391	0.00209	0.0122	0.0517
	(0.0762)	(0.0556)	(0.0834)	(0.0939)	(0.0617)
Log(Population)	−0.0461	−0.177***	−0.0841	−0.0776	−0.0268
	(0.0473)	(0.0501)	(0.0667)	(0.0637)	(0.0211)
Constant	0.956***	0.915***	0.846*	1.077**	−1.288**
	(0.347)	(0.303)	(0.503)	(0.485)	(0.548)
Observations	1,202,245	68,418	93,784	860,188	179,855
R-squared	0.006	0.004	0.007	0.007	0.033
Number of firms	318,167	25,382	43,287	252,404	53,519
Clustered at	Region	Region	Region	Region	Region
Year dummy	Yes	Yes	Yes	Yes	Yes

COEs = collectively owned enterprises.
FIEs = foreign-invested enterprises.
GDP = gross domestic product.
POEs = privately owned enterprises.
SOEs = state-owned enterprises.
*** $p < 0.01$
** $p < 0.05$
* $p < 0.1$
Notes: The dependent variable is the log of TFP. Robust standard errors in parentheses.
Source: Li and Huang (forthcoming).

But how does foreign bank entry affect firms' productivity? What are the detailed mechanisms through which the policy takes effect? Since POEs in China are widely considered to be subject to lack of credit, one possible channel could be its role in the improvement of financing conditions. Li and Huang (forthcoming) further exploit this by introducing an index used in Rajan and

Zingales (1998),[3] which represents the demand for external funds of the industry of which the firm is part. In addition, they construct its interaction term with the dummy variable *Foreign* to capture the different impact that foreign bank entry could exert on enterprises with different levels of demand for external financing. With other control variables staying the same as those in Table 4.3, they estimate the model using the full sample as well as subsamples again, and the results are presented in Table 4.4. As expected, the significantly positive coefficient of the interaction term for POEs indicates that the impact of foreign bank entry on POEs' TFP will be larger in industries that have more demand for external funds. In other words, one possible channel is that foreign bank entry enhances POEs' TFP by easing their credit constraints. The insignificant coefficients in the other three groups are a natural consequence since SOEs and COEs generally do not suffer from financing constraints, and FIEs are neither substantially discriminated against nor substantially favoured under the financial repression in China.

The case study of Li and Huang (forthcoming) above lends strong support to the positive effects foreign bank entry has on industrial efficiency at the aggregate level, which conforms to prior expectations. Additionally, this policy takes effect through easing the financing constraints on private firms, which are heavily discriminated against by banks and have limited access to credit before foreign bank entry. Combined with the analysis in the previous section that shows foreign bank entry can improve bank efficiency, this easing effect could be ascribed to the fact that by competing for the same businesses with local banks, foreign banks force local banks to deflect their services to those clients not previously covered, and thus improve the financing conditions of private firms.

Therefore, the introduction of foreign banks to China benefits domestic enterprises by enhancing overall productivity, and it improves POEs' efficiency by easing their credit constraints. As a result, the previous effects of financial repression can be reduced or even reversed. We could gain some insights—though admittedly there are some limitations when applying this specific case study to a more general case—that this reversal effect will play an essential role in leading Chinese financial reform to a more market-oriented stage and facilitating the healthy development of the Chinese real economy, of which domestic enterprises, especially POEs, are important driving forces.

---

3   The index was originally used to capture the dependence of US firms on external financing, but is also justified as a reasonable proxy for external financing dependence in developing countries (Rajan and Zingales 1998).

Table 4.4 Financial constraints and foreign bank entry (TFP)

	SOEs	COEs	POEs	FIEs
Foreign×Index	0.107	−0.00472	0.0493**	0.0182
	(0.0668)	(0.0380)	(0.0201)	(0.0232)
Foreign	0.000327	−0.0272*	0.0460***	−0.00534
	(0.0147)	(0.0146)	(0.0131)	(0.0236)
Index	−0.138*	0.0917*	0.0314	−0.0162
	(0.0724)	(0.0470)	(0.0203)	(0.0282)
Age	0.000690	−0.000610	0.000306	0.00223
	(0.000863)	(0.000767)	(0.000415)	(0.00141)
Log(Assets)	−0.101***	−0.0976***	−0.0699***	0.00428
	(0.0156)	(0.0147)	(0.00748)	(0.0138)
Log(GDP)	0.0151	−0.0269	−0.00111	0.0506
	(0.0679)	(0.102)	(0.0948)	(0.0663)
Log(Population)	−0.156**	−0.0771	−0.0640	−0.0314
	(0.0635)	(0.0707)	(0.0612)	(0.0243)
Constant	1.607***	2.086***	1.663***	0.686*
	(0.371)	(0.599)	(0.463)	(0.367)
Observations	41,192	73,705	761,091	164,304
R-squared	0.018	0.012	0.009	0.012
Number of firms	15,969	33,598	218,458	48,377
Clustered at	Region	Region	Region	Region
Year dummy	Yes	Yes	Yes	Yes

COEs = collectively owned enterprises.
FIEs = foreign-invested enterprises.
GDP = gross domestic product.
POEs = privately owned enterprises.
SOEs = state-owned enterprises.
*** $p < 0.01$
** $p < 0.05$
* $p < 0.1$
Notes: The dependent variable is the log of TFP. Robust standard errors in parentheses.
Source: Li and Huang (forthcoming).

Conclusion

Since China's accession to the WTO in late 2001, the Chinese Government has been incrementally relaxing restrictions on foreign banks—a process that continues. Initially, this raised some concerns among participants in the Chinese financial sector. The fear was that foreign banks would crowd out domestic banks, and also that foreign banks would be under the control of their parent corporations rather than responsive to China's monetary authorities, and this would be a source of financial instability for China. Would incremental liberalisation of the banking sector prove to be a case of 'barbarians at the gate' or a positive opportunity for China?

Our empirical analysis shows that liberalising foreign bank lending benefits China's economy, at least in the case of the non-state banking sector. Despite their small market share in China, foreign banks help to improve the efficiency and competition of the Chinese banking sector. This in turn alleviates the financial constraints of firms, especially private firms that are less connected to the government—a finding that is consistent with the literature. The evidence above lends some support to the view in favour of achieving greater financial openness.

Liberalisation, however, is never a single-edged sword. Although foreign banks are under domestic regulation and rely on Chinese financial stability to generate profits, risk regulation should be undertaken with care. The right framework by which to rationalise the generally positive policy effects above is that of financial repression. In an economy with seriously repressive financial policies—which is a reasonable depiction of the current situation in China—the state sector is often strongly favoured, while the private sector (the focus of this study) is discriminated against.

Research has identified that the arrival of foreign banks in China appears to be associated with reduced repression in the banking sector, and therefore should reverse earlier adverse policy effects. This could mean hurting state enterprises while benefiting private enterprises, other things being equal. Reform programs should be designed with caution to ensure a smooth transition. While the case of foreign bank entry is useful for thinking about future reform steps, it is important to remember that our case study of opening-up foreign banks' RMB business is quite different from opening up the entire banking sector. However, this risk–reward framework and the positive results for competition in the banking sector offer the basis for broader policy deliberation.

Another crucial question for future research is that, although foreign bank entry can be beneficial in the current stage, will it be different if foreign banks are ever to take a much larger share of the financial market? Our answer is: possibly. The size of foreign banks in China will increase dramatically in the future and the domestic banking sector will face great challenges.

The decline of the size of foreign banks in China since 2008 was largely due to the GFC and the increasing liquidity challenges facing foreign parent companies. The current Chinese Government has shown great determination to implement reforms. Even though economists expect China's 'new normal' growth rate to be 7 per cent, well down from the first decades of the reform era, this still points to a vast opportunity given the size of China's economy. Moreover, the Chinese Government has a sound fiscal system. An economic crush is unlikely to happen in the near future. Foreign banks will most likely seize this opportunity.

If our prediction of a big advance of foreign banks turns out to be true, domestic banks, especially large SOBs, will face the biggest challenges. Preparing the domestic banking sector is especially critical for China, a bank-centred economy. But reform in the banking sector is deeply intertwined with reforms in other areas. The NPLs of SOBs are largely from SOEs and local government financing vehicles. The new 'one belt and one road' policy could induce more long-term loans backed up by the government. The ongoing interest rate liberalisation further decreases banks' profit margins, leaving them less room to handle the challenges. The situation is tough, but the appropriate timing and sequencing of comprehensive reforms will help the Chinese economy smoothly adapt to its new normal.

However, foreign banks in China will also face tough competition; their Chinese counterparts are giants, and there is a large, established domestic customer base. Similarly, Chinese banks have rich experience in screening and monitoring Chinese customers. Without further reforms, implicit discrimination against foreign banks will persist.

References

Abiad, A, Detragiache, E. and Tressel, T. (2008), *A new database of financial reforms*, Working Paper No. 2008-2266, Washington, DC: International Monetary Fund.

Barajas, A., Steiner, R. and Salazar, N. (2000), The impact of liberalization and foreign investment in Columbia's financial sector, *Journal of Development Economics*, 63(1): 157–96.

Berger, A., Hasan, I. and Zhou, M. (2009), Bank ownership and efficiency in China: What will happen in the world's largest nation?, *Journal of Banking and Finance*, 33(1): 113–30.

Blomström, M. and Kokko, A. (1998), Multinational corporations and spillovers, *Journal of Economic Surveys*, 12(3): 247–77.

Bonin, J. and Huang, Y. (2001), Dealing with the bad loans of the Chinese banks, *Journal of Asian Economics*, 12(2): 197–214.

Caves, R. (1974), The distinctive nature of multinational enterprise, in Dunning, J. (ed.), *Economic analysis and the multinational enterprise*, London: Allen & Unwin.

CEIC, a standing online commercial data service provider.

China Banking Regulatory Commission (CBRC) (2006), *Annual report 2006*, Beijing: CBRC.

China Banking Regulatory Commission (CBRC) (2011), *Annual report 2011*, Beijing: CBRC.

China Banking Regulatory Commission (CBRC) (2013), *Annual report 2013*, Beijing: CBRC.

Chung-Hua, S., Lu, C.H. and Wu, M.W. (2009), Impact of foreign bank entry on the performance of Chinese banks, *China & World Economy*, 17(3): 102–21.

Claessens, S., Demirgüc-Kunt, A. and Huizinga, H. (2001), How does foreign entry affect domestic banking markets?, *Journal of Banking and Finance*, 25(5): 891–911.

Clarke, G., Cull, R., D'Amato, L. and Molinari, A. (1999), *The effect of foreign entry on Argentina's domestic banking sector*, Policy Research Working Paper No. 158, Washington, DC: The World Bank.

Dell'Ariccia, G. and Marquez, R. (2004), Information and bank credit allocation, *Journal of Financial Economics*, 72(1): 185–214.

Dunning, J. (1980), Toward an eclectic theory of international production: Some empirical tests, *Journal of International Business Studies*, 11(1): 9–31.

Dunning, J. (1983), Market power of the firm and international transfer of technology: A historical excursion, *International Journal of Industrial Organization*, 1(4): 333–51.

Gang, F., Wang, X. and Zhu, H. 2003. NERI Index of Marketization for China's Provinces: 2003 Report. Beijing: Economic Science Press.

Gang, F., Wang, X. and Zhu, H. 2004. NERI Index of Marketization for China's Provinces: 2004 Report. Beijing: Economic Science Press.

Gang, F., Wang, X. and Zhu, H. 2007. NERI Index of Marketization for China's Provinces: 2007 Report. Beijing: Economic Science Press.

Gang, F., Wang, X. and Zhu, H. 2010. NERI Index of Marketization for China's Provinces: 2010 Report. Beijing: Economic Science Press.

Giannetti, M. and Ongena, S. (2009), Financial integration and firm performance: Evidence from foreign bank entry in emerging markets, *Review of Finance*, 13(2): 181–223.

Huidan, L. (2011), Foreign bank entry and firms' access to bank credit: Evidence from China, *Journal of Banking & Finance*, 35: 1,000–10.

Hymer, S.H. (1960), The international operation of national firms: A study of direct foreign investment, Cambridge, Mass.: Massachusetts Institute of Technology Press.

Leung, M.K. and Chan, R. (2006), Are foreign banks sure winners in post-WTO China?, *Business Horizons*, 49(3): 221–34.

Leung, M.K., Rigby, D. and Young, T. (2003), Entry of foreign banks in the People's Republic of China: A survival analysis, *Applied Economics*, 35(1): 21–31.

Levine, R. (1996), Foreign banks, financial development, and economic growth, in Barfield, C. (ed.), *International financial markets: Harmonization versus competition*, Washington, DC: AEI Press, pp. 224–54.

Li, R. and Huang, Y. (forthcoming), How does financial opening affect industrial efficiency? The case of foreign bank entry in the People's Republic of China, *Asian Development Review*.

Mao, Z., Wu, J. and Liu, M. (2010), An empirical study of foreign banks' effect on Chinese credit supply, *Journal of Financial Research*, 1: 106–16.

Miller, T., Holmes, K.R. and Kim, A. (2015), *Index of economic freedom*, Washington, DC: The Heritage Foundation.

Olley, G.S. and Pakes, A. 1996. The dynamics of productivity in the telecommunications equipment industry. *Econometrica*, 64: 1263–1297.

Petersen, M. and Rajan, R. (1995), The effect of credit market competition on lending relationships, *Quarterly Journal of Economics*, 110(2): 407–43.

Rajan, R. and Zingales, L. (1998), Financial dependence and growth, *American Economic Review*, 88(3): 559–86.

Sarma, M. and Prashad, A. (2013), Do foreign banks in India indulge in cream skimming?, Paper presented at the Annual International Studies Convention, 10–12 December, Jawaharlal Nehru University, New Delhi.

Sengupta, R. (2007), Foreign entry and bank competition, *Journal of Financial Economics*, 84(2): 502–28.

Shen, Y., Shen, M., Xu, Z. and Bai, Y. (2009), Bank size and small- and medium-sized enterprise (SME) lending: Evidence from China, *World Development*, 37(4): 800–11.

Unite, A. and Sullivan, M. (2003), The effect of foreign entry and ownership structure on the Philippine domestic banking market, *Journal of Banking and Finance*, 27(12): 2323–45.

WIND, Wind Information Co., Ltd (Wind Info), a leading integrated service provider of financial data, information and software.

World Bank (various years), *World development indicators*, Washington, DC: The World Bank.

Xu, Y. (2011), Towards a more accurate measure of foreign bank entry and its impact on domestic banking performance: The case of China, *Journal of Banking and Finance*, 35(4): 886–901.

5. Destination Consumption

Enabling migrants' propensity to consume

Meiyan Wang and Cai Fang

Introduction

The 2014 Central Economic Working Conference emphasised that China's economy has a 'new normal', characterised mainly by slower growth. One approach to fostering new sources of growth is to enable consumption to play a more significant role in boosting economic development in China. That potential is large, as the proportions of final consumption expenditure and household consumption expenditure in gross domestic product (GDP) have significantly declined since the period of reform and opening-up. In 2013 these two proportions were 48.2 per cent and 34.1 per cent respectively. In comparison, the proportions of final consumption expenditure and household consumption expenditure in GDP in the United States and Japan are both higher and have been increasing. For the United States in 2013, these rates were 83 per cent and 68 per cent and for Japan 82 per cent and 61 per cent, respectively.[1]

There are many possible approaches to achieving the target of expanding consumption in China. Releasing migrant consumption potential is one of the most important. This relates, first, to the fact that the number of migrants and migrant income per capita have recently increased rapidly (Cai and Du 2011; Cai and Wang 2013; DRS NBS 2014; Li 2013). The resulting total migrant income pool is huge, and this offers large potential consumption. Second, the new generation of migrants has a higher marginal propensity to consume than the previous generation of migrants (Project Team on 'New Generation of Migrant Workers' 2011; Wang 2013). In this way, migrants are an emerging new consumer group whose impact on the shape of the new normal could be significant.

A number of factors could, however, be suppressing migrant consumption. The leading factor is that compared with urban residents, migrants are disadvantaged in employment conditions, income levels and access to social welfare and public services. Specifically, they usually do not have stable jobs, they earn lower incomes and they have fewer social security and public service entitlements (China Development Research Foundation 2010; Fan et al. 2013).

---

1   Data are from World Bank (various years).

Yet microeconomics informs us that income is the fundamental determinant of consumption. Less directly, employment conditions, social security and public services have also been shown to affect consumption.[2]

This gulf between urban residents and migrants is driven by the strictures of China's *hukou* system, which has been hindering migration from rural to urban areas. Migrants do not have equitable access to education, health care, social welfares and public services with urban residents (Fan et al. 2013; Research Group of Development Research Center of the State Council 2010), though many reforms of the *hukou* system have been implemented in the past three decades (Cai 2011b). The gulf in migrants' rights could also be indicative of the potential to increase urban consumption levels via migrants. Cai (2011a) found that migrants' propensity to consume would increase were they able to obtain permanent and full rights in their adopted urban home.

Comparative analysis of migrant consumption potential requires micro-survey data from both migrants and urban residents. Unfortunately, most studies use the data compiled from surveys that exclusively sample migrants (for example, Cao et al. 2012; Kong and Su 2013; Su and Kong 2012). The work of Song et al. (2010) is an exception. Macroeconomic linkages between migrant rights and consumption demand and economic development were explored using a computable general equilibrium (CGE) model (Research Group of Development Research Center of the State Council 2010). Unfortunately, the macroeconomic focus hid microeconomic considerations. The CGE model also forces a lot of assumptions.

This study uses micro-survey data that include migrants and urban residents to explore the consumption potential of migrants if they enjoy comprehensive urban rights, taking urban residents as the reference group. It compares the consumption level and patterns of migrants and urban residents and explores the determinants of consumption for the two groups. The study also estimates the consumption potential of migrants if they are granted equivalent status to and consume the same as urban residents. Migrants in cities can be divided into rural-to-urban migrants and urban-to-urban migrants. This study focuses on rural-to-urban migrants.

The rest of this study is organised as follows: the second section introduces the data used for this analysis and analyses empirical trends in the consumption level and patterns of migrants, using urban residents as the benchmark. The third section examines the determinants of consumption for migrants and

---

2   For example, many studies show that social security coverage can promote consumption (Feldstein 1974; Munnell 1974; Zhang 2008). In contrast, a lower social security coverage rate generates unstable expectations for the future, which can restrict consumption.

urban residents and estimates both the income elasticity of consumption and the marginal propensity to consume for the two groups. The fourth section estimates the consumption level and consumption pattern of migrants in the case of this group enjoying comprehensive urban rights; and the last section offers conclusions and policy suggestions.

Consumption levels and consumption patterns of migrants and urban residents

This section introduces the data used for the analysis, describing the sampling method for the data and the main information included, as well as discussing the advantage of using these data for the analysis. It also analyses the consumption level and pattern of migrants, taking urban residents as the reference group.

The data

This study uses the data from the China Urban Labour Survey (CULS). The CULS was conducted in 2010 in six cities—Shanghai, Wuhan, Shenyang, Fuzhou, Xi'an and Guangzhou—by the Institute of Population and Labour Economics of the Chinese Academy of Social Sciences. There are two advantages of using these survey data. First, the survey includes both migrants and urban residents, which can be used for comparative analysis and prediction of the consumption potential of migrants using urban residents as the reference group. Second, the survey includes detailed information on employment, income, consumption and social security, which offers the possibility of examining the determinants of consumption for migrants and urban residents.

The CULS used population-sampling techniques to identify 700 representative urban households in each city, and then applied a two-stage interview procedure. First, each household head was questioned about the household and then all household members were interviewed individually. In each city, that process was repeated in interviews with 600 migrant households. Migrants included those who had moved from rural areas and those who had moved from one urban hub to another—that is, migrants in the survey held both agricultural and non-agricultural *hukou*. This study exclusively utilises the survey results of the migrant households holding an agricultural *hukou*. In other words, this study analyses rural-to-urban migrants.

Information captured by the survey can be divided into two categories: individual information of household members and household information. The individual information includes the basic demographics of household members such as human capital characteristics, employment situation, income and consumption at the individual level, and social security situation. The household information includes housing, income and consumption at the household level and some other information. This study focuses on consumption results, which are very detailed. Samples from 4,148 urban households and 2,428 migrant households from the CULS are used.

Comparative descriptive analysis of migrant consumption

The categories of consumption involved in the CULS study include food, clothing, household facilities, articles and services, health care and medical services, transport and communications, education, culture and recreation, and other articles and services. For simplicity, we combine these categories as follows. First, clothing, transport and communications, and cultural and recreation consumption are combined into work-related consumption; second, household facilities, articles and services and other articles and services are combined into facilities and services; third, health care and medical services and education are combined into human capital consumption. The four categories of consumption used in this study are thus food consumption, work-related consumption, facilities and services consumption, and human capital consumption.

The average yearly consumption per capita of migrants is RMB8,627, which is, on average, 22 per cent lower than that of urban residents (Table 5.1). The gap may relate to differences in facilities, services and human capital consumption between migrants and urban residents. Migrant facilities and services consumption is 37.6 per cent lower than that of urban residents, while human capital consumption is 47.9 per cent lower than that of urban residents. The difference between migrants and urban residents for food and work-related consumption is smaller. Migrants' food consumption is lower than that of urban residents by 14.7 per cent, and migrants' work-related consumption is 19.6 per cent lower than that of urban residents.

Table 5.1 Yearly consumption per capita of migrants and urban residents

Consumption category	Migrants (1) (RMB)	Urban residents (2) (RMB)	(1)–(2) (RMB)	[(1)–(2)]/(2)*100 (%)
Food	4,620	5,416	−796	−14.7
Work-related	2,707	3,367	−660	−19.6
Facilities and services	554	888	−334	−37.6
Human capital	747	1,433	−686	−47.9
Total	**8,627**	**11,104**	**−2,477**	**−22.3**

Source: Authors' calculations based on the China Urban Labour Survey (CULS) (2010).

For both migrants and urban residents, the proportion of food consumption in total consumption is about 50 per cent. The proportion of work-related consumption ranks second, and the proportions of other categories of consumption are all relatively low (Table 5.2). The proportions of work-related consumption and that of facilities and services are similar for migrants and urban residents, but there are some differences in the consumption patterns between the two groups. For example, the proportion of migrants' food consumption is higher than that of urban residents by 4.8 percentage points, while the proportion of migrants' human capital consumption is lower than that of urban residents by 4.2 percentage points.

Table 5.2 Consumption patterns of migrants and urban residents

Consumption category	Migrants (1) (%)	Urban residents (2) (%)	(1)–(2) (%)
Food	53.6	48.8	4.8
Work-related	31.4	30.3	1.1
Facilities and services	6.4	8.0	−1.6
Human capital	8.7	12.9	−4.2
Total	100	100	0.0

Source: Authors' calculations from CULS (2010).

The analysis above reveals differences in the consumption levels and patterns of migrants and urban residents. Descriptive analysis, however, cannot reveal if these differences are significant. The consumption level and patterns of a household are affected by many factors, such as household income level, social security coverage rate of household members, household size, age structure of household members, gender of household head, age of household head and educational level of household head. Use of an econometric model enables better exploration of the determinants of consumption for migrants and urban residents.

The determinants of consumption for migrants and urban residents

This section uses an econometric model to analyse the determinants of consumption for migrants and urban residents. Specifically, it examines whether there is a significant difference in consumption level, income elasticity of consumption and marginal consumption propensity between the two groups. The model utilised is ordinary least squares (OLS).

Income elasticity of consumption for migrants and urban residents: Sub-sample analysis

The household is the unit of analysis. The dependent variable is the log of consumption per capita of a household. Income is the fundamental factor affecting consumption, which is first included among independent variables in the model. The rate of coverage of social security of household members is an important factor affecting consumption, which is also included in the model. In addition, household size, the age structure of household members, individual characteristics of the household head and city dummy variables are included in the model. The model is specified as follows (Equation 5.1).

Equation 5.1

$$\ln conpc = \alpha + \beta \ln incpc + \psi ssp + \gamma hhsize + \eta pold + \lambda HEAD + \phi CITY + u$$

In Equation 5.1, ln$conpc$ is the log of consumption per capita of a household; ln$incpc$ is the log of disposable income per capita of a household; β (the coefficient of ln$incpc$) is the income elasticity of consumption; ssp is the pension coverage rate of household members; $hhsize$ is household size; $pold$ is the proportion of household members aged 65 and above; $HEAD$ is a vector of individual characteristics of the household head (including gender, age and years of schooling); $CITY$ is a group of city dummy variables (the reference group is Shanghai); and u is the error term. The independent variables in the model are listed in Table 5.3.

Table 5.3 Independent variables in the model

Independent variable	Variable type	Explanation
Disposable income per capita	Continuous	Household disposable income per capita
Coverage rate of pension	Continuous	Coverage rate of pension among household members aged 16 and above
Household size	Continuous	Number of household members
Proportion of household aged 65 and above	Continuous	Proportion of household members aged 65 and above
Household head is female	Dummy	Household head is female=1; household head is male=0
Age of household head	Continuous	Age of household head
Years of schooling of household head	Continuous	Years of schooling of household head
Wuhan	Dummy	Wuhan=1, otherwise=0
Shenyang	Dummy	Shenyang=1, otherwise=0
Fuzhou	Dummy	Fuzhou=1, otherwise=0
Xi'an	Dummy	Xi'an=1, otherwise=0
Guangzhou	Dummy	Guangzhou=1, otherwise=0

Income level is the fundamental factor affecting consumption. Disposable income per capita is included in the model to capture the effect of income on consumption. The positive effect of income on consumption has been proven by previous studies (for example, Feldstein 1974; Song et al. 2010). We can expect that income has affected consumption positively.

The coverage rate of social security has also affected consumption (Munnell 1974; Zhang 2008). We include the pension coverage rate of household members aged 16 and above in the model to capture the effect of social security coverage on consumption, which could be mixed. On the one hand, people covered by social security might have more stable expectations of future income, which could increase current consumption. On the other hand, expenditure on social security reduces current disposable income, which could reduce current consumption.

Variables relating to household size and the age structure of household members could also affect consumption. Household size is included in the model to capture whether there are economies of scale in household consumption. The proportion of those aged 65 and above is included in the model to capture the effects on some categories of consumption. For example, households with a higher proportion of members aged 65 and above might have higher levels of consumption of health care and medical services and less consumption of education.

A vector of variables of individual characteristics of the household head, including gender, age and years of schooling, is included in the model. These are all important characteristics of the household head, which could affect consumption decisions. For example, households whose head has more years of schooling might have greater consumption. Finally, a group of city dummy variables is included to reflect the city where the sample points were collected: Wuhan, Shenyang, Fuzhou, Xi'an and Guangzhou. This captures the regional factors that could affect consumption, and takes Shanghai as the reference group. The descriptive statistics on the independent variables are in Table 5.4.

Table 5.4 Descriptive characteristics of migrants and urban residents

Independent variable	Migrants	Urban residents
Disposable income per capita (RMB)	19,559	20,995
Coverage rate of pension	0.11	0.70
Household size	2.29	2.89
Proportion of household aged 65 and above	0.01	0.16
Proportion of households whose head is female	0.33	0.31
Age of household head	35	52
Years of schooling of household head	9.7	11.1

Source: Authors' calculations from CULS (2010).

Table 5.5 presents the regression results. From the descriptive analysis, we saw that food consumption is an important part of total consumption, occupying about 50 per cent of total consumption. We thus run regressions on total consumption and food consumption. The R squared for all regression models is above 20 per cent, and the regression results are basically in line with our expectations.

Table 5.5 Income elasticity of consumption for migrants and urban residents (sub-sample)

Dependent variable: Log of consumption per capita	Total consumption		Food consumption	
	Migrants	Urban residents	Migrants	Urban residents
Log of disposable income per capita	0.247	0.279	0.189	0.201
	(10.21)***	(18.35)***	(8.55)***	(14.29)***
Coverage rate of pension	0.109	0.020	0.078	0.002
	(2.89)***	(0.91)	(1.81)*	(0.09)
Household size	−0.033	−0.087	−0.053	−0.124
	(3.01)***	(11.74)***	(4.64)***	(16.17)***
Proportion of household aged 65 and above	0.149	0.037	−0.094	0.045
	(0.81)	(1.09)	(0.72)	(1.30)
Household head is female	0.048	0.045	−0.006	0.031
	(2.05)**	(2.84)***	(0.23)	(1.85)*
Age of household head	−0.004	−0.002	0.001	−0.000
	(3.60)***	(2.86)***	(0.63)	(0.17)
Years of schooling of household head	0.031	0.028	0.025	0.018
	(7.97)***	(11.47)***	(6.00)***	(6.99)***
City dummy variables	Omitted	Omitted	Omitted	Omitted
Constant term	6.515	6.559	6.507	6.852
	(25.49)***	(42.49)***	(26.86)***	(47.74)***
R squared	0.29	0.36	0.23	0.31
Number of observations	2428	4148	2428	4148

*** significant at 1 per cent.
** significant at 5 per cent.
* significant at 10 per cent.
Note: t statistics in parentheses.
Source: Authors' calculations from CULS (2010).

The dependent variable of the model is log of consumption per capita. The coefficient of log of disposable income per capita is income elasticity of consumption. The income elasticity of total consumption for migrants is 0.247, which indicates that, if migrants' income per capita increases by 1 per cent, 0.247 per cent of this will be used for consumption. Similarly, the income elasticity of food consumption for migrants is 0.189, which indicates that, if migrants' income per capita increases by 1 per cent, 0.189 per cent of this will be used for food consumption. For migrants and urban residents, both income elasticity of total consumption and income elasticity of food consumption are significantly positive.

The pension coverage rate has a positive effect on both total consumption and food consumption for migrants, but almost no effect on total consumption and food consumption for urban residents. This implies that pension coverage expansion would promote migrants' consumption. This is consistent with conclusions of the existing literature (for example, Feldstein 1974; Munnell 1974). Therefore, expanding pension coverage is an important way to promote migrants' consumption.

Household size has a negative effect on total consumption and food consumption for both migrants and urban residents. This indicates that total consumption per capita and food consumption per capita are lower in larger households. This suggests that households enjoy economies of scale in total consumption and food consumption. For example, the coefficient on household size for migrants' total consumption is −0.033, which indicates that migrants' total consumption per capita decreases by 3.3 per cent with one additional household member. The coefficient of household size for migrants' food consumption is −0.053, which indicates that migrants' food consumption per capita decreases by 5.3 per cent with each additional household member.

Compared with households whose heads are males, in households whose heads are females total consumption per capita is higher, for both migrant and urban households. The age of the household head has a consistent effect also, but this is negative, which indicates that the total per capita consumption of households whose head is older is less. The age of the household head does not, however, have a significant effect on food consumption.

The years of schooling of the household head have a positive effect on total consumption and food consumption, for both migrants and urban residents. This indicates that, after controlling for other factors, total consumption per capita and food consumption per capita of households whose heads have had more years of schooling are higher for both migrants and urban residents. Therefore, improving educational levels is an important way to promote consumption.

Income elasticity of consumption for migrants and urban residents: Pooled sample

As has been pointed out, due to the different characteristics of migrants and urban residents, migrant attitudes to consumption could be different from those of urban residents. In order to examine this prospective difference, we pool the samples of migrants and urban residents and add a dummy variable, M ($M=1$ if migrant, $M=0$ otherwise) to run the regressions. This model is specified as follows (Equation 5.2).

Equation 5.2

$$\ln conpc = \alpha + \sigma M + \beta \ln incpc + \psi ssp + \gamma hhsize + \eta pold + \lambda HEAD + \phi CIT$$

Furthermore, to examine for any difference in the income elasticity of consumption of migrant and urban residents, we add a term (M^*ln$incpc$) to Equation 5.2, which is the interaction of M and the log of disposable income per capita, forming Equation 5.3.

Equation 5.3

$$\ln conpc = \alpha + \sigma M + \beta \ln incpc + \omega M * \ln incpc + \psi ssp + \gamma hhsize + \eta pold + \lambda HEAD + \phi CITY + u$$

If the coefficient of the interaction term (ω) is significant, it means there is a difference in income elasticity of consumption between migrants and urban residents. Positive ω means the income elasticity of consumption for migrants is higher than for urban residents, and negative ω means the income elasticity of consumption for migrants is lower than for urban residents.

The regression results of Equations 5.2 and 5.3, which use pooled samples of migrants and urban residents on total consumption per capita and food consumption per capita, respectively, are shown in Table 5.6. The regressions results are basically in line with our expectations.

For Equation 5.2, we focus on the dummy variable M. The coefficient of M is negative for both total consumption and food consumption. This means that, compared with urban residents, for migrants, total consumption per capita and food consumption per capita are both less. Specifically, total consumption per capita for migrants is lower than for urban residents by 24.4 per cent, and food consumption per capita for migrants is lower than for urban residents by 14.5 per cent.

In Equation 5.3, we focus on the interaction term of M and log of disposable income per capita. If the coefficient of the interaction term is significant, it means there is a difference in the income elasticity of consumption of migrants and urban residents. The regression results show that the coefficient of the interaction term is not significant for total consumption and food consumption, which means there is no difference in income elasticity of consumption between migrants and urban residents.

Table 5.6 Income elasticity of consumption for migrants and urban residents (pooled sample)

Dependent variable: Log of consumption per capita	Equation 5.2		Equation 5.3	
	Total consumption	Food consumption	Total consumption	Food consumption
Migrant	−0.244	−0.145	0.106	−0.000
	(12.47)***	(7.14)***	(0.45)	(0.00)
Log of disposable income per capita	0.266	0.195	0.281	0.201
	(19.93)***	(16.03)***	(19.29)***	(14.94)***
Interaction term			−0.036	−0.015
			(1.48)	(0.67)
Coverage rate of pension	0.046	0.023	0.047	0.024
	(2.50)**	(1.21)	(2.55)**	(1.24)
Household size	−0.064	−0.094	−0.065	−0.094
	(10.37)***	(14.50)***	(10.41)***	(14.49)***
Proportion of household aged 65 and above	0.076	0.058	0.072	0.056
	(2.41)**	(1.80)*	(2.25)**	(1.73)*
Household head is female	0.047	0.015	0.047	0.014
	(3.58)***	(1.01)	(3.57)***	(1.00)
Age of household head	−0.003	0.000	−0.003	0.000
	(4.25)***	(0.58)	(4.32)***	(0.56)
Years of schooling of household head	0.030	0.021	0.029	0.020
	(14.49)***	(9.52)***	(14.29)***	(9.39)***
City dummy variables	n.a.[1]	n.a.	n.a.	n.a
Constant term	6.605	6.748	6.473	6.694
	(47.86)***	(52.13)***	(44.05)***	(48.73)***
R squared	0.36	0.28	0.36	0.28
Number of observations	6576	6576	6576	6576

[1] n.a. = not applicable.
*** significant at 1 per cent.
** significant at 5 per cent.
* significant at 10 per cent.
Notes: t statistics in parentheses.
Source: Authors' calculations from CULS (2010).

Marginal consumption propensities for migrants and urban residents: Sub-sample

In the previous sections, we discussed income elasticity of consumption for migrants and urban residents. In addition, we would like to understand the marginal propensity to consume of the two groups. From Equation 5.1, if both log of consumption per capita and log of disposable income per capita are changed to their original values but other variables remain as they are, Equation 5.4 is formed as follows, in which the coefficient of disposable income per capita (β) is marginal consumption propensity (Equation 5.4).

Equation 5.4

$$conpc = \alpha + \beta incpc + \psi ssp + \gamma hhsize + \eta pold + \lambda HEAD + \phi CITY + u$$

We run regressions on migrants and urban residents respectively, using Equation 5.4. The regression results are shown in Table 5.7 and are basically in line with our expectations. We focus on the variable capturing disposable income per capita and its coefficient, the marginal consumption propensity. We do not discuss results of other independent variables in detail.

Table 5.7 Marginal consumption propensities of migrants and urban residents (sub-sample)

Dependent variable: Consumption per capita	Total consumption		Food consumption	
	Migrants	Urban residents	Migrants	Urban residents
Disposable income per capita	0.161	0.102	0.065	0.024
	(5.64)***	(3.23)***	(4.16)***	(2.75)***
Coverage rate of pension	1,214.369	71.024	774.982	40.777
	(1.50)	(0.18)	(1.54)	(0.18)
Household size	−426.084	−1,314.904	−406.435	−945.193
	(2.54)**	(8.37)***	(5.23)***	(9.88)***
Proportion of household aged 65 and above	1,556.470	935.788	−558.701	404.275
	(1.18)	(1.55)	(1.01)	(1.32)
Household head is female	282.475	368.961	−19.287	−52.010
	(0.75)	(1.34)	(0.12)	(0.37)
Age of household head	−71.971	−24.857	−13.790	−0.897
	(4.14)***	(1.84)*	(1.56)	(0.11)
Years of schooling of household head	221.350	390.871	96.130	135.229
	(4.15)***	(7.09)***	(3.32)***	(6.26)***
City dummy variables	Omitted	Omitted	Omitted	Omitted

Dependent variable: Consumption per capita	Total consumption		Food consumption	
	Migrants	Urban residents	Migrants	Urban residents
Constant term	7,424.812	10,555.847	4,425.996	7,309.175
	(5.38)***	(9.29)***	(5.53)***	(11.54)***
R squared	0.19	0.22	0.19	0.14
Number of observations	2428	4148	2428	4148

*** significant at 1 per cent.
** significant at 5 per cent.
* significant at 10 per cent.
Notes: t statistics in parentheses.
Source: Authors' calculations from CULS (2010).

The marginal propensities of total consumption and food consumption are positive for both migrants and urban residents. The marginal propensity of total consumption for migrants is 0.161, which means that RMB0.161 is used for total consumption if migrants' disposable income per capita increases by RMB1. Marginal propensity of food consumption for migrants is 0.065, which means that RMB0.065 is used for food consumption if migrants' disposable income per capita increases by RMB1.

Marginal consumption propensities of migrants and urban residents: Pooled sample

To further examine marginal propensity of consumption, we pool together the samples of migrants and urban residents and add a dummy variable (M) to examine the differences in consumption of migrants and urban residents to Equation 5.4, which forms Equation 5.5.

Equation 5.5

$$conpc = \alpha + \sigma M + \beta incpc + \psi ssp + \gamma hhsize + \eta pold + \lambda HEAD + \phi CITY + u$$

In order to examine whether there is a difference in the marginal consumption propensities of migrants and urban residents, we add a term ($M*incpc$) to Equation 5.5, which is the interaction of M and disposable income per capita, forming Equation 5.6. If the coefficient of the interaction term (ω) is significant, this means there is a difference in marginal consumption propensities between migrants and urban residents. A positive ω means that the marginal consumption propensity for migrants is higher than for urban residents, while a negative ω means that the marginal consumption propensity of migrants is lower than that of urban residents.

Equation 5.6

$$conpc = \alpha + \sigma M + \beta incpc + \omega M * incpc + \psi ssp + \gamma hhsize + \eta pold + \lambda HEAD + \phi CITY + u$$

The regression results of Equations 5.5 and 5.6 are shown in Table 5.8. We use pooled samples of migrants and urban residents to run regressions on total consumption per capita and food consumption per capita, respectively. The regression results are basically in line with our expectations.

Table 5.8 Marginal consumption propensities of migrants and urban residents (pooled sample)

Dependent variable: Consumption per capita	Equation 5.5		Equation 5.6	
	Total	Food	Total	Food
Migrant	−2,500.342	−750.115	−3,473.584	−1,537.236
	(7.32)***	(3.87)***	(4.38)***	(5.04)***
Disposable income per capita	0.119	0.035	0.107	0.026
	(4.16)***	(3.36)***	(3.32)***	(2.85)***
Interaction term			0.044	0.036
			(1.12)	(2.14)**
Coverage rate of pension	446.476	331.065	352.477	255.042
	(1.24)	(1.52)	(1.01)	(1.26)
Household size	−964.451	−738.352	−945.096	−722.699
	(7.73)***	(11.20)***	(8.05)***	(11.28)***
Proportion of household aged 65 and above	1,316.799	521.165	1,413.048	599.008
	(2.35)**	(1.93)*	(2.55)**	(2.22)**
Household head is female	237.770	−108.936	262.247	−89.140
	(1.08)	(0.96)	(1.19)	(0.79)
Age of household head	−39.120	−3.900	−39.296	−4.043
	(3.68)***	(0.63)	(3.71)***	(0.66)
Years of schooling of household head	333.261	119.996	340.017	125.460
	(7.81)***	(6.34)***	(7.95)***	(7.01)***
City dummy variables	Omitted	Omitted	Omitted	Omitted
Constant term	10,162.353	6,397.481	10,338.443	6,539.897
	(9.91)***	(11.39)***	(10.01)***	(12.17)***
R squared	0.22	0.15	0.22	0.16
Number of observations	6576	6576	6576	6576

*** significant at 1 per cent.
** significant at 5 per cent.
* significant at 10 per cent.
Notes: t statistics in parentheses.
Source: Authors' calculations from CULS (2010).

In Equation 5.5, we focus on the dummy variable M. The coefficient of M is negative for both total consumption and food consumption. This means that, compared with urban residents, for migrants, total consumption per capita and food consumption per capita are both less.

In Equation 5.6, we focus on the interaction term of M and disposable income per capita. If the coefficient of the interaction term is significant, it means there is a difference in marginal consumption propensity between migrants and urban residents. The regression results show that the coefficient of the interaction term is not significant for total consumption; however, the coefficient of the interaction term is significant and positive for food consumption. This means that there is no difference in the marginal propensities of total consumption between migrants and urban residents, but the marginal propensity of food consumption for migrants is higher than for urban residents.

Consumption potential of migrants: Taking urban residents as a reference group

The analysis above informs us that across all categories of consumption migrant consumption is lower than that of urban residents. After controlling for other factors, however, there is no significant difference in the marginal propensity of total consumption between migrants and urban residents, but the marginal propensity of food consumption for migrants is higher than for urban residents. Since migrant incomes have been increasing rapidly in recent years, we can expect that, if migrants are able to enjoy resident rights in terms of access to services and facilities, social security and so on in their adopted urban home, their consumption potential is huge.

To estimate how huge, we assume that migrants will follow the same consumption patterns as urban residents when they have access to the same rights and benefits. We can use the regression model of consumption for urban residents (Equation 5.4) to calculate the consumption of migrants under that assumption (Table 5.9).

If migrants consume like urban residents, their consumption level will become similar to that of urban residents. Examining by category, we find that migrants' estimated consumption of food and of facilities and services will be very similar to those of urban residents. Estimated work-related consumption for migrants will be higher than that of urban residents, by 9.1 per cent. Meanwhile, the estimated human capital consumption for migrants will be much lower—28.4 per cent lower—than that for urban residents.

Table 5.9 Estimation of consumption potential of migrants

Category	Estimation for migrants (1) (RMB)	Urban residents (2) (RMB)	(1)–(2) (RMB)	(1)–(2)/(2)*100 (%)
Food	5,393	5,416	−23	−0.4
Work-related	3,674	3,367	307	9.1
Facilities and services	868	888	−20	−2.3
Human capital	1,026	1,433	−407	−28.4
Total	10,960	11,104	−144	−1.3

Note: Estimates for migrants refer to migrants' yearly consumption per capita if they follow the same paths to consumption as urban residents.
Source: Authors' calculations from CULS (2010).

If migrants consume the same as urban residents, their consumption will increase by a large extent—compared with their actual consumption (Table 5.10). Specifically, total consumption per capita of migrants will increase by RMB2,333, or by about 27 per cent. Food consumption will increase by 16.7 per cent, which is the lowest increase among all categories of consumption. Work-related consumption and human capital consumption will increase by 35.7 per cent and 37.3 per cent, respectively. Facilities and services consumption will increase by a massive 56.7 per cent.

Table 5.10 Consumption per capita of migrants: Actual and estimated

Category	Estimated (1) (RMB)	Actual (2) (RMB)	(1)–(2) (RMB)	(1)–(2)/(2)*100 (%)
Food	5,393	4,620	773	16.7
Work-related	3,674	2,707	967	35.7
Facilities and services	868	554	314	56.7
Human capital	1,026	747	279	37.3
Total	10,960	8,627	2,333	27.0

Note: 'Estimated' refers to migrants' yearly consumption per capita if they follow the same paths to consumption as urban residents. 'Actual' refers to migrants' actual yearly consumption per capita.
Source: Authors' calculations from CULS (2010).

A monitoring survey of migrants conducted in 31 provinces by the National Bureau of Statistics of China (NBS) shows that the number of those having migrated beyond their home township for a period longer than six months reached 145 million in 2009 (DRS NBS 2014). Our analysis shows that migrants' yearly consumption per capita is RMB8,627. Total consumption of migrants was thus RMB1.251 trillion in 2009.

Similarly, our analysis finds that if migrants consume the same as urban residents, their consumption per capita will increase by RMB2,333. The total consumption of migrants will also increase, by RMB338.3 billion, and reach RMB1.589 trillion. Since GDP was RMB34.090 trillion in 2009, total consumption of migrants thus occupied 4.7 per cent of GDP.

Estimation of migrants' consumption potential in this chapter is based on the assumption that migrants' characteristics remain as they are. The regression results show that income, pension coverage and educational level can promote migrants' consumption levels. For migrants, income has been increasing rapidly, pension coverage has been expanding and the educational level has been improving in recent years. If improvements in these aspects are considered, the potential consumption of migrants is more substantial.

Conclusions and policy suggestions

This study used China Urban Labour Survey data from 2010 to compare the consumption level and patterns of migrants and urban residents. It analysed the determinants of consumption and examined the income elasticity of consumption and the marginal propensity to consume of the two groups. Using the regression results, it estimated the consumption potential of migrants under the assumption that migrants achieve full residency and access rights in their adopted home and that their characteristics are otherwise unchanged.

This study shows that migrants' total consumption per capita is 22 per cent lower than that of urban residents. The income elasticity of total consumption and the income elasticity of food consumption are positive for both migrants and urban residents. There is no difference between the two groups in income elasticity of total consumption and income elasticity of food consumption.

Factors affecting consumption include pension coverage, which has a positive effect on total consumption per capita and food consumption per capita for migrants. Household size negatively affects total consumption and food consumption per capita, for both migrants and urban residents, possibly due to scale effects. The years of schooling of the household head affect total consumption and food consumption per capita positively for both migrants and urban residents. The marginal propensities of total consumption and of food consumption are positive for both migrants and urban residents. There is no significant difference between migrants and urban residents in the marginal propensity of total consumption. The marginal propensity of food consumption is higher for migrants than for urban residents.

If migrants are granted equivalent status and consume the same as urban residents, and other characteristics are held constant, total migrant consumption per capita will increase by 27 per cent—to a level similar to that of urban residents. The regression results suggest that increases in income, pension coverage and educational attainment can promote migrant consumption.

Through the urbanisation process of recent years, these characteristics have been improving rapidly for migrants. The combination of implied changes in consumption levels that would be enabled through improvements in areas of these demographic characteristics could in turn produce an enormous lift to aggregate consumption—that is, migrants have the potential to become a huge emerging consumer group and to play an important role in boosting domestic demand and promoting China's economic development.

Therefore, granting migrants full residency rights, such as access to education, health care and social security, is not only an important task and challenge of urbanisation, but also appears to be an intrinsic requirement for China's economic development. In recent years, China has made great efforts to provide more and better public services and social welfare for migrants (Cai 2011b; China Development Research Foundation 2010). Several documents have been issued to elaborate issues concerning rural-to-urban migrants since 2014. Continued promotion of migrant livelihoods is crucial to further tap the economic benefits of their consumption potential.

References

Cai, F. (2011a), Citizenization of rural migrant workers and development of new consumers, *Journal of Graduate School of Chinese Academy of Social Sciences*, (3): 5–11.

Cai, F. (2011b), Hukou system reform and unification of rural–urban social welfare, *China & World Economy*, 19(3): 33–48.

Cai, F. and Du, Y. (2011), Wage increase, wage convergence and Lewis turning point, *Economic Perspectives*, (9): 9–16.

Cai, F. and Wang, M. (2013), Consumption of new generation of migrants, *Chinese Cadres Tribune*, (11): 25–8.

Cao, G., Li, K. and Liu, T. (2012), Chinese migrant workers' household consumption structure and urbanization, Paper for the annual conference of the Geographical Society of China, Kaifeng City and Zhengzhou City, Henan Province.

China Development Research Foundation (2010), *China development report 2010: New urbanization strategy of promoting human development*, Beijing: People's Publishing House.

Department of Rural Surveys, National Bureau of Statistics (DRS NBS) (2014), *China rural household survey yearbook 2014*, Beijing: China Statistics Press.

Du, Y. and Wang, M. (2010), New estimate of surplus rural labor force and its implications, *Journal of Guangzhou University (Social Sciences Edition)*, 9(4): 17–24.

Fan, G. and Guo, W. (2013), *Migrant workers early withdrawal from urban labour market: Theory, evidence and policies*, Beijing: China Economic Publishing House.

Feldstein, M. (1974), Social security, induced retirement and aggregate capital accumulation, *Journal of Political Economy*, 82(5): 905–26.

Kong, X. and Su, J. (2013), An analysis of the elements affecting farmer workers' consumption in our country: A study based on the data from 1860 samples in the 28 provinces and regions across the country, *Journal of Shaanxi Normal University (Philosophy and Social Sciences Edition)*, 42(1): 24–33.

Li, S. (2013), Current situation of rural migrant workers in the Chinese labor market, *Studies in Labor Economics*, 1(1): 51–68.

Munnell, A. (1974), *The effect of social security on personal saving*, Cambridge, Mass.: Ballinger.

Project Team on 'New Generation of Migrant Workers' (2011), New generation of migrant workers: Number, structure and characteristics, in Cai, F. (ed.), *China population and labor report no. 12: Challenges during the 12th Five-Year Plan period—Population, employment, and income distribution*, Beijing: Social Sciences Academic Press.

Research Group of Development Research Center of the State Council (2010), The effect of citizenization of rural migrant workers on the domestic demand and economic growth, *Economic Research Journal*, (6): 4–41.

Song, L., Wu, J. and Zhang, Y. (2010), Urbanization of migrant workers and expansion of domestic demand, *Social Sciences in China*, XXXI(3): 194–216.

Su, J. and Kong, X. (2012), The analysis of Chinese peasant workers' consumption structure characteristics and urbanization: Based on 1249 valid samples of 28 provinces, *Statistics & Information Forum*, 27(12): 96–101.

Wang, M. (2013), Changes of migrants' consumption and its determinants, in Cai, F. (ed.), *China population and labor report no. 14: From demographic dividend to institutional dividend*, Beijing: Social Sciences Academic Press.

World Bank (various years), *Development indicators*, Washington, DC: The World Bank.

Zhang, J. (2008), *A study on the effect of social security on China's urban residents' consumption and saving behavior*, Beijing: China Social Sciences Press.

6. National Energy Market Integration

A study of energy price convergence in China

Qing King Guo, Chi Keung Marco Lau, Kunwang Li and Ligang Song

Introduction

Energy price convergence is one of the leading indicators for understanding market liberalisation and integration. The first contribution to the literature on the success of Chinese market reform and market integration is Young (2000). The author uses simple trends in the regional variance of prices to quantify market liberalisation and integration. Fan and Wei (2006), however, cast doubt on Young's controversial finding that China's internal markets became less rather than more integrated during the reform period. Fan and Wei used a nonlinear panel unit root test and found 'strong evidence of price convergence and hence market integration in China. Such a finding is in favour of the view that China's transition to a market economy has been quite successful during the last two decades' (2006: 692).

Following the method of Fan and Wei (2006), Ma et al. (2009) use a linear panel unit root test and focus on the energy market; they found evidence that energy prices are mostly converging to the national average price. They further suggested that 'if policymakers actually want to control energy markets in the future, they need to devise new ways to intervene in the energy sector, otherwise the reforms they have introduced have clearly led to a more market-oriented energy sector' (Ma et al. 2009: 4848). The work of Fan and Wei (2006) and Ma et al. (2009) links price convergence to market liberalisation and internal market integration by adopting the 'law of one price' (LOP) and arbitrage behaviour.

The LOP implies that identical goods sold in different locations tend to converge to the same price if markets for those goods are fully developed and transport costs are controlled for, indicating purchasing power parity (PPP) in the international context. In the 1980s, a vast literature studied price convergence and the speed of adjustment for international markets, using unit root and cointegration techniques. In the 1990s, researchers shifted their focus and interest from international to intra-national studies of price convergence, in part because the latter are subject to less restrictive assumptions for PPP[1] (Parsley and Wei 1996). Many intra-country studies have examined whether the LOP holds (for example, Fan and Wei 2006; Lan and Sylwester 2010).

It is the conventional view that arbitrage opportunity among regions exists such that for the same good, trade will take place for agents to make a profit. In the long run, prices in different regions should converge to a single level, assuming zero or negligible transaction costs—say, transportation costs. In the literature, only nonlinear unit root tests can release the non-zero transaction cost assumption. Some recent examples of convergence studies that link convergence phenomena and policy reform, market integration and marketisation include Lau et al. (2015) for military expenditure convergence for the world; Lau et al. (2014) for healthcare expenditure in the European Union; Bilgin et al. (2010) for rental price convergence in Turkey; Akhmedjonov et al. (2013) for income convergence in Russia; and Suvankulov et al. (2012) for gasoline price convergence in Canada.

Empirical literature devoted to price convergence of energy markets in China remains limited (Ma et al. 2010). Fan and Wei (2006) are the first to investigate internal market integration in China using the unit root test. Their empirical results provide evidence for the proposition that gradualist reform has been quite successful in effecting the transformation from a planned to a market-oriented economy.[2]

Since a free and competitive market with a price mechanism underlies efficient resource allocation, this is of central concern for a transitional and per capita resource-poor economy such as China. The price dynamics of China's energy sector in particular are critical to market integration, not only because the energy market has been closely associated with manufacturing activities and environmental issues, but also because these are exposed to international energy price fluctuations. Moreover, China has 30 provinces and provincial-level municipalities, and each of these is unique in terms of demographic structure, geography and level of development. This also suggests that these characteristics may affect the market integration for goods and energy products, and vice versa.[3]

---

1   For example, the theory assumes that the transaction for mobile goods takes place converging towards PPP only under competitive market conditions for both countries without incurring transportation costs, barriers to trade and other transaction costs. It can be argued that these conditions are more valid in intra-national than international settings.

2   In this chapter, we denote the success of this transformation as 'marketisation'.

3   Fan and Wei (2006) found evidence of a higher degree of market integration for major cities in the coastal region for commodities including raw industrial materials, processed industrial materials, durable goods and vehicles, and services. Moreover, we cannot exclude the possibility that a higher degree of market integration (that is, allocative efficiency) affects the development level.

The purpose of this chapter is to examine price convergence among key energy products, such as gasoline, diesel, coal and gas across different regions in China over the sample period. This exercise helps shed light on the marketisation process in China, which has been being introduced incrementally for some three decades now. In addition, understanding whether domestic energy markets are more integrated across different regions can retrospectively and prospectively inform the reform process in China. Where a lack of evidence of price convergence is found for key energy products between regions in China, this could imply that Chinese domestic markets are not closely integrated, and that central and local governments should persist in extending relevant policy designs and implementation. Finally, a clear understanding of the price dynamic is important for designing economic policies, such as setting the level of the minimum wage in different locations across China.

China's industrialisation massively increased demand for energy. By 2005, and immediately following the annual growth of 3 per cent in energy intensity of gross domestic product (GDP) (the ratio of energy consumption per unit of GDP) during 2002–05 (Zhou et al. 2010), the government reached a consensus that rapid increases in energy demand were unsustainable. A decision was taken to reduce the energy intensity of GDP, via improved energy efficiency, and this in turn would be driven in part by marketisation of energy prices. With the energy intensity of China's GDP in 2007 being almost three times higher than the world average (Ma et al. 2009),[4] a series of goals was set to improve China's energy efficiency levels.

Table 6.1 Recent key energy policies supporting China's 20 per cent reduction goal

Energy policies	Date effective	Responsible agency
Fuel consumption limits for passenger cars	2004	
Medium and long-term plan for energy conservation	2005	National Development and Reform Commission (NDRC)
Renewable Energy Law	2005	
Government procurement program	2005	NDRC and Ministry of Finance (MoF)
National energy efficient design standard for public buildings	2005	Ministry of Construction (MoC)
Eleventh Five-Year Plan	2006	NDRC
State Council decision on strengthening energy conservation	2006	State Council
Reduced export tax rebates for many low value-added but high energy-consuming products	2006	MoF
Top 1,000 Energy-Consuming Enterprise program	2006	NDRC

---

4   For China, the energy intensity was 0.91 tonnes of oil equivalent per US$1,000 GDP (at 2000 prices) in comparison with 0.32 for the world average and 0.19 in Organisation for Economic Cooperation and Development (OECD) countries as reported by NBS (2007).

Energy policies	Date effective	Responsible agency
'Green Purchasing' program	2006	Ministry of Environment Protection (MEP) and MoF
Revision of Energy Conservation Law	2007	National People's Congress and NDRC
Allocation of funding on energy efficiency and pollution abatement	2007	MoF and NDRC
China energy technology policy outline	2007	NDRC and the Ministry of Science and Technology
Government Procurement program	2007	NDRC and MoF
National Phase III Vehicle Emission Standards	2007	
Interim administrative method for incentive funds for heating and metering and energy efficiency retrofit for existing residential buildings in China's northern heating area	2007	MoF
Law on Corporate Income Tax (preferential tax treatment for investment in energy-saving and environmentally friendly projects and equipment)	2008	NDRC
Allocation of funding on energy efficiency and pollution abatement	2008	MoF and NDRC
Appliance standards and labelling	Various years	General Administration of Quality Supervision, Inspection and Quarantine

Source: Zhou et al. (2010).

The reforms instigated in 2005 were both broad and deep. Table 6.1 outlines a selection of the key policies, providing background to the direction of those reforms and also to the governance of that reform element. Energy-related quantitative goals agreed in November 2005 included a 20 per cent reduction of energy intensity of GDP by 2010, part of which could be achieved by closing small plants and phasing out outdated capacity in high-consumption industry sectors.[5] Subsequent measures were designed and implemented, including laws, regulations and tax incentives to increase energy efficiency (Table 6.1) (Zhou et al. 2010). For such market-oriented measures to work effectively, parallel energy market reforms are required to allow energy product prices to move towards market-determined prices—a process that would also reduce differences in energy prices across different regions. This study explores that process of energy price convergence within China.

A sample period spanning 2006–12 is chosen for the study. This period begins one year after the initial set of energy pricing reforms began, in 2005, allowing for a time lag in policy outcomes. The time structure also implicitly allows for study of the impact of the energy pricing mechanism on energy efficiency (Ma et al. 2009) in testing the spatial convergence of energy prices during the

---

5   The 10 industries of iron, steel, cement, coal-fired power, coking, ferrous metal, glass, paper, ethanol and coal production.

key period in which energy reform policies applied, and especially the target of 20 per cent energy efficiency improvement by 2012 as set in 2005. The rationale for analysing the energy price convergence trend between Chinese regions is that segmentation of energy markets across the country is likely to undermine energy-related reforms.

Further, to date there has been insufficient attention in the literature to China's energy markets. This means there is insufficient evidence on energy price convergence in China and, accordingly, little is known about the efficiency of reforms. Ma et al. (2009), for example, studied the spot price for four energy products—coal, electricity, gasoline and diesel—but only covering 35 provincial (or autonomous region and municipality) capital cities across one decade from 1995. This study utilises a richer and updated dataset, and studies the energy market landscape following recent reforms.

Data

Data used are collected from the Price Supervision Centre of the National Development and Reform Commission (NDRC). These data cover 20 types of energy products from the five key energy product categories: coal, gasoline, diesel, electricity and gas. Moreover, these data were collected at 10-day intervals, on the 5th, 15th and 25th of each month, from 2006 to 2012. The advantage of high-frequency data is that they contain more information regarding arbitrage opportunities and convergence speed (Bachmeier and Griffin 2006; Ma et al. 2009; Taylor 2001). Setting the sample period to coincide with the key energy market reform era also provides scope to examine the degree of regional energy price convergence during the implementation phase of important energy policies in China. Detailed descriptions of data and the number of cities and provinces involved in each energy product are provided in the Appendix for this chapter.

Finally, the sample period coincides with the large fiscal stimulus package implemented by China's government in response to the global financial crisis (GFC). This sought to boost demand, impacting both energy prices and energy efficiency. If substantial variation in energy prices between regions in China in the post-crisis period is uncovered, this could be related to the large scale of the fiscal stimulus package. In this case, the stimulus may have been effective in boosting domestic demand, but it could also have served to undermine energy market integration in the process. The design of this study is expected to reveal useful information on energy markets in China, and also on the wider issues within that market of spatial convergence or divergence over time and between locations.

Preliminary analysis: Historical average energy product price trend

Gasoline and diesel

We first individually examine the pattern of price change over time for each energy product. Figure 6.1 shows the trend in average price—the mean of spot price at time 't' across all regions—for each product. We observe that after 2009 the average price of gasoline products was more volatile. From 2009 to 2012, that price also rose far more sharply than from 2006 to 2008. Specifically, from 2009 to 2012, the average price climbed by RMB4,000 per tonne—double the rate of the earlier period, 2006–08.

Price movement of diesel products is similar to that of gasoline products. This could relate to the oil price reform launched in 2009, under which domestic fuel prices were adjusted over a 22-day working period in response to a 4 per cent increase in Brent, Dubai and Cinta crude oil prices. A policy of explicit market response was linked to participants being free to set prices below the maximum retail price regulated by the government. This could also have contributed to higher price volatility after 2009. Finally, in 2013 the market was liberalised further and the prices of oil products were allowed to be adjusted every 10 working days, instead of every 22 days, to better reflect global oil price movement.

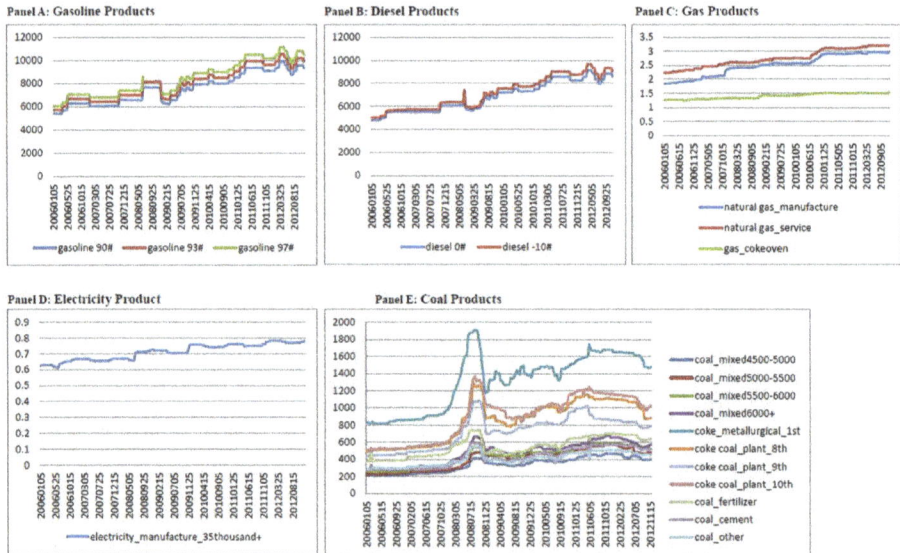

Figure 6.1 Historical average prices of energy products in China

Source: Plotted using the survey data.

Gas, electricity and coal

There is less movement in the gas price than in the prices of gasoline and diesel. Price changes that did take place in 2007 and 2010 are probably attributable to reform policies, including the 2007 price adjustment policy and energy intensity reduction reforms that were adopted in 2010.

Coal product prices show a similar pattern of gradual increase before 2007, followed by a dramatic increase, and finally a substantial drop during the GFC. Since the beginning of 2009, all coal product prices remained steady, until the second half of 2011, when prices tended to decrease gradually.

Preliminary analysis: Comparison of energy price trend

Table 6.2 presents the average spot prices and their changes for 20 energy products. The price of coal shows higher volatility than other energy products. For many coal products, the price in 2012 was double that in 2006—the result of an annual growth rate for coal products that was mostly above 11 per cent across the sample period. For diesel products, the price in 2012 was about 67 per cent more than the price in 2006. For gasoline products, the price in 2012 was 57 per cent more than the price in 2006, reflecting an annual average growth rate of 7.8 per cent.[6] Finally, compared with coal, gasoline and diesel, the prices of gas and electricity rose less rapidly. Gas increased by 40 per cent and electricity increased by an annual rate of 3.4 per cent, or 22 per cent over the sample period.

In addition to such price variation between different energy categories, price variation within energy product category groups is phenomenal. Coal and gas in particular have many subcategory products, and these have different growth rates. In the case of coal, the 2006–12 change in the price of 'coal_mixed5000-5500'[7] was a striking 1,275 per cent, while that for 'coal fertiliser' was only 35 per cent. Similar observations are found within gas product prices; however, this is not the case for gasoline or diesel products. The price changes of all gasoline and diesel subcategories are the same. This could imply that the markets for gasoline, diesel and electricity are subjected to greater regulation than the markets for coal and gas.

---

6 By coincidence, China's growth trajectory depending on political calibrations is also 7.8 per cent GDP growth.

7 '5000-5500' refers to the calorific value; this category belongs to the 'sub-bituminous' rank and the moisture content is 20–40 per cent. For more information, see: www.coalmarketinginfo.com/coal-basics.

Table 6.2 Aggregate price of energy products, 2006–12

Products	2006	2007	2008	2009	2010	2011	2012	2006–12 % change	2006–12 % yearly growth rate
coal_mixed4500-5000 (RMB/t)	211	236	337	332	374	430	426	102	12.4
coal_mixed5000-5500 (RMB/t)	231	264	374	416	462	550	524	127	14.6
coal_mixed5500-6000(RMB/t)	281	314	485	487	526	602	602	114	13.5
coal_mixed6000+ (RMB/t)	321	347	547	534	571	644	629	96	11.9
coal_metallurgical_1st(RMB/t)	803	869	1,489	1,400	1,500	1,719	1,702	112	13.3
coke coal_plant_8th (RMB/t)	529	558	911	860	966	1,062	972	84	10.7
coke coal_plant_9th (RMB/t)	481	515	809	759	832	913	815	69	9.2
coke coal_plant_10th (RMB/t)	527	566	969	900	1,009	1,154	1,063	102	12.4
coal_fertiliser (RMB/t)	485	530	672	508	573	667	653	35	5.1
coal_cement (RMB/t)	335	289	438	384	437	509	495	48	6.7
coal_other (RMB/t)	296	322	438	382	429	494	467	58	7.9
gas_manufacture (RMB/cu m)	1.9	2.11	2.43	2.56	2.68	2.92	2.96	56	7.7
gas_service (RMB/cu m)	2.29	2.48	2.61	2.73	2.88	3.11	3.2	40	5.7
gas_cokeoven (RMB/cu m)	1.27	1.31	1.33	1.42	1.47	1.5	1.51	19	2.9
electricity_manufacture_35 thousand+ (RMB/kWh)	0.64	0.66	0.69	0.71	0.75	0.76	0.78	22	3.4
gasoline90# (RMB/t)	5,956	6,128	7,088	7,011	8,027	9,085	9,361	57	7.8
gasoline93# (RMB/t)	6,336	6,525	7,493	7,465	8,532	9,671	9,958	57	7.8
gasoline97# (RMB/t)	6,702	6,898	7,442	7,912	9,031	10,224	10,532	57	7.8
diesel_0# (RMB/t)	5,238	5,586	6,109	6,332	7,329	8,315	8,575	64	8.6
diesel_10# (RMB/t)	5,382	5,828	6,393	6,584	7,724	8,751	9,094	69	9.1

Source: Assembled using the survey data.

Preliminary analysis: Trend for coefficient of variation

The coefficient of variation is defined as the standard deviation over the mean price over each region at time 't', and shows the extent of price variability across regions. Figure 6.2 shows coefficients of variation for energy products in China, which we explored next.

Gasoline

Panel B of Figure 6.2 shows the trend for the coefficient of variation attached to gasoline products. First, we observe more frequent regional variation after 2009, which may be attributable to market reform policies launched in 2009 that allowed greater arbitrage activity in the gasoline products market. Second, after mid-2009, the coefficient was not only subject to more variation, but also demonstrated a consistent pattern of increase.

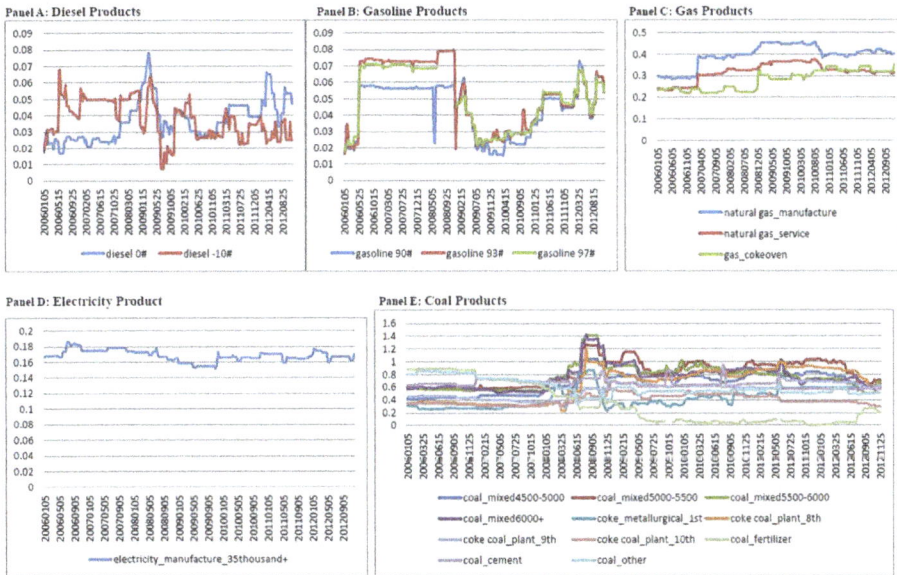

Figure 6.2 Coefficient of variation for energy products in China

Source: Plotted using the survey data.

Diesel

For product line 'diesel 10#', the coefficient of variation stabilised after 2009. As in the case of gasoline products, this could be the result of oil price reforms that were launched in 2009. There were differences, however, between the variation of gasoline products and that of diesel products. The coefficients of variation for diesel and gasoline were both about 0.03 in 2009. For diesel products, price divergence across major cities is not obvious; however, the price variation of gasoline products started to climb after 2009, indicating that the price stabilisation program is not very efficient.

Gas and electricity

For both service gas and manufacturing gas, the coefficient of variation jumped in 2007, and continued to rise slowly until the end of 2010, when it began to fall. These turning points in 2007 and 2010 could be attributed to government price adjustment in 2007 and broader price reforms in 2010. The coefficient of variation attached to electricity decreased slowly from 2006 to 2010, and remained relatively stable thereafter.

Coal

Several observations can be made about the coefficient of the variation trend attached to coal products. First, the coefficient had more frequent ups and downs after 2008 than before 2008; also from 2008, the level of the coefficient was higher than before 2008. Second, the gap in the coefficient of variation between different coal products became larger after 2008. These observations could be linked to reforms in 2008 that deregulated the market for coal by allowing prices to better reflect supply and demand. Third, it is interesting to see the coefficient for fertiliser coal hitting zero from 2009.[8] Fourth, we note that prices for coal, gasoline and diesel all became more volatile after the reform period, implying that market reforms in the energy sector in general have produced more frequent arbitrage activities.

Finally, we observe that the coefficient of variation attached to coal product prices changed substantially after the GFC. This could reflect outcomes attached to government fiscal stimulus policy that sought to boost crisis-affected demand.

---

8   For details, see: www.fertmarket.com/newsabout.aspx?id=37. The reason for this trend is not clear; however, fertiliser coal is the raw material for most of China's nitrogen fertiliser, and nitrogen fertiliser received subsidies of about US$7.46 billion during 2008–09 (Heffer and Olegario 2010).

In sum, these preliminary observations provide evidence of price change within energy product markets in China between 2006 and 2012. In the next section, we test to see if the direction of these energy price changes is towards convergence or divergence across different regions in China and over the sample period.

Testing for energy price convergence: A series-specific nonlinear panel unit root test

We use a nonlinear panel unit root test that is series specific (see Breuer et al. 2002; Kapetanios et al. 2003; Lau et al. 2012; Wu and Lee 2009). This series-specific nonlinear panel unit root test model (hereinafter NNSS) has several advantages over the conventional panel unit root tests. The NNSS is advantageous in testing for stationarity for each city, while the model itself accounts for nonlinearity and contemporaneous correlation among cross-section series—statistical features that are widely identified in financial and economic datasets.

In the case of our dataset, cross-sectional dependence is a distinctive feature. Cities are heterogeneous—that is, in the culture of doing business, local governmental policies, languages, consumer preferences, and market structure and international exposure—but to some extent they are affected by common factors, such as using the same currency, the same time zone and the same written language. External shocks to the foreign exchange rate and the international oil price, for example, will in turn uniquely influence energy prices in different cities.

The most significant common factors between Chinese cities—but which differ from other major economies—are China's unique political institutions. China operates with a unique intra-provincial political system known as the Regionally Decentralised Authoritarian System (Xu 2011). Most influentially, this serves to link regional economic performance to the career promotion of officials—that is, regional competition provides incentives to sub-national officials to initiate and implement market-oriented reforms (Xu 2011). Under this institutional arrangement, sub-national officials tend to accept and implement (rather than resist and initiate) policies formulated by the central government. These policies work as common factors that influence every city to a certain degree. When conducting research in this political institutional setting, the issue of cross-sectional dependence should not be ignored.

We use the seemingly unrelated regression (SUR) method in this study, with N cities and T time periods. The following simultaneous equations form the nonlinear SUR model, as in Equation 6.1.

Equation 6.1

$$\Delta y_{1,t} = \delta_1 y_{1,t-1}^3 + \sum_{j=1}^{\rho_1} \eta_{1,j} \Delta y_{1,t-j} + \varepsilon_{1,t}$$

$$\Delta y_{2,t} = \delta_2 y_{2,t-1}^3 + \sum_{j=1}^{\rho_2} \eta_{2,j} \Delta y_{2,t-j} + \varepsilon_{2,t}$$

$$\Delta y_{N-1,t} = \delta_{N-1} y_{N-1,t-1}^3 + \sum_{j=1}^{\rho_{N-1}} \eta_{N-1,j} \Delta y_{N-1,t-j} + \varepsilon_{N-1,t}$$

$$\Delta y_{N,t} = \delta_N y_{N,t-1}^3 + \sum_{j=1}^{\rho_N} \eta_{N,j} \Delta y_{N,t-j} + \varepsilon_{N,t} \quad (1)$$

In Equation 6.1, t=1, 2, ..., T; $p_{k,t}$ is the original price of a specific good for city k at time t; $y_{k,t}$ is the relative price defined as $y_{k,t} = \ln\left(\frac{p_{k,t}}{\bar{p}_t}\right)$; and $\bar{P}_t$ is the average price of a specific good for all cities at time t. $\Delta y_{k,t} = y_{k,t} - y_{k,t-1}$. ρ_k is thus the number of augmentations or lags for goods k. The null and alternative hypotheses to be tested are in Equation 6.2.

Equation 6.2

$$H_0^k: \delta_k = 0; \quad H_1^k : \delta_k < 0 \quad \forall k = 1,2,\dots, N$$

The critical values are generated using a bootstrapping method because of the non-standard distribution of the test statistics.[9] Here we modify the Gauss code provided by Wu and Lee (2009),[10] and for each series, $y_{k,t}$, report t-statistic (SURt$_{NL}^k$ statistic) results and the critical values at 5 per cent and 10 per cent. If the t-statistic is less than the 5 per cent SURt$_{NL}^k$ critical value, the null hypothesis of having a unit root is rejected; results reported in Table 6.3 are based on the 10 per cent SURt$_{NL}^k$ significance level.[11]

The rejection of the unit root hypothesis, H_0^k, implies that the time series of price differentials is stationary; if tests fail to reject the null hypothesis, the price differentials follow a random walk. This means we can proceed to calculate the price differentials. To do this, we use the group average price (the mean of all the regions concerned for each product) as the benchmark. Hypothesis tests

---

9   A bootstrap-after-bootstrap method (Berkowitz and Kilian 2000) is applied to obtain the effective empirical sizes of bootstrap tests given the nominal size of 5 per cent.

10 We thank Jyh-Lin Wu for making the Gauss code available online. A sample code can be downloaded from Jyh-Lin Wu's homepage: econ.nsysu.edu.tw/files/11-1124-1326-1.php.

11 Detailed convergence test results for all energy products and regions are available on request.

are conducted for a spot price panel dataset relating to each energy product. There are 20 energy products within five energy categories: gasoline, diesel, coal, gas and electricity.

This approach enables us to use time series analysis to test whether each region is converging to group average price. We can use some major cities as benchmarks—for example, we can examine whether prices in different cities converge with those in Shanghai or Guangzhou. We use a cross-sectional mean as the benchmark in our chapter because the coverage of reform policy is nationwide, and we intend to provide a more complete picture of the impact of reform policy on energy price convergence. More importantly, it was suggested in the literature that using a cross-sectional mean as the benchmark is preferable from an econometrics point of view for consistency (for details, see Akhmedjonov et al. 2013; Evans 1998; Lau 2010).

The study makes a unique contribution to the literature on energy price convergence as follows: first, the econometric model captures the characteristics of nonlinearity and cross-sectional dependence across regions; second, the study applies to a wider coverage of energy products than has previously been explored. On the latter, Fan and Wei (2006) tested only two energy products: gasoline and diesel. Ma et al. (2009) extended this to four energy products: gasoline, coal, diesel and electricity. This research covers 20 energy products from the five broad energy categories: gasoline, coal, diesel, electricity and gas. Third, this study covers the period after 2005, which is during the energy reform process. All previous studies were undertaken before 2005. Finally, earlier studies covered only 35 Chinese provinces, while ignoring the effects of energy prices in non-capital cities. Ours is not only the most recent such study undertaken, it is also the most comprehensive in terms of city coverage, and is unique in being able to capture the effects of ongoing energy reforms since 2006.

Empirical results

Price convergence by energy category and product

Table 6.3 summarises the share of cities showing evidence of nonlinear convergence to the average cross-regional energy price for all energy products. These suggest that, on average, 39.2 per cent of the sample cities exhibit nonlinear convergence and hence imply a level of energy price integration across regions in China. An earlier study concluded that more than 80 per cent of regions showed price convergence (Fan and Wei 2006).[12] That study, however, only included gasoline and diesel products, and also covered only 36 major cities. The present study is more comprehensive along regional and product lines, and the results are thus more convincing that while energy market reforms are progressing, they are not yet effective enough to lead to more widespread convergence in energy prices.

A study by Ma et al. (2009), meanwhile, suggested that convergence applied to a lower share of cities: only 26 per cent. Unfortunately, their conclusion was based on a univariate augmented Dickey–Fuller (ADF) test. This is widely criticised for its lack of statistical power in rejecting the null hypothesis of a unit root. The empirical findings of this research—that 39.2 per cent of cities exhibit convergence—are more reliable as our testing method incorporates panel data, nonlinearity and cross-sectional dependence.

Table 6.3 Percentage of nonlinear convergence by product type

All	Coal	Diesel	Electricity	Gas	Gasoline
39.2%	28.3%	67.7%	11.1%	26.0%	44.8%

Source: Authors' own calculations.

Table 6.4 presents the results by significant region by the five category types. The results show that the price of diesel is converging most, specifically across 67.7 per cent of regions sampled. The remaining products by order of degree of convergence are gasoline, coal, gas and electricity—a result that merges perfectly with Ma et al. (2009).

For the above results, we conclude that coal and gas markets are less integrated than those of diesel and gasoline, leaving the electricity market as the least integrated of the five categories. According to these results, we cannot conclude that China's energy markets are well integrated. In contrast, these results highlight the limited convergence achieved by the energy reform agenda.

---

12 The authors claimed that 31 of 35 cities (88.6 per cent) were convergent for gasoline and 30 of 34 cities (88.2 per cent) for diesel, which suggests some degree of market integration for gasoline and diesel. Meanwhile, the study of Ma et al. (2009) and our current research suggest that the diesel market is much more integrated than the gasoline market.

Table 6.4 Percentage of significant regions by energy product

	Category	Product	Number of regions (provinces or cities)	Number of significant regions at 5%	Number of significant regions at 10%	Percentage of significant regions by product
1	Coal	coal_cement	3	2	3	100.0
2	Coal	coal_fertiliser	2	0	0	0.0
3	Coal	coal_metallurgical_1st	5	0	0	0.0
4	Coal	coal_mixed4500-5000	8	3	3	37.5
5	Coal	coal_mixed5000-5500	7	2	2	28.6
6	Coal	coal_mixed5500-6000	6	2	2	33.3
7	Coal	coal_mixed6000+	5	3	3	60.0
8	Coal	coal_other	4	0	0	0.0
9	Coal	coal_plant_10th	6	0	0	0.0
10	Coal	coal_plant_8th	4	0	1	25.0
11	Coal	coal_plant_9th	3	1	1	33.3
12	Diesel	diesel_0#	46	27	28	60.9
13	Diesel	diesel_10#	19	16	16	84.2
14	Electricity	electricity_manufacture_35thousand+	36	3	4	11.1
15	Gas	gas_cokeoven	19	2	3	15.8
16	Gas	gas_manufacture	28	2	3	10.7
17	Gas	gas_service	26	11	13	50.0
18	Gasoline	gasoline90#	31	28	29	93.5
19	Gasoline	gasoline93#	48	9	10	20.8
20	Gasoline	gasoline97#	46	15	17	37.0
	Sum		**352**	**126**	**138**	

Source: Authors' calculations.

An additional contribution of this study is that we provide detailed information on the percentage of converging major cities for each subcategory of energy product. These results are presented in Table 6.4, several observations from which are worth highlighting. First, the prices of some products demonstrate a far higher level of regional convergence than for other products. At the extreme, price convergence is taking place among 93.5 per cent of cities for 'gasoline90#', where that level of convergence is 0 per cent for 'coal_plant_10th'.

Second, the level of price convergence across products in the same energy category is different across each of the five energy categories. For example, within the gas category, 'gasoline93#' and 'gasoline97#' show a similar degree of regional price integration, but that level is much lower for 'gasoline90#'. This could be because 'gasoline93#' and 'gasoline97#' display a similar degree of market integration, while 'gasoline90#' exhibits the highest level of integration in this energy category.

Overall, our empirical findings suggest China's energy market is characterised by a low degree of domestic price integration. This implies that despite the implementation of a number of policies and reform mechanisms to encourage reform of the energy sector, the reform process is either incomplete or not comprehensive. It is also possible that significant transaction costs due to institutional factors, such as local protection, may contribute to this phenomenon of price divergence.[13]

Coal products, for example, dominate China's energy market. Coal met some 70 per cent of China's energy needs in 2009, and thanks to energy reforms this level of dependence is expected to fall to 62 per cent by 2035 (EIA 2012). In China's case, coalmine methane (CMM) recovery projects across the country have been playing an important role in coal-related power generation, town gas projects, as well as energy efficiency enhancement programs (US EPA 2012). CMM is, however, according to the US Environmental Protection Agency (US EPA), also associated with cross-regional integration barriers, including low-quality drained CMM, and explosive gas mixtures that make handling and transportation risky. In addition, there are inconsistent laws between provinces in terms of the level of methane concentration required for the use of CMM, which typically pivots about 30 per cent. Such factors reduce the ease with which energy reforms can stimulate cross-regional energy market integration in China.

---

13 For instance, the band of inaction could be widened by recent increases in salaries and transportation costs in China, especially in coastal regions.

Overall energy marketisation by province

A final area of analysis of this chapter is to shed light on the literature on overall energy marketisation at the province level. Previous research examines the marketisation of certain energy categories or the general marketisation for a given province, as shown in column 7 in Table 6.5 (Fan et al. 2011). However, the criteria for assessing the general marketisation index published by Fan et al. (2011) is not transparent. There is limited evidence for energy marketisation at the province level. We therefore propose a new index for measuring marketisation within the energy industry for each province, as follows (Equation 6.3).

Equation 6.3

$$MI = \frac{NTR}{NTT}$$

In Equation 6.3, MI is the proposed index to proxy the degree of marketisation, as Fan and Wei (2006) also use the proportion of converging cities to quantify the effectiveness of transformation from a planned to a market-oriented economy for a specific commodity category in a particular city. NTR is the number of times convergence is detected (that is, the number of times the unit root test rejects the null of having a unit root test), and NTT is the number of appearances of cities in our study. Therefore MI (as shown in column C in Table 6.5) is the measure to proxy, and quantifies the effectiveness of market reform for the energy sector.[14] A high index result thus implies a high level of marketisation in terms of a more market-oriented energy sector, as suggested by Ma et al. (2009). A high index ratio indicates that a province's energy market is characterised by a higher degree of marketisation in terms of a more market-oriented energy sector, and this is quantified, proxied by the province's average fuel price convergence level.

Table 6.5 Comparison of energy marketisation with general marketisation by province

ID	Province	A[a]	B[b]	C[c]	D[d]	E[e]	F[f]
1	Jilin	13	10	77%	1	18	17
2	Qinghai	9	6	67%	2	30	28
3	Guizhou	17	11	65%	3	26	23
4	Tianjin	8	5	63%	4	6	2
5	Hebei	17	10	59%	5	17	12
6	Liaoning	16	9	56%	6	9	3

---

14 Ma et al. (2009) is the first study to use the unit root test methodology to examine the effect of policy reforms on energy price convergence, and they conclude that reforms have led to a more market-oriented energy sector in China (p. 4848).

ID	Province	A[a]	B[b]	C[c]	D[d]	E[e]	F[f]
7	Ningxia	13	6	46%	7	25	18
8	Hunan	11	5	45%	8	16	8
9	Chongqing	7	3	43%	9	10	1
10	Heilongjiang	14	6	43%	10	22	12
11	Henan	7	3	43%	11	12	1
12	Guangdong	12	5	42%	12	4	−8
13	Shanghai	8	3	38%	13	2	−11
14	Beijing	6	2	33%	14	5	−9
15	Gansu	6	2	33%	15	29	14
16	Jiangxi	9	3	33%	16	15	−1
17	Shandong	33	11	33%	17	8	−9
18	Yunnan	9	3	33%	18	24	6
19	Shanxi	16	5	31%	19	23	4
20	Guangxi	10	3	30%	20	21	1
21	Jiangsu	10	3	30%	21	3	−18
22	Sichuan	10	3	30%	22	13	−9
23	Anhui	11	3	27%	23	11	−12
24	Fujian	8	2	25%	24	7	−17
25	Hainan	4	1	25%	25	19	−6
26	Hubei	12	3	25%	26	14	−12
27	Zhejiang	16	4	25%	27	1	−26
28	Inner Mongolia	22	5	23%	28	20	−8
29	Xinjiang	5	1	20%	29	28	−1
30	Shaanxi	12	2	17%	30	27	−3
31	Tibet	1	0	0%	31	31	0

[a] Number of times cities appear.
[b] Number of times convergence is detected.
[c] Percentage (= column B, column A).
[d] Energy marketisation ranking using MI indicator.
[e] General marketisation index ranking, 2006–09 (Fan et al. 2011).
[f] Difference between ranking of energy marketisation and that of general marketisation (= column E − column D).
Notes: There are 31 provinces investigated. The Province column lists all the provinces. The data in column A indicate how many times they appear in all 352 hypothesis tests. The data in column B indicate how many times the corresponding hypothesis testing rejects the null hypothesis. Column C is generated as the ratio of column B over column A. Take Jilin Province as an example: it appears 13 times (see column A) in all 352 hypothesis tests among which 10 times found evidence of convergence (see column B). Column C is equal to 10, 13 or 77 per cent. Column D ranks all provinces based on the data in column C. Column E lists the ranking of the general marketisation based on the average marketisation index (2006–09) created by Fan et al. (2011). The lower the data are, the higher is the level of general marketisation. In column D, the datum for Zhejiang Province is 1, which means the general market of Zhejiang is most developed during the period 2006–09. Column F is equal to column E minus column D.
Source: Authors' own calculations.

The overall indices ranks derived for each province are presented in column C of Table 6.5, and the ranking of general marketisation for each province is presented in column D. Jilin Province, in China's far north-east on the border with North Korea, and which experiences severe cold weather, is ranked first among China's provinces as the most market-oriented energy market. The reason for this observation is not clear, but it is interesting to note that the top 10 regions in terms of MI measures are all coastal provinces located north of the Yangtze River,[15] and are classified as 'severely cold' heating zones. One reason for their successful implementation of price reform could be local government prioritisation as heating is required by law. Heating consumption in these regions accounts for about 7 per cent of aggregate gas demand compared with a national average of 2 per cent (Chen 2014). In contrast, Zhejiang Province, a coastal frontier south of Shanghai, was identified as the overall most integrated market using the published ranking of Fan et al. (2011).

Table 6.5 demonstrates that there is a lack of correlation between energy market convergence and the overall degree of commodity marketisation—the latter as identified by Fan et al. (2011), which fills the last column of Table 6.5. For example, one of China's most economically advanced provinces, Zhejiang, ranks first in terms of general marketisation, but 27th for energy sector marketisation. Similar results are identified for developed markets such as Shanghai, Jiangsu, Guangdong and Beijing. In contrast, provinces considered to have the highest level of market integration in the energy sector are mostly on the coast north of the Yangtse River, and are classified as 'severely cold' heating zones—such as Hebei, Tianjin, Liaoning, Jilin and Heilongjiang—where heating supply is required by law.

There may be several reasons for divergence between the marketisation process of the energy market and the general market across regions of China. First, our definition of 'marketisation' is different from that used by Fan et al. (2011): we use an econometrics test to define marketisation, while Fan et al.'s (2011) definition is comprehensive but ambiguous. Second, the source of a high degree of price convergence for less-developed provinces could be the intervention from the central government, rather than free-market arbitrage activities.

Energy products are among the most important inputs for economic development. Recent studies argue that local governments in China, especially those of more developed provinces, have incentives to control the price in the energy sector (Young 2000; Xu 2011). Further research is needed, however, to examine why these more developed regions are not exhibiting a high degree of price convergence, and hence a market-oriented energy sector. The lack of correlation between the results of our indices for energy and general market

---

15 They are Hebei, Tianjin, Liaoning, Jilin and Heilongjiang.

integration also calls for further research so as to better understand the role of energy markets in the general marketisation index ranking constructed by Fan et al. (2011). It could also be useful to calculate the same marketisation index of this study for single durable goods, non-durable goods and services in China, so as to have a better understanding of the marketisation process for different products across different cities and provinces.

Conclusion

Energy price convergence is one of the leading indicators for understanding market liberalisation and integration. Studies examining energy price convergence in China are limited in both quantity and findings. This study has added to the existing literature in several aspects. First, the dataset used here covers a previously unstudied period, despite its centrality within ongoing energy market reforms. Our dataset also offers higher data frequency and has wider regional coverage. Second, the methodology used in this study is more robust in capturing nonlinearity and cross-sectional dependence of the pricing process. Third, this research extends the range of energy products investigated to cover all the critical energy categories in the economy. It thus provides the most comprehensive analysis to date of pricing in China's energy sector.

We find little evidence of price convergence, as measured by convergence to the average price across provinces, between cities in Chinese energy markets from 2006–12. We take this to mean that China's domestic energy market is not well integrated across the country's cities. Examination of detailed energy categories finds few cities are moving towards price convergence for electricity, gas and coal. There is greater price convergence in gasoline and diesel, but these markets are far from perfectly integrated as far as the existence of a unified price would indicate.

The study also finds that the level of market integration varies between different products within the same broader energy type category. Similarly, the coefficients of variation in the price of some key energy products, such as gasoline, diesel, coal and gas, have changed substantially since the GFC. This could indicate that the combination of international volatility in prices and the large domestic fiscal stimulus package implemented by the Chinese Government in response to the GFC has caused variations in both energy prices and energy efficiency.

Moreover, by augmenting the general marketisation index ranking constructed by Fan et al. (2011), we find little association between energy marketisation and general marketisation across numerous provinces. That is, there are cases where provinces considered to be highly developed and integrated in general—such as Zhejiang, Shanghai, Jiangsu, Guangdong and Beijing—display an unexpectedly low level of energy market price integration. In contrast, provinces with a high level of energy market integration are mostly in areas with lower rankings in the general marketisation index: China's poorer provinces, including Qinghai and Guizhou, in the west and south-west of the country.

One reason for this inconsistency could be that provinces with low marketisation are followers of the price set by the central government. That is, local governments cannot influence prices according to local conditions or interests. Provinces with a higher degree of marketisation, however, are typically more developed, and this comes with greater rights to intervene in—or to allow markets to decide—local energy markets.

Further research is required to provide more detailed explanations of the different levels of marketisation of different energy categories in different provinces in China. One suggestion would be to calculate a marketisation index, as proposed in this study, for single durable goods, non-durable goods and services across China. Only with this type of panel data study that captures market price integration across regions, time and products in China will it be possible to better understand the marketisation process in China.

Finally, the study focuses on internal integration and does not discuss the impact of international integration of energy markets. With reform and opening one would expect price movements to be influenced by international price movements. The global price of coal, gas and oil varied enormously over the period of the study (see Figures 2.3 and 2.4 in Chapter 2 of this volume) and so could be expected to influence domestic movements of energy prices. This too would be an avenue for future research.

References

Akhmedjonov, A., Chi Keung Lau, M. and İzgi, B.B. (2013), New evidence of regional income divergence in post-reform Russia, *Applied Economics*, 45(18): 2675–82.

Bachmeier, L.J. and Griffin, J.M. (2006), Testing for market integration: Crude oil, coal, and natural gas, *The Energy Journal*, 27: 55–71.

Berkowitz, J. and Kilian, L. (2000), Recent developments in bootstrapping time series, *Econometric Reviews*, 19(1): 1–48.

Bilgin, M.H., Lau, C.K.M., Demir, E. and Astrauskienė, N. (2010), Rental price convergence in a developing economy: New evidence from nonlinear panel unit root test, *International Journal of Strategic Property Management*, 14(3): 245–57.

Breuer, J.B., McNown, R. and Wallace, M. (2002), Series-specific unit root tests with panel data, *Oxford Bulletin of Economics and Statistics*, 64(5): 527–46.

Chen, M. (2014), *The development of Chinese gas pricing*, OIES Paper NG 89, Oxford: Oxford Institute for Energy Studies.

Energy Information Administration (EIA) (2012), China Country Analysis Brief. Energy Information Administration. www.eia.doe.gov. Retrieved October 2012.

Evans, P. (1998), Using Panel Data to Evaluate Growth Theories, *International Economic Review*, 39: 295–306.

Fan, C.S. and Wei, X. (2006), The law of one price: Evidence from the transitional economy of China, *The Review of Economics and Statistics*, 88(4): 682–97.

Fan, G., Wang, X. and Zhu, H. (2011), *NERI index of marketisation of China's provinces 2011*, Beijing: Economic Science Publishing House.

Heffer, P. and Olegario, A. (2010), *Fertilizer subsidy situation in selected countries: 2008/09*, Paris: International Fertiliser Industry Association. Available from: www.fertilizer.org.

Kapetanios, G., Shin, Y. and Snell, A. (2003), Testing for a unit root in the nonlinear STAR framework, *Journal of Econometrics*, 112(2): 359–79.

Lan, Y. and Sylwester, K. (2010), Does the law of one price hold in China? Testing price convergence using disaggregated data, *China Economic Review*, 21(2): 224–36.

Lau, C.K.M. (2010), New evidence about regional income divergence in China, *China Economic Review*, 21(2): 293–309.

Lau, C.K.M., Demir, E. and Bilgin, M.H. (2015), A nonlinear model of military expenditure convergence: Evidence from Estar nonlinear unit root test, *Defence and Peace Economics*: 1–12.

Lau, C.K.M., Fung, K.W.T. and Pugalis, L. (2014), Is health care expenditure across Europe converging? Findings from the application of a nonlinear panel unit root test, *Eurasian Business Review*, 4(2): 137–56.

Lau, M.C.K., Suvankulov, F. and Ogucu, F. (2012), Price regulation and relative price convergence: Evidence from the retail gasoline market in Canada, *Energy Policy*, 40: 325–34.

Ma, H., Oxley, L. and Gibson, J. (2009), Gradual reforms and the emergence of energy market in China: Evidence from tests for convergence of energy prices, *Energy Policy*, 37(11): 4834–50.

Ma, H., Oxley, L. and Gibson, J. (2010), China's energy economy: A survey of the literature, *Economic Systems*, 34(2): 105–32.

National Bureau of Statistics (NBS) (2007), *China Energy Statistical Yearbook 2007*, Beijing: China Statistics Press.

Parsley, D. and Wei, S.J. (1996), Convergence to the law of one price without trade barriers or currency fluctuations, *Quarterly Journal of Economics*, 111(4): 1211–36.

Suvankulov, F., Lau, M.C.K. and Ogucu, F. (2012), Price regulation and relative price convergence: Evidence from the retail gasoline market in Canada, *Energy Policy*, 40: 325–34.

Taylor, A.M. (2001), Potential pitfalls for the purchasing-power-parity puzzle? Sampling and specification biases in mean-reversion tests of the law of one price, *Econometrica*, 69(2): 473–98.

United Nations Conference on Trade and Development (UNCTAD) (2012), *Special challenges facing emerging market and least developed countries owing to the volatility in commodity prices*, Geneva: UNCTAD. Available from: dgff.unctad.org/chapter3/3.5.html. Retrieved 6 April 2013.

United States Environmental Protection Agency (US EPA) (2012), *China's energy markets: Anhui, Chongqing, Henan, Inner Mongolia, and Guizhou Provinces*, December, Washington, DC: US EPA. Available from: epa.gov/cmop/docs/2012ChinaEnergyMarket.pdf.

Wu, J.L. and Lee, H.Y. (2009), A revisit to the non-linear mean reversion of real exchange rates: Evidence from a series-specific non-linear panel unit-root test, *Journal of Macroeconomics*, 31(4): 591–601.

Xu, C. (2011), The fundamental institutions of China's reforms and development, *Journal of Economic Literature*, 49(4): 1076–151.

Young, A. (2000), The razor's edge: Distortions and incremental reform in the People's Republic of China, *The Quarterly Journal of Economics*, 115(4): 1091–135.

Zhou, N., Levine, M.D. and Price, L. (2010), Overview of current energy-efficiency policies in China, *Energy Policy*, 38(11): 6439–52. doi: dx.doi.org/10.1016/j.enpol.2009.08.015.

Appendix

Table A6.1 Detailed description of dataset by product

Product	Regions in original dataset
Natural gas manufacture	28 cities: Beijing, Chengdu, Harbin, Haikou, Hangzhou, Hefei, Hohhot, Jinan, Lanzhou, Nanjing, Nanning, Ningbo, Qingdao, Xiamen, Shanghai, Shenyang, Shijiazhuang, Taiyuan, Tianjin, Urumqi, Wuhan, Xi'an, Xining, Yinchuan, Changchun, Changsha, Zhengzhou, Chongqing
Natural gas_service	28 cities: Beijing, Chengdu, Harbin, Haikou, Hangzhou, Hefei, Hohhot, Jinan, Lanzhou, Nanjing, Nanning, Ningbo, Qingdao, Xiamen, Shanghai, Shenyang, Shijiazhuang, Taiyuan, Tianjin, Urumqi, Wuhan, Xi'an, Xining, Yinchuan, Changchun, Changsha, Zhengzhou, Chongqing
Gas_cokeoven	22 cities: Dalian, Guiyang, Harbin, Hangzhou, Hohhot, Jinan, Kunming, Nanchang, Nanjing, Ningbo, Qingdao, Shanghai, Shenyang, Shijiazhuang, Taiyuan, Tianjin, Wuhan, Xi'an, Yinchuan, Changchun, Changsha, Zhengzhou
Electricity_manufacture_35k+	36 cities: Beijing, Chengdu, Dalian, Fuzhou, Guangzhou, Guiyang, Harbin, Haikou, Hangzhou, Hefei, Hohhot, Jinan, Kunming, Lhasa, Lanzhou, Nanchang, Nanjing, Nanning, Ningbo, Qingdao, Xiamen, Shanghai, Shenzhen, Shenyang, Shijiazhuang, Taiyuan, Tianjin, Urumqi, Wuhan, Xi'an, Xining, Yinchuan, Changchun, Changsha, Zhengzhou, Chongqing
Gasoline90#	60 cities: Baotou, Baoji, Beijing, Chengdu, Dalian, Daqing, Datong, Fuzhou, Ganzhou, Golmud, Guangzhou, Guiyang, Harbin, Haikou, Hangzhou, Hefei, Hengyang, Hohhot, Jilin, Jinan, Jiaxing, Jiangmen, Jingmen, Kunming, Lhasa, Lanzhou, Liuzhou, Nanchang, Nanjing, Nanning, Ningbo, Qingdao, Qujing, Quanzhou, Sanya, Xiamen, Shanghai, Shenzhen, Shenyang, Shijiazhuang, Taiyuan, Tianjin, Tongling, Urumqi, Wuzhong, Wuhan, Xi'an, Xining, Xingtai, Xuzhou, Yantai, Yili, Yinchuan, Changchun, Changsha, Zhengzhou, Chongqing, Zhoukou, Zigong, Zunyi
Gasoline93#	60 cities: Baotou, Baoji, Beijing, Chengdu, Dalian, Daqing, Datong, Fuzhou, Ganzhou, Golmud, Guangzhou, Guiyang, Harbin, Haikou, Hangzhou, Hefei, Hengyang, Hohhot, Jilin, Jinan, Jiaxing, Jiangmen, Jingmen, Kunming, Lhasa, Lanzhou, Liuzhou, Nanchang, Nanjing, Nanning, Ningbo, Qingdao, Qujing, Quanzhou, Sanya, Xiamen, Shanghai, Shenzhen, Shenyang, Shijiazhuang, Taiyuan, Tianjin, Tongling, Urumqi, Wuzhong, Wuhan, Xi'an, Xining, Xingtai, Xuzhou, Yantai, Yili, Yinchuan, Changchun, Changsha, Zhengzhou, Chongqing, Zhoukou, Zigong, Zunyi
Gasoline97#	59 cities: Baotou, Baoji, Beijing, Chengdu, Dalian, Daqing, Datong, Fuzhou, Ganzhou, Golmud, Guangzhou, Guiyang, Harbin, Haikou, Hangzhou, Hefei, Hengyang, Hohhot, Jilin, Jinan, Jiaxing, Jiangmen, Jingmen, Kunming, Lanzhou, Liuzhou, Nanchang, Nanjing, Nanning, Ningbo, Qingdao, Qujing, Quanzhou, Sanya, Xiamen, Shanghai, Shenzhen, Shenyang, Shijiazhuang, Taiyuan, Tianjin, Tongling, Urumqi, Wuzhong, Wuhan, Xi'an, Xining, Xingtai, Xuzhou, Yantai, Yili, Yinchuan, Changchun, Changsha, Zhengzhou, Chongqing, Zhoukou, Zigong, Zunyi

Product	Regions in original dataset
Diesel_0#	60 cities: Baotou, Baoji, Beijing, Chengdu, Dalian, Daqing, Datong, Fuzhou, Ganzhou, Golmud, Guangzhou, Guiyang, Harbin, Haikou, Hangzhou, Hefei, Hengyang, Hohhot, Jilin, Jinan, Jiaxing, Jiangmen, Jingmen, Kunming, Lhasa, Lanzhou, Liuzhou, Nanchang, Nanjing, Nanning, Ningbo, Qingdao, Qujing, Quanzhou, Sanya, Xiamen, Shanghai, Shenzhen, Shenyang, Shijiazhuang, Taiyuan, Tianjin, Tongling, Urumqi, Wuzhong, Wuhan, Xi'an, Xining, Xingtai, Xuzhou, Yantai, Yili, Yinchuan, Changchun, Changsha, Zhengzhou, Chongqing, Zhoukou, Zigong, Zunyi
Diesel_10#	41 cities: Baotou, Baoji, Beijing, Dalian, Daqing, Datong, Ganzhou, Golmud, Guiyang, Harbin, Hangzhou, Hefei, Hohhot, Jilin, Jinan, Jingmen, Jiaxing, Lhasa, Lanzhou, Liuzhou, Ningbo, Qingdao, Shanghai, Shenyang, Shijiazhuang, Taiyuan, Tianjin, Tongling, Urumqi, Wuzhong, Xi'an, Xining, Xingtai, Xuzhou, Yantai, Yili, Yinchuan, Changchun, Zhengzhou, Zhoukou, Zunyi
Coal_mixed4500-5000	8 provinces: Guizhou, Hebei, Henan, Heilongjiang, Inner Mongolia, Shandong, Shanxi, Sichuan
Coal_mixed5000-5500	7 provinces: Guizhou, Henan, Heilongjiang, Inner Mongolia, Shandong, Shanxi, Shaanxi
Coal_mixed5500-6000	6 provinces: Guizhou, Henan, Heilongjiang, Inner Mongolia, Shandong, Shanxi
Coal_mixed6000+	5 provinces: Guizhou, Heilongjiang, Inner Mongolia, Shandong, Shaanxi
Coal_metallurgical_1st	5 provinces: Guizhou, Hebei, Inner Mongolia, Shandong, Shanxi
Coal_plant_8th	4 provinces: Guizhou, Hebei, Inner Mongolia, Shandong
Coal_plant_9th	3 provinces: Guizhou, Inner Mongolia, Shandong
Coal_plant_10th	7 provinces: Guizhou, Henan, Heilongjiang, Inner Mongolia, Shandong, Shanxi, Sichuan
Coal_fertiliser	2 provinces: Guizhou, Shandong
Coal_cement	3 provinces: Anhui, Guizhou, Inner Mongolia, Shandong
Coal_other	4 provinces: Guizhou, Inner Mongolia, Shandong, Sichuan

7. China's Gas Market Liberalisation
The impact on China–Australia gas trade

Xunpeng Shi and Hari Malamakkavu Padinjare Variam

Introduction

The regional and global impacts of activity in China's gas sector have become increasingly significant but are a relatively new issue for most energy researchers. Building on the remarkable growth of its economy since the 1980s, China has been an engine for the world economy. China's impact on the global energy and commodity markets has also been growing and has become significant since the 2000s. While much attention has been focused on the case of oil and minerals such as copper, nickel and iron ore, the emerging impact is evident in the world's natural gas and liquefied natural gas (LNG) markets in the past decade. With current consumption of about 180 billion cubic metres (bcm), China is the world's third-largest gas consumer and its gas consumption is projected to grow to about 600 bcm by 2035 (BP 2015). Given it is set to see the largest single volume of growth for any nation in the world in the next two decades, any swings in Chinese gas demand and supply options will affect the global gas market and gas trade. Thus, the Chinese gas sector should be an object for future energy study.

In addition to its size and growth prospects, two other factors in the Chinese gas sector have earned global attention. The ongoing domestic gas market liberalisation, which started in the past decade, may also have a significant impact on the world gas market. In the effort to establish a market-orientated economy, significant changes have been made in the past five years aimed at liberalising the gas sector. With the introduction of market forces, it is possible to generate prices that reflect the fundamentals of China's supply and demand. If successful, the ongoing efforts to create an independent pipeline operator will have a significant impact on future Chinese gas prices. Moreover, access to transport and storage infrastructure would lead to changes in Chinese market patterns at the national and provincial levels. Here, the literature has demonstrated that the evolution of market structure and organisation in gas-importing countries results in their domestic markets becoming increasingly subject to market forces, which further become a key determinant of international gas pricing.

The second factor is the effort to create gas trading hubs and gas benchmark pricing. As a result, China's gas liberalisation will improve in terms of infrastructure, size and liquidity of the market, as well as regulations, which are some of the prerequisites for trading hub formation (IEA 2002). A deregulated and competitive gas market would result in competitive price formation and the inception of financial contracts based on hub prices. Shanghai has announced its plans to create the Chinese 'Henry Hub' (China Securities Newspaper 2015). These efforts will create the dynamics for hub-building efforts in other countries such as Singapore and Japan. Moreover, China's gas pricing could be an important benchmark for the East Asian region, as it has the largest importing capacity in Asia, the most diversified (and relatively balanced) portfolios of supplies and the most diversified means of transport and transport routes (Chen 2014).

This chapter aims to examine the liberalisation of the Chinese gas market in terms of its domestic, regional and global impacts. The contribution of this report is fourfold: 1) it is potentially the first model to address the impact of Chinese gas market liberalisation on both domestic and international gas markets; 2) it will quantify the regional impact of China's gas market development on other regions, with a focus on Australia, which will be new to the literature; 3) the impact of the Chinese domestic market on Australia offers a new angle to study Chinese gas market issues; and 4) the study offers additional reference for market players, including policymakers, in the East Asian region as they develop their policy towards LNG trading hubs.

The chapter is structured as follows. It first introduces the motivations for the study, with a focus on the current situation in China's gas sector, placing it in a global context and its relationship with Australia's gas sector. Section three explains the methodology and data for further analyses. Section four reviews key features of the Chinese gas market and progress in gas market liberalisation policies against the backdrop of creating competitive markets. Section five explains the modelling methods and results, followed by the conclusion.

Motivations for the study

Overview of China's natural gas sector

As stated in the introduction, given its size, growth prosperity and ongoing efforts in liberalisation and building trading hubs, China will be a game changer in the regional and global gas markets. For almost four decades during China's rapid industrialisation, natural gas remained a secondary consideration as an energy source behind coal, oil and hydropower. The growth in natural gas consumption was slow in the period 1980–95 (with an annual growth rate of 1.5 per cent) and modest from 1996–2002 (with an annual growth rate of 7.9 per cent). The twenty-first century, however, witnessed an emphasis on developing natural gas as the 'fuel of the future', with stress on its environmental benefits and promotion of it as a solution to urban pollution. Growth in natural gas consumption was dramatic from 2003 (with an annual growth rate of 16.9 per cent). Gas consumption increased from just 24.5 bcm per year in 2000 to 182.4 bcm in 2014. The share of China's gas consumption experienced a dramatic increase in the 2000s—up to 4.8 per cent in 2013. From 2007, China became a net gas importer. In 2012, China became the world's third-largest gas consumer after the United States and Russia (Figure 7.1). However, despite rapid growth in recent years, the level of gas consumption in China (5.9 per cent of total primary energy supply in 2014) is still below the government target and the international average.

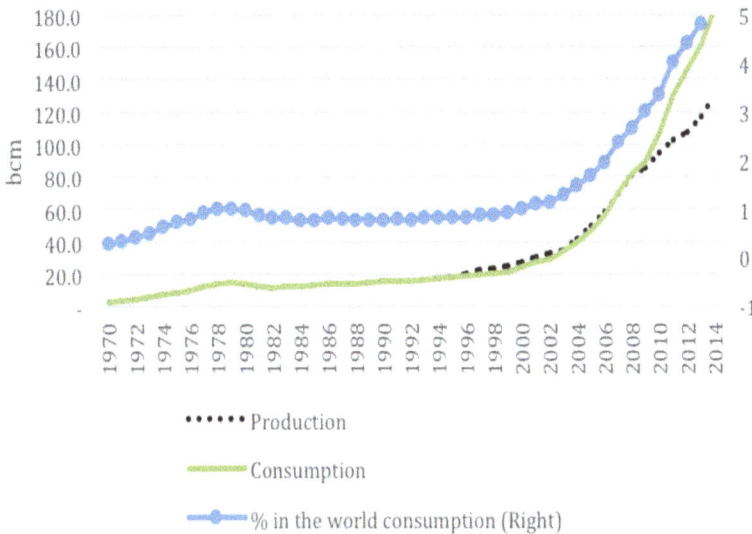

Figure 7.1 Evolution of the gas sector in China

Sources: BP (2014); NBS (2015).

According to the new Energy Development Strategy Action Plan (2014–20) released by the State Council (2014) in November 2014, the share of natural gas will be raised above 10 per cent, or 360 bcm p.a. Many observers (BP 2015; Reuters 2012) predict that gas consumption in 2035 will be about 608 bcm/p.a., with natural gas representing 12 per cent of the global energy mix by 2035.

As China's domestic production gradually lagged behind consumption, importation of gas started in 2006 and grew dramatically. The first import was of LNG, which amounted to 20.16 megatonnes (Mt) in 2014. Pipeline gas imports started in 2010, bringing gas from Turkmenistan and other Central Asian countries, and from Myanmar in 2014. In 2013, pipeline gas (PPG) imports overtook LNG imports, and in 2014 PPG accounted for 52.5 per cent of the total natural gas imports (Figure 7.2).

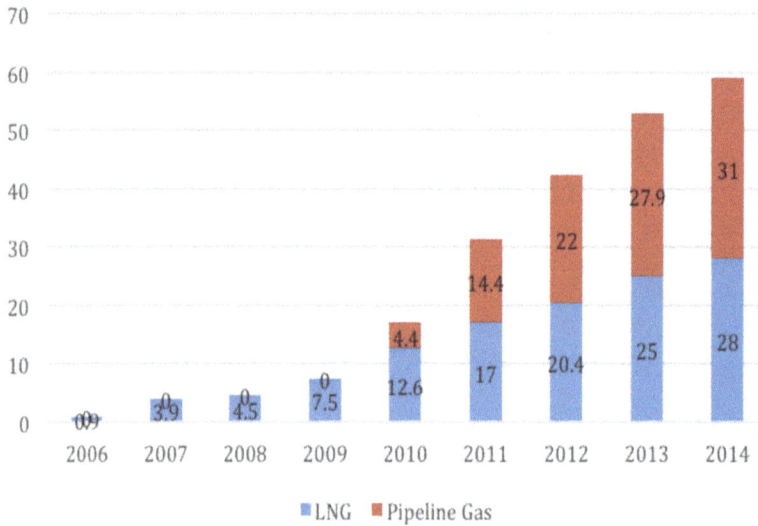

Figure 7.2 China's imports of natural gas, 2006–14

Source: China Customs data, cited from (Qian and Jiang 2015).

Qatar and Australia are China's major LNG import sources. In 2014, China imported 19.84 Mt of LNG. Representing the largest shares of supply are the four countries that have signed long-term contracts with China: Australia, Qatar, Indonesia and Malaysia. The remaining 18 per cent of supply share was purchased from Yemen, Equatorial Guinea, Nigeria and other countries through the spot market (Figure 7.3).

As a result of recent deals with Russia, more PPG is expected from the 'Power of Siberia' pipeline, as early as 2018. China's pipeline import capacity is projected to increase from 77 bcm in 2015 to 160 bcm in 2035 (Table 7.1). In comparison with our estimates, Henderson (2014) estimate a total of 165 bcm pipeline import capacity by 2030, with increased flows from Russia (68 bcm) and less from Central Asia (85 bcm). Central Asia (Turkmenistan) remains the largest pipeline import source. Based on forecasts from the International Energy Agency (IEA), US Energy Information Administration (EIA) and China National Petroleum Corporation (CNPC), China's LNG imports in 2030 are forecast to reach 120 bcm, while the assumed regasification capacity in 2030 is forecast to reach 157 bcm (ESI unpublished).

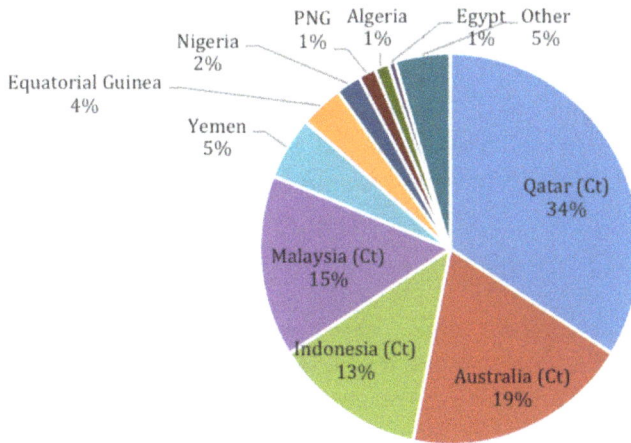

Figure 7.3 China LNG import sources, 2014

Source: Pang (2015).

Table 7.1 Pipeline gas imports into China

From	2015	2025	2035
Russia	0	38	58
Central Asia	65	90	90
Myanmar	12	12	12
Total	**77**	**140**	**160**

Source: ESI unpublished.

China and Australia's gas sector

Australia holds great potential resources for conventional gas (mainly offshore) and unconventional gas onshore. Estimated proven gas reserves are estimated to be 3.84 trillion cubic metres (tcm) (EIA 2014). Economically recoverable reserves of conventional gas are estimated to be 2.9 tcm. A recent study places technically recoverable reserves of shale gas at 12.4 tcm. If confirmed, this would place Australia on par with the United States, albeit with a much lower level of consumption: 25 bcm p.a. in Australia compared with 720 bcm p.a. in the United States in 2012.

Australia was the second-largest source of China's LNG imports as of 2014, and is expected to be the largest soon. China's first LNG import was from Australia in 2006. Since then, Chinese LNG imports from Australia have increased significantly, from less than 1 bcm in 2006 to about 5.3 bcm in 2014, which makes it the world's second-largest importer of Australian LNG. Moreover, China's 'Big Three' oil companies—China National Petroleum Corporation (CNPC),

China Petroleum & Chemical Corporation (Sinopec) and China National Offshore Oil Corporation (CNOOC)—have acquired interests in Australian LNG projects and have secured long-term purchase agreements. The total contracted LNG volume between Australia and China was only 3.5 Mt in 2014, and is expected to increase to 13.5 Mt in 2016 and to a maximum of 16.8 Mt in 2019. LNG trade could be further boosted by the Chinese–Australian free trade agreement.

Brief review of the literature

China's gas market and its regional impact have been intensively studied in recent years. Market-based pricing is a fundamental part of market liberalisation (IEA 2012). As a symbolic indicator of liberalisation, gas pricing was given particular attention. Zhang (2014) calls for a gas pricing system in which global pricing cues together with domestic supply and demand signals drive price formation. Furthermore, Chen (2014) discusses the implications of pricing reform for gas demand. In a report by the IEA (2002), reform in natural gas pricing and taxation policy was advocated as the best policy drivers in the national quest to increase the share of natural gas in the energy mix. The importance of supply diversity in price formation and supply security was addressed by Fernandez and Palazuelos (2011), Li and Bai (2010), Shi et al. (2010) and Lin et al. (2010), for whom competition between Russian gas and LNG prices relative to coal prices is seen as critical in price formation, creating incremental demand and the development of infrastructure, and attracting new investment. These studies can be summarised as eventual development of a pricing system based on market fundamentals with short-term contracts with flexible terms, influenced by gas and competing fuel prices in the domestic and world markets.

Gas market liberalisation is generally positive but could have a negative impact on some sectors. Economic theories often favour a market-pricing mechanism, as it is deemed to remove price distortions, improve efficiency of supply and use, and thus maximise the net benefits of gas. In gas markets, deregulation and gas-on-gas competition in a key market such as Shanghai are seen as benefiting the policy goals of liberalisation (Manuhutu and Owen 2010). A gradual breakdown of monopoly power in the three national oil and gas corporations in production, exploration, imports and transportation of gas was also seen as beneficial. Experience from studying liberalisation in other sectors has demonstrated that market liberalisation could have both positive and negative impacts. In the study of the deregulation of electricity markets in China, Chen and He (2013) demonstrated that deregulation has improved the efficiency of electricity production, employment and social welfare, but has also caused job disruption.

However, studies on the future of gas market liberalisation in China and its regional and global impacts are rare in the literature. The market-based discovery of natural gas prices and deregulated gas markets are extensively covered in the North American and European context, but are rare in terms of East Asian perspectives. No efforts have been made to simulate the impact of China's domestic market reforms on the regional and global gas markets. The lack of study on competitive pricing, however, is expected, as competitive pricing of natural gas is yet to be seen in China and even East Asia. Further studies of China's gas market liberalisation and associated issues would be valuable to the literature and to policymakers inside and outside China.

Given the likelihood of creating a competitive gas market and competitive prices in China, it would be interesting to examine the following questions:

1. What is the effect of a liberalised Chinese market on China's imports?

2. What is the effect of China's gas market liberalisation on Chinese spot market prices and key benchmark spot gas prices (Henry Hub, National Balancing Point, Australia Spot and Japan Spot)? Will the 'Asian premium' decline?

3. Will Australian LNG remain competitive against other major producers in a hub-indexed pricing system in China?

4. Will gas market liberalisation in China provide incentive for domestic production? Will the marginal cost of extraction of domestic gas increase in a liberalised market?

Methodology and data

This chapter consists of two main interrelated parts. The first part is a qualitative study. Here, relevant policies that have been implemented in the past decade are carefully surveyed to capture the development of gas sector policy. An analytical framework for studying the competitive market is proposed based on an IEA report. This analytical framework is employed to assess China's gas market liberalisation. The liberalisation efforts and associated increasing liquidity make it possible to create at least one gas trading hub in China. If the hub prices are deemed creditable, this hub may be used as a trade benchmark in China given the current efforts in Europe and East Asia to move away from oil-indexed prices in traded contracts.[1] The consequences of applying the Chinese hub prices as a benchmark for Chinese gas trade will be further examined in the second part of the chapter.

---

1 As discussed in Stern (2012), the rationale for oil-indexed contract pricing is not tenable in a hub-price market.

The second part of the chapter focuses on modelling. The impact of China's gas market liberalisation on the trade flows and prices of pipeline gas and LNG was examined with the Asian Gas Trade Model (AGTM), which is based on the Nexant World Gas Model (WGM) (Nexant 2013). The WGM covers every country in the world that consumes or produces natural gas. The historical data are available for 2006–13 and the outlook period is up to 2035. The model captures flows at the country-to-country level by pipeline and LNG, with contracted and uncontracted flows identified separately.

Supply and demand for piped gas and LNG are balanced on a quarterly basis and include seasonal demand variations, supply swing and storage capacities (working volume and deliverability). Demand forecasts for each node are exogenously estimated based on considerations of gross domestic product (GDP) and population growth, usage share and energy intensity in each sector. Supply data are included as a cost curve for each of the natural gas fields for the producing country. Production capacity and forecasting data list all active and potential natural gas production fields in all natural gas producing countries.

The model includes all known sales contracts, and active and planned infrastructure (pipelines and LNG liquefaction and regasification terminals). Contract data include the source and destination of contracts, annual contract quantity (ACQ), contract start and end dates, and price formulae. The infrastructure information includes location, start and end dates of operation, source and destination, pipeline capacity, start and end dates of pipelines, and transportation tariffs.

The oil price assumption used in all our cases was based on World Bank (2015) and EIA (2014) forecasts of the Brent Crude average spot price. Previously, it has been reported that observed import gas prices follow developments in the oil price with a lag of about four to eight months (Siliverstovs et al. 2005). In order to capture this, we employed a three-month lag (one-quarter) whenever there is indexation to previous prices. For ease of analysis for our study, we have classified regions as in the Appendix (Table A7.1).

Flows within nodes were constrained according to the available infrastructure and within the bounds of long-term contracts where appropriate. If the export and import nodes were both specified, the model delivered at least the take-or-pay (TOP) level from the export node to the import node. Volumes above the TOP level could be delivered to the import node, diverted to another location or even shut in (not produced) based on least-cost grounds. Such contestable volumes were priced on a spot basis. The pricing of gas also took into account the tightness of the market (for spot contracts) and, in the case of contracts, the linkage with oil/oil product prices. For any demand above contracted gas delivery, spot (uncontracted gas) trades occur subject to infrastructure availability. Hence changing the terms of contracts can influence the amount of spot trade in the future.

Using the scenario assumptions, the model matched supply to demand taking into account production costs, contract costs and transportation costs by pipe and LNG with the cost minimisation as the optimisation objective. For more details on the specifications of the model, please refer to the AGTM (Andrews-Speed et al. 2015; ESI n.d.).

China's market reforms towards a competitive gas market

This section introduces market liberalisation from the perspective of policy and regulation, gas pricing reform, infrastructure and market structure. Economic theory and past experience suggest that market liberalisation requires openness of the whole supply chain of the gas sector, from licensing and exploration in the upstream sector to trade and transportation and to the final customer (IEA 2012). An IEA analysis provides a useful framework to assess the development of gas liberalisation. According to this report, the initial steps to create gas markets include four goals: open access to infrastructure—that is, unbundling of transport and marketing functions and third-party access (TPA); introduction of consumer choice; reduction of regulation of wholesale prices; and application of competition policy in the sector (IEA 2013). Based on this framework, we provide a brief assessment of liberalisation efforts so far.

Policy and regulation

China's national gas policy emerged in the past decade with the rapid development of the natural gas sector. The policies include upstream development such as of shale gas and coalbed methane (CBM), liberalisation of LNG imports, midstream regulation featuring TPA, and downstream regulations such as environmental projects that require substitution of coal with natural gas. Involvement of the private sector and liberalisation of pricing are applied to the whole supply chain. These policies aim to encourage exploration, production, infrastructure development, efficient utilisation and competition in the gas sector.

Earlier policies focused on generating adequate supply of natural gas and efficient utilisation. For example, on 30 August 2007, China released its National Gas Utilisation Policy, which was intended to ease natural gas supply and demand, and optimise the structure of natural gas utilisation (NDRC 2007).

In line with the overall policy of marketisation and establishing a market economy that was promoted in the past five years, the focus of recent natural gas policy has shifted from gas supply and consumption to the gas market, with liberalisation the highlight. Measures promoted in these policies include pricing reform, opening up of the sector to private investors and TPA. For example, the State Council's policy on private investment issued in May 2010 explicitly encourages private investment in oil and gas exploration and production, storage and pipeline development for oil, gas and refined oil products (State Council 2010).

According to a reform package issued after the Third Plenary Session of the Eighteenth Communist Party of China (CPC) Central Committee in November 2013, the principles related to the natural gas sector and their implications are that the administrative monopoly will be removed and thus access to some upstream resources for non-state-owned companies will be improved; the government's role will be regulation and not the operation of monopoly industries, thus creating a level playing field between state and private companies; network and operations (marketing) will be separated and thus could encourage private investment in monopoly sectors such as pipelines; restrictions on market access to competition-based operations will also be removed, such as those in the downstream gas sector; pricing of gas will be liberalised and there will be no intervention in any prices that can be determined by the markets (except network prices) (Central Committee of the CPC 2013). In mid-2014, the 'Energy Revolution' advocated calls for restoration of the commodity characteristics of energy products, which indicates that gas may be depoliticised and become a product open to more competition; market-based energy pricing mechanisms could be established; and there will be changes in governance and improvements in the regulatory system.

In the latest policy on energy issued by the State Council (2014)—that is, the Energy Development Strategy Action Plan (2014–20)—pricing reform and liberalisation for competitive prices are specified: ex-plant prices and retail prices will be determined by the markets while network transmission prices will be regulated by the government; network infrastructure and its transparent and non-discriminatory TPA will be gradually established; and laws and regulations on gas pipeline projection will be advanced.

A legal framework and a regulator are still absent from China's gas regulatory framework. In particular, there is a lack of independent and holistic gas regulators The regulation for natural gas is divided between the central government and local governments along the supply chain—the central government, with the National Development and Reform Commission (NDRC) as the administrative agency, regulates gas prices from wellhead to city-gate terminals (wellhead prices, processing fees and transportation tariffs);[2] while provincial and local governments regulate local distribution charges (including connection fees) and end-user prices (Chen 2014). After the wholesale transaction, the price is adjusted by the provincial government with consideration given to economic disparities and local distribution costs (IEA 2013). As residential gas tariffs are regulated by local governments, uniform reforms are not possible and the central government's policy goals may not be achieved at the local level.

Some recent environmental policies will likely have a significant impact on the gas sector. The first is climate change policy. China has a target to reduce carbon dioxide emission intensity by 40–45 per cent in the period 2005–25, and a national carbon market is expected to be launched within two years. Both policies will boost future demand for natural gas. Another policy relates to air pollution control. In 2013, the Chinese Government set ambitious targets to reduce air pollution by 2017; fine particulate matter (PM2.5) is targeted to fall by 25 per cent, 20 per cent and 15 per cent, respectively, in the three economically developed coastal areas of Beijing–Tianjin–Hebei, Yangtze River Delta and Pearl River Delta from their 2012 levels, while all other cities must reduce their levels of PM10 by 10 per cent. Given the relative cleanliness of gas over coal in terms of carbon emissions and air pollutants, the replacement of coal with gas is promoted as a key solution (NDRC and NEA 2014).

Gas pricing reform

Like the pricing of other energy commodities, gas pricing has experienced transformation from the planned to the market economy. The extent of regulations on gas pricing varies according to a few factors, such as the source of supply, the means and routes of transportation, and the type of end use of the specific region. Before 2011, when a trial market mechanism was introduced, there were four stages of gas pricing similar to other typical pricing of key commodities in China. The fifth stage featured market-based pricing; it started in 2011 and has continued (Table 7.2). A detailed account of the gas pricing mechanism can be found in the recent literature (Chen 2014; IEA 2014).

2   Offshore gas prices, which accounted for 10 per cent of domestic gas output, at the wellhead are not strictly regulated by the NDRC as offshore acreage has been open to foreign cooperation since the 1980s and therefore is subject to a more market-driven pricing system. Similarly, LNG prices are not subject to regulation. However, the sale of LNG (after regasification) via long-distance pipeline would be subject to the uniform city-gate price regulation (Chen 2014).

Table 7.2 Evolution of gas pricing reforms in China

Stage	Year	Event
I	1957–81	Gas production quotas and prices were set by the government. At this stage, gas prices were low
II	1982–92	Also featured 'dual pricing'. Production beyond quotas was allowed and was priced higher than that within the quota (not exceeding 10 per cent). This change in pricing aims to encourage investment in gas exploration and production
III	1993–2005	Along with the marketisation process, a government-guided price was introduced alongside the government-set price. Ex-factor prices were introduced to combine the wellhead price and processing fees in 2001
IV	2006–11	The dual pricing system was abolished and a guided-pricing system was implemented. A two-tier (classified according to the geological locations of the fields) price was introduced during this period. According to the plan, an annual adjustment not exceeding 8 per cent of the wellhead price for tier-two gas fields was allowed.[a] In reality, however, there was no annual adjustment

[a] The reference is a five-year moving weighted-average price of crude oil, LPG and coal prices, weighted at 40 per cent, 20 per cent and 40 per cent, respectively.
Sources: Authors' summary based on various studies (Chen 2014; IEA 2013).

Under the cost-plus pricing mechanisms that prevailed until 2011, the ex-factory prices,[3] including wellhead prices and processing fees, were often set according to production costs and could differ among producers (Chen 2014). The transmission prices were guided by government regulations. The city-gate price was calculated as the ex-plant price plus the pipeline tariff, and thus could be different for each sector in each city or region (Chen 2014). Cost-plus pricing was also used in the United States in the 1950s to 1970s; however, it changed from a wellhead to an area approach to reduce the burden on regulators. It is useful in maintaining low gas prices when the level of marketisation is low (IEA 2012).

Cost-plus pricing mechanisms have many shortcomings. The pricing mechanism can lead to market distortions—either too generous or too parsimonious—because it is almost impossible to reveal the true costs of gas production. The prices also will not reflect the market fundamentals and fail to send the appropriate market signals for upstream development and demand response (IEA 2012). Under the cost-plus gas pricing mechanisms, final gas prices are fragmented among different kinds of consumers and different regions, and cannot accommodate increasing imports of LNG (IEA 2013). Such divergences can be unfair and ineffective. Fragmented and uneven pricing regulation created tensions among producers and distributors, and discouraged investment in production and infrastructure, which are needed to meet demand and enhance market access

---

3   Currently, gas prices include ex-factory (plant) prices, transmission prices, city-gate prices and end-user prices. In this chapter, unless mentioned otherwise, 'gas price' refers to the wholesale price.

and regional connectivity. The increasing gap between regulated prices and supply costs causes significant financial losses for gas importers (Chen 2014). Moreover, government-regulated gas pricing will lead to less transparent price signals and an unstable investment climate, as government policy objectives to meet desired political, social, economic or environmental outcomes can easily change (IEA 2013).

To address these challenges, the Chinese Government introduced a trial netback market-value pricing mechanism at the end of 2011 to replace the fragmented, cost-plus onshore gas pricing regime. The trial was initially launched in Guangdong and Guangxi provinces, where a single regulated price ceiling for all piped gas supply to the provinces replaced previous cost-plus wellhead price controls (IEA 2014). This reform also indicates that the pricing control point was moved from the wellhead to the city gate. The purpose of the reform is to allow market forces to play a bigger role in determining the level of domestic upstream investment and the volume of imports (Chen 2014). Effectively, it is expected to generate more liquidity and help development of a nascent gas market without compromising sustainability and affordability (Chen 2014).

In July 2013, in order to facilitate pricing reform, secure gas supplies, promote energy efficiency and control emissions, the Chinese Government started to use a market-oriented approach by linking the price of incremental gas volume to the import prices of alternatives (40 per cent of LPG and 60 per cent of heavy fuel oil), which is an expansion of the pilot program (NDRC 2013). The reform introduced two categories of gas—existing gas volumes and incremental gas volumes—and planned a gradual transition of cost-plus pricing for city-gate gas to netback pricing for non-residential sectors (mainly industrial users and power generators), which accounted for 80 per cent of the total consumption in 2012 (NDRC 2013). In this initial adjustment, only 9 per cent of gas demand was affected and the industrial sector bore the majority of impacts (Chen 2014).

From 1 April 2015, netback pricing replaced the cost-plus pricing as the mechanism to price gas for non-residential use. In 2013 and 2014, the government steadily raised the prices of existing volumes three times, and the price levels in both categories eventually converged to a fully oil-linked gas price from 1 April 2015. With the introduction of such a market-oriented pricing mechanism, Chinese gas demand will become more closely correlated with pricing reform and natural gas will be able to compete against oil products across non-residential end-user sectors.

However, some issues with the netback pricing mechanisms remain. First, it is still arguable that this mechanism does not necessarily reflect the true gas market fundamentals. For example, this methodology fails to account for coal, which is the true competitor of gas for power generation. This will become relevant when gas starts to compete with coal for power generation. The second issue is how to manage affordability under market mechanisms. Third, is how to differentiate city-gate prices among different regions, which differ in their ability to pay, the size of their resource endowment and seasonality. Fourth, what are the threshold and frequency of adjustment?

It is also not clear whether the government will follow the netback when oil prices return to high levels, such as above $80 a barrel. Current low oil prices provide a chance to implement netback gas prices without a huge surge in gas prices; however, continuous application of market-oriented pricing will lead to a price surge when oil prices are high. Given the sensitivity of gas demand to gas prices, whether the netback pricing will be maintained in that scenario is an important question.

Pricing reform for the residential sector was announced in March 2014, although still not market oriented. According to this reform, gas for the residential sector will be priced progressively—the price will be higher the greater is consumption, and all cities connected to gas pipelines must establish the three-tiered tariff by the end of 2015 (NDRC 2014). The regulation of prices—and thus limited pass-through of gas costs to residential end-users—will remain a long-term challenge to market liberalisation. This prevailing cross-subsidisation among gas end-users could distort the markets and could be counterproductive for gas use in the industry and commercial sectors (IEA 2012).

Pipeline and third-party access

The midstream, the pipeline, is dominated by national oil companies and provincial grid companies. China's limited long-distance and high-pressure transmission network is still being expanded (IEA 2012). China's pipeline transmission is neither sufficient nor open. China had more than 75,000 km of long-distance gas transmission pipelines by late 2014 (Su 2014). Although the Energy Development Strategy Action Plan (2014–20) projects that the backbone of natural gas pipelines will extend to at least 120,000 km by 2020, China seems to have a long way to go to develop its network infrastructure to the level of Germany or the United States. Furthermore, CNPC is the dominant player here, owning 80 per cent of the pipeline network (IEA 2012). As for LNG receiving terminals, the first privately owned LNG import terminal, the Zhoushan LNG terminal, owned by ENN, was approved in January 2015 and may be completed by 2017 (Platts 2015).

The midstream is still in the early days of privatisation and plans for full ownership unbundling. According to the decisions of the Central Committee of the CPC (2013), privatisation is the politically preferred direction for state-owned companies, creating momentum for privatisation of the Big Three.

For example, Sinopec announced in September 2014 that it had sold almost 30 per cent of its retail unit, comprising a wholesale business, more than 30,000 petrol stations, more than 23,000 convenience stores, as well as oil-product pipelines and storage facilities (Aldred and Zhu 2014).

CNPC has also made moves to privatise its pipeline assets and its recent privatisation plan is quite radical. East–West Pipelines (EWPs) started to undergo privatisation by PetroChina, a subsidiary of CNPC, in 2012. It was further reported in January 2015 that the PetroChina board had approved the plan to fully privatise its Shanghai-based PetroChina Eastern Pipelines (CNPC News Centre 2015). Once completed, the pipelines would be completely unbundled from PetroChina's market activities. This separation of pipeline activities from CNPC's production and marketing activities makes it possible for the private sector to invest in pipelines and for independent gas producers to bypass PetroChina and make deals directly with consumers. However, the unbundling does not necessarily improve TPA, thus continuous development of TPA policy and enhancement of regulatory capacity are still needed.

The regulation of TPA was announced in February 2014, mandating gas pipeline operators to provide non-discriminatory TPA whenever they have spare capacity. The regulation also allows downstream distributors to negotiate directly with upstream suppliers over gas supply, while pipeline operators may provide only transmission services (NEA 2014). The TPA regulation, however, has a major limitation in that it mandates TPA only when the operator has spare capacity, which is difficult for third parties to monitor. The current shortage of network capacity renders the concept of TPA useless. It is also not clear who will judge where there is a surplus capacity. Furthermore, process, terms of conditions and tariffs for the TPA are not publicly available (and may have not been determined by the NEA). Nevertheless, in the case of LNG import terminals, the first successful TPA happened in December 2014, when EEN received 6 Mt of LNG through the PetroChina-operated Rudong LNG terminal in China's eastern Jiangsu Province (Platts 2014).

Market structure and number of players

The Chinese gas industry is dominated by the Big Three national oil companies (NOCs): CNPC, CNOOC and Sinopec.[4] About 75 per cent of China's natural gas is produced by CNPC, which is also the biggest owner and operator of pipelines, in which it has a share of about 90 per cent. CNOOC was the first company to import LNG and it is likely to remain the main LNG importer (IEA 2014). CNOOC

---

4 While the major oil and gas companies are partially privatised, the state is still the majority shareholder of these companies.

also has exclusive marketing rights and buys offshore gas from its production-sharing contract partners at the wellhead (Chen 2014). Shaanxi Yanchang Petroleum (Group) is the only local oil and gas enterprise apart from the Big Three that is qualified to undertake exploration and development (IEA 2012). Other small and medium-sized gas producers have a small share in production due to their limited market access—they have to either sell their supplies to CNPC or develop the gas for local consumption. Gas imports, such as LNG, are, however, not restricted (IEA 2012).

In the downstream sector, there are no nationally dominant players. A variety of domestic suppliers with various ownership structures[5] exist, often supported by local governments. These distribution companies usually receive gas at the city gate and have limited direct access to gas sources (IEA 2012). These distribution companies may have monopoly power in their local market, often owning the local gas pipeline, as is the case with ENN Energy Holdings. These distributors face new competition from the Big Three NOCs, which are currently trying to take over some of the domestic markets (IEA 2012). Such integration attempts may give the Big Three larger market power and thus impede competition.

Overall, the number of market players is still not sufficient for meaningful market competition even at the wholesale level. To achieve a fully competitive market, the gas industry will have to transfer its vertically integrated structure to smaller, less vertically integrated energy companies. Experience from the IEA countries suggests that in closed markets with one or only a few dominant market players on the supply side, market openness along the whole gas value chain—in particular, in transmission—is necessary because it takes time for new entrants to build up confidence, set up business and gain market share (IEA 2012). The US experience suggests that liberalisation and open access to pipelines starting in 1985 are what led to the creation of the competitive wholesale gas market (IEA 2012).

Long-term structural reforms, such as the privatisation of existing gas business, opening up TPA and the emergence of new LNG importers, will increase the number of market players so that more liquid and thus price-competitive gas markets can be generated. The development of shale gas will provide an option not available in the past to create new market players. Shale gas may increase competition because private firms, as well as non-oil companies, are participating in the development of this sector.

---

5   Some companies are privately owned—such as ENN Energy Holdings and China Gas—while others belong to local governments.

Simulating the impact of China's gas market liberalisation

The scenario setting

For the current study, a baseline scenario is developed as a reference case to study how the international gas market might evolve to 2035. Policy changes were simulated in policy scenarios. The differences between the impacts of the baseline scenario and the policy scenarios on regional trade patterns, prices, production and consumption are then analysed in detail to understand the effects of liberalisation, from which we draw our conclusions.

In the *baseline scenario*, we have all active LNG contracts in China, of which 94 per cent are indexed to Japan Customs-cleared Crude (JCC) and only one contract is indexed to Henry Hub (HH). For pipeline gas, all contract prices are indexed to oil products. Thus, 98.4 per cent by volume of LNG and 100 per cent of the pipeline gas are indexed to oil products. All the contracts have 'take-or-pay' (TOP) and destination clauses built in. This is the reference case with which we compare the results from our policy scenario simulations. Details can be found at Andrews-Speed et al. (2015).

In the natural gas liberalisation *Scenario I – 'China spot'*, China's Shanghai spot prices become the benchmark for both pipeline gas and LNG trading in China—a pricing mechanism that is similar to how natural gas is currently priced in the United States and the United Kingdom. The Shanghai spot price is formed within the range of the marginal cost of supply of gas (shadow price) in Shanghai and gas-on-gas competition with LNG prices in the region.[6] All new contracts starting from 2020, and all existing contacts from 2025, will be indexed to the regional benchmark.

In the 'China spot, no TOP' scenario, in addition to the assumptions of Scenario I, TOP and destination clauses are removed for all contracts in China (post-2025), effectively making China a spot-only market.[7]

Baseline scenario

A detailed explanation of the baseline scenario can be found at Andrews-Speed et al. (2015). In this section, we report results relating to China and Australia.

---

6   The competing fuel prices used in calculation were average China LNG Contract DES price; Japan spot price; and average LNG contract price from Australia.

7   Removing TOP and destination clauses from a contract makes that supply contestable by other demand regions. Hence, removing the contract clauses is similar to making all purchases in a spot-only market.

Prices

A decline in oil prices is the main reason for a decline in spot and shadow prices[8] for consumers (China, India and Japan) until about 2020 (Figure 7.4). This is due to 1) spot gas competing with oil and oil products in the region; and 2) predominantly oil-indexed long-term contracts in the region. The increasing cost of gas extraction in China (unconventional gas) is the reason for an increase in shadow prices in China. Increased shadow prices and increased domestic demand is expected to make the Chinese market the highest spot-price market in the region by 2035. Ample supply of shale gas and moderately rising demand result in a less tight market in the United States. This leads to steady HH prices. Spot prices in Russia and Australia increase due to increased tightness in the domestic market and increased costs of gas extraction.

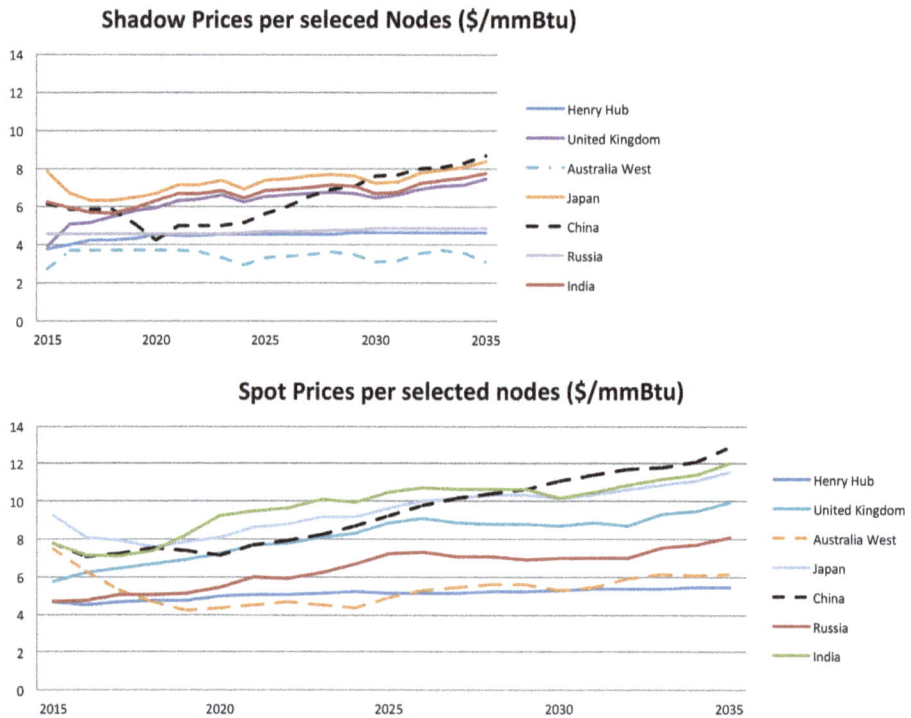

Shadow Prices per seleced Nodes ($/mmBtu)

Spot Prices per selected nodes ($/mmBtu)

Figure 7.4 Spot price and shadow price (all prices in 2012 US$ per mmBtu)[a]

[a] mmBtu = one million British thermal units.
Source: Authors' projections.

---

8   The shadow price is the marginal cost of gas supply to each node and is thus indicative of the true cost of gas. Spot prices are market-driven prices that customers pay for consumption of the gas. The spot price is dependent on the cost of procurement (shadow price) and the tightness of the market. Tightness of the market is a measure of overall flexibility of supply in relation to demand in a regional market. In a market with fewer supply options, market tightness will be high if supply is relatively constrained. The exact position within this range is determined according to the state of supply and demand assumed for the model run. In an oversupplied market, the spot price should lie close to the marginal cost and in a tighter market the spot price will be influenced more strongly by competing fuel prices (Nexant 2013).

Production & consumption in China

China sees a more than twofold jump in total production from 149 bcm in 2015 to 341 bcm in 2035, and the increase in consumption is projected to be 256 per cent, from 207 bcm in 2015 to 532 bcm in 2035 (Figure 7.5). The weighted average cost of production increases from \$1.32 per mmBtu in 2015 to \$2.54 per mmBtu in 2035.

Chinese Gas Market Balance

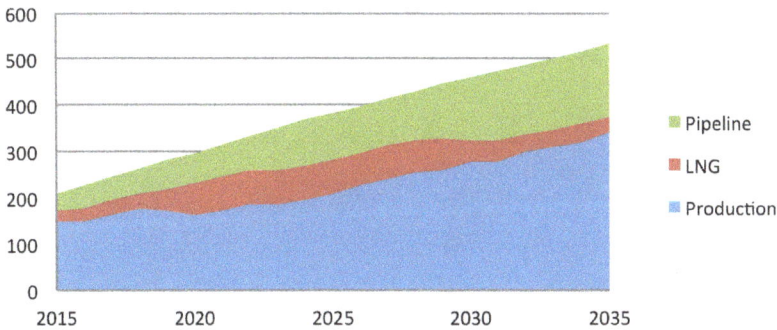

Figure 7.5 Chinese gas market balance (production and imports) (bcm)

Source: Authors' projections.

Australia's LNG production and exports will also dramatically increase. Production is expected to increase from 72 bcm in 2015 to 126 bcm in 2019 and to stay relatively stable in the forecast period. LNG exports is projected to increase from 26 Mt in 2015 to 62 Mt in 2019, and decline slightly to 55 Mt, on average, in the period 2030–35. Meanwhile, domestic consumption is expected to be relatively stable with a mild growth trend. About 60 per cent of production will be exported, even in 2035 (Figure 7.6).

Australia Market Balance

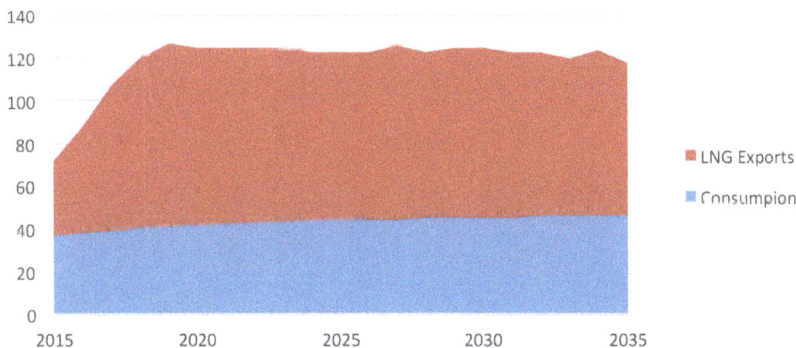

Figure 7.6 Australia's gas market balance (production and exports) (bcm)

Source: Authors' projections.

Inter-regional trade flows for China and Australia

There is a significant increase in pipeline imports to China, from 37 bcm in 2015 to 156 bcm in 2035, and PPG remains the largest source of imports. This increase in pipeline imports and increased domestic production (341 bcm in 2035) result in decreased dependence on LNG imports, as seen in Figure 7.7. Australia remains the dominant supplier to China after 2030, while South-East Asian exporters (mainly due to their decreased export capacity) are expected to lose market share.

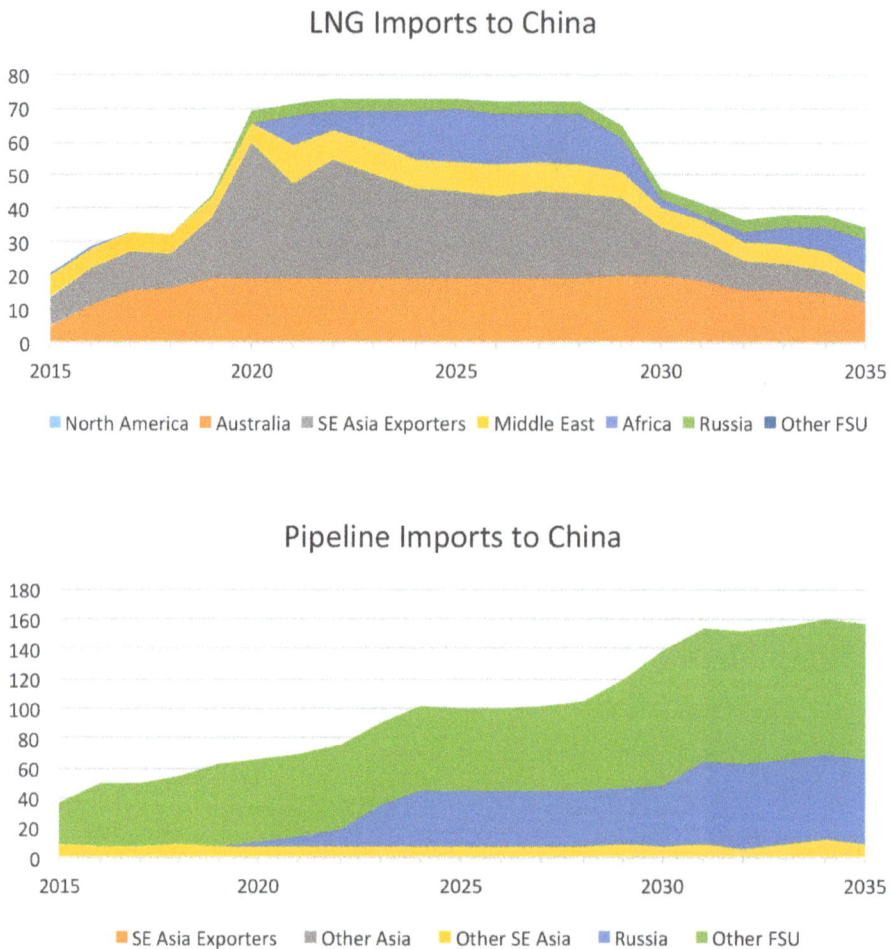

LNG Imports to China

Legend: ■ North America ■ Australia ■ SE Asia Exporters ■ Middle East ■ Africa ■ Russia ■ Other FSU

Pipeline Imports to China

Legend: ■ SE Asia Exporters ■ Other Asia ■ Other SE Asia ■ Russia ■ Other FSU

Figure 7.7 China's pipeline and LNG imports (bcm)

FSU = Former Soviet Union.
Source: Authors' projections.

In this baseline scenario, Australia remains the overall largest exporter of LNG to China in the forecast period (2015–35). Australia exports the majority of LNG to China and North-East Asia during our forecast period. Exports to China will decline after 2030 due to competition from Russia and Central Asia (Figure 7.8).

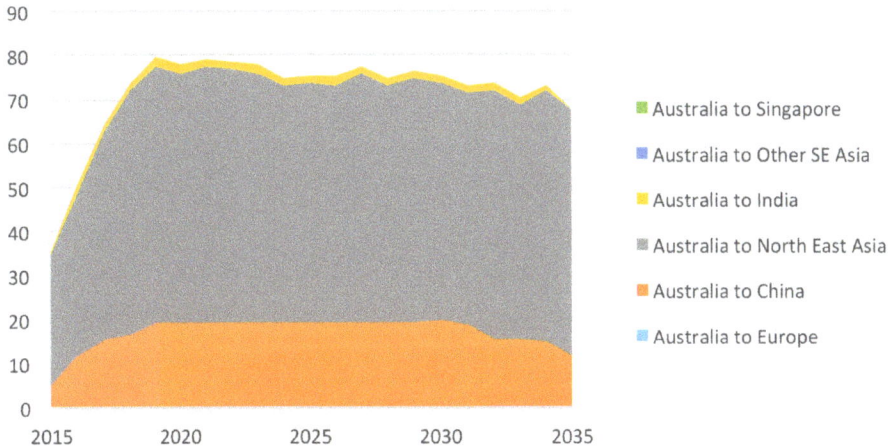

Figure 7.8 Australia's LNG exports: baseline scenario (bcm)

Source: Authors' projections.

Modelling results

Impact of China's gas market liberalisation on China's gas sector

As seen in Figure 7.9, Chinese spot prices start to decline (with reference to the baseline scenario) from 2025—the start of hub-based pricing—while hub prices in all other major markets remain largely the same. This is due to 1) gas-on-gas competition leads to lower competing prices in China; and 2) domestic market is less tight due to increased supply options from contract and spot LNG and pipeline gas. The same market price for both contracted and spot gas is more efficient in bringing in supplies to match demand, resulting in lower spot prices.

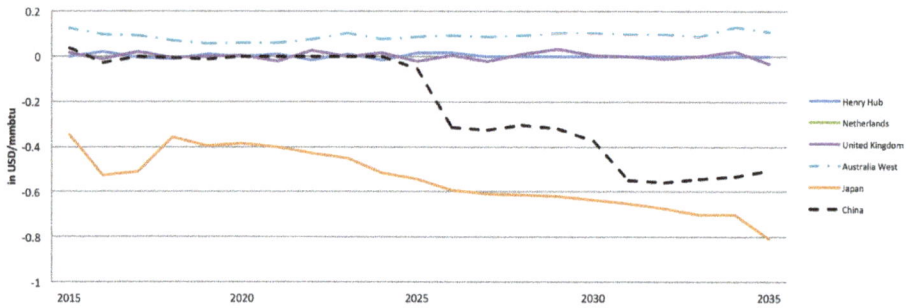

Figure 7.9 Selected spot price comparison: baseline versus China spot price

Source: Authors' projections.

Production and consumption patterns remain unchanged. LNG and pipeline trade patterns are also largely unchanged in such a scenario. This is to be expected as demand is unchanged and supply through contracts is also unchanged as contract terms remain the same, leading to similar levels of spot purchases (both pipeline and LNG) in China, as in the baseline scenario. Total LNG and pipeline trade flow patterns to China are therefore relatively unaffected in the 'China spot' scenario (Figures 7.10 and 7.11).

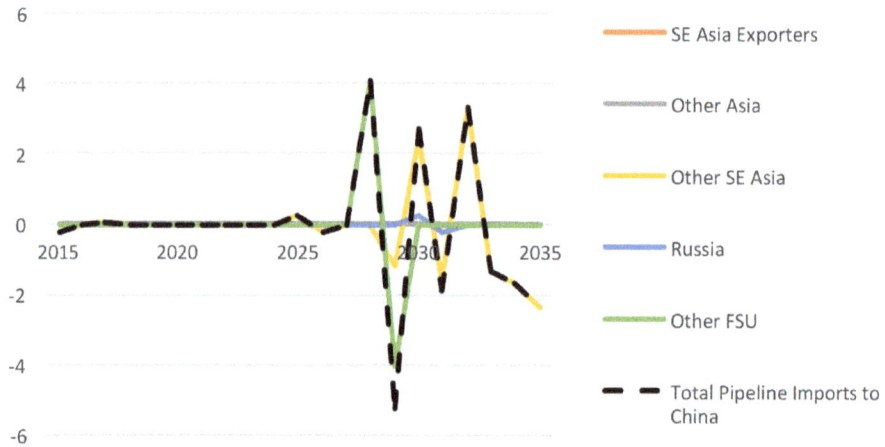

Figure 7.10 Pipeline imports to China: baseline versus China spot (bcm)

Source: Authors' projections.

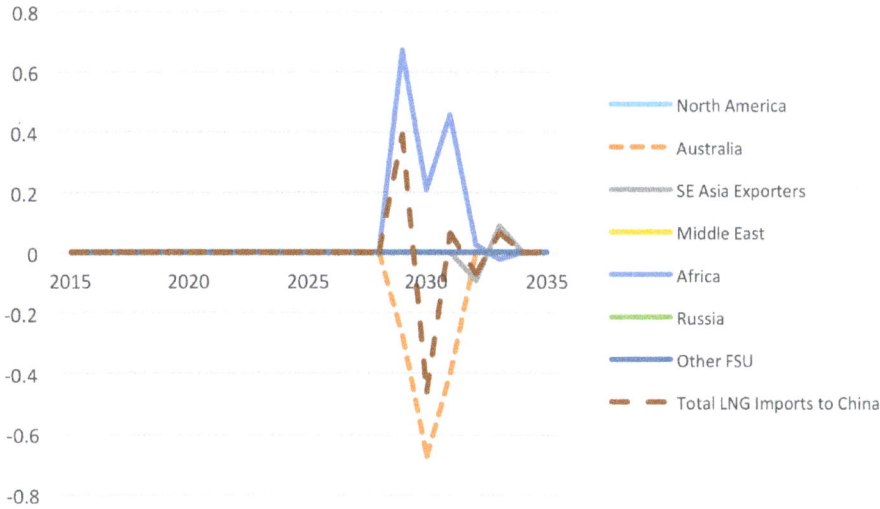

Figure 7.11 LNG imports to China: baselines versus China spot (bcm)

Source: Authors' projections.

In the second scenario, in this spot-only market (without TOP and destination clauses), China has to compete for spot gas (both pipeline and LNG) to satisfy all its demand, and demand may only marginally decline (<1 per cent). Here the optimisation of costs sees China developing more of its costlier unconventional gas resources compared with the baseline scenario.

The spot price in China increases in a market where all Chinese imports are procured from spot rather than the baseline scenario (Figure 7.12). This is due to the fact that in a market where all import purchases are from spot market supply, security is reduced. This provides incentives for domestic production from new, unconventional sources at higher cost. This leads to the marginal cost of gas production (shadow price) increasing in China after 2025, and in Asia after 2030 (Figure 7.12). Second, competition for spot gas from the market increases the tightness of the domestic gas market in China. Therefore, in a spot-only market, where China is forced to compete for contestable gas volumes at higher prices and also produce gas at higher cost, the spot price in China increases. This increase in China spot price leads to increase in spot prices in the region due to trade arbitrage.

Spot price

Shadow price

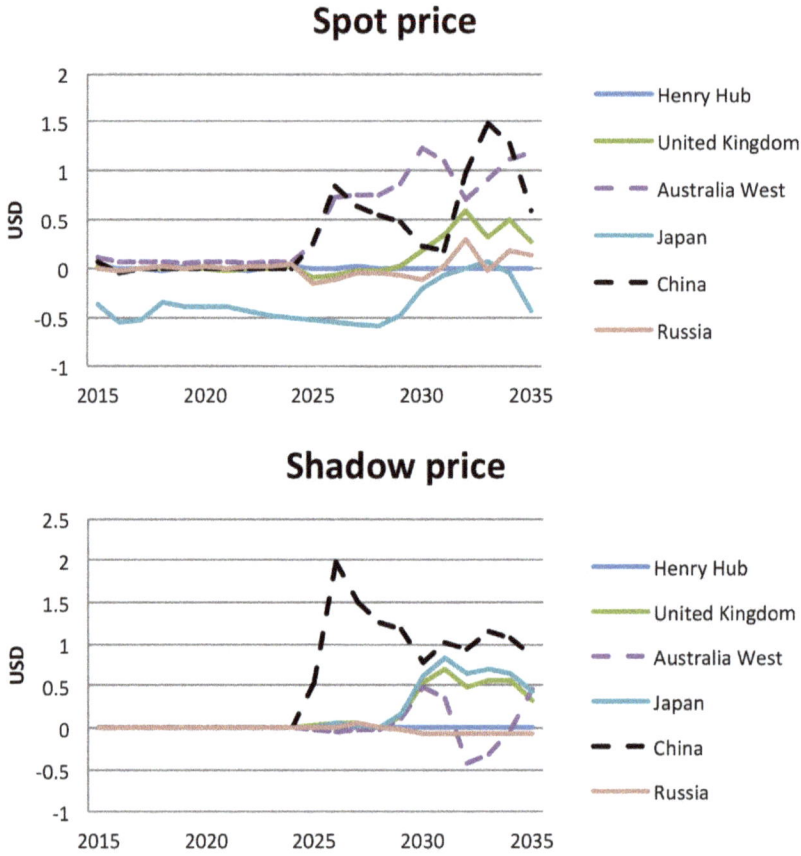

Figure 7.12 Spot and shadow prices: 'China spot, no TOP' versus baseline (US$)

Source: Authors' projections.

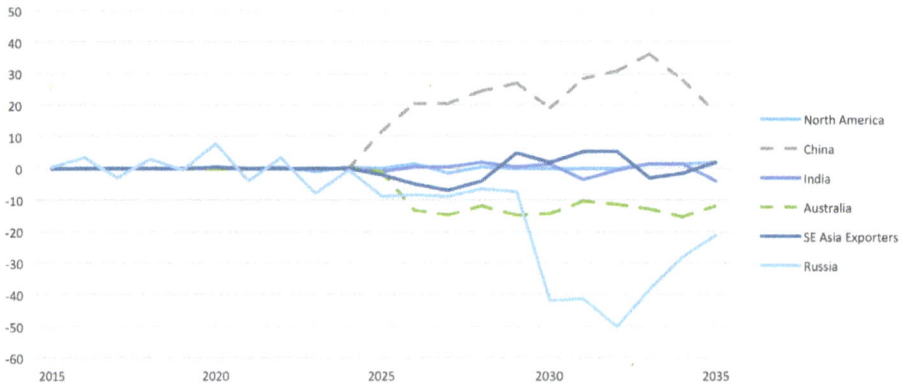

Figure 7.13 Production comparison: baseline versus 'China spot, no TOP' (bcm)

Source: Authors' projections.

Domestic production of natural gas increases, on average, by 7.4 per cent, while the production cost rises by 13.1 per cent (Figure 7.13).

This increase in production (and therefore less dependence on contestable spot gas from global markets) leads to changes in trade patterns, for both LNG and pipeline gas.

Overall, there is *only* marginally lower import of LNG compared with the baseline scenario during this period. Hence LNG import is seen as favorable in a fully liberalised market. Although the impact is different among different LNG producers. China imports more LNG from South-East Asia, the Middle East and Africa and less from Australia and Russia. LNG imports from the first three regions are favoured due to the fact that 1) a higher spot price means marginal LNG volumes from South-East Asia, Africa and the Middle East are no longer priced out; 2) as contracted voumes are displaced by spot gas, cost competitive regions (Table 7.3) are expected to dominate the market; and, most importantly, 3) the decrease in cost of LNG is higher than decrease in cost of pipeline gas, as compared to base case scenario. Australian LNG exports to Asia decrease, on average, by 20 bcm, while Russia is able to compensate for the loss of Chinese exports by exporting more LNG to North-East Asia (Figure 7.14).

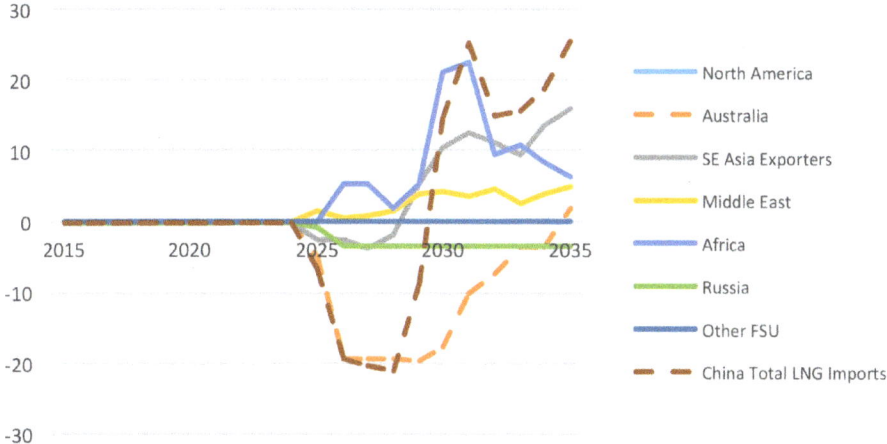

Figure 7.14 LNG imports to China: baseline versus 'China spot, no TOP' (bcm)

Source: Authors' projections.

Increased domestic production leads to less demand for piped gas, and most of the curtailment applies to Russian gas. Russian gas imports to China decrease, on average, by 40 bcm from 2025 to 2035. In contrast, there is an increase, on average, of 23 bcm in gas exports from Central Asia, which compensates for Russian gas until about 2030. Thereafter, Russian gas is compensated by an increase in production than an increase in imports. Other pipeline imports to

China are mostly unchanged (Figure 7.15). There are three reasons for this. First, Russian piped gas is costlier (at $12.33 per mmBtu) than Central Asian piped gas ($12.07 per mmBtu) during the period 2025–35. Second, China buys gas in the market for contestable pipeline spot gas. The Russian spot gas market is expected to be more competitive as Russian gas can be sold in Europe, the former Soviet Union (FSU) and Asia. The marginal cost of procuring spot gas away from the Russian pipeline is therefore higher compared with the Central Asian gas market. Third, when the incremental Central Asian contestable gas capacity that can be cost effectively diverted to China is exhausted, it is more economical to develop domestic resources for production.

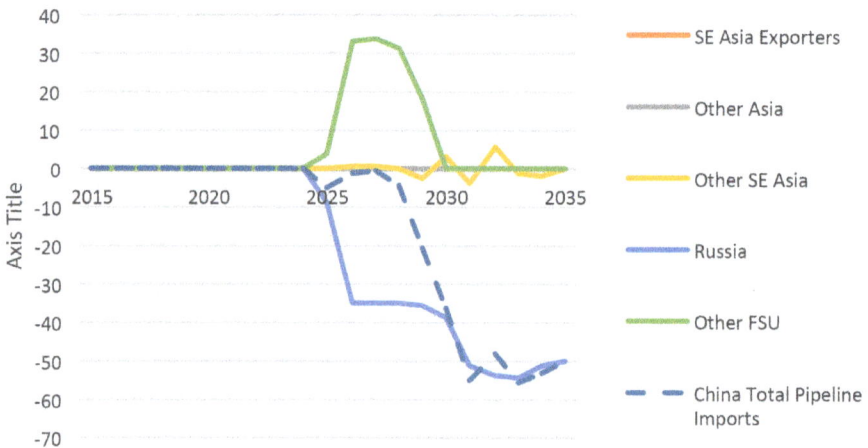

Figure 7.15 Pipeline imports to China: baseline versus 'China spot, no TOP' (bcm)

Source: Authors' projections.

Impact of China's gas market liberalisation on Australia's LNG exports

In a contracted world, due to TOP and destination clauses, Australia sees a very small (less than 0.1 per cent) change in overall production and exports to Asia even with a spot-indexed market. Therefore, in the 'China spot' case, the trading pattern remains unchanged. The total change in export volume is not more than 1 bcm during the study period (Figure 7.16). Despite the low spot prices in China, due to contractual obligations, the demand for contestable gas is lower, and Australia with its proximity and cost competitiveness compared with North America can supply it at the margin.

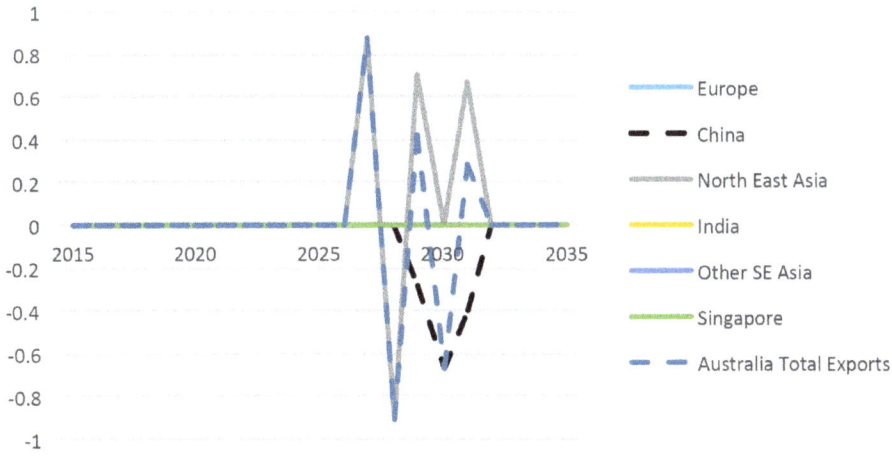

Figure 7.16 Australian LNG exports: 'China spot' scenario

Source: Authors' projections.

In a market where the demand for spot gas is high and flexibility of supply is also high ('China spot, no TOP' scenario), higher-cost producers such as Australia could, however, lose some of their export volumes to lower-cost producers supplying in the region. When all Chinese contracts change to pure spot (without TOP and destination clauses), Australia's LNG is displaced from China (all contracted flows) and there is little compensation from increased flows to North-East Asia. Total Australian production therefore decreases by 8.5 per cent and exports decrease by 28 per cent, on average (Figure 7.17).

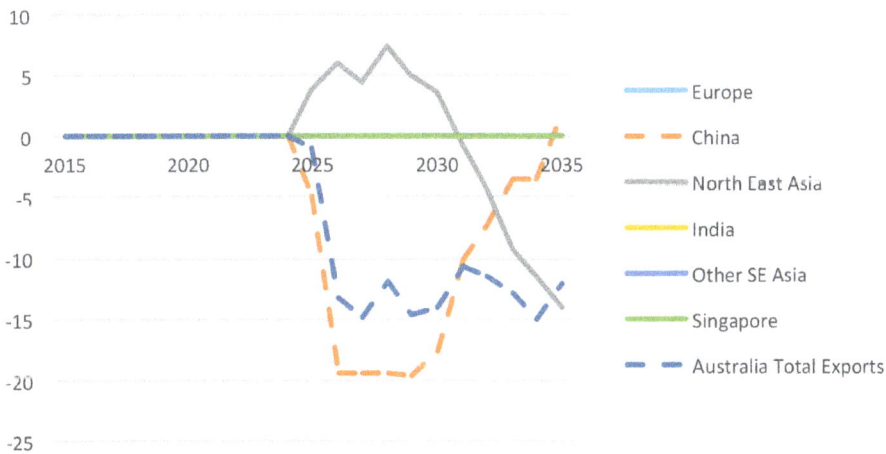

Figure 7.17 Australian LNG exports: baseline versus 'China spot, no TOP' scenario

Source: Authors' projections.

The decline can be explained by the marginal cost and average cost of production of gas from Australia compared with other major producers. Australian gas is of comparable cost with that of the United States and Russia, while disadvantaged against that from Qatar, Nigeria and other major producers in South-East Asia (Table 7.3). Moreover, factoring in the transportation cost to Asian markets, Australia will lose out to Middle Eastern producers (Qatar, United Arab Emirates), Africa and South-East Asia, and is at a slight disadvantage compared with Russian gas due to the lower transportation costs for Russian LNG from Sakhalin through the pipeline to China (Ledesma et al. 2014). It is seen as competitive with North American gas in Asia, hence Australia (with contracted gas) continues to supply all of its exports to Asia.

Table 7.3 Marginal cost of production of gas[a]

$ mmBtu	2015	2020	2025	2030	2035
Australia	2.79	4.56	4.34	4.19	3.70
Qatar	1.99	1.99	1.99	1.99	1.99
United States	3.73	4.40	4.44	4.45	4.45
Russia	3.36	3.62	4.31	4.41	4.45
Nigeria	1.69	1.07	1.35	2.20	2.20
South-East Asia exporters	3.12	3.62	3.43	4.67	5.69

[a] Shadow price at the node = marginal cost of production of gas for producers.
Source: Authors' calculations.

Financial impact assessment

In the 'China spot' scenario, liberalisation of the gas market leads to lower procurement costs for China (Table 7.4). It is instructive to compare the total cost of gas in China during the forecast period in the baseline scenario with that in the 'China spot' case—total consumption is the same, but the procurement costs are reduced. Due to lower domestic spot prices for the same demand, pipeline costs are lower by 5.9 per cent and LNG contract and spot purchase costs are lower by 11.7 per cent. Overall procurement costs are lower by 6.3 per cent. Uncontracted volumes increase and contracted volumes are kept to the minimum TOP amount.

In the 'China spot, no TOP' scenario, the total cost of procuring gas for China during the forecast period increases by 6.8 per cent compared with the baseline scenario. There is a production cost increase of 13 per cent due to increased production from higher-cost fields, a 10.5 per cent increase in total pipeline procurement costs (even though total pipeline deliveries decline), and an 11 per cent decrease in LNG import costs due to reduced imports from Australia and Russia.

Table 7.4 Total production, import and procurement costs for China across scenarios, 2015–35

Cost calculation	Volume (bcm)			Procurement cost[a] (US$ million)		
	Baseline	Spot	Spot, no TOP	Baseline	Spot	Spot, no TOP
Production	4,732	4,735	4,997	353,114.40	353,378.20	399,398.00
PPG contracted	4,337	4,435	1,886	780,341.50	689,221.40	279,063.60
PPG uncontracted	4,439	4,447	6,194	1,618,756.00	1,566,592.00	2,373,357.00
LNG contracted	690	688	350	463,525.20	394,801.80	208,463.40
LNG uncontracted	416	417	810	141,484.40	139,285.70	329,525.60
Regasification	n.a.[b]	n.a.	n.a.	28,805.57	28,924.07	30,125.56
Consumption	7,938	7,938	7,927	3,386,027.00	3,172,203.00	3,619,933.00

[a] Production cost = production per field; LRMC, contract price = delivered quantity; Contract price, spot price = spot quantity; Spot price, calculated for each production field, contracts and spot purchases for the duration of forecast in the case of China.
[b] n.a. = not applicable.
Source: Authors' projections.

Chinese liberalisation is expected to cause a net profit loss to Australia's LNG exports, caused by a decrease in export prices as well reductions in volume of exports. In the 'China spot' scenario, Australia's LNG export volumes do not change, but average prices will decrease. With the removal of TOP and destination clauses, Australian LNG exports further reduces with little in compensation from an increase in spot prices.

As we analyse the export revenue for Australia (Table 7.5) under different scenarios of Chinese market liberalisation, in the 'China spot' scenario total export revenue declines by 4.1 per cent, while in the 'China spot, no TOP' scenario total export revenue declines by 9.4 per cent. Contracted and uncontracted export volumes remain unchanged in the 'China spot' scenario, while decline in prices result in decline of overall revenue. An increase in spot prices is more than compensated by a decline in the export volumes 'China spot no TOP' scenario, resulting in decline of overall revenue.

Overall net profits, accounting for costs of production and liquefaction,[9] show that profits are expected to decline when China liberalises the market (price and volume flexibility). Average LNG prices ($ per cm) are $0.5209, $0.4999 and $0.5149 under the three scenarios of baseline, 'spot' and 'spot, no TOP', respectively.

9   Price DES = cost of production + cost of liquefaction + cost of transportation + profit.

Table 7.5 Export revenue for Australia in different scenarios, 2015–35

	Exports (bcm)			Revenue ($ billion)/average price		
	Baseline	Spot	Spot, no TOP	Baseline	Spot	Spot, no TOP
LNG contracted exports	1,251.6	1,250.3	1,072.3	697.0	670.9	601.1
LNG uncontracted exports	321.2	322.6	368.7	122.3	115.4	140.9
Total LNG exports	1,572.8	1,572.9	1,441.0	819.3	786.3	742.0
Production	2,481.6	2,481.6	2,349.7	n.a.	n.a.	n.a.
Production and liquefaction costs	n.a.[a]	n.a.	n.a.	485.6	486.9	441.9
Profit	n.a.	n.a.	n.a.	333.7	299.4	300.0

[a] n.a. = not applicable.
Source: Authors' projections.

In contrast with the mixed results for China and Australia, the world is better off in China liberalised market scenarios, as seen in the global system cost. Global costs for 'China spot' and 'China spot, no TOP' are lower—1.24 per cent and 1.18 per cent respectively—compared with the baseline scenario. The procurement costs for major importers in East Asia are, on average, lower by 2.12 per cent for 'China spot' and 0.84 per cent for the 'China spot, no TOP' scenario (Table 7.6). This is due mainly to reduced LNG import costs in all countries (similar to China), while being independent of pipeline imports (in China, pipeline import costs substantially increase in the 'no TOP' scenario).

Table 7.6 Optimised system cost, 2015–35 (US$ million)

	Baseline	Spot	Spot, no TOP
Procurement costs: India	568,988.8	562,563.4	570,893.1
Procurement costs: Japan	1,131,709.0	1,107,390.0	1,117,638.7
Procurement costs: Korea	549,608.0	538,492.7	544,446.3
Procurement costs: Taiwan	190,362.1	184,361.8	187,490.6
Global optimised system cost	13,157,315.0	12,994,139.0	13,000,958.0

Source: Individual country costs are calculated similar to China cost calculation, and global cost is an output of the optimiser of the World Gas Model.

Summary and implications

In an importing region with a marked dependence on long-term contracts (North-East Asia) and with China as the only fully deregulated market, China could potentially be worse off. This is due to a potential increase in the spot price due to demand for contestable gas. Concern for supply security[10] and the level and volatility in price for and supply of spot gas could potentially be a good incentive to develop costlier unconventional production, which would otherwise be shut down. Even with less import dependence, the overall procurement cost could potentially be driven up due to the twin effects of higher uncontracted pipeline gas and LNG spot purchases.

Australian LNG could face competition from a surge in the supply of piped gas from Russia and Central Asia. Australian LNG is, however, seen as competitive with North American LNG in the baseline scenario simulation. Both in the baseline scenario and in the 'China spot price' scenario, most of the Australian LNG is contracted and Australian LNG is cost competitive with spot gas from Russia, North America and South-East Asia by the end of 2030.

Australian exports could reduce in cases where China's gas market is fully liberalised in the 'China spot' scenario (Scenario I). The future of Chinese gas supply is well diversified, with an emphasis on domestic production and pipeline imports from Russia and Central Asia. This well-supplied market with liberalised prices could lead to lower spot prices in North-East Asia. In this market, Australian gas with higher marginal costs is expected to be priced out at the margin. Moreover, remaining contracted exports to China are transacted at this lower spot price, leading to lower export revenue. However, the TOP clause in contracts allows Australia to continue to export at least up to the TOP level.

In the scenario in which the Chinese gas market is fully liberalised 'China spot, no TOP' (Scenario II), the twin effects of increased domestic production and competition for spot gas from lower-cost producers in Africa, the Middle East and South-East Asia result in a decline in Australian exports to China. Here the impact on exports is due to competition with other producing regions (for both piped gas and LNG) to supply spot gas (contestable volumes) to China. Reduced supply security in an 'all-spot' market would provide incentives for domestic production in China, thereby reducing import dependence. Also, pipeline gas from Central Asia and Russia is cheaper than LNG. However, in this tight 'spot-only' market, higher spot prices would compensate for the drop in volumes.

Nevertheless, the world and the major East Asian buyers are better off, which justifies the liberalisation efforts. Comparing the two policy scenarios, however, a fully deregulated Chinese market increases the total global system cost and procurement costs for the major East Asian gas importers.

---

10 Supply security is reflected in the model as the tightness of the domestic market.

The simulations suggest that, first, for China, a market with a mix of contracted purchases (with TOP and destination clauses) and spot purchases at a single price is the most effective form of regulation. We have seen one possibility in which, in a balanced market (based on production and consumption forecasts), the optimum response for China is to take contracted supplies up to the level of TOP and bridge the gap with lowest-cost spot purchases, with a single price driven by local supply and demand characteristics.

In contrast, for Australia, from the perspective of maintaining export volumes, keeping TOP and destination clauses is in Australia's economic interest. However, when judged against total profit, the benefit becomes small. In any case, to compete in a scenario of full liberalisation of key consumer markets such as China, with a corresponding impact on domestic prices and emphasis on shorter-term contracts, Australia can look at 1) alternative key markets where spot prices are higher than Japanese and Chinese prices; and 2) retaining contract terms with some conditions on TOP and destination clauses.

Conclusion

Given the importance of China's current and future gas demand, its liberalisation efforts and the prospect of a hub of Chinese benchmark prices, Chinese liberalisation is an important topic for natural gas researchers and policymakers at home and abroad. Against the IEA's assessment criteria, it is clear that China's gas market is still developing and is therefore not ready for wholesale competition. Although non-residential gas prices are linked to oil products, they are still regulated. And although large customers are allowed to choose their suppliers in the full netback pricing from April 2015, TPA is a challenge due to the inadequacy of transmission capacity. Short transmission capacity will still prevent the access of third parties. Moreover, residential gas pricing is still regulated; and the current oil indexation for gas pricing will not lead to the more ambitious goal of establishing a spot market and competitive prices. The insufficient number of market players in the oligopolistic market structure will prevent the formation of a competitive gas market, even at the wholesale level. The dominance of NOCs also casts a shadow over market competition, if there is any.

The gas market liberalisation process in China, despite recent momentum, may require a few decades to be completed. To establish a spot market, the Chinese Government will need to take additional measures, including institutional changes such as wholesale price deregulation, separation of transmission and marketing activities, sufficient network capacity with TPA, creation of a sufficient number of market players to enable competition, and the involvement of financial institutions.

Despite the challenges, looking forward a decade, a competitive market in China is possible. It is possible to develop a deregulated market through either pipeline-to-pipeline competition or wholesale market competition in a developing stage (IEA 2013). Gas market liberalisation has been reaffirmed by the current leadership and could be expedited in coming years. With the determination of the Communist Party to liberalise markets, more wholesale competition reforms—such as pricing liberalisation, separation of pipelines and building gas trading hubs—are on the way. Gas trading hubs, building on wholesale competition, could emerge in the coming decade.

Immediate improvements in the gas pricing mechanisms could extend the netback to other alternatives, such as coal; allow the publication of price-adjustment criteria and procedures; specify regional differentiation formulas; apply market prices to the residential sector; and redirect subsidies from distribution companies to underprivileged households. For the long term, improvement in gas pricing could be achieved by moving the pricing mechanism away from the netback and towards competitive hub prices.

The emergence of hub-based prices will have an impact on world trade, and prices and demand for natural gas. The emergence of competitive market (gas-to-gas) prices, if adopted as a trade benchmark, will have a significant impact on other gas producing and consuming countries.

Our estimations show that in an importing region with a marked dependence on long-term contracts (North-East Asia), with China as the only fully deregulated market, could potentially make China worse off. Even with less import dependence, overall procurement costs could potentially be driven up due to the twin effects of higher volume and prices for uncontracted pipeline gas and LNG spot purchases. A market with a mix of contracted purchases (with TOP and destination clauses) and spot purchases at a single price is seen as the most effective form of regulation.

Based on the modelling exercise and the nature of Chinese and Australian markets, the optimum response for China is to take contracted supplies up to the level of TOP and bridge the gap with lowest-cost spot purchases, with a single price driven by local supply and demand characteristics. Similarly, Australia would also potentially be better off in a predominantly long-term contract market.

The ongoing liberalisation process is important in achieving China's gas demand targets, which, in turn, is important to achieve its critical goals of improving air quality and reducing carbon dioxide emissions. Regulated and often capped gas prices make it difficult to pass through high gas prices to consumers and reward the comparative advantages of gas over coal in reducing carbon dioxide emissions and air pollutants. On the contrary, in a deregulated gas market, the prices of gas could be adjusted with oil prices. In this context, pricing carbon makes natural gas more competitive over coal in power generation and other industrial usage, and carbon taxes will be more effective. The liberalised gas market will make it possible to fully utilise the potential of gas in carbon-abatement technology, and thus could reduce carbon prices. These issues, although important, will have to be left for future study.

References

Aldred, S. and Zhu, C. (2014), Sinopec to sell $17.5 billion retail stake in privatization push, *Reuters*, Hong Kong/Beijing.

Andrews-Speed, P., Yao. L., bin Zahur, N., Rohatgi, A., M.P., H., Regan, T., Linga, P., (2015), *International outlook for unconventional gas and implications for global gas markets*, Singapore: Energy Studies Institute, National University of Singapore.

Asche, F., Misund, B. and Sikveland, M. (2013), The relationship between spot and contract prices in Europe, *Energy Economics,* 38: 212–17.

BP (2014), *Statistical review of world energy 2014*, London: British Petroleum.

BP (2015), *Energy outlook 2035*, London: British Petroleum. Available from: www.bp.com/en/global/corporate/about-bp/energy-economics/energy-outlook.html. Accessed 26 February 2015.

Central Committee of the Communist Party of China (CPC) (2013), *Decision of the Central Committee of the Communist Party of China on some major issues concerning comprehensively deepening the reform*, Beijing: Central Committee of the Communist Party of China.

Chen, M. (2014), *The development of Chinese gas pricing: Drivers, challenges and implications for demand*, Oxford: Oxford Institute for Energy Studies.

Chen, S. and He, L. (2013), Deregulation or governmental intervention? A counterfactual perspective on China's electricity market reform, *China & World Economy,* 21: 101–20.

China Securities Newspaper (2015), Xinhua Newsagency is leading the efforts to set up the Shanghai Oil and Gas Trading Centre [in Chinese], *China Securities Newspaper.*

CNPC News Centre (2015), *To gradually advance mixed ownership for network assets, CNPC plans to sell the Eastern Pipeline Company* [in Chinese], Beijing: China National Petroleum Corporation. Available from: news.cnpc.com.cn/system/2015/01/07/001523904.shtml. Accessed 3 March 2015.

Energy Information Administration (EIA) (2014), *Annual energy outlook 2014*, Washington, DC: EIA.

Erdos, P. (2012), Have oil and gas prices got separated?, *Energy Policy*, 49: 707–18.

Energy Studies Institute (ESI) (n.d.), Asia gas trade model, Unpublished ms, Singapore: Energy Studies Institute, National University of Singapore.

Fernandez, R. and Palazuelos, E. (2011), The future of Russian gas exports to East Asia: Feasibility and market implications, *Futures*, 43: 1069–81.

Foss, M.M. (2014), Natural gas pricing in North America, in Stern, J. (ed.), *The pricing of internationally traded natural gas*, Oxford: Oxford Institute for Energy Studies, pp. 85–144.

Henderson, J. (2014), *Russian gas matrix*, Oxford: Oxford University Press.

International Energy Agency (IEA) (2002), *Developing China's natural gas market: The energy policy challenges*, Paris: IEA.

International Energy Agency (IEA) (2012), *Gas pricing and regulation: China's challenges and IEA experience*, Paris: IEA.

International Energy Agency (IEA) (2013), *Developing a natural gas trading hub in Asia*, Paris: IEA.

International Energy Agency (IEA) (2014), *The Asian quest for LNG in a globalizing market*, Paris: IEA.

Ledesma, D., Palmer, N. and Henderson, J. (2014), *The future of Australian LNG exports: Will domestic challenges limit the development of future LNG export capacity?* Oxford: Oxford Institute for Energy Studies.

Li, Y. and Bai, F. (2010), A policy study examining the use of imported LNG for gas fired power generation in south east coast of China, *Energy Policy*, 38: 896–901.

Lin, W., Zhang, N. and Gu, A. (2010), LNG: A necessary part in China's future energy infrastructure, *Energy*, 35: 4383–91.

Manuhutu, C. and Owen, A.D. (2010), Gas on gas competition in Shanghai, *Energy Policy,* 38: 2101–6.

Maxwell, D. and Zhu, Z. (2011), Natural gas prices, LNG transport costs and the dynamics of LNG imports, *Energy Economics,* 33: 217–26.

National Bureau of Statistics of China (NBS) (2015), *Statistical communiqué of the People's Republic of China on the 2014 National Economic and Social Development*, Beijing: NBS.

National Development and Reform Commission (NDRC) (2007), *National gas utilisation policy*, Beijing: NDRC.

National Development and Reform Commission (NDRC) (2013), *Circular on natural gas price adjustments* [in Chinese], No. 1246, Beijing: NDRC.

National Development and Reform Commission (NDRC) (2014), *Guiding opinions of NDRC on improving tier gas prices for the residential sector*, Beijing: NDRC. Available from: www.sdpc.gov.cn.

National Development and Reform Commission (NDRC) and National Energy Administration (NEA) (2014), *Energy sector's action plan of strengthening air pollution prevention and control*, No. 56, Beijing: NDRC and NEA.

National Energy Administration (NEA) (2014), *Administrative measures on opening up fair access to the oil and gas pipeline*, Beijing: NEA.

Nexant (2013), *User manual (Version 3.05 for Office 2010)*, London: Nexant.

Pang, M. (2015), *Review of China's gas imports in 2014*, [in Chinese]. Available from: www.wusuobuneng.com/archives/16453. Accessed 21 February 2015.

Platts (2014), *China's ENN receives first LNG cargo*, New York: Platts. Available from: www.platts.com/latest-news/natural-gas/singapore/chinas-enn-receives-first-lng-cargo-21755210. Accessed 4 March 2015.

Platts (2015), *China's first private LNG import terminal project in Zhejiang delayed*, New York: Platts. Available from: www.platts.com/latest-news/natural-gas/singapore/chinas-first-private-lng-import-terminal-project-27129958. Accessed on 4 March 2015.

Qian X. and Jiang X. (2014), *Development Report for Oil and Gas Industry in China and Abroad*. Beijing: Oil Industry Press.

Reuters (2012), CNPC sees China's gas consumption trebling by 2030, *Reuters,* 7 June. Available from: in.reuters.com/article/2012/06/07/china-gas-consumption-idINL3E8H74O720120607. Accessed 26 February 2015.

Schultz, E. and Swieringa, J. (2013), Price discovery in European natural gas markets, *Energy Policy*, 61: 628–34.

Shi, G.-H., Jing, Y.-Y., Wang, S.-L. and Zhang, X.T. (2010), Development status of LNG industry in China, *Energy Policy*, 38: 7457–65.

Siliverstovs, B., L'Hegaret, G., Neumann, A. and von Hirschhausen, C. (2005), International market integration for natural gas? A cointegration analysis of prices in Europe, North America and Japan, *Energy Economics*, 27(4): 603–15.

State Council (2010), *Opinions of the State Council on encouraging and guiding the healthy development of private investment*, Beijing: The State Council of the People's Republic of China. Available from: www.gov.cn.

State Council (2014), *Energy development strategy action plan (2014–2020)* [in Chinese], Beijing: General Office, The State Council of the People's Republic of China.

Stern, J.P. (ed.) (2012), *The pricing of internationally traded gas*, Oxford: Oxford University Press.

Su, N., 2014. Major Energy Infrustructure Accellerated, *China Energy Newspaper*, Beijing. Available at: http://paper.people.com.cn/zgnyb/html/2014-12/08/content_1508629.htm [19 May 2015].

World Bank (2015), *World Bank commodities price forecast (January 2015)*, Washington, DC: The World Bank. Available from: www.worldbank.org/content/dam/Worldbank/GEP/GEP2015a/Price_Forecast.pdf.

Zhang, Z. (2014), Energy price subsidies and resource tax reform in China, *Asia & Pacific Policy Studies*, 1: 439–54.

Appendix

Table A7.1 Regional specifications used in the study

Regions	Countries
Australia	Australia
China	China
India	India
Russia	Russia
Singapore	Singapore
North-East Asia	Japan, South Korea, Chinese Taipei
Asia-Pacific exporters	Brunei Darussalam, Malaysia, Indonesia, Papua New Guinea
Rest of South-East Asia	Cambodia, Myanmar, Philippines, Thailand, Vietnam
Other Asia	Bangladesh, Hong Kong, Mongolia, Nepal, Pakistan, Sri Lanka, DPRK, Afghanistan, New Zealand
Africa	Algeria, Angola, Benin, Botswana, Cameroon, Congo, Côte d'Ivoire, DR Congo, Egypt, Equatorial Guinea, Eritrea, Ethiopia, Gabon, Ghana, Kenya, Libya, Morocco, Mozambique, Namibia, Nigeria, Senegal, South Africa, Sudan, Togo, Tunisia, Tanzania, Zambia, Zimbabwe
Europe	Austria, Belgium, Czech Republic, Denmark, Finland, France, Germany, Greece, Hungary, Iceland, Italy, Luxembourg, Netherlands, Norway, Poland, Portugal, Slovak Republic, Spain, Sweden, Switzerland, Turkey, United Kingdom, Albania, Bosnia and Herzegovina, Bulgaria, Croatia, Cyprus, Macedonia (FYROM), Romania, Serbia, Slovenia, Estonia, Latvia, Lithuania
Former Soviet Union	Armenia, Azerbaijan, Belarus, Georgia, Kazakhstan, Kyrgyzstan, Moldova, Tajikistan, Turkmenistan, Ukraine, Uzbekistan
Latin America	Argentina, Bolivia, Brazil, Chile, Colombia, Cuba, Dominican Republic, Peru, Trinidad and Tobago, Venezuela, Uruguay, Jamaica, Puerto Rico, Panama
Middle East	Bahrain, Iraq, Iran, Israel, Jordan, Kuwait, Lebanon, Oman, Qatar, Saudi Arabia, Syria, UAE, Yemen
North America	Canada, Mexico, United States

8. China's Electricity Sector

Powering growth, keeping the lights on and prices down

Stephen Wilson, Yufeng Yang and Jane Kuang[1]

Introduction and historical context

Electricity is essential for both human and national development. China's leaders—many of them engineers—have long understood this. Indeed, improved and increased electricity supply were integral to at least two of the 'four modernisations' in Deng Xiaoping's landmark closing speech at the Third Plenary Session of the Eleventh Party Congress on 18 August 1977.

At the founding of the People's Republic in 1949, China had just 1.85 GW of installed electricity generation capacity and a population of more than 540 million (Jowett 1984). To put this in context, 1.85 GW is less than 2,000 MW—the capacity of a typical modern large coal-fired or nuclear power plant with two units. By 1982, China's installed power generation capacity had reached 50 GW for a population that passed the 1 billion mark in that census year (Jowlett 1984), about 800 million of whom lived in rural areas with limited or no access to electricity (Peng and Pan 2006, citing the in-depth chapter on China in IEA 2002).

By 1990, according to UN data, installed generation capacity had reached 138 GW, and according to the World Bank, more than 94 per cent of the population had access to electricity. In 2011, China's installed generation capacity passed the 1,000 GW mark, and has since overtaken the United States to become the largest power system in the world. By 2010, the World Bank reported near-universal electricity access of 99.7 per cent in China—equal to the rate across Organisation for Economic Cooperation and Development (OECD) countries.

---

1   This chapter is dedicated to the memory of Wang Leiping (1963–2015), a former energy specialist at the World Bank in Washington, DC. Stephen Wilson first met Leiping in 1997 while he was director of the Beijing Economic Research Institute for Water Resources and Electric Power (BERI), where he provided expert advice on the planning of much of China's generation and transmission system. This chapter reflects a number of things Leiping taught Stephen about China's power sector when they worked together at ERM Energy, and which have stood the test of time. The authors also acknowledge research support on the international comparators from Parth Goyal of Rio Tinto India. Any errors are the responsibility of the authors.

China's electricity sector faces the competing challenges of powering economic growth and development, and keeping the lights on and prices down. To explore how China's policymakers and companies respond to these challenges and to understand the likely future development of China's electricity sector, it is helpful to review how China made the journey from extremely limited electricity availability to universal access, driving a modern-day industrial revolution in the process.

A hydrothermal power system

While coal is the foundation fuel of China's power system today—and coal has been a vital energy source in China for hundreds of years—China's national vision for electricity has long included hydropower as a key source of supply, along with electricity for all and to power modern industry. Sun Yat-sen originally envisioned a large dam across the Yangtze River in 1919, and estimated its capacity as 22 GW. The 22.5 GW Three Gorges Dam is the world's largest power station and China's flagship hydropower project. Construction began in 1994 and the dam opened in 2008. The importance of hydropower was reflected in the name of the former Ministry of Water Resources and Electric Power, which was responsible for the electrification of the People's Republic of China (PRC) as a catalyst for industrialisation.

China has a hydrothermal power system: approximately 75 to 80 per cent coal-fired (thermal) and 15 to 20 per cent hydropower. While this chapter is about electricity, it is important to note that large-scale hydropower in China is not primarily about electricity generation. The dams are first and foremost about flood control—China has had devastating floods, killing large numbers of people and destroying livelihoods.

During the more than 2,000 years between the Han Dynasty (206 BC – 220 AD) and the Qing Dynasty (1644–1911), floods occurred on the Yangtze River nearly once every 10 years. During the past 300 years, severe floods breached the Jingjiang Dam 60 times, and disastrous floods struck twice in the past 100 years. Floods have been a persistent problem for residents and businesses along the Yangtze and for the Chinese Government (Chinese Embassy to the United States n.d.).

The dams are secondarily about irrigation and then about improved river navigation. Finally, electricity generation provides a revenue stream that enables the financing of the major capital works required to build the multipurpose dams on China's many rivers.

The purely hydrothermal structure of China's power sector has begun to change with the introduction of other forms of generation, including nuclear and gas-fired power plants and various forms of intermittent renewable energy, including solar and wind power. The first nuclear power plant was built at Daya Bay in Guangdong, near Hong Kong, in the 1990s. Yet even with the largest nuclear building program the world has yet seen planned or in progress, nuclear today comprises only a few per cent of national generation capacity. Similarly, natural gas-fired capacity—complementing coal in the thermal side of the system—is used mainly for electricity generation at peak times, due to the limited supply of gas from domestic sources and the relatively high cost of gas imported as liquefied natural gas (LNG) or via long-distance pipelines from Central Asia, South-East Asia and, in the future, from Russia. China's policies to provide financial encouragement for wind and solar power have stimulated one of the largest renewable energy programs in the world, but these sources also provide a small share of overall electricity generation.

Structure of this chapter

This chapter is organised as follows:

- The current situation and some of the challenges facing China's power sector are described, the evolution of China's electricity sector in the past 30 years and reforms undertaken to date are summarised, and the key policy issues facing the sector and how they have been managed so far are discussed.

- Selected international comparisons are drawn between China and other significant countries both in terms of the physical power systems and in terms of approaches to policy and regulation, with a particular focus on the experience of the United Kingdom and reference also to Australia.

- A framework for analysing ownership structures and regulatory approaches is defined.

- The chapter concludes with the policy choices available for China's power sector.

The current situation and some of the challenges facing China's power sector

The physical system

China, with 1.4 billion people, already has the largest power system in the world, with 1,260 GW of installed generation capacity (as of June 2014), having overtaken the United States, which has 1,040 GW for 325 million people. And yet, based on international electricity per capita indices (see Wensley et al. 2013) and conservative projections of gross domestic product (GDP) growth and energy efficiency improvements, China's system is still only half-developed, if that.

Zhou, X. (n.d.) noted that '[t]he construction of the Three Gorges Hydropower Project will further push forward the implementation of the nationwide interconnection program'. Not only is the Three Gorges power station large and, like all hydropower projects, fully flexible in its ability to ramp its output up and down almost instantaneously, it is also located in an advantageous central position in the emerging national grid (Figure 8.1).

Figure 8.1 The central location of the Three Gorges Dam

Source: image.baidu.com/.

Zhou, X. (n.d.) went on to write that '[t]he first 10–15 years of the 21st century will be a key period to form a nationwide interconnected grid. By the year[s] 2010–2020, a nationwide interconnected grid will be basically established, which will cover major regional and provincial power grids.' This transpired as expected: substantial progress has been made towards the vision of a single national grid, with alternating current (AC) interconnectors between a number of the regional grids, as well as long-distance ultra-high voltage (UHV) direct current (DC) lines, particularly from hydro projects in the south-west to large coastal demand centres, including Shanghai and Guangzhou.

Yet, in common with most other Chinese and foreign experts at the time, Zhou, X. (n.d.) also wrote, '[i]t is predicted that the nation's total installed capacity will reach 500GW in the year 2010 … [and] a total installed capacity of about 750GW by the year 2020'. The 2010 estimate turned out to be about half of the actual result, and the 2020 projection also looks like being only half or less of the likely outcome.

The sectoral structure of electricity consumption in China is approximately 70 per cent industrial, 20 per cent commercial and 10 per cent residential. In developed economies, the shares are approximately equal. Commercial and residential loads are more temperature sensitive and also vary more by season and throughout 24 hours in a day than does industrial load, which is relatively constant in aggregate.

With commercial and residential consumption expected to grow faster than industrial consumption in China in coming decades, proportionately greater demands will be placed on generation and transmission capacity, which consequently will become more valuable. The ability of the system to cope with seasonality and peak demands will become increasingly important.

Compounding these challenges, an increasing proportion of electricity coming from intermittent (wind and solar) and non-variable (nuclear) sources generates challenges for stability of the grid (Garnaut 2014: 11). Also with China moving to the new model of economic growth, it envisages a decline in the contribution of growth in the labour force and capital stock, leading to overall growth several percentage points lower than in the first decade of the century. The focus on increased productivity includes efforts to improve the efficiency with which energy is used, to reduce the amount of energy consumed in producing each unit of economic output.

Many of the structural changes embodied in the new model of economic growth have large and favorable implications for greenhouse gas emissions (Garnaut 2014: 7). Hence any reforms and regulatory mechanisms implemented will need to be appropriate for this reality.

Development of the regulatory system and reforms to date

Xu and Chen (2005) identify three phases in the development of the regulatory system of the power industry in China:

- phase I, 1949–85—power industry as state monopoly: the unification of government and business functions
- phase II, 1985–97—the unification of government and business functions with the gradual opening of the power generation market
- phase III, 1998–2002—separating the functions and responsibilities of the government from those of commercial enterprises, and establishing market mechanisms for the power industry in some pilot provinces and cities.

As Deng Xiaoping said, '[r]eform is China's second revolution'. Since the mid-1980s, the Chinese Government has carried out a series of power sector reforms. Xu and Chen (2005) comment on the success of these reforms:

> In China, the power industry has gone through a series of changes since 1985, including: the termination of the monopoly of 'exclusive investment in power generation', which existed for over 30 years during China's planned economy period; the gradual opening of the power generation market; and the introduction of new investment and operation entities to relieve the power shortage that had been hindering the development of the Chinese economy. Such changes led to the remarkably rapid development of China's power industry. For example, the demands for electricity have been largely met. (pp. 2458–2459)

The first major step in the reform process was corporatisation. Following the enactment of the Electric Power Law of the PRC in 1996:

> In 1997, the Chinese government took more radical steps to reform the power industry, particularly with respect to separating business operations and management from government oversight and guidance. The governmental functions of the former Ministry of Electric Power were divided between the State Power Corporation of China (which was newly established) and the State Economic and Trade Commission. (Xu and Chen 2005: 2459)

Towards the end of phase I, in 1980, during the early years of Deng's 'second revolution', the first China–Hong Kong power sector joint venture was proposed, which led to the 1,980 MW Daya Bay nuclear power plant in Guangdong with CLP Group and CGN Power.

The early stages of phase II saw five projects for a total of 3,950 MW by about 1991. All of these were greenfield projects, and most were joint ventures (JVs), including Shiajiao B by the Hopewell Corporation from Hong Kong, the first build-operate-transfer (BOT) power project in China. The latter part of phase II, from the early 1990s to the late 1990s, saw a stampede of foreign independent power producers (IPPs) into China, including Intergen (Shell and Bechtel), Mirant (Southern Company) from the United States, AES (also from the United States) and Meiya Power from Hong Kong. During the 'big rush', more than 100 memoranda of understanding (MoUs) were signed between foreign companies and Chinese partners for the development of power plants, and 29 large, mostly greenfield projects totalling more than 22 GW were developed. Milestones in this period included the first privatisation of an existing plant, when 55 per cent of a 2 × 200 MW plant in Liaoning Province was sold to a Hong Kong company; the first New York listing, by Huaneng, Naimeng Huadian renminbi-listing of Shanghai A-shares; the first competitively bid BOT project, Laibin 2 × 360 MW; and Zhejiang Southeast US dollar listing of Shanghai B-shares (Wilson and Wang 2002).

At this time, Guangdong was suffering power capacity shortages due to rapid growth in industrial demand, and self-generation—much of it by high-emission diesel generators and small, poorly controlled coal plants—was proliferating. Some of this was on-grid and some off-grid. As Figure 8.2 shows, 14 of 31 GW were not centrally dispatched at that time, including 10 GW of thermal plant and 4 GW of hydro plant.

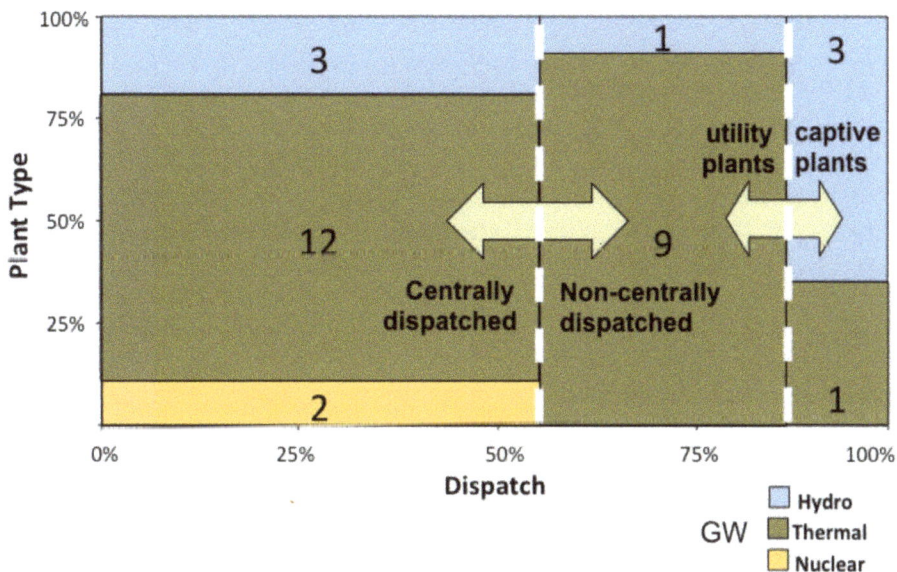

Figure 8.2 The Guangdong electricity sector in late 2002

Source: Wilson and Wang (2002).

Not long after, as China's electricity demand growth rate started to accelerate, Zhejiang Province would suffer severe capacity shortages and rolling blackouts during the peak summer season. One of the present authors was asked to assist Zhejiang Energy to forecast the 2003 summer peak demand. Distinguishing seasonal fluctuations from the suddenly accelerating underlying demand was a difficult task. Ironically, a year or two earlier, foreign investors such as National Power had looked at a power plant investment in Zhejiang, and decided against it, having doubted the demand outlook (Gordon 2005).

Such lack of foreign confidence in China's continued economic growth and development, and need for electricity—which appears rather quaint from the comfortable perspective of 2015—was perhaps a factor in China's lack of confidence in seeking foreign investors as the answer to the country's power needs. By the early 2000s, a number of foreign IPPs were watching and waiting and some were already withdrawing from the Chinese market. This followed the 1996–97 reforms heralding the beginning of phase III, and disappointments on the part of a number of Western IPPs arising from misunderstandings about the terms and status of their power purchase agreements (PPAs) with their local counterparts and the system operators in the power grids hosting their power plants. The backdrop to this was a regional investment climate clouded by the aftermath of the Asian Financial Crisis, and such high-profile figures as the last governor of Hong Kong, Chris Patten (1998), openly questioning 'Asian values' in print and through a television documentary series.

Before his departure from Hong Kong in mid-1997, Patten had asked whether there might be scope for competition in Hong Kong's electricity sector to replace the Scheme of Control agreements with the government that were used to regulate Hong Kong's two vertically integrated investor-owned power utilities. The resulting study, presented to the Legislative Council under Chief Executive Tung Chee-hwa's post-handover government concluded that genuine competition would not be feasible in Hong Kong's power sector without the existence of a competitive market in Guangdong (Wilson et al. 1999). Hong Kong was not to be a laboratory for Chinese power sector reform.

By the end of phase III of its reform process, China had less and less need for any of the three things that foreign IPPs could bring: capital, technology and management skills. China was well on the way to becoming an exporter not an importer of capital. With the exception of certain gas-turbine technology (not particularly relevant in a country with limited availability of high-cost gas) and some nuclear technology, China already had world-class, highly competitive power plant manufacturers. And imported Western managers, in most cases with very limited Chinese language and cultural skills, could hardly be considered competitive candidates to run power plants in China.

Figure 8.3 presents the ownership structure of the generation sector in China in late 2002, just before the break-up of the State Power Corporation (SPC) monopoly, showing the role of the SPC, other Chinese state-owned enterprises (SOEs), privately controlled Chinese companies and foreign private companies.

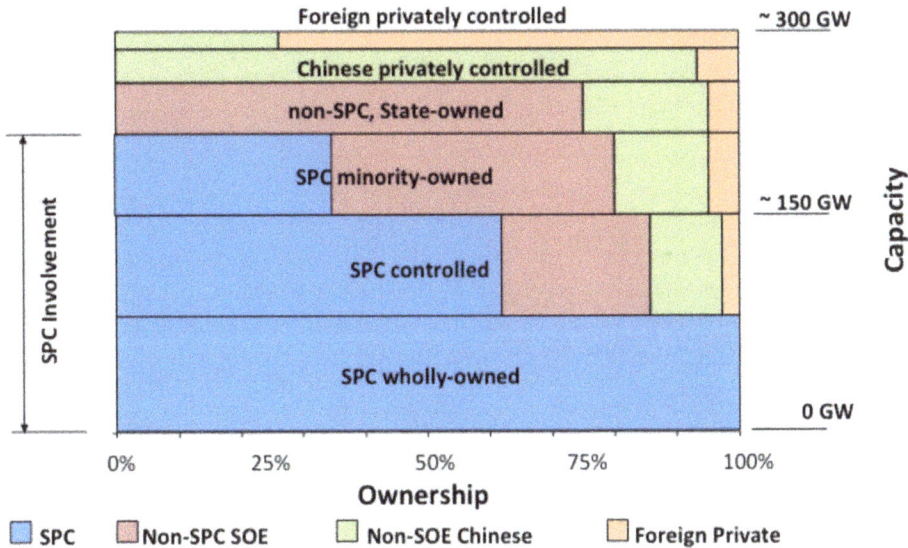

Figure 8.3 Structure of generation capacity ownership in China in late 2002

Source: Wilson and Wang (2002).

A key question at the time was would the privatisation trend continue, with the role for foreign private companies and Chinese non-SOEs extending from the margins at the top right of the diagram towards the bottom left? Or would the trend be reversed?

An industry structure for a future competitive market

The beginning of 2003 marks what we might call phase IV of China's power sector reforms: putting in place the architecture for future competition. A major restructuring of the SPC, separating generation from transmission, had put in place an industry structure to enable wholesale competition:

> China dismantled the State Power Corporation on December 29, 2002 and set up 11 new companies in a move to end the corporation's monopoly of the power industry. The former State Power Corporation owned 46% of the country's electricity generation assets and 90% of the electricity supply assets.

> The new companies include two power grid operators, namely the State Power Grid and China South Power Grid. Each of the five electricity generation companies own[s] less than 20% of China's market. They will compete with each other for signing contracts with the power grid operators. (Xu and Chen 2005: 2462)

The 'big-five gencos' (generation companies) are as follows:

- **China Huaneng Group** is the largest and oldest power generation company in China, established in 1985. By the end of 2014, Huaneng had 130 plants, more than 110 GW of generation capacity and more than 60 Mt of annual coal production.

China Datang Corporation, Huadian Group, China Guodian Corporation and China Power Investment Corporation (CPI Corp) were all incorporated in 2002 from the former SPC as part of the restructuring.

- **China Datang** has China's largest coal-fired power plant (Inner Mongolia Tuoketuo), the world's largest wind farm (Inner Mongolia Chifeng) and the second-largest hydropower project (Longtan Hydro). By the end of 2014, Datang had 68 plants and more than 120 GW of power generation capacity.
- **Huadian Group** has 70 plants with 123 GW of capacity.
- **China Guodian** has 94 plants with a total capacity of 123 GW.
- **CPI** has the highest proportion of clean energy of the Chinese generation companies, which accounts for 30 per cent of its generation capacity. It has participated in nine nuclear power projects in China and has also developed downstream industries including alumina refineries. CPI has 65 plants with a combined 90 GW of capacity.

A number of the big-five gencos have integrated up the value chain by acquiring coalmines to secure and manage the fuel supply to their power plants.

- **Shenhua Group**, meanwhile, has integrated down the value chain by developing power plants in addition to its complex of 70 operational coalmines, including some of the largest open-cut and underground mines in the world, 1,765 km of railway lines, 185 Mt of coal port and wharf capacity, 30 coal vessels and coal-to-liquids plants. Through its 21 wholly owned and holding subsidiaries, the group has 68 GW of power plant, of which 61 GW is coal-fired.
- **China National Nuclear Corporation** (CNNC) and **China General Nuclear Corporation** (CGN; formerly China Guangdong Nuclear Power Corporation or CGNPC) are the main companies investing in nuclear power plants in China. More recently, the **State Nuclear Power Technology Corporation**

(SNPTC) has had a key role as the partner with Toshiba-Westinghouse in the construction and development of third-generation advanced-passive (AP) reactor technology in China. In early 2015, it was announced that SNPTC and CPI will merge to form the State Power Investment Group, which will have assets equivalent in size to the sum of CNNC and CGN assets.

On 30 December 2002, the government also set up the State Electricity Regulatory Commission (SERC), to supervise market competition and issue licences to operators in the power industry (Xu and Chen 2005). SERC was responsible for administration and regulation of the electricity and power industry, including regulating the development of electricity markets and advising the National Development and Reform Commission (NDRC) on setting tariffs, while the NDRC actually sets the tariffs, transmission, distribution, safety and technical standards, issues business licences, establishes environmental laws and supervises development of the industry. In March 2008, the National Energy Administration (NEA) was established under the NDRC, and on 26 March 2013, Xinhua reported that SERC was to be dissolved and its functions incorporated within the NEA. Its main responsibilities would include drafting and implementing energy development strategies, plans and policies; advising on energy system reform; and regulating the sector (Xinhua 2013).

Bordie et al. (2014) observed that the rail sector, which plays a key role in transporting coal—by far the major fuel used in power generation—is the last of China's large network or infrastructure industries previously organised as government ministries to be reformed. Network and infrastructure sectors in China that were reformed previously include airlines, telecommunications, power and water, oil and gas, and highways.

In the case of the power sector, China's reforms have not yet proceeded to the extent of the reforms in the United Kingdom, Australia and parts of the United States. In China, state ownership retains a dominant role, although through a number of 'competing' corporate entities rather than the semi-monopolistic former SPC. The structure of the industry, its ownership and the role of competitive forces and regulation remain largely the same as those put in place in 2002, as described by Xu and Chen (2005). There are good reasons for this, which we return to later in this chapter.

Meanwhile, China has greatly expanded the capacity, efficiency and reliability of its power supply. With the emerging challenges of increasing power costs, security, power demand growth and environmental issues related to both the consumption of electricity generation and the production of coal in particular, the government has actively developed programs to increase energy efficiency and minimise emissions.

The 'golden decade' from 2003–04 to 2012–13 saw unprecedented rates of electricity demand growth, generation capacity additions, coalmine developments, production and consumption, and associated rail, port and transmission infrastructure development. By 2010, China had a 1,000 GW power system, when a 500 GW system had been anticipated a decade earlier. Its coal industry had grown from 1 billion tonnes to more than 3 billion tonnes, when a 2 billion tonne coal and coal-rail system had been considered a challenge a decade earlier. This development path has raised questions about environmental impacts, amid the constant challenges of economic competitiveness and energy security.

Yet these questions are relevant to all energy sources and power generation technologies, although not in similar degree. China has the world's largest hydropower plant and hydropower sector, which are not without environmental issues—some with international dimensions in the region. China was on the way to having the world's largest and most rapid nuclear power plant construction program when the East Japan earthquake, tsunami and subsequent decisions led to the destruction of the Fukushima nuclear power plant in Japan. The program has been slowed, but is still likely to become the world's largest sometime in the 2020s. China also has the world's largest installed capacity of wind and solar power.

Parallel reforms and regulation in related industries

In addition to its role as electricity price regulator through the NEA, the NDRC plays a key role in regulating prices in other industries, a number of which are closely related to electricity, including the coal market and the rail freight sector. Since the major power sector reforms of 2002, China's coal market has undergone substantial reform, prices are now essentially determined by market competition between large SOEs, provincial SOEs, private companies and small local township and village enterprises, as well as by imported coal. As a result, coal prices have become much more volatile, rising to very high levels when the market was tight several years ago, and to well below the cost of production for many producers in the currently oversupplied market.

When coal prices were high, power generators' margins were severely squeezed or negative. The NDRC revised wholesale power tariffs accordingly, but electricity prices have remained 'ratcheted' at about that level, after coal prices declined.

Rail freight transport, which accounts for a significant part of the value chain for coal delivered to power plants, particularly in coastal and southern China, is in the early stages of reform (Bordie et al. 2014). The current healthy margins for power generators provide an opportunity to ratchet up rail freight tariffs to reduce the financial challenges facing the rail sector.

The gas sector has undergone some reform of pricing, but the high-pressure transmission pipeline network is not yet fully open to third-party access. The relatively limited availability and high delivered cost of natural gas in China, and the policy priorities for its use in sectors other than electricity generation, mean that gas sector reform is not likely to be as high a priority for the power sector in China as it has been in other countries.

Looking to the future, the key to economic reform is to properly handle the relationship between government and the market. As China is transforming itself from a highly power-centralised planned economy to a market-led economy, this implies a gradual process of government devolving decision-making back to enterprises. This has been the key topic in electricity sector reform in China.

In 2002, the State Council issued a 'Proposal for Power Sector Structural Reform', which marked the beginning of the last round of power sector reform. The key achievement of this round of reform is that it has led to competition in the power generating industry. According to the proposal, there is a separation of power generation and power transmission. The State Electricity Company (SEC) has been divided into power generation and transmission businesses. The objective set out in the proposal is also to 'gradually realise the separation of transmission and distribution service[s] of State Grid and also introduce competition in power retailing'. However, State Grid has entrenched its monopoly in dispatch management, transmission and market transactions. This has greatly hindered the interaction between power users and power producers. Reform of the State Grid is therefore the most important step in the next round of electricity market reform.

Separation of transmission ownership from system operation (generation dispatch) is likely to be key to the success of these reforms. Woolf (1996) has made the case for a genuinely independent system operator (ISO).

On 18 March 2012, the State Council stressed again that the key to deepening power sector reform is to carry out trials for separation of transmission and distribution, and to ensure that distributed energy power generation can access the grid without 'bias', which will ensure continuous reform of the power sector.

Selected international comparator countries

Before discussing alternative industry and regulatory frameworks and the choices available to China, it is helpful to review the electricity sector in other countries and their experience of reform.

- **The United States** has a number of weakly interconnected or unconnected regional grids, ageing infrastructure, and is a laboratory of regulatory arrangements in a federal system.

- **Japan** has one of the world's largest power systems, but its grid is fragmented among the vertically integrated regional Japanese power utilities, each with its own franchise monopoly, protected by grid frequency incompatibility—some operate at 50 Hz, others at 60 Hz. The vertical franchise monopolies are now under pressure from the government to reform after the Fukushima shock to the system.

- **India** has a coal-dominated hydrothermal system. Unlike China, in India, the electrification rate is very low.

- **Russia** has abundant gas reserves and generally poor resource utilisation and conversion efficiency. China is a neighbour and customer of Russian energy.

- **Germany** is generally considered to be a model of industrial efficiency. Its power system is one of the largest in Europe and is central to the European grid, on which it relies to balance its large proportion of intermittent wind and solar renewable energy.

- **Canada** has an eclectic system, with ownership and regulatory framework varying across Provinces, with parts integrated into adjacent United States systems.

- **France** has a nuclear-dominated power system complemented by gas, with extensive interconnections with neighbouring countries. Government-controlled Electricité de France dominates the market in an example of the state-owned corporate model within a wider competitive market according to EU rules.

- **Brazil** has a hydro-reliant system vulnerable to drought.

- **The United Kingdom** was the pioneer in privatising electricity markets and attempting to introduce competition to reduce the need for regulation. In more recent years, numerous centrally planned mandates, particularly on renewable energy and nuclear power, have in practice squeezed the role of competition in the power market.

- **Australia** has the longest interconnected electricity market and was an early follower of the United Kingdom in electricity reform, with the state of Victoria moving first and far on privatisation.

China plus these 10 comparator countries account for two-thirds of the global installed power generation capacity (including self-generation) and span a wide range of industry and regulatory models. Most of the 1.25 billion people currently without electricity are outside the 11 comparator countries (825 million), except for India (400 million). Table 8.1 shows the data. Table 8.2 provides a summary of the industry structure, ownership, forms of regulation and extent of competition for the 10 comparator countries.

Table 8.1 Electricity sector of China and 10 comparator countries

Country	Land area	Pop'n 2010	Access 2010	Capacity 2010	GDP	Ownership
	(m sq km)	(million)	(%)	(GW)	(US$ b)	(type)
China	9.60	1,360	99.7	999	5.9	Mixed
United States	9.63	312	100	1,041	15.0	Varietya
Japan	0.38	127	100	287	5.5	Private
Russia	17.1	144	100	223	1.5	State
India	3.29	1,206	75	207	1.7	Mixed
Germany	0.36	83	100	163	3.4	Mixed
Canada	9.98	34	100	132	1.6	Mixed
France	0.55	63	100	125	2.6	State
Brazil	8.51	195	98.9	112	2.1	Mixed
United Kingdom	0.24	62	100	94	2.4	Privateb
Australia	7.74	22	100	60	1.1	Mixed
Subtotal	67.38	3,609	91.5	3,443	43.0	
RoW	67.04	3,307	74.0	1,672	22.2	
World	134.42	6,916	83.1	5,115	65.2	

a From private to state to cooperative.
b Includes foreign state entities.
Sources: Land area, UN FAO; population, UNDP (data.un.org); capacity, UNDP; electricity access, World Bank database.

Table 8.2 Electricity industry structures and forms of ownership, regulation and competition

Country	China	Japan	Russia
Industry model	Corporatised	Corporatised	Corporatised
Ownership of generation	State	Mix of private and state governments	Mixed private and government
Ownership of transmission	State	As above	State
Ownership of distribution	State	As above	State
Key legislation	State and federal	Federal	Federal
Form of regulation	Price regulation	Competitive market oversight	Price regulation
Regulator/s	NDRC, State Electricity Regulatory Commission	METI, ESCJ, NRA	Ministry of Energy, Federal Tariff Service, FAS
Extent of competition	Competition to build new power plants, but not for dispatch	Limited to very large customers	None

Country	Brazil	India	Germany
Industry model	Corporatised	Corporatised	Regulated market
Ownership of generation	Mixed private and government	Mixed private and government	Mix of private and state governments
Ownership of transmission	Federal and state	Federal govt	As above
Ownership of distribution	Mixed	Mixed	As above
Key legislation	Federal	State and federal	State and federal
Form of regulation	Competitive market oversight	Price regulation	Competitive market oversight
Regulator/s	MME, ANEEL, CNPE and CMSE	MoP, CERC	Federal Network Agency, Federal Cartel Office, state regulatory authorities
Extent of competition	Limited: periodic auctions held for new generation capacity	No competitive market. Capacity shortages and substantial self-generation	Wholesale and retail markets, under EU law

Country	France	United States	Canada
Industry model	Regulated market	Varies by state	Varies by province
Ownership of generation	Mix of private and state governments	Mix: investor-owned, state govt, coops	Mixed: investor-owned, state govt
Ownership of transmission	Federal	As above	As above
Ownership of distribution	State and federal	As above	As above
Key legislation	Federal	State and federal	Provincial and federal
Form of regulation	Competitive market oversight	Price regulation and market oversight: varies by state/region	Varies by province
Regulator/s	CRE, FCA	FERC, NERC, plus regulators in each state, members of NARUC	NEB plus regulators in each province
Extent of competition	As required by EU law	Varies from state to state from full competition to no choice	Varies between provinces, includes competitive markets, some US-integrated

Country	United Kingdom	Australia
Industry model	Market model	Market model in NEM states
Ownership of generation	Mix of private and state governments	Mix of private and state governments
Ownership of transmission	Federal	As above
Ownership of distribution	Private	As above
Key legislation	Electricity Act (1989)	National Electricity Law, plus various state laws
Form of regulation	Competitive market oversight	Competitive market oversight
Regulator/s	OFGEM, GEMA, CMA, ONR	AEMO, AER, ACCC, AEMC, plus state regulatory oversight
Extent of competition	Wholesale and retail markets	Wholesale and retail markets

China's profile in the global power industry

China today has the largest power system in the world. As Figure 8.4 shows, while China has close to universal electricity access, China's power system development measured in kilowatts of generation capacity per capita and economic development measured in GDP per capita are still far below the levels of the seven developed countries in the sample.

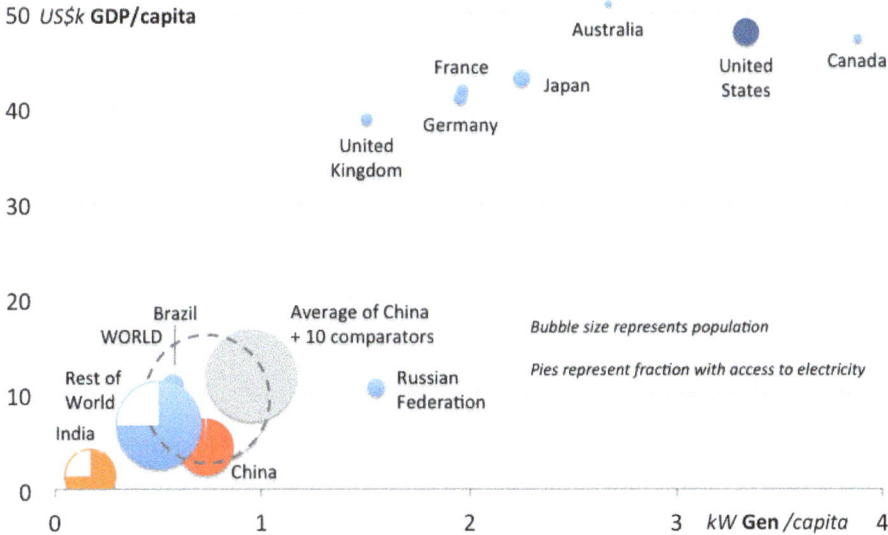

Figure 8.4 Global comparison of power systems (2010 data)

Source: Authors' analysis using data from UNDP and World Bank.

Let us take a closer look at systems which have relevance to China's efforts to build a more competitive electricity market. We have selected the United Kingdom and Australia with its National Electricity Market (NEM), with a particular emphasis on the state of Victoria, as the examples. The United Kingdom was the pioneer in introducing privatisation and competition to large, national-scale electricity systems. Victoria was an early follower, while the other states in Australia have a variety of ownership structures, which, like China, include continued government ownership of generation, transmission and distribution assets.

The United Kingdom's history of electricity ownership and structure

Historically, the electricity sector in most countries was perceived to be a public good or was seen primarily as an essential service. Electricity transmission and distribution networks tended to be viewed as having strong natural monopoly characteristics. It does not make economic sense to duplicate network infrastructure because of their public goods character. This thinking was not limited to the networks transmitting and distributing the electricity, but extended to the power plants generating the electricity. The economies of scale available from large, centralised power plants tended to reinforce the view of the entire system as one large, natural monopoly.

This thinking is evident in the long history of the UK electricity industry. By World War II, the United Kingdom had more than 600 electric power companies, both 'local authority undertakings' (electricity distribution businesses belonging to local governments) and private companies— constituting quite a decentralised system. After the war, the political climate tended to favour nationalisation and centralisation. This had not always been the prevailing thought.

In 1831, Michael Faraday discovered electric induction, and then magneto-electric induction. He produced the first electric generator in his laboratory in London, and laid the basis for the transformer and the electric motor. By 1879, Thomas Edison in the United States had perfected a practical electric light bulb. The first legislative milestone in the UK electricity industry was *The Electric Lighting Act 1882*, which allowed the setting up of supply systems by individuals, companies or local authorities. Numerous amendments and new acts followed, including the 1909 Act regulating planning consent for building power stations; the 1919 Act, passed during the reconstruction of the nation's industries after World War I, which rejected the recommendations of two committees to effectively nationalise the industry and to unify generation, transmission and distribution; the 1922 Act; the 1926 Act creating the Central

Electricity Board and the National Grid operating at 132 kV and 50 Hz AC; *The Electricity Supply (Meters) Act 1936*; and *The Hydro-Electric Development (Scotland) Act 1943*.

The Electricity Act 1947 established the British Electricity Authority (BEA), responsible for bulk electricity generation and transmission, and nationalised and merged the more than 600 small electricity companies into 12 'area electricity boards'. *The Electricity Reorganisation (Scotland) Act 1954* moved responsibility for Scottish electricity supply to the Scottish Office, replacing the BEA with the Central Electricity Authority (CEA). *The Electricity Act 1957* dissolved the CEA and replaced it with the Central Electricity Generating Board (CEGB) and the advisory and supervisory Electricity Council.

Various other amendments and acts on electricity (and gas) were passed in 1961, 1963, 1968, 1972 and 1979. All of these—a large body of incrementally evolving legislation, representing the journey from small, entrepreneurial, private and local authority electricity supply businesses—were repealed by *The Electricity Act 1989*, which was a revolutionary piece of legislation that swept away the nationalised structure and (re-)privatised the industry.[2]

> The [government] White Paper 'Privatising Electricity' published in February 1988 proposed splitting the CEGB into a transmission system operator, eventually called The National Grid Company (which was transferred to the joint ownership of the 12 Area Boards, who were retitled 'Regional Electricity Companies') and two generators called Big G, which eventually became National Power (40GW) and Little G, which eventually became PowerGen (16GW). The rationale for this split was the hope that National Power would be big enough to absorb the uncertainties of the operating performance of Britain's idiosyncratic nuclear reactors, and also bear the capital cost and operational risks of the 1200MW Sizewell B pressurised water reactor being built, together with three more units which the government hoped would be built. (Henney 1994, summarised in Henney 2011)

A major lesson in the United Kingdom was that the nuclear sector could not thrive under competitive market conditions without some form of government support. This was a big factor in the way the generation sector ended up being structured at the time of privatisation. Henney continues:

---

2 A list of major events in the history of the United Kingdom's electricity supply is available from: en.wikipedia.org/wiki/Timeline_of_the_UK_electricity_supply_industry.

But while the government could manipulate the valuation and finances of the existing nuclear plants, it could not obscure the future construction cost risks, nor the high cost of electricity from Sizewell B. The financial advisers concluded that the nuclear plants could not be sold and eventually the government was forced to put them in Nuclear Electric, which would remain in public ownership. By now there was no time to split up National Power and PowerGen, and the industry started its existence with a most unsatisfactory generation structure of a dominant price setting duopoly, which was … to cause many problems and costs. (Henney 1994, summarised in Henney 2011)

National Power and PowerGen were both privatised in a 60 per cent float in March 1991, and the balance in 1995. Nuclear Electric, formed in 1990 as a government-owned corporation to remove the 11 GW of nuclear assets from National Power's portfolio, was privatised as British Energy in 1995, without Magnox Electric, which became part of BNFL in 1998. Electricité de France (EdF), a corporation largely owned by the French Government, acquired British Energy in 2009. North Scotland Hydro-Electric board became Scottish Hydro-Electric, and was privatised in 1991. The South of Scotland Electricity Board's non-nuclear plants became Scottish Power and the nuclear plants were put into Scottish Nuclear. The 1989 Act created 12 regional electricity companies (RECs) from the area electricity boards, which were each then sold in 1990 in a public float.

Lessons from the history of electricity in the United Kingdom

The above summary of the history of legislation in the electricity industry in the United Kingdom paints a picture of constant evolution and organisational change. The changes from 1882 to 1989 reflect the evolution of society and technology and the tide of prevailing political philosophy during that century.

State ownership, which has been adopted in the United Kingdom and many other countries, is one remedy to the natural monopoly problem, but other models are possible, including regulated private ownership. By the late 1980s, leading economists and engineers had recognised that electricity generation and retail supply need not necessarily be considered natural monopolies.

Modern information technology and control systems (which were still in their infancy in 1989) today enable electricity to be competitively generated, centrally scheduled and dispatched according to a set of market rules, subject to technical engineering constraints in power stations and throughout the network.

Henney's (2011) view of the initial outcomes of UK electricity privatisation listed a number of 'clear political gains' as well as economic gains from cost reductions, along with identification of serious flaws. In his words, privatisation:

[A]ppeared to free [electricity] generation from government imposed fuel policies; reduced the political power of the electric industry and its political dependents, British [power] plant manufacturers and British Coal; increased the industry's accountability because the government had not been particularly competent at controlling what it owned; freed the industry from public sector constraints; and allowed government to focus on tasks which only it could fulfil. There were significant cost gains from stopping the construction of three [nuclear] PWRs [pressurised water reactors] and four 900MW coal plants that had been planned. Manpower reduced by 40% by April 1993 compared with 1990, and equipment buying was more careful and more cost conscious. But there were serious flaws with privatisation, notably the creation of a duopoly of price setting generators, and customers got a poor initial deal—most customers' prices increased to pay for the generous financing of the industry, which resulted in major gains for shareholders. (Henney 2011)

Competition policy and electricity reform in Australia

The first moves to define and establish a national grid in Australia followed the Special Premiers Conference in 1991, where:

Discussions … focussed on measures to increase national efficiency and international competitiveness and to move towards a single national economy. The focus was on micro-economic reform in the areas of regulatory reform; road and rail transport; electricity generation, transmission and distribution; and reform of Government Trading Enterprises. (COAG 1991)

This followed the then prime minister Bob Hawke's 12 March ministerial statement, 'Building a competitive Australia', which noted that:

The Trade Practices Act is our principal legislative weapon to ensure consumers get the best deal from competition. But there are many areas of the Australian economy today that are immune from that Act: some Commonwealth enterprises, *State public sector businesses*, and significant areas of the private sector, including the professions. (Hawke 1991, emphasis added)

A subsequent meeting of the premiers and chief ministers in November endorsed the need for a national competition policy and an independent review of the *Trade Practices Act 1974*. On 26 February, shortly after taking office as prime minister, Paul Keating tabled the major ministerial statement 'One nation' (Keating 1992), foreshadowing the prominence that the Commonwealth would give to competition policy as one of seven elements of its economic and social strategy for the 1990s. On 4 October, Keating appointed Professor Fred Hilmer to head the National Competition Policy Review, which delivered its report on 25 August 1993.

The evolution and operation of Australia's national competition policy are well summarised by Kain et al. (2001) and provide the national context for the reform of state public sector businesses in Victoria, including the then State Electricity Commission of Victoria (SECV).

Victoria's experience of UK-inspired reforms

As it turned out, the State Government of Victoria led by example the introduction of Australia's competitive NEM, and retail customer choice of supplier by rapidly restructuring and privatising the state's electricity sector. This program was driven by the premier Jeff Kennett and treasurer Alan Stockdale, who set out to privatise assets as a means of retiring the state government debt of \$32 billion. During its time in office, Kennett's government raised more than \$30 billion by selling businesses in energy, transport and other areas.

In the words of Kennett's pre-election energy policy of 1992, they would 'implement structural changes in the energy industry necessary to promote economic prosperity and job opportunities for more Victorians'. The reforms therefore represented a combination of pragmatism (reducing government debt) and political philosophy—specifically, the view that private businesses, motivated by profit and constrained by competitive forces, with regulatory supervision where required, would use capital and operate more efficiently than government-owned monopoly corporations. The Kennett government split the privatised businesses into competing units whenever possible, to facilitate commercial rivalry.

The UK reforms under *The Electricity Act 1989* provided the inspiration and general template, and a number of advisors who had worked on the UK electricity privatisation also worked on the Victorian electricity privatisation.

In the late 1980s and early 1990s, reports by the Industry Commission, the Tasman Institute, the Business Council and the Review Committee of the Victorian Parliament had critically reviewed the performance of the SECV. The industry had pursued efficiency improvements through outsourcing, transfer pricing, downsizing and internal power pool arrangements, albeit within the constraints of an integrated monopolistic industry structure (Fearon and Moran 1999).

In October 1994, Victoria's electricity industry was again restructured, largely into the final form for privatisation. Transmission was disaggregated into the Victoria Power Exchange (VPX), a non-commercial body responsible for system operation and control, transmission planning and market operations; and Power Networks Victoria (PNV), responsible for transmission assets, maintenance and operations. Five businesses responsible for distribution networks and retail energy supply to customer accounts were created. Generation Victoria was separated into four individual baseload power stations (including Loy Yang B, then under construction), one portfolio of hydro-plant and one of intermediate and peaking gas plant. During 1995–97, all of these businesses, except the gas portfolio, were privatised. Proceeds amounted to $24 billion—some $13 billion in excess of the SECV's book value of assets recorded in 1993.

Australia's NEM today

The NEM itself began operations in 1998, with three states—Victoria, New South Wales and South Australia—followed by Queensland. Tasmania joined in 2005, with the commissioning of Basslink.

> Australia's NEM is the world's [longest] interconnected system. It stretches for more than 4000 kilometres from Port Douglas in the north of Queensland, to Port Lincoln in South Australia and via the Basslink undersea cable between Victoria and Tasmania … The NEM was designed to include six distinct regions, represented by the five states, with the addition of the Snowy Mountains Hydro-Electricity Scheme as the sixth region (the Australian Capital Territory is incorporated into NSW). Each of these regions operates their own market for the supply and demand of electricity. However, every region is connected through at least one interconnector that allows for electricity to be imported or exported between regions. (NERA Economic Consulting 2007: 3)

Figure 8.5 shows the generation and transmission topology of the physical system in which the NEM operates. NERA Economic Consulting (2007: Figure 2.1) shows interconnection capacity between the states. Figure 8.6 shows the geographic coverage of the NEM in the context of Australia and the other smaller systems that are not part of the NEM.

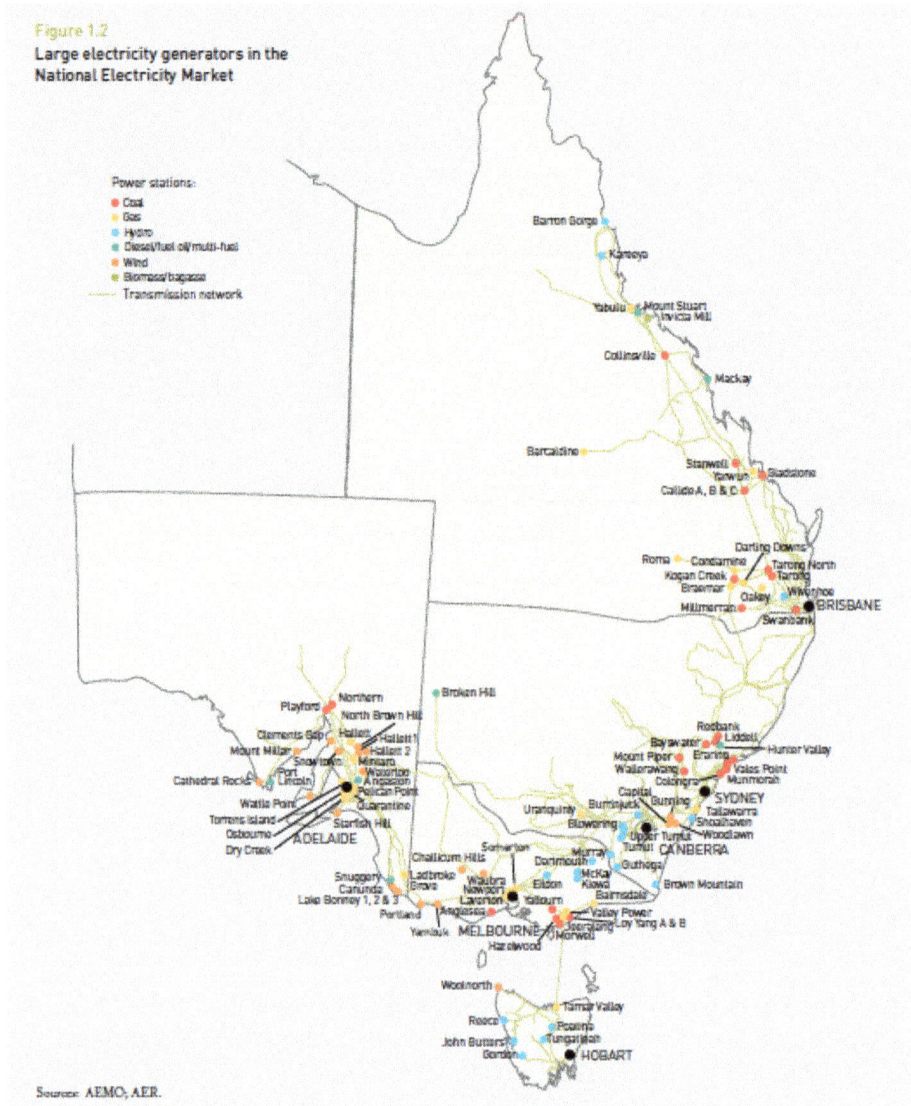

Figure 1.2

Large electricity generators in the
National Electricity Market

Source: AEMO; AER.

Figure 8.5 Generation and transmission map of the NEM

Source: AEMO (2015).

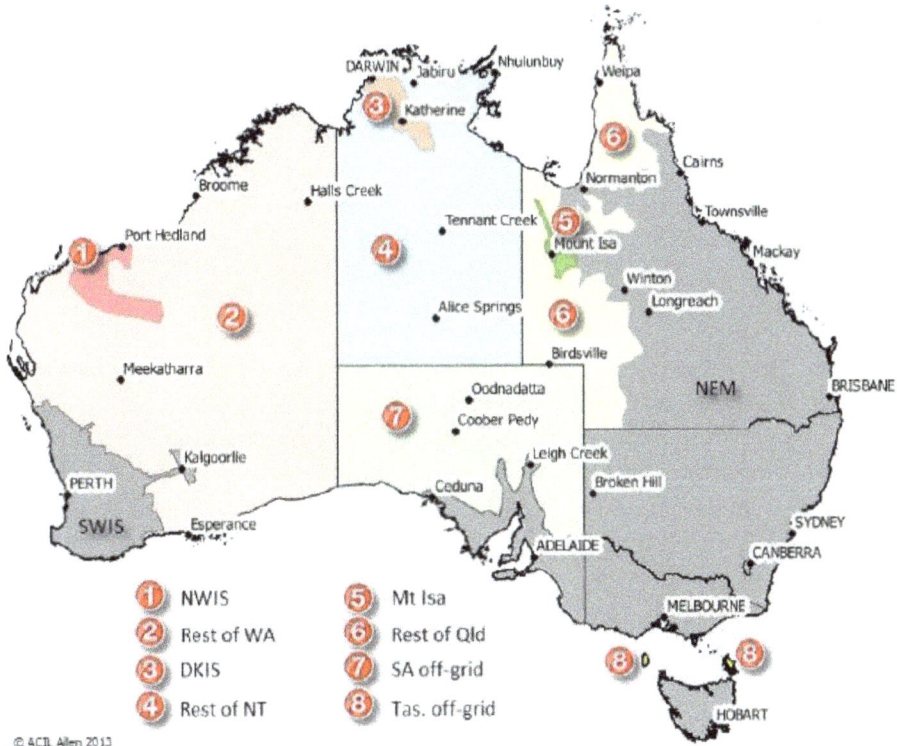

Figure 8.6 Australia's NEM and other electricity markets

Notes: Region 1, NWIS, is the North-West Interconnected System. Region 9 includes off-grid areas of New South Wales, Victoria, the Australian Capital Territory and external territories. These areas are too small and geographically scattered to present on this map. 'Rest of WA' excludes the South-West Interconnected System (SWIS) connected areas of Western Australia. 'Rest of Qld' excludes NEM-connected areas of Queensland.
Source: Hyslop et al. (2014).

South Australia followed Victoria's lead in privatising its generation, transmission and distribution assets, but the other states have largely retained electricity assets in state ownership as government corporations.

After the Victorian privatisation, it turned out that a number of foreign companies had significantly overbid in the tenders for the generation assets, based on the expectation that wholesale prices would be approximately double the level they turned out to be. This later led to a number of bankruptcies and debt writedowns.

Policy goals and a framework for analysing ownership structures and regulatory approaches

Drivers of electricity reform vary from one jurisdiction to another. While policy goals also vary, they almost universally include the goal to ensure consumers and businesses have a safe, reliable and efficiently priced supply of electricity that does not adversely affect the natural environment. While specific to electricity, this is consistent with the universal framework of the more general 'energy policy trilemma', as described by Wensley et al. (2013).

Cost-efficiency is required for efficient pricing. Installed capacity—in generation, transmission and distribution—is an important part of the cost of electricity supply. Therefore, the market and regulatory arrangements need to avoid overinvestment (or premature investment) in capacity, which raises costs above their efficient level, and at the same time avoid underinvestment (or late investment) in capacity, which compromises the reliability of supply.

Issues with competitive electricity market models

The introduction of competition to electricity markets requires careful consideration and design. Competition between generators over common transmission networks and competition between retailers over common distribution networks do not arise spontaneously, but need to be created by design, through a set of market rules by which all market participants are bound, and an appropriate initial industry structure. This requires substantial expert input from engineers, economists and legal experts.

Transmission and distribution networks have significant natural monopoly characteristics, and need to be regulated accordingly, with the policy objectives in mind.

It is essential to consider the initial conditions in the market. Whether the market has excess capacity, demand balanced with capacity including sufficient reserve margin for the desired level of reliability or insufficient capacity will have an enormous bearing on market outcomes.

When competition was introduced to the UK and Victorian power markets in the 1990s, there was more than sufficient generation and transmission capacity, and despite this, the generation planning and design departments in the former state-owned monopoly companies (CEGB in the United Kingdom and SECV in Victoria) were planning major plant additions. The introduction of market discipline prevented the construction of overcapacity, and competitive forces squeezed economic inefficiencies out of the operation of the existing fleet.

If, however, competition was introduced to a market with insufficient capacity, wholesale prices could rise dramatically, which may or may not be acceptable to policymakers. High prices would send a strong signal to build more plants, but could lead to bankruptcies if retailers were not able to pass the costs on to end consumers, or to political instability if end prices became very high. This would be a particular risk, and potentially damaging to the credibility of policymakers, particularly if the introduction of competition had been promoted to citizens and electricity consumers as a way to drive down prices.

At the same time as competition can drive down prices, it tends to increase price uncertainty. Depending on the characteristics and design of the market, it can also increase price volatility. The value of lost load (VoLL) is the economic or financial opportunity cost of electricity supply interruption. VoLL varies by customer type, but for most customers is tens or hundreds of times the delivered economic cost of the electricity itself. Therefore, it can easily be a thousand times or thousands of times the value of savings to customers from increased economic efficiency. Therefore, a single interruption to electricity supply of several hours' duration can wipe out the gains from lower prices accumulated over an entire year.

Designers of competitive markets need to consider how reliability, including sufficient generation reserve margin (as well as sufficient transmission capacity), will be assured in the absence of central planning. Capacity reliability margins require investments of the appropriate quantity, location (for both generation and transmission), timing, type (whether generation and/or transmission as well as fuel and plant choices) and environmental impact including emissions.

Companies investing in competitive markets take into account the return they expect to achieve, and make decisions according to their assessment of whether this is commensurate with the level of risk. If assets have the potential to become stranded in the future, the level of investment risk increases.

In some circumstances, privatisation can relieve capital constraints, particularly where government-owned entities have been subject to public sector borrowing requirements. Government borrowing limits have led to underinvestment, for example, in rural distribution networks in New South Wales in the 1990s, where projects to reduce line losses that would have paid back the investment rapidly could not be undertaken.

Financial risk tends to be higher in competitive markets than in non-competitive markets, due to price and volume risk. This is in addition to the fact that the cost of capital for private companies is higher than for government corporations.

Organisational models and a broad analytical framework

The general classification typology introduced by Bordie et al. (2014) to describe models for the organisation of the rail sector can be adapted and applied to the electricity sector. It adopts a two-axis categorisation, providing a matrix framework for the various models of ownership, organisational structures and regulation of the electricity industry around the world (Figure 8.7).

On one axis, we consider the *ownership* of the power sector, distinguishing state-owned from privately owned companies, and acknowledging that in some countries there is a mix of the two, whether from one region of the country to another, for different parts of the system (for example, generation, transmission, distribution and retail energy supply) or through partial floats of shares in companies.

On the other axis, we consider the *structure* of the industry in terms of the degree of vertical integration or separation, and the extent of *regulation*. We note that models can exist with either no formal regulation (of private electricity companies) or no notion of a separation between the ownership of electricity assets and their regulation—for example, where a self-regulating government ministry owns the assets. So, the regulation axis also embodies the concept of separation between the ownership and regulation of assets.

Five major organisation models are identified: the ministry model, the corporatised model, the regulated model, the market model and the laissez-faire model. These ownership and regulatory models occupy the edges and corners of the diagram.

Because of the natural monopoly characteristics of transmission and distribution networks, the need for electricity markets to be created by a government imposing by law a set of market rules, the desire of most governments to regulate the environmental impacts of the industry, and the political importance of reliable, accessible and affordable electricity supply, there is a variety of approaches to electricity sector governance, and few examples of uncomplicated 'textbook' models. This is particularly so for the market model.

The United Kingdom and some sub-national jurisdictions experimented with the full market model in the 1990s. Barker et al. (1997) discussed in detail power market governance and regulation by comparing the governance and regulatory arrangements of power pools operating at the time in England and Wales, Victoria (Australia), Alberta (Canada) and Scandinavia. Since the turn of the century, new goals—including on renewable energy, facilitating new nuclear build and climate mandates—have increasingly been implemented via additional regulatory or fiscal constraints.

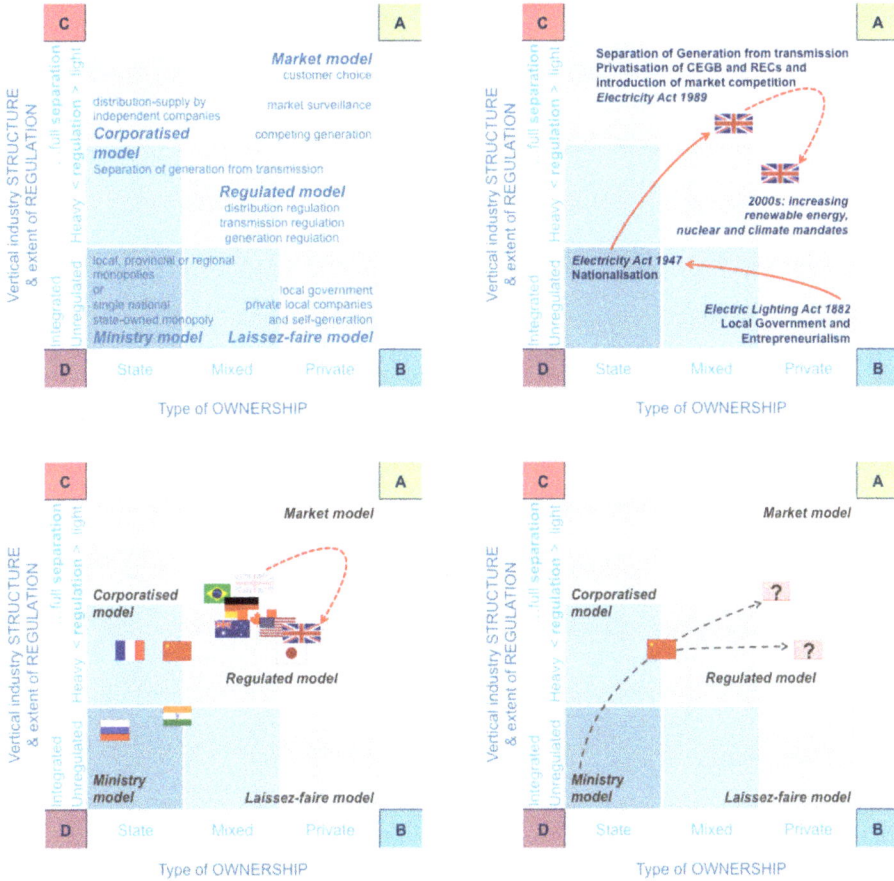

Figure 8.7 Power sector models, 10 comparator countries, UK pathway since 1882 and recent and possible future pathways for China

Source: Authors' diagrams, based on industry knowledge and publicly available information.

Conditions required for a competitive wholesale market

The industry structure and requirements for true competitive conditions in the wholesale market include the following.

Competitive sourcing of fuel

If there is no competitive choice of upstream fuels for power generation, competition between generators will be less effective.

More than adequate generation capacity

If the system reserve is not greater than the size of the smallest generation company in the system, generation companies can bid strategically to drive up the price, thereby gaming the market. Explicit collusion, or price-fixing, which would be illegal, is not required. Publicly available information on the capacities and technical and economic characteristics of other plants, and observation of one another's behaviour in the bidding process, which is repeated every day, is enough. Even if this behaviour only applies for a relatively few peak demand hours on the system, the extremely high prices resulting at those times have the potential to cancel out the gains from competitive forces driving down prices at other times of the year.

Sufficient capacity at the transmission level

Sufficient capacity at the transmission level is needed so that energy can flow unconstrained from generators to the areas of demand. Woolf (2002) argues that underinvestment in transmission costs much more than marginal overinvestment. If transmission capacity is insufficient, generators can gain monopoly pricing power in the constrained parts of the system. Transmission is widely considered to remain a natural monopoly, in any given geographic area, after the introduction of competition. However, it is possible to have 'merchant transmission' projects, where an investor builds a new transmission line to earn a return based on relieving congestion in the grid. Woolf (2002) set out 'recipes' for performance-based (incentive) regulation for regulators concerned about inadequate transmission investment, with the aim being a transmission system that reduces congestion and other costs for the consumer, improves reliability and reduces the potential for the abuse of market power.

Controlled demand growth

Demand growth must not be so rapid as to erode the reserve margin, otherwise competitive conditions will disappear faster than the industry is able to plan, build and bring online new capacity. This would likely have been a serious problem in China if market competition had been introduced in the early 2000s, for example.

Conditions required for a competitive retail market

Competitive sourcing of wholesale electricity

Competitive sourcing of wholesale electricity is required if customers are to be offered prices that reflect competitive wholesale prices. This was not the case, for example, in New Zealand in the early 1990s, when retail electricity competition was introduced.

Regulation of distribution costs

Appropriate regulation of distribution ('poles and wires') costs is required, as this remains a natural monopoly, for similar reasons that transmission is generally considered to have strong natural monopoly characteristics.

The policy choices for China's power sector

In the late 1990s and early 2000s, a number of international advisors and agencies, including the World Bank, encouraged China to reform its power sector by increasing the role of the private sector and introducing competition. China's 2002 reforms were influenced to a large degree by the UK example, as Zhang (2012) has said:

> The grid company's natural geographical monopoly has not changed as, no matter what, you cannot get grid companies [to] build transmission lines like a spider web everywhere. Hence how to enhance supervision and ensure fair transactions becomes [a] must. After a study trip by the then 'infrastructure department' to the UK, the Chinese government felt that the separation between power generation and the grid, as well as setting up an electricity supervision council is suited to China's situation. Hence, China's power sector reform has largely borrowed [from] the UK model and experience.

However, having put in place the industry structure that would enable full wholesale competition along the lines of the then UK power pool, or the Australian NEM, China has paused in its reforms. The electricity crisis and market failure in California in 2000–01—which involved blackouts, market manipulation, declaration by the state governor of a state of emergency, and several major corporate bankruptcies—were probably influential in this respect. In any case, the Chinese Government's decision not to press blindly ahead with full-blown electricity market competition, or large-scale privatisation of the generation sector, now appears wise, given the challenges of the investment that was required to meet double-digit demand growth during the 'golden decade' that followed, and the success of the industry in meeting that challenge. It would have been difficult to meet the policy goals of ensuring a safe, reliable and efficiently priced supply of electricity under such conditions. In the meantime, in markets from Australia to the United Kingdom and the United States, the role of the competitive market has become increasingly constrained by policies to promote renewable energy, to reduce carbon dioxide emissions and, in the case of the United Kingdom, to underwrite new nuclear power investment.

In the past few years, the rate of growth of China's economy, energy system and electricity demand has slowed to more moderate levels. Power demand is still growing faster than in developed economies. Many developed countries, including Australia, have recently been experiencing a decline in power consumption and peak demand, due to a combination of policy support for distributed renewable energy, improved energy efficiency and the closure of energy-intensive industrial facilities no longer able to compete.

While China's annual growth rate has slowed, and energy efficiency continues to improve, its low electricity intensity per capita compared with other countries suggests that considerable generation and transmission capacity investment will still be required before the power system is mature (Wensley et al. 2013). Estimates vary, but this point is unlikely to be reached before 2025, and possibly not until 2035 or later.

Yang (2015) identifies the current period, from 2008 to 2020, as a transition from the first 30 golden years after Deng's second revolution to the 30 years from 2020 to 2050 in which China will achieve major milestones in energy, the economy and the environment.

As this chapter goes to press:

> China's top planning body has published multiple documents stressing that market forces should decide how electricity is generated, transmitted and distributed. Specifics are still missing, and internal contradictions are still rife—the documents, for instance, push renewable energy that currently survives by government rules that subvert market forces. But if enacted, these ideas would mark the next step in electricity reform after Beijing in 2002 cleaved transmission and distribution away from generation. In theory, that allowed generation companies to compete, though in practice, Beijing dictated electricity prices. (Bhattacharya 2015: 28)

As it moves towards phase V of its power sector reforms, China is now in a good position to benefit from the evolving experience of other countries' experiments with power sector markets. Given the scale, geographic extent, regional nature and different stages of development across China's power system, it could be possible to experiment further with market approaches and enhanced regulation in some of the more mature parts of China's power sector and move to national implementation later. Such an approach would build on the foundation of the earlier reforms, and be consistent with China's general economic, political and social philosophy of making changes carefully and gradually—'crossing the river by feeling the stones', as Deng famously said.

References

Australian Energy Market Operator (AEMO) (2015), *About the National Electricity Law*, Canberra: AEMO. Available from: www.aemo.com.au/About-the-Industry/Legislation/National-Electricity-Law. Retrieved 11 May 2015.

Barker, J., Jr, Tenenbaum, B. and Woolf, F. (1997), *Governance and regulation of power pools and system operators: An international comparison*, World Bank Technical Paper No. WTP 382, Washington, DC: The World Bank. Available from: documents.worldbank.org/curated/en/1997/09/441122/governance-regulation-power-pools-system-operators-international-comparison.

Bhattacharya, A. (2015), China fires away at coal operators, *The Wall Street Journal*, Asia edn, 15–17 May: 28.

Bordie, R., Wilson, S. and Kuang, J. (2014), The importance, development and reform challenges of China's rail sector, in Song, L., Garnaut, R. and Fang, C. (eds), *Deepening reform for China's long-term growth and development*, Canberra: ANU Press.

Chinese Embassy to the United States (n.d.), *Chronology of Three Gorges project*, Washington, DC: Chinese Embassy. Available from: www.china-embassy.org/eng/zt/sxgc/t36515.htm.

Commonwealth of Australia (1974), *Trade Practices Act*, Canberra: Commonwealth of Australia. Available from: australiancompetitionlaw.org/legislation/1974tpaoriginal.html.

Commonwealth of Australia (2010), *Competition and Consumer Act*, Canberra: Commonwealth of Australia. Available from: australiancompetitionlaw.org/legislation/2010cca.html.

Council of Australian Governments (COAG) (1991), *Special Premiers Conference communiqué*, 30 July, Sydney. Available from: archive.coag.gov.au/coag_meeting_outcomes/1991-07-30/index.cfm.

Energy Policy Institute of Australia (EPIA) (2014), *Second submission to the energy white paper process: The institute's detailed comments and submissions on the EWP 'Issues Paper'*, Sydney: EPIA.

Fearon, P. and Moran, A. (1999), *Privatising Victoria's electricity distribution*, Melbourne: Institute of Public Affairs. Available from: ipa.org.au/publications/483/privatising-victoria's-electricity-distribution.

Gordon, A. (2005), Private conversation with Andrew Gordon, then a senior executive with International Power of the UK, responsible for China development.

Henney, A. (1994), *The privatisation of the electricity supply industry in England & Wales*, London: EEE Limited.

Henney, A. (2011), *The British electric industry 1990–2010: The rise and demise of competition*, London: EEE Limited.

Hyslop, P., Kelp, O. and Dundas, G. (2014), Modelling assumptions stakeholder workshop, ACIL Allens Consulting for the Warburton RET Review, Department of Premier and Cabinet, 23 April, Sydney.

Garnault, R. (2014), China's Role in Global Climate Change Mitigation, *China & World Economy*, 22 (5): 2-18.

Gillard, G. (1999), *Powercor Australia Ltd v Pacific Power* [1999], Victorian Supreme Court judgment, Melbourne. Available from: jade.barnet.com.au/Jade.html#!a=outline&id=72814. Retrieved 4 May 2015.

Government of South Australia (1996), *National Electricity (South Australia) Act 1996*, Adelaide: Attorney-General's Department. Available from: www.legislation.sa.gov.au/LZ/C/A/NATIONAL%20ELECTRICITY%20(SOUTH%20AUSTRALIA)%20ACT%201996.aspx.

Hawke, R.J.L. (1991), Building a competitive Australia, Ministerial statement, 12 March, Parliament House, Canberra. Available from: parlinfoweb.aph.gov.au/piweb/view_document.aspx?id=220386&table=hansardr.

Hilmer, F. (1993), *National competition policy review*, 25 August, Canberra: Commonwealth of Australia.

International Energy Agency (IEA) (2002), *World energy outlook 2002*, Paris: IEA. Available from: www.iea.org.

Jowett, A.J. (1984), The growth of China's population, 1949–1982 (with special reference to the demographic disaster of 1960–61), *The Geographical Journal*, 150(2): 155–70. Available from: www.jstor.org/stable/634995.

Kain, J., Kuruppu, I. and Billing, R. (2001), *Australia's national competition policy: Its evolution and operation*, E-Brief, Canberra: Parliament House. Updated 2003. Available from: www.aph.gov.au/About_Parliament/ Parliamentary_Departments/Parliamentary_Library/Publications_Archive/ archive/ncpebrief.

Keating, P.J. (1992), One nation, Prime Ministerial statement, 26 February, Parliament House, Canberra. Available from: parlinfoweb.aph.gov.au/piweb/ view_document.aspx?id=446942&table=hansardr.

NERA Economic Consulting (2007), *The wholesale electricity market in Australia*, June, Report to Australian Energy Market Commission, Canberra. Available from: www.aemc.gov.au/Media/docs/The%20Wholesale%20Elec%20 Market%20in%20Aust%20-%20NERA-dfc9ce45-8398-4d43-896b- 1fca0311779e-0.pdf.

Parliament of the United Kingdom (1947), *The Electricity Act*, Westminster. Available from: www.legislation.gov.uk/ukpga/1947/54/pdfs/ ukpga_19470054_en.pdf.

Parliament of the United Kingdom (1957), *The Electricity Act*, Westminster. Available from: www.legislation.gov.uk/ukpga/1957/48/pdfs/ ukpga_19570048_en.pdf.

Parliament of the United Kingdom (1989), *The Electricity Act*, Westminster. Available from: www.legislation.gov.uk/ukpga/1989/29/contents.

Patten, C. (1998), *East and west: China, power, and the future of Asia*, London: Times Books.

Peng, W. and Pan, J. (2006), Rural electrification in China: History and institution, *China & World Economy*, 14(1): 71–84.

People's Republic of China (PRC) (1996), *Electric Power Law*, Beijing. English translation available from: www.lehmanlaw.com/resource-centre/laws-and- regulations/environment/electric-power-law-of-the-peoples-republic-of- china-1996.html.

Pritchard, B. (2015), Private communications, Resources Law International, Sydney.

Sun, Y.-S. (1922), *The international development of China*, New York and London: The Knickerbocker Press. Available from: www.gutenberg.org/ebooks/45188.

United Nations Food and Agriculture Organization Statistics. Available from www.fao.org.

Unite Nations Development Program Statistics. Available from data.un.org.

Wensley, S., Wilson, S. and Kuang, J. (2013), China's energy demand growth and the energy policy trilemma, in Garnaut, R., Fang, C. and Song, L. (eds), *China: A new model for growth and development*, Canberra: ANU E Press.

Wilson, S. and Wang, L. (2002), Implications for Hong Kong of China power market development, China Light and Power 'Regulating Electricity' Conference, 17 October, Hong Kong. Slides available on request from the author.

Wilson, S., Nair, C., Schmieg, M. and Lewington, P. (1999), *Interconnection and competition study*, November, ERM Energy for the Hong Kong Government Economic Services Bureau, Hong Kong.

Woolf, F. (1996), The unbundling and rebundling of transmission and market related functions, *The Electricity Journal*, 9(10): 44–51.

Woolf, F. (2002), *Global transmission expansion: Recipes for success*, Tulsa, Okla.: PennWell.

World Bank Database. Available from: data.worldbank.org.

Xinhua (2013), Former electricity regulator leads national energy watchdog, *Xinhua*, 26 March. Available from: www.china.org.cn/china/2013-03/26/content_28361852.htm.

Xu, S. and Chen, W. (2005), The reform of electricity power sector in the PR of China, *Energy Policy*, 34(2006): 2455–65. Available from: probeinternational. org/library/wp-content/uploads/2010/10/The-reform-of-electricity-power-sector-in-the-PR-of-China.pdf.

Yang, Y. (2012), *China energy outlook*, Beijing: Energy Research Institute, National Development and Reform Commission.

Yang, Y. (2015), China's energy outlook, Keynote address to Energy State of the Nation Conference: Energy Policy, Energy Markets—Getting the Priorities Right, 20 March, Energy Policy Institute of Australia, Sydney.

Zhang, G. (2012), Interview, 12 March, *South China Energy Observation*, [in Chinese]. Translated by the authors. Original available from: i.ifeng.com/news/news?ch=rj_bd_me&vt=5&aid=32928811&mid=20nbxI&p=10.

Zhou, X. (n.d.), *Power system development and nationwide grid interconnection in China*, Beijing: Electric Power Research Institute.

Zhou, X. (2010), An overview of power transmission systems in China, *Energy*, 35(11): 4302–12.

Part II: China's participation in global integration

9. Financial Integration and Global Interdependence

Rod Tyers[1]

Introduction

Fundamental to China's global impact is the 'unbalanced' nature of its growth surge since the 1990s. The expansion of merchandise production at a faster rate than consumption in particular has had direct, and much analysed, effects on the terms of trade facing other regions.[2] By having created a parallel excess supply of savings, however, this also changed the global financial terms of trade. That in turn contributed to the observed trend decline in asset yields in the same period.[3] These improvements in both the product and the financial terms of trade of the advanced economies have, however, been partially offset by structural unemployment.[4]

Since the global financial crisis (GFC), there has been a decline in the level of imbalance in China's growth. It is likely that we have seen the beginning of the inevitable transition process whereby China's production structure diversifies away from export-oriented light manufacturing into sectors of rising demand domestically, and also higher value-added exports. This change is much anticipated,[5] yet it is also non-neutral from the view of the other large

1   Funding for the research described in this chapter is from Australian Research Council Discovery Grant No. DP0557885. Useful discussions on the topic with Dong He, Song Ligang, Paul Luk and Wenli Chen are acknowledged, along with comments received at seminars at The Australian National University, the China Center for Economic Research, Peking University and the Hong Kong Institute of Monetary Research. Thanks for assistance with data gathering for this research are due to Ying Zhang.
2   The literature on the terms-of-trade consequences for the advanced economies began in the 1990s with the debate over the poor performance of unskilled US workers (Bound and Johnson 1992; Wood 1994; Berman et al. 1994; and Leamer 1996) and extended into a more complex debate over the apparently declining performance of all but the most highly paid US workers (Haskell et al. 2012; Helpman et al. 2010; Autor et al. 2013). It has also included global modelling studies that kicked off with Krugman (1995) and proceeded to the decomposition studies by Tyers and Yang (1997) and Francois and Nelson (1998), with more detailed follow-up of labour effects by Tyers and Yang (2000); Winchester and Greenaway (2007); Francois and Wignaraja (2008); Harris et al. (2011); Harris and Robertson (2013); Levchenko and Zhang (2012); and di Giovanni et al. (2013). Diversity in method notwithstanding, all the global modelling studies find net gains to the rest of the world transmitted via terms-of-trade effects.
3   The terms-of-trade gain transmitted financially has been commonly referred to as the Asian 'savings glut'. See Bernanke (2005); Chinn and Ito (2007); Choi et al. (2008); Ito (2009); Chinn et al. (2012); and Arora et al. (2015).
4   For a survey and analysis of the neoclassical and Keynesian effects abroad, see Tyers (2015b).
5   See, for example, Lardy (2006).

economies. Although growth in physical capital and productivity is expected to continue, albeit at slower rates than previously, the relative growth in Chinese consumption will see a decline in its excess saving.

The international effects of this transition depend on trade and financial openness—both in advanced economies and in China. Trade openness has been shown to be extensive throughout the regions of focus in this chapter. Financial openness has, however, varied through time. Sensitivity to the effects of China's financial openness of the change in China's growth regime in advanced economies has not yet been widely studied. It is the focus of the research presented in this chapter.

A parsimonious global macroeconomic model is employed. It incorporates bilateral linkages across six regions via both trade and financial flows, in combination with a number of innovative mechanisms for characterising financial and macroeconomic interactions. The latter include allowing for asset differentiation so as to include optimising financial portfolio management in each region. This serves to direct savings from each into investments across all regions according to expected rates of return, with the degree of regional asset differentiation quantified to reflect financial integration. Second, long-maturity assets are central to global financial behaviour and, recently, also to unconventional monetary policy (UMP), which places direct demands on global markets for these assets.[6] In reality and in the modelling, this tends to enhance the spillover effects of monetary policy.[7] This proves important during China's period of high growth because substantial monetary expansions were induced in the advanced economies by the deflationary effects of increased supply of Chinese products. By contrast, China's transition to the new model of growth increases its consumption and so is inflationary in the advanced economies. When we consider the effects of nominal wage rigidities in the advanced economies, the Chinese surge and transition shocks are, respectively, contractionary and expansionary.

Overall, the results suggest that China's earlier growth and ongoing structural transition have significant implications for the advanced economies, in terms of both financial flows and international terms of trade.[8] Given nominal rigidities,

---

6   Conventional monetary policy focuses on short maturity assets that serve domestic financial industries and are not held in great volume abroad.

7   See, for example, Chen et al. (2014); and Lin and Ye (2015).

8   Advanced economies here refer specifically to the United States, Japan, the European Union and Australia.

these changes are shown to affect their levels of employment.[9] With compensation for the displaced and unemployed, the results suggest China's growth surge yielded net real income gains in advanced economies driven primarily by the terms-of-trade change. On the other hand, the more balanced new growth regime also offers net benefits, though driven primarily by increases in employment. Both results are sensitive to China's financial integration because this increases flexibility in management of China's collective asset portfolio.

The next section offers an introduction to China's international macroeconomic impacts and their determinants. Section three describes the model used for quantitative analysis. Section four presents numerical analysis of the foreign effects of China's growth surge and transition. Section five considers the sensitivity of these effects to financial integration, and section six concludes.

The global impact of China's growth surge

A significant share of the macroeconomic literature on China's growth has its genesis in concern about the imbalances associated with excess savings (the 'savings glut') and the 'upstream' financial flows that stem from them.[10] China's contribution to these upstream financial flows has been variously attributed, including to capital market distortions, exchange rate management and myriad other Chinese state interventions that confer unfair advantage on selected Chinese firms while also raising export and investment levels at the expense of household consumption.[11]

China's growth surge

Adopting the standard Lewis model of growth that also reflected growth patterns in other East Asian growth transformations, China's growth model involved the shift of hundreds of millions of workers from informal rural to urban

---

9   Empirical analysis also reveals large macroeconomic effects, as found, for example, by Eickmeier and Kuehnlenz (2013). The results are contrary to those of N'Daye et al. (2010) and Genberg and Zhang (2010), who find that the international effects of increased Chinese consumption are small. Their conclusions stem from the use of a model in which spillover effects stem primarily from trade, and financial flows are only weakly represented.

10 The literature asserting, and depending on, the 'savings glut' hypothesis is now extensive. Contributions include Bernanke (2005, 2011); Caballero et al. (2008); Caballero (2009); Chinn and Ito (2007); Choi et al. (2008); Chinn et al (2012); Eichengreen (2004); and Lee and McKibbin (2007).

11 The American literature critical of China's macroeconomic policies is also extensive. Bernanke (2005, 2011) offers the outline and Krugman (2010) declares that 'China is making all of us poorer'. The US macroeconomic position is put in more detail by, among others, Lardy (2006, 2012) and Bergsten et al. (2008). Similar advocacy of policy-induced 'balance' in China's growth can be found, still more formally, in Blanchard and Giavazzi (2006), while it is also recognised that some of the US reaction is mercantilist (Ito 2009).

employment, where their labour could be combined with capital and imported technology, yielding rapid productivity growth. The modest skill level of these workers shifted production towards light (labour-intensive) manufactures. In the absence of a parallel increase in consumer and investment demand, this required a rapid expansion in trade. The related growth, without parallel reform to social and industrial institutions, induced very high rates of household and corporate savings, the latter via rising state-owned enterprise (SOE) profits. Until China's World Trade Organization (WTO) accession in 2001, the modest size of the Chinese economy limited its effects on the advanced economies.

Given the relocation of much of the world's light manufacturing to China during its growth surge, it is unsurprising that, for advanced economies, the flipside was downward pressure on real wages growth. Moreover, the excess saving and associated cheap credit presumably contributed to asset price booms that in turn ultimately destabilised banking systems. And yet the bulk of the literature quantitatively exploring this issue finds a net gain for advanced economies, albeit with the caveat of increased *structural* unemployment.[12]

The transition to inward-focused growth

Since the global financial crisis (GFC), demand for China's exports has declined. Diversification of patterns of production specialisation, however, is neither automatic nor straightforward from a policy standpoint. Moreover, the comparative growth required in heavy manufacturing and services is constrained by the tendency for these industries to be oligopolistic and thus to offer considerable rents associated with entrenched interests.

Despite such challenges, there is considerable potential for growth from these previously suppressed sectors (Song et al. 2011; Tyers 2014). Along with reforms to social policy that have the ultimate impact of reducing the need for precautionary household savings, there are already signs of an emerging, larger role for consumption growth in China. Recent studies go so far as to question whether China's official statistics on consumption expenditure are underestimating the underlying extent of consumption that is already taking place (Ma and Yi 2010). Huang et al. (2013) use a weighted average of consumption-related retail sales growth and service sales growth to project the consumption share of gross domestic product (GDP). Their results suggest that the consumption share of GDP *climbed*, from 49 to 54 per cent during 2008–10, while China's National

---

12 See the survey by Tyers (2015b).

Bureau of Statistics (NBS) had it falling, from 48 to 47 per cent.[13] This suggests a continuing decline in the relative size of China's current account surplus (Arora et al. 2015).

Excess saving and yields

Of the growth in global GDP since 1980 as measured in US dollars at current exchange rates, one-third is due to Asian growth, the scale of which has been emphasised by the World Bank (2013). The contribution of Asian economies to global savings has been even larger. They have supplied about half of the corresponding increment to global saving in the same period, with China contributing fully one-third of the total increment since 1990. These proportions imply that the shift in global growth towards high-saving Asia, which occurred in the 1980s, accelerated the rate at which the global savings supply curve shifted to the right. If, as the data suggest, the corresponding global investment demand curve shifted by less, there would have been a decline in the Wicksellian (Wicksell 1936) 'natural' rate of interest at the global level.[14] Such a shift has significant implications for the international financial market.

The global financial market

Consistent with the segmentation theory of the yield curve (Johnson et al. 2010), long rates are more than the commonly claimed (Borio and Disyatat 2011) expectational extensions of short policy rates. Specifically, since the transaction cost of financing long-term investments via a succession of short contracts is prohibitive, short and long-maturity instruments trade at prices and yields that differ beyond what would be expected from time preference and expectation forces (Shiller et al. 1983; He and McCauley 2013). Short bonds are instruments of conventional domestic monetary policy that primarily serve the domestic financial sector. Their yield movements are clearly linked to region-specific business cycles (Arora et al. 2015). In contrast, long bonds arbitrage with major instruments of private saving and investment, and are widely traded internationally. Their yields therefore tend to follow a smoother path through time than yields on short instruments and the trend of this path is indicative of movements in the equilibrium between global saving and investment, as is suggested in Figure 9.1—the case of the financially dominant United States.

---

13 Huang et al. (2013) start with the official consumption share in 2000 and derive the GDP shares in remaining years using real GDP growth and their estimated consumption growth rates. Using similar data, Garner and Qiao (2013) suggest that Chinese consumption expenditure is officially underestimated by US$1.6 trillion, also concluding that its GDP share is expanding.
14 Ex ante shifts in saving supply and investment demand cannot be observed. See Tyers (2015b) for a discussion of this.

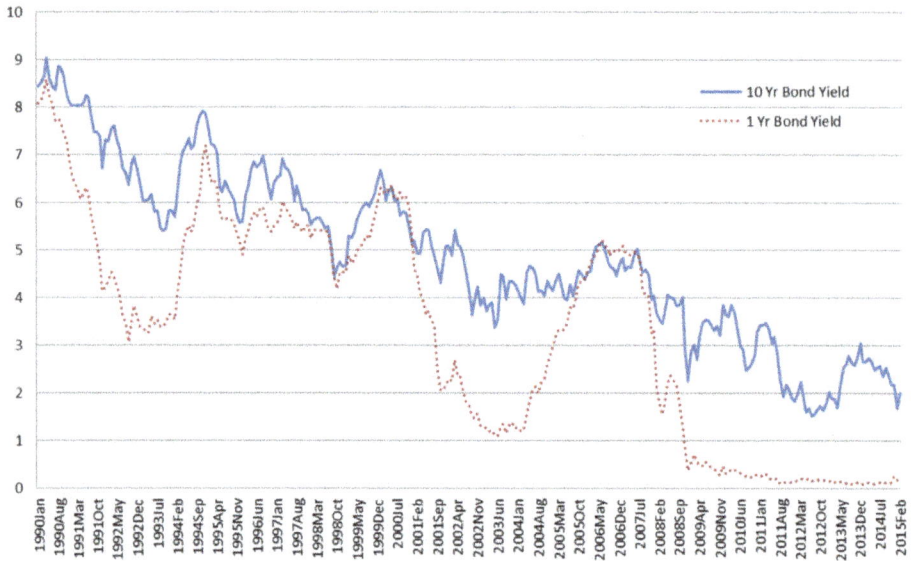

Figure 9.1 US Treasury bond short and long yields over two decades

Source: US Treasury.

He and McCauley (2013) use their evidence of 'imperfect substitutability along the yield curve' to explore monetary policy spillover effects. They consider the latter to be enlarged by the global integration of long bond markets. That view is supported by Ito (2013: 8), who argues that financial globalisation has made domestic financial markets more vulnerable to international factors. This in turn tends to decouple short-term and long-term rates. Consistent with Bernanke (2005), Ito (2013) concludes that the long-term interest rate is tied to global saving imbalances, and hence reflects the natural rate of interest.

The reasoning of He and McCauley, and Ito, along with the findings of Rey (2013), imply that given free capital mobility, inter-regional arbitrage will take place at the long end of the yield curve while the short end of the yield curve is, more conventionally, controlled by monetary authorities.[15] The time paths of the advanced economies' long yields in Figure 9.2 offer support for this idea of international arbitrage. It follows that the contemporary increase in Asian savings is a potential explanation for the persistent downward trend in long-term bond rates since the 1980s that is also apparent from Figure 9.2.[16]

---

15 I thank Paul Luk for clarifying this point.

16 The separation of the series for Japan is associated with its long-term current account surplus and the major yen appreciation shocks of the late 1980s and early 1990s, which established a negative risk premium among Japanese savers. In all regions, inflation rates were low throughout the period shown in the figure and so the trend of nominal long rates reflects that of corresponding real rates.

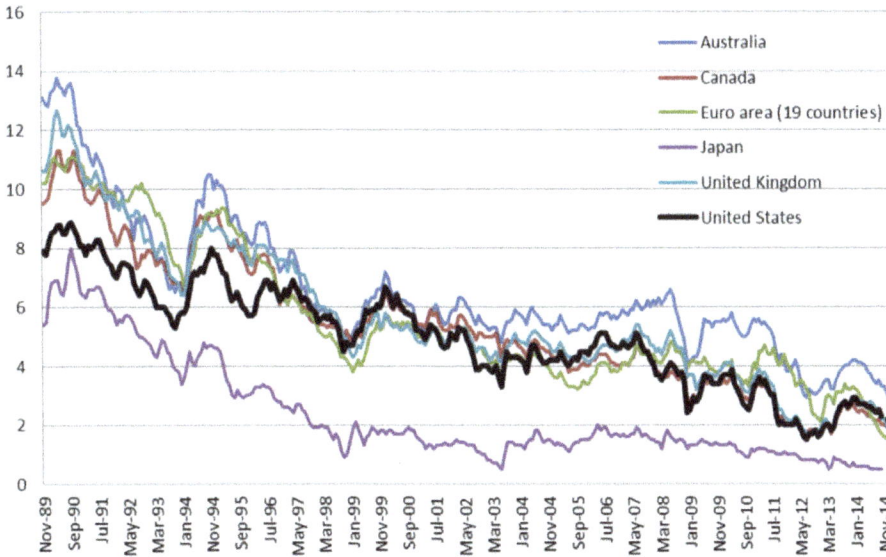

Figure 9.2 Long-term bond yields in advanced economies

Source: OECD (2015).

Implications

The trends and research presented so far in this chapter suggest changes in China's savings level contribute to trends in the underlying Wicksellian interest rate at the global level and therefore to the yields in long bond markets that reflect it, now that it has become 'macroeconomically' large. It follows that the current transition in the pattern of Chinese growth, and its consumption behaviour, has important implications for global financial markets and for the economic performance of advanced economies, the more so as China's financial sector deepens and becomes more internationally integrated. Second, it follows that the emergence of UMP in the large regional economies is also placing important demands on long bond markets. These demands, like China's excess saving, tend to reduce yields on long-term debt globally and so the impacts of these two forces are difficult to separate. One way to study this is to model the global economy numerically, and thereby enable the decomposition of observed change among its determinants and the evaluation of the sensitivity of outcomes to factors such as financial integration.[17]

---

17 For a comparison of the global effects of the change of China's growth regime with those of the current US recovery and the continuing EU and Japanese monetary expansions, see Tyers (2015a).

Modelling global macro-interdependence

A multi-region general equilibrium structure that centres on the global financial capital market is used for this analysis.[18] In it, the financial products of each region are differentiated and portfolio managers assign new net savings across regions so as to maximise expected portfolio returns. This retains Feldstein and Horioka (1980) home investment bias while allowing significant redirections of financial flows at the margin in response to changes in expected yields. It also allows the level of global financial market integration to be parameterised by varying this degree of differentiation. By implication, the scale of short-run spillover effects associated with growth performance, excess saving and monetary policy therefore also depends on it.

There is a tendency for flows between integrated financial markets to move the global economy towards interest parity. Asset differentiation, however, helps reflect true differences in the properties and riskiness of debt and equity contracts across regions, ensuring that interest parity is realistically incomplete. At the same time, the expected regional rates of return that drive investment flows depart from regional bond yields. The former reflect anticipated rates of return on installed capital and the latter reflect short-run equilibrium in regional financial markets between savers, indebted governments and investors.

Within each region the demand for money is driven by a 'cash in advance' constraint applying across the whole of GDP. For any one household, home money is held in a portfolio with long-maturity bonds, which comprise claims over physical capital and government debt across the regions.[19] On the supply side of the money market, in regions with UMP, expansions raise demand for long maturity bonds, reducing their yield and hence also reducing the opportunity cost of holding money.

Six economic regions are identified in the present study—the United States, the European Union, Japan, China, Australia and the Rest of the World— though the focus of this chapter is on the first four.[20] Each of these economies supplies a single unique product. On the supply side, there are three primary factors, with production labour variable and partially employed. The stocks of

---

18 The model used is a more advanced variant of that used in Tyers (2015c). That model assumed a perfectly integrated global bond market and so tended to generate unrealistically large spillover effects. Here, all financial products, including government bonds, are represented as regionally differentiated and so there is no perfectly integrated global market for any asset class. Also, this model introduces unconventional monetary policy, which sees monetary expansions directly affecting the markets for long-maturity assets.

19 Expectations are exogenous in the model and are formed over future values of home nominal disposable income, the rate of inflation, the real rate of return on home assets and bilateral real exchange rate alignment.

20 The European Union is modelled as the full 26 countries and it is assumed that this collective has a single central bank.

physical capital and skill are exogenous in the short run and fully employed. The collective household is a net saver, with reduced-form real consumption depending on current and expected future real disposable income and the home real interest rate. Aggregate consumption is subdivided between the products of all regions via a single constant elasticity of substitution (CES) nest. Further details of the aspects of the model central to this analysis are provided in Tyers (2015a: 4).

Model database, parameters and operation

National accounts, international trade and financial data for the global economy in 2011 are used to assemble the database used. The implications of changes in China for the three advanced economies are emphasised here and the scale of these economies, as represented in the database, is indicated in Table 9.1. Of particular interest are the financial flows between the regions in question—a pattern of which is suggested in Table 9.2. In interpreting the analysis to follow, it is important to note the substantial share of the United States in financial outflows from China.[21]

Table 9.1 Relative economic sizes of China and the other large regions, ca 2011

% of world	China	US	EU(26)	Japan
GDP	11	22	26	9
Consumption, C	8	27	26	9
Investment, I	20	15	22	8
Government spending, G	7	20	30	10
Exports, X	17	17	25	7
Imports, M	15	21	23	8
Total domestic saving, S^D	19	13	20	9

Sources: National accounts data supply most of the elements though adjustments have been required to ensure that current accounts sum to zero globally, as do capital/financial accounts. The IMF database (n.d.) is the major source but there is frequent resort to national statistical databases.

---

21 Further details as to the sources and construction of the database can be obtained from Tyers (2015c: Appendix 2).

Table 9.2 Shares of total domestic savings directed to investment in each region, 2011[a]

% of row total saving	US	EU(26)	Japan	China	Australia	Rest of World
US[b]	68.0	13.3	6.4	6.4	1.5	4.4
EU(26)[c]	12.9	80.1	2.3	2.3	0.9	1.5
Japan[d]	14.0	3.3	72.2	6.2	0.7	3.6
China[c]	9.2	0.6	0.9	81.1	0.1	8.0
Australia[e]	13.0	4.8	2.3	2.1	77.3	0.4
Rest of world[f]	3.4	3.9	2.6	2.8	0.1	87.2

[a] These shares sum to 100 horizontally. They are based on 2011 investment flows. The original flow matrix is inconsistent with data on savings and investment from national accounts and so an RAS algorithm is used to ensure that row and column sums are consistent with other data. The row sums of the original flow matrix are total savings by region and the column sums are total investment by region. These sums are sourced from the IMF (n.d.) database and the World Bank (n.d.) database.
[b] United States: Values are based on official statistics, BEA.
[c] European Union and China: Indirect information from US, Australian and Japanese statistics.
[d] Japan: Estimated based on foreign direct investment (FDI) data, assuming investment outflow = FDI*1.6. The ratio 1.6 is that of US-reported inward investment from Japan divided by Japanese reported outward FDI to the United States.
[e] Australia: ABS (2013).
[f] Rest of World is a residual. Its saving is inferred from national accounts estimates and its investment abroad is determined to balance the matrix of financial flows.
Sources: As per the notes above.

Primary results: Growth surge and transition effects

Two sets of comparative static experiments are undertaken in which shocks are applied to the Chinese economy that represent changes over a single year. These are stylised representations of actual changes during the growth surge period, on the one hand, and the subsequent transition to the new growth model on the other. For each, a set of assumptions is required about labour markets, fiscal policy and the target of monetary policy in all the regions. These are short run and Keynesian in flavour, and are detailed in Table 9.3.[22] The stylised annual growth surge shocks are listed in Table 9.4 and they represent the comparative performance of the Chinese economy in the surge

---

22 Keynesian and neoclassical assumptions about behaviour in response to the Chinese shocks are compared using a similar model by Tyers (2015b). While there are key differences in financial market structure between the two models, the contrasts that emerge are similar to those that would stem from the model used here.

period: 2002–07.[23] The particular shock to consumption behaviour represents the observed decline in the share of consumption expenditure and the rise in the share of private savings in GDP over those years.

Table 9.3 Key assumptions about labour markets, fiscal and monetary policy[a]

Closure	
Labour market	Exogenous nominal production (unskilled) wage with endogenous production employment
Fiscal policy	Exogenous nominal government spending and endogenous government revenue at fixed rates of tax on income, consumption and trade
Monetary policy targets[b]	China and the Rest of the World: Fixed exchange rates against the US$[c]
	US, EU and Japan: Fixed monetary bases[d] Producer price level targets Consumer price level targets

[a] Since the model is a system of nonlinear simultaneous equations and more variables are specified than equations in the system, there is flexibility as to the choice of those to make exogenous. This choice mirrors assumptions about the behaviour of labour markets, fiscal deficits and monetary policy targets.
[b] Money supplies can be set to target any of the three price levels (consumer, producer and GDP), nominal exchange rates against the US dollar or nominal GDP levels.
[c] Australia is a small region also identified in the model. Its monetary policy targets the producer price level, which ensures no change in employment.
[d] No changes in commercial bank reserve behaviour are assumed so that money multipliers remain constant.

In the case of the transition, the first signs of which appeared after 2009, slower productivity and factor accumulation rates are combined with a single change in Chinese preferences that boosts consumption and reduces saving.[24] The preference shock might be thought of as stemming from the combination of life-cycle changes and the social and industrial reforms discussed in earlier sections, and it is set at a level sufficient to raise the consumption share of GDP by about one-tenth (from 45 to near 50 per cent), which is representative of the change suggested by Huang et al. (2013).

---

23 The capital accumulation and productivity shares of China's recent growth are controversial (Krugman 1994). The separate roles these played are examined using a similar model by Tyers (2015a). The shock values used here are consistent with the meta-analysis by Wu (2011).
24 The slowdown assumed here is consistent with the analysis by Feng and Yang (2013), though this is not to deny that considerable potential remains for further productivity growth, even in China's manufacturing sector (Hsieh and Klenow 2009).

The growth surge

The numerical simulation results are summarised in Table 9.5. The simulation is repeated for three different monetary policy settings for the United States, the European Union and Japan, as described in Table 9.3. China's growth surge, combined with its imbalance between production and consumption, created excess supply in the advanced economies, so was deflationary in the absence of money supply adjustment.[25] In the simulation, US dollar appreciation ensures that US consumer prices deflate by more than producer prices,[26] so monetary targeting of the consumer price level requires the largest expansion of the US monetary base. Unsurprisingly, the resulting greater liquidity yields the best short-run outcome for the advanced economies in general, although the monetary expansion, which includes UMP, places further demands on long bond markets and exacerbates the decline in their yields.

In the case where the advanced economies target their monetary bases, and hence do not respond with monetary expansions, it is noteworthy that the decline in bond yields does not occur in all regions. This is because the deflations that result are contractionary, reducing both output and saving. This in turn places offsetting upward pressure on domestic yields. The net effect depends on the intensity of financial interaction with China.

As we have seen, this interaction is far more intense between China and the United States than between China and the other advanced economies. In the European Union, therefore, reduced home saving tends to dominate the opposing downward force due to the financial influx from China. For this reason, the simulated net change in the domestic real interest rate in the European Union is positive in the absence of a domestic monetary expansion sufficient to avert the contraction.

Real domestic investment rises in the advanced economies with the influx from China, but where deflation is not eliminated by monetary expansion, insufficiently to sustain domestic labour demand. The net effects on real GDP depend on the level of employment, which declines where deflation is allowed to persist. Historically, deflation occurred only briefly in the United States and Europe during the surge period, but it has been a persistent feature in Japan. The results therefore suggest that China's growth surge ultimately contributed to the slow real GDP growth observed in the United States and the European Union and the stagnation in Japan during this period.

---

25 Another way to think of this is that lower interest rates raise the demand for money relative to goods, thus reducing the prices of goods in terms of money.

26 This is because the consumption basket includes imported products not included in the calculation of the producer or GDP prices.

In more general terms, however, these economies experienced real appreciations relative to China, of a scale roughly equivalent to the terms-of-trade gains reflected in this model. The welfare effect of these real income gains can be incorporated by deflating nominal GDP by the domestic consumer price level to obtain the real purchasing power of home income at home consumer prices. This measure shows consistent net gains, suggesting that the overall effect of China's surge in the advanced economies was positive but it was distributed in favour of capital owners rather than workers, so it caused distributional stress.

The transition

Both the surge and the transition shocks indicated in Table 9.4 embody productivity and factor endowment changes. At their core, however, they differ in that the transition offers a reversal of the change in consumption behaviour. There is in the transition a rise in Chinese consumption expenditure and a decline in savings. This reduces the structural imbalance substantially, so the transition's effects on global financial markets are opposite to those of the growth surge. That is, bond yields in the advanced economies rise as China's excess savings are reduced. Because of incomplete financial integration, however, yield rises abroad are smaller than within China. This ensures that the simulated change in international financial flux is reversed, reducing Chinese net outflows and increasing Chinese investment domestically. In the absence of monetary contractions in the advanced economies, these shocks are modestly inflationary. This stimulates employment and real GDP growth. Real purchasing power of income at consumer prices is boosted in the European Union and Japan—though not in the United States. This is because the transition shocks have caused the advanced economies to suffer terms-of-trade losses. Because China is more financially integrated with the United States, these are more than fully offset by increased employment only in the European Union and Japan.[27]

---

27 These results differ in detail, though not in bottom-line magnitudes of net effects, from the Keynesian outcomes of the analysis by Tyers (2015b). This is because the assumption of a fully integrated global bond market, made in that paper, yields considerably larger financial spillover effects than obtained with the model adopted here.

Table 9.4 Experimental shocks[a]

Scenario	Shocks, %	
Growth surge	Productivity, A^Y	3
	Consumption constant, A^C	−10
	Capital stock, K	8
	Skill stock, S	10
Transition	Productivity, A^Y	1
	Consumption constant, A^C	15
	Capital stock, K	3
	Skill stock, S	10
	Nominal wage, W^b	4

[a] All shocks are to the Chinese economy only. They are considered representative of annual shocks in the growth surge and transition periods.
[b] The Chinese nominal wage is shocked with the transition case only to allow for accelerated relative production wage growth in the transition, fostering consumption.
Sources: Calibration to observed changes, combined with the meta analysis of productivity change by Wu (2011).

Sensitivity to financial integration

Financial integration can be thought of in several ways, even within the confines of the model adopted here. One possibility is to regard greater financial integration as being indicative of a more fluid substitution process between assets across all regions. This is readily reflected by a rise in all the regions' elasticities of asset substitution, σ_i^I.[28] Since Chinese financial development is more recent than corresponding developments in China's product markets or in the financial markets of advanced economies, it is here represented as a progression in the value of China's σ_i^I from small values to full parity with the advanced economies.[29]

For low values of σ_i^I, China's financial outflows adhere to the original pattern of these flows, as reflected in the 2011 database. When its substitution elasticity rises, the distribution of these outflows across regional assets is more responsive to relative yield changes. This includes greater flexibility of the share in China's collective portfolio of China's own domestic assets. To explore the effects

---

28 In the model, described in detail by Tyers (2015a), financial integration is indexed by the preparedness of asset holders to substitute the assets of one region with those of another, represented by an elasticity of substitution. When the value of that elasticity is large, portfolio managers rebalance across regions on fine movements in expected rates of return on investment. When it is small, portfolio compositions are comparatively stable.

29 The values of the substitution elasticity used in generating the results in the previous section are 15 for the United States and the European Union, 10 for Japan and five for China. These values reflect numerical measures of comparative financial openness (Tyers 2015c: Appendix 2). Here the analysis sets them as constant at 20 for all the advanced economies and examines the effects of allowing China's elasticity to rise from two to 20.

of integration, the growth surge and transition shocks are introduced with values of σ_i^I that range from the very small to those representing integration at the level of the advanced economies. The effects of the surge and transition on regional bond yields, real GDP and the real purchasing power of regional income at consumer prices are assessed for China and the advanced economies. For economy of illustration, only the cases in which the advanced economies hold constant their money supplies are presented.

Sensitivity during the growth surge

More flexible Chinese portfolio management alters the effects of the growth surge, causing departures from the results in Table 9.5 in ways that can be seen in Figure 9.3. Not surprisingly, given that the shocks arise from the Chinese economy, Chinese performance indicators are the most strongly affected by changes in financial integration. Increases in it make China's outbound investment easier and more flexibly distributed across the other economies. Since the growth surge caused a substantial rise in excess saving, the more readily that saving can be shifted abroad, the smaller is its tendency to suppress Chinese home bond yields and the greater is its tendency to suppress yields in regions with which China has intensive financial exchange. In the end, the modelling suggests that these changes in the degree of Chinese integration have, in themselves, only small effects on global bond yields. Of course, these experiments have common shocks to Chinese output and excess saving, the average international effects of which have already been indicated in Table 9.5. The marginal effects of greater flexibility of direction of financial flows are what are comparatively small.

Table 9.5 Effects of the growth surge with moderate financial integration[a]

% changes	US, EU, Japan monetary target	US	EU(26)	Japan	China
Real bond yield, r					
	Monetary base	−0.21	0.07	−0.20	−2.43
	Producer price level	−1.23	−0.82	−1.22	−3.33
	Consumer price level	−3.23	−2.84	−3.15	−4.94
Consumer price level, P^c					
	Monetary base	−0.20	−0.16	−0.12	−6.19
	Producer price level	0.00	0.00	0.00	−5.74
	Consumer price level	0.31	0.64	0.19	−5.02
Producer price level, P^p					
	Monetary base	−0.67	−0.81	−0.37	−1.58
	Producer price level	−0.39	−0.74	−0.21	−1.17
	Consumer price level	0.00	0.00	0.00	−0.59
Exchange rate versus US$, E					
	Monetary base	0.00	−0.32	−0.83	0.00
	Producer price level	0.00	0.03	−0.63	0.00
	Consumer price level	0.00	−0.24	−0.28	0.00
Real investment, I/P^p					
	Monetary base	0.36	0.11	0.2	10.86
	Producer price level	0.54	0.83	0.32	11.63
	Consumer price level	1.05	2.19	0.65	13.09
Production employment, L					
	Monetary base	−0.24	−0.19	−0.14	3.68
	Producer price level	0.00	0.00	0.00	4.35
	Consumer price level	0.38	0.78	0.23	5.44
Real output (GDP), Y/P^y					
	Monetary base	−0.04	−0.03	−0.03	10.52
	Producer price level	0.00	0.00	0.00	10.71
	Consumer price level	0.07	0.14	0.04	11.01
Real income, Y/P^c					
	Monetary base	0.55	0.86	0.25	4.15
	Producer price level	0.48	0.99	0.24	4.35
	Consumer price level	0.44	0.89	0.25	4.77

[a] These results are from the model described in the text with the closures and shocks listed in Tables 9.3 and 9.4. The 'moderate' financial integration parameters referred to are values of the elasticity of substitution between assets for each region, σ_i^f. These are United States: 15; European Union: 15; Japan: 10; China: 5; Australia: 15; Rest of World: 5.

Source: Simulations of the model described in the text.

Table 9.6 Effects of the transition with moderate financial integration[a]

% changes	US, EU, Japan monetary target	US	EU(26)	Japan	China
Real bond yield, r					
	Monetary base	0.62	0.54	0.63	3.05
	Producer price level	2.61	2.22	2.69	4.94
	Consumer price level	2.00	1.63	1.89	4.42
Consumer price level, P^c					
	Monetary base	0.37	0.23	0.31	−1.47
	Producer price level	0.00	0.00	0.00	−2.36
	Consumer price level	0.07	0.15	0.28	−2.19
Producer price level, P^p					
	Monetary base	0.46	−0.15	−0.03	0.65
	Producer price level	−0.07	−0.16	−0.47	−0.13
	Consumer price level	0.00	0.00	0.00	−0.07
Exchange rate versus US$, E					
	Monetary base	0.00	0.84	1.31	0.00
	Producer price level	0.00	0.00	1.22	0.00
	Consumer price level	0.00	−0.06	0.45	0.00
Real investment, I/P^p					
	Monetary base	−0.91	−0.62	−0.78	2.64
	Producer price level	−1.18	−1.99	−0.81	1.25
	Consumer price level	−1.03	−1.59	−1.11	1.67
Production employment, L					
	Monetary base	0.45	0.28	0.37	−0.93
	Producer price level	0.00	0.00	0.00	−2.15
	Consumer price level	0.08	0.19	0.34	−1.91
Real output (GDP), Y/P^y					
	Monetary base	0.08	0.05	0.07	4.57
	Producer price level	0.00	0.00	0.00	4.23
	Consumer price level	0.01	0.03	0.06	4.29
Real income, Y/P^c					
	Monetary base	−0.08	0.47	0.41	4.10
	Producer price level	0.05	0.15	0.40	3.70
	Consumer price level	0.06	0.16	0.34	3.89

[a] These results are from the model described in the text with the closures and shocks listed in Tables 9.3 and 9.4. The 'moderate' financial integration parameters referred to are values of the elasticity of substitution between assets for each region, σ_i^f. These are United States: 15; European Union: 15; Japan: 10; China: 5; Australia: 15; Rest of World: 5.
Source: Simulations of the model described in the text.

Real long bond yield　　**Real purchasing power of income**　　**Real GDP**

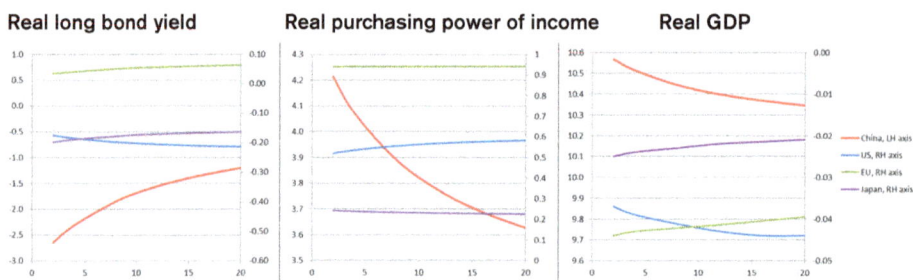

Figure 9.3 Effects of the growth surge: sensitivity to China's financial integration (percentage changes)

Source: Simulations of the model described in the text.

The expected movement towards convergence of bond yields occurs between China and the United States, but, while Japan also sees its yield declining, the effects of integration are opposite in direction in both Japan and the European Union relative to the United States. This occurs for the reasons discussed in the previous section—namely, there is a mismatch between the intensities of trade and financial flows to Japan and the European Union. Strong trading relationships cause major terms-of-trade effects and deflation, while weak financial relationships (Table 9.2) mean effects on European and Japanese bond markets are comparatively small. So, home bond markets in these regions are primarily affected by their deflation-induced domestic supply (and hence saving) contractions. Even where proportional changes to the initial shares of Chinese outflows to the European Union and Japan are substantial, the small base tends to push most of the additional outflow to the United States.

The effect of China's financial integration on its own real GDP and on the purchasing power of its income at domestic prices is to impair its short-run economic performance. This is because greater integration increases financial outflows from China and hence reduces domestic investment. This further depreciates China's real exchange rate, exacerbating the terms-of-trade shift against it. Even so, the net effect for China of the surge shock remains very positive. Internationally, the tendency for China's financial outflows to be US-focused serves to appreciate the US real exchange rate relative to the European Union and Japan. On the one hand, this exacerbates the employment contraction and hence the effects of the surge on US GDP. On the other hand, it increases the terms-of-trade gain and so enhances the real purchasing power of US income.

Sensitivity during the transition

The results from the transition shocks taken over the same range of levels of Chinese financial integration (asset substitutability) have a pattern that is generally the opposite of the surge shocks. This time the reduction in excess saving ensures that the higher returns are available within China. As can be seen from Figure 9.4, at higher levels of integration, China's portfolio rebalances more fully towards domestic assets and away from foreign ones. Home yields end up lower, and those in the United States—from whence the rebalance is resourced—rise. More minor redistributions also favour the European Union and Japan, whose yields fall slightly. Bringing expenditure back home improves both real GDP and the purchasing power of national income in China. Removing it from the United States reduces the US terms-of-trade gain and hence impairs the real purchasing power of US income. On the other hand, the higher US bond yield that stems from Chinese integration raises liquidity, while higher inflation—though still modest—improves employment, lifting real GDP. These effects are reduced in the European Union and Japan because of the effect Chinese integration has in reducing their bond yields. On the one hand, this causes less inflation and less employment uptake, but on the other, it tends to appreciate their real exchange rates, conferring larger terms-of-trade gains.

Real long bond yield   **Real purchasing power of income**   **Real GDP**

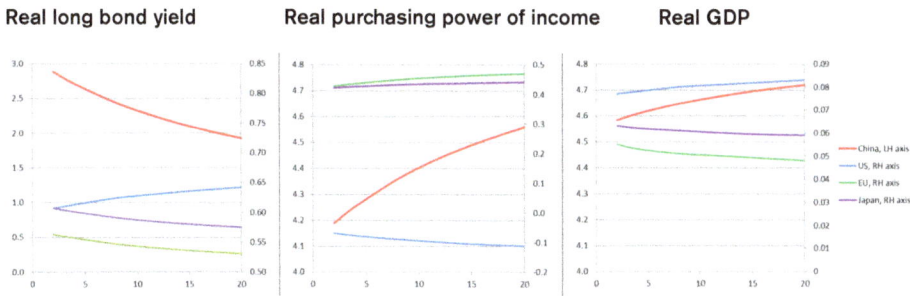

Figure 9.4 Effects of the transition: sensitivity to China's financial integration (percentage changes)

Source: Simulations of the model described in the text.

Conclusion

This chapter introduces an elemental global macroeconomic model with national asset portfolio rebalancing and explicit representation of unconventional monetary policy. It is used to evaluate the international effects of changes in China's growth regime. The post-WTO accession growth surge and the subsequent and ongoing structural transition are shown to have important implications for the United States, the European Union, Japan and Australia. The scale of these effects is further shown to depend on the level of China's financial integration with these advanced economies.

Even though the growth surge caused considerable structural change in the advanced economies—as manufacturing employment relocated to China, contributing to increased unemployment—this growth conferred on the advanced economies considerable terms-of-trade gains. The results from this analysis suggest that these gains outweighed the losses associated with increased unemployment. Had China been more financially integrated at the time, it is further shown that the financial influx, particularly into the United States, would have been larger. This would have made the US terms-of-trade gain larger, but its domestic bond yields would have been lower and the effects more deflationary, further reducing US employment and real GDP growth.

China's ongoing structural transition is relaxing its previous consumption repression and this is likely to continue to reduce its excess saving over time. The result is a tightening of global financial markets and some still modest increases in inflation in the advanced economies, therefore tending to restore employment in those economies.

On the other hand, reduced financial outflows from China depreciate real exchange rates in the advanced economies and redistribute investment towards China. This brings terms-of-trade losses in the advanced world and the moderating investment could slow growth there. As measured by the purchasing power of national incomes at home consumer prices, the employment gains appear to outweigh the terms-of-trade losses, at least for Europe and Japan. Increasing Chinese financial integration is shown to exacerbate these effects, particularly for the United States, since Chinese financial outflows have tended to be focused on US asset markets.

References

Arora, V., Tyers, R. and Zhang, Y. (2015), Reconstructing the savings glut: The global implications of Asian excess saving, *International Journal of Economics and Finance*, 7(7).

Australian Bureau of Statistics (ABS) (2013), *International investment position, Australia: Supplementary statistics, 2011*, Cat. no. 5352.0, Canberra: ABS.

Autor, D.H., Dorn, D. and Hanson, G.H. (2013), The China syndrome: Local labor market effects of competition in the United States, *American Economic Review*, (103)3: 220–25.

Bergsten, C.F., Freeman, C., Lardy, N.R. and Mitchell, D.J. (2008), *China's rise: Challenges and opportunities*, Washington, DC: Peterson Institute for International Economics.

Berman, E., Bound, J. and Griliches, Z. (1994), Changes in the demand for skilled labour within US manufacturing: Evidence from the annual survey of manufactures, *Quarterly Journal of Economics*, 109(2): 367–97.

Bernanke, B.S. (2005), Remarks by the governor, Federal Reserve Board, Sandridge Lecture, Virginia Association of Economists, March, Richmond, Va.

Bernanke, B.S. (2011), Global imbalances: Links to economic and financial stability, Speech given at the Banque de France Financial Stability Review Launch Event, 18 February, Paris.

Blanchard, O. and Giavazzi, F. (2006), Rebalancing growth in China: A three-handed approach, *China and the World Economy*, 14(4): 1–20.

Bound, J. and Johnson, G. (1992), Changes in the structure of wages in the 1980s: An evaluation of alternative explanations, *American Economic Review*, 82(3): 371–92.

Borio, C. and Disyatat, P. (2011), *Global imbalances and the financial crisis: Link or no link*, BIS Working Paper 346, May, Basel: Bank for International Settlements.

Caballero, R.J. (2009), *The 'other' imbalance and the financial crisis*, MIT Working Papers in Economics 9-32, December, Cambridge, Mass.: Massachusetts Institute of Technology.

Caballero, R.J., Farhi, E. and Gourinchas, P.O. (2008), An equilibrium model of 'global imbalances' and low interest rates, *American Economic Review*, 98(1): 358–93.

Chen, Q., Filardo, A., He, D. and Zhu, F. (2014), Financial crisis, unconventional monetary policy and international spillovers, Presentation at the ECB-IMF Conference on International Dimensions of Conventional and Unconventional Monetary Policy, 29–30 April, Frankfurt.

Chinn, M.D. and Ito, H. (2007), Current account balances, financial development and institutions: Assaying the world 'saving glut', *Journal of International Money and Finance*, 26: 546–69.

Chinn, M.D., Eichengreen, B. and Ito, H. (2012), Rebalancing global growth, in Canuto, O. and Leipziger, D. (eds), *Ascent after descent: Regrowing economic growth after the great recession*, Washington, DC: The World Bank, pp. 35–86.

Choi, H., Mark, N.C. and Sul, D. (2008), Endogenous discounting, the world saving glut and the US current account, *Journal of International Economics*, 75: 30–53.

di Giovanni, J., Levchenko, A.A. and Zhang, J. (2013), Global welfare effect of China: Trade integration and technical change, *AER Macroeconomics*, October.

Eichengreen, B. (2004), *Global imbalances and the lessons of Bretton Woods*, NBER Working Paper 10497, Cambridge, Mass.: National Bureau of Economic Research.

Eickmeier, S. and Kuehnlenz, M. (2013), *China's role in global inflation dynamics*, Discussion Paper 7-2013, Frankfurt: Deutsche Bundesbank.

Feldstein, M. and Horioka, C.Y. (1980), Domestic saving and international capital flows, *Economic Journal* [Royal Economic Society], 90(358): 314–29.

Feng, C. and Yang, L. (2013), The end of China's demographic dividend, in Garnaut, R., Fang, C. and Song, L. (eds), *China: A new model for growth and development*, Canberra and Beijing: ANU E Press & Social Sciences Academic Press, pp. 55–74.

Francois, J.F. and Nelson, D. (1998), Trade, technology and wages: General equilibrium mechanics, *Economic Journal*, 108: 1483–99.

Francois, J.F. and Wignaraja, G. (2008), Economic implications of Asian integration, *Global Economy Journal*, 8(3): 1–48.

Garner, J. and Qiao, H. (2013), China: Household consumption most likely US1.6 trillion larger than officially stated, *Asian Insight*, 28 February, Morgan Stanley Research. Available from: www.morganstanleychina.com/views/121217.html.

Genberg, H. and Zhang, W. (2010), Can China save the world by consuming more?, *VOX EU*, 25 April.

Harris, R.G. and Robertson, P.E. (2013), Trade, wages and skill accumulation in the emerging giants, *Journal of International Economics*, 89(2): 407–21.

Harris, R.G, Robertson, P.E. and Xu, J. (2011), The international effects of China's trade and education booms, *The World Economy*, 34(10): 1703–25.

Haskel, J., Lawrence, R.Z., Leamer, E.E. and Slaughter, M.J. (2012), Globalization and US wages: Modifying classic theory to explain recent facts, *Journal of Economic Perspectives*, 26(2): 119–40.

He, D. and McCauley, R.N. (2013), *Transmitting global liquidity to East Asia: Policy rates, bond yields, currencies and dollar credit*, Hong Kong Institute for Monetary Research Working Paper No. 15/2013, BIS Working Papers 431, October, Basel: Bank for International Settlements.

He, D., Cheung, L., Zhang, W. and Wu, T. (2012), How would capital account liberalization affect China's capital flows and *renminbi* real exchange rates?, *China and the World Economy*, 20(6): 29–54.

Helpman, E., Itskhoki, O. and Redding, S.J. (2010), Inequality and unemployment in a global economy, *Econometrica*, 78(4): 1239–83.

Hsieh, C.T. and Klenow, P. (2009), Misallocation and manufacturing TFP in China and India, *Quarterly Journal of Economics*, 124(November): 1403–48.

Huang, Y., Chang, J. and Yang, L. (2013), Consumption recovery and economic rebalancing in China, *Asian Economic Papers*, 12(1): 47–67.

International Monetary Fund (IMF) (n.d.), *International financial statistics*, Washington, DC: International Monetary Fund.

Ito, H. (2009), US current account debate with Japan then, and China now, *Journal of Asian Economics*, 20: 294–313.

Ito, H. (2013), Monetary policy in Asia and the Pacific in the post, post-crisis era, Presented at the 36th Pacific Trade and Development Conference: Financial Development and Cooperation in Asia and the Pacific, Hong Kong Monetary Authority, 19–21 November.

Johnson, R.S., Zuber, R.A. and Gandar, J.M. (2010), A re-examination of the market segmentation theory as a pedagogical model, *Journal of Financial Education*, 36(1–2): 1–37.

Krugman, P. (1994), The myth of Asia's miracle, *Foreign Affairs*, 73(6): 62–78.

Krugman, P. (1995), Growing world trade: Causes and consequences, *Brookings Papers*, 1: 327–77.

Krugman, P. (2010), Capital export, elasticity pessimism and the *renminbi* (wonkish), *The New York Times* [blog], 16 March.

Lardy, N.R. (2006), *Toward a consumption-driven growth path*, Policy Brief 06-6, Washington, DC: Peterson Institute for International Economics.

Lardy, N.R. (2012), *Sustaining China's growth after the global financial crisis*, January, Washington, DC: Peterson Institute for International Economics.

Leamer, E.E (1996), Wage inequality from international competition and technological change: Theory and country experience, *American Economic Review*, 86(2): 309–14.

Lee, J.W. and McKibbin, W.J. (2007), *Domestic investment and external imbalances in East Asia*, CAMA Working Paper 4-2007, Canberra: The Australian National University.

Levchenko, A.A. and Zhang, J. (2012), The global labor market impact of emerging giants: A quantitative assessment, Presented at the 13th Jacques Polak Annual Research Conference, hosted by the International Monetary Fund, 8–9 November, Washington, DC.

Lin, S. and Ye, H. (2015), *The international transmission of U.S. monetary policy: New evidence from trade data*, Working Paper No. 08/2015, Hong Kong: Hong Kong Institute for Monetary Research.

Ma, G. and Yi, W. (2010), China's high saving rate: Myth and reality, *International Economics*, 122: 5–40.

N'Daiye, P., Zhang, P. and Zhang, W. (2010), Structural reform, intra-regional trade, and medium-term growth prospects of East Asia and the Pacific: Perspectives from a new multi-region model, *Journal of Asian Economics*, 21: 20–36.

Organisation for Economic Cooperation and Development (OECD) (2015), *Long-term interest rates (indicator)*, Paris: OECD. Available from: doi:10.1787/662d712c-en. Accessed 23 March 2015.

Rey, H. (2013), Dilemma not trilemma: The global financial cycle and monetary policy independence, Federal Reserve Bank of Kansas City Economic Symposium, August, Jackson Hole, WY.

Rogoff, K. (2013), Inflation is still the lesser evil, *Project Syndicate*, 6 June. Available from: www.project-syndicate.org/commentary/. Accessed 12 June 2013.

Shiller, R.J., Campbell, J.Y. and Schoenholtz, K.L. (1983), Forward rates and future policy: Interpreting the term structure of interest rates, *Brookings Papers on Economic Activity*, 1983(1): 173–223.

Shin, H.S. (2011), Global banking glut and loan risk premium, Presented at the 12th Jacques Polak Annual Research Conference hosted by the International Monetary Fund, 10–11 November, Washington, DC.

Song, L., Yang, J. and Zhang, Y. (2011), State-owned enterprises' outward investment and the structural reform in China, *China and the World Economy*, 19(4): 38–53.

Tyers, R. (2014), Looking inward for transformative growth, *China Economic Review*, 29: 166–84.

Tyers, R. (2015a), *China and international macroeconomic interdependence*, CAMA Working Paper No. 9-2015, April, Canberra: The Australian National University.

Tyers, R. (2015b), International effects of China's rise and transition: Neoclassical and Keynesian perspectives, *Journal of Asian Economics*, 37: 1–19. Available from: doi:10.1016/j.asieco.2015.01.002.

Tyers, R. (2015c), Pessimism shocks in a model of global macroeconomic interdependence, *International Journal of Economics and Finance*, 7(1): 37–59.

Tyers, R. and Yang, Y. (1997), Trade with Asia and skill upgrading: Effects on labor markets in the older industrial countries, *Review of World Economics*, 133(3): 383–418.

Tyers, R. and Yang, Y. (2000), Capital–skill complementarity and wage outcomes following technical change in a global model, *Oxford Review of Economic Policy*, 16: 23–41.

Tyers, R. and Zhang, Y. (2011), Appreciating the renminbi, *The World Economy*, 34(2): 265–97.

Tyers, R. and Zhang, Y. (2014), Real exchange rate determination and the China puzzle, *Asian-Pacific Economic Literature*, 28(2): 1–32.

Wicksell, K. (1936) [1898], *Interest and prices: A study of the causes regulating the value of money*, London: Macmillan.

Winchester, N. and Greenaway, D. (2007), Rising wage inequality and capital–skill complementarity, *Journal of Policy Modeling*, 29(1): 41–54.

Wood, A. (1994), *North–South trade, employment and inequality*, Oxford: Clarendon Press.

World Bank (n.d.), *World Bank Open Data*, Washington, DC: The World Bank. Available from: data.worldbank.org/.

World Bank (2013), *Capital for the future: Saving and investment in an interdependent world*, Washington, DC: The World Bank.

Wu, Y. (2011), Total factor productivity growth in China: A review, *Journal of Chinese Economic and Business Studies*, 9(2): 111–26.

Yang, D.T. (2012), Aggregate savings and external imbalances in China, *Journal of Economic Perspectives*, 26(4): 125–46.

10. Capital Account Liberalisation in China[1]

Reform sequence, risks and selective policy issues

Liqing Zhang and Qin Gou

Introduction

Recent decades have witnessed a global wave of financial liberalisation unprecedented in both intensity and scope. This follows the breakdown of the Bretton Woods fixed exchange rate system in the early 1970s. The wave first appeared in high-income economies, following which, during the 1990s, a large number of emerging economies undertook profound financial reforms. Most but not all high-income economies introduced gradual reforms implementation characterised by domestic financial reforms and then capital account opening. In contrast, the process of reforms for developing economies lacked a clear sequence (see Figure 10.1).

As the 1990s unfolded, some developing economies undertook rapid, aggressive reforms at about the same time, and some relaxed capital controls during the very early stages of the reform process. On the one hand, the aggressive approach suggests an element of reform efficiency. On the other hand, this approach is typically accompanied by short-term pain that results from the relatively high risk of financial turbulence. In the second half of the 1990s and early 2000s, most of the countries that adopted the aggressive approach to financial reform experienced deep and traumatic financial crises, such as Mexico's 'Tequila' crisis and the East Asian Financial Crisis (World Bank 2001). In contrast, countries that adopted a gradual approach seldom faced such crises, but paid efficiency costs for delaying the reform process.

1   Note: The chapter is jointly sponsored by the Chinese Ministry of Education (MOE) project 'China's
    capital account liberalization: sequences and risks' (approval number: 14JZD016).

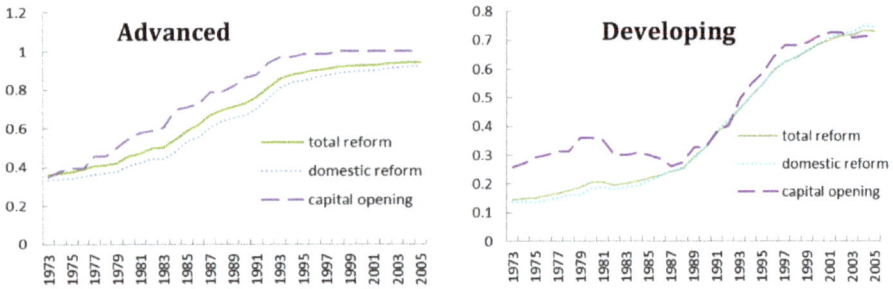

Figure 10.1 Trends in global financial reform

Notes: Total reform is defined as reform of the domestic financial system concurrent with opening of the capital account, and refers to the financial reform index constructed by Abiad et al. (2008). Domestic reform is defined as those reforms applying to the intra-country financial system, including interest rate controls, credit controls, prudential regulations, supervision of the banking sector and equity market policy. Capital reforms specifically measure the liberalisation of the capital account. Along each reform dimension, Abiad et al. (2008) allocate a country a score from zero to three, increasing the scale as liberalisation increases. Inverse scoring is used in constructing the index of banking system regulation and supervision.
Sources: Abiad et al. (2008); and authors' calculations.

In parallel with the varying stylised facts associated with different financial reform sequencing strategies among countries runs a longstanding heated debate on this topic in the academic literature. Some economists argue that correct sequencing, staggered over time, is important to avoid financial instability and minimise the risk of crisis that has been attached to free capital mobility (Edwards 1984, 1990; Funke 1993; McKinnon 1973, 1991; Stiglitz 2002). On the other hand, economists have also argued for simultaneous reform so as to improve economic and reform efficiency, including via interest rate liberalisation and exchange rate flexibility (Choksi and Papageorgiou 1986; Quirk and Evans 1995).

Within this broader debate, China, like many other developing economies, confronts a complex set of questions related to the desirability and mode of implementing capital account liberalisation as well as to domestic financial reform. In the past 15 years, incremental progress has been made in liberalisation of the capital account. Recent liberalisation measures include the launch of the Shanghai–Hong Kong Stock Connect program, amendment of foreign investment law and an increase in the scale of Qualified Foreign Institutional Investor (QFII), Renminbi Qualified Foreign Institutional Investor (RQFII) and Qualified Domestic Institutional Investor (QDII) schemes.

Following such progress in China's financial reform program, the 2014 *Annual Report on Exchange Arrangements and Exchange Restrictions* (*AREAER*) (IMF 2014) considered that of China's 40 capital account transaction items, 14 (some 35 per cent) have essentially been liberalised, 23 (57.5 per cent) have been partially liberalised and three (7.5 per cent) remain restricted. The last three items relate mainly to controls on capital and money market instruments, and controls on derivatives and other instruments.

Inward foreign direct investment (FDI) was among the earliest items to be liberalised in China—a process that began in the mid-1980s and accelerated in the early 1990s. The stock of inward FDI stood at US$1.8 trillion in 2014—equivalent to almost 20 per cent of China's gross domestic product (GDP). Outward FDI and portfolio flows, in comparison, remain restricted. Stocks of outward FDI, as well as inward and outward portfolio investments, amounted to about 7 per cent of GDP or less in 2014. While there has been some progress in capital account liberalisation in recent decades, the degree of capital account convertibility in China remains low compared with high-income economies and also some developing economies.

At the Third Plenary Session of the Eighteenth Central Committee of the Chinese Communist Party in late 2013, a comprehensive market-oriented reform program was authorised.[2] Financial reform is a significant component of these planned reforms. It comprises some 11 items of the newly authorised reform agenda, including the opening up of both foreign and private financial institutions; establishing a system of market-based interest rates, exchange rates and of the official yield curve; developing multilayered capital markets; capital account convertibility; and improved financial regulation (Central Committee of the Chinese Communist Party 2013).

While most of these items individually are in urgent need of reform, unavoidably, related reforms can only be pushed through simultaneously or in sequence. A heated debate has ensued as to the right approach to take in implementing China's financial reforms. Some economists believe a precondition for capital account convertibility should be reforms that deliver a strong domestic banking system, relatively developed domestic financial markets, interest rate liberalisation and exchange rate flexibility (Lardy and Douglass 2011; Prasad et al. 2005; Yu 2013). Other economists and policymakers argue for the acceleration of capital account convertibility in order to reap its growth benefit, removing capital control costs or even pushing back domestic financial reforms.

This chapter reviews the issues involved in moving towards deeper domestic financial liberalisation and capital account liberalisation in China. Despite the extensive literature on financial reform sequencing, empirical evidence on the crisis risks of alternative sequencing strategies is relatively limited. In this

---

2   The decision involved several aspects including society, politics, economy, culture and ecological civilisation. Decisions of the Central Committee of the Communist Party of China at the Third Plenum of the Eighteenth Party Congress are available from: www.china.org.cn/. Retrieved 16 January 2014.

chapter, we use experience of financial reforms to investigate the crisis risks of alternative financial reform sequencing, using a cross-country panel-data analysis for 50 economies in the years 1973–2005.

The second section of the chapter reviews the related literature. In the third section, we lay out the empirical model used to analyse financial crisis risks around alternative sequencing of financial reforms. In the fourth section, we apply these empirical results to a scenario-based study of the implications for China's onward financial reform, before offering some concluding remarks.

A brief literature review of capital account liberalisation

The theoretical literature suggests that there are several benefits of capital account liberalisation. First, liberalisation improves capital allocation efficiency and risk diversification, and fosters financial development, which in turn stimulate economic growth (Kose et al. 2009). Second, it avoids the transaction cost of capital controls, which in any case are not perfectly effective.

There are also several arguments in favour of capital controls. First, extreme flows of capital are likely to induce excessive fluctuations in liquidity and to render monetary policies ineffective. Second, large capital flows help to synchronise the domestic and international business cycles, implying the domestic economy risks unpredictable capital flow reversals and severe financial instability, even financial distress and crises (Bhagwati 1998; Levy Yeyati et al. 2009; Rodrik 1998; Stiglitz 2002).

Empirical studies, however, find little conclusive evidence for growth-enhancing effects (Edison et al. 2002; Quinn and Toyoda 2008; Rodrik 1998). Nor has consensus been reached on the net effects of the volatility and crisis risks induced by free capital flows across countries (Edwards 2007, 2008; Glick and Hutchison 2001; Glick et al. 2006; Hutchison and Noy 2005).

A more nuanced literature exploring the effects of financial reform according to their sequence offers some insight into how countries can reap the benefits and minimise the costs of capital account liberalisation (IMF 2012). Sequencing here is defined as the setting of a clear order among financial sector liberalisation measures (IMF 2012). There are three different views on the importance of sequencing.

The first view favours gradual reform that incrementally implements reforms in an appropriate sequence. This is usually called the 'gradualist approach'. Three main reasons why the appropriate sequencing and coordination of reforms are important are summarised by the IMF (2012: 317):

> Inappropriate sequencing of reforms could cause excessive risk taking and financial instability; limited institutional capacity necessarily requires some prioritization of reform elements; given the numerous policy and operational reforms in each area of financial policy, setting priorities could facilitate and encourage the adoption of reforms; hence, this aspect of financial sector assessments is important.

Before this note from the IMF, sequencing of financial reforms had been of less concern since the early stages of the post-fixed exchange rate financial and capital account liberalisation process (Edwards 1984, 1990; Funke 1993; McKinnon 1973, 1991; Prasad et al. 2005; Stiglitz 2002). In general, these authors argue that eliminating capital restrictions too early can be costly because of the effects on the (real) exchange rate and on international competitiveness, and also the potential short-term effect of instigating an asset-price boom. More dangerously again, the country may be subject to 'sudden stops' of capital inflow, and also to large-scale capital flight when capital inflows are unexpectedly withdrawn by foreign investors (speculators). In such circumstances, the country is forced to devalue its currency and can suffer a costly monetary crisis. Such a crisis can also spread to other countries and result in a severe international or regional crisis.

The East Asian currency crisis provides an example that is suggestive of a pattern of inappropriate sequencing of capital account liberalisation that contributed to both the speed and the severity of the crisis in many countries (Edwards 2009; World Bank 2001). Development of adequate institutional capacity appears to be an important and necessary precondition for coping with capital account liberalisation volatility, and thus for reaping net gains from that process (IMF 2012; Obstfeld and Taylor 2004). This thus raises the issue of the institutional design and scope of reform strategies for safeguarding macroeconomic and financial stability (IMF 2003, 2012).

This further raises the question of what is the appropriate sequence. McKinnon (1993) offers a widely influential argument that reform of the domestic financial sector and trade liberalisation should precede liberalisation of the capital account. The reason is that in a distorted domestic financial system with interest rate regulations and credit controls that lack sufficient supervision, opening of the capital account will either lead to capital flight that in turn erodes the domestic deposit base or lead to over-borrowing foreign currency, which is also risky.

In contrast, the 'interest group theory', proposed by Rajan and Zingales (2003), suggests that trade and capital account openness should instead precede domestic financial liberalisation (Hauner and Prati 2008). Their logic relates to the fact that in a closed economy, interest groups oppose financial development because they benefit from preventing the entrance of new competitors. In this way, early trade and capital liberalisation introduce new external competition that challenges the rents enjoyed by local interest groups in the closed economy, and thus facilitates financial development.

Another body of thought argues for simultaneous reforms—that is, for no sequencing at all. There are three points of logic behind these arguments. The first is that full liberalisation of the capital account can promote flexibility in both the exchange rate and the interest rate, which could in turn support capital account reforms (Quirk and Evans 1995). Second, simultaneous reform has no reform cost but brings great economic benefit in the absence of market distortions and externalities (Choksi and Papageorgiou 1986). Finally, a 'big-bang' reform can avoid the delays brought by interest groups and thus reduce the costs of reform.

Capital account liberalisation, sequence and crisis: An empirical investigation

We investigate the effects of financial reform sequencing on the likelihood of experiencing financial crisis. Following Edwards (2009), Ghosh et al. (2014) and others, we specify the following benchmark variance component panel probit model (Equations 10.1 and 10.2).

Equation 10.1

$$Crisis_{it} = \begin{cases} 1, & if \ Crisis_{it}^* > 0 \\ 0, & otherwise \end{cases}$$

Equation 10.2

$$Crisis_{it}^* = \beta_0 + \beta_1 Kaopen_{it} + \beta_2 Kaopen_{it} * Fin\_domestic_{it} + X_{it} + \varepsilon_{it}$$

In Equations 10.1 and 10.2, $Crisis_{it}$ is a dummy variable that takes the value of one if country i in period t experiences a financial crisis (banking, currency or debt crisis), and zero otherwise. Whether a country experiences a crisis is the result of an unobserved latent variable, $Crisis_{it}^*$, which is a function of the degree of capital opening ($Kaopen_{it}$) and domestic financial system liberalisation, and a group of other controlled variables within the vector X_{it}, including GDP per capita (in log term), the annual growth rate of GDP per capita, the inflation rate based on the consumer price index (CPI), the growth rate of the ratio of broad money to foreign reserves, the real interest rate, the real exchange rate overvaluation, the current account surplus over GDP, financial development measured as the ratio of private credit to GDP, and government deficit over GDP.

Crisis data are sourced from Laeven and Valencia (2013), whose dataset comprises all systemic banking, currency and sovereign debt crises during the period 1970–2011. They define a systemic banking crisis as either significant signs of financial distress in the banking system or severe banking policy intervention, while currency crisis is defined as a nominal depreciation of the currency via the US dollar of at least 30 per cent that is also at least 10 percentage points higher than the rate of depreciation in the year before; a sovereign debt crisis is defined as sovereign debt default and restructuring. $Crisis_{it}$ takes a value of one if at least one of these events happens, and zero otherwise. All controlled variables are lagged one year in order to control for potential endogeneity issues arising from a reverse causal effect from crisis to the control variables, and thus omitting the variable effects.

The capital account liberalisation indicator used, $Kaopen_{it}$, is constructed by Quinn and Toyoda (2008), and is a standard indicator used in the literature. This measures de jure restrictions on cross-border financial transactions based on detailed information on restrictions on capital transactions collected by *AREAER* (IMF 2014). The data are constructed around an index range of 0–100, where a higher value implies a higher degree of capital account liberalisation. We construct our own index of capital account liberalisation by dividing the Quinn and Toyoda (2008) indicator by 100 to obtain an index scaled from zero to one.

The domestic financial reform indicator, $Fin\_domestic_{it}$, is constructed by aggregating domestic financial system reform indicators from the financial reform dataset of Abiad et al. (2008). That dataset captures the degree of liberalisation in five dimensions: 1) credit controls and reserve requirements; 2) interest rate controls; 3) entry barriers to the banking industry; 4) state ownership of banks; and 5) regulations and supervision of the banking sector. Along each dimension, a country was given a score between zero and three, with zero corresponding to repression and three indicating full liberalisation. For banking system regulation and supervision, the opposite scoring is true. These scores were normalised to a range from zero to one. This index is available for a sample of 91 countries in the period 1973–2005.

Since domestic financial reform is a multifaceted phenomenon, we further divide domestic financial reforms by three sub-dimensions: banking system reform, which includes entry barriers to the banking industry; state ownership of banks and regulation and supervision of the banking sector (Fin_bank_{it}); interest rate control (*Fin_interest$_{it}$*) and credit controls (*Fin_credit$_{it}$*). Definitions of all the variables and their sources are summarised in Table A10.1 in the Appendix, while descriptive statistics are reported in Table A10.2.

Baseline empirical results

To examine the impact of domestic financial reform and capital account liberalisation on the probability of financial crisis, we start with a baseline model covering the entire sample. We run panel data regressions using a random effects probit model, the results of which are reported in Table 10.1.

The significantly positive coefficient of Kaopen and the significantly negative coefficient of its cross-term with domestic financial reform in column (1) indicate that capital opening (Kaopen) increases the likelihood of experiencing a crisis, while domestic financial system reform facilitates in reducing the crisis-inducing effect of capital account opening.

For the three types of financial crisis, the results are mostly consistent: the coefficient of Kaopen is positive and significant, except in the case of currency crisis; and the coefficient on the cross-term with domestic financial reform is significant and negative. Moreover, the coefficients are very stable, varying from 1.32 to 1.61 for Kaopen and −1.68 to −1.89 for the cross-term. This means a 1 per cent increase in capital opening is associated with an increase in the propensity of experiencing a crisis by 1.4 per cent, while a 1 per cent increase in domestic financial reform is associated with a 1.7 per cent increase in crisis propensity. Therefore, a more open domestic financial system helps buffer an economy from financial risks caused by capital account opening. The influence of other variables is as predicted.

Table 10.1 Marginal effects and predicted probabilities of financial crisis: The role of capital account opening and domestic financial reform

Variables	(1) Crisis	(2) Banking crisis	(3) Currency crisis	(4) Sovereign debt crisis
Kaopen	1.6143**	1.4802**	1.3246	1.4275**
	(0.6269)	(0.7137)	(0.8767)	(0.7085)
Kaopen*Fin_domestic	−1.8841***	−1.8197***	−1.6881**	−1.7650***
	(0.5745)	(0.6457)	(0.8288)	(0.6420)
Fixed EXR	−0.6132	−0.0733	−1.1383*	−0.0786
	(0.4152)	(0.4549)	(0.6711)	(0.4508)
Intermediate EXR	−0.0042	0.0276	0.0323	0.0111
	(0.2974)	(0.3497)	(0.4559)	(0.3475)
GGDP	−2.6722	1.6215	−6.2185**	1.5592
	(2.1325)	(2.6016)	(2.7526)	(2.6023)
Log(GDP)	−0.2202	−0.1259	−0.2200*	−0.1214
	(0.0823)	(0.0984)	(0.1131)	(0.0981)
Inflation	0.1674	0.2051	0.1561	0.1926
	(0.1738)	(0.2198)	(0.2176)	(0.2206)
M2_reserve	0.3974**	0.1170	0.7054***	0.1040
	(0.1734)	(0.2336)	(0.2206)	(0.2196)
Real interest	0.4298	1.9737**	−0.6393	1.8595*
	(0.8549)	(0.9891)	(1.2086)	(0.9821)
Real exchange rate overvaluation	0.0114**	0.0072	0.0151***	0.0067
	(0.0046)	(0.0064)	(0.0054)	(0.0065)
Current account surplus (% of GDP)	−2.4192	−2.4621	−2.4595	−2.2879
	(1.8413)	(2.0962)	(2.7738)	(2.0847)
Financial development	0.0047*	0.0048	0.0029	0.0044
	(0.0028)	(0.0033)	(0.0043)	(0.0032)
Predicted probabilities	5.20%	3.41%	2.56%	3.25%
Observations	890	890	890	890
No. of countries	50	50	50	50
R-squared	0.148	0.102	0.266	0.096

*** $p < 0.01$
** $p < 0.05$
* $p < 0.1$
Note: Standard errors are in parentheses.
Source: Authors' estimations.

To analyse the influence of the specific domestic financial reforms on the consequences of capital account opening, we separately examine the three areas of domestic financial reform—namely, domestic banking sector reform, interest rate liberalisation and credit reform (Tables 10.2–10.4). We find similar results in Table 10.2, as domestic banking sector reforms are associated with reduced capital account opening crisis risks, for each type of financial crisis. Specifically, a 1 per cent increase in capital opening is associated with an increase in the propensity of experiencing a crisis by about 1 per cent, while a 1 per cent increase in domestic financial reform is associated with a decrease in crisis risk of some 1.4 per cent. The effects of other controlling variables still hold.

The results suggest that banking system reform—which mainly refers to reducing entry barriers to the banking sector, allowing greater development of private banks—and strengthening regulation and supervision of the banking sector play an important role in mitigating the financial risks of capital account opening. This is possibly because greater supervision and competition increase the risk-management capacities of the domestic banking sector and thus increase domestic market resilience in the face of external economic and financial shocks that could trigger capital outflows on the level of a financial crisis.

Table 10.2 Marginal effects and predicted probabilities of financial crisis: The role of capital account opening and banking sector reform

Variables	(1) Crisis	(2) Banking crisis	(3) Currency crisis	(4) Sovereign debt crisis
Kaopen	1.1356**	1.0073*	0.8902	0.9702*
	(0.5119)	(0.5815)	(0.7166)	(0.5779)
Kaopen_bank	−1.5203***	−1.4754***	−1.3338**	−1.4341***
	(0.4640)	(0.5242)	(0.6711)	(0.5215)
Fixed EXR	−0.5585	−0.0232	−1.0806	−0.0278
	(0.4096)	(0.4514)	(0.6577)	(0.4474)
Intermediate EXR	−0.0241	0.0089	0.0121	−0.0058
	(0.2950)	(0.3478)	(0.4481)	(0.3459)
GGDP	−2.8479	1.4437	−6.4181**	1.4010
	(2.1270)	(2.6105)	(2.7475)	(2.6082)
Log(GDP)	−0.2193***	−0.1250	−0.2157*	−0.1209
	(0.0828)	(0.0992)	(0.1135)	(0.0990)
Inflation	0.1390	0.1742	0.1322	0.1629
	(0.1779)	(0.2286)	(0.2204)	(0.2290)
M2_reserve	0.3933**	0.1090	0.7011***	0.0954
	(0.1731)	(0.2341)	(0.2197)	(0.2200)
Real interest	0.2173	1.7482*	−0.8488	1.6421*
	(0.8578)	(0.9877)	(1.2170)	(0.9806)
Real exchange rate overvaluation	0.0113**	0.0074	0.0150***	0.0069
	(0.0046)	(0.0063)	(0.0055)	(0.0063)

	(1)	(2)	(3)	(4)
Variables	**Crisis**	**Banking crisis**	**Currency crisis**	**Sovereign debt crisis**
Current account surplus	−2.4341	−2.4079	−2.6362	−2.2437
(% of GDP)	(1.8323)	(2.0850)	(2.7740)	(2.0744)
Financial development	0.0043	0.0044	0.0025	0.0040
	(0.0028)	(0.0032)	(0.0042)	(0.0032)
Predicted probabilities	5.19%	3.40%	2.57%	3.25%
Observations	817	795	803	813
No. of countries	50	50	50	50
R-squared	0.148	0.103	0.265	0.097

*** $p<0.01$
** $p<0.05$
* $p<0.1$
Note: Standard errors are in parentheses.
Source: Authors' estimations.

For the other two dimensions of domestic financial reform, we find that while credit reform is associated with decreasing the crisis risks of capital account opening (Table 10.3), interest rate liberalisation unexpectedly has a positive but insignificant effect (Table 10.4). Eliminating credit controls meanwhile facilitates capital allocation efficiency and removes distortions in the domestic financial system—a result supported by (McKinnon 1991).

Table 10.3 Marginal effects and predicted probabilities of financial crisis: The role of capital account opening and credit distribution

	(1)	(2)	(3)	(4)
Variables	**Crisis**	**Banking crisis**	**Currency crisis**	**Sovereign debt crisis**
Kaopen	0.5847	0.4140	0.5201	0.3961
	(0.4722)	(0.5526)	(0.6279)	(0.5529)
Kaopen_credit	−0.7845**	−0.6642	−0.8760*	−0.6363
	(0.3696)	(0.4285)	(0.5138)	(0.4274)
Fixed EXR	−0.4757	−0.0067	−0.9618	−0.0107
	(0.3934)	(0.4309)	(0.6401)	(0.4273)
Intermediate EXR	−0.0335	−0.0119	−0.0022	−0.0245
	(0.2919)	(0.3407)	(0.4498)	(0.3392)
GGDP	2.8711	1.3334	−6.3950**	1.2590
	(2.1179)	(2.5673)	(2.7565)	(2.5684)
Log(GDP)	−0.1827**	−0.0946	−0.1820*	−0.0927
	(0.0799)	(0.0956)	(0.1091)	(0.0954)
Inflation	0.2078	0.2504	0.1803	0.2358
	(0.1649)	(0.1994)	(0.2116)	(0.1998)

Variables	(1) Crisis	(2) Banking crisis	(3) Currency crisis	(4) Sovereign debt crisis
M2_reserve	0.4102**	0.1480	0.7017***	0.1266
	(0.1714)	(0.2281)	(0.2165)	(0.2138)
Real interest	0.7513	2.2359**	−0.3327	2.1078**
	(0.8536)	(0.9949)	(1.2073)	(0.9873)
Real exchange rate overvaluation	0.0111**	0.0067	0.0147***	0.0063
	(0.0046)	(0.0065)	(0.0054)	(0.0065)
Current account surplus (% of GDP)	−2.5391	−2.6568	−2.4772	−2.4821
	(1.7814)	(2.0272)	(2.7011)	(2.0148)
Financial development	0.0034	0.0034	0.0021	0.0030
	(0.0027)	(0.0032)	(0.0042)	(0.0031)
Predicted probabilities	5.21%	3.41%	2.57%	3.26%
Observations	817	795	803	813
No. of countries	50	50	50	50
R-squared	0.128	0.077	0.259	0.072

*** $p < 0.01$
** $p < 0.05$
* $p < 0.1$
Note: Standard errors are in parentheses.
Source: Authors' estimations.

Table 10.4 Marginal effects and predicted probabilities of financial crisis: The role of capital account opening and interest rate liberalisation

Variables	(1) Crisis	(2) Banking crisis	(3) Currency crisis	(4) Sovereign debt crisis
Kaopen	0.0617	0.2639	−0.3028	0.2702
	(0.7140)	(0.7766)	(1.0331)	(0.7752)
Kaopen_int	−0.1202	−0.3835	0.1529	−0.3847
	(0.5540)	(0.5875)	(0.8283)	(0.5864)
Fixed EXR	−0.4989	−0.0953	−0.8611	−0.0942
	(0.3947)	(0.4321)	(0.6324)	(0.4298)
Intermediate EXR	−0.0087	0.0090	0.0420	0.0003
	(0.2856)	(0.3334)	(0.4349)	(0.3325)
GGDP	−2.9846	1.2262	−6.5579**	1.1574
	(2.0975)	(2.5474)	(2.7354)	(2.5490)
Log(GDP)	−0.1959**	−0.1116	−0.1886*	−0.1095
	(0.0802)	(0.0959)	(0.1098)	(0.0957)
Inflation	0.1972	0.2401	0.1615	0.2271
	(0.1614)	(0.1928)	(0.2043)	(0.1930)

Variables	(1) Crisis	(2) Banking crisis	(3) Currency crisis	(4) Sovereign debt crisis
M2_reserve	0.4096**	0.1553	0.6873***	0.1331
	(0.1697)	(0.2247)	(0.2123)	(0.2111)
Real interest	0.5988	2.0538**	−0.5212	1.9387**
	(0.8407)	(0.9776)	(1.1824)	(0.9698)
Real exchange rate overvaluation	0.0105**	0.0060	0.0141***	0.0056
	(0.0046)	(0.0063)	(0.0054)	(0.0063)
Current account surplus (% of GDP)	−2.6725	−2.6763	−2.8106	−2.5335
	(1.7495)	(2.0008)	(2.6414)	(1.9927)
Financial development	0.0025	0.0028	0.0004	0.0025
	(0.0027)	(0.0031)	(0.0041)	(0.0031)
Predicted probabilities	5.19%	3.39%	2.56%	3.25%
Observations	817	795	803	813
No. of countries	50	50	50	50
R-squared	0.114	0.069	0.243	0.065

*** $p < 0.01$
** $p < 0.05$
* $p < 0.1$
Note: Standard errors are in parentheses.
Source: Authors' estimations.

Evaluation of the early warning system

We test the predictive power of our empirical model following the methods of the early warning system literature (Qin and Luo 2014). To identify risks of a financial crisis, we first need to set a parameter threshold so that the model can signal when the estimated probability of a crisis exceeds that threshold. Typically, the in-sample crisis probability is chosen as the threshold. The in-sample probabilities of financial crisis, banking crisis, currency crisis and sovereign debt crisis are 5.14 per cent, 3.27 per cent, 2.49 per cent and 3.63 per cent, respectively, as shown in Table 10.5.

The model has correctly signalled a crisis for 82 per cent of financial crises, 81 per cent of banking crises, 95 per cent of currency crises and 78 per cent of sovereign debt crises, and in the same order has successfully predicted non-crisis for 76 per cent, 77 per cent, 58 per cent and 77 per cent, respectively. The Type I error—that is, the probability of incorrect rejection of financial crisis when crisis actually occurs—is between 5 per cent and 22 per cent, while that of a Type II error (failure to reject a financial crisis when crisis does occur) is between 23 per cent and 42 per cent. Generally speaking, the predictive power of our model is good, especially for the currency crisis model that predicted correctly 95 per cent of the time.

Table 10.5 Performance of the early warning system

	Crisis	Banking crisis	Currency crisis	Sovereign debt crisis
Threshold	5.14%	3.27%	2.49%	3.63%
(a) No crisis occurs				
(i) No signal	633	621	458	617
(ii) Signal	142	148	325	170
(b) Crisis occurs				
(i) No signal	10	6	1	6
(ii) Signal	32	20	19	20
Statistics				
(1) The percentage of correct classification	76	77	59	77
(2) The proportion of signals conditional on crises occurring	82	81	95	78
(3) Type I error	18	19	5	22
(4) Type II error	24	23	42	23

Source: Authors' summary.

Robustness check

Our baseline results could be subject to statistical error, which affects the reliability of the findings.

To understand these risks, we conduct some robustness checks. First, we substitute the indicator for capital account liberalisation with the one constructed by Abiad et al. (2008) (*Kaopen2*) for the index constructed by Quinn and Toyoda (2008) to reduce the risk of measurement error. The results are reported in Table 10.6. The results are similar to the benchmark model, in which the coefficient on capital account opening is positive and significant, and its cross-term with domestic financial liberalisation is negative and significant. This reconfirms the earlier result that indicates greater reform of the domestic financial system serves to decrease the crisis risks attached to capital account opening. We also check the influence of different types of domestic financial reforms, and find that banking system reform appears to be important in its association with reducing the harmful risks of capital account opening—confirming the results of the basic model.

The second robustness check is to add more control variables to the baseline model. In this case, we focus on the government deficit.[3] Results of this new model, presented in Table 10.7, show that financial reform is associated with

---

3   This is not included in the basic model because this variable greatly reduces our final sample.

different outcomes of capital account liberalisation, except that in the case of the currency crisis that association is not significant. Therefore, we believe our basic model is robust.

Table 10.6 Robustness check: Alternative indicators

Variables	(1) Crisis	(2) Banking crisis	(3) Currency crisis	(4) Sovereign debt crisis
Kaopen2	0.3613**	0.3543*	0.3134	0.3302
	(0.1791)	(0.2065)	(0.2446)	(0.2056)
Kaopen2_domestic	−1.6786***	−1.7735**	−1.4610*	−1.7154**
	(0.6025)	(0.6894)	(0.8596)	(0.6887)
Fixed EXR	−0.4949	0.0212	−1.0102	0.0038
	(0.4062)	(0.4600)	(0.6400)	(0.4562)
Intermediate EXR	0.0116	0.0621	0.0343	0.0371
	(0.2987)	(0.3615)	(0.4493)	(0.3581)
GGDP	−2.8160	1.2572	−6.2683**	1.1852
	(2.1244)	(2.5853)	(2.7557)	(2.5815)
Log(GDP)	−0.1668**	−0.0731	−0.1869*	−0.0670
	(0.0755)	(0.0893)	(0.1058)	(0.0888)
Inflation	0.1808	0.2117	0.1573	0.1988
	(0.1648)	(0.2085)	(0.2066)	(0.2095)
M2_reserve	0.3913**	0.1093	0.6866***	0.0936
	(0.1736)	(0.2363)	(0.2187)	(0.2216)
Real interest	0.5818	2.0562**	−0.5710	1.9475**
	(0.7869)	(0.9120)	(1.0913)	(0.9040)
Real exchange rate overvaluation	0.0110**	0.0065	0.0145***	0.0060
	(0.0046)	(0.0065)	(0.0053)	(0.0065)
Current account surplus (% of GDP)	−2.5654	−2.6430	−2.6088	−2.4709
	(1.8175)	(2.0860)	(2.7121)	(2.0766)
Financial development	0.0033	0.0037	0.0018	0.0034
	(0.0027)	(0.0032)	(0.0041)	(0.0031)
Predicted probabilities	5.19%	3.40%	2.55%	3.25%
Observations	817	795	803	813
No. of countries	50	50	50	50
R-squared	0.140	0.102	0.260	0.096

*** $p<0.01$
** $p<0.05$
* $p<0.1$
Note: Standard errors are in parentheses.
Source: Authors' estimations.

Table 10.7 Robustness check: Alternative control variables and samples

Variables	(1) Crisis	(2) Banking crisis	(3) Currency crisis	(4) Sovereign debt crisis
Kaopen	5.5497*	7.2340*	78.9570	7.1280*
	(2.9560)	(4.2125)	(0.0000)	(4.2784)
Kaopen_domestic	−7.0235**	−8.7139**	−77.5441	−8.4916**
	(2.7593)	(3.9870)	(0.0000)	(4.0445)
Fixed EXR	2.5600	2.6641	−77.8428	2.7100
	(461.3604)	(624.5154)	(0.0000)	(732.6701)
Intermediate EXR	3.5700	3.6512	−17.3689	3.6532
	(461.3589)	(624.5133)	(0.0000)	(732.6683)
GGDP	−4.3000	−6.4972	−183.6347	−6.8148
	(8.0252)	(9.4391)	(0.0000)	(9.3527)
Log(GDP)	0.1214	0.1800	−6.6217	0.2203
	(0.3811)	(0.4933)	(0.0000)	(0.4926)
Inflation	−0.0475	−0.1484	−45.8003	−0.1721
	(0.4666)	(0.4530)	(0.0000)	(0.4645)
M2_reserve	0.1466	−2.4797*	21.6464	−2.6337*
	(0.3573)	(1.3089)	(0.0000)	(1.3714)
Real interest	−1.1628	−0.5035	29.2760	−0.5415
	(2.5250)	(2.8508)	(0.0000)	(2.8854)
Real exchange rate overvaluation	0.0379	0.0263	3.8286	0.0258
	(0.0346)	(0.0425)	(0.0000)	(0.0430)
Current account surplus (% of GDP)	−12.3877	−16.5165	88.5961	−16.7613
	(7.5535)	(11.7872)	(0.0000)	(12.1869)
Financial development	0.0073	0.0111	0.1996	0.0077
	(0.0081)	(0.0113)	(0.0000)	(0.0102)
Gov_deficit	−0.0644	−0.0758	0.6441	−0.0828
	(0.0677)	(0.0798)	(0.0000)	(0.0811)
Predicted probabilities	1.50%	2.54%	1.64%	1.58%
Observations	315	311	312	314
No. of countries	45	45	45	45
R-squared	0.487	0.497	1.000	0.483

*** p<0.01
** p<0.05
* p<0.1
Note: Standard errors are in parentheses.
Source: Authors' estimations.

Four scenarios for China by 2020: Probability of financial crisis under different reform sequences

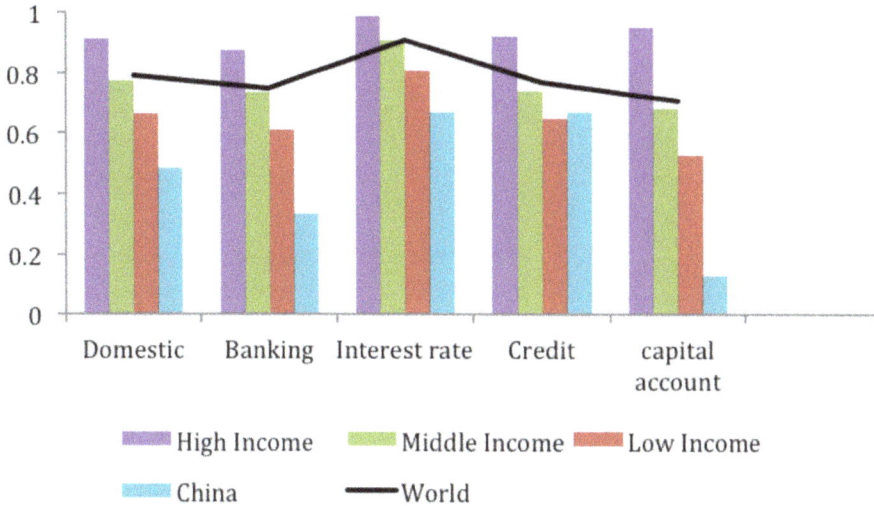

Figure 10.2 China's financial reform: Cross-country comparison

Sources: Abiad et al. (2008); and authors' calculations.

China's financial system is relatively repressed in several dimensions, even when compared with low-income economies, as shown in Figure 10.2. The degree of capital account opening and domestic financial system liberalisation, including the banking system, interest rate formation and credit allocation, is low.

China is on track to speed up implementation of market-oriented reforms in the financial system, both internally and externally. It is therefore important to understand whether the sequence of domestic financial reforms and capital account opening is important. To more specifically draw policy implications for China, we analyse a multi-country dataset to investigate how the sequence of financial reform affects financial risk.

Based on our empirical model and results, we also predict the probabilities of financial crisis under different scenarios of reform sequencing.

In the first instance, we explore the different sequences of domestic financial reforms as a whole and with capital account opening. We assume four related scenarios as follows:

- **Scenario one** assumes that capital account opening precedes liberalisation of the domestic financial system, and also that the capital account is opened in a single period following a big-bang pattern. Specifically, we assume

China fully liberalises the capital account to the average level of high-income economies in 2015 while domestic financial reform retains its present status.

- **Scenario two** assumes that capital account opening precedes liberalisation of the domestic financial system but capital account opening takes place gradually. Specifically, we assume that China gradually liberalises the capital account to the average current opening level of high-income economies by 2020 while putting domestic financial reforms on hold.

- **Scenario three** assumes that China gradually and concurrently liberalises the capital account and the domestic financial system to the current average opening level of high-income economies by 2020.

- **Scenario four** assumes that China liberalises its domestic financial system before achieving full capital account opening. Specifically, we assume that China gradually liberalises the domestic financial sector to the current average opening level of high-income economies by 2017, while gradually liberalising its capital account to the current average opening level of high-income economies by 2020.

The assumptions of all the other variables used in the perdition model are described in Appendix Table A10.3. Table 10.8 reports the predicted probabilities of experiencing a financial crisis in the years 2015–20 under the four scenarios. In our empirical model, the probability of crisis is regressed on lagged capital account opening and domestic financial reform variables—that is, reform in 2015 affects the crisis propensity in 2016, and so on.

Table 10.8 Scenario analysis: Sequence and speed of domestic financial reform and capital account opening–Percentage chance of experiencing crisis

Type of crisis	2015	2016	2018	2020	2016–20 average
Scenario 1: Big-bang reform of capital accounts in 2015 without domestic financial system reform					
Crisis	9	14	14	14	14
Banking crisis	8	11	11	11	11
Currency crisis	27	3	3	3	3
Sovereign debt crisis	7	10	10	10	10
Scenario 2: Gradual reform of capital accounts until 2020 without domestic financial system reform					
Crisis	9	10	12	14	12
Banking crisis	8	8	9	10	9
Currency crisis	2	2	3	3	3
Sovereign debt crisis	7	7	8	9	8
Scenario 3: Gradual reforms of both capital account and domestic financial system until 2020					
Crisis	9	9	8	6	7
Banking crisis	8	7	6	4	6
Currency crisis	2	2	2	1	1

Type of crisis	2015	2016	2018	2020	2016–20 average
Sovereign debt crisis	7	7	5	4	5
Scenario 4: Gradual reform of capital account until 2020 and gradual reform of domestic financial system until 2017 (achieving full liberalisation of domestic financial system earlier than of capital account)					
Crisis	9	7	5	5	6
Banking crisis	8	6	4	3	4
Currency crisis	2	2	1	1	1
Sovereign debt crisis	7	6	3	3	4

Source: Authors' summary.

Under scenario one, when a big-bang opening of the capital account takes place without additional reforms to the domestic financial system, the model predicts a big jump in the likelihood of China experiencing a financial crisis in 2015–16. The likelihood rises further—to 14 per cent—by 2020. Applying the same reform assumptions to each type of crisis delivers similar predictions. China is somewhat likely to experience a banking crisis and a sovereign debt crisis during 2016–20, with an average probability of 11 per cent and 10 per cent, respectively. Following the sequencing assumptions of scenario one would be relatively risky for China.

The model predicts smaller probabilities of experiencing each type of financial crisis under scenario two than under scenario one. The difference lies in the much more gradual capital account liberalisation for China, though the difference does not eliminate the probability of China experiencing a crisis. In scenario two, the likelihood of China experiencing a financial crisis is 12 per cent, on average, in 2016–20. Moreover, there is lower likelihood under these assumptions that China will experience a banking and sovereign debt crisis.

The picture changes dramatically under scenario three and scenario four. When China reforms its domestic financial system at least as soon as it reforms the capital account, the probability of crisis falls significantly. Compared with scenario two, China is assumed to gradually liberalise its domestic financial system concurrently with a gradual liberalisation of the capital account from 2015 to 2020. Reform of the domestic financial system appears to serve as a buffer against the risk of shocks, which then leads the likelihood of crisis to fall annually, and reach less than 6 per cent by 2020. China similarly faces a smaller likelihood of experiencing each type of crisis under scenario three.

Under scenario four, China realises full liberalisation of the domestic financial system in 2017, ahead of realising full liberalisation of the capital account, which happens in 2020. The model predicts that crisis probability falls to an average of 6 per cent. The likelihood of experiencing each type of crisis also decreases. In other words, a more liberalised domestic financial system, with a more competitive banking system, more liberalised interest rates and a more market-oriented credit allocation mechanism, serves to increase the overall stability of China's financial system.

Trends among the predicted probabilities of experiencing different types of financial crises are depicted in Figure 10.3. This shows clearly that from scenario one to scenario four, the probabilities decrease by year for each type of crisis from 2016. This offers striking evidence that gradual liberalisation in China's case would be safer than a big-bang reform of the capital account (see the difference between scenario two and one), and also that advanced or concurrent domestic financial system liberalisation would serve to buffer against capital account opening shocks and similarly to reduce related crisis probabilities (the difference between scenarios two and three). This is more clearly so where full domestic liberalisation is achieved in advance of capital account opening (the difference between scenarios three and four).

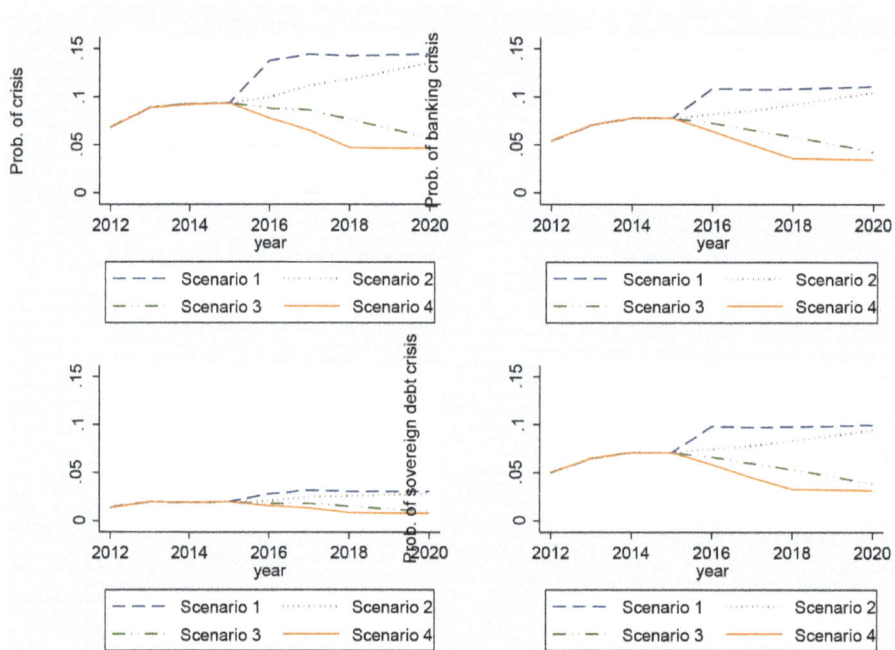

Figure 10.3 Scenario analysis: Domestic financial reform and capital account opening

Notes: Scenario one assumes big-bang reform of the capital account in 2015 without domestic financial system reform; scenario two assumes gradual reform of the capital account until 2020 without domestic financial system reform; scenario three assumes gradual reform of both the capital account and the domestic financial system until 2020; scenario four assumes gradual reform of the capital account until 2020 and gradual reform of the domestic financial system until 2017, which means China achieves full liberalisation of the domestic financial system earlier than of the capital account.
Source: Authors' summary.

We further examine the effects of different sequences and speeds for banking system reform and capital account opening. As before, we assume four scenarios and predict crisis probabilities. The only difference is that here we substitute reform of the whole domestic financial system for domestic banking sector reform. The predicted probabilities under four scenarios are depicted in Figure 10.4.

Figure 10.4 shows a similar pattern: from scenario one to scenario four, crisis probabilities become lower and lower. This again supports two propositions. First, gradual liberalisation is much safer than big-bang reform in capital account opening. Second, domestic banking system reform is important in reducing the financial risks of further capital account liberalisation.

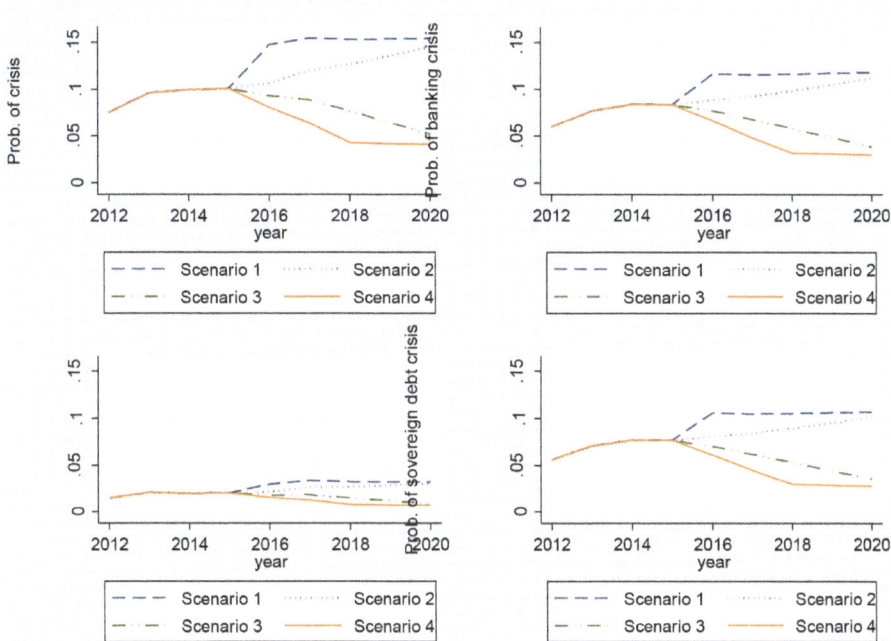

Figure 10.4 Scenario analysis: Banking system reform and capital account opening

Notes: Scenario one assumes big-bang reform of the capital account in 2015 without domestic banking system reform; scenario two assumes gradual reform of the capital account until 2020 without domestic banking system reform; scenario three assumes gradual reform of both the capital account and the domestic banking system until 2020; scenario four assumes gradual reform of the capital account until 2020 and gradual reform of the domestic banking system until 2017, which means China achieves full liberalisation of the domestic banking system earlier than of the capital account.
Source: Authors' summary.

Finally, we predict probabilities of crisis under similar scenarios for different sequences of credit allocation reform and capital account opening. The results are shown in Figure 10.5. Although the difference of the predicted crisis probabilities is smaller between different scenarios, scenarios three and four are still much safer policy paths than scenarios one and two. Therefore, gradual reform of the capital account and earlier domestic financial reform are important.

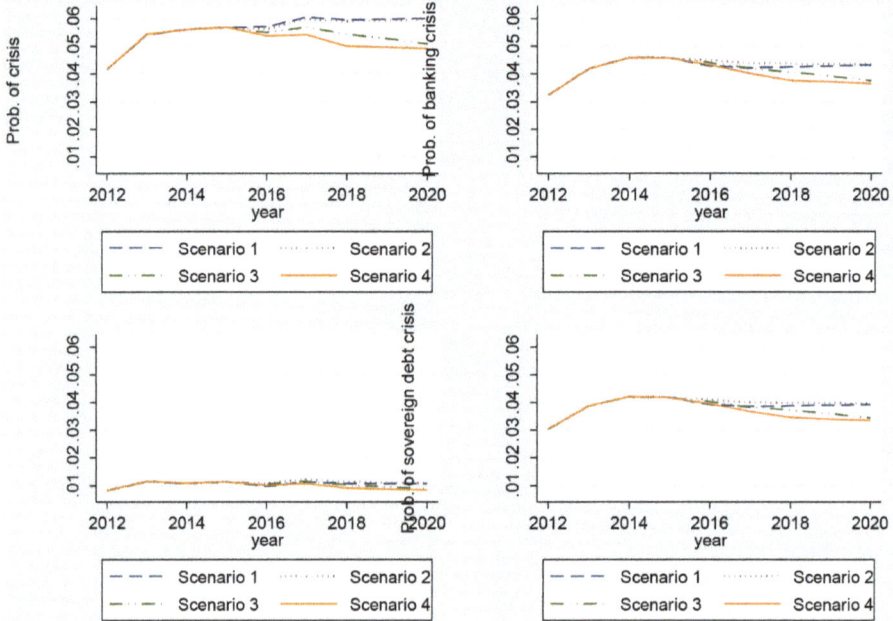

Figure 10.5 Scenario analysis: Credit allocation reform and capital account opening

Notes: Scenario one assumes big-bang reform of the capital account in 2015 without domestic credit allocation system reform; scenario two assumes gradual reform of the capital account until 2020 without domestic credit allocation system reform; scenario three assumes gradual reforms of both the capital account and the domestic credit allocation system until 2020; scenario four assumes gradual reform of the capital account until 2020 and gradual reform of the domestic credit allocation system until 2017, which means China achieves full liberalisation of the domestic credit allocation system earlier than of the capital account.
Source: Authors' summary.

In summary, the results suggest that the financial risks that China could suffer during the process of financial reform would be lower if China were to implement domestic financial system reform before capital account liberalisation, and also to achieve capital account liberalisation gradually. Among domestic financial system reforms, banking system reform appears to be especially important.

This refers to lowering banking market entry barriers, improving the equality of access to private capital, and strengthening the regulation and supervision of banks.

Conclusion

Within the financial liberalisation sequencing literature there are different schools of thought. In one, economists believe that the opening of the capital account should be the last step of economic liberalisation in transitional economies so as to avoid risks of financial instability—that is, policy sequencing should be used in the process of financial reform, meaning that domestic financial reform can be pursued in advance of full removal of capital controls. This relates to the fact that premature liberalisation of the capital account can invite excessive capital inflows that ultimately produce a boom–bust cycle in economies where the domestic financial sector is sufficiently distorted and constrained, or simply underdeveloped.

Another school of thought argues that trade reforms and capital account liberalisation should precede the entire process of economic reform because foreign competition and related spillovers reduce the resistance of interest groups that stand against domestic financial and other internal economic reforms. Finally, one group of economists believes that no sequence at all should be followed—that is, emerging market economies can undertake all reforms, domestic and external, simultaneously. This is because this dramatic reform strategy removes all market distortions in a single shot and therefore significantly reduces the costs associated with reforms and allows the benefits of reform to come earlier.

Using a cross-country panel dataset of 50 economies during the period 1973–2005, our empirical study identified substantial effects of the sequencing of financial reforms on the likelihood of an economy experiencing a financial crisis. Specifically, the liberalisation of the capital account can increase the likelihood of experiencing a crisis, while domestic financial system reforms reduce the risks of a crisis resulting from the potential volatility of an open capital account. Specifically, reform of the domestic banking sector and removal of credit controls tend to have a substantial impact on the mitigation of financial risks induced by capital account opening, while the impact of interest rate liberalisation remains unclear.

After three decades of economic transition that have left the financial sector comparatively untouched, China has pledged to deepen its financial sector reforms. At the Third Plenary meeting of the Eighteenth National Congress of the Chinese Communist Party in November 2013, a comprehensive plan for these reforms was announced, to take place from now until 2020. Among these reforms, financial sector liberalisation is obviously one of the more significant. Related policy areas include lowering market entrance to the banking sector, interest rate liberalisation, capital market development, establishment of a deposit insurance system, improvement of financial regulation, increased exchange rate flexibility and capital account convertibility. It is widely believed that success in financial sector reform is of great importance to China's structural adjustment and long-term economic development.

To reduce the associated risks and increase the chance of success of China's financial reforms, the right policy sequence is crucial. Our scenario analysis suggests that if China fully liberalises its capital account using a big-bang model in 2015 in the absence of sufficient domestic financial sector reform, especially reform of the banking sector, there is about a 14 per cent probability of experiencing a financial crisis during 2016–20. The likelihood falls to 12 per cent if China gradually liberalises its capital account, without domestic financial reforms. And, finally, gradual reform of the capital account combined with advanced completion of domestic financial reforms reduces the predicted probability of crisis—to 6 per cent during 2016–20 in our model.

Although there has been a strong push to fully liberalise the capital account, this study suggests that acceleration of domestic financial reforms is a more urgent task. Among others, state-owned banking reforms, interest rate liberalisation, together with building up a deposit insurance system and enhancing the role of capital markets, should be policy priorities. To maintain the independence of monetary policy and to mitigate currency speculation under a more open capital account, a significant increase in the flexibility of the renminbi exchange rate is also imperative.

A contrasting argument—one in favour of accelerating capital account liberalisation—is that it will benefit the process of renminbi internationalisation, and that this is good for building a new international monetary system as well as for China (Zhang and Tao 2015). It is true that a more open capital account is necessary for the internationalisation of the renminbi, particularly where the renminbi will serve as an international reserve currency. It is not necessarily the case, however, that there will be no progress on renminbi internationalisation until China has fully liberalised its capital account. The rapid development of the Hong Kong offshore renminbi market in recent years has shown that renminbi internationalisation can progress even where China retains selective capital controls. In fact, the euro dollar market in the 1950s and 1960s provides an interesting historical precedent for such a process. In that case, the US dollar became much more influential as an invoice and settlement currency through the offshore market, while the US domestic financial market retained many restrictions, including controls on cross-border capital movement.

Prudent strategy in capital account liberalisation is advised not only on the basis of this chapter's risk assessments, but also in the context of China's less stable macroeconomic situation. Risks include rapid increases in local government debt, a fragile shadow banking system and continuous cooling of the real estate market. Moreover, fake invoicing of cross-border trade transactions and fictional outward service payments have combined to allow capital flight in the past year or so. In the context of these potentially unstable macroeconomic and financial circumstances, the findings of this study suggest that rapid and full removal of capital controls could induce serious challenges to China's financial stability in the short run. Research towards better understanding the effects of financial policy sequencing on the soundness of financial opening, especially in the case of a large economy like China's, is required urgently.

References

Abiad, A., Detragiache, E. and Tressel, T. (2008), *A new database of financial reforms*, IMF Working Paper, Washington, DC: International Monetary Fund.

Bekaert, G., Harvey, C.R. and Lundblad, C. (2005), Does financial liberalization spur growth?, *Journal of Financial Economics*, 771: 3–55.

Bekaert, G., Harvey C.R. and Lundblad, C. (2006), Growth volatility and financial liberalization, *Journal of International Money and Finance*, 25: 370–403.

Bhagwati, J. (1998), Capital myth: The difference between trade in widgets and dollars, *Foreign Affairs*, 77: 7.

Cai, F. and Lu, Y. (2012), At what rate can the Chinese economy grow in the next 10 years?, in Chen, J., Li Y., Liu S. and Wang T. (eds), *Chinese economy blue cover book 2012* [in Chinese], Beijing: Social Science Literature Press.

Central Committee of the Chinese Communist Party (2013), The decision on major issues concerning comprehensively deepening reforms (in brief), *China Daily*, 16 November.

Choksi, A. and Papageorgiou, D. (eds) (1986), *Economic liberalization in developing countries*, New York: Basil Blackwell.

Edison, H.J., Levine, R., Ricci, L. and Sløk, T. (2002), International financial integration and economic growth, *Journal of International Money and Finance*, 216: 749–76.

Edwards, S. (1984), *The order of liberalization of the external sector in developing countries*, Princeton Essays in International Finance No. 156, December, Princeton, NJ: International Finance Section, Princeton University.

Edwards, S. (1990), The sequencing of economic reform: Analytical issues and lessons from Latin American experiences, *The World Economy*, 13(1): 1–14.

Edwards, S. (2007), Capital controls, sudden stops, and current account reversals, in *Capital controls and capital flows in emerging economies: Policies, practices and consequences*, Chicago: University of Chicago Press, pp. 73–120.

Edwards, S. (2008), Financial openness, currency crises, and output losses, in *Financial markets volatility and performance in emerging markets*, Chicago: University of Chicago Press, pp. 97–120.

Edwards, S. (2009), Sequencing of reforms, financial globalization, and macroeconomic vulnerability, *Journal of the Japanese and International Economies*, 23(2): 131–48.

Funke, M. (1993), Timing and sequencing of reforms: Competing views and the role of credibility, *Kyklos*, 46(3): 337–62.

Ghosh, A.R., Ostry, J.D. and Mahvash, S.Q. (2014), *Exchange rate management and crisis susceptibility: A reassessment*, IMF Working Papers 14/11, Washington, DC: International Monetary Fund.

Glick, R. and Hutchison, M.M. (2001), Banking and currency crises: How common are twins?, in Glick, R., Moreno, R. and Spiegel, M.M. (eds), *Financial crises in emerging markets*, New York: Cambridge University Press.

Glick, R., Guo, X. and Hutchison, M. (2006), Currency crises, capital-account liberalization, and selection bias, *The Review of Economics and Statistics*, 884: 698–714.

Hauner, D. and Prati, A. (2008), *Openness and domestic financial liberalization: Which comes first?*, IMF Working Paper, Washington, DC: International Monetary Fund.

Hutchison, M.M. and Noy, I. (2005), How bad are twins? Output costs of currency and banking crises, *Journal of Money, Credit and Banking*: 725–52.

Ilzetzki, E.O., Reinhart, C.M. and Rogoff, K.S. (2011), Exchange rate arrangements entering the 21st century: Which anchor will hold?. Available from: www.wam.umd.edu/~creinhar.

International Monetary Fund (IMF) (2003), *World economic outlook, April 2003: Growth and institutions. World economic and financial surveys*, Washington, DC: International Monetary Fund.

International Monetary Fund (IMF) (2012), Sequencing financial sector reform, in *Financial sector assessment: A handbook*, Washington, DC: International Monetary Fund. Available from: www.imf.org/external/pubs/ft/fsa/eng/pdf/ch12.pdf.

International Monetary Fund (IMF) (2014), *Annual report on exchange arrangements and exchange restrictions*, Washington, DC: International Monetary Fund.

Kose, M.A., Prasad, R., Rogoff, K. and Wei, S.J. (2009), *Financial globalization: A reappraisal*, IMF Staff Papers 561, Washington, DC: International Monetary Fund, pp. 8–62.

Laeven, L. and Valencia, F. (2013), Systemic banking crises database, *IMF Economic Review*, 61(2): 225–70.

Lardy, N. and Douglass, P. (2011), *Capital account liberalization and the role of the renminbi*, Working Paper 11-6, Washington, DC: Peterson Institute for International Economics.

Levy Yeyati, E., Schmukler, S.L. and van Horen, N. (2009), International financial integration through the law of one price: The role of liquidity and capital controls, *Journal of Financial Intermediation*, 183: 432–63.

McKinnon, R.I. (1973), *Money and capital in economic development*, Washington, DC: The Brookings Institution.

McKinnon, R.I. (1993), *The order of economic liberalization: Financial control in the transition to a market economy*, Baltimore: Johns Hopkins University Press.

Obstfeld, M. and Taylor, A.M. (2004), *Global capital markets: Integration, crisis, and growth*, Cambridge: Cambridge University Press.

Prasad, E., Rumbaugh, T. and Wang, Q. (2005), *Putting the cart before the horse? Capital account liberalization and exchange rate flexibility in China*, IMF Policy Discussion Paper No. 05/1, Washington, DC: International Monetary Fund.

Qin, X. and Luo, C. (2014), Capital account openness and early warning system for banking crises in G20 countries, *Economic Modelling*, 39: 190–4.

Quinn, D. and Toyoda, A.M. (2008), Does capital account liberalization lead to growth?, *Review of Financial Studies*, 21: 1403–49.

Quirk, P.J. and Evans, O. (1995), *Capital account convertibility: Review of experience and implications for IMF policies*, IMF Occasional Paper No. 131, Washington, DC: International Monetary Fund.

Rajan, R.G. and Zingales, L. (2003), The great reversals: The politics of financial development in the twentieth century, *Journal of Financial Economics*, 69: 5–50.

Rodrik, D. (1998), *Who needs capital-account convertibility?*, Essays in International Finance No. 207, Princeton, NJ: International Finance Section, Economics Department, Princeton University.

Stiglitz, J.E. (2002), *Globalization and its discontents*, New York: W.W. Norton.

World Bank (2001), *Finance for growth: Policy choices in a volatile world*, World Bank Policy Research Report, New York: The World Bank and Oxford University Press.

World Bank (2014), *World development indicators*, Washington, DC: The World Bank.

Yu, Y. (2013), *China's capital account liberalization*, PAFTAD Working Paper Series, Canberra: Pacific Trade and Development Conference.

Zhang, L. and Tao, K. (2015), The benefits and costs of renminbi internationalization, in Eichengreen, B. and Kawai, M. (eds), *Renminbi internationalization: Achievements, prospects, and challenges*, Washington, DC: Brookings Institution Press and Asian Development Bank.

Appendix

Table A10.1 Variables definition and data sources

Variable	Definition	Source
Crisis	Dummy variable taking a value of one if at least one of systemic banking, currency or sovereign debt crisis arises, and zero otherwise	Laeven and Valencia (2013)
Banking crisis	A systemic banking crisis is defined as either a significant sign of financial distress in the banking system or a severe banking policy intervention. A dummy variable is equal to one where any of these arise, and zero otherwise	Laeven and Valencia (2013)
Currency crisis	A currency crisis is defined as a nominal depreciation of the currency against the US dollar of at least 30 per cent that is also at least 10 percentage points higher than the rate of depreciation in the preceding year. A dummy variable is equal to one in these cases, and zero otherwise	Laeven and Valencia (2013)
Sovereign debt crisis	A sovereign debt crisis is defined as a sovereign debt default and where there is a need for sovereign debt restructuring. A dummy variable is equal to one in these cases, and zero otherwise	Laeven and Valencia (2013)

Variable	Definition	Source
Kaopen	Measures the degree of liberalisation of the capital account	Quinn and Toyoda (2008)
Kaopen2	A measure of the degree of liberalisation of the capital account	Abiad et al. (2008)
Fin_domestic	Captures domestic financial reform along five different dimensions: credit controls and reserve requirements, interest rate controls, entry barriers, state ownership, and banking regulations	Abiad et al. (2008)
Fin_bank	A measure of banking system reform, including entry barriers to the banking sector, state ownership of banks and regulations, and supervision of the banking sector	Abiad et al. (2008)
Fin_interest	A measure of the liberalisation of the interest rate	Abiad et al. (2008)
Fin_credit	A measure of the liberalisation of credit allocation	Abiad et al. (2008)
Fixed EXR	A dummy variable equal to one in cases of a fixed exchange rate regime, defined to include classification of 1) no separate legal tender; and 2) a pre-announced peg or currency board arrangement, and equal to zero otherwise	Ilzetzki et al. (2011)
Intermediate EXR	A dummy variable indicating an intermediate exchange rate regime, defined to include classification of 3, pre-announced horizontal band ≤ +/−2%; 4, de facto peg; 5, pre-announced crawling peg; 6, pre-announced crawling band ≤ +/−2%; 7, de facto crawling peg; 8, de facto crawling band ≤ +/−2%; 9, pre-announced crawling band ≥ +/−2%; 10, de facto crawling band ≤ +/−5%; 11, moving band ≤ +/−2%; and 12, managed floating	Ilzetzki et al. (2011)
Float EXR	Dummy variable indicating a floating exchange rate regime. It includes classification of 13, freely floating	Ilzetzki et al. (2011)
GGDP	Growth rate of real GDP per capita (purchasing power parity)	World Bank (2014)
LogGDPP	Log term of real GDP per capita (purchasing power parity)	World Bank (2014)
Inflation	Inflation rate as measured by the consumer price index	World Bank (2014)
M2_reserve	M2/reserve	World Bank (2014)
Real interest	Real interest rate	World Bank (2014)
Real exchange rate overvaluation	Deviation of real effective exchange rate from trend (obtained from HP filter, smoothing parameter 100)	World Bank (2014)
Current account surplus	The surplus of current account/GDP	World Bank (2014)
Financial development	Private credit/GDP	World Bank (2014)
Gov_deficit	Government fiscal deficit/GDP	World Bank (2014)

Table A10.2 Statistical description of variables

Variable	Obs	Mean	Median	Std dev.	Min.	Max.
Crisis	820	0.05	0	0.21	0	1
Banking crisis	796	0.03	0	0.17	0	1
Currency crisis	800	0.02	0	0.14	0	1
Sovereign debt crisis	816	0.03	0	0.17	0	1
Kaopen	820	0.74	0	0.27	0.125	1
Kaopen2	820	0.74	1	0.35	0	3
Fin_domestic	820	0.66	0.73	0.26	0	1
Fin_bank	820	0.59	0.67	0.29	0	1
Fin_interest	820	0.82	1	0.34	0	3
Fin_credit	820	0.69	0.67	0.32	0	3
Fixed EXR	820	0.14	0	0.34	0	1
Intermediate EXR	820	0.74	1	0.44	0	1
GGDP	820	0.02	0.02	0.04	−0.15	0.30
LogGDPP	820	8.69	9.31	1.48	5.13	10.61
Inflation	820	0.09	0.05	0.39	−0.03	10.58
M2_reserve	820	0.06	0.01	0.38	−0.94	3.58
Real interest	820	0.07	0.06	0.10	−0.71	0.94
Real exchange rate overvaluation	820	−8.94	−0.06	102.71	−1,678.56	153.44
Current account surplus	820	−0.01	−0.01	0.06	−0.18	0.33
Financial development	816	58.05	49.48	40.61	2.21	196.48
Gov_deficit	286	0.42	0.41	4.60	−15.79	11.26

Note: The definition and data source of each variable correspond with those described in Table A10.1.

Table A10.3 Assumptions for projecting financial crisis

Variable	Assumption
Kaopen	The index from Quinn and Toyoda (2008) is updated only until 2011. According to the IMF's *AREAER* (IMF 2014), China has only had one major policy change in the capital account transactions from 2012 to 2014, which was the relaxing of controls on derivatives and other instruments. Using this as a reference, we augment the Quinn and Toyoda (2008) database for 2011–14, via a marginal increase in China's capital account opening score, from 0.5 in 2011 to 0.55 in 2014. From 2015 to 2020, this is assumed to follow each of four scenarios, which are described in detail in section four
Fin_bank	The index from Abiad et al. (2008) is updated only up to 2005. We update the series, including an adjustment to the banking sector-controlling index proportionally to reflect the large state-owned banks' market share of loans from 2005 to 2014, as sourced from the China Banking Regulatory Commission. From 2015 to 2020, this is assumed to follow each of four scenarios, which are described in detail in section four

Variable	Assumption
Fin_interest	The index from Abiad et al. (2008) is updated only to 2005. We adjust the interest rate liberalisation index to 2.25 in 2014 from 2.0 in 2005—an augmentation that reflects the expansive floating range of the interest rate in 2012 and the removal of the floor on the baseline loan rate in 2013
Fin_credit	The index from Abiad et al. (2008) is updated only to 2005. We adjust the credit liberalisation index to 2.5 in 2014 from 2.25 in 2005. From 2015 to 2020, this is assumed to follow each of four scenarios, which are described in detail in section four
Fin_domestic	We update the index based on the updated index of banking, interest rate and credit controls to 2014. From 2015 to 2020, this is assumed to follow each of four scenarios, which are described in detail in section four
Intermediate EXR	We assume China maintains its current exchange rate regime until 2020
GGDP	The World Bank (2014) reports data until 2013. Growth rate of GDP per capita data for 2014 are obtained from the National Bureau of Statistics. We assume the GDP per capita growth rate will be 7 per cent in 2015 and 6.1 per cent from 2016 to 2020, based on Cai and Lu (2012)
LogGDPP	We predict GDP per capita during 2015–20 according to the predicted growth rate of GDP per capita based on Cai and Lu (2012)
Inflation	The World Bank (2014) reports data until 2013. We assume an inflation rate of 2.6 per cent from 2015 to 2020, which is average inflation between 2008 and 2013, and obtain the inflation rate for 2014 from the National Bureau of Statistics
M2_reserve	The World Bank (2014) reports data until 2013. From 2014 to 2020, we assume the ratio of M2 over reserves will grow at 2.5 per cent year-on-year, which is the average growth of the ratio between 2008 and 2013
Real interest	The World Bank (2014) reports data until 2013. We assume the rate to be 4.2 per cent from 2014 to 2020 onwards, which is the rate in 2013
Real exchange rate overvaluation	The World Bank (2014) reports data until 2013. We assume this rate to be 0.74 annually from 2014 to 2020, the period average value from 2008 to 2013
Current account surplus	The World Bank (2014) reports data until 2013. For 2014, we use data directly from the National Bureau of Statistics. Global economic prospects from the World Bank indicators predict the ratio of China's current account surplus over GDP until 2017, which is 2 per cent. And we assume it stays constant from 2018 to 2020
Financial development	The World Bank (2014) reports data until 2013. From 2014 to 2020, we assume the ratio of credit over GDP will grow at 1.27 per cent year-on-year, which is the average growth of the ratio between 2004 and 2013

11. The Offshore Renminbi Market and Renminbi Internationalisation

William Nixon, Eden Hatzvi and Michelle Wright[1]

Introduction

The status of the Chinese renminbi (RMB) as an 'international' currency has developed considerably over recent years. This is evidenced by the increasing use of the RMB as a settlement currency for transactions between Chinese residents and non-residents. To date, the internationalisation process has been largely policy-driven. Chinese authorities are, for example, actively encouraging residents to increase their use of RMB in international trade transactions and, more recently, providing non-residents with greater access to RMB investment in the Chinese mainland (and vice versa).

It is apparent, however, that there is still a considerable way to go before the RMB becomes a truly international currency. The RMB, for example, is not yet widely used in transactions between non-residents—a key reason for which is that China's capital account remains partially closed. It follows, then, that the success of the RMB internationalisation agenda will be determined in large part by China's broader path towards capital account liberalisation. That said, the development of an offshore RMB market is also an important part of this process, in that it provides ready access to RMB for use in transactions between non-residents—should there be demand to do so.

There are a number of motivations for RMB internationalisation. One of these is largely symbolic—namely, to ensure that the international usage of the RMB better reflects China's global economic weight. But there are also some other, more direct benefits that could be associated with RMB internationalisation. In particular, greater international usage of the RMB may reduce the currency risk and cost of international trade for Chinese exporters and importers (Frankel 2012). More specifically, if Chinese residents are able to *invoice* their cross-border transactions in local currency, they will be less exposed to increasing exchange

---

1   The authors are from the International Department of the Reserve Bank of Australia. The views expressed in this chapter are the authors' own and do not necessarily reflect those of the Reserve Bank of Australia. The authors are solely responsible for any errors.

rate volatility if China continues to transition from a managed to a freely floating exchange rate regime. This could help to alleviate some of the 'fear of floating' concerns that can arise for many emerging economies during the capital account and exchange rate liberalisation process (Calvo and Reinhart 2002). Further, if Chinese residents are able to *settle* cross-border transactions in RMB, they will be able to avoid the transaction costs associated with converting RMB into foreign currency (and vice versa).

RMB internationalisation thus also has the potential to reduce the aggregate currency mismatch on China's international balance sheet. As outlined in Cheung et al. (2011), the combination of China's large and persistent current account surpluses, its managed exchange rate regime and its openness to (mostly RMB-denominated) foreign direct investment (FDI) has led to a large—and rapidly increasing—long foreign currency position. By internationalising the RMB, Chinese residents can potentially increase their RMB-denominated claims on the rest of the world, which would diversify the currency risk embedded in China's overall international asset position.

A final possible motivation for RMB internationalisation is related to there being a close link between RMB internationalisation and capital account liberalisation. Policy initiatives that seek to internationalise the RMB may also have the effect of increasing the flow of RMB between the onshore and offshore markets. Given that there continues to be some debate in China about the merits of capital account liberalisation per se, some commentators consider the goal of RMB internationalisation to be a politically more palatable way for proponents of capital account liberalisation to achieve this objective (Yu 2014).

In light of the important role played by the offshore RMB market in facilitating China's progress towards currency internationalisation, this chapter begins with a brief overview of the features of the offshore market in section two. Drawing on Hatzvi et al. (2014), the chapter then outlines a range of recent policy initiatives that seek to further develop the offshore market, in section three, before discussing their implications for various metrics of RMB internationalisation in section four.

Although there has been significant progress in internationalising the RMB, this does not yet appear to have translated into a reduction in currency mismatch. This conclusion, consistent with Cheung et al. (2011), is explored further in section five. We specifically propose that the internationalisation of the RMB to date could have actually increased the currency mismatch on China's international balance sheet, as the widely held perception (until recently) that the RMB would continue to appreciate steadily against the US dollar is likely to have discouraged non-residents from denominating their liabilities in RMB. However, we also suggest that, in the future, there may be some scaling back in these expectations; indeed, there has already been some evidence of this throughout much of 2014 and 2015. If increased two-way flexibility in the RMB is sustained, this could mean that the RMB internationalisation process may become increasingly associated with a reduction in China's long US dollar position over time.

Overview of the offshore RMB market

Since the announcement of a pilot scheme for RMB trade settlement in mid-2009, the Chinese authorities have been gradually easing restrictions on the use of RMB outside mainland China. Since mid-2010, the original RMB trade settlement scheme has specifically been expanded to encompass all trade between China and the rest of world, and the RMB has also become fully convertible *outside* China. This has enabled the creation of a pool of RMB outside the mainland and the development of an offshore RMB market.

Hong Kong initially provided the sole connection between the onshore RMB market and the rest of the world, making it the primary hub of offshore RMB activity. In recent years, several additional official offshore 'RMB centres' have emerged. Although the flow of RMB between the Chinese mainland and the offshore market remains subject to a number of restrictions, RMB is permitted to flow freely *between* the various official offshore centres, which means that the offshore RMB market is best described as comprising the sum of all activity in these centres (even though most offshore RMB activity continues to occur in Hong Kong). Given that the offshore pool of RMB is freely accessible to market participants outside mainland China, the offshore RMB market can be thought of as providing an environment in which a range of RMB banking products can be developed and in which firms outside mainland China can begin to use the currency, even if they do not have direct access to the onshore market. The ultimate source of both onshore and offshore RMB, however, remains the People's Bank of China (PBC).

There are three main channels through which the size of the offshore pool of RMB can change: trade, income and capital flows (described in further detail in Table 11.1).[2] To date, RMB payments by Chinese importers have been the primary source of RMB liquidity for the offshore market. This is not surprising, as foreign exporters have an incentive to receive RMB from their Chinese counterparts so long as there is an expectation that the RMB will continue to appreciate (discussed further in section five).

---

2 This abstracts from the money multiplier effect where RMB loans offshore would increase the amount of offshore RMB deposits. There are also 'informal' channels that are created by attempts to evade existing capital controls.

Table 11.1 RMB flows between mainland China and the offshore market

	Current account		Capital account	
	Trade in goods and services	Income flows	Direct and portfolio investment	Other
Flows to offshore market	Chinese importers paying offshore exporters Chinese tourists converting RMB abroad	Individuals' remittances Corporate cross-border RMB 'pooling'	RMB-denominated FDI Shanghai–Hong Kong Stock Connect program RMB Qualified Domestic Institutional Investor program	Foreign central banks activating currency swaps with PBC Cross-border RMB loans
Flows to mainland China	Offshore importers paying Chinese exporters Foreign tourists converting RMB outside China for use in the mainland	Individuals' remittances Corporate cross-border RMB 'pooling' Repatriated dim sum bond issuance[a]	RMB-denominated overseas direct investment Shanghai–Hong Kong Stock Connect program RMB Qualified Institutional Investor program	Foreign central banks unwinding currency swaps with PBC Cross-border RMB loans

[a] Issuance of RMB-denominated bonds in the offshore market, where the funds raised are repatriated back to the mainland. 'Panda' bonds are where foreign firms issue bonds in mainland China, but these cannot generally be repatriated offshore.
Source: Authors' own summary.

Although the capital account liberalisation process to date has led to an increase in RMB-denominated capital flows, the onshore and offshore pools of RMB continue to be partly separated by the capital controls that remain in place. This also means that there are two distinct exchange rates for the RMB: the onshore spot rate (where RMB is denoted as yuan, CNY), which is managed by the PBC and is accessible only to participants in the mainland market; and the spot rate in offshore markets—the most important of which is Hong Kong (where RMB is denoted CNH)—which is freely floating and accessible to all offshore participants.[3] The offshore rate tends to track the onshore rate relatively closely, although the two rates can diverge at times (Figure 11.1).

---

3   Other offshore centres sometimes refer to their own exchange rate—for example, CNT is used to define RMB exchange rates in Taiwan. However, as there are few restrictions on the flow of RMB offshore, the value of offshore RMB should be equivalent at any point regardless of the location within the offshore market.

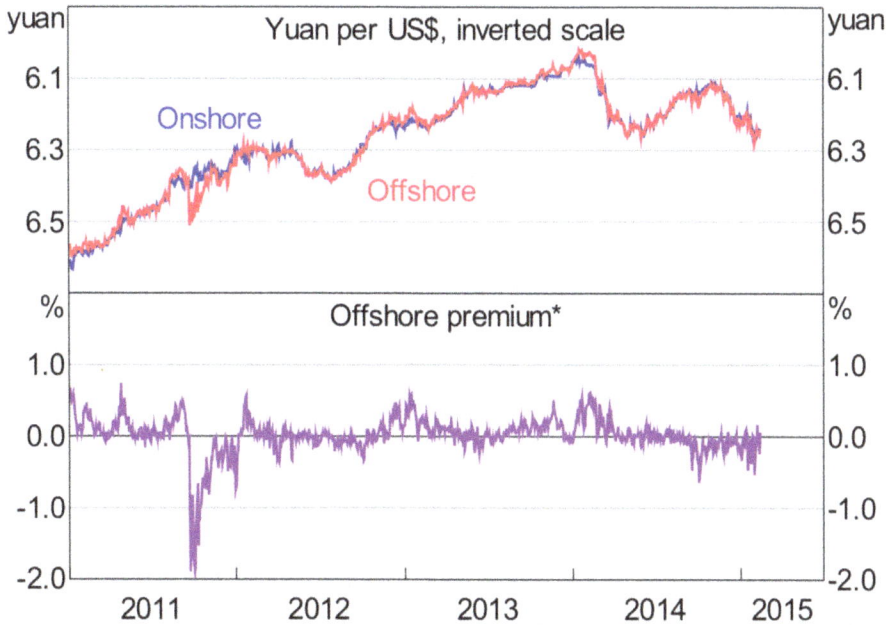

Figure 11.1 Chinese renminbi (RMB per US dollar, inverted scale)

* Negative spread indicates that US$1 buys more RMB offshore than onshore.
Sources: Bloomberg; RBA.

Recent policy initiatives in the offshore RMB market

In recent years, a range of policy initiatives has been introduced to further develop the offshore RMB market. These include initiatives that are designed to increase the efficiency of payment system linkages between the onshore and offshore markets—most notably through the establishment of official RMB clearing banks. Other such initiatives seek to increase non-resident participation in RMB markets, such as the Renminbi Qualified Foreign Institutional Investor (RQFII) program, central bank investment in RMB assets, cross-border RMB lending schemes and, most recently, the Shanghai–Hong Kong Stock Connect program.

Official RMB clearing banks

As with any currency, with the RMB, international use requires the cooperation of domestic banks in China. In particular, offshore banks need access to clearing balances with onshore banks in order to facilitate RMB transactions in the offshore market.

With that in mind, the internationalisation of the RMB began in late 2003 when the Chinese authorities appointed the Bank of China, Hong Kong (BOCHK), the first official 'RMB clearing bank' outside mainland China. This meant BOCHK could accept RMB deposits from offshore banks and place them with the PBC's Shenzhen sub-branch. In turn, BOCHK could clear and settle RMB transactions in the offshore market. As part of its clearing bank status, BOCHK was also granted a quota to transact directly within China's onshore interbank foreign exchange (FX) market, enabling it to square foreign currency positions arising from 'participating' bank transactions.[4] Alongside BOCHK's new rights, foreign branches and subsidiaries of mainland Chinese banks began to offer 'correspondent' banking services to offshore banks. Those services provide offshore banks with an additional channel via which to clear and settle RMB transactions with their mainland Chinese counterparts, essentially by allowing offshore banks to open RMB accounts at banks in mainland China.

In recent years, the Chinese authorities have designated official RMB clearing banks in a wide range of jurisdictions outside Hong Kong. As of April 2015, there were 15 official clearing banks worldwide, all of which are offshore branches of Chinese banks, including one in Australia (Table 11.2). The primary purpose of these clearing banks is to facilitate cross-border RMB payments between the onshore and offshore RMB markets, and within the offshore market itself. Similar to BOCHK, these clearing banks are permitted to maintain onshore RMB balances to facilitate RMB transactions on behalf of their local participating banks. They also have more direct access to RMB liquidity from the PBC and are permitted to transact directly within China's onshore interbank foreign exchange market, subject to a quota.

Table 11.2 RMB clearing banks, as of 4 May 2015

Centre	Date announced	Bank
Hong Kong	Dec 2003	Bank of China
Macau	Jun 2004	Bank of China
Taipei	Dec 2012	Bank of China
Singapore	Feb 2013	ICBC
London	Mar 2014	China Construction Bank
Frankfurt	Mar 2014	Bank of China
Luxembourg	Jun 2014	ICBC
Paris	Jun 2014	Bank of China
Seoul	Jul 2014	Bank of Communications
Doha	Nov 2014	ICBC

---

4 Participating banks hold accounts with a clearing bank for the purpose of clearing RMB transactions.

Centre	Date announced	Bank
Toronto	Nov 2014	Bank of China
Kuala Lumpur	Nov 2014	Bank of China
Sydney	Nov 2014	Bank of China
Bangkok	Dec 2014	ICBC
Zurich	Jan 2015	–

Sources: RBA; SAFE.

Prior to the establishment of RMB clearing banks in these other offshore centres, local banks were able to effect RMB transactions through two channels: by participating in another offshore clearing bank's payments system (most likely BOCHK); or by making use of 'correspondent banking' relationships with banks in mainland China (discussed above). The primary benefit of using a *local* official clearing bank rather than a non-local offshore clearing bank or a correspondent banking relationship is that it can provide a more direct method of effecting payments (for example, a reduction in settlement delays). Over time, this could improve the efficiency and/or lower the transaction costs of such payments. The official status of these clearing banks also means that they play an important symbolic role in establishing recognised offshore RMB centres, especially by raising awareness and confidence among firms in these jurisdictions about their local financial sectors' capacity to facilitate RMB transactions.

That said, it is possible that the role of clearing banks (along with the other alternative mechanisms for effecting cross-border RMB payments) could diminish over time. Chinese authorities are in the process of developing the China International Payments System (CIPS), which is expected to give *all* offshore banks the opportunity to acquire access to China's domestic payments system and foreign exchange market. The development of CIPS, therefore, has the potential to foster significant further development of the offshore market. The process, however, may take some time to complete. Hence, offshore RMB clearing banks are likely to play a central role in connecting offshore financial institutions and their non-financial customers to their counterparts in China for some time yet.

Central bank initiatives

Central banks have also undertaken a number of initiatives that seek to support the development of the offshore RMB market, including bilateral currency swap agreements, RMB liquidity facilities and RMB investments.

The PBC has, as of February 2015, signed bilateral currency swap agreements with 28 central banks (Figure 11.2). Under these agreements, foreign central banks can exchange their local currency for RMB with the PBC (that is, RMB obtained from the onshore market) for mutually agreed purposes. This enables foreign central banks to provide RMB liquidity to the offshore market during times of market stress or, in some cases, simply to promote the development of the offshore RMB market. By providing an assurance that market participants can approach their local central bank to access RMB liquidity if required, central bank swap lines support the development of the local RMB market. Swap lines range in size from RMB700 million (Uzbekistan) to RMB400 billion (Hong Kong). There is relatively little publicly available information on the extent to which these swap lines have been activated. It is, however, known that Hong Kong, Singapore, South Korea and Argentina have all activated their swap lines (for non-test purposes).

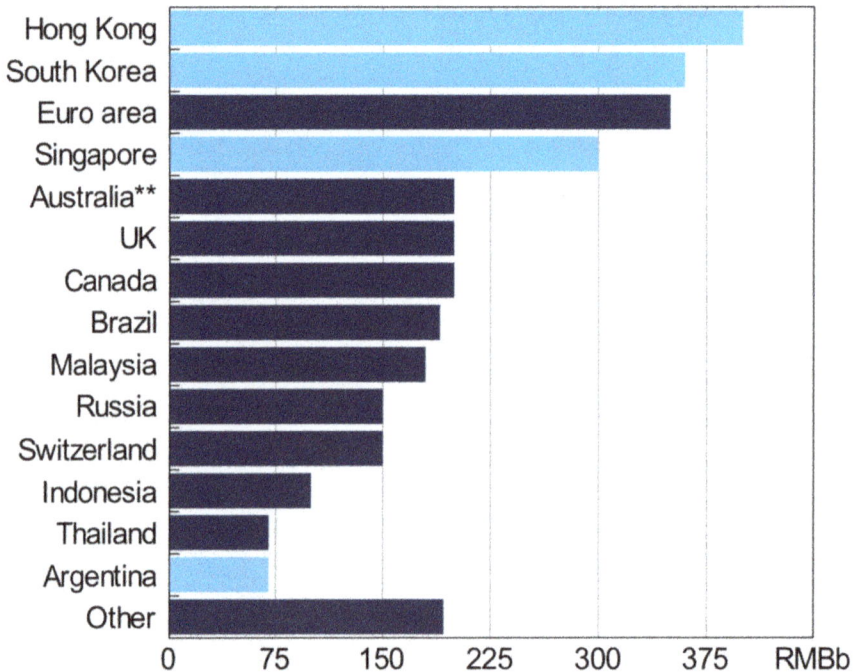

Figure 11.2 PBC local currency swap agreements

Note: A light-blue bar indicates that some portion of the swap line has been activated as of February 2015 (based on publicly available information).
Sources: PBC; RBA.

Some central banks have also established RMB liquidity facilities to provide short-term RMB funds to offshore market participants, in some cases using their swap agreements with the PBC. These additional measures are designed to further ensure market participants have confidence in the availability of liquidity in the offshore RMB market. Specifically, the Hong Kong Monetary Authority (HKMA) and the Monetary Authority of Singapore (MAS) both offer eligible financial institutions access to overnight RMB loans. The MAS also allows participants in Singapore's payments system to access three-month RMB loans for trade-related purposes. Further, in anticipation of additional demand for offshore RMB following the launch of the Shanghai–Hong Kong Stock Connect program (discussed below), the HKMA has introduced an *intraday* RMB repurchase agreement (repo) facility to provide up to RMB10 billion to banks in Hong Kong.[5]

In recent years, at least 40 central banks have also begun to invest a portion of their foreign exchange reserves in RMB-denominated assets (BOCHK 2014). For example, the Reserve Bank of Australia (RBA) now holds 5 per cent of its total foreign exchange reserves in RMB-denominated assets (RBA 2014).[6] While this does not directly influence the offshore RMB market per se, as these reserves are typically held in the form of RMB-denominated assets in mainland China, it is an important component of the broader RMB internationalisation process. Reserve asset holdings are a key characteristic of an international currency.

The RMB Qualified Foreign Institutional Investor (RQFII) program

The expansion in the number of official RMB clearing banks and currency swap agreements should increase demand for offshore RMB by increasing market participants' confidence that cross-border RMB transactions can be effected efficiently and predictably. Chinese authorities have recently taken a number of further steps to increase the investment options available to offshore holders of RMB, and thereby support the development of the market by increasing market participants' willingness to take on RMB exposures. For example, offshore RMB can now be used to make investments in mainland China, primarily via the RQFII program. This allows approved foreign investors to buy and sell designated assets in China's onshore equity and bond markets. The RQFII program can thus be thought of both as being part of China's broader capital account liberalisation process and as an initiative that is designed to encourage broader participation in the offshore RMB market.

Importantly, the RQFII program is only available to investors with operations in a jurisdiction that has been granted an RQFII quota by the Chinese authorities. The RQFII program was initially made available only to Hong Kong-domiciled

---

5   Additionally, the HKMA designated a number of banks as primary liquidity providers (PLPs). The HKMA will offer PLPs an RMB repo line (to obtain both intraday and overnight funds) to ensure that they have sufficient liquidity available to perform market-making functions in Hong Kong's offshore market.

6   The Reserve Bank's investment makes use of a scheme commonly known as the China Interbank Bond Market scheme, which is separate to the QFII and RQFII programs (discussed below) and is typically used by central banks and sovereign wealth funds.

investors, with a quota of RMB20 billion granted in 2011. Hong Kong's quota has since been incrementally raised to RMB270 billion. From the middle of 2013 to April 2015, RQFII quotas totalling RMB600 billion (A\$123 billion) have also been granted to a range of other offshore centres, including Australia (Table 11.3).

Table 11.3 RQFII quotas, as at 4 May 2015

Centre	Quota (RMB b)	Date announced	Allocation to date[a] (RMB b)
Hong Kong	270	Dec 2011	270.0
Singapore	50	Oct 2013	26.0
United Kingdom	80	Oct 2013	15.2
France	80	Mar 2014	6.0
Germany	80	Jul 2014	6.0
South Korea	80	Jul 2014	30.5
Qatar	30	Nov 2014	n.a.[b]
Canada	50	Nov 2014	n.a.
Australia	50	Nov 2014	10.0
Switzerland	50	Jan 2015	n.a.
Luxembourg	50	Apr 2015	n.a.

[a] The activation of Taiwan's RQFII quota is conditional on the finalisation of the Cross-Strait Trade in Service Agreement.
[b] n.a. = not applicable.
Sources: PBC; SAFE.

As of April 2015, about 80 Hong Kong-domiciled entities had been granted RQFII licences. Outside Hong Kong, about 40 firms have acquired quotas, although more are in the process of applying (the process typically takes about six months). Once a firm has acquired a quota, it is able to offer RMB investment products to a broad range of investors, including those located outside its original jurisdiction. For example, some Hong Kong-domiciled firms have partnered with US and Europe-domiciled financial institutions to launch exchange-traded funds on foreign stock exchanges, including the New York Stock Exchange and the London Stock Exchange. This allows investors without an RQFII quota to gain exposure to China's equity and bond markets.

The RQFII program is in addition to the Qualified Foreign Institutional Investor (QFII) program, which has been in place since 2003. The QFII program permits approved foreign investors to use *foreign currency* to invest in designated Chinese financial assets. Unlike the RQFII program, the QFII program has no jurisdiction-specific quotas. From an investor's perspective, however, the RQFII program has several potential advantages over the QFII program—among them, greater discretion in portfolio allocation and less restrictive rules regarding the repatriation of funds. The RQFII program also permits authorised investors to invest part of their RQFII quota in China's fixed-income interbank bond market, whereas QFII-approved investors must apply for an additional quota to access this market. As of the end of April 2015, the total value of allocated quotas under the RQFII program was about RMB364 billion, with an additional RMB506 billion worth of aggregate global RQFII quotas yet to be allocated. This compares with about RMB457 billion of allocation for the QFII program (Figure 11.3). As investors utilise their jurisdictions' quotas, the RQFII program is likely to account for more foreign investment in Chinese financial assets than the QFII program.

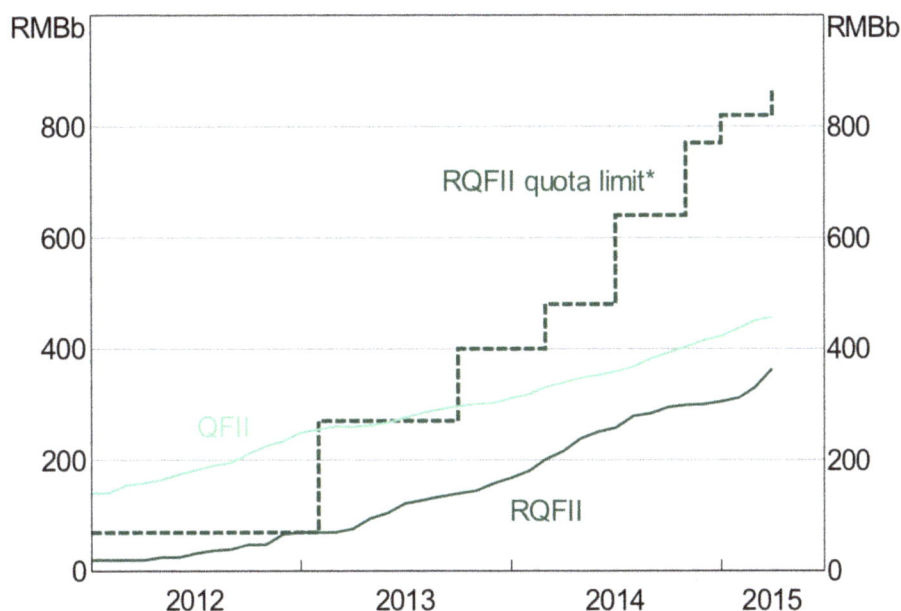

Figure 11.3 Foreign investment in Chinese financial assets (accumulated approved quotas)

* Excludes Taiwan's RQFII quota.
Sources: CEIC Data; RBA, SAFE.

Shanghai–Hong Kong Stock Connect program

In addition to the RQFII program, the other key policy initiative aimed at increasing the attractiveness of offshore RMB (from the perspective of foreign investors) is the Shanghai–Hong Kong Stock Connect program. The program, which began operating in November 2014, allows offshore investors to purchase approved (RMB-denominated) stocks listed on the Shanghai Stock Exchange (SSE)—known as 'northbound' trading. Similarly, eligible mainland investors are able to purchase (Hong Kong dollar-denominated) stocks listed on the

Hong Kong Stock Exchange (HKEx)—known as 'southbound' trading. In other words, the Stock Connect program provides an additional avenue through which offshore (onshore) investors can buy and sell Chinese (Hong Kong) equities in addition to the RQFII and QFII programs, and therefore is an additional link between the offshore and onshore RMB markets.

Purchases in both exchanges are subject to total and daily quotas (Table 11.4). Offshore investors are permitted to purchase a total of RMB300 billion worth of SSE stocks (daily quota of RMB13 billion). Mainland Chinese investors are permitted to purchase a total of RMB250 billion worth of HKEx stocks (daily quota of RMB10.5 billion) (Table 11.4). Like the RQFII program, the currency exchange takes place in the offshore market, so investors must purchase (sell) RMB in the offshore market in order to buy mainland (Hong Kong) stocks.

Table 11.4 Features of the Stock Connect program

	Northbound trading Hong Kong to Shanghai	Southbound trading Shanghai to Hong Kong
Daily quota[a]	RMB13 billion	RMB10.5 billion
Aggregate quota	RMB300 billion	RMB250 billion
Eligible investors	All foreign investors	Institutional Chinese investors, mutual funds and high net-worth Chinese individuals[b]
Eligible index constituents	SSE 180 Index and SSE 380 Index	Hang Seng Composite LargeCap Index and Hang Seng Composite MidCap Index

[a] Daily limits operate on a 'first come, first served' basis. Daily quota balances are calculated on a 'net buy' basis and are adjusted when a buy order is cancelled, rejected by the other exchange or executed at a better price.
[b] Individuals with more than RMB500,000 in their brokerage accounts.
Source: Hong Kong Exchanges and Clearing Limited (HKEx).

Early trading via the Stock Connect program was heavily skewed towards Shanghai-listed stocks. The daily northbound quota was exhausted on the first day of trading, while less than 20 per cent of the daily southbound quota was used. However, southbound trading increased markedly in April 2015 alongside a broadening of eligible mainland investors to include mutual funds. As of April 2015, investors have used some 43 per cent of the aggregate northbound quota and 34 per cent of the aggregate southbound quota (Figure 11.4).

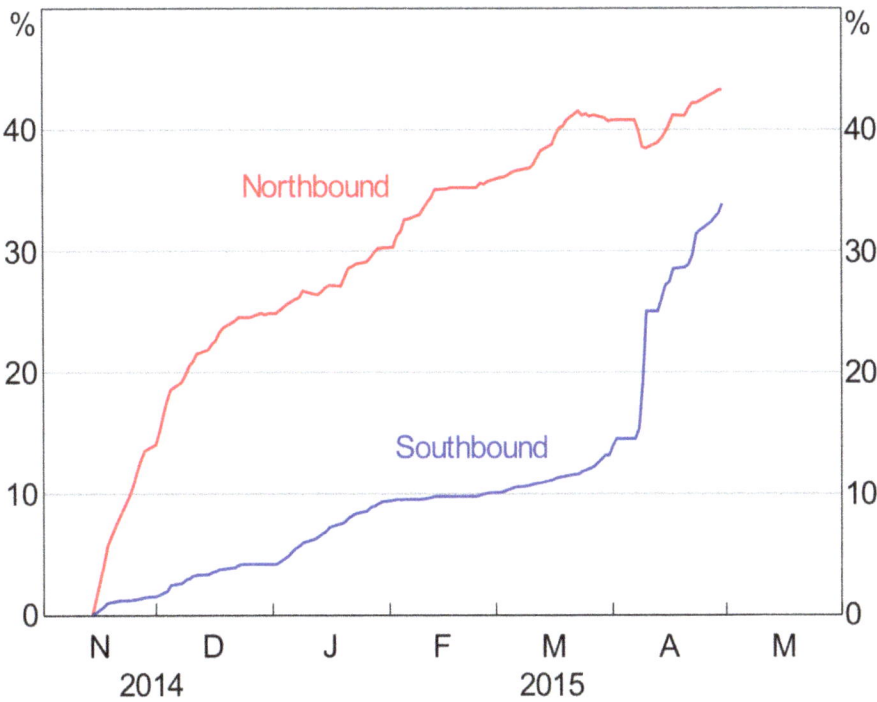

Figure 11.4 Shanghai–Hong Kong Stock Connect program (aggregate quota used)

Source: Hong Kong Exchanges and Clearing Limited (HKEx).

The primary advantage of the Stock Connect program over the RQFII program is that it is open to all foreign investors, whereas the RQFII program is restricted to financial institutions domiciled in countries that have been granted RQFII quotas (although once an institution obtains an RQFII quota, it can use this to set up RMB products elsewhere). Moreover, gaining an RQFII licence and quota for individual institutions is a comparatively lengthy process.

Nevertheless, the RQFII program is likely to continue to be used as it has some advantages over the Stock Connect program. Importantly, institutions with an RQFII quota can invest in mainland fixed-income assets and a broader range of mainland stocks. In addition, while Stock Connect investors are subject to an aggregate daily quota (for the market as a whole) and execution queues, RQFII investors can transact subject only to their own individual quotas. The two programs are nonetheless partial substitutes. Since Hong Kong has exhausted its aggregate RQFII quota, some Hong Kong-based entities have reportedly requested to be allowed to transfer stocks bought under the RQFII program to the Stock Connect program in an attempt to free up space in their existing RQFII quotas.

RMB cross-border lending schemes

In addition to the RQFII and Stock Connect programs—which seek to increase the cross-border flow of RMB-denominated portfolio investment—there are a number of pilot schemes that permit RMB-denominated lending flows. Such schemes typically only permit flows between designated mainland Chinese cities or regions and specific offshore centres, and are therefore not available to all offshore market participants. The first of these schemes, established in January 2013, allows companies incorporated in Qianhai—a special economic zone (SEZ) within the Chinese city of Shenzhen—to borrow RMB from banks in Hong Kong to fund investment projects within Qianhai. As interbank RMB interest rates have typically been noticeably lower in Hong Kong than in the mainland (notwithstanding some narrowing in the onshore–offshore spread in the latter half of 2014), it is possible the scheme has provided Qianhai firms with access to cheaper funding.[7]

In 2014, similar schemes were established between Singapore-based banks and firms in China's Suzhou Industrial Park, in Jiangsu Province, and Tianjin Eco-City, as part of a broader range of initiatives between the Chinese and Singaporean governments to develop these two innovation-oriented initiatives. Entities within the zone of both initiatives have also been permitted to issue RMB-denominated bonds in Singapore and to undertake direct investment in Singapore-based corporations.

Another scheme, with Taiwan, was established in late 2013 and follows a slightly different model. Under this scheme, subsidiaries of Taiwanese firms in the Jiangsu city of Kunshan, near Shanghai, are permitted both to borrow RMB from their offshore parent companies and to extend RMB loans to them. In addition, and most recently, non-bank financial institutions and enterprises domiciled in the Shanghai Free Trade Zone have been permitted to borrow RMB from any offshore centre, subject to certain conditions.[8]

Recent progress towards RMB internationalisation

Partly through the policy initiatives outlined above, China has made significant progress in internationalising its currency in the past few years. This is evident in part by the fact that China's RMB-denominated current account transactions

---

7   Interest rates are privately negotiated between borrowers and lenders and are therefore not publicly available.
8   The funds must be put towards manufacturing operations and project construction within the zone and their value cannot exceed specified limits.

have grown rapidly, and now account for about one-fifth of China's total current account transactions (Figure 11.5). RMB-denominated investment (particularly inward investment) has also increased noticeably in recent years, but remains small relative to the value of RMB-denominated trade settlement.

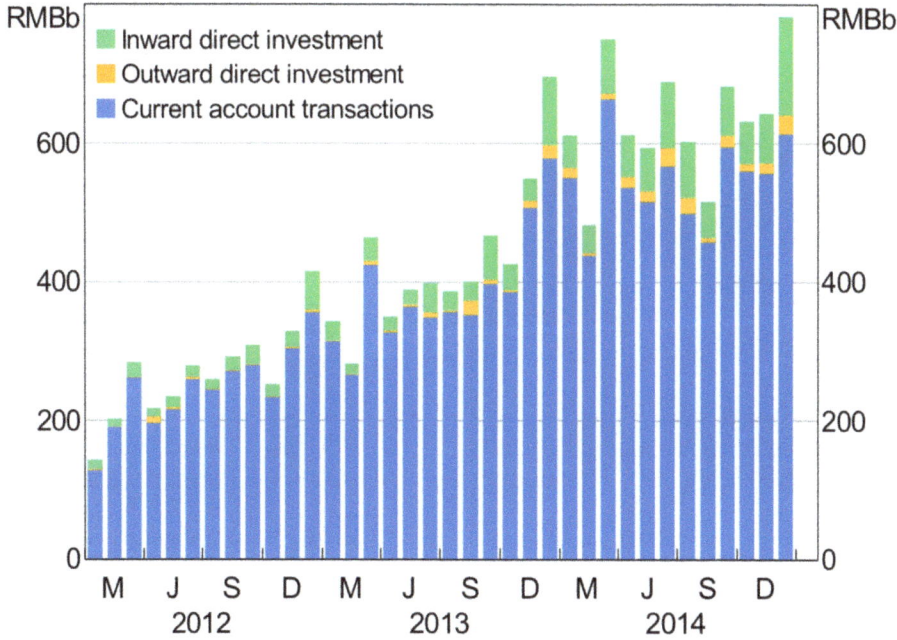

Figure 11.5 Cross-border RMB settlement

Sources: CEIC Data; RBA.

By economic jurisdiction, Hong Kong continues to account for the majority of China's RMB-denominated cross-border transactions, followed by Singapore and Taiwan. This is unsurprising given that Hong Kong remains the centre of the offshore RMB market. Nevertheless, the launch of official RMB clearing banks in Singapore and Taiwan in early 2013 coincided with a substantial increase in the RMB-denominated share of each economy's bilateral merchandise trade with China in 2013 (Figure 11.6). The share of China's merchandise trade settled in RMB with economies excluding Hong Kong, Taiwan and Singapore increased slightly in 2013, but, in comparison, remained relatively low at about 3 per cent.

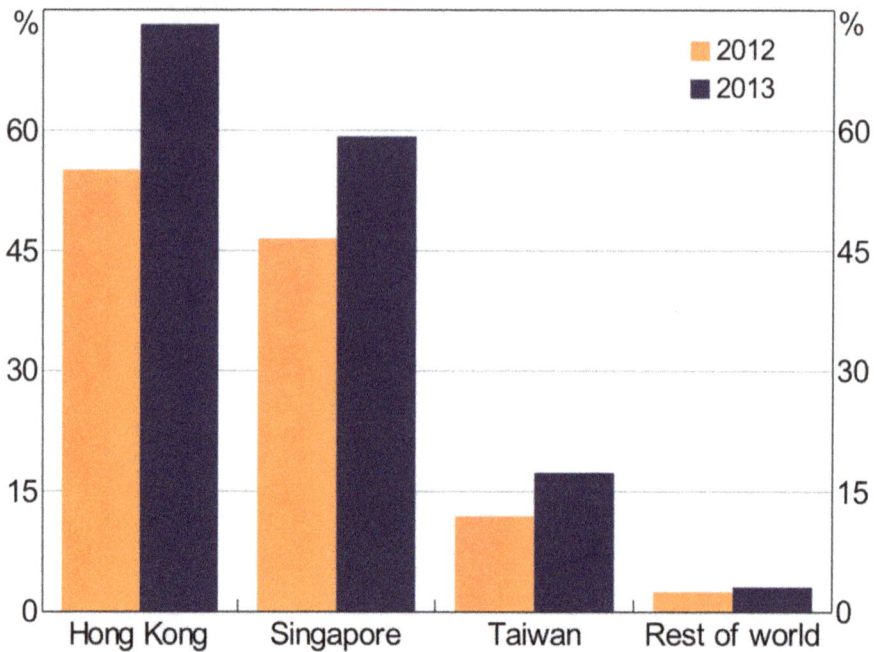

Figure 11.6 Bilateral RMB trade settlement, as a share of total bilateral merchandise trade with China

Sources: CEIC Data; PBC; RBA.

Importantly, while the share of trade *settled* in RMB has increased markedly, it is not clear whether the share of trade *invoiced* in RMB has increased to the same extent. Relatively few data are available on invoicing. The distinction is important because the extent of trade settlement in RMB could partly reflect differences in the value of onshore and offshore RMB. This could mean the settlement data are overstating underlying demand for RMB.

Notwithstanding China's overall current account surplus, the value of China's cross-border RMB *payments* (for example, for imports) typically exceeds the value of China's cross-border RMB *receipts* (for example, from exports) (Figure 11.7). In other words, China runs a current account surplus but an RMB-denominated deficit for trade denominated in RMB. One potential reason for this is that Chinese firms may have been attempting to benefit from the typically higher value of offshore RMB relative to onshore RMB (also known as the offshore premium, and shown in Figure 11.1). For example, when the RMB buys more US dollars in the offshore market than in the onshore market, Chinese importers have an incentive to exchange RMB for US dollars in the offshore market to meet

US dollar payments. From China's perspective, such a transaction will be counted as RMB trade settlement even though, from the perspective of the foreign firm, the underlying trade flow is both settled and invoiced in US dollars.[9]

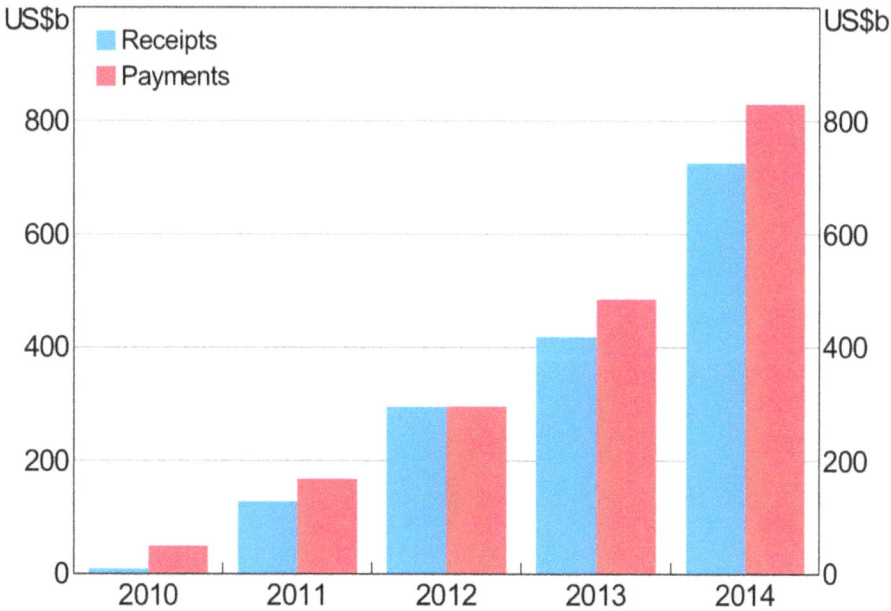

Figure 11.7 Cross-border RMB receipts and payments

Sources: CEIC Data; RBA; SAFE.

In any case, the net outflow of RMB from China in recent years has led to a rapid increase in the stock of RMB deposits in offshore centres, although growth slowed somewhat in 2014 (Figure 11.8). While Hong Kong continues to account for the majority of offshore RMB deposits, the stock of deposits in Taiwan and Singapore has increased rapidly since early 2013, respectively rising to about RMB300 billion and RMB280 billion at the end of December 2014.

---

9 Likewise, when the RMB buys *fewer* US dollars in the offshore market, Chinese exporters have an incentive to exchange their US dollar receipts for RMB in the offshore market (rather than the onshore market) before sending the receipts back to the mainland. Again, this will count towards RMB trade settlement even though the underlying trade flow is settled and invoiced in RMB from the foreigner's perspective.

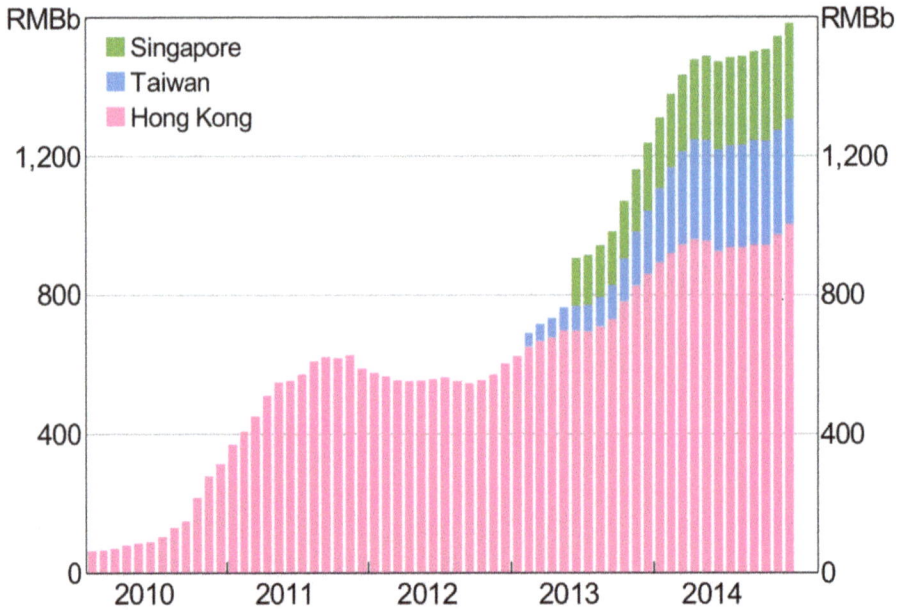

Figure 11.8 Value of RMB deposits

Sources: CEIC Data; MAS.

As the pool of offshore RMB deposits has grown, so too has the offshore RMB-denominated bond market. Hong Kong remains the prime location for offshore RMB bond—or 'dim sum' bond—issuance, but the market is also growing rapidly in Singapore, Taipei and Luxembourg. The majority of issuers continue to be mainland Chinese companies or offshore subsidiaries of mainland Chinese companies (Figure 11.9). Funds raised are typically repatriated back to mainland China. Most of the dim sum bond issuance by other firms has also been used to fund their operations in mainland China.

One reason for the prevalence of mainland Chinese issuers in the dim sum bond market is that the cost of funding has typically been lower in the offshore market than on the mainland. This is evidenced, for example, by the consistently lower yield paid on Chinese government bonds issued in the offshore market relative to those issued in the onshore market (Figure 11.10). This is partly because capital account restrictions limit the flow of offshore RMB back to the mainland, such that there is a large pool of RMB in offshore markets with relatively limited investment opportunities (and therefore strong demand for dim sum bonds from offshore investors). However, recent policy initiatives aimed at increasing the flow of RMB between the offshore and onshore markets (for example, the Stock Connect program and cross-border lending schemes) have begun to reduce this gap.

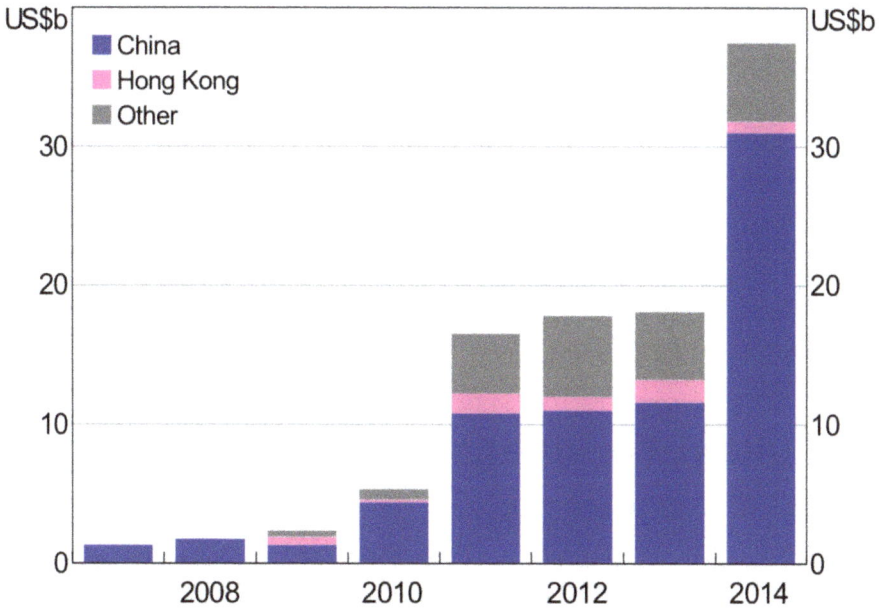

Figure 11.9 Dim sum bond issuance, by nationality of parent issuer

Source: Dealogic.

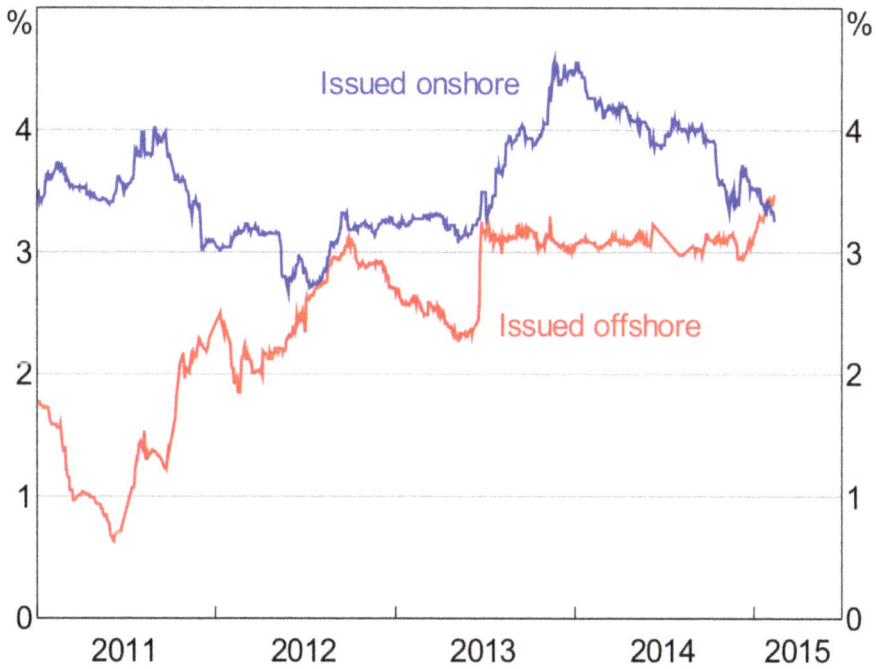

Figure 11.10 Chinese five-year government bond yields

Sources: Bloomberg; RBA.

There have also been a small number of offshore RMB bond issues by foreign governments, with the UK Government raising RMB3 billion in October 2014 and the NSW Treasury Corporation raising RMB1 billion in November 2014. This followed the Canadian Province of British Columbia's issuance of an RMB2.5 billion dim sum bond in late 2013. Some foreign banks have also tapped the market. ANZ, for example, became the first foreign issuer to sell a Basel III-compliant RMB-denominated capital instrument when it issued an RMB2.5 billion dim sum bond in January 2015. Moreover, bond issuers have used the offshore RMB swap market to hedge their foreign currency risk. For example, the NSW Treasury Corporation swapped the proceeds from its RMB bond issue into Australian dollars.

RMB internationalisation and currency mismatch

As outlined in Cheung et al. (2011), the combination of China's large and persistent current account surpluses, its managed exchange rate regime and its openness to (mostly RMB-denominated) FDI has led to a large currency mismatch in the past decade. The value of China's foreign currency assets has correspondingly far exceeded the value of its foreign currency liabilities. In other words, years of foreign currency reserve accumulation by the PBC have produced a substantial long US dollar position (Figure 11.11). As a result, an appreciation of the RMB against the US dollar leads to a decline in the value of China's net international asset position (in RMB terms).

Against this background, one potential motive for RMB internationalisation is to increase China's *RMB-denominated* foreign assets and thus reduce China's exposure to an appreciation of the RMB. For example, if a Chinese resident purchased a dim sum bond issued by a non-resident, and the non-resident used the proceeds to purchase goods from a Chinese exporter, China's RMB-denominated claims on the rest of the world would increase (all else remaining constant).

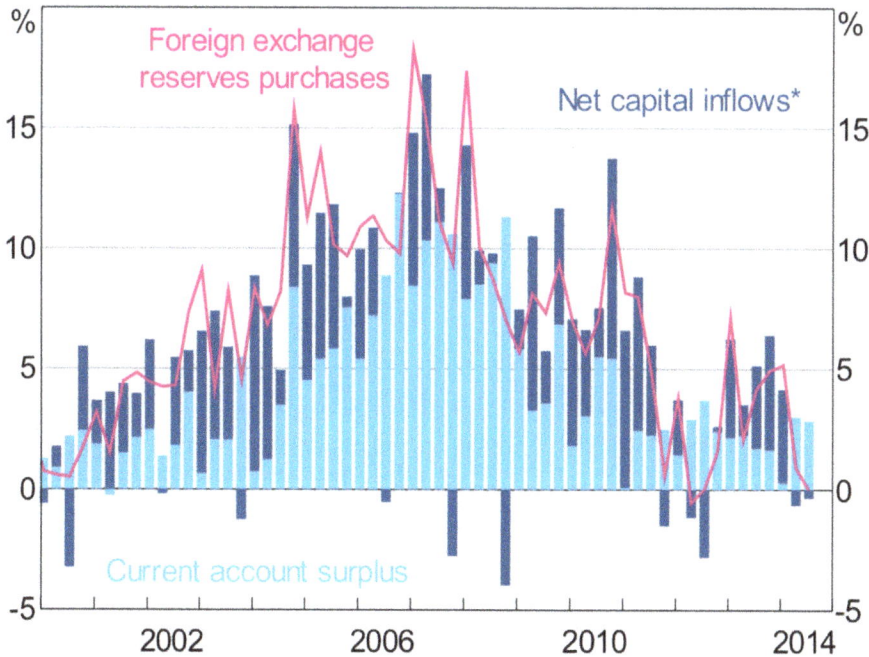

Figure 11.11 China's balance of payments (quarterly flows, percentage of GDP)

* Excluding foreign exchange reserves.
Sources: CEIC Data; IMF; RBA.

The RMB internationalisation process to date has, however, likely worsened the currency mismatch between China's international assets and liabilities. One reason for this is that, by design, the policy initiatives so far announced (such as RQFII and Stock Connect) have had the effect of increasing China's RMB-denominated foreign liabilities, rather than increasing its RMB-denominated foreign assets.[10] Another reason is that the net outflow of RMB from China's cross-border trade in recent years has led to an increase in the stock of RMB deposits in offshore centres, which has also increased China's RMB-denominated foreign liabilities. This outcome likely reflects the fact that, until recently, market participants have typically expected the RMB to continue to appreciate against the US dollar. In effect, foreigners have been discouraged from denominating their liabilities in RMB because they expect the RMB to experience a significant real appreciation against the US dollar. (For a full discussion of the relationship between RMB trade settlement, RMB appreciation and currency mismatch, see the Appendix for this chapter.)

---

10 The Stock Connect program also increases China's FX-denominated foreign assets.

Against this background, the extent to which market participants perceive the RMB to be undervalued or overvalued is an important consideration when trying to assess the outlook for RMB internationalisation—and is especially so of the extent to which this process is likely to translate into a reduction in aggregate currency mismatch on China's international balance sheet. Specifically, if firms continue to view RMB appreciation against the US dollar as a 'one-way' bet, there would likely be a continuation of the trend of recent years of net RMB outflows from trade settlement, net RMB capital inflows and a further increase in the degree of currency mismatch. This trend could reverse if participants come increasingly to expect greater two-way movements in the RMB exchange rate.

A number of reports suggest that market participants have either scaled back their expectations for future RMB appreciation against the US dollar or now expect the RMB to depreciate against the US dollar (Figure 11.12) (see, for example, Wildau 2015). These expectations may have arisen for a number of reasons, but have likely been reinforced by the fact that the RMB has increasingly been trading near the lower bound of its daily trading band against the US dollar in the onshore market. Relatedly, there has been a marked slowdown in the pace of PBC reserve accumulation. Moreover, Chinese officials have indicated their desire to see greater two-way volatility in the RMB's exchange rate (PBC 2014).

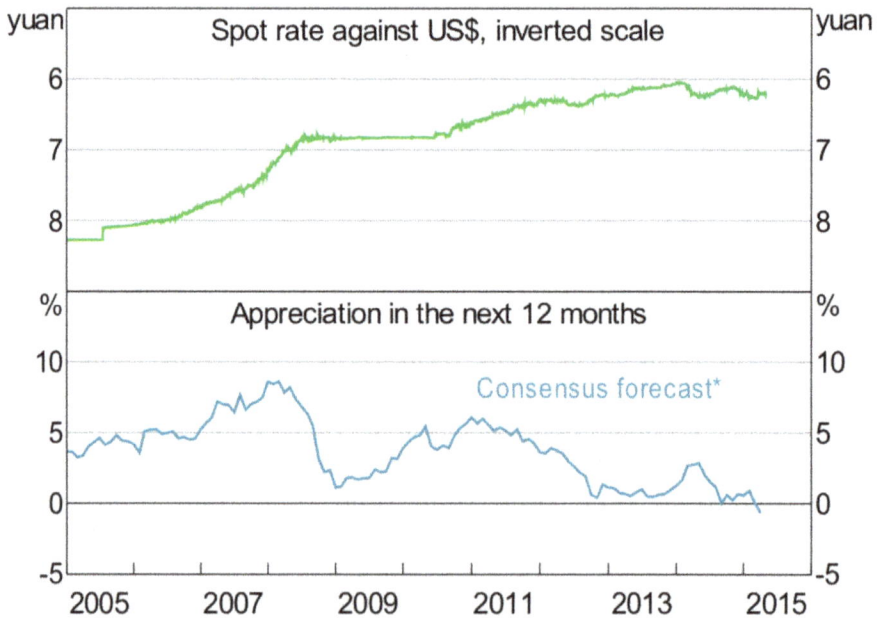

Figure 11.12 Chinese RMB (spot rate against US dollar, inverted scale)

* Mean estimate of forecasters polled by Consensus.
Sources: Bloomberg, Consensus Economics; RBA.

Conclusion

The international use of the RMB has continued to increase in the past few years, facilitated by policy initiatives applying within mainland China and to several offshore centres. For example, the designation of official RMB clearing banks has provided more direct mechanisms for settling offshore entities' RMB transactions with their Chinese counterparts. By facilitating RMB transactions, these clearing banks establish the necessary infrastructure for future progress in RMB internationalisation. The expansion of the RQFII program and the launch of the Stock Connect program have also increased the extent to which cross-border flows of RMB are liberalised, particularly flows *into* China.

There are a number of possible reasons why China is pursuing RMB internationalisation. These include ensuring that the status of the RMB reflects China's global economic weight, and also to reduce the currency risk faced by individual Chinese entities as the exchange rate regime is progressively liberalised. In addition, China may be pursuing RMB internationalisation to reduce the extent of currency mismatch on its aggregate balance sheet. To date, however, RMB internationalisation has instead tended to increase the degree of currency mismatch, partly because of pervasive expectations of future one-way RMB appreciation. Nevertheless, recent experience of greater two-way volatility in the RMB—and a growing market consensus that the RMB is unlikely to continue to appreciate monotonically against the US dollar—could change this over time. In any case, given that RMB internationalisation is closely related to the broader capital account liberalisation process, it is likely to continue to be pursued as a policy objective for some time. Until this broader capital account liberalisation process is completed—and potentially beyond then—the offshore RMB market is likely to have an important role to play in RMB internationalisation.

References

Bank of China, Hong Kong (BOCHK) (2014), *Offshore RMB Express*, January, Honk Kong: BOCHK.

Calvo, G. and Reinhart, C. (2002), Fear of floating, *The Quarterly Journal of Economics*, 117(2): 379–408.

Cheung, Y.-W., Ma, G. and McCauley, R. (2011), Why does China attempt to internationalise the renminbi, in Golley, J. and Song, L. (eds), *Rising China: Global challenges and opportunities*, China Update Series, Canberra: ANU E Press.

Frankel, J. (2012), Internationalization of the RMB and historical precedents, *Journal of Economic Integration*, 27(3): 329–65.

Hatzvi, E., Nixon, W. and Wright, M. (2014), The offshore renminbi market and Australia, *RBA Bulletin*, December, Sydney: RBA, Available from: www.rba.gov.au/publications/bulletin/2014/dec/bu-1214-7a.html.

People's Bank of China (PBC) (2014), Media Release No. 5, 15 March, Beijing: PBC.

Reserve Bank of Australia (RBA) (2014), *Annual Report 2014*, Sydney: RBA, Available from: www.rba.gov.au/publications/annual-reports/rba/2014/pdf/2014-report.pdf.

Wildau, G. (2015), Renminbi not immune from emerging market outflows, *Financial Times*, 29 January.

Yu, Y. (2014), *How far can renminbi internationalisation go?*, ADBI Working Paper Series 461, Tokyo: Asian Development Bank Institute.

Appendix

To illustrate the relationship between RMB trade settlement and currency mismatch, we can consider three different states of the world:

1. China settles all of its trade in US dollars

2. China settles all of its trade in RMB

3. China settles more imports than exports in RMB
    (that is, the current situation).

For simplicity, in each scenario it is assumed the Chinese authorities maintain an independent monetary policy and a hypothetical fixed exchange rate of US\$1 = RMB5 (note that this highly stylised example implies that China must be closed to *private* capital flows, as per the standard 'trilemma' of international finance). China is also assumed to run a current account (trade) surplus of US\$5 billion (US\$10 billion of exports and US\$5 billion of imports).

In the first scenario—in which all current account transactions are settled in US dollars—the PBC must increase its foreign exchange reserves by US\$5 billion to maintain the RMB's fixed exchange rate against the US dollar (Table A11.1). This is equivalent to the PBC lending US dollars to the rest of the world to finance the rest of the world's current account deficit (relative to China). This increases China's international asset position by US\$5 billion. Regardless of whether the PBC chooses to sterilise its purchases of US dollars, its liabilities will increase by RMB25 billion (in the form of newly printed RMB or RMB loans from domestic entities).

Table A11.1 China's international assets and liabilities[a]

	Exports	Imports	Change in China's net international asset position	Change in China's foreign currency reserves
Scenario 1	US$10 billion	US$5 billion	+ US$5 billion	+ US$5 billion
Scenario 2	RMB50 billion	RMB25 billion	+ RMB25 billion	0
Scenario 3	US$10 billion	US$4 billion + RMB5 billion	+ US$6 billion – RMB5 billion	+ US$6 billion

[a] Assuming the PBC maintains its fixed exchange rate of US$1 = RMB5.

In the second scenario—in which all current account transactions are settled in RMB—the PBC must (on net) loan RMB25 billion to finance the rest of the world's RMB25 billion current account deficit. In turn, China's net international asset position increases by RMB25 billion. Unlike the first scenario, here, the PBC's assets and liabilities are both denominated in RMB, so there is no currency mismatch.

In the third scenario, we assume that all exports are denominated in US dollars (US$10 billion), but the US$5 billion worth of imports are partly denominated in US dollars (US$4 billion) and partly in RMB (RMB5 billion). This means that there is a net US dollar inflow of US$6 billion and a net RMB outflow of RMB5 billion (through trade). This RMB outflow is a liability on the PBC's balance sheet (for example, held as RMB deposits offshore), but the PBC must purchase the US$6 billion inflow to maintain the fixed exchange rate, implying additional liabilities of RMB30 billion.

The currency composition of China's international assets and liabilities is different in scenario three (assets of US$6 billion and a liability of RMB5 billion) to that in scenario one (assets of US$5 billion). China's long foreign currency position, in fact, increases by more in scenario three, as the partial RMB denomination of imports means that there is a greater net inflow of foreign currency from trade. As a result there is a greater need for the PBC to acquire foreign currency reserves to offset this inflow. This demonstrates—in a highly stylised way—how the internationalisation of the RMB can result in a greater degree of currency mismatch on China's aggregate balance sheet than otherwise—*if it results in a higher value of RMB outflows than inflows.*

12. China's Manufacturing Performance and Industrial Competitiveness Upgrading

International comparison and policy reflection

Kevin H. Zhang[1]

Introduction

China's sustained economic growth in the 37 years from 1978 is a story of manufacturing industry success. China has enjoyed rapid structural transformation and a process of deep development (Gereffi 2009; Lin and Wang 2012; Zhang 2006). As a factory to the world, China is also the world's number one producer of manufactured goods and manufactured exports. Recently, China has also been seeking to upgrade its production frontier towards more capital and technology-intensive industries.

China is evidently a manufacturing giant, but is it really an industrial power? And if it is an industrial power, what drives its industrial competitiveness? While there have been some studies on Chinese industry and manufacturing exports in general, the literature focusing on these questions has so far been limited.[2] One evident gap in the literature is inadequate measurement of manufacturing performance (MP) and the identification of MP determinants. Working in this direction, this chapter aims to advance the existing literature as follows. First, it studies eight indicators of three MP dimensions (capacity, intensity and quality) in both domestic and world markets, as suggested by UNIDO (2013), we provide more comprehensive measures of MP in China. Second, in addition to manufacturing drivers at the micro level of firms and industries, it examines macro-drivers of China's industrial development against international benchmarks, including development strategies and industrial policy. Third, we assess the role played by foreign trade and foreign direct investment (FDI) in China's MP and IC by focusing on their impact on industrial

---

1   This chapter is a revised version of a paper presented at the CESA-RDI Conference on Deepening Reform for China's Long-Term Growth and Development, Chinese Academy of Social Sciences, Beijing, 11–12 December 2014. I thank the participants of the conference for their helpful comments. Of course, any errors remain my own.
2   The studies on Chinese industry and manufacturing development include Brandt and Thun (2010); Gereffi (2009); Lin and Wang (2012); Nahm and Seinfeld (2014); Zhang (2006); Zhao and Zhang (2007, 2010).

capacity, intensity and quality, especially technology upgrading. Fourth, we use more recent data (up to 2013) to complement the cross-country ranking in 1992–2010 by UNIDO (2013).

Section two provides the analytical framework on which China's industrial competitiveness is assessed and against which its performance is compared internationally. Section three examines the drivers of China's industrial success by first distinguishing initial conditions and causes and then by identifying their main drivers. Two drivers, industrial policy and export FDI, are then discussed in sections four and five, and conclusions are drawn in the final section.

An analytical framework for study of China's industrial competitiveness

Industrialisation—structural transformation from traditional agriculture to modern manufactures and services—has been considered a key to economic growth and development since the Industrial Revolution in the eighteenth century. Industrial development is desirable not only as a source of higher productivity growth and per capita income, but also to achieve greater diversity in economic structure. The latter helps to reduce a country's vulnerability to poverty and external shocks.

To better illustrate China's industrial performance, Figure 12.1 and Table 12.1 lay out some basic related indicators. As the data in the table illustrate, in the 35 years from 1978 to 2013 China's gross domestic product (GDP) grew 26 times over. The industrial sector, however, grew the fastest and also made the largest contribution to growth (growing 42 times over), as shown in Figure 12.1. By 2014, China had become the second-largest economy in the world at current exchange rates, but number one in purchasing power parity (PPP) terms. As the most populous country, however, China's GDP per capita lags far behind the United States and other high-income economies, including South Korea, Taiwan, Singapore and Hong Kong.

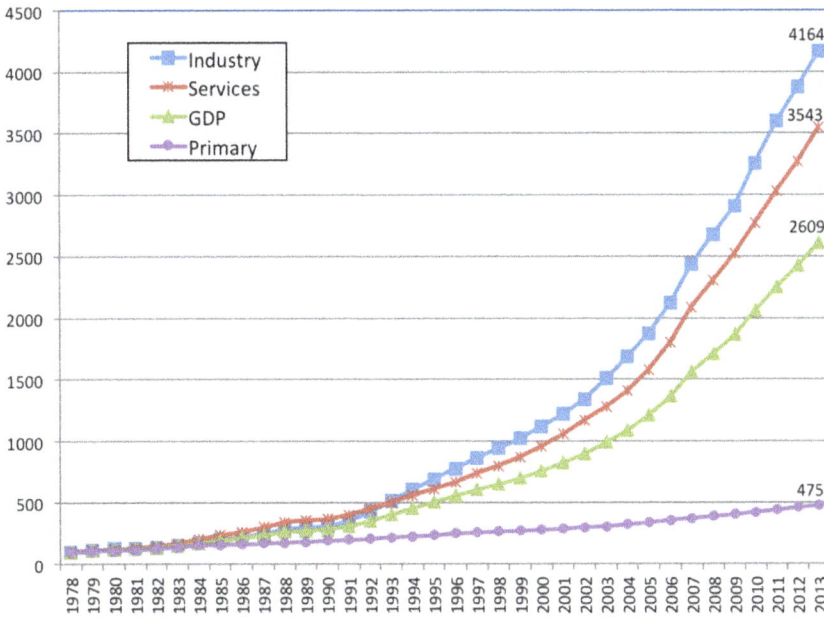

Figure 12.1 Growth of China's GDP and its component sectors, 1978–2013 (1978=100)

Sources: National Bureau of Statistics various years[a].

Table 12.1 China's position in the top-10 economies, 2014

Economy	GDP (US$b)	GDP (PPP $b)	Population (million)	GDP per capita (US$)	GDP per capita (PPP $)
United States	17,416(1)	17,416(2)	316(3)	53,670(1)	53,960(1)
China	10,361(2)	17,617(1)	1,357(1)	7,635(9)	12,982(9)
Japan	4,770(3)	4,750(4)	127(6)	46,140(2)	37,630(3)
Germany	3,820(4)	3,722(5)	80(7)	46,100(3)	44,540(2)
France	2,902(5)	2,580(8)	66(8)	42,250(4)	37,580(4)
United Kingdom	2,848(6)	2,549(9)	64(9)	39,110(5)	35,760(5)
Brazil	2,244(7)	3,264(7)	200(4)	11,690(8)	14,750(8)
Russia	2,057(8)	3,565(6)	144(5)	13,860(7)	23,200(7)
Italy	2,129(9)	2,120(10)	60(10)	34,400(6)	34,100(6)
India	2,048(10)	7,376(3)	1,252(2)	1,570(10)	5,350(10)

Notes: Ranking for each indicator in the table is given in parentheses after the figure. According to the World Bank's International Comparison Program, China passed the United States to become the world's number one economy in purchasing power parity (PPP) GDP in 2014.
Sources: World Bank (2015); and CIA (2015).

Based on a method developed by UNIDO (2013), a country's industrial competitiveness (IC) can be assessed via eight indicators that are grouped along three dimensions, as shown in Table 12.2. The first dimension relates to a country's capacity to produce and export manufactures. Unlike measures used before, we include total output as well as output per capita to capture the manufacturing scale in the context of China's population. Output per capita can understate the capacity of populous countries like China, India and the United States relative to small ones. Including total output might not only correct such understating, but also reflect economies of scale derived from the large amount of output. The second dimension covers a country's industrial intensity in terms of manufacturing value added share in GDP and manufactured export share in total exports. The third IC dimension captures a country's industrial quality in terms of technological deepening and upgrading in domestic manufacturing output and exports. In contrast with other available indices, the IC index provides a unique cross-country industrial performance benchmark and rank based on quantitative indicators of industrial performance. These rankings are provided for 135 countries for the years 1992–2010 (UNIDO 2013).[3]

Table 12.2 Industrial competitiveness: Three dimensions and eight indicators

Industrial capacity	Manufacturing value added per capita (MPC) Manufactured exports per capita (MXPC) Manufacturing value added share in world (MWS) Manufactured exports share in world (MXWS)
Industrial intensity	Manufacturing value added share in GDP (M/GDP) Manufactured exports share in total exports (MX/X)
Industrial quality	Medium and high-tech manufacturing value added share in total (MQ) Medium and high-tech manufactured export share in total (MXQ)

Source: Author's reorganisation based on UNIDO (2013).

Table 12.3 reports the top 15 of the world IC ranking in 1992–2010, which reveals a pronounced yet familiar pattern. The most industrially competitive nations in the world are those with high-income industrialised economies. The top-three positions are occupied by Japan, Germany and the United States, which have headed the rankings since 1992. China has ascended rapidly to its rank of seventh.

---

3   In contrast with other indices currently available, the IC index provides a unique cross-country industrial performance benchmark and ranking based on quantitative indicators of manufacturing development. Rankings are provided at global levels for 135 countries in 1992–2010 (UNIDO 2013).

Table 12.3 Rank of top-15 economies for industrial competitiveness, 1992–2010

Economy	2010	2009	2008	2007	2006	2005	2000	1995	1992	Change in 1992–2010
Japan	1	2	2	2	1	1	1	1	1	0
Germany	2	1	1	1	2	2	3	2	2	0
United States	3	3	3	3	3	3	2	3	3	0
Korea	4	4	4	4	4	4	12	13	15	+11
Taiwan-China	5	5	5	5	5	10	10	12	11	+6
Singapore	6	7	9	9	7	9	11	10	12	+6
China	7	10	14	15	16	18	23	26	30	+23
Switzerland	8	9	10	12	13	13	14	7	7	−1
Belgium	9	6	7	8	9	6	9	8	8	−1
France	10	8	6	6	6	5	5	6	5	−5
Italy	11	11	8	7	10	8	7	5	6	−5
Netherlands	12	13	12	13	14	14	15	11	9	−3
Sweden	13	15	11	10	11	12	13	14	13	0
United Kingdom	14	14	13	11	8	7	4	4	4	−10
Ireland	15	12	15	14	12	11	8	15	17	+2

Note: UNIDO's ranking, published in 2014, runs only to 2010.
Source: UNIDO (2014).

Selected details capturing China's industrial growth are presented in Table 12.4, including eight IC component indicators for the period 1990–2010. Within each of UNIDO's nominated eight indicators, China has evidently made significant progress. Looking to the indicators that have been augmented here to adjust for China's population size, manufacturing value added per capita (MPC) has increased eight times and manufactured exports per capita (MXPC) are up an extraordinary 19 times. In parallel, China's share of manufacturing value added in the world (MWS) rose by 13 percentage points, from 2.6 per cent in 1990 to 15.3 per cent in 2010, and its share in world manufactured exports (MXWS) rose by 12 percentage points, from 2.2 per cent to 14.1 per cent. In parallel, in 2010 China surpassed Germany to become the world's largest manufactured goods exporter, and in 2011 it replaced the United States as the largest producer of manufactured goods in the world.

Table 12.4 China's industrial competitiveness and eight indicators, 1990–2010

Indicators	1990	1995	2000	2005	2010	Change in 1990–2010
Industrial capacity						
MPC (US$)	100.3	199.4	303.1	480.4	820.0	+$719.7
MXPC (US$)	58.2	108.9	179.9	550.4	1,123.6	+$1,065.4
MWS (%)	2.6	5.0	6.7	9.4	15.3	+12.7
MXWS (%)	2.2	3.4	4.7	9.3	14.1	+11.9
Industrial intensity						
M/GDP (%)	25.9	30.5	32.1	33.0	34.2	+8.3
MX/X (%)	72.5	88.8 91	91.7	94.8	96.2	+23.7
Industrial quality						
MQ (%)	37.8	38.0	42.9	41.6	40.7	+2.9
MXQ (%)	26.7	35.4	45.5	57.7	59.8	+33.1
IC index value	0.08	0.13	0.16	0.24	0.33	+0.25

Source: Computed from UNIDO (2015).

Table 12.5 presents cross-country comparisons of the eight IC indicators for the top 15 economies for industrial competitiveness in 2010. Given its population size and stage of development, China, of the 15 countries listed, is the country with the lowest per capita values for MPC and MXPC, but the country with the highest values for the aggregate items, including MWS and MXWS. China outperforms most of the other 14 economies in industrial intensity, as measured by M/GDP and MX/X, but rates poorly by the share of medium and high-tech manufacturing value and exports in total, respectively.

Table 12.5 Top 15 economies for industrial competitiveness in 2010

Rank	IC index	Economy	Capacity				Intensity		Quality	
			MPC (US$)	MXPC (US$)	MWS (%)	MXWS (%)	M/GDP (%)	MX/X (%)	MQ (%)	MXQ (%)
1	0.54	Japan	7,994	5,521	14.1	6.5	20.4	91.6	53.7	79.7
2	0.52	Germany	4,667	13,397	5.3	10.2	18.6	86.8	56.8	72.3
3	0.48	United States	5,522	2,736	24.0	8.0	14.9	76.8	51.5	64.7
4	0.40	Korea	4,783	9,280	3.2	4.2	29.1	96.9	53.4	75.8
5	0.36	Taiwar	6,153	10,825	2.0	2.3	29.9	96.0	61.9	72.4
6	0.35	Singapore	8,198	35,709	0.5	1.5	24.5	89.7	73.4	69.0
7	0.33	China	820	1,124	15.3	14.1	34.2	96.2	40.7	60.5
8	0.31	Switzerland	7,168	23,652	0.7	1.7	18.4	91.5	34.9	69.7
9	0.31	Belgium	3,794	34,138	0.5	3.3	15.0	87.4	42.3	54.9
10	0.31	France	2,885	7,237	2.5	4.2	12.2	88.4	45.4	65.8
11	0.29	Italy	2,848	6,935	2.3	3.8	14.9	91.6	39.3	53.9
12	0.29	Netherlands	3,325	22,081	0.8	3.4	1258	74.0	4017	55.0
13	0.29	Sweden	6,559	15,376	0.8	1.3	20.0	89.7	47.0	57.7
14	0.28	United Kingdom	3,162	5,248	2.7	3.0	11.4	79.5	42.0	63.2
15	0.27	Ireland	6,507	23,960	0.4	1.0	23.1	91.7	64.1	53.8

Notes: same as in Table 12.5.
Source: UNIDO (2015).

A summary of China's position in global industry can be derived for industrial capacity, industrial intensity and industrial quality. First, China has raised its industrial capacity by an unprecedented amount in a short time, in both manufacturing output and manufacturing exports. Due to its scale, no country is likely to challenge China seriously on these dimensions in the near future. Second, China's industrial intensity has grown to a level that is comparable with or even higher than many industrialised economies. Third, China has made significant progress in industrial quality, although it still has a long way to go to catch up with the leading economies. China is continuing a process of upgrading its manufacturing exports from simple, labour-intensive products to capital and technology-intensive goods. It should be noted, however, that the high ratios of MQ and MXQ—40.7 per cent and 59.8 per cent respectively (Table 12.5)—overstate China's performance in technological upgrading due to the extensive role played by China in vertical integrated global value chain and processing exports, which is discussed later.

In sum, China's manufacturing success is mainly due to extraordinary performance in aggregate *capacity* and *intensity*, but not yet in *quality*.

Why was China's performance extraordinary?

A range of factors influences industrial development. These include the macro and microeconomic environments and the policy environment. To understand which combinations lead to successful industrial performance, it is essential to distinguish between endowments or conditions and the causes of industrial performance. A country's advantageous (disadvantageous) endowments or conditions relative to other countries can be viewed as its comparative advantages (disadvantages) in industrial development. These, however, are not the causes of good (bad) industrial performance. Causes of a particular outcome are instead generative forces or events that are the origin of the outcome or the factor that make it happen.

The initial advantages China had for industrial development included abundant cheap labour; huge potential markets; a high saving rate; a culture of patience, persistence and learning; good relations with the Western, economically developed world in 1978; and an efficient, centralised governance system (although this is open to debate). China's disadvantages included low labour quality; low industrial technology; poor infrastructure; an inefficient planned economic system; a weak market system; and shallow human capital. These endowments or conditions had existed for some time, but cannot be attributed to China's industrial success. There are instead two driving causes: a well-designed development strategy and industrial policy, and an effective export and FDI attraction strategy.

China's development strategy was one of a mixed-economic transition that gradually introduced market elements into the pre-existing planned economy, including and especially by opening up to foreign trade and FDI. This export-led and FDI-led industrial development approach served as a catalyst for the effective utilisation of China's then advantages so as to offset or transform its disadvantages. For example, cheap labour was utilised in processing exports and foreign-invested labour-intensive manufacturing enterprises; the large domestic market was used to attract foreign investors; industrial upgrading took place over time via rising foreign trade and FDI; and so on.

China is unique in its endowments, especially in having been the world's most populous country and also one of its poorest, in addition to being an economy that was autarkic before 1978. In being a low-income country, however, China did share many features in common with other developing economies. What China did differently from others are its market-oriented reforms, which led to an effective development strategy and industrial policy and its opening to trade and FDI, which helped build up industrial competitiveness, especially industrial upgrading.

China's export structure changed dramatically, as suggested by data in Tables 12.6 and 12.7. In 1985, exports of primary products and resource-based manufactures specifically represented 49 per cent of all exports. By 2013, less than 30 years later, that share had fallen to 7.5 per cent. In contrast, the share of non-resource-based manufactures rose from 50 per cent to 92 per cent (Table 12.6). Within that category, the share of high-technology exports jumped from 3 per cent in 1985 to 34 per cent in 2013, and for medium-technology exports the share increased from 8 per cent to 29 per cent. Table 12.7 reports export structure by Standard International Trade Classification (SITC) in 1984–2013. The biggest change took place in SITC 7 (machinery and transport equipment), which now makes up almost half of China's exports (about $1 trillion in 2013), compared with less than 6 per cent ($1.5 billion) in 1984.

Table 12.6 China's export structure: 1985–2013 (percentage)

Sectors	1985	1995	2002	2013	Changes in 1985-2013
Primary products	35.0	7.0	4.1	3.3	-31.7
Manufactures based on natural resources	13.6	7.4	4.7	4.2	-9.4
Manufactures not based on natural resources	50.0	84.6	91.2	92.1	+42.1
Low technology	39.7	53.5	44.7	29.8	-9.9
Medium technology	7.7	16.9	19.8	28.6	+20.9
High technology	2.6	14.2	26.7	33.7	+31.1
Others	1.4	1.0	1.0	0.4	-1.0
Total Exports	**100**	**100**	**100**	**100**	**100.0**

Sources: UNCTAD (2002a and 2002b) and WTO (2014).

Table 12.7 Export upgrading by SITC, 1984–2013 (percentage)

SITC	Description	1984	1986	1990	1995	1998	2001	2007	2013
0+1	Food, animals + beverages, tobacco	13.7	12.1	11.3	7.5	6.3	4.7	2.6	2.6
2+3+ 4+5	Crude materials + mineral fuels, lubricants + animal & vegetable oils + chemicals	37.3	27.0	21.1	12.5	11.5	10.3	7.4	7.6
3	Mineral fuels, lubricants							1.6	1.5
5	Chemicals							5.0	5.4
6	Goods classified chiefly by materials	18.8	17.3	20.2	22.0	16.7	17.5	18.1	16.4
7	Machinery and transport equipment	5.8	2.6	17.7	20.0	25.1	33.0	47.4	47.1
8	Miscellaneous manufactured articles	17.1	15.4	25.2	38.8	37.0	36.1	24.3	26.2
9	Not classified elsewhere in the SITC	7.3	24.5	2.0	0.4	0.2	0.11	0.2	0.1
Total		**100.0**	**100.0**	**100.0**	**100.0**	**100.0**	**100.0**	**100.0**	**100.0**

Source: Author's calculations based on UN (2015).

China's process of industrial upgrading displayed several turning points since the inception of reforms in 1978. The first of these appeared in 1986, when exports of textiles and clothing exceeded those of crude oil, indicating the transition from exporting resource-intensive products to labour-intensive manufactured goods. The second turning point was in 1995, when exports of machinery and electronics overtook those of textiles and clothing. This signified the transition from exporting labour-intensive goods to capital-intensive products. China's entry to the World Trade Organization (WTO) in 2001 indicated the third wave of upgrading, after which not only did product sophistication increase, but also high and new technology exports grew rapidly. Many Chinese exporters have through these transitions become an integral part of the global supply chains of large multinationals that lead the automobile, computer and aviation industries (Lin and Wang 2012). In 2014, China initiated several programs that worked on not only increasing value-added exports and moving up global value chains, but also encouraging firms to go global. Such programs include the 'one belt and one road' strategy, and supporting financial organisations proposed mainly by China: the Asia Infrastructure Investment Bank, Silk Fund and the New Development Bank.

Development strategy and industrial policy

The role of development strategy and industrial policy in China's structural upgrading is impossible to ignore (Ahrens 2013; Harrison and Rodriguze-Clare 2010). Strategy and policy here refer to the ways in which and policy tools with which China's government aims to build up the country's manufacturing competitiveness.

The key to China's development strategy is following, not defying, comparative advantage (Lin and Wang 2012). This type of policy enabled China to selectively promote certain industries or activities with the aim of encouraging them to develop their latent/potential comparative advantage. The comparative advantage-following strategy should be taken not in a static but in a dynamic way, and a nation should not only follow the initial comparative advantages, but also create new comparative advantages over time. The Chinese Government has been playing a pivotal role in industrial development in developing such dynamic comparative advantages, although the importance of the market economy has grown. The government has, in particular, directed both domestic and foreign investment towards specifically targeted sectors as soon as the latent/potential comparative advantages began to appear. Investment promotion has mainly assumed the form of (public) investment in physical infrastructure, the provision of credit at preferential interest rates and fiscal incentives.

Compared with many developing economies, China's strategy and industrial policy seem to be successful in enhancing industrial development and manufacturing upgrading. Before 1978, China's comparative advantage was suppressed by its heavy industry-oriented development strategy. As heavy industries are capital intensive and incapable of absorbing more workers, employment opportunities in the industrial sector were limited in spite of large investments. The economic reforms introduced since 1978 put China's development strategy more in line with its comparative advantages, in which priority was given to labour-intensive manufactures in order to take advantage of its abundant cheap labour (Lin and Wang 2012).

In addition to the comparative advantage-following strategy, China's industrial policy in the past three decades emphasised principles of developing through industrialisation and long-term policy goals rather than random and short-term behaviours. The policy contains the following elements: market-oriented industrial development, export-led manufacturing, FDI-led manufacturing, investing in infrastructure, and innovation through industrial agglomeration and large market-led business models. The current policy targets include developing the higher end of the global industry chain; promoting technological innovation and investing in research and development (R&D); increasing China's discourse power in the global supply chain; raising the value of made-in-China brands through improving technology, management and marketing; changing from original equipment manufacturer (OEM) to original design manufacturer (ODM) and original brand manufacturer (OBM); changing from parts manufacturing to machine manufacturing; and changing from single-business globalisation to multiple-business globalisation.

China's development strategy is premised on leveraging its advantages, including the size of its potential market and the low cost of its factor inputs—chiefly labour, but also the cost of land, electricity and raw materials. Over time, China has sought to add to these advantages by seeking to minimise its weaknesses (bureaucratic red tape, low-quality labour), upgrade its logistics capabilities and move up the technology value chain. China also seeks to leverage economies of scale, and it has made major investments in infrastructure and logistics to lower transportation costs and to speed the time to market for export products. The growth of China's supply-chain cities—led by FDI-driven clusters in Guangdong and single-product clusters in Zhejiang—is a perfect illustration of how China's government and enterprises are turning scale-driven specialisation into a persistent competitive advantage for the country. China has a coherent and multidimensional upgrading strategy to diversify its industrial mix and to add high-value activities. China is developing high-tech exports in a regionally integrated fashion, based on complex networks of export production that link leading electronics multinational enterprises (MNEs) and their first-tier suppliers and global contract manufacturers.

Exports and foreign direct investment

China and many other developing countries have pursued export-oriented and FDI-oriented strategies, but with different implications for industrial upgrading. While many developing countries followed a model associated with extensive privatisation and open markets, China has attained record levels of export growth and FDI inflows through a more statist approach to its industrial development. Liberalising imports alone was not considered to be sufficient to jump-start exports. The Chinese way has two equally important parts: economic system reform and the gradual opening of its markets to the outside world. Both are indispensable for achieving industrial growth.

The opening up of China's trade and FDI occurred in five stages. The first (1979–87) was characterised by reforms to break the state monopoly in trade, to experiment with special economic zones (SEZs) and to provide incentives for exporters. Foreign borrowing and FDI were encouraged. In the second stage (1988–93), the responsibility system and the shared foreign exchange revenue system were introduced to promote exports, and the dual exchange rate system was implemented and import tariffs began to be reduced. The third stage (1994–2001) witnessed further liberalisation in trade and FDI to prepare for WTO entry, including unifying the foreign exchange rate and reducing the tariff rate unilaterally from 40 per cent to 16 per cent. China's entry to the WTO was the start of the fourth stage (2001–14). As China's laws and institutions were conforming to international standards, trade and FDI inflows expanded dramatically (at an average annual rate of 35 per cent until 2007), and trade value exploded from $510 billion in 2001 to $2.174 trillion in 2007, and more than $4 trillion in 2014. The export structure was upgraded rapidly as well, making it comparable with that of a high-income rather than a developing economy (Rodrik 2006). The last stage began in 2014, with China 'going global': China overtook the United States as the largest trading nation; its outward FDI exceeded inward FDI; it proposed and established the Asia Infrastructure Investment Bank; and initiated the 'one belt and one road' program to encourage closer links with the rest of the world.

Foreign investors played a vital role in providing the market connections for the types of products needed by the international market, and for accessing orders for exports and the technology suitable for the development stage of the country. Thus, labour-intensive industries were able to expand rapidly. China's success has been a unique form of industrial organisation called supply-chain cities

(Gereffi 2009), which has permitted it to achieve economies of both scale and scope in global value chains. China's unique path is fascinating in its own right, but China's escalating importance as a supplier, a market and recently as a source of outward FDI makes many countries in the world highly dependent on China's future economic performance.

China also uses FDI to accelerate learning in new industries and knowledge spillovers in its domestic market. Despite restrictions imposed by the WTO against domestic performance requirements for MNEs, China's local market is sufficiently attractive for multinational manufacturers that they are willing to comply with the wishes of local, regional and national government authorities, despite stringent technology transfer requirements.

Caveats for export structure and industrial upgrading

The title of 'world's factory' was first applied to the United Kingdom during the Industrial Revolution, when that country was dominant in global industry. As the United States took off in the 1870s and surpassed the United Kingdom in terms of GDP, the United States became the world's factory, especially after World War II, when the United States made up almost half of global GDP. The strong manufacturing performance of Germany and Japan (especially the latter's industrial miracle in the 1970s) won the description of 'world manufacturing centres' for those countries.

How can China's world-factory position and advanced export structure be assessed relative to traditional industrial powers. According to the data, China's export composition resembles that of a country with an income per capita level three times higher than China's (Rodrik 2006). The overlap between China's exports to the United States and those of Organisation for Economic Cooperation and Development (OECD) countries to the United States increased from 15 per cent in 1994 to 21 per cent in 2005 (Schott 2008). Two caveats should be noted. One is that foreign-invested enterprises (FIEs) have played a very important role in China's expansion and industrial upgrading. The FIE share of China's exports rose from less than 10 per cent to 60 per cent in 1985–2007, and fell but remained at 50 per cent in 2013. FIE export share in high-technology goods is even higher. More than 90 per cent of China's high-tech exports to the United States were produced by FIEs, and about 65 per cent of China's high-tech exports to the United States were from various policy zones in China (Schott, 2008).

Another caveat relates to processing trade. A large share of China's exports involves assembling duty-free imported inputs for export in processing trade zones. The share of processing trade in China's exports rose from 47 per cent in 1992 to 55 per cent in 2007, before falling to 42 per cent in 2013. In the high export growth machinery sector, most of this growth is indeed due to growth in processing trade. More than 95 per cent of China's high-tech exports were processing exports during 1995–2006, and 90 per cent of China's expanding high-tech exports to the United States are in processing trade (Rodrik 2006 and Schott 2008).

Nevertheless, even after taking account of these caveats—that is, small value added in vertical integration and processing trade—China is still likely to outperform all other countries in export structure and industrial upgrading.

In sum, China has come a long way in upgrading, but it has been only partially successful. China has become competitive with industrial countries in high-tech sectors, but it still has a long way to go to climb the technological ladder.

Conclusion

This chapter studies China's manufacturing performance and industrial development in 1978–2014, focusing on two issues: the global position of Chinese industry and the main drivers of China's rapid industrial growth. Taking advantage of recent UNIDO (2015) data on cross-country industrial competitiveness, we assess China's industrial development based on eight indicators grouped into three dimensions (industrial capacity, industrial intensity and industrial quality). The main conclusions from this work are 1) China's large manufacturing success is manifested mainly in volume, although further development will depend on industrial quality; and 2) China's industrial development has been driven by development strategy and industrial policy, and success in exports and FDI.

International comparisons suggest advantages and disadvantages for China in industrial development. The advantages include strong and effective central government, abundant and cheap but productive labour, a huge and growing domestic market, high quality of infrastructure, and a culture of patience, persistence, innovation and frugality. The disadvantages include lack of innovation and therefore dependence on Western technology, low value added due to processing/assembly manufacturing at the bottom of the 'smiling curve', and weaknesses in logistics, marketing and sales channels. The future of China's manufacturing represents the future of emerging economies and the future of the world. There is still a long way to go for China to transform from a manufacturing giant to a centre of manufacturing quality. Innovation and operational excellence are the keys to the transformation.

References

Ahrens, N. (2013), *China's industrial policymaking process*, Washington, DC: Center for Strategic and International Studies.

Baily, M.N. and Bosworth, B.P. (2014), US manufacturing: Understanding its past and its potential future, *Journal of Economic Perspectives,* 28(1): 3–26.

Barro, R. and Sala-i-Martin, X. (1995), *Economic growth*, Cambridge, Mass.: MIT Press.

Brandt, L. and Thun, E. (2010), The fight for the middle: Upgrading, competition, and industrial development in China, *World Development,* 33(11): 1555–74.

Brandt, L., Rawski, T.G. and Sutton, J. (2008), China's industrial development, in Brandt, L. and Rawski, T.G. (eds), *China's great economic transformation,* New York: Cambridge University Press, pp. 569–632.

Central Intelligence Agency (CIA) (2015), *World factbook*, Langley, Va: CIA.

Gereffi, G. (2009), Development models and industrial upgrading in China and Mexico, *European Sociological Review*, 25(1): 37–51.

Harrison, A. and Rodriguez-Clare, A. (2010), Trade, foreign investment, and industrial policy for developing countries, *The Handbook of Development Economics*, 5: 4039–214.

Lin, J.Y. and Wang, Y. (2012), China's integration with the world: Development as a process of learning and industrial upgrading, *China Economic Policy Review*, 1(1): 1–33.

Markusen, J. and Venables, A. (1999), Foreign direct investment as a catalyst for industrial development, *European Economic Review*, 43(2): 335–56.

Nahm, J. and Steinfeld, E.S. (2014), Scale-up nation: China's specialization in innovative manufacturing, *World Development*, 54: 288–300.

National Bureau of Statistics (NBS) (various years[a]), *China statistical yearbook* [2004–12], Beijing: China Statistics Press.

National Bureau of Statistics (NBS) (various years[b]), *China industrial economy and statistical yearbook* [2004–12], Beijing: China Statistics Press.

Rodrik, D (2006), What's so special about China's exports?, *China & World Economy*, 14 (5): 1-19.

Schott, P. (2008), The relative sophistication of Chinese exports, *Economic Policy*, 23: 5-49.

United Nations (UN) (2014), *Comtrade database*, New York: UN.

United Nations Conference on Trade and Development (UNCTAD) (2002a), *Trade and development report 2002*, Geneva: UNCTAD.

United Nations Conference on Trade and Development (UNCTAD) (2002b), *World investment report 2002*, Geneva: UNCTAD.

United Nations Industrial Development Organization (UNIDO) (2002), *Industrial development report 2002/2003*, Vienna: UNIDO.

United Nations Industrial Development Organization (UNIDO) (2005), *Western China: Enhancing industrial competitiveness and employment*, Vienna: UNIDO.

United Nations Industrial Development Organization (UNIDO) (2012), *Structural change, poverty reduction and industrial policy in BRICS*, Vienna: UNIDO.

United Nations Industrial Development Organization (UNIDO) (2013), *Industrial competitiveness of nations: Looking back, forging ahead*, Vienna: UNIDO.

United Nations Industrial Development Organization (UNIDO) (2015), *UNIDO database*, Vienna: UNIDO.

World Bank (2014a), *Purchasing power parities and real expenditures of world economies*, Washington, DC: The World Bank.

World Bank (2014b), *World development indicators 2014*, Washington, DC: The World Bank.

World Bank (2015), *World development indicators 2015*, Washington, DC: The World Bank.

World Trade Organization (WTO) (2005), *World trade report 2005*, Geneva: WTO.

Zhang, K.H. (2006), *China as the world factory*, London: Routledge, Taylor & Francis.

Zhang, K.H. (2007), International production networks and export performance in developing countries: Evidence from China, *The Chinese Economy*, 40(6): 83–96.

Zhang, K.H. (2009), FDI and export performance, in Reinert, K. and Rajan, R. (eds), *The Princeton encyclopedia of the world economy*, Princeton, NJ: Princeton University Press, pp. 454–6.

Zhang, K.H. (2014), How does FDI affect industrial competitiveness? Evidence from China, *China Economics Review*, 30: 530–9.

Zhang, K.H. (forthcoming), What drives export competitiveness? Role of FDI in Chinese manufacturing, *Contemporary Economic Policy*.

Zhao, Z. and Zhang, K.H. (2007), China's industrial competitiveness in the world, *The Chinese Economy*, 40(6): 6–23.

Zhao, Z. and Zhang, K.H. (2010), FDI and industrial productivity in China: Evidence from panel data in 2001–2006, *Review of Development Economics*, 14(3): 656–65.

13. China Becomes a Capital Exporter

Trends and issues

Mei (Lisa) Wang, Zhen Qi and Jijing Zhang

Introduction

The rapid rise of China's outbound direct investment (ODI) in the past decade is a significant economic phenomenon. According to China's Ministry of Commerce, in 2014 Chinese companies invested US$116 billion in 156 countries—about 45 times more than in 2002. If new investments by Chinese companies with an existing foreign presence abroad were included, China's ODI in 2014 would have exceeded inbound FDI by about US$20 billion—that is, China became a net capital exporting country in 2014 (Ministry of Commerce 2015).

The surge in China's ODI has in fact encountered a lot of resistance in some destination countries. Questions arise about Chinese companies' investment motivations, and there are concerns expressed about Chinese ODI approaches. Moreover, some consider Chinese investment a threat. Former minister of commerce Deming Chen suggests that only one-third of China's intended investments in the United States receive approval from authorities (Hornby 2013). In other words, there is a large share of potential Chinese ODI that has failed to go abroad. Similarly, there is the potential of significant benefit, for China and destination countries, in better understanding China's ODI.

This chapter addresses selective concerns about Chinese companies and the resistance they have encountered in their ODI experiences. It particularly focuses on the fact that a significant share of China's outbound investment is by state-owned firms. The background to China's state-owned enterprise (SOE) reform process explains why and how SOEs have behaved in making ODI. The chapter also discusses the new round of SOE reforms and the implications for the future development of China's ODI. The aim of this is both to facilitate China's globalisation process and to enable destination countries to benefit from Chinese ODI potential by having a clear understanding of the institutional background against which Chinese SOEs have participated in ODI.

The chapter has three further sections. Section two analyses trends and discusses issues in Chinese ODI focusing on SOEs' motivations and political connections in determining ODI. Section three discusses the new round of SOE reform and the implications for Chinese ODI. We then discuss and conclude in section four.

Trends and issues in China's ODI

Trends in China's ODI

Recent trends

Since the period of opening-up and reform, China's outbound FDI has moved in four phases. The first, early in the reform period, from 1980 to 1990, was when ODI was negligible (Figure 13.1). China's goal at that time was solely to attract inbound investment. From 1991 to 2000, ODI was similarly limited, reaching just US$2.3 billion in the period (Figure 13.1).

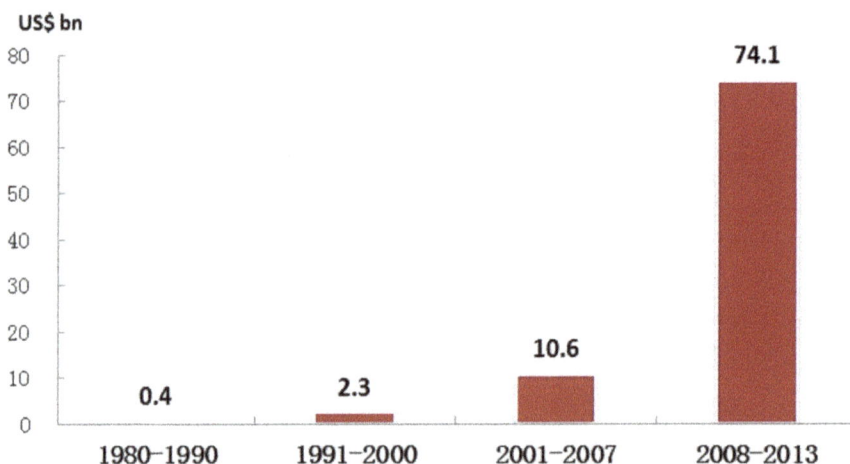

Figure 13.1 Four stages of China's ODI

Source: Foreign direct investment data set compiled by United Nations Conference on Trade and Development (UNCTAD).

In 2001, China's economy shifted from being just 'open' towards also being outbound. First, China became a member of the World Trade Organization (WTO). Second, the Chinese Government launched its 'going out' policy, which encouraged ODI via selective incentives. This marks the third phase of China's ODI development (Figure 13.1). Specifically, from 2001 to 2007, China's ODI rose to US$10.6 billion. This is 4.6 times the level of ODI in 1991–2000. In the years since the global financial crisis (GFC), however, China's ODI has grown at an extraordinary rate (Figure 13.1).

Figure 13.2 illustrates the dramatic rise in China's ODI flows. From 2002 to 2013, it grew at a compound rate of some 40 per cent (Figure 13.2).[1] Average annual ODI since the GFC has reached US$74 billion—seven times the level of ODI in 2001–07 (Figure 13.2). Since some research has highlighted that a good share of China's ODI passes through Hong Kong or is otherwise excluded from national statistics, these levels could be far higher.

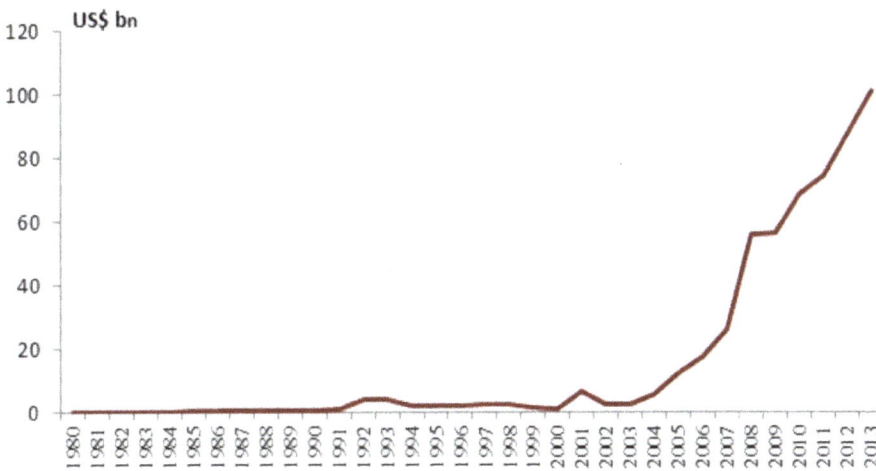

Figure 13.2 China's ODI flows, 1980–2013

Source: UNCTAD.

By the end of 2013, China's ODI flow and stock were US$101 billion and US$614 billion, respectively, ranking China at number three and number 12 in the world, respectively. China ranks first among developing countries in both categories.

Future prospects[2]

China's ODI has developed rapidly in the past decade. There is vast potential for additional ODI growth.

The 'investment development path' theory is based on an empirical analysis of 67 countries in the period 1967–78 (Dunning 1981), which found a tendency for net ODI to be cyclical around the level of economic development. Between a gross

---

1 Because the flow was unusually low in 2000 and unusually high in 2001, the flow in 2002 was used.
2 The work is based on Professor Fan Gang's advice.

national product (GNP) per capita range of US$5,000 and US$10,000, ODI tends to reach a transition point where it surpasses the level of inbound investment—that is, the net outward investment (NOI) becomes positive, and the country becomes a net direct investment exporter.

In China's case, GNP per capita reached US$5,680 in 2012, at which point China's outbound investment was still less than its inbound FDI by US$27.5 billion. It was not until 2014, when China's gross domestic product (GDP) per capita reached $7,485, that China's NOI become positive. In line with the per capita range identified by Dunning (1981), China's ODI surge is in the mid range of the theory's predictions.

Looking forward, it is estimated that China's ODI will increase at the annual compound growth rate of 19–22 per cent in the decade from 2013 (Wang 2014).[3] This would make the total increased volume of China's ODI during 2013–20 between US$2.5 trillion and US$3.6 trillion (Figure 13.3). The estimates of Wang (2014) are higher than Rhodium Group's estimate of US$1–2 trillion, but lower than that of the Hong Kong Institute for Monetary Research (HKIMR), which puts the figure at US$4.6 trillion (Figure 13.4).[4]

Whatever the precise level, China's ODI is set to keep growing rapidly in the next decade.

---

3 See detailed analysis in Wang (2014).

4 HKIMR's estimation is based on very optimistic assumptions. For example, they assume that China's average GDP growth rate is 8.4 per cent during 2012–15 and 7 per cent during 2016–20. The authors' assumption is 7 per cent during 2013–17 and 6.5 per cent during 2018–22.

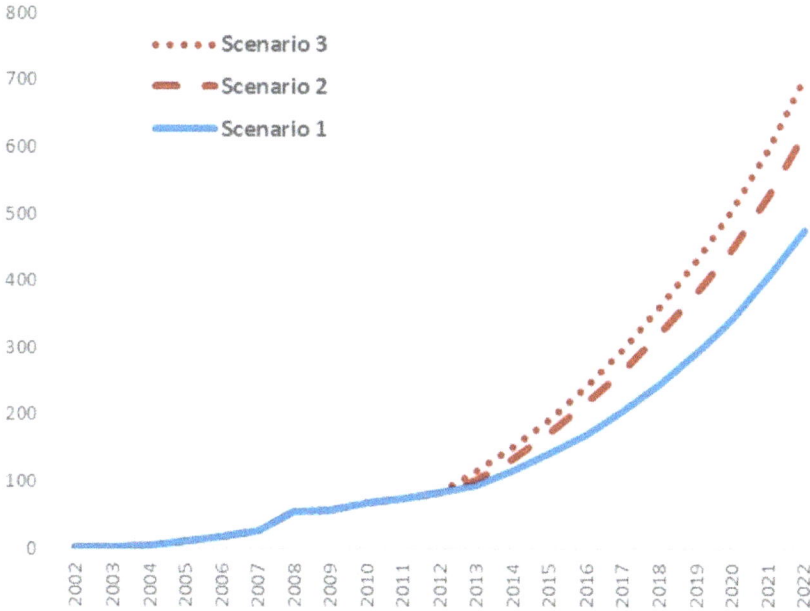

Figure 13.3 Estimated annual flow of Chinese ODI, 2013–22 (US$ billion)

Source: Wang (2014).

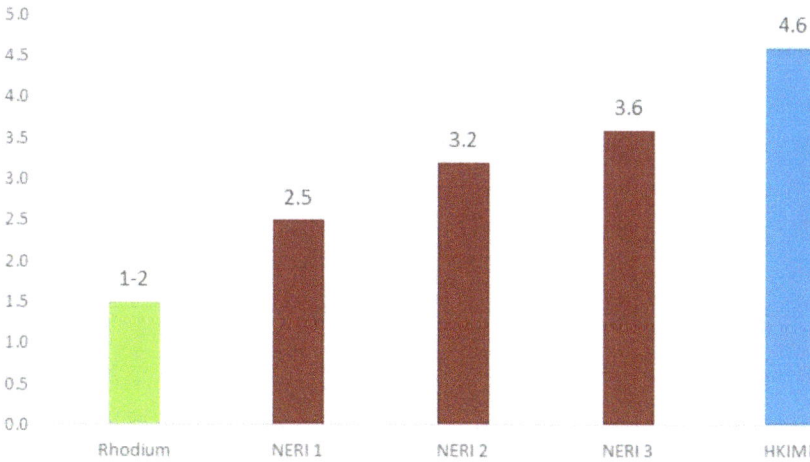

Figure 13.4 Comparison of China's future ODI estimations, 2013–22
(US$ trillion)

NERI = National Economic Research Institute.
Note: Estimation by Rhodium and HKIMR is for the period 2011–20.
Sources: Rhodium from Rosen and Hanemann (2011); Hong Kong Institute for Monetary Research
(HKIMR) from He et al. (2012).

China is not the only developing country with surging ODI levels. As the share of global GDP of developing economies has grown and per capita incomes have risen into the US$5,000–10,000 range identified by Dunning (1981), so too has their collective ODI. Figure 13.5 charts developing-country ODI across 40 years—from almost nothing to more than one-third of total global ODI.

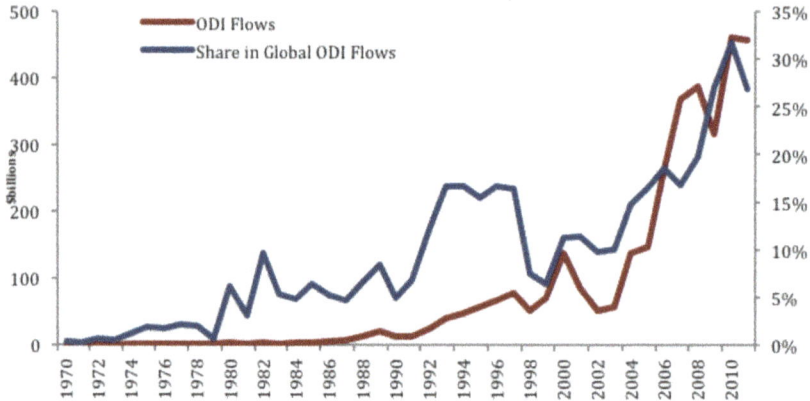

Figure 13.5 ODI of developing countries

Source: UNCTAD.

Figure 13.6 illustrates ODI trends among several of the largest emerging market economies, the BRIC countries (Brazil, Russia, India and China), in particular after the GFC. About the time of the GFC, China's ODI surpassed Russia's to become number one amongst these four countries.

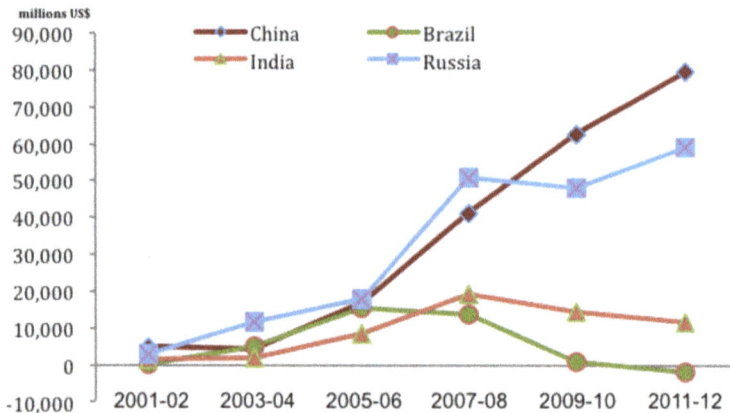

Figure 13.6 BRIC ODI

BRIC = Brazil, Russia, India and China.
Source: UNCTAD.

Traditional ODI theories were developed primarily around developed-country ODI as, until the turn of the century, these ODI flows dominated global ODI. There is an insufficient comparative body of research on ODI between developing countries to understand whether these earlier theories still provide an ideal framework for analysis in this new, more varied global ODI landscape. Indeed, in this new landscape, there are cases where developing countries have become the largest investors in developed economies—for example, the case of Chinese ODI into Australia.

Issues in China's ODI

Dominance of SOEs

As noted earlier, the rapid growth of China's ODI has led to concern in some host destinations. These concerns come from not only the media and the general public, but also governments, scholars and other analysts. A leading concern is the high share of China's ODI by Chinese SOEs.

The ODI of China is in fact dominated by SOEs, even though it is not easy to confirm this using official data. Specifically, China's official ODI data list numerous state-owned or state-controlled corporations under the broader classification of 'corporation', from which it is not possible to distinguish whether these corporations are state or privately owned.

Our attempt to explore SOE ODI relies on data compiled by the US-based Heritage Foundation's *China global investment tracker* (HF 2015), which has recorded Chinese ODI and contracts of more than US$100 million since 2005. That this series from the HF tracks only transactions of more than US$100 million suggests that non-SOEs' investment—mostly smaller transactions—is under-represented. On the other hand, as an unofficial tracker, it could also miss some SOE investments. We assume the HF data are representative.

By the end of 2013, according to the foreign direct investment dataset compiled by United Nations Conference on Trade and Development (UNCTAD), China's ODI stock was US$614 billion, while HF records China's ODI (excluding the contracts) as US$476 billion between 2005 and 2013. This suggests the HF data capture some 78 per cent of China's ODI, even though its record starts only from 2005. It is not known whether the difference relates to large investments that were not included in the HF dataset or whether the difference is made up of ODI transactions below the US$100 million limit of the tracker.

Based on the HF dataset, we identify companies one by one and categorise them as SOEs and non-SOEs. The dominance of SOEs within Chinese ODI is obvious, especially before 2009 (Figure 13.7). According to our calculations, between 2005 and 2013, 89.4 per cent of the US$807.5 billion of Chinese ODI and contracts were linked to SOEs.

With an estimated 90 per cent of China's ODI from SOEs, demystifying SOEs is the key to understanding Chinese ODI. Among the concerns of ODI recipient countries is that SOE ODI is driven by the Chinese Government, and in turn motivated by political and state-based strategic considerations, not commercial ones. That generates fear that SOE investment is potentially harmful to the national interest of destination countries.

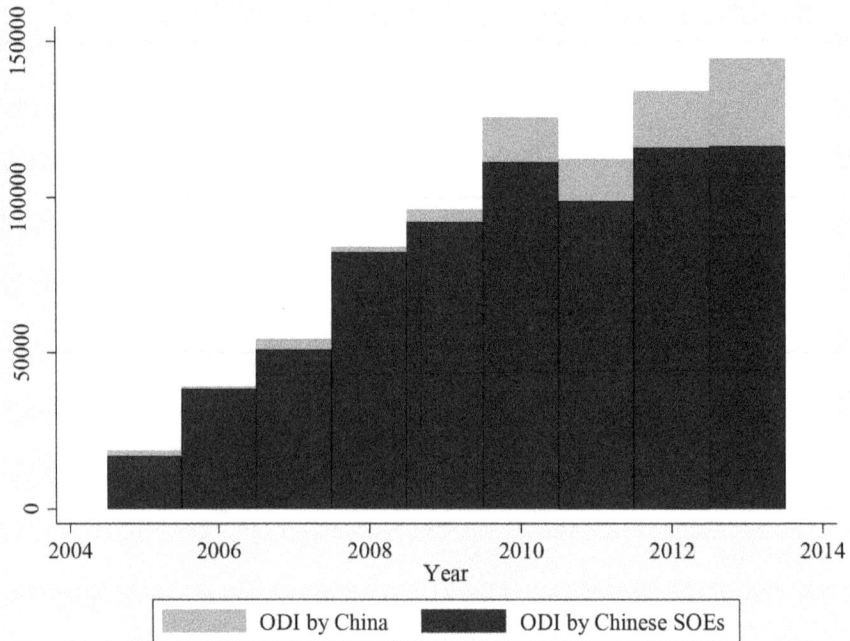

Figure 13.7 ODI by China and Chinese SOEs above US$100 million

Note: The value here includes both investments and contracts, so the value here is larger than the UNCTAD data. On average, 59 per cent is investments and the rest are contracts.
Source: Heritage Foundation (2015); and authors' calculations.

These concerns are understandable. China's rising ODI is new. Traditionally, ODI has moved between Organisation for Economic Cooperation and Development (OECD) countries, and from OECD countries to developing countries. In the case of China's ODI, China is not only a developing country but also a transitional economy. It is not a member of the OECD. This means that China's ODI comes from an economy with a unique system that is not easy to understand. Understanding it demands energy, time and interest in learning about it. Of course, some concerns could be protectionism in disguise.

Regulatory environment confronting China's ODI

In response to such concerns, the overseas regulatory environment confronting China's ODI is getting tougher, especially towards SOEs. For example, following the passage of the *US Foreign Investment and National Security Act* of 2007, Australia also issued new foreign investment guidelines, in 2008, while Canada introduced an amendment to the *Investment Canada Act* in 2009. All have made SOEs' investments in their domestic markets more difficult.

In the United States, 2012 marked a shift in the apparent scrutiny of Chinese investment in that country. That year, the number of Chinese transactions reviewed by the Committee on Foreign Investment in the United States (CFIUS) jumped 109 per cent—from 11 transactions in 2011 to 23 in 2012 (CFIUS 2012). China accounted for 20 per cent of the total transactions covered by CFIUS (Figure 13.8) (CFIUS 2012). In comparison, China's investment in the United States comprised only 2.5 per cent of total FDI in the United States that year (UNCTAD).

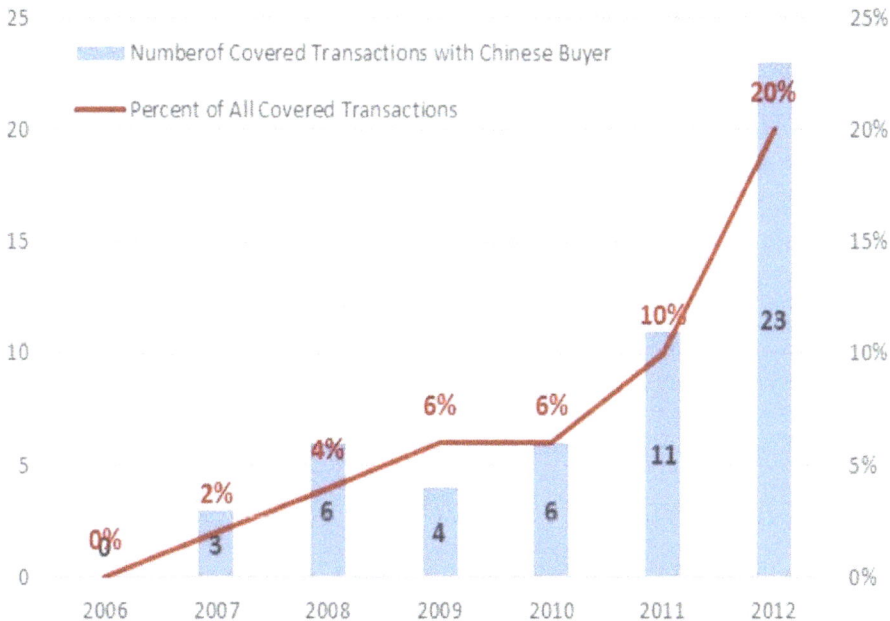

Figure 13.8 Chinese transactions covered by the Committee on Foreign Investment in the United States

Sources: US Treasury Department; Rhodium Group; authors' calculations.

Figure 13.9 illustrates the characteristics of Chinese ODI in the United States in the third quarter of 2014, which is after the investment review process was tightened. In this quarter, SOEs' investment in the United States almost disappeared (Hanemann and Gao 2014).

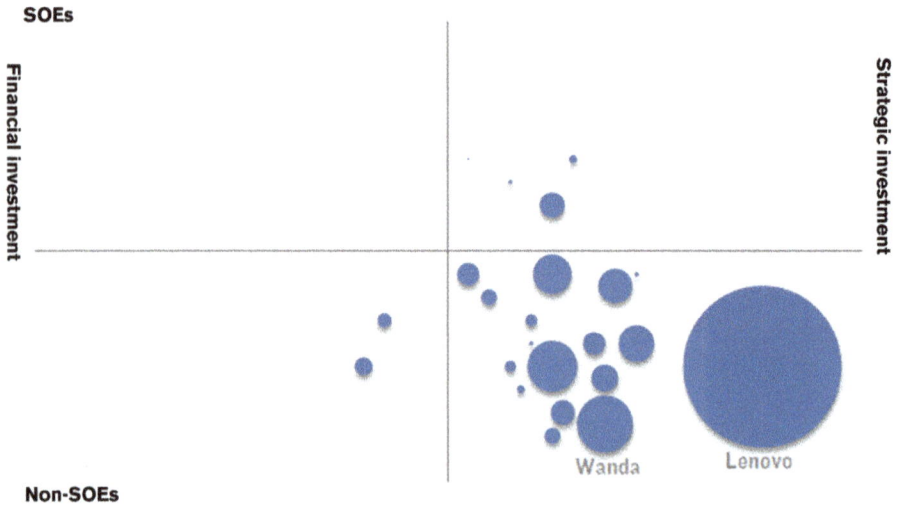

Figure 13.9 Typology of Chinese entities investing in the United States, Q3 2014

Source: Hanemann and Gao (2014).

In addition to investments reviewed by CFIUS, many proposed transactions were withdrawn by Chinese companies before the review stage, after informal exchanges with regulatory agencies or their legal advisors. These abandoned bids are unknown to the public. Deming Chen, former Chinese minister of commerce, said in March 2013, '[r]oughly one dollar of every three dollars we want to invest in the U.S. gets approved' (Hornby 2013).

Let us take an example of how process affects Chinese investment attempts in the United States. In July 2012, CITIC Securities, the biggest securities house in China, announced that it had approved its subsidiary, CITIC Securities International, to purchase 100 per cent of equity in Credit Lyonnais Securities Asia (CLSA),[5] for US$1.25 billion. The transaction was closed a year later, in late July 2013. One of the main causes of the delay was that the US Government was against the transaction—because CITIC Securities' biggest shareholder was CITIC Group (which owns 20 per cent of CITIC Securities) and CITIC Group is owned by China's Ministry of Finance. The US Government does not want a US company—CLSA Americas LLC—to be controlled by the Chinese Government.

---

5   CLSA is a brokerage firm that used to be owned by Credit Lyonnais, a French company.

The deal was only approved when China's Vice-Premier Wang Yang personally raised the issue during the fifth round of the US–China Strategic and Economic Dialogue, held in early July 2013.

In 2012, a US$15 billion acquisition of Canadian company Nexen by China's third-largest oil company, China National Offshore Oil Corporation (CNOOC), was considered by many as a breakthrough for China's overseas investment. Canadian Prime Minister Stephen Harper, when announcing approval of the deal in December 2012, said that the government had been making efforts to reduce state ownership in economic sectors, but the energy sector had been made an exception in being bought and controlled by foreign governments instead. Although China's CNOOC, as an SOE, has received approval for the Nexen deal, it was followed by the Canadian Government indicating that it intends to impose stricter rules in future for foreign state-owned companies acquiring Canadian companies. CFIUS has also barred CNOOC from operating Nexen's Gulf of Mexico oilfields. In 2013, Lenovo, a leading private computer company in China, which some consider a state-supported enterprise (*The Economist* 2012), attempted to acquire Blackberry, but the deal was rejected by the Canadian Government.

There is new uncertainty about trade and investment policies. The United States is leading the formation of Asia's biggest trade and investment agreement, the Trans-Pacific Partnership (TPP), but without the inclusion of China—the region's largest economy. An article in *The Economist* considers this initiative nonsensical (*The Economist* 2014). A former US undersecretary of state Robert Hormats has linked the TPP to restrictions on investments by SOEs and SSEs [state-supported enterprises] that, he says, may have an unfair competitive advantage in the US or in third countries, through anti-competitive practices which require 'a robust and effective policy response'. The TPP, in his view, is a significant opportunity to move the SOE issue forward (Hormats 2011).

In order to clarify SOEs' motivations in ODI, it is necessary to investigate SOE reform and the principal–agent problem.

The evolving role of SOEs

At the end of 2013, there were 156,000 SOEs (incorporated enterprises, not corporation groups) in China. Among them, 52,000 were central SOEs (some of them are subsidiaries of 112 central SOE groups, which are under the supervision of the State-Owned Assets Supervision and Administration Commission; some were SOEs affiliated with central ministries, such as the Ministry of Finance), and 104,000 were provincial or other local SOEs. The total number of SOE employees was about 37 million, 18 million of whom were employed by central SOEs, and 19 million by local SOEs (Ministry of Finance 2014).

At the end of 2013, the combined assets of SOEs stood at RMB104 trillion (US$17 trillion)—up 16.3 per cent year-on-year (yoy); and the total outstanding debt was RMB67.1 trillion (US$10.9 trillion)—up 16.7 per cent yoy. In 2013, SOEs' operating revenue rose 10.8 per cent to RMB47.1 trillion (US$7.7 trillion), and profits increased 5.3 per cent to RMB2.6 trillion (US$400 billion). The companies paid a total of RMB3.8 trillion (US$620 billion) in taxes in 2013—up 5.4 per cent yoy (Ministry of Finance 2014).

In the past 30 years, Chinese SOEs have undergone a series of reforms, including on bankruptcy, mergers and acquisitions. From the first SOE bankruptcy, of Shenyang Explosion in 1986, to the first SOE listing, of China Communications Construction Company, on the Hong Kong Stock Exchange in 2006, and the first SOE (CITIC) moving its headquarters to Hong Kong in 2014, the Chinese SOEs have undergone profound changes.

At the core of this is change to the management system and operating modality. At the beginning of the 1980s, Chinese SOEs were directly attached to the government bodies that, in turn, were deeply involved in SOE operations. During the 1980s and 1990s, initial reforms were carried out to separate the government's ownership from management's operating role. Early last decade, nine government bodies engaged in managing SOEs were abolished. The resistance to these reforms was immense. Then Premier Zhu Rongji declared 'I am willing to risk my life to carry this reform through'.

From 1998 to 2006, the number of SOEs decreased by 59 per cent, from more than 60,000 to less than 30,000. The number of people employed by SOEs fell from about 37 million to about 18 million (Shao 2007). Many small and medium SOEs have been privatised.

In 2003, the Chinese Government established the State-Owned Assets Supervision and Administration Commission (SASAC). SASAC is the SOE empowered to execute regulatory authority over and determine the rights of SOEs. Unlike former regulators, SASAC enjoys consolidated powers over SOE regulation—there has been a massive shift from fragmented to concentrated regulatory power. This new regulatory regime exerts a subtle influence on SOEs' behaviour, the detailed mechanism for which will be discussed in the section exploring SOEs' motivations.

In 2006, SASAC issued the 'Guiding Opinions on Pushing Forward the Adjustment of State-Owned Capital and Merger and Acquisition of State-Owned Enterprises'. The document made it clear that if central SOEs did not rank among the top three of their industry, they would be merged and acquired. The goal then was to reduce the number of central SOEs from 155 to between 80 and 100.

Eight years later, in 2014, there were 112 central SOE groups. In the intervening years, the SOE performance evaluation criteria set up by SASAC was revised several times, with profit-making at its core. By 2013, there were about 260 SOEs listed overseas, and 953 SOEs listed on the domestic stock market (*People's Daily* 2013).

Therefore, after a series of reforms, SOEs' motivations and political connections have been reshaped.

Is SOE ODI commercially motivated?

Many scholars have undertaken comprehensive analyses of whether SOEs are commercially motivated (for example, Cornish 2012; Downs 2007; Drysdale 2011; Drysdale and Findlay 2009; Hanemann and Rosen 2012; Rosen and Hanemann 2011). These scholars have concluded that that SOEs are generally commercially motivated, but concerns remain. There is a spectrum of SOE behaviours, and this leads to a spectrum of different views.

Central SOEs: China CNR versus China CSR

China CNR and China CSR are both leading companies in the rail rolling stock industry in China. Both are centrally owned SOEs and both are listed on the Hong Kong and Shanghai stock exchanges.

In the second half of 2012, Argentina announced a decision to purchase a fleet of city rail cars. China CNR, Alstom and several other companies participated in the bid. China CNR's bid price was US$2.3 million per car, and other companies' bid prices were about US$2 million per car. This prompted China CSR to approach Argentina with a lower bid, of US$1.27 million per car. Ignoring the Chinese Government's request that it should first register at the China Chamber of Commerce for the Import and Export of Machinery and Electronic Products (CCCME), China CSR ultimately won the contract to supply 409 cars to Argentina for a total of US$514 million.

The reason for China CSR's bid being much lower was that its car design was for an older model and its car parts would be made in China, while China CNR's bid was for a newer car model and the car parts would be imported. As a result, China CSR was able to make a profit at its low bid price. Furthermore, China CSR was at the time short of orders and facing operating difficulties.[6]

---

6   The two companies were merged by the end of 2014. One of the purposes was to avoid the harmful cut-throat competition between them.

SOE versus a privately owned enterprise: Zoomlion and Sany

Zoomlion and Sany are both leading public companies in the construction machinery industry in China. Zoomlion is listed on both the Hong Kong and the Shanghai stock exchanges. Sany is listed only on the Shanghai Stock Exchange.

Zoomlion is a provincial government company, operating under the auspices of the Hunan Assets Supervision and Administration Commission. Zoomlion was established in 1992. It had been growing at a compound annual rate of 65 per cent for 20 years.

Sany is a privately owned enterprise (POE)—that is, founded and owned by private individuals, with chairman Liang Wengen as its controlling shareholder. Sany was established in 1994 and has been growing at about 50 per cent annually. It was selected by the *Financial Times* as one of the FT Global 500 in July 2011, becoming the only Chinese machinery company on the list.

In November 2007, the Italian company CIFA, the world's third-largest concrete machinery company, launched a public auction for its shares. Zoomlion and Sany both submitted bids in January 2008. Zoomlion partnered with Goldman Sachs and won the bid. Afterwards, the chairman of Zoomlion said that even though the timing of the bid was not good (on the eve of the GFC), it could not let CIFA fall into the hands competitors.

Another example from Europe is from late 2011. When German company Putzmeister, the world's number one brand in concrete machinery, was looking for a buyer in December 2011, Zoomlion and Sany both received invitations to bid. Even though Zoomlion was the only company with approval from the National Development and Reform Commission (NDRC) to participate in the bid, Sany partnered with CITIC PE and succeeded in acquiring Putzmeister in a record 33 days.

These two cases are examples of Chinese SOEs competing fiercely with each other and with POEs. They also illustrate how SOEs and POEs do not necessarily follow the coordinating efforts of the Chinese Government to enhance their own business as independent commercial entities.

How do political elements influence SOEs' ODI?

Being state-owned, SOEs are clearly connected closely with the government and politics. However, this does not necessarily mean that SOEs' behaviour reflects their owners' policy purposes. Twisted by the complicated principal–agent problem, SOEs tend to pursue their own rather than their owners' objectives.

It is essential to understand SOEs' principal–agent problem. There are three tiers to the SOE principal–agent system: the nation or all people as principal are located on the top; as agents, the SOEs' managers are at the bottom of the three tiers; the regulators, who exercise SOE owners' authority and rights on behalf of the principal, are in the middle.

Within this system, regulators play multiple and significant roles. On behalf of the whole nation, they scrutinise SOE investment proposals, select and assign SOE managers, inspect SOE productivity, examine SOE restructuring plans, and evaluate senior managers' performances, as well as other performance or proposals. In other words, the regulators are involved in and exert subtle influence on SOEs' operation.

As the bridge connecting the SOE owners with SOE managers, regulators have dual characters: economic and political. By changing the regulatory structure and political environment, the nation or government can exert influence on regulators' incentives and also constrain their behaviour. The changed behaviour of regulators in turn affects the SOEs' behaviour and performance.

Regulatory regime change

We divide the regulatory regime into 'separated regime' and 'integrated regime' according to the degree of concentration of regulatory power. The regulatory regime is integrated where fewer regulators enjoy a higher concentration of power. The regime is regulated where there are more regulators and a lower concentration of power.

Since the market-oriented reforms introduced in 1978, Chinese SOEs' regulatory regime has been changing dramatically. The main trend since the reforms began in 1978 is towards consolidating what were decentralised regulatory powers. There has been incremental transition from a separated regime to an integrated regime.

The regulatory regime transition since 1982 can be divided into two periods that pivot around 2003, the year in which the creation of SASAC led to greater concentration of regulatory power. From 1982 to 2003, there were for the most part four SOE regulators: the State Economic and Trade Commission for examining SOEs' reform and reconstruction; the Ministry of Finance for asset management and financial supervision; the Ministry of Organisation for selecting and assigning SOE managers; and the Central Work Committee for Large Enterprises, ensuring the implementation of the party's policies. There were also 10 specialised industrial ministries depending on the year, including the Ministry of Textiles, Ministry of Coal and Ministry of Mechanical Engineering Industry. These took responsibility for their corresponding industry's planning, coordination and supervision. Generally, before 2003, the regulatory power was distributed among various regulators, which can be called 'a separated regulatory regime' as compared with 'an integrated regime', to be discussed next.

In 2003, SASAC was established, consolidating all the powers of the State Economic and Trade Commission, Ministry of Finance, Central Work Committee for Large Enterprises, Ministry of Organization, and so on. This in turn means that SASAC monopolises all regulatory powers over SOEs. Consequently, the period after 2003 can be viewed as an integrated regulatory regime, taking the concentration of regulatory power into consideration.

According to Qi et al. (2015), there is a trade-off in these regime choices. A more decentralised, separated regime has comparative advantage in reducing the risks of collusion between regulators and SOEs. An integrated and more centralised regime has comparative advantage in effective use of regulatory powers.

There is a free-riding problem in the separated regulatory regime. When regulatory powers are shared by several regulators, responsibility for success and failure is diffused amongst all players. In the separated or decentralised regulatory regime, Chinese SOEs repeatedly complained that all the regulators would claim success when their SOEs outperformed expectations, but avoid responsibility when SOEs underperformed. Regulators in the separated regime do not have sufficient incentive to promote good performance in the SOE, including when that would involve expanding domestically or internationally.

The establishment of SASAC resolved the problem of free-riding, because reward or punishment for good or bad performance goes to the sole regulator. Regulators' reputations for competence are enhanced by successful expansion into more mature and competitive foreign markets. Promoting ODI is also a way for regulators to respond to the national strategy of 'going out', and by so doing, to accumulate credits for future promotion.

The Chinese national strategy of 'going out' was initiated in the late 1990s, but was not implemented effectively until a decade later. According to the mechanism described above, only if the related government departments' incentive problems were solved properly could the 'going out' strategy be implemented effectively. The establishment of SASAC solved the incentive problems, assisting the acceleration of SOEs' ODI after the mid-2000s.

Another concern of SOE regulation is the need for mechanisms to prevent collusion between regulators and SOEs. The state delegates to regulators so that they can supervise SOE behaviour. This in turn mitigates the SOE principal–agent problem, although it does not completely remove it. In the process of regulation, the regulators can potentially collude with the SOEs they regulate for their own benefit and at the expense of the state. For regulators, collusion has at least two faces: bribery and the 'revolving door'.

Corruption related to a regulator's abuse of power is not uncommon in the Chinese state sector. This can be indirectly demonstrated by the dozens of SOE officials who have been investigated and charged during the national anti-corruption campaign that was instigated in 2013. The revolving-door phenomenon is also a salient problem in the Chinese state sector. According to the Unirule Institute of Economics (2011), among 19 ministries and commissions, 30.6 per cent of the 183 leaders with at least the rank of Vice Minister have at some point been employed by an SOE. Zhou (2010) shows that among the SOEs listed on the Chinese A Share Market, 1,142 senior corporate executives—some 50 per cent—used to serve as government officials.

The revolving door gives regulatory officials an incentive to collude with SOEs. They can, for example, avoid strictly imposing regulation to keep a friendly relationship with their potential SOE's colleagues.

While the integrated regulator has a stronger incentive to perform well and is less constrained than separated regulators in using regulatory powers, the separated regime regulators can check and balance one another. The checks and balances reduce the risk of collusion (Qi 2015).

Collusion, causes losses to the SOE owners—for example, through approval of inefficient investments. However, extra costs are incurred when owners try to police this kind of collusion.

As the Chinese regulatory regime changed from a separated to an integrated regime, SOE regulators had stronger incentives to promote SOEs' ODI. SOEs' investments have increased dramatically since the establishment of SASAC in 2003. However, possible collusion between the regulator and SOE under the SASAC regime can lead to lower quality ODI. Low-quality ODI could contribute to SOE ODI growth, but lower the efficiency of Chinese ODI as a whole.

Political environment

The second factor that influences regulator incentives and constraints is the political environment. Currently, the biggest factors that influence government officials' inventiveness and constraint are the breadth and depth of the ongoing national anti-corruption effort.

China's corruption problem is severe. In 2014, China ranked 100th among 175 countries on the Transparency International's Corruption Perceptions Index—on par with Algeria and Suriname. Corruption can lead to low-quality investment—domestically and internationally—and so impose a cost on the SOE owner and the Chinese economy.

Since 2013, Chinese President Xi Jinping has overseen a high-profile anti-corruption campaign. This has targeted hundreds of thousands of officials at all levels of government and in the state-owned sector. As of 2015, it had executed cases involving 100 high-level officials, including several very senior executives of SOEs, and punished more than 70,000 officials for violations of the eight-point anti-graft rules. More than 200,000 petty officials have also been targeted. Considering the number of officials punished and the scale of scrutiny, this anti-corruption campaign is considered the toughest in China for 30 years.

The scale of this anti-corruption action has had several consequences for China's SOE ODI. It slows SOE ODI growth, but ultimately enhances its efficiency. According to the analysis framework we have applied here, the regulator's incentive for promoting ODI partially comes from benefits from collusion. In an environment with intense anti-corruption efforts, regulators' and SOEs' collusive behaviour is easier to investigate—that is, regulator incentives to collude with SOEs have been compressed by anti-corruption actions. Reduction of the expected benefits from collusion discourages regulator and SOE collusion, and reduces inefficient investments.

Our analysis shows that SOE behaviour is affected by political elements such as the regulatory regime and the political environment. The perceptions of some destination countries differ from the actual behaviour of SOEs not only because the State sees value in good commercial performance of the companies which it owns, but also because principal–agent problems means the managers do not always follow the objectives of the State.

Chinese SOEs cannot be compared with those three decades ago during the central planning era. Moreover, SOEs keep changing as the reforms grow broader and deeper over time.

SOE reform: Implications for China's ODI

At the Third Plenary Session of the Eighteenth Communist Party of China Central Committee, held in November 2013, 'The Decision on Major Issues Concerning Comprehensively Deepening Reforms' was adopted. SOE reforms make up a key element of reforms within the decision.

The main components of this next round of SOE reforms include developing a mixed-ownership economy, improving the state-owned asset management system, improving SOE governance and management systems, and strengthening the budget system for state-owned capital operation.

Developing a mixed-ownership economy, in particular, is central to the new round of SOE reforms. Mixed ownership refers to allowing more SOEs and enterprises of other ownership types to develop into mixed-ownership enterprises. This means allowing private capital to invest in state-owned capital investment projects, and allowing mixed-ownership enterprises to adopt employee stock ownership so as to align the interests of capital owners and workers.

Currently, the overall design of the SOE reform is being studied and developed under the leadership of a unit within the Central Leading Group for Comprehensively Deepening Reform,[7] chaired by President Xi. Key questions of the reform being discussed and explored include how and what share private capital can take in SOEs, how senior management might be allowed to hold stocks, and how state-owned capital investment and operating companies can be established. On the final point, the question is whether to transform existing central SOEs into separate holding and operating companies, or to divide central SOEs into different groups, with the larger and stronger ones sponsoring and establishing holding and operating companies.

A number of central SOEs have already started reforms within the new policies. For example, the board of China Petroleum & Chemical Corporation (Sinopec)—China's largest manufacturer and supplier of petroleum products and major petrochemical products—approved a plan to restructure its fuel retail business and invite private capital to form a mixed-ownership company. The shareholding percentage allocated to private capital is up to 30 per cent (*Shanghai Securities Daily* 2014).

Separately, in October 2013, Sinopec announced it would look for investors for its Monteny and Duvernay shale gas projects in Canada, which Sinopec acquired in 2011. The hope is that this will lower Sinopec's own capital requirement and also speed up development of the projects. The Canadian Minister of National Resources commented that this SOE was operating just like a commercial entity, in buying, selling and bringing in investors (Reuters 2013).

A second example is from China's largest oil and gas producer and distributor, PetroChina. In March 2014, PetroChina announced it would establish six separate platforms for its undeveloped reserves, unconventional oil, gas, transmission, refinery (onshore and offshore) and financial businesses. It plans

---

7   The unit's name is Economic System and Ecological Civilization System Reform Group.

to use the production share model to bring in private capital and push for a mixed-ownership system. This reform reflects PetroChina's desire to open the entire business chain, and also to outcompete Sinopec.

In the power sector, China Power Investment Corporation (CPI Corp), one of the five largest state-owned electricity producers in China, announced in March 2013 that it would allow private capital to invest in some of its subsidiaries and projects. This would extend to up to one-third of the total share capital.

CITIC Pacific's acquisition of CITIC Limited in March 2013 caught the market's attention. The acquisition process involved CITIC Group injecting most of its operating businesses, currently held by CITIC Limited, into its Hong Kong-listed subsidiary company, CITIC Pacific (Figure 13.10). The deal would be the largest asset injection into a Hong Kong-listed company from the Chinese mainland.

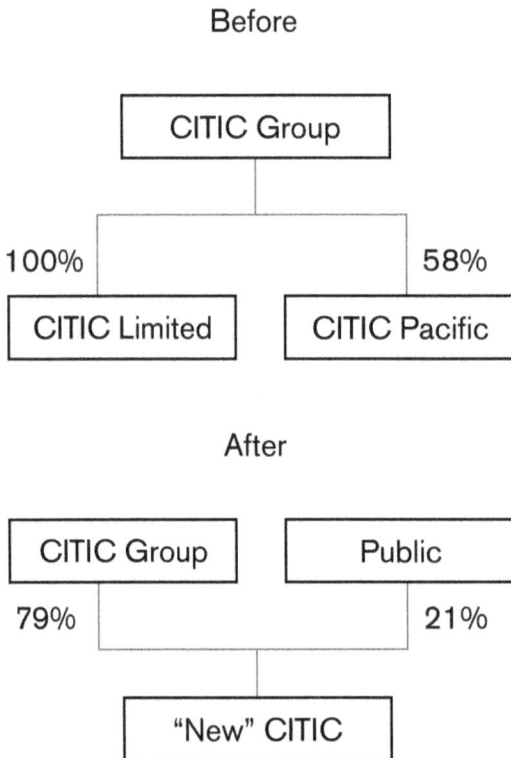

Figure 13.10 CITIC before and after the acquisition
Source: CITIC.

The 'new' CITIC headquarters will be in Hong Kong. As a Hong Kong-listed company, the new CITIC will be subject to the more mature legal system of Hong Kong and similarly to the higher supervision standards of Hong Kong regulators and media. This will help make its operations and finances more transparent, and will also improve its management system and corporate governance. Changes will include adopting an employee stock option plan, recruiting senior management from the market, lowering the government's ownership share and attracting more private and overseas capital.

On 15 July 2014, SASAC announced pilot reforms applying to six central SOEs, including State Development and Investment Corp, China National Cereals, Oils and Foodstuffs Corporation (COFCO), Sinopharm, China Construction, China Energy Conservation and Environmental Protection Group, and Xinxing Cathay International Group. The pilot projects include 1) transforming central SOEs into state-owned capital investment companies; 2) developing central SOEs into mixed-ownership companies; and 3) giving central SOE boards the right to recruit senior management personnel from the market, and to assess their performance and determine compensation independently.

At the provincial level, almost all of the 32 provinces and municipalities have publicly announced SOE reform plans. For example, Gree Electric Appliances Inc., a provincially owned entity in Guangdong and a leading electric appliances company in China, will transfer up to 49 per cent of its shares to investors through an open bidding process. These plans received positive reactions from capital markets.

What's new in this round of SOE reform?

Mixed ownership is not a new concept in China. It was in use more than two decades ago, in 1993. Central SOEs' mixed-ownership practices have been continuing over the years, through public listing and introducing strategic investors, and so on. More than 60 per cent of the subsidiaries of central SOEs are now structured in ways that include some level of mixed ownership.

Several differences can be identified between this new round of SOE reform and previous ones. First, the status of mixed ownership has been elevated and is now considered the basic form of the socialist economic system—and, as a result, the majority of SOEs can now become mixed-ownership entities. Second, private capital is encouraged to take controlling shares. Third, employees of mixed-ownership enterprises will be permitted to hold stocks (*China Securities Daily* 2014).

The SOE reforms, as difficult and complicated as they are, will bring profound changes to the Chinese economy, as well as to Chinese enterprises and their overseas investments. As the SOE reforms evolve, so should the world's views on them.

Concluding Remarks

China's ODI, like ODI from any other country, aims to make profits, and to do so seeks sound investment environments with fair and transparent regulatory rules. As China's economy continues to grow at a slower, 'new normal' rate in the next decade, the rate of China's outbound FDI, by SOEs and privately owned firms, is likely to continue to be buoyant. In parallel, their economic efficiency will be enhanced by broader economic reforms, and also SOE reforms.

Through this growth process, misunderstandings, fear and protectionism will hinder the execution and success of China's ODI, while also preventing host countries from benefiting from the contributions that Chinese ODI could make to economic growth and employment. To that end, '[s]uccumbing to the nationalist response to foreign investment would, based on all the evidence, be extremely damaging economically as well as have political ramifications' (Drysdale 2011: 70). Similarly, *The Economist* has noted that 'to reject China's advances would thus be a disservice to future generations, as well as a deeply pessimistic statement about capitalism's confidence in itself' (*The Economist* 2010).

References

China Securities Daily (2014), Peng Jianguo, Deputy Director of the Research Center of SASAC: First break up monopoly, then adopt mixed ownership; refine implementation plan to avoid loss of assets [in Chinese], *China Securities Daily*, 21 August.

Committee on Foreign Investment in the United States (CFIUS) (2012), *CFIUS annual report to Congress for CY2012*, Washington, DC: CFIUS.

Cornish, M. (2012), *Behaviour of Chinese SOEs: Implications for investment and cooperation in Canada*, Ottawa: The Canadian International Council. Available from: opencanada.org/author/margaretcornish/.

Downs, E. (2007), The fact and fiction of Sino–African energy relations, *China Security*, 3(3). Available from: www.brookings.edu/views/articles/fellows/downs20070913.pdf.

Drysdale, P. (2011), A new look at Chinese FDI in Australia, *China & World Economy*, 19(4).

Drysdale, P. and Findlay, C. (2009), Chinese foreign direct investment in Australia: Policy issues for the resources sector, *China Economic Journal*, 2(2).

Dunning J.H. (1981), Explaining the international direct investment position of countries: Towards a dynamic or development approach, *Review of World Economics*, 117(1): 30–64.

Feng, Q. (2003), Two challenges of Zhu Rongji: SOE reform and system reform, *Southern Weekend*, 8 March.

Graham, E. and Marchick, D. (2006), National security issues related to investments from China, *National security issues and foreign direct investment*, Washington, DC: Peterson Institute for International Economics.

Hanemann, T. and Gao, C. (2014), *Chinese FDI in the United States: Q3 2014 update*, Policy report, New York: Rhodium Group.

Hanemann, T. and Rosen, D.H. (2012), China invests in Europe: Patterns, impacts and policy implications, New York: Rhodium Group. Available from: rhg. com/wp-content/uploads/2012/06/RHG_ChinaInvestsInEurope_June2012. pdf.

He, D., Cheung, L., Zhang, W. and Wu, T. (2012), How would capital account liberalization affect China's capital flows and the renminbi real exchange rates?, *China & World Economy*, 20(4).

Heritage Foundation (HF) (2015), *China global investment tracker*, Washington, DC: Heritage Foundation.

Hormats, R. (2011), Ensuring a sound basis for global competition: Competitive neutrality. Available from: blogs.state.gov/stories/2011/05/06/ensuring-sound-basis-global-competition-competitive-neutrality.

Hornby, L. (2013), China commerce minister seeks clearer U.S. investment guide, *Reuters*, 8 March. Available from: cn.reuters.com/article/companyNews/idC NL4N0C02Y520130309?symbol=CCE.N.

Ministry of Commerce (2015), Press speaker of Ministry of Commerce, Mr. Sun Jiwen at http://finance.chinanews.com/cj/2015/01-19/6983545.shtml.

Ministry of Finance (2014), The national state-owned enterprises financial statements in 2013. Available from: http://www.mof.gov.cn/preview/qiyesi/ zhengwuxinxi/gongzuodongtai/201407/t20140728_1118640.html.

People's Daily (2013), New SOEs, new starting point, *People's Daily*. 15, 16, 17 and 18 April.

Qi, Z., Song, L. and He, F. (2015), Chinese style regulation: Incentive, collusion and competition, Working paper.

Qi, Z. (2015), Chinese State-owned enterprise' regulation, outward investment and anti-corruption, Working paper.

Reuters (2013), In rare Chinese move, Sinopec seeks partner for Canada Shale, *Reuters*, 25 October. Available from: www.reuters.com/article/2013/10/25/us-sinopec-canada-idUSBRE99O03R20131025.

Rosen, D.H. and Hanemann, T. (2011), *An American open door? Maximizing the benefits of Chinese foreign direct investment*, Washington, DC: Center on US–China Relations Asia Society and Kissinger Institute on China and the United States, Woodrow Wilson International Center for Scholars. Available from: asiasociety.org/policy/center-us-china-relations/american-open-door.

Rosen, D.H. and Houser, T. (2007), China energy: A guide for the perplexed, *China Balance Sheet*, Washington, DC: Peterson Institute for International Economics. Available from: www.iie.com/publications/papers/rosen0507.pdf.

Shanghai Securities Daily (2014), Sinopec initiated mixed ownership reform, selling shares not exceeding 30 per cent [in Chinese], *Shanghai Securities Daily*, 20 February.

Shao, N. (2007), The prospect of China's SOE reform and its challenges, *Theory Frontier* [in Chinese], 20.

The Economist (2010), China buys up the world: And the world should stay open for business, *The Economist*, 11 November.

The Economist (2012), New masters of the universe, *The Economist*, 21 January.

The Economist (2014), What China wants, *The Economist*, 23 August.

Unirule Institute of Economics (2011), *The nature, performance, and reform of the state-owned enterprises*, Research Report, Beijing: Unirule Institute of Economics.

United Nations Conference on Trade and Development (UNCTAD). UNCTADSTAT foreign direct investment data set. Geneva, Switzerland.

Wang, L.M. (2014), *China overseas investment: Concerns, facts and analysis*, [in Chinese], Beijing: CITIC Press.

Zhou, J. (2010), Officials in China's listed enterprises, *Investor China*, 5 July.

14. The Impact of Coastal FDI on Inland Economic Growth in China

Chunlai Chen

Introduction

One of the most successful aspects of China's economic reform and open-door policy implemented since late 1978 has been attracting inflows of foreign direct investment (FDI). By the end of 2014, China had attracted US$1.5 trillion in FDI inflows, making it the largest FDI recipient in the developing world. Coastal and inland regions vary in their attractiveness as locations for FDI, and Chinese policies have favoured coastal regions through the establishment of special economic zones (SEZs) and various preferential treatments (Chen 2011). FDI inflows have therefore been concentrated in the coastal regions, which account for about 80 per cent of total FDI inflows into China.

That spatial concentration of FDI within China could have consequences for inland regions. On the one hand, it could be drawing factors of production away from inland regions and providing competition in product markets, both domestic and international. This would produce unbalanced regional growth and widen income inequality between coastal and inland regions. On the other hand, inland regions less well-served by FDI could benefit from coastal FDI if there are inter-regional knowledge spillovers from coastal to inland regions.

This chapter aims to investigate whether the dense concentration of FDI in China's coastal regions has boosted or undermined the economic growth of inland regions. Specifically, the study uses Chinese province-level data to test whether there are inter-regional knowledge spillovers from FDI concentrated in coastal regions and also how these spillovers are affected by FDI directed to different trade activities—processing trade[1] versus ordinary trade. This study

---

1   There are two kinds of processing trade: processing or assembling with imported materials; and processing or assembling with supplied materials. For the first, the processing firms import—free of customs duty—materials and components that are used to produce finished goods and export them to international markets. In the case of the second, the processing firms process or assemble duty-free materials and components supplied by foreign firms and export finished products. They are paid a fee for the processing or assembling activities. The foreign firms control both the supply of the materials and the entire international marketing of the processed or assembled products.

makes two contributions to the literature. First, it tests directly inter-regional knowledge spillovers from FDI—specifically, spillovers from coastal FDI to inland provinces. This serves to add new empirical evidence to the sparse literature on inter-regional knowledge spillovers of FDI. Second, the study tests how FDI in different types of trade activities—processing versus ordinary trade—in coastal regions affect the economic growth of inland provinces. This could shed light on the effectiveness of processing trade policies implemented in coastal regions since the mid-1980s.

The study finds that, on average, coastal FDI has had a negative impact on economic growth in inland provinces. By further dividing coastal FDI into northern and eastern FDI and southern FDI, based on the depth of engagement in processing trade, the study finds that FDI in the northern and eastern coastal provinces (which are moderately engaged in processing trade) has positive spillovers on the economic growth of inland provinces, while FDI in southern coastal provinces (those heavily engaged in processing trade) has had a negative effect on the economic growth of inland provinces. It is also interesting to note that FDI in other inland provinces that are less engaged in processing trade is found to have positive spillovers on the economic growth of inland provinces. One explanation for this could be that ordinary trade generates larger industrial linkages with inland regions than does processing trade, as the latter is based largely on processing imported inputs.

The rest of this chapter is structured as follows: the second section discusses the theoretical explanations of how knowledge spillovers from FDI contribute to developing host countries' economic growth and presents a brief literature review. Section three sets out the theoretical framework of this analysis and specifies the empirical model; section four describes the data and specifies the variables; section five presents the results of the regression analysis and explains the estimation results. Section six provides the conclusion and policy implications.

Literature review

FDI is one of the most important means through which international knowledge spillovers take place. Because of ownership advantages and the possession of firm-specific intangible assets, FDI can generate knowledge spillovers to domestic firms (Caves 1996; Dunning 1993). FDI knowledge spillovers are regarded as an important source of knowledge in developing countries. Demonstration effects, human resource movement, vertical industrial linkages, technical assistance and information flows are examples of knowledge spillovers via which FDI can improve the productivity and competitiveness of local firms, and thus promote economic growth in the host country.

FDI knowledge spillovers can be horizontal or vertical. Horizontal spillovers take place within the same industry through demonstration effects and labour turnover. FDI can, however, also impose competition on domestic firms, crowding them out of product markets and competing with them in labour and resource markets (for example, Aitken and Harrison 1999; Chen 2011; Chen et al. 2013; Fu 2011; Hu and Jefferson 2002; Hu et al. 2005).

Vertical FDI knowledge spillovers arise through forward and backward industrial linkages between FDI firms and domestic firms within the supply chain (for example, Chen et al. 2013; Girma et al. 2004; Javorcik 2004; Kneller and Pisu 2007). When FDI firms provide higher-value intermediate materials for their customers or when they transfer product knowledge to their suppliers, they contribute to domestic firms' productivity and competitiveness in upstream and downstream industries, in turn increasing local economic growth.

Do FDI knowledge spillovers also take place between regions within a country? Theoretically, inter-regional knowledge spillovers of FDI could take place via at least four channels. The first is inter-regional movement of labour: FDI stimulates inter-regional labour migration, and when employees trained by FDI firms move back to their own regions, they can bring knowledge to local firms and thus knowledge diffusion takes place (Fosfuri et al. 2001; Holger and Strobl 2005).[2] Second are inter-regional backward and forward industrial linkages: FDI firms may develop inter-industry linkages with local firms in other regions, providing those firms with greater opportunities in economies of scale and productivity improvement (Chen et al. 2013; Javorcik 2004; Kugler 2006; Liu 2008). Third, the innovations and research and development (R&D) activities of FDI firms might generate inter-regional knowledge spillovers through imitation and reverse engineering by firms in other regions (Bronzini and Piselli 2009; Funke and Niebuhr 2005; Keller 2002; Kuo and Yang 2008). The fourth channel is formed by the macroeconomic consequences of increased demand for products from other regions as a result of the increased income generated by FDI (Brun et al. 2002; Zhang and Felmingham 2002). FDI could, however, also impose competition on other regions—for example, crowding them out of product

---

2   Cai and Wang (2003) show that in 2000 there were 124.6 million internal migrants in China, of whom 73.4 per cent were inter-provincial migrants. The eastern provinces are the main destination for inter-regional migrants. More than 60 per cent of immigrants in eastern provinces were from inland regions. Bao et al. (2007) find that when real FDI rose by 1 per cent, internal migration rose by more than 1.25 per cent during the 1990s. The workers returning from the coastal foreign firms accelerated the inland regions' processes of imitation of advanced technologies brought by coastal foreign firms (Du et al. 2005; Rozelle et al. 1999).

markets and competing with them in labour and resource markets (Aitken and Harrison 1999; Branstetter and Feenstra 2002; Fu 2011; Hu and Jefferson 2002; Hu et al. 2005).

The literature on knowledge spillovers from FDI is extensive and growing. Studies on the inter-regional knowledge spillovers of FDI, however, remain few. Girma and Wakelin (2007) find that while domestic firms in the United Kingdom benefit positively from foreign firms in the same region and that FDI spillovers do occur within regions, they find no relationship (even a negative relationship) between productivity in one region and FDI in other regions. Halpern and Murakozy (2007) examine firm-level data for Hungary and find that the effect of regional and county boundaries is insignificant.

In the case of China, a few studies have used firm-level data to test regional spillovers from FDI, but reached inconsistent conclusions. Girma and Gong (2008) use data for state-owned enterprises (SOEs) from 1999 to 2002 and find that the activities of foreign firms do not benefit SOEs in other regions. Liu et al. (2009) find backward and forward FDI spillovers among firms at the regional level only. Xu and Sheng (2012) use firm-level census data from the manufacturing industry for 2000–03 and find that domestic firms benefit more from the presence of foreign firms in the same sector within the same region than either between sectors or between regions.

However, a few studies find positive inter-regional spillovers from FDI. Madariaga and Poncet (2007) use city-level data for 1990–2002 and find that FDI inflows affect economic growth in surrounding cities. Ouyang and Fu (2012) use city-level data for 1996–2004 and find that FDI in coastal regions has positive inter-regional spillovers on the economic growth of inland regions. In contrast, using provincial industry-level data for the period 1990–2005, Wang et al. (2013) find that inter-regional FDI spillovers are consistently negative—that is, foreign investment in one region attracts resources away from regions with less FDI, and thus has a negative influence on the growth of industrial output in neighbouring regions. Additional study of the impact of FDI on inter-regional knowledge spillovers is evidently required in order to better understand its role in the economic growth of host countries.

This study adds to the existing literature by examining inter-regional knowledge spillovers from FDI in China—the largest developing country and also the largest FDI recipient among the developing economies. This study specifically investigates and answers two questions: 1) are there inter-regional knowledge spillovers from coastal FDI on the economic growth of inland regions; and 2) do different types of FDI in coastal regions have different impacts on the economic growth of inland provinces?

The model

We use the following aggregate production function to estimate the impact of coastal FDI on the economic growth of inland provinces (Equation 14.1).

Equation 14.1

$$Y_{it} = A_{it} L_{it}^{\beta_1} DK_{it}^{\beta_2} FK_{it}^{\beta_3}$$

In Equation 14.1, Y_{it} is the real gross domestic product (GDP) of inland province i in year t; A_{it} is the total factor productivity (TFP) level of inland province i in year t; L_{it} is total labour input of inland province i in year t; DK_{it} is domestic capital stock of inland province i in year t; and FK_{it} is the foreign capital stock of inland province i in year t.

Under these assumptions, within the aggregate production function, FDI is treated as a separate factor of capital input (FK) alongside domestic capital input (DK) and labour input (L).

Theoretically, because FDI brings into the host country a package of capital, technology, production knowhow, management skills, marketing skills and information, competition, and so on (Caves 1996; Dunning 1993), it is expected that FDI can increase the host country's economic growth by a number of means.

First, FDI inflows will increase demand for labour and create employment in a host country, especially a developing country. The increase in employment will contribute to an increase in total output, thus leading to a higher output level along the existing production function. It is expected that the higher the level of employment created by FDI, the higher will be the output growth of the host economy.

Second, FDI inflows increase the host country's fixed capital formation. FDI is believed to be a leading source of technology transfer and human capital augmentation in developing countries. Technological progress takes place through a process of capital deepening through the introduction of new varieties of knowledge-based capital goods. It also proceeds via specific productivity-increasing labour training and skill acquisition promoted by multinational enterprises (MNEs). Therefore, through capital augmentation in the recipient economy, FDI is expected to be growth enhancing by encouraging the incorporation of new inputs and technologies into the production function, thus shifting the production function of the host country. This positive shifting effect is the contribution to output growth of FDI as a capital input. It is expected that the higher the foreign capital input, the higher will be the output growth of the host economy.

Third, through knowledge spillovers such as learning by doing or learning by watching (demonstration effects), R&D, human resource movement, training courses, vertical industrial linkages, technical assistance and exposure to fierce competition, FDI is expected to increase the productivity and efficiency of local firms in the host country. As a result, FDI can shift the production function of the host economy to a higher level. It is expected that the greater the presence of FDI, the higher will be the spillover effects of FDI on local economic growth.

Fourth, FDI can generate inter-regional knowledge spillovers to increase the productivity and efficiency of firms in other regions through the inter-regional movement of labour, inter-regional backward and forward industrial linkages, inter-regional imitation and reverse engineering, and inter-regional macroeconomic consequences, such as increased market demand for products from other regions as a result of increasing incomes generated by FDI. As a result of inter-regional knowledge spillovers, FDI in one region can shift the production function of another region to a higher level. It is expected that the higher the regional FDI stock to which a region is exposed, the higher the inter-regional knowledge spillovers of FDI on that region's economic growth will be. However, FDI in one region may also impose competition on other regions, crowding them out of the product market and competing with them in the labour and resource markets. So, the net effect of inter-regional spillovers from FDI in one region on the economic growth of other regions is inconclusive, subject to empirical investigation. In this study, to investigate the inter-regional knowledge spillovers of FDI on inland provinces, we define two kinds of inter-regional FDI knowledge spillovers. One is the inter-regional knowledge spillover of FDI from coastal regions on an inland province, and the other is the inter-regional knowledge spillover of FDI on an inland province from other inland provinces.

Given our assumptions of the model of the spillover channels of FDI, TFP, $A_{it'}$ can be defined as in Equation 14.2.

Equation 14.2

$$A_{it} = B_{it} CRFK_{it-1}^{\alpha_1} OIRFK_{it-1}^{\alpha_2} e^{g(SFK_{it-1}, t, HK)}$$

In Equation 14.2, A_{it} is the TFP level of inland province i in year t; B_{it} is the residual TFP level of inland province i in year t; SFK_{it-1} is the presence of FDI in inland province i in year $t-1$, which captures the spillovers from FDI within inland province i; $CRFK_{it-1}$ is coastal region FDI stock exposed by inland province i in year $t-1$, which captures the inter-regional spillovers of coastal province FDI on inland province i; $OIRFK_{it-1}$ is other inland region FDI stock exposed by inland province i in year $t-1$, which captures the inter-regional spillovers of FDI from other inland provinces on inland province i; t is a time trend, which captures the Hicks-neutral technological progress in inland province i; and HK is human capital in inland province i in year t, which is expected to have a positive impact on economic growth.

Incorporating Equation 14.2 into the aggregate production function Equation 14.1, and rearranging the items on the right-hand side, with the addition of a constant term (β_0) and an error term (ε_{it}), we obtain the following empirical regression (Equation 14.3).

Equation 14.3

$$LnY_{it} = \beta_0 + \beta_1 LnL_{it} + \beta_2 LnDK_{it} + \beta_3 LnFK_{it} + \beta_4 SFK_{it-1} + \beta_5 LnCRFK_{it-1} + \beta_6 LnOIRFK_{it-1} + \beta_7 HK_{it} + \beta_8 t + \varepsilon_{it}$$

In Equation 14.3, i ($i = 1, 2, ..., 20$) and t ($t = 1987, ..., 2010$) denote inland province i and year t; Y is real provincial GDP; L and DK are labour and domestic capital stock;[3] FK is foreign capital stock, which serves to capture the contribution of FDI to economic growth through capital augmentation; SFK is the presence of FDI in an inland province (share of foreign capital stock in total capital stock), which captures the spillover effects of FDI within an inland province; $CRFK$ is the coastal region foreign capital stock to which an inland province is exposed, which captures the inter-regional spillovers of coastal FDI; $OIRFK$ is other inland foreign capital stock to which an inland province is exposed, which captures the inter-regional spillovers of other inland FDI; HK is human capital; and t is a time trend, which captures the Hicks-neutral technological progress.

This specification allows not only testing of the direct contribution of FDI to provincial economic growth (if coefficient β_3 is positive and statistically significant then it can be ascertained that FDI has directly contributed to inland province economic growth through capital input), but also further tests undertaken on the spillover effects of FDI on inland province economic growth in three aspects. First, we can test the spillover effects of FDI on economic growth within an inland province. If the coefficient β_4 is positive and statistically significant, there is evidence that FDI has generated positive spillover effects within an inland province. Second, we can test the inter-regional spillover effects of FDI from coastal provinces on inland province economic growth. If the coefficient β_5 is positive and statistically significant, there is evidence that FDI in coastal provinces has generated positive inter-regional spillovers on the economic growth of inland provinces. Third, we can test the inter-regional spillover effects of FDI from other inland provinces on the economic growth of

---

3 Official data of labour employed by FDI at the provincial level are not available, so the total numbers for labour in each province are used in the regression.

an inland province. If the coefficient β_6 is positive and statistically significant, there is evidence that FDI in other inland provinces has generated positive inter-regional spillover effects on an inland province's economic growth.

Equation 14.3 is an augmented production function that we use to estimate the intra-provincial and inter-regional spillover effects of FDI on China's inland provinces' economic growth. The first part of the analysis is to investigate whether there are inter-regional spillover effects on inland provinces from FDI in coastal provinces. The second part of the analysis is to investigate whether FDI in different trade activities generates different inter-regional spillover effects on inland provinces' economic growth by dividing coastal FDI into northern and eastern coastal FDI and southern coastal FDI based on the level of engagement in processing trade. The following section outlines the data and specifies the variables.

Data and variable specification

This study uses province-level data covering China's 31 provinces and the period 1987–2010. The 31 provinces are divided into 11 coastal provinces[4] and 20 inland provinces.[5] The data for provincial GDP (Y) and provincial total capital stock (billion RMB at 1978 prices) are from Wu (2009).[6] Wu uses the conventional perpetual inventory method by employing the recently released national accounts figures to derive a capital stock series for China's 31 provinces and three economic sectors (that is, agriculture, manufacturing and services) for the period 1977–2010. This produces one of the most comprehensive datasets of capital stock series for China's 31 provinces and three economic sectors.

Calculating foreign capital stock

The data for FDI stock (FK) are calculated in several steps. First, the US dollar value of annual FDI inflows is converted into a renminbi (RMB) value by using the annual average official exchange rate. Second, the RMB value of annual FDI inflows is deflated into the real value at 1978 prices by using China's national consumer price index (CPI). Third, a 5 per cent depreciation rate is assumed for foreign capital (FDI). Finally, FDI stock is accumulated for each year end measured in billion RMB at 1978 prices.

---

4   The 11 coastal provinces are Beijing, Fujian, Guangdong, Hainan, Hebei, Jiangsu, Liaoning, Shandong, Shanghai, Tianjin and Zhejiang.

5   The 20 inland provinces are: Anhui, Chongqing, Gansu, Guizhou, Guangxi, Heilongjiang, Henan, Hubei, Hunan, Inner Mongolia, Jiangxi, Jilin, Ningxia, Qinghai, Shaanxi, Shanxi, Sichuan, Tibet, Xinjiang and Yunnan.

6   Data for 2007–10 are provided by Wu (2009).

Calculating the share of foreign capital

The presence of FDI in an inland province is measured as the share of FDI stock in the total capital stock of an inland province (*SFK*) to capture the intra-province spillover effects of FDI on provincial economic growth. The share of FDI stock is calculated as FDI stock over total capital stock of an inland province. It is reasonable to assume that FDI inflows and spillover effects have a time lag, so the value of one year lag of *SFK* is used in the model. The use of the lagged value of *SFK* also can reduce the potential problem of endogeneity in the regression. The hypothesis is that provinces with a higher share of FDI stock in total capital stock will have higher spillover effects from FDI to the local economy, thus increasing the productivity and efficiency of local firms and promoting provincial economic growth.

Measuring coastal region FDI

We use the formula $\Sigma_{jt} FDI_{jt} \times e^{-Dij}$ to measure the coastal region FDI stock (*CRFK*) to which an inland province is exposed,[7] where FDI_{jt} is the amount of FDI stock in coastal province j in year t; D_{ij} is the distance in 1,000 km between inland province i and coastal province j; and e^{-Dij} works as a discount factor, since greater distance implies higher transaction and transportation costs, which make inter-regional migration and access to coastal markets more difficult. Therefore, $FDI_{jt} \times e^{-Dij}$ measures the amount of FDI stock in coastal province j that might affect inland province i, and $\Sigma_{jt} FDI_{jt} \times e^{-Dij}$ is the total amount of FDI stock from all coastal provinces that might affect inland province i in year t.

Different coastal regions attract different types of FDI. FDI in southern coastal provinces is mainly directed towards processing trade, while FDI in northern and eastern coastal provinces is moderately engaged in processing trade (Chen 2011). In addition to estimating the average inter-regional spillovers, we also estimate inter-regional spillovers of FDI from different coastal regions. We use the same formula as above to calculate the amount of FDI stock in the northern and eastern coastal provinces (*N&ECRFK*)[8] and the amount of FDI stock in the southern coastal provinces (*SCRFK*)[9] to which an inland province is exposed. Using the same reasoning as for the share of foreign capital, the value of one year lag is used for all coastal region FDI stock variables in the model.

---

7   Keller (2002) uses a similar method to measure the effective foreign-country R&D to which a country is exposed.
8   The northern and eastern coastal provinces are Beijing, Hebei, Jiangsu, Liaoning, Shandong, Shanghai, Tianjin and Zhejiang.
9   The southern coastal provinces are Fujian, Guangdong and Hainan.

Controlling for FDI in other inland provinces

FDI in other inland provinces may also generate inter-regional spillovers and influence the economic growth of the inland province. To control for the potential inter-regional spillovers from other inland provinces on an inland province's economic growth, we use the same formula to calculate the FDI stock of other inland provinces ($OIRFK$) to which an inland province is exposed. As above, the value of one year lag is used for the other inland region FDI stock variable ($OIRFK$) in the model.

Measuring other inland province variables

The domestic capital stock (DK) of each inland province is obtained by deducting the FDI stock (FK) from the total capital stock. Labour (L) is the total number of people employed in each province measured as million persons. Human capital (HK) is measured as the ratio of the number of university students to the total population of each inland province.

The dependent and independent variables and the data sources are summarised in Table 14.1.

Table 14.1 Variables of the impact of FDI on the economic growth of China's inland provinces

Variable name	Specification of variables	Sources
Dependent variable		
Y_{it}	GDP of inland province i in year t. RMB billion at 1978 prices	Wu (2009) and NBS (various issues)
Independent variables		
L_{it}	Total number of employed people of inland province i in year t. Million persons	NBS (various issues)
DK_{it}	Domestic capital stock of inland province i in year t. RMB billion at 1978 prices	Calculated from Wu (2009) and NBS (various issues)
FK_{it}	FDI stock of inland province i in year t. RMB billion at 1978 prices	Calculated from, for before and including 2005, NBS (various issues); after 2005, PBS (various issues of each province)
SFK_{it-1}	Share of FDI stock in total capital stock of inland province i in year $t-1$. Percentage	Same as above
$CRFK_{it-1}$	Coastal region FDI stock exposed by inland province i in year $t-1$. RMB billion at 1978 prices	Same as above
$OIRFK_{it-1}$	Other inland region FDI stock exposed by inland province i in year $t-1$. RMB billion at 1978 prices	Same as above

Variable name	Specification of variables	Sources
$N\&ECRFK_{it-1}$	Northern and eastern coastal region FDI stock exposed by inland province i in year $t-1$. RMB billion at 1978 prices	Same as above
$SCRFK_{it-1}$	Southern coastal region FDI stock exposed by inland province i in year $t-1$. RMB billion at 1978 prices	Same as above
HK_{it}	Human capital of inland province i in year t measured as the ratio of the number of university students to total population. Percentage	NBS (various issues)

Estimation Results

Estimates of average inter-regional spillover effects

The data used in the regression are a panel dataset at the province level, containing China's 19 inland provinces for the period 1987–2010.[10] We first conduct a Hausman test to choose between the random-effects model and the fixed-effects model for the regression. The Hausman test prefers the fixed-effects model. Therefore, we estimate Equation 14.3 under the fixed-effects model in order to eliminate the province-specific and time-invariant factors that could affect economic growth. The regression results are reported in Table 14.2.

The regression results show that domestic capital input (DK) is positive and statistically significant at the 1 per cent level, while labour input (L) is negative but insignificant. This implies that the marginal product of domestic capital is much higher than that of labour due to the relatively abundant labour supply and scarcity of capital in inland provinces. The variable of human capital (HK) is positive and statistically significant at the 1 per cent level, which provides empirical evidence that human capital contributes to economic growth. The Hicks-neutral technological progress represented by the coefficient on a time trend (t) is positive and statistically significant at the 1 per cent level, indicating that inland provinces experience technological progress and move onto a higher steady-state technology over time.

---

10 Tibet is excluded from the regression because of a lack of data.

Table 14.2 Estimating inter-regional spillovers of FDI on inland province economic growth, 1987–2010 (dependent variable: *LnY*)

Independent variables	Fixed effects
Constant	1.7583 (9.13)***
LnL	−0.0442 (−0.83)
LnDK	0.4095 (15.98)***
LnFK	0.0615 (9.09)***
HK	0.0570 (3.44)***
t	0.0545 (16.07)***
SFKt−1	−0.0021 (−0.43)
LnCRFKt−1	−0.2103 (−9.17)***
LnOIRFKt−1	0.1541 (6.74)***
No. of observations	446
No. of groups	19
R^2	0.75
F-statistics	9288***

* Statistically significant at 0.10 level.
** Statistically significant at 0.05 level.
*** Statistically significant at 0.01 level.
Note: t-statistics are in parentheses.
Source: Author's own estimations.

Turning to the variables of our main interest: first, the variable of foreign capital stock (*FK*) is positive and statistically significant at the 1 per cent level, which provides strong support for the idea that FDI as a factor of capital input directly contributes to inland province economic growth. The estimation results imply that inland provinces with higher FDI inflows will have higher economic growth as a direct result of the increase in foreign capital input.

Second, the variable of the share of FDI stock in total capital stock (*SFK*)— the spillovers of an inland province's own FDI—is negative and insignificant. This finding is consistent with Chen (2013, 2014), who finds that FDI in China's inland provinces has not generated significant spillovers on the local economy due to the low level of FDI. Nunnenkamp and Stracke (2007) also find that FDI in poor regions in India is too small to generate spillover effects to boost local economic growth.

Third, the variable of *OIRFK*—the FDI stock of other inland provinces—is positive and significant at the 1 per cent level, which implies that FDI in other inland provinces has generated positive spillovers on inland provinces. This may be because of technology spillovers through backward and forward industrial linkages, information flows and the movement of labour between FDI firms in inland provinces and local economies, thus increasing the economic growth of inland provinces.

Fourth, on the other hand, the variable of *CRFK*—the FDI stock in coastal provinces—is negative and significant at the 1 per cent level, which implies that FDI in coastal provinces has had a negative impact on the economic growth of inland provinces. This might be explained by the following two points.

The first is competition between coastal FDI firms and inland provinces. Coastal FDI firms compete with inland provinces in both factor markets and product markets. Although competition can force inland provinces to improve their efficiency and increase productivity, inland provinces are at a competitive disadvantage when facing superior technology, modern management methods, advanced marketing skills and extensive international market networks, high product quality, and high wages and other compensation provided to employees of FDI firms in the coastal regions.

In the factor markets, attracted by greater employment opportunities and the higher wages offered by coastal FDI firms, tens of millions of young and more productive non-skilled workers flow from inland to coastal regions. This is evidenced by the massive flows of migrant workers from inland to coastal regions. Second, attracted by a set of preferential policies, including tax policies, offered to FDI firms, especially in the coastal regions, capital flows from inland provinces to the coastal regions for FDI joint ventures. Third, because of high incomes, high living standards and more carrier development opportunities, skilled labour also flows from inland provinces to coastal regions to work in FDI firms.

In the product markets, because of high quality, famous brand names, advanced domestic and international marketing skills and extensive market networks, as well as good post-sales customer service, coastal FDI firms outperform inland provinces not only in the domestic market by stealing domestic market share from the inland provinces, but also in international export markets by squeezing out inland provinces.

The second point is the lack of industrial linkages between coastal FDI and inland provinces. This may be because coastal FDI firms, on average, are heavily engaged in processing trade, which is based largely on processing imported inputs and exporting final products to world markets. Therefore, backward and forward industrial linkages may be absent or very weak between coastal FDI and inland provinces. For example, Fu (2004) uses Chinese province-level data for 1990–99 and finds no evidence of spillovers from coastal export activity into inland regions. She argues that this is because nearly half of export activity in coastal provinces is processing trade that does not provide inter-industry linkages to inland regions. Chen et al. (2013) use Chinese firm-level data from 2000 to 2003 and find that high-exporting FDI firms do not generate technology spillovers to domestic firms because the former are heavily engaged in processing exports and have no backward and forward industrial linkages with domestic firms.

The above analysis has revealed that, on average, coastal FDI has negative impacts on the economic growth of inland provinces because of intense competition in factor and product markets and because of the lack of industrial linkages between coastal FDI firms and inland provinces. However, different coastal provinces attract different types of FDI, especially in the level of engagement in processing trade, which may have different impacts on the economic growth of inland provinces. Therefore, in addition to estimating the average inter-regional spillovers of coastal FDI, it is necessary to estimate the impact of inter-regional spillovers of FDI from different coastal regions on the economic growth of inland provinces.

Estimating the impact on inland provinces of FDI in different coastal regions

The northern and eastern coastal region and the southern coastal region are the two main destinations for FDI inflows into China. In terms of the level of engagement in processing trade, however, FDI in these two regions is different. Table 14.3 presents the shares of processing trade in the total trade of selected provinces for the period 2003–10. As the table shows, the southern coastal provinces have the highest shares of processing trade, the northern and eastern coastal regions have moderate shares of processing trade and the inland provinces have the lowest shares. On average, FDI firms' trade accounts for more than 50 per cent of China's total trade and is directed heavily towards processing trade, particularly in the southern coastal provinces. Therefore, in terms of trade patterns, FDI in the southern coastal region is mainly engaged in processing trade, FDI in the northern and eastern coastal region is moderately engaged in processing trade and FDI in inland provinces is less engaged in processing trade.

Table 14.3 Shares of processing trade in selected provinces, 2003–10

	2003	2004	2005	2006	2007	2008	2009	2010
Coastal provinces								
North and east								
Beijing	23.38	23.11	24.20	22.57	24.26	34.62	39.60	34.31
Shanghai	40.76	43.02	45.47	44.88	43.42	41.81	40.92	37.92
Jiangsu	54.83	58.82	62.58	61.23	58.80	52.50	52.83	50.66
South								
Fujian	42.40	44.09	43.35	41.52	38.97	38.47	33.69	34.37
Guangdong	68.96	67.65	67.26	46.27	62.73	58.96	70.58	42.68
Inland provinces								
Shanxi	2.95	5.12	9.49	12.65	23.55	15.35	11.45	13.95
Inner Mongolia	7.22	7.59	14.52	6.25	3.38	5.97	2.77	7.70
Heilongjiang	4.76	5.01	4.31	3.52	3.91	4.06	6.29	3.95
Anhui	12.62	16.41	17.92	21.99	20.14	17.76	17.18	17.65
Jiangxi	9.23	12.93	15.41	23.26	22.69	25.59	23.61	23.35
Henan	22.87	29.83	31.49	25.82	17.67	13.01	15.02	15.71
Hubei	15.99	14.74	13.84	17.57	17.88	15.72	6.13	4.77
Hunan	7.55	10.06	8.19	10.64	11.88	5.99	10.69	17.33
Chongqing	3.56	2.76	1.21	8.21	7.12	6.41	8.23	13.41
Sichuan	28.15	20.91	14.33	22.40	27.83	33.54	37.23	41.83
Shaanxi	11.06	12.84	12.37	16.74	18.54	15.48	19.00	36.02
Gansu	27.16	22.55	19.87	17.14	5.28	4.83	7.36	7.12
Xinjiang	3.63	3.29	2.40	1.80	1.11	0.66	2.15	1.53

Sources: Calculated from Qiu (2013); and NBS (various issues).

Knowledge spillovers through backward and forward industrial linkages are among the most important channels through which technology, management skills and marketing information are transferred from FDI firms to the local economy. Therefore, we can hypothesise that FDI in coastal regions engaged in different trade activities—processing and ordinary trade—could have different impacts on inland provinces. FDI firms engaged mainly in processing trade would have no impact on inland provinces because of the lack of industrial linkages or a negative impact by reducing demand for intermediate inputs from and competing in world export markets with inland provinces. FDI firms engaged mainly in ordinary trade would generate positive knowledge spillovers to inland provinces through industrial linkages by sourcing raw materials and intermediate inputs from inland provinces.

We also use Equation 14.3 to conduct the regression; however, the variable of coastal region FDI stock (*CRFK*) is replaced with two variables: the northern and eastern coastal region FDI stock (*N&ECRFK*) and the southern coastal region FDI stock (*SCRFK*). The estimation results (see Table 14.4) show that FDI in the northern and eastern coastal region (*N&ECRFK*) generates positive and statistically significant (at the 5 per cent level) spillovers on the economic growth of inland provinces, while FDI in the southern coastal region (*SCRFK*) has a negative and statistically significant (at the 1 per cent level) impact on the economic growth of inland provinces.

Table 14.4 Estimating inter-regional spillovers from coastal FDI in different trade activities on inland province economic growth, 1987–2010 (dependent variable: *LnY*)

Independent variables	Fixed effects
Constant	1.8028 (10.08)***
LnL	−0.0865 (−1.65)*
LnDK	0.3969 (15.99)***
LnFK	0.0530 (8.45)***
HK	0.0035 (0.21)
t	0.0496 (13.99)***
SFK_{t-1}	0.0052 (1.15)
$LnN\&ECRFK_{t-1}$	0.1053 (2.43)**
$LnSCRFK_{t-1}$	−0.3066 (−8.44)***
$LnOIRFK_{t-1}$	0.1334 (5.16)***
No. of observations No. of groups R^2 F-statistics	446 19 0.66 8966***

* Statistically significant at 0.10 level.
** Statistically significant at 0.05 level.
*** Statistically significant at 0.01 level.
Note: t-statistics are in parentheses.
Source: Author's own estimations.

Why does FDI in the southern coastal region have a negative spillover on inland provinces while FDI in the northern and eastern region generates positive spillovers on inland provinces? Because FDI in the southern coastal region is heavily engaged in processing trade, it not only reduces demand for intermediate inputs from firms in inland provinces, due to a lack of backward and forward industrial linkages, it also competes in world export markets with inland firms, generating a negative impact on their economic growth. FDI in the northern and eastern coastal region is moderately engaged in processing trade, and although it also competes with firms in inland provinces, it does have a certain level of backward and forward industrial linkages with inland provinces through sourcing raw materials and intermediate inputs from inland firms and selling intermediate inputs to those firms, thus generating some positive spillovers on inland provinces. Therefore, the empirical estimation results support our hypothesis that FDI in coastal regions engaged in different trade patterns—processing versus ordinary trade—has different impacts on the economic growth of inland provinces.

It is also interesting to note that the variable of $OIRFK$—FDI stock in other inland provinces—is consistently positive and significant in all regressions, implying that FDI in other inland provinces generates positive spillovers on the economic growth of inland provinces. As discussed above, FDI in inland provinces is less engaged in processing trade and more engaged in ordinary trade. Therefore, FDI in inland provinces has extensive backward and forward industrial linkages with firms in other inland provinces, which enhance the transfer of knowledge spillovers from FDI to local economies, thus contributing to the economic growth of inland provinces. This finding provides further evidence of the importance of industrial linkages in enhancing knowledge spillovers from FDI to the local economy.

Conclusion

The main purpose of this study is to investigate empirically the impact of inter-regional spillovers from coastal FDI on the economic growth of China's inland provinces, with a particular emphasis on how this impact is affected by the level of engagement of FDI in processing trade in different coastal regions. The study finds that, on average, coastal FDI has a negative impact on the economic growth of inland provinces. However, by dividing coastal FDI into a northern and eastern region and a southern region, the study finds that FDI in southern coastal provinces still has a negative impact on the economic growth of inland provinces because of intense competition in both factor markets and product markets, and because of a lack of backward and forward industrial linkages with inland provinces because of heavy engagement in processing trade. FDI in the northern and eastern coastal provinces, however, has positive spillovers through backward and forward industrial linkages with inland provinces because of moderate engagement in processing trade and a certain level of local sourcing. FDI in other inland provinces has positive spillovers on the economic growth of inland provinces through backward and forward industrial linkages due to the low level of engagement in processing trade and a high level of local sourcing. Therefore, this study provides further evidence of the importance of industrial linkages in enhancing knowledge spillovers from FDI to the local economy. The study also finds that spillovers from inland province FDI are absent because of the low level of FDI inflows into those provinces.

The findings of this study imply that China's inland provinces still have a lot of benefits to gain from the inflow of FDI. First, China should design policies to help inland provinces improve local economic and technological conditions and their overall investment environment in order to attract more FDI inflows. The implementation of the 'Western Development Strategy' and the 'One Belt and One Road Development Strategy' will greatly improve the investment environment of inland provinces. Second, China should redesign processing trade policies to focus on increasing local sourcing and enhancing industrial linkages through economic structural reform and industrial upgrading. Third, China should encourage contact, information exchange, production and technological cooperation, and joint R&D activities between FDI firms and domestic firms in general and between coastal FDI firms and inland firms in particular, in order to enhance and accelerate the diffusion of positive knowledge spillovers from FDI to China's economy.

References

Aitken, B. and Harrison A. (1999), Do domestic firms benefit from direct foreign investment? Evidence from Venezuela, *American Economic Review*, 89(3): 605–18.

Bao, S., Bodvarsson, O., Hou, J. and Zhao, Y. (2007), *Interprovincial migration in China: The effects of investment and migrant networks*, IZA Discussion Paper No. 2924, Bonn: Institute for the Study of Labor.

Branstetter, L. and Feenstra, R. (2002), Trade and foreign direct investment in China: A political economy approach, *Journal of International Economics*, 58(2): 335–58.

Bronzini, R. and Piselli, P. (2009), Determinants of long-run regional productivity with geographic spillovers: The role of R&D, human capital and public infrastructure, *Regional Science and Urban Economics*, 39(2): 187–99.

Brun, J., Combes, J. and Renard, M. (2002), Are there spillover effects between coastal and noncoastal regions in China?, *China Economic Review*, 13(2–3): 161–9.

Cai, F. and Wang, D. (2003), Migration as marketisation: What can we learn from China's 2000 census data?, *China Review*, 3(2): 73–93.

Caves, R. (1996), *Multinational Enterprise and Economic Analysis*, 2nd edn, Cambridge: Cambridge University Press.

Chen, C. (2011), *Foreign Direct Investment in China: Location determinants, investor differences and economic impacts*, Cheltenham, UK, and Northampton, Mass.: Edward Elgar.

Chen, C. (2013), FDI and economic growth, in Wu, Y. (ed.), *Regional Development and Economic Growth in China*, Series on Economic Development and Growth No. 7, Singapore: World Scientific, pp. 117–40.

Chen, C. (2014), The impact of FDI on China's regional economic growth, in Song, L., Garnaut, R. and Cai, F. (eds), *Deepening Reform for China's Long-Term Growth and Development*, Canberra: ANU Press, pp. 407–27.

Chen, C., Sheng, Y. and Findlay, C. (2013), Export spillovers of FDI on domestic firms, *Review of International Economics*, 21(5): 841–56.

Du, Y., Park, A. and Wang, S. (2005), Migration and rural poverty in China, *Journal of Comparative Economics*, 33(4): 688–709.

Dunning, J. (1993), *Multinational Enterprises and the Global Economy*, Wokingham, UK: Addison-Wesley.

Fosfuri, A., Motta, M. and Ronde, T. (2001), Foreign direct investment and spillovers through workers' mobility, *Journal of International Economics*, 53(1): 205–22.

Fu, X. (2004), Limited linkages from growth engines and regional disparities in China, *Journal of Comparative Economics*, 32(1): 148–64.

Fu, X. (2011), Processing trade, FDI and the exports of indigenous firms: Firm-level evidence from technology-intensive industries in China, *Oxford Bulletin of Economics and Statistics*, 73(6): 792–817.

Funke, M. and Niebuhr, A. (2005), Regional geographic research and development spillovers and economic growth: Evidence from West Germany, *Regional Studies*, 39(1): 143–53.

Girma, S. and Gong, Y. (2008), FDI, linkages and the efficiency of state-owned enterprises in China, *Journal of Development Studies*, 44(5): 728–49.

Girma, S. and Wakelin, K. (2007), Local productivity spillovers from foreign direct investment in the UK electronics industry, *Regional Science and Urban Economics*, 37(3): 399–412.

Girma, S., Gorg, H. and Pisu, M. (2004), *The role of exporting and linkages for productivity spillovers*, GEP Research Paper No. 2004/30, Nottingham: Nottingham Centre for Research on Globalisation and Economic Policy.

Halpern, L. and Murakozy, B. (2007), Does distance matter in spillover?, *Economics of Transition*, 15(4): 781–805.

Holger, G. and Strobl, E. (2005), Spillovers from foreign firms through worker mobility: An empirical investigation, *The Scandinavian Journal of Economics*, 107(4): 693–709.

Hu, A. and Jefferson, G. (2002), FDI impact and spillover: Evidence from China's electronic and textile industries, *World Economy*, 38(4): 1063–76.

Hu, A., Jefferson, G. and Qian, J. (2005), R&D and technology transfer: Firm-level evidence from Chinese industry, *The Review of Economics and Statistics*, 87(4): 780–6.

Javorcik, B. (2004), Does foreign direct investment increase the productivity of domestic firms? In search of spillovers through backward linkages, *The American Economic Review*, 94(3): 605–27.

Keller, W. (2002), Geographic localization of international technology diffusion, *American Economic Review*, 92(1): 120–42.

Kneller, R. and Pisu, M. (2007), Industrial linkages and export spillovers from FDI, *The World Economy*, 30(1): 105–34.

Kugler, M. (2006), Spillover from foreign direct investment: Within or between industries, *Journal of Development Economics*, 88(2): 444–77.

Kuo, C. and Yang, C. (2008), Knowledge capital and spillover on regional economic growth: Evidence from China, *China Economic Review*, 19(40): 594–604.

Liu, X., Wang, C. and Wei, Y. (2009), Do local manufacturing firms benefit from transactional linkages with multinational enterprises in China?, *Journal of International Business Studies*, 40(7): 1113–30.

Liu, Z. (2008), Foreign direct investment and technology spillovers: Theory and evidence, *Journal of Development Economics*, 85(1–2): 176–93.

Madariaga, N. and Poncet, S. (2007), FDI in Chinese cities: Spillovers and impact on growth, *World Economy*, 30(5): 837–62.

National Bureau of Statistics of China (NBS) (various issues), *China Statistical Yearbook*, Beijing: China Statistics Press.

Nunnenkamp, P. and Stracke, R. (2007), *Foreign direct investment in post-reform India: Likely to work wonders for regional development?*, Working Paper No. 1375, Kiel: Kiel Institute of World Economics.

Ouyang, P. and Fu, S. (2012), Economic growth, industrial development and the inter-regional spillovers from foreign direct investment: Evidence of China, *China Economic Review*, 23(2): 445–60.

Provincial Bureau of Statistics (PBS) (various issues for each province), *Provincial National Economic and Social Development Statistical Bulletin*, Beijing: China Statistics Press.

Qiu, W. (2013), *Situation of China's processing trade and strategies*, Paper, Available at paper.people.com.cn/rmlt/html/2013-08/11/content_1295002.htm. Accessed 30 January 2015.

Rozelle, S., Taylor, E. and Brauw, A. (1999), Migration, remittances, and agricultural productivity in China, *American Economic Review*, 89(2): 287–91.

Wang, L., Meijers, H. and Szirmai, A. (2013), *Technological spillovers and industrial growth in Chinese regions*, UNU-MERIT Working Paper Series No. 2013-044, Tokyo: United Nations University.

Wu, Y. (2009), *China's capital stock series by region and sector*, Discussion Paper No. 09.02, Perth: Business School, University of Western Australia, Available at www.business.uwa.edu.au/__data/assets/pdf_file/0009/260487/09_02_Wu.pdf. Accessed 30 January 2015.

Xu, X. and Sheng, Y. (2012), Are FDI spillovers regional? Firm-level evidence from China, *Journal of Asian Economics*, 23(3): 244–58.

Zhang, Q. and Felmingham, B. (2002), The role of FDI, exports and spillover effects in the regional development of China, *Journal of Development Studies*, 38(4): 157–78.

15. China's Trade Negotiation Strategies

Matters of growth and regional economic integration

Fan He and Xiaoming Pan[1]

Introduction

China's opening and reform process that began in the late 1970s has induced a great era during which the Chinese economy has been incrementally integrating with the world economy. Outbound trade and inbound foreign direct investment (FDI) served as the twin engines of growth. China's contemporary economic story is 'a classical demonstration of the potential of export-oriented industrialization' (Krugman and Obstfeld 1991: 247). An acceleration of that process arrived with China's accession to the World Trade Organization (WTO) in 2001. China enjoyed tremendous gains by facing lower tariffs and fewer trade restrictions in accessing the extensive markets of WTO member countries and by reducing its own restrictions on trade. China became the 'factory of the world'.

China's reliance on export-oriented growth now faces challenges. The global financial crisis (GFC) of 2008 hit developed countries—the most important markets for Chinese export goods. The consequent sluggish demand for Chinese products forced many small and medium enterprises to close, especially in south-eastern China where most light manufactured goods for export are made. Guangdong was hit especially hard, as was China's aggregate export level. While the US economy has somewhat recovered from the turmoil that began in 2008, structural challenges in the European Union paint a gloomy economic picture. External demand for Chinese products has not rebounded to pre-GFC levels. On the supply side, too, wage gains in China are making labour-intensive production more expensive. Manufacturing industries seeking lower labour costs have already begun to move to other Asian countries, such as Vietnam and Indonesia. The 'world's factory', therefore, faces overcapacity within many export-oriented industries.

---

1   The views expressed in this chapter do not necessarily represent the views of the institutions for which the authors work. The authors are responsible for any errors.

In terms of its continuing economic development, China also faces the 'middle-income trap'—few countries have smoothly transitioned from middle to high-income status. Acknowledging the need for a change of growth model, the Third Plenary Session of the Eighteenth Communist Party Central Committee in November 2013 clearly highlighted that China will need to shift from a fast-growing economy that is essentially dependent on 'investment in heavy industry and low-cost, manufactured exports to a more mature economy driven by domestic consumption and the production of higher-value goods and services' (Wharton Business School 2015).

In addition to the endogenous challenge of a growth model transition, China is also facing an exogenous international dynamic where the current international trade rules are under negotiation. New rules are being called for so as to adjust for the expansion of global value chains. Thanks to the more than a decade-long stalemate of the WTO's multilateral Doha Round negotiations, countries are now seeking to reform current trade rules through mega-regional negotiations. This is the first time regionalism has prospered over multilateralism since the establishment of the WTO in 1995. The negotiations for mega-regional trade agreements—especially the Trans-Pacific Partnership (TPP), the Transatlantic Trade and Investment Partnership (TTIP) and the Regional Comprehensive Economic Partnership (RCEP)—have attracted a lot of attention. These delineate the general outlook of international trade rules in the twenty-first century. While these persist with seeking to liberalise trade in goods, they involve trade discrimination and therefore rules of origin. There is greater focus on liberalisation of services and investment protection. They also expand the current trade agenda by incorporating new issues—such as the environment and labour—into negotiations.

Given these potential shifts in trade governance, as part of the transition to a new growth model, China must also reconsider its approach to trade agreements. Under the old growth model, trade agreements played a critical role in facilitating the export of goods made in China and also in allowing Chinese manufacturers to successfully plug into East Asian production networks. China could reconsider its entire negotiation approach in the face of a weakening WTO-based multilateral trading system and the emergence of exclusive mega-regional negotiations. Fully utilising multilateral and regional trade negotiation platforms and participating in the process of international trade rule-making are significant to how China defines its role in international economic governance. A comprehensive and sophisticated negotiation strategy will help China to confront domestic economic challenges and to accelerate its steps to further integrate with the world economy.

This chapter explores Chinese trade negotiation strategy in response to its domestic reform as well as its changing role in the world economy. Section two briefly introduces China's export-oriented economic model and points to the need for new methods of navigation in the world economy. Section three discusses the changing dynamics of the international trading system and the implications for China in a geopolitical context and with regard to its trade negotiation agenda. Based on the analyses of China in the world economy and international trade rule-making process, section four focuses on the discussion of Chinese trade negotiation strategies. Given the three perspectives discussed—the failure of the Doha Round, the proliferation of regional trade agreements and calls for new trade rules in the Pacific Rim—this chapter offers a comprehensive overview of Chinese trade negotiation strategies. The chapter finally suggests that China will work with other countries towards convergence of the different trade agendas of mega-regional agreements and in so doing play a bigger role in shaping the international trading system.

Changing relations between China and the world economy

Challenge for the traditional export-oriented growth model

The opening-up policy from the late 1970s transformed China from a planned economy towards a market-oriented economy. In the early stages of that process, a fundamental policy element was the pioneering opening up of selective coastal areas of China, which in turn helped to fire up the economic growth of other regions in the country.

First, China's government boosted its investment in these coastal regions. The share of the central government's investment in these regions increased from 39.5 per cent during 1953–78 to 53.5 per cent during 1979–91 (Yao 2008). That surge in investment was used mainly to construct infrastructure. Favourable policies also sought to attract FDI. The rapid development of infrastructure and favourable treatment for foreign investors, together with cheap local labour, helped China to become the largest developing country FDI destination. During these years, China received about 20 per cent of total inbound FDI into developing countries. Through 2006–10, FDI accounted for nearly 2.5 per cent of China's average gross domestic product (GDP) (World Bank 2010). The majority of foreign companies that flooded into China set up factories that produce goods for export. In turn, foreign-invested enterprises came to produce nearly half of all China's exports. China in turn rose to become a significant global trade participant.

Figure 15.1 displays the evolution of the trade volume of China, from 1978 to 2013. It illustrates that the levels of imports and exports have risen since 1990. The year 2001, when China joined the WTO, marks an acceleration point, especially in China's exports. The financial crises of 1997 and 2008 each reduced demand for China's exports. China was, however, hit more severely by the latter than the former. Having experienced a temporary fall in demand in 2009, Chinese exports have, however, continued to increase, helped by the post-GFC economic stimulus package. The graphs of both imports and exports are less steep in the period after 2011.

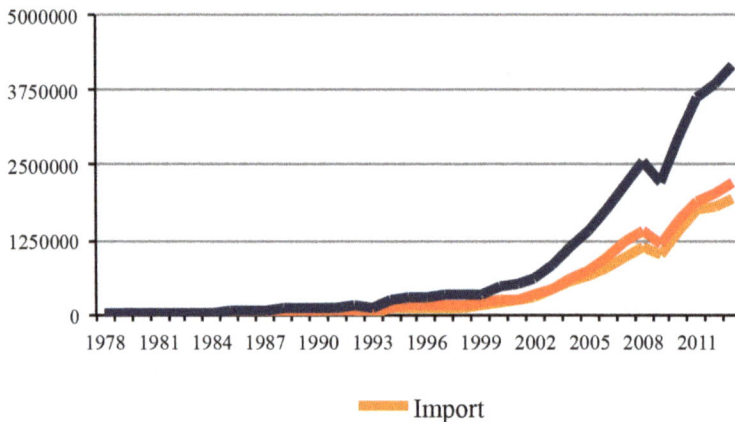

Figure 15.1 Chinese trade volume, 1978–2013 ($ million)

Source: NBS (2015).

Figure 15.2 illustrates the share of GDP in exports since 1978. The mainly rising trend demonstrates how trade became an important endogenous component of China's economic growth, especially from the mid-1990s. The importance of exports to China's economy, in particular, was accentuated after China's accession to the WTO. During 2002–07, the average share of exports in GDP peaked at 30 per cent, in 2007. Exports became the 'engine' of Chinese economic growth. Since the GFC in 2008 exports have not returned to pre-crisis levels, and instead have contributed less and less annually to GDP. In 2013, the ratio of exports to GDP reached 23.3 per cent—close to the ratio of 2003. While still making a great contribution to GDP, exports evidently no longer serve as China's economic engine.

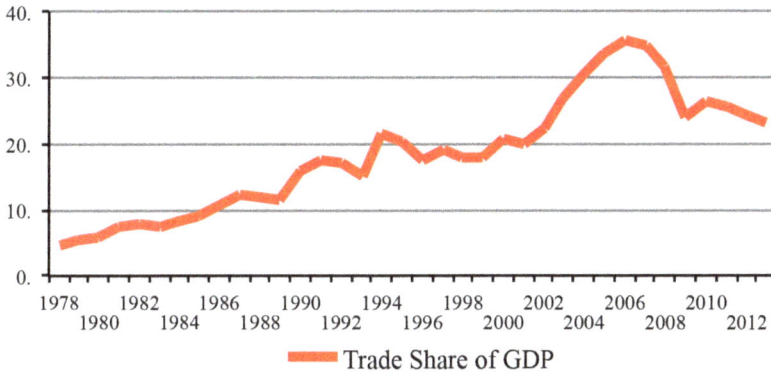

Figure 15.2 Export trade share of GDP, 1978–2013

Source: NBS (2015).

Sluggish world demand is one of the main explanations for China's export slowdown. While the uncertain recovery of the US economy is somewhat positive news for Chinese exporters, the US Government's measures to minimise its trade deficit with China serve to curb the scale of rebound in demand for Chinese exports. The pace of export increase is slow. In contrast, China's demand for US exports is rising relatively rapidly. China became the United States' largest export destination in 2013. That year, China imported goods to the value of $122.1 billion—up 10.4 per cent year-on-year (US Trade Representative 2015). China's exports to the United States in 2013 increased $14.9 billion, with a more moderate rate of 3.4 per cent from 2012.

China's exports to the European Union face challenging conditions. A stalled recovery, ageing population, monetary challenges and high unemployment prevent the European Union from rebounding as a major importer. According to EU statistics, from 2009 to 2013, the average growth rate of imports from China was 6.8 per cent, against an average growth rate of its exports to China of 15.6 per cent. In fact, the growth rate of imports from China was negative in 2009, 2012 and 2013, at −13.6 per cent, −1 per cent and −4.1 per cent respectively (EC 2015). The drawn-out economic recovery of the European Union hardly offers a promising future for bilateral trade.

Emerging economies' growth has decelerated to their slowest pace since 2008, or pre-GFC. Weak domestic demand and currency depreciation since May 2013 leave even emerging economies unable to import at previous levels. In sum, China's export-oriented growth model faces an unprecedented challenge in the face of shrinking global demand.

Domestically, China also faces the challenge of adjusting to a new balance between investment and consumption. In the past three decades, investment has served as the other engine of Chinese economic growth. Investment currently accounts for nearly half of GDP—well above the peak of about 40 per cent at a similar stage in South Korea and Taiwan. While investment remains high, 'the marginal contribution of an extra unit of investment to growth has been falling, necessitating ever larger increases in investment to generate an equal amount of growth' (Lee et al. 2012: 16). Over-reliance on investment offers diminishing returns, and is unsustainable especially following the excessive investment induced by the RMB400 trillion stimulus program implemented in the aftermath of the GFC in 2008.

While greater domestic consumption is being encouraged, this will hardly ignite economic growth. Household final consumption in China in 2012 was 38.2 per cent of GDP—up only marginally from 36.7 per cent in 2006, despite rapid economic growth (OECD 2014: 39). This level is much lower than the average for OECD countries. Striking a sustainable balance between investment and consumption is a focus of China's ongoing domestic economic reforms.

In light of this challenging set of conditions, official figures suggest China's economic growth rate in 2014 was 7.4 per cent—the lowest since the 1990s. The current economic slowdown, however, could benefit China in the long run if it is used as a springboard for reforms that successfully and sustainably shift the country's growth model. In this way, the 'new normal' era requires adjustments in domestic economic policies and also in externally oriented trade policies and strategies. Moreover, trade strategies that are compatible with these domestic conditions will help China to achieve a stable and successful growth model shift. Areas of relevance to these adjustments are explored in the next section.

Changing facets of the Chinese economy

The GFC in 2008 has deeply changed the shape of the global economy. For China, it forced a reconsideration of its growth model and pushed forward related domestic reforms. Indeed, it is also offers a turning point through which China is renavigating its role in the world economy.

Moving up global value chains

The proliferation of multinational companies investing in China not only drove China's economic growth, but also created opportunities for Chinese businesses to plug into global value chains (GVCs). Components were exported to China and final products were cased in China, and vice versa. As a result, China has become an integral part of Asia's regional production networks.

Early in China's broader economic transition, Chinese exports were famously characterised as cheap clothes, shoes and low-value-added products. Chinese industries were therefore positioned at the low end of the GVCs, with the interest margin for Chinese companies being accordingly minimal; however, 'benefiting from GVCs depends on how much value a country creates in the GVCs' (OECD 2013). In the face of sluggish demand for those products, the Chinese economy and Chinese companies now need to figure out how to add more value to the GVCs.

Innovation is part of the story of moving upwards in GVCs. This also helps Chinese companies maintain competitive advantage in the face of increasing pressure from labour costs. Chinese companies are already successfully taking action in pushing for higher status within GVCs. The 2014 world intellectual property report, the flagship publication of the Geneva-based World Intellectual Property Organization (WIPO), notes that China filed 32.1 per cent of the 2.6 million global patent applications in 2013, making it the greatest total patent filer in the world, followed by the United States (22.3 per cent) and Japan (12.6 per cent) (WIPO 2014: 12). In addition, Chinese foreign-oriented patents have surged since 2000, by an average annual growth rate of 40 per cent between 2000 and 2005, and 23 per cent since 2005 (WIPO 2014: 2).

The significance of innovation has, in fact, been written into China's national economic strategy. Innovation is intended to be a new driving force for growth and for increasing Chinese competitiveness in the world economy. Accordingly, subsidies and policy support from both the central and local governments are intended to encourage companies to increasingly engage in research and development (R&D) activities.

Becoming an outbound investor as well as a recipient investor

Inbound FDI has served as an important driver of China's economic growth in the past three decades. China became one of the hottest investment destinations in the world. In 2014, China attracted US$128 billion in foreign investment, reflecting a moderate increase of 3 per cent on the previous year. That year, China also surpassed the United States to become the largest recipient of investment in the world (UNCTAD 2015: 1).

In parallel, the recent rapid increase in Chinese outward foreign direct investment (OFDI) is also striking. In 2014, Chinese OFDI reached US$102.9 billion—up 14.1 per cent on the previous year. At this rate, Chinese OFDI will soon exceed its FDI. Having been a large capital-recipient country, China has become an important investor in the world economy.

Within that broader trend are tendencies that reflect Chinese companies seeking to develop advanced technologies through a merger and acquisition (M&A) process. For example, it is reported that PetroChina and China National Offshore Oil Corporation (CNOOC) have signed a few agreements with Western transnational corporations (TNCs), including Shell. Some of these agreements include articles on technological assistance and support (UNCTAD 2014b: 12). Concurrent with expanding market size and maximising business opportunities, Chinese companies are investing globally in a manner that emphasises narrowing the technology and management gaps with companies in developed countries. This is a critical step for Chinese companies undergoing a process of globalisation.

At the national level, Chinese OFDI is also expected to grow with the implementation of the 'one road and one belt' initiative. A $40 billion 'Silk Road Fund' has been founded to support investment in the infrastructure of developing countries. In general, Chinese companies are being encouraged to invest abroad and compete in the global market. It is hoped that massive investment by Chinese companies abroad will unlock opportunities for China to evolve from a country that is 'merchandise exporting' to one that is 'capital exporting'.

Free trade zones and other opening-up measures

Transition from export orientation poses many challenges for China's economy. There is no single prescription that can offer a detailed picture of what China's economy will become in the future, so China's government continues its usual practice of learning by doing.

One such area of experimentation is the practice of free trade zones (FTZs), which set aside an area for trial of innovative trade, investment and financial policies. The idea is to provide 'replicable experience' for other regions and the national economy as a whole for further liberalisation. The Shanghai Pilot Free Trade Zone, which was approved by the State Council in August 2013, is the pioneer for exploring approaches to achieving deepening reform and further opening in the current economic context. Its practices include granting investors 'national treatment' except for investment items listed in the 'negative list', and also simplifying customs procedures. These are novel policy instruments for both national and local governments.

Particularly noteworthy is the approach to the 'negative list', which has been explicitly written into the draft Foreign Investment Law. This approach fundamentally changes the traditional Chinese system of governing foreign investment. Under the new rules, foreign investors can enjoy pre-national treatment unless they fall into a category on the negative list. That is, a clear and transparent framework is now provided for foreign investment. In parallel, foreign investors can also benefit from a simplified registration system that removes the traditional lengthy approval process. Despite some criticism, the draft Foreign Investment Law indicates the arrival of a more transparent, stable and sophisticated system of governance of foreign investment (Pan 2015).

In the footsteps of Shanghai, Fujian, Guangdong and Tianjin are the recently announced second group of experimental FTZs. In addition to replicating the successful experience of Shanghai, these zones are expected to contribute to a more open Chinese economy, and to explore a new model of regional cooperation and a rule-based business environment. It is also hoped these three new FTZs will serve as hubs of regional economic growth and offer useful experience to facilitate regional development. In so doing, they should also be able to provide experience in responding effectively to the changing dynamics of international trade.

Changing dynamics of international trade rules

Failure of Doha Round negotiations in the WTO

At the end of the twentieth century, the establishment of the WTO was one of the greatest achievements of the international economic system. The agreements made under this multilateral trading system have had extensive influence on its 160 member countries. Under three pillars—trade in goods, services and intellectual property rights—the WTO has brought high-level liberalisation to international trade rules. In addition, the WTO's rule-based dispute-settlement system has earned a reputation for efficiency and effectiveness in settling trade-related disputes between member countries.

On the other hand, and as highlighted by Petersmann (2005: 649), multilateral trading is like a bicycle that has one wheel subject to regular negotiation. Through WTO negotiations, trade rules are updated and member countries can be motivated to seek changes in the multilateral trading system. The stalemate of Doha Round negotiations, however, has stalled that system. Confident of success more than a decade ago, negotiators proposed an agenda based on development issues for the Doha Round negotiations. Yet, the round has run into problems due to the divergent interests between developed and developing countries (Cho 2010: 574). Moreover, the 'single undertaking' principle—which requires universal agreement of member countries on an issue—makes the negotiations extremely difficult. At the ministerial conference in Bali in 2013, however, some modest progress was achieved on trade facilitation, reduction of import barriers from least-developed countries (LDCs) and on food security programs in developing countries. The reality is, however, that member countries are struggling to wrap up the Doha Round, and hope among members for agreement on substantial rules is slim. The multilateral trading system is struggling to provide new trade rules.

The proliferation of regional trade negotiations

In the last decades of the twentieth century, another remarkable, new phenomenon in the global economy was the emergence of GVCs. As they change the shape of global trade and investment, GVCs are now among the leading causes of the proliferation of regional trade negotiations.

With advances in technology reducing transportation and communication costs, multinational companies have in recent decades been able to operate with branches across countries, including developing countries. Specifically, production lines are split across countries with the location of each process based on comparative advantage, such as in cheap labour. In turn, a single product is no longer made within one country. Rather, production is an incremental process across many countries that provide different components of the production process.

Removing barriers to customs and investment, and facilitating the activities of value chains, is thus now essential to creating trade and bolstering the prosperity of the economy in the twenty-first century. It is estimated that reducing barriers in GVCs could increase global GDP by nearly 5 per cent and global trade by 15 per cent (World Economic Forum et al. 2013: 13). Existing trade rules, however, are built on the perception of trade 'at the border'. Concepts such as tariffs, rules of origin and so on reflect a way of thinking in which products are labelled as being from a single country, rather than the combined effort of many countries. In the twenty-first century, trade rules that advocate tariff reductions and quota elimination are important, but insufficient to bolster trade. The expansion of GVCs has thus led to calls for changes to create new rules that better suit the structure and needs of global trade (Baldwin 2011: 8–9).

Amid this dynamic, the deadlock of the Doha Round of negotiations has helped create a trend among member countries to turn to regional trade negotiations. The world's greatest traders—China, Japan, the European Union and the United States—have all sought solutions in regional talks. As noted earlier, there are three leading regional negotiation initiatives under way: the RCEP, TPP and TTIP. Two of them—RCEP and TPP—are concentrated on the Asia-Pacific, reflecting the well-developed and lucrative supply chains in the region, and creating common interest for countries to push for the negotiation of more sophisticated trade rules that are compatible with local production networks.

In contrast, the TTIP focuses on divergence within and duplication of regulatory policies. It seeks to create a more specific and subtle set of trade rules based on business sectors that reduce divergence and duplication across domestic laws. The European Union and the United States are already working on divergence within related issues, such as food safety and automobile parts. They hope to use the TTIP as the 'standard makers, rather than standard takers' (Bollyky and Bradford 2013). Through a more united regulatory approach, the European Union and the United States hope to ensure other countries gravitate towards their joint standards, despite the shift of economic power to emerging economies.

As of April 2015, none of these three negotiation platforms has borne substantial fruit. Although the TPP is moving towards a conclusion, its content is still unclear due to issues with the Trade Promotion Authority and disagreement within the US Democratic Party. The RCEP agenda also seeks to conclude negotiations by the end of 2015; however, there are many issues needing resolution before a final deal can be reached. The TTIP appears to be a secondary priority on the United States' trade agenda this year—after the TPP deal.

A call for new trade rules in the Pacific Rim

In the Pacific Rim, while RCEP and TPP complement each other in terms of their membership scope and issue coverage, they are in competition to be the first to offer an update to the international trade rules of the WTO. In turn, the outlook for international trade rules varies greatly, depending on whether the RCEP or the TPP is signed first.

RCEP negotiations include 10 Association of South-East Asian Nations (ASEAN) members and Australia, China, India, Japan, New Zealand and South Korea. These are big trading partners within the region. The negotiation agenda covers an extensive range of issues, such as tariff reduction, services, investment and intellectual property rights protection. RCEP's aim is to further reduce tariffs among member countries, to grant more market access within service sectors and to create a liberal, facilitative and competitive regional investment environment. Negotiations are taking place based on the current structure of the ASEAN+1, but with improvements in many aspects. The RCEP negotiations engage 16 countries so as to make RCEP rules comprehensive and of high quality, reflecting the collective determination to more deeply integrate the various national economies. The negotiation agenda incorporates sensitive issues, including competition. The competition issue was once raised in multilateral trade discussions in the Singapore Round of negotiations of the WTO. It was removed from the agenda, however, due to opposition from developing countries. It represents remarkable progress that it can now appear on the agenda of RCEP, even though most of the participants are developing countries. Despite the pursuit of comprehensive liberalisation, the guidelines of the RCEP also address the issue of flexibility by 'taking into consideration … the different levels of development of participating countries'.[2] The negotiations will consider country differences and allow special and differentiated treatment for LDCs.

Unlike the RCEP, the TPP purports to create 'twenty-first-century high-level international trade rules'. Led by the United States, the TPP is being negotiated by 11 other Asia-Pacific countries: Australia, Brunei, Canada, Chile, Japan, Malaysia, Mexico, New Zealand, Peru, Singapore and Vietnam. The TPP seeks comprehensive coverage of issues, including services, investment, intellectual property rights, state-owned enterprises (SOEs), the environment and labour. While improving the level of rights based on WTO rules, such as protection for investors and intellectual property rights, it also intends to reduce tariffs to zero and expand market access in service sectors.

More ambitiously, the TPP aims to write new disciplines into international trade rules. It addresses competitive neutrality and regulates SOEs. It also imports environmental and labour-related elements into trade law frameworks. Specifically, it attempts to add the environment and labour costs into the cost of products so as to factor these impacts into the competitiveness level of products. Developing countries have expressed concern that TPP negotiation areas will make them less competitive. Concerns have also arisen about selective rule proposals, such as the extension of intellectual property right protection to pharmaceutical products, which could favour developed countries. The TPP is being pushed by the United States, and this makes it a struggle for developing countries to protect their interests. Negotiators are still working towards a final deal.

If agreed by negotiating countries, the TPP could become the template for future international trade rules. By utilising the TPP, the United States could maintain its lead in international trade rule-making. In this way, the TPP serves as a critical instrument for the United States to achieve its goal 'to be involved in

---

2   Guiding Principles and Objectives for Negotiating Regional Comprehensive Economic Partnership, November 2013.

the discussions that could shape the future of this region and to participate fully in appropriate organizations as they are established and evolve'.[3] These rules are used to secure the competitiveness of American companies globally and to regain leverage for the US economy. In a geopolitical sense, the TPP also serves to unite the United States and its allies through economic ties and adds momentum to political bilateral and regional relationships. It is understood to be the economic pillar of the United States' 'rebalancing' policy in the Pacific Rim.

Despite its increasing trade power and enthusiasm to join international trade rule-making, China is currently excluded from TPP negotiations. Chinese high-level officials have expressed interest in joining the negotiations to deepen China's integration with other economies (Tiezzi 2014). Despite this, it is appears China will not be allowed to join in drafting the new international trade rules under the framework of the TPP.

The RCEP serves as an alternative for China, though China and other negotiating countries have a long way to go to reach an agreement. The rules of RCEP will be not as ambitious as the TPP's, but this could serve as a middle ground towards consensus on a more ambitious trade package like the TPP. In his address to the 2015 Boao Forum for Asia, Chinese President Xi Jinping re-emphasised the significance of concluding the RCEP deal by the end of 2015. Hopefully, Chinese facilitation can help to induce accelerated negotiation of the RCEP towards agreement. We will see which is the first agreement to update the trade rules in the Pacific Rim.

Chinese trade negotiation options

Cards in China's hands

Multilateral approaches

Joining the WTO in 2001 has significantly benefited Chinese economic growth in the past decade. It also saw China deepen its integration with the global economy. As the world's largest exporter, China should now be part of trade negotiations and write its will into the system of international trade rules. It wishes to seize the opportunity during this round of mega-regional trade rule negotiations by joining the various negotiating arenas.

---

3   Remarks of President Barack Obama at Suntory Hall, Tokyo, 14 November 2009.

The WTO is the fundamental platform for negotiating new trade rules. As a proponent of multilateralism, China supports the significance of the WTO's legislative function in evolving new rules. China has actively participated in the Doha Round negotiations. It has also worked closely with the United States and India on the divergence between developed country and developing country issues. It signed the agreement on trade facilitation at the Bali ministerial conference and pushed for its conclusion when the agreement was struck in 2014.

China is also an active participant of plurilateral agreement negotiations inside the WTO. Given the stalemate of the Doha Round, the plurilateral approach has emerged in the form of groups of like-minded WTO member countries negotiating on selected issues. Thus far China has entered into negotiations for the Information Technology Agreement and Government Procurement Agreement. China has also expressed its interest in the Trade in Services Agreement (TISA) and hopes to become a negotiating member. It has, however, so far been excluded due to the concerns of some developed countries, including the United States. Indeed, some of the issues covered in these negotiations are also sensitive for the Chinese economy and could pose challenges to the current structure of Chinese governance. The Chinese Government has realised that being among the rule-makers is essential to protecting its own interests in the global context. Being a signatory to negotiations within the WTO would allow China to be present when the important issues are being considered. The plurilateral agreements negotiated by a group of members will apply to all WTO members, if accepted by all the other WTO members. Multilateral negotiations, despite their slowness, can be effective instruments for advancing trade-related issues.

Regional approach

Given its core interest in the Asia-Pacific, China also actively participates in regional negotiations of new trade rules. It engages in discussions towards building free trade areas with neighbouring countries with a view to having a positive impact on both regional economics and geopolitics.

In East Asia, free trade agreement (FTA) negotiations between China, Japan and South Korea began in 2012. The seventh round of negotiations was completed in April 2015. China and South Korea were able to reap an early harvest by signing a bilateral FTA—China's most substantive FTA, covering the largest trade volume and the most comprehensive range of issues.

In addition, China is negotiating an FTA with the Gulf Cooperation Council, which consists of Bahrain, Oman, Kuwait, Qatar, Saudi Arabia and the United Arab Emirates (UAE). The negotiations were stopped after being launched in 2009, but resumed in 2013. Bilateral negotiations between China and each Gulf Cooperation Council country continue. FTAs serve as important instruments for strengthening economic ties between China and signatory countries. Under the 'one belt and one road' initiative, it could be expected that there will be a proliferation of FTAs and bilateral investment treaties (BITs) between China and its neighbours in the near future. Of course, preferential trade is not multilateral free trade and cannot substitute for its benefits.

The RCEP is another trade-related negotiating platform in the Asia-Pacific, incorporating 16 countries. Production networks within this region are tightly interconnected. China has put great emphasis on RCEP negotiations to facilitate further expansion of regional production networks and strengthen China's ties with South-East Asian countries in particular. It might not be easy to wrap up these negotiations quickly, however, due to the different development levels and interests of the countries involved. An alternative accelerated track lies in China having started negotiations with ASEAN countries on an upgraded version of the ASEAN–China FTA, which is at the top of the Chinese trade negotiation agenda.

At the 2014 Asia-Pacific Economic Cooperation (APEC) leaders' gathering in Beijing, China addressed the importance of building a free trade area among APEC member countries. The feasibility study on an FTA for the Asia-Pacific (FTAAP) will be launched in response. In addition to the RCEP, therefore, through the FTAAP and the ASEAN–China FTA, China could play a bigger role in shaping trade rules and the regional economic architecture in the ongoing process of Asia-Pacific economic integration.

China's FTAAP initiative also highlights that China is willing to work with the United States on drafting new trade rules towards broader Asia-Pacific economic integration. Although the original FTAAP idea was first proposed by the United States, the United States is now preoccupied with concluding the TPP. Even where the negotiations for an FTAAP are launched, the United States would have these built on the TPP negotiations—that is, with its clear emphasis on the TPP, the United States seeks to influence the general structure of the FTAAP and apply the TPP's rules to a larger group of APEC countries. Since the FTAAP's negotiation agenda has not yet been clarified, it will require a lot of collaboration between China and other countries to make the FTAAP a reality.

Bilateral approaches

Among 15 FTAs signed by China as of April 2015, almost all are bilateral agreements, except the FTAs agreed with Hong Kong, Taipei (China) and Macau (Table 15.1). China has signed FTAs with a broad range of Asian countries, including ASEAN, Australia, Korea, Pakistan and Singapore. China also has FTAs with Chile, Costa Rica, New Zealand and Switzerland. FTAs now in the pipeline will boost Chinese economic integration with Japan and Norway.

Table 15.1 FTAs signed by China as of April 2015

Asia-Pacific (1976)	Developing–developed
China–Thailand (2003)[a]	Developing–developing
China–Hong Kong, China (2003)	
ASEAN–China (2004)	Developing–developing
China–Chile (2006)	Developing–developing
China–Pakistan (2006)	Developing–developing
China–New Zealand (2008)	Developing–developed
China–Singapore (2008)	Developing–developed
China–Peru (2009)	Developing–developing
China–Macau, China (2009)	
China–Taipei, China (2010)	
China–Costa Rica (2010)	Developing–developing
China–Iceland (2013)	Developing–developing
China–Switzerland (2013)	Developing–developed
China–Australia	Developing–developed
China–Korea (2015)	Developing–developed

[a] It was later included in the ASEAN+China.
Source: Authors' compilation based on information from China's Ministry of Commerce.

Chinese experience as a WTO member, which helped to massively increase China's exports in the past decade, made it an enthusiast for free trade. While preferential trade agreements have few of the advantages of genuine free trade, and have disadvantages as well, China has tended to seek to replicate that success by gaining more market access and by further reducing tariff levels through bilateral FTAs with countries in the region. In the early days of these FTA negotiations, China applied an individual approach to negotiations on goods, services and investments to accelerate implementation, including in the ASEAN–China FTA's Early Harvest Program. During this period, Chinese FTA emphasis was on trade in goods, particularly tariff reductions. The more complicated Singapore Round issues—referring to an earlier WTO multilateral negotiation round, including government procurement, competition and trade facilitation—received little attention.

A more proactive stance by China emerged in FTAs signed with New Zealand and Singapore in 2008. These negotiations had multiple focuses in addition to the liberalisation of trade in goods. In particular, China put more emphasis on the negotiation of services and Singapore Round issues. The coverage of services and liberalisation steps was more vigorous and comprehensive compared with earlier negotiations. Several Singapore Round issues, such as trade facilitation, were on the negotiation agenda, although competition and government procurement proved too sensitive to address. China has, however, recently taken a more comprehensive and vigorous approach to FTAs signed with developed countries. For example, China's FTAs with Iceland and Switzerland, each signed in 2013, and with South Korea in 2015, have more comprehensive coverage in goods, services and investments, especially with respect to Singapore Round issues.

Chinese issue-related FTA strategies

Bilateral investment treaties

Following China's shift towards becoming an important outbound investor, it urgently needs to update its BITs with its trade and investment partners. As of April 2015, China has signed 145 BITs with a wide array of countries (UNCTAD 2014a). Many of these BITs—particularly those signed in the early days of China's opening-up—were drafted from the stance of protecting China's inbound investment recipient interests. For instance, the BITs intentionally narrowed the scope of arbitration and restricted the availability of use of ad hoc arbitration in the International Centre for Settlement of Investment Disputes (ICSID), unless disputes were related to compensation over expropriation and nationalisation (Heymann 2008: 515).

China's BITs have evolved significantly in the past decade, offering more balance between investor and recipient protections, including a more fully fledged dispute-settlement provision. 'While it has not yet converged on U.S. "high-standard" BIT practice, it has come closer' (Gantz 2014: 28). Recent BITs signed with developed countries, such as Canada in 2012, represent remarkable progress in the way China addresses national treatment, most-favoured nation (MFN) treatment and dispute settlement, though there have been some reservations. The enlarged scope of these BITs indicates a clear shift for China in its negotiating stance, based on its role changing from being merely a recipient to being also a major outbound investor. The ongoing BIT negotiations with the United States will, when completed, reflect China's most advanced such regulations.

The negotiations for BITs or for investment chapters within FTAs will be among the priorities of Chinese trade negotiations in the future, especially under the umbrella of the 'one road and one belt' strategy. Cautious agreement on reciprocal national treatment, MFN and dispute-settlement mechanisms in host countries will benefit Chinese investors in the long run by offering accessible, stable and predictable investment environments. This will also help to ensure a successful transition from the tradition of government-led overseas investment to private outward investment while adhering to the relevant international rules.

Last, China's change in its stance in BIT negotiations leaves room for it to join high-level FTAs. Building a predictable and stable, investment-friendly environment will be in China's and China's investors' favour. Despite many contentious issues in the high-level trade rules, the shared concern over protections for investors could create common ground for China and other developed countries to work together. The consensus on investment issues will pave the way for China to join the negotiations for high-level international trade rules.

Services

According to WTO statistics, China's services exports reached $205 billion in 2013. With a steady annual rate of increase of nearly 8 per cent, Chinese exports in services cover 4.4 per cent of total world services exports. China's imports of services in the same year were $329 billion, reflecting a higher share—some 7.52 per cent—of total world imports. China's services imports also increased more sharply, at an annual rate of 18 per cent (WTO 2014).

Transportation and travel explain most of the increase in services trade. More importantly, value-added services are contributing increasingly to GDP—up to 46 per cent in 2013 from 32 per cent in 1992 (World Bank 2015). The expansion of GVCs integrates not only Chinese component manufacturers into the global economy, but also the service providers of these production lines. As a huge market that holds much promise for China's middle class, there is great potential for a boom in trade in services, both domestically and globally. This is particularly true in the global context given that China's advantage in providing cheap labour is diminishing. Indeed, China faces a great opportunity to expand its services into the region and the world.

In that context, China will also embark on negotiating service agreements with its trading partners. Its activeness in participating in the TISA, as mentioned above, is part of this story. The emphasis in negotiations for services is first on opening market access in the transportation and travel sectors; the Chinese Government faces few difficulties to open domestically. Liberalisation of the financial and telecommunications sectors is expected to gradually increase in the pace and prioritisation of domestic reforms. This liberalisation of services trade also could provide China with a new engine for its economic growth.

New sensitive issues

Some new sensitive issues—such as SOEs, the environment and labour—pose challenges for China in twenty-first-century trade negotiations. As outlined above, these issues are important impediments to China joining high-level trade negotiations such as those of the TPP. Handled badly, they can also be impediments to genuinely free trade. Environment was once an area in which

Chinese standards once diverged from most developed countries, but today Chinese standards in many areas exceed those of some countries, including Australia, which are expected to be members of the TPP. If the TPP is concluded, the pressure for China to tackle labour standards in particular will increase. China's commitment to addressing these issues, however, is also subject to progress in Chinese domestic reforms in each relevant sector. If the TPP cannot be concluded in the near future, this will buy China time to proceed at its own pace on domestic reforms in related issues.

It is noted, however, that Chinese negotiators will pay more attention to the regulation of these new issues in such high-level trade negotiations. Due to the sensitivity of these issues, the TPP, even were it to be concluded, might not be able to set binding rules for members. China could address these rules as non-binding, or seek a transitional period in which to adapt to relevant rules, in order to minimise its exposure to any negative consequences. Despite the sensitivity and complexity of these issues, China might consider adjusting by putting emphasis on domestic reform and negotiation strategies.

Conclusion: To work towards converging on a trade deal

The international trading system is at a crossroad, thanks to deadlock in the multilateral Doha Round of WTO negotiations and the parallel emergence of a few mega-regional trade negotiation platforms. The mega-regionals, which have attracted a lot of attention, could turn out to be a stumbling block for genuinely global free trade, or could pave the way to reaching a multilateral deal within the WTO's frameworks. It is important that they pave the way, and that major participants in regional preferential trading areas keep this at the front of their minds. Divisions among trading blocks, as reflected in the shape of these mega-regional negotiations, pose uncertainty for the international trading system and suggest there could be delays in adapting to these trading dynamics. Though geopolitical concerns could justify such divisions, large traders need to work together to converge on a trade deal towards the goal of evolving the new trade rules that are needed for twenty-first-century prosperity and economic security. Through this process, China will play an active role and seek to expand its influence to match its economic power. Any attempt to exclude China is unwise and would be unsuccessful, as the story of the Asian Infrastructure Investment Bank proves.

China seeks to work with its large trading partners, such as the United States and the European Union, towards taking responsibility for collectively upgrading international trade rules. The internal reform of the Chinese economy and its changing role in the global economy provide common ground for China, a large developing country, and developed countries to work on their divergence and to agree to a new set of rules. As an important and indispensible player in the Pacific Rim as well as the world, China is expected to take on a more active role in the evolution of a twenty-first-century trading system.

References

Baldwin, R. (2011), *21st century regionalism: Filling the gap between 21st century trade and 20th century trade rules*, WTO Staff Working Paper, ERSD-2011-08, 23 May, Geneva: World Trade Organization.

Bollyky, T.J. and Bradford, A. (2013), Getting to yes on transatlantic trade: Consistent US–EU trade could remake global commerce, *Foreign Affairs*. Available from: www.foreignaffairs.com/articles/139569/thomas-j-bollyky-and-anu-bradford/getting-to-yes-on-transatlantic-trade. Retrieved 16 April 2015.

Cho, S. (2010), The demise of development in the Doha round negotiations, *Texas International Journal of Law*, 45: 573–601.

European Commission (EC) (2015), *European Union, trade in goods with China*, Brussels: Directorate-General for Trade, European Commission. Available from: trade.ec.europa.eu/doclib/docs/2006/september/tradoc_113366.pdf. Retrieved 23 March 2015.

Gantz, D.A. (2014), *Challenges for the United States in negotiating a BIT with China: Reconciling reciprocal investment protection with policy concerns*, Arizona Legal Studies Discussion Paper no. 14-03, Tucson: University of Arizona.

Heymann, M.C.E. (2008), International law and the settlement of investment disputes relating to China, *Journal of International Economic Law*, 11(3): 507–26.

Krugman, P. and Obstfeld, M. (1991), *International economics: Theory and policy*, 2nd edn, New York: Harper Collins.

Lee, I.H., Syed, M. and Xueyan, L. (2012), *Is China over-investing and does it matter?*, IMF Working Paper 12/277, Washington, DC: International Monetary Fund.

National Bureau of Statistics (NBS) (2015), Beijing.

Organisation for Economic Cooperation and Development (OECD) (2013), *Global value chains: China*, Paris: OECD Publishing. Available from: www.oecd.org/sti/ind/GVCs%20-%20CHINA.pdf. Retrieved 26 March 2015.

Organisation for Economic Cooperation and Development (OECD) (2014), *National accounts at a glance*, Paris: OECD Publishing.

Pan, X. (2015), Chinese new governance of foreign investment, *China US Focus*, 17 March. Available from: www.chinausfocus.com/finance-economy/chinas-foreign-investment-law-regulations-for-chinas-foreign-investment-governance-in-the-new-era/. Retrieved 30 March 2015.

Petersmann, E.-U. (2005), Addressing institutional challenges to the WTO in the new millennium: A longer-term perspective, *Journal of International Economic Law*, 8(3): 647–65.

Tiezzi, S. (2014), Will China join the trans-Pacific partnership?, *The Diplomat*, 10 October. Available from: thediplomat.com/2014/10/will-china-join-the-trans-pacific-partnership/. Retrieved 15 April 2015.

United Nations Conference on Trade and Development (UNCTAD) (2014a), *Total number of bilateral investment treaties concluded [by China]*, 5 May, Geneva: UNCTAD. Available from: investmentpolicyhub.unctad.org/IIA/CountryBits/42. Retrieved 20 April 2015.

United Nations Conference on Trade and Development (UNCTAD) (2014b), *World investment report 2014: Investing in the SDGs—An action plan*, Geneva: UNCTAD.

United Nations Conference on Trade and Development (UNCTAD) (2015), Global FDI flows declined in 2014 and China becomes the top FDI recipient, *Global Investment Trend Monitor* no. 18, Geneva: UNCTAD.

US Trade Representative (2014), *US–China trade facts*, Washington, DC: Office of the US Trade Representative. Available from: ustr.gov/countries-regions/china-mongolia-taiwan/peoples-republic-china. Retrieved 23 March 2015.

Wharton Business School (2015), *China in 2015: Gauging the new normal*, Philadelphia: Wharton School, University of Pennsylvania. Available from: knowledge.wharton.upenn.edu/article/gaging-the-new-normal-in-china/. Retrieved 16 March 2015.

World Bank (2010), Foreign direct investment: The China story, *News*, 16 July, Washington, DC: The World Bank. Available from: www.worldbank.org/en/news/feature/2010/07/16/foreign-direct-investment-china-story. Retrieved 23 March 2015.

World Bank (2015), *World databank*, Washington, DC: The World Bank. Available from: databank.worldbank.org/data/views/reports/tableview. aspx. Retrieved 20 April 2015.

World Economic Forum, Bain & Company and World Bank (2013), *Enabling trade: Valuing growth opportunities*, Geneva: World Economic Forum.

World Intellectual Property Organization (WIPO) (2014a), *International patenting strategies of Chinese residents*, Geneva: WIPO.

World Intellectual Property Organization (WIPO) (2014b), *World intellectual property indicator 2014*, Geneva: WIPO.

World Trade Organization (WTO) (2014), *China: Statistics*, Geneva: WTO. Available from: stat.wto.org/CountryProfile/WSDBCountryPFView. aspx?Country=CN&. Retrieved 20 April 2015.

Yao, Y. (2008), The political economy of government policies toward regional inequality in China, in Huang, Y. and Bocchi, A.M. (eds), *Reshaping economic geography in East Asia*, Washington, DC: The World Bank.

16. Boom to Cusp

Prospecting the 'new normal' in China and Africa

Lauren Johnston

Introduction

Multiple domestic structural factors underlie China's lower 'new normal' growth target of 7 per cent: reduced export demand growth, an ageing and higher-cost workforce, environmental priorities and constraints, and diminishing returns to physical capital relative to human capital. With the middle-income trap still to be avoided and China home to some 100 million citizens living below the RMB2,300 per annum national poverty line at the end of 2012 (World Bank 2015), finding ways to ensure growth is sustainable and delivers the livelihoods of a high-income country is now an objective of government.

Economic ties with Africa are one source of growth for China. China–Africa trade reached almost US$200 billion in 2013—up from about US$10 billion in 2000 (IMF 2015a). Realised annual foreign direct investment (FDI) in Africa in 2013 surpassed US$3 billion—up from US$317 million a decade earlier (NBS 2014). Total Chinese investment stock in Africa exceeded US$26 billion in 2013 (NBS 2014).

Despite the slowing of China's own growth, China–Africa growth prospects remain buoyant. By 2020, intra-developing country trade is forecast to have increased tenfold over a decade, with China–Africa trade leading the way (Fletcher and Ahmed 2012). China's investment in Africa is also set to expand dramatically. Chinese state media announced in late 2013 a national decision to provide US$1 trillion in financing to Africa by 2025 (Xinhuanet 2013). These growth trajectories will not only shape China's international integration and Africa's economic development prospects, but also come to shape features of the world economy.

Internal debate in Africa about China's rising economic ties with the continent is intense. At the political level, in 2006 Zambian presidential candidate the late president Michael Sata famously accused the Chinese of being 'infestors' rather than investors. South African President Jacob Zuma has been more circumspect, suggesting in 2012 that 'Africa's commitment to China's development has been demonstrated by supply of raw materials, other products and technology transfer', adding that '[t]his pattern of trade is unsustainable in the long term. Africa's past economic experience with Europe dictates a need to be cautious when entering into partnerships with other economies' (Hook 2012).

There are governance issues also. In a 2014 transparency index, China was ranked last of 62 donor agencies (Publish What You Fund 2014). The home regions of African presidents are found to receive three to four times more Chinese aid than other regions, leading to accusations that China plays patronage politics (Dreher 2014). Trade with China is also found to be proportionately greater to African countries with a poor governance record (de Grauwe et al. 2012).

In the *Financial Times* in March 2013, the Central Bank Governor of Africa's largest economy, Nigeria's Sanusi Lamido, wrote that Africa should:

> [R]ecognize that China—like the US, Russia, Britain, Brazil and the rest—is in Africa not for African interests but its own. Romance must be replaced by hard-nosed economic thinking. Engagement must be on terms that allow the Chinese to make money while developing the continent, such as incentives to set up manufacturing on African soil and policies to ensure employment of Africans. (*Financial Times* 2013)

The stakes are high, for both China and Africa. In 2010, current Chinese President and then vice-president, Xi Jinping, promised Africa that China would 'enlarge the scale of China–Africa trade, and optimize the trade structure' (Pang 2010). This is important—during 2005–12, China accounted for some 30 per cent of sub-Saharan Africa's export growth (Drummond and Liu 2013: 10).

China's 'new normal' growth era is, however, now ending the decade-long China-led commodities price boom (Garnaut 2012), which in turn will affect China–Africa economic ties. The majority of Africa's exports to China are raw commodities, especially oil. Visiting Africa in early 2015, International Monetary Fund (IMF) Managing Director Christine Lagarde warned, '[m]omentum is slowing in many advanced and emerging economies, including in China—one of Africa's main trading partners' (Ochelle 2015).

The effects for Africa's commodity and non-commodity exporters alike could be extensive. Dramatic falls in the iron ore price, for example, are a significant factor in the IMF in April 2015 lowering its annual growth forecasts for Guinea, Liberia and Sierra Leone—from 6 to 1 per cent, from 11 to 6 per cent and from 5.4 per cent to 1 per cent respectively (IMF 2015b). The falling iron ore price has delivered an especially harsh blow to the fiscal positions of the three least-developed countries (LDCs) that are battling the aftermath of the worst-ever Ebola virus outbreak.

This chapter focuses on the evolution of China–Africa economic ties. It sheds light on the importance of China to Africa, and also of Africa to China. The chapter also draws attention to a series of factors that highlight ways in which China's slowdown may not be all bad news for African economies. The end of the commodities boom could instead give rise to gradual investment and trade expansion outside the resources sector—a case of 'boom to cusp'—that could place the continent in a better position for more broadly based growth.

The second section of this chapter presents a short chronological introduction to China–Africa relations, with a focus on economics. The third section presents the stylised facts of contemporary economic ties. The fourth section outlines issues in China–Africa ties, with a focus on trade, especially in oil. The final section draws together the preceding discussion to highlight uncertainty amid potential for the emergence of new sources of growth in China and Africa.

China–Africa: Return of a fleeting 'old normal'

China's ties with Africa date back to the three fifteenth-century visits of Admiral Zheng He's fleets to the East African coastline (Dreyer 2007). On these visits, Chinese porcelains, silks and crafts were exchanged for African products, fauna and flora (Levathes 2014).

When the People's Republic of China (PRC) was formed in 1949, most of Africa remained under European colonial rule. The first independent African country to establish official diplomatic ties with Beijing was Egypt, in 1956. This marks also the beginning of China's direct aid to Africa (Mao 2011). Other post-independence early movers to recognise Beijing include Guinea and Sudan (in 1959), Ghana (1960), Democratic Republic of the Congo (DR Congo, 1961), Kenya (1963), and Benin and Republic of the Congo (Congo Republic, 1964) (Brautigam 2009: 68).

Premier Zhou Enlai's 1963 visit to 10 mostly newly independent countries was another turning point in Sino–African political economic ties.[1] The visit delivered the formal launch of China's aid policy for Africa, including a promise of help to construct a railway from Zambia to Tanzania, enabling landlocked Zambia's copper to be exported around Zimbabwe and South Africa. In the years thereafter, African votes were instrumental in Beijing's 1971 win over Taiwan in acquiring China's seat on the UN Security Council (Brautigam 2009).

---

[1] Including United Arab Republic (now Egypt), Algeria, Morocco, Tunisia, Ghana, Mali, Sudan, Ethiopia and Somalia (MFA 2000).

As Beijing launched its opening and reform policies in the late 1970s, African growth performance was mostly poor to disastrous. Examples include the 1980s economic crises in Guinea and Tanzania. From the mid-1970s to mid-1990s, almost all economies in sub-Saharan Africa (SSA) had zero or negative economic growth per capita (Radelet 2010: 1). Just one African economy made *The Growth Report*'s list of 13 sustained high-growth economies of the later twentieth century: Botswana (World Bank Staff 2008). China's ongoing transformation, in contrast, took place within a neighbourhood of high-performing economies; more than half the economies listed were East Asian.[2]

Macroeconomic conditions in Africa, however, have changed. The majority of economies in SSA have performed better since 1996 (Arbache and Page 2007). The 1994 end of Apartheid in South Africa allowed SSA's then largest economy to reintegrate with the region, while also helping to stabilise regional politics (Carmody 2009). Chinese President Jiang Zemin's visit to Africa in 1996 marks a shift in the driver of Sino–African ties from politics towards economics (Alden 2007: 15).

For China, those changes in Africa and Jiang's official visit came at a ripe time. China's exports of machinery and electronics exceeded those of textiles and clothing in 1995 (Lin and Wang 2014: 4). That rapid industrial growth saw China become a net oil importer in 1991, prompting an international quest for energy and other raw material supplies. Africa was seen as a potential source of undeveloped resources.

In extended outreach to Africa, China also sought support for Chinese policies in international affairs, acceptance of the RMB as an international currency, and the creation of new markets for Chinese goods and services. China offered willingness to invest in Africa's infrastructure and capacity to follow through (Brautigam 2009; Broadman 2007: 11; Pannell 2013). Jiang's visit coincided with a decision of China's State Council to 'combine aid to Africa, mutual co-operation, and trade together' (Brautigam 2009: 80).

For these reasons, Africa is also a focus of China's national-level outbound investment policy. Officially launched in 2000, the 'Going Out' policy aims to gain access to natural resources that are in short supply domestically, to forge international brand names of Chinese origin, and to diversify investments utilising China's trillion-dollar foreign exchange reserves.

Since 2000, growing China–Africa ties are coordinated through the Forum on China and Africa Cooperation (FOCAC), which China instigated in the footsteps of the Europe–Africa Summit and the Tokyo International Conference on

---

2 The 13 are Botswana, Brazil, China, Hong Kong (China), Indonesia, Japan, Korea, Malaysia, Malta, Oman, Singapore, Taiwan (China) and Thailand.

African Development (TICAD). Via FOCAC, a triennial head-of-state forum rotate between China and an African host. The sixth such summit will be hosted by South Africa in November 2015. FOCAC is also the umbrella under which more regular ministerial and working groups between Chinese and African governments take place.

Not all African countries are part of FOCAC. Burkina Faso and Swaziland are excluded from FOCAC because China insists that all participants adhere to the One China Policy. Gambia is also excluded as, although in late 2014 it ceased recognising Taipei, it has not agreed to diplomatic ties with Beijing.

FOCAC politically formalised ties between China and Africa in 2000, and since 2009 China has grown to become Africa's largest bilateral trade partner. Since 2009 Africa's trade with China exceeds in value the sum of all intra-African trade (IMF 2015a). The rapid expansion of economic ties helped to transform Africa from the 'hopeless continent' (*The Economist* 2011) into a new pole of global growth, and home to some of the world's fastest growth rates (*The Economist* 2011; Wang 2007).

China–Africa economics overview

Sino–African economic ties run in three interconnected channels: aid, investment and trade. This section provides an overview of those flows, and also outlines their interlaced structure.

China's aid data are presented using a different methodology to that of the Organisation for Economic Cooperation and Development (OECD). This makes it difficult to draw international comparisons (Brautigam 2011a: 203–22; Brandt 2013).

According to the *2014 China White Paper on Foreign Aid*, from 2010 to 2012, China provided RMB89.3 billion (US$13.4 billion) in foreign aid, through grants, interest-free loans (8.1 per cent of total foreign aid) and concessional loans (55.7 per cent of total foreign aid). This three-year sum is equivalent to about one-third of China's entire pre-2009 foreign aid to all countries, according to figures in the first aid white paper of 2011 (Zhou 2014). The amount suggests annual foreign aid of about $5 billion, making China the world's tenth-largest provider of foreign aid (Zhou 2014).

The white paper also reveals that about half of China's foreign aid goes to countries in Africa (MOFCOM 2011, 2013). That aid prioritises agricultural development, followed by infrastructure, health, capacity building (education) and climate change (MOFCOM 2011, 2013). There were 86 aid-related infrastructure projects under way that seek to better integrate domestic and regional economies (MOFCOM 2011, 2013).

Towards mitigating and adjusting to climate change, China has built several meteorological monitoring stations in African countries, and is active in supporting the development and utilisation of new energy on the continent. Recent projects receiving Chinese state financial support include a 400-megawatt solar power plant in Ghana at a cost of US$1 billion. Negotiations are in progress around a US$140 million solar power station in Garissa, Kenya (Tsagas 2013), and a US$132 million wind farm in Tanzania. Such investments help to address Africa's power gap in a more sustainable way than via old energy models. They also create an international market for Chinese new energy companies. This type of exchange reflects the principle of mutual development that is an explicit founding principle of China's foreign aid program.

And so the line between Chinese aid and investment is a murky one (see Brautigam 2011). The evolution of China's development financing between aid and commercial investment is introduced by Lin and Wang's (2014: 8) summary of China's financing mechanisms available to Africa:

> Other Official Flows [OOF] (large but less concessional loans and export credit provided by China EXIM [Export–Import Bank of China]); resource for infrastructure packages; equity investment by China–Africa Development (CAD) fund; infrastructure investment by the China Development Bank (CDB) and other commercial banks (which are OOF-like loans and investments with the intention for development, but non-concessional, and suitable for long-term infrastructure investment).

As a result of economics and of Chinese policy, China's FDI stock in Africa has risen rapidly in the past decade—from US$900 million in 2004 to US$3.37 billion by 2013 (Figure 16.1). Until 2013, the largest single investment made by China in Africa took place in 2008, a year in which China's FDI flow, stock and single largest investment item were comparable in level. FDI stock has since accumulated to vastly exceed any single project or annual flow. The majority of all such Chinese FDI into Africa is loan financed (MOFCOM 2013). It is noted that since government statistics have been found to underestimate the size of outward FDI (Shen 2015), the actual flow and stock levels are probably significantly higher than these official statistics.

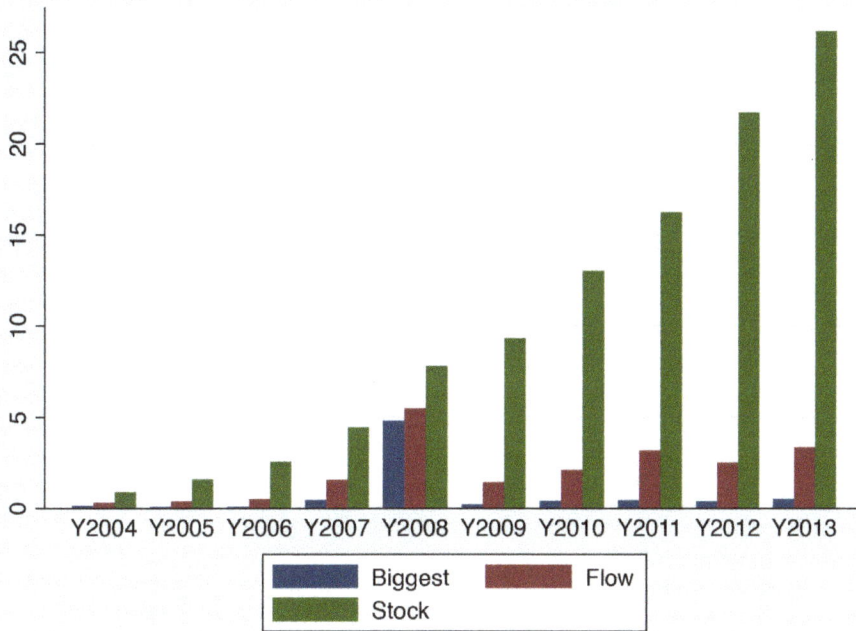

Figure 16.1 Mainland Chinese FDI stock in Africa (US$ billion)

Sources: NBS (2013, 2014).

Table 16.1 Bilateral Chinese FDI into Africa, 2013 (US$ million)

Country	Flow	Stock
Algeria	191.3	1,497.2
Angola	224.5	1,634.7
Benin	8.4	49.9
Botswana	10.2	230.9
Burkina Faso	4.3	4.3
Burundi	1.1	9.8
Cameroon	57.2	148.4
Cape Verde	0.1	15.2
Central African Republic	1.3	60.4
Chad	121.0	321.3
Comoros	–	4.5
Congo Republic	110.0	695.4
Congo, DR	121.3	1,091.8
Côte d'Ivoire	−4.8	35.0
Djibouti	2.0	30.6
Egypt	23.2	511.1

Country	Flow	Stock
Equatorial Guinea	22.4	260.9
Eritrea	0.9	104.6
Ethiopia	102.5	771.8
Gabon	32.1	168.5
Gambia	-	1.2
Ghana	122.5	834.8
Guinea	100.1	338.6
Guinea-Bissau	-	27.0
Kenya	230.5	636.0
Lesotho	-	9.1
Liberia	30.3	196.1
Libya	0.5	108.8
Madagascar	15.5	286.1
Malawi	8.3	253.8
Mali	108.1	316.7
Mauritania	15.3	108.3
Mauritius	61.1	850.0
Morocco	7.7	103.1
Mozambique	131.9	508.1
Namibia	7.1	349.5
Niger	116.4	241.9
Nigeria	209.1	2,146.1
Rwanda	−6.0	73.3
São Tomé and Príncipe	-	0.4
Senegal	10.4	83.3
Seychelles	17.7	103.5
Sierra Leone	40.0	108.4
South Africa	−89.2	4,400.4
South Sudan	11.5	26.5
Sudan	140.9	1,507.0
Tanzania	150.6	716.5
Togo	23.6	123.1
Tunisia	7.1	13.9
Uganda	60.6	383.8
Zambia	292.9	2,164.3
Zimbabwe	517.5	1,520.8
Africa total	3,370.6	26,185.8

- = not available.
Source: (MOFCOM 2014).

Lumpy across time and countries, official Chinese FDI data (Table 16.1) for 2013 reveal the consistent recent tendency for fuel and metal suppliers to receive the lion's share of China's Africa-bound FDI. Across the past decade, the largest annual recipients of Chinese FDI in Africa were Nigeria in 2003; Sudan in 2004, 2005 and 2011; Algeria in 2006, 2009 and 2012; South Africa in 2007, 2008 and 2010; and Zimbabwe in 2013. Countries in recent years that have received more than 5 per cent of total Chinese FDI into Africa include Kenya, Angola and Sudan—the last two being China's most important African oil suppliers.

Despite this prominence of commodities in China–Africa ties, neither of the largest two single investments by China in Africa arose within the commodities sector; they were in finance and in infrastructure. In 2008 the Industrial and Commercial Bank of China (ICBC) acquired 20 per cent of South Africa's Standard Bank for US$5.6 billion (Standard Bank 2011), while in November 2014, Africa became home to China's largest-ever outbound FDI transaction. That deal is between Nigeria, Africa's largest economy, and state-owned China Railway Construction Corporation Limited. When complete, the 22-stop, 1,400-kilometre railway line will connect Nigeria's most populous city, Lagos, in the west, along the coast to Calabar in the east, creating 200,000 construction jobs in Nigeria and generating US$4 billion in Chinese equipment exports.[3]

Non-commodity investments in general—including in wholesale trade, retail catering and textiles—often fall outside China's official investment statistics, the reliability of which generally remain of concern (Rosen and Hanemann 2009: 3). The scale of mainland Chinese FDI into Africa that passes via Hong Kong and other offshore centres is similarly not known, but is significant.

Structural factors also help to explain these patterns. China became dependent on foreign sources of energy from the early 1990s and its 'going out' policy explicitly prioritised investment in natural resources in which Chinese import demand was strong. More recently, labour in China has also become relatively scarce and more expensive. Selective African countries, in contrast, offer young, rapidly increasing and, on average, lesser-educated populations, in an environment that is more politically and macroeconomically stable than in earlier decades. Rising Chinese investment interest in Africa is what one would expect from analysis based on relative factor endowments and costs (see Krueger 1977).

The commodity-focused pattern of investment supports resources serving as collateral for high-risk investment financing—a model of Chinese investment known as 'Angola terms'. However, the presence of resources seems to affect only the level of investment, not the decision to invest (Cheung et al. 2012). A link between commodity wealth and corruption in Africa (see Leite and

---

3 See: www.out-law.com/en/articles/2014/november/china-signs-contract-for-coastal-rail-project-in-nigeria/.

Weidmann 1999) could also help explain why, from 2003 to 2006, China's foreign investment in 26 African countries was biased towards natural resources and poor governance (Kolstad and Wiig 2011).

The associated increase in Chinese investor interest in such diverse countries as Vietnam, Bangladesh, Ethiopia and Tanzania reflects a new phase in an old process in which China itself served as a low-cost investment destination. This process of transfer of industrial processes from higher to lower-wage countries is described by the multi-tiered, hierarchical 'flying geese' model (Akamatsu 1961, 1962). The model traces the spread of industrialisation from more to lesser developed economies—the initial 'goose' (the more advanced economy) leads the second-tier 'geese' (lesser advanced economies), which are followed by third-tier geese (least-developed economies) through a process of gradual production transfer.

While the model describes the iterative industrialisation process that was followed by Japan, South Korea and Taiwan in their investments in China and elsewhere in Asia, Lin and Wang (2014) compare the different scale of China's flying geese potential with that of Japan and Korea at a similar stage. According to their numbers, Japan in 1960 had 9.7 million workers in manufacturing and in 1980 Korea had 2.3 million. China, by comparison, is presently home to something closer to 100 million factory jobs. A comparable transfer of factory jobs abroad could thus logically be an immense driver of employment and industrialisation in today's poor countries.

There are an increasing number of examples from China in Africa of this potentially greatest-ever gander of flying geese. Textile giant China JD Group's textile factory now produces textiles once produced in China for export to the United States—from Tanzania. In Ethiopia, China's Huajian Group plans to invest some US$2 billion in the coming decade, expanding a nascent shoe-manufacturing cluster that exports within Africa, and also to Europe and North America. The plan makes use not only of Ethiopia's comparatively low wages, but also of intra-African trade preferences and its LDC trade preferences.

Investments in the automotive sector similarly seek to utilise low wages and intra-African trade preferences. A US$50 million Foton Motors vehicle assembly plant in Nairobi, Kenya, opened in 2012. The plant has capacity to manufacture up to 10,000 pick-up trucks and light commercial vehicles annually, and targets its output to the emerging East African market. Similarly, state-led Beijing Automotive Industry Holding Company, one of China's largest automotive manufacturers, and South Africa's Industrial Development Corporation, since 2013, together run Beijing Automotive Works (BAW) South Africa. The joint US$17.8 million minibus assembly line brings South Africa closer to its goal of full domestic manufacture of minibus taxis (*Global Post* 2015).

Table 16.2 Geographic distribution of China's outbound FDI flows, 2013

Continent	Amount	Share (%)	Annual growth
Asia*	75.60	70.1	16.7
Europe	5.95	5.5	−15.4
Latin America	14.36	13.3	132.7
North America	4.90	4.5	0.4
Africa	3.37	3.2	33.9
Oceania	3.66	3.4	51.6
Total	107.84	100.0	22.8

* Includes investment channelled through Hong Kong to third destinations.
Source: NBS (2014: 85).

Despite an ever-increasing number of such investment projects, China's outbound FDI to African destinations is small relative to China's total outbound FDI and to total inbound FDI into Africa. In 2013 Africa attracted just 3.2 per cent of total Chinese outbound FDI (Table 16.2). And yet, few topics in applied development economics attract more media scrutiny, and less attention from empirical economists.

Future directions in China's investments in Africa can be deduced from political speeches and the combination of excess supply capacity in China and large development needs, suggesting that a good proportion of China's US$1 trillion investment target for Africa will focus on infrastructure.

Visiting Africa in May 2014, Premier Li spoke directly of connecting African capitals using China's high-speed rail technology. In Africa in January 2015, Chinese Foreign Minister Wang Yi reiterated China's commitment to helping Africa build the 'three major networks': railway, road and regional aviation. In Ethiopia at the 2015 heads-of-state meeting of the 54-member African Union (AU), China signed the 'African Union–China deal'. This is billed as the most substantive project the AU has ever signed with a partner, and promises to connect the continent by road, rail and air transportation.

In aviation, privately owned Hainan Airlines agreed to inject US$50 million into Kenya's Astral Aviation in 2014. The memorandum agrees to develop Kenya's Nairobi Jomo Kenyatta airport into a regional East African aviation hub using funds from China's China–Africa Development Fund. Senegal, Sudan, Togo and Djibouti are among countries that have ongoing airport construction projects that include a Chinese partner (Radliki 2015).

Under China's flagship 'One Belt and One Road' initiative, several deep-water coastal ports in Africa are also in progress: Bizerte in Tunisia; Dakar, Senegal; Dar es Salaam, Tanzania; Djibouti, Djibouti; Libreville, Gabon; Maputo, Mozambique;

and Tema, Ghana. These are intended to facilitate Africa's own economic development, as well as to serve as locations for transcontinental trade between Chinese and African economies, along the 'maritime Silk Road'.

The focus on infrastructure reflects the importance of easing 'bottle-necks in domestic and intra-regional economic development' (Lin and Wang 2014: 13). China's high level of foreign exchange reserves, coupled with excess capacity and competitive strength in infrastructure and related industries, can convert Africa's development requirements into new sources of foreign income and international brand recognition. It can also help to realise China's geo-economic and geopolitical ambitions via railway and maritime trade routes.

Chinese investors are similarly investing in downstream infrastructure-related industries. In late 2014, Hebei Iron & Steel, China's largest steelmaker, announced plans to relocate 5 million tonnes of production (roughly 11 per cent of its annual output) to South Africa. In March 2015, state-owned giant steelmaker Sinosteel signed a memorandum of understanding with the Government of Kenya to build a 'steel city' outside Nairobi towards meeting Kenya's rising domestic and regional steel demand (Muhoro 2015).

At the raw commodities level, in 2014 China was also party to a US$20 billion agreement with Rio Tinto, Chinese state-owned aluminium giant Chinalco, the Government of Guinea and the International Finance Corporation. The deal will develop Guinea's Simandou iron ore deposits—home to almost 2 billion tonnes of mostly high-grade iron ore. It is the largest combined iron ore and infrastructure project ever attempted in Africa.

Similarly, in April 2015, Shandong Iron and Steel Group reported acquiring the remaining 75 per cent share of Sierra Leone's Tonkolili iron ore mine, and the associated infrastructure company, African Port and Railway Services. Shandong plans to lift production at the mine to 25 million tonnes per year (Cornish 2015; Macrobusiness 2015). The academic literature has considered the potential for Africa's iron ore reserves to supply Chinese demand (Hurst 2013). The potential to supply rising steel demand in Africa is of increasing importance to Africa, China and the global mining industry.

Across Africa, urbanisation and infrastructure development are increasing demand for steel.[4] In Kenya, government projections suggest that domestic demand for steel will rise, from 1.8 million metric tonnes in 2013 to 2.5 million tonnes by 2020, and then to double by 2030 (Ministry of Industrialisation and Enterprise Development of Kenya 2015). These developments are being assisted by Chinese infrastructure investments, including the Chinese-led East

---

4　From Nairobi, the railway line will extend to Uganda, Rwanda, Burundi and South Sudan.

African standard-gauge railway that is under construction, to be completed by early 2018. This project will link five East African countries: Kenya, Uganda, Rwanda, Burundi and South Sudan. The nascent Chinese-founded multilateral Asian Infrastructure Investment Bank has received support from the President of the African Development Bank for institutional cooperation to provide the capital and support for such growth forecasts.

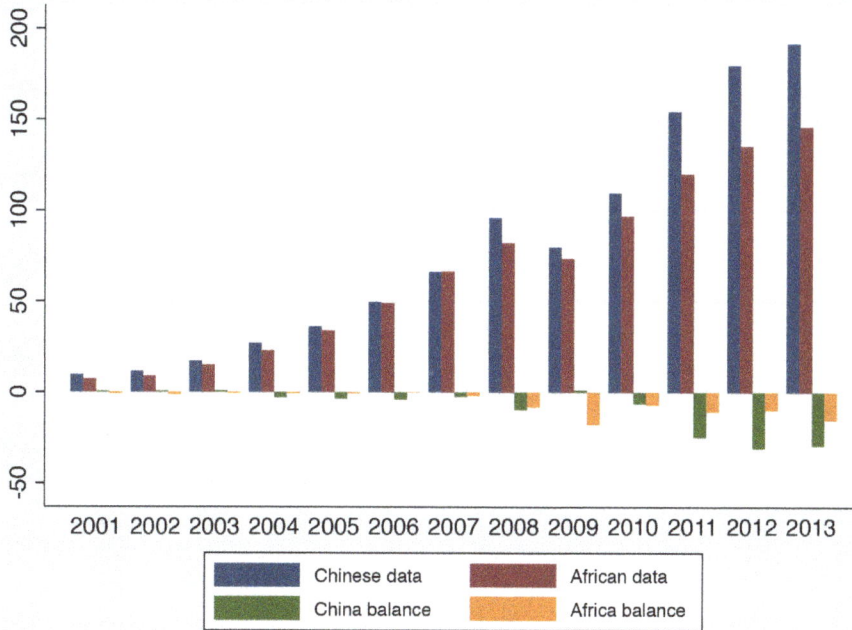

Figure 16.2 China–Africa trade (US$ billion)

Source: IMF (2015a). Trade balances reflect the author's own calculations.

While Chinese FDI in Africa is expected to rise rapidly, presently China–Africa trade levels dwarf those of aid and FDI combined. According to Chinese data, total Sino–African trade value reached US$192 billion in 2013 (Figure 16.2). This comprised Chinese imports of US$111 billion from Africa and exports of US$81 billion—a figure more than 10 times higher than the US$10 billion value of trade in 2000 (IMF 2015a). Aggregated African data, however, report a lower total trade level for 2013, of US$146.1 billion.

Sino–African trade is proportionately more important to Africa than to China. Trade with China made up 14 per cent of total African reported trade in 2013. China's trade with Africa, however, made up just 4.6 per cent of total reported Chinese trade that year (IMF 2015a). African data point to a trade deficit with China of US$15.2 billion in 2013. That year, China reported a deficit in trade with Africa, of US$29.4 billion (ibid).

Oil makes Chinese imports larger than exports in trade with Africa (Ademola et al. 2009; Thomson and Horii 2009). Oil imports have risen significantly in recent years. In 1990, China imported no oil from Africa. By 2010, roughly one-quarter of its foreign oil supply was being sourced from the continent (Thompson and Horii 2009: 648).

Table 16.3 Selective 'top-10' Africa–China export indicators, 2013

Country	Export volume (US$b)	Country	Export intensity (%)
Angola	29.0	Sierra Leone	78.1
South Africa	11.8	Gambia	57.0*
Congo Republic	5.2	Mauritania	55.5
Congo, DR	2.5	Congo Republic	53.5
Zambia	2.4	Angola	45.9
Mauritania	1.6	Congo, DR	42.2
Nigeria	1.4	Mali	30.1
Sierra Leone	1.3	Zambia	25.5
Gabon	0.8	Burkina Faso	24.8
Ghana	0.7	Rwanda	24.3
Zimbabwe	0.6	Zimbabwe	23.6
Egypt	0.6	Benin	21.2
Africa	65.4	Africa	14.3

* A significant share of which are re-exports from other West African countries.
Note: Author's own calculations, and where export intensity is weighted by country, not by travel level.
Source: IMF (2015a), where export intensity is defined as the ratio of exports to China over a country's total exports.

Data in Table 16.3 make the point that of China's top-10 African exporters, half have oil as the main export—Angola, Republic of the Congo, Ghana, Nigeria and Gabon. The remainder of the top 10 are minerals exporters. Countries in Africa with fewer minerals and fuel exports have much less favourable trade complementarities and thus lower export intensities with China. Countries exporting less than 1 per cent of their total exports to China in 2013 include Kenya, Senegal, Tunisia, Morocco, Djibouti and the island nations of Mauritius, São Tomé and Príncipe, Comoros and Cape Verde (IMF 2015a).

These trade tendencies are congruent with old trade theory. A condition of trade under the Heckscher-Ohlin (1991) model is that trade should arise between two countries that differ with respect to their relative factor endowments—primarily labour, capital and natural resources. The model demonstrates that the gains to trade around specialisation are greatest when the country with abundant capital and scarce labour specialises in the production of goods that utilise capital most intensively, and vice versa.

Accordingly, China is not alone in having imports from Africa dominated by fuels and minerals. Even where oil and gas-rich North African countries are excluded, imports to the European Union and the United States from sub-Saharan Africa are still dominated by minerals and fuels (see Gualberti et al. 2014). According to the study by Gualberti et al. (2014), in 2012 fuel represented some 76 per cent of the United States' imports from SSA—more than China's 72 per cent. Africa's imports from China, in contrast, are driven mainly by machinery, chemicals and manufactured goods, though patterns vary somewhat among importers (Drummond and Liu 2013).

Strong export specialisation in commodities can have negative externalities, including through 'Dutch disease'. Dutch disease arises when a surge in the value of commodity exports pushes up the real exchange rate, reducing the competitiveness of other, including industrial, sectors (Corden and Neary 1982).

China–Africa economics research

Alongside hope for greater African international economic integration, there is cynicism about China's growing investment and trade ties with Africa. The worry is that what is perceived as the colonial outcome will be repeated—large-scale extraction of resources for little indigenous return.

While it is early days yet for assessing the long-run nature of the return of the 'fleeting old normal', it is not too early to assess some impacts. The China–Africa literature identifies both positive and negative effects of expanding Sino–African economic ties. These depend to a large extent on mineral resource endowments (Jenkins and Edwards 2005; Kaplinsky 2005; Zafar 2007).

China led strong growth in demand for energy and metals over the first decade of this century, causing a rapid rise in related prices from 2003 to 2011, with a brief interlude for the global financial crisis (GFC) (Garnaut, forthcoming). Declining prices since 2011, however, reflect China's progress towards its goal of using less energy, especially coal, per unit of GDP.

China's demand growth for energy and metals decelerated just as global supply growth was building strong momentum. Oil and copper are among China's important imports from Africa, the latter especially in trade with Zambia. The prices of both oil and copper peaked in 2011, before declining through to early 2015 (Chapter 2 in this volume).

Prior to the passing of the peak of the China-led commodities boom, research had identified some of the impacts of China's trade and investment ties on African economies. Indirect trade impacts, including the diversion of investment and labour to the extractive sector at the expense of manufacturing (Dutch disease), is found to have adversely affected the horticulture and textiles sectors of Zambia (Bova 2008), and Africa's resource exporters more generally (Kaplinsky and Morris 2008). Commodity trade with China has also displaced light manufacturing in selected African countries (Giovannetti and San Filippo 2009; Kaplinsky and Morris 2008; Khan and Baye 2008). At least during the years of the commodities boom, African countries that were strongly specialised in exports of commodities tended to experience stronger and more broadly based growth than countries with more diverse exports (Baliamoune-Lutz 2011). Change under way in China's own economy, however, means that the China-led resources boom is now fading, and may narrow that gap.

Imports from China have contributed to African development (Baliamoune-Lutz 2011; Maswana 2010). Low-cost Chinese manufactures suit average income levels and thus consumption budgets in many African economies. Intensity of import trade with China varies less across countries than intensity of exports to China (Johnston et al. 2014: 6).

The 50 per cent fall in the oil price, from June 2014 to March 2015, is explored by Hou et al. (2015). For the continent as a whole, the report cites research suggesting that a 30 per cent drop in oil prices (smaller than the recent decline) is projected to directly reduce the value of oil exports in SSA by US$63 billion and reduce imports by an estimated US$15 billion.

Table 16.4 Oil importer and exporter groupings, top 10, Africa, 2013[a]

Oil exporters	
Net oil exporters	Nigeria, Angola, Algeria, Libya, Equatorial Guinea, Congo Republic, Gabon, Sudan, Chad, Ghana
Oil export dependency	Chad, Angola, Libya, Gabon, Nigeria, Congo Republic, Sudan, Equatorial Guinea, Algeria, Cameroon
Oil exports as share of GDP	Equatorial Guinea, Angola, Congo Republic, Gabon, Libya, Chad, Nigeria, Algeria, Côte d'Ivoire, Sudan
Oil importers	
African net oil importers	South Africa, Morocco, Tanzania, Kenya, Egypt, Ethiopia, Zimbabwe, Mozambique, Uganda, Senegal
Oil import dependency	Tanzania, Guinea, Mali, Côte d'Ivoire, Senegal, Gambia, Burkina Faso, Kenya, Mauritania, São Tomé and Príncipe
Oil imports as a share of GDP	Liberia, Mauritania, Tanzania, Seychelles, São Tomé and Príncipe, Zimbabwe, Senegal, Guinea, Mali and Mozambique

[a] Listed in order of magnitude.
Source: Hou et al. (2015).

The effects at the country level depend primarily on whether a country is an oil exporter or importer. Table 16.4 lists countries in order of the scale of oil exports and imports, and shows the relative importance of oil in trade value, fiscal revenues and production (GDP). Countries listed in the top half of the table—oil exporters—are suffering a loss of direct revenues from oil sales. The result is a painful revision of budget plans, with Ghana, Gabon, Angola and the Republic of the Congo all reported to be cutting back on national expenditure plans this year (Games 2015). For those in the bottom half of Table 16.5, however, the drop in oil price provides an improvement in the terms of trade.

Hou et al.'s (2015) overview of the impacts of the oil price crash on Africa also shows how declining resources exports lead to real exchange rate depreciation in many countries. This expands opportunities for trade and investment in other sectors, with favourable development effects. There is a chance of a long-run positive story for Africa, and China–Africa—the chance of a 'boom to cusp'. The opportunity is for movement from a commodities boom to the cusp of a sustainable industrial transition and integration with the world economy.

Table 16.5 Selective net oil importer economic ties with China

Country	Export dependence	FDI stock	BIT in force	Infrastructure[a]
Tanzania	13.2	717	2014	Port
Kenya	0.9	636	2001	Rail
Ethiopia	12.8	772	1998	Rail[b]

[a] Not a complete list of China-invested infrastructure projects.
[b] Associated with a port extension in Djibouti, at a port that is relied on by landlocked Ethiopia.
Sources: IMF (2015a); MOFCOM (2014); Johnston and Yuan (2014); UNCTAD (2015); various news sources.

Table 16.5 highlights selected stylised facts about China's economic ties with three net oil importers in Africa. These countries are especially important to the idea of 'boom to cusp' because they are three economies that China has nominated to become hubs for its outbound investment in Africa. All are in East Africa and currently have low export intensities with China as against more resource-rich countries. All have signed a bilateral investment treaty with China and are direct or indirect beneficiaries of China's infrastructure investments in Africa.

Advantageously in a context of long-run economic development, two of the three economies are also classed as coastal and resource-poor (CRP) economies (Collier and O'Connell 2007). The significance of CRP status relates to recent findings on the relationship between sustainable economic transformation between countries and over time. Specifically, in the second half of the twentieth century, it was when CRP countries began to sustainably industrialise that growth elsewhere in a region/continent—in resource-rich economies and in landlocked resource-poor economies—was likely to produce a broader, more sustainable transformation (World Bank Staff 2008) than is more typical of growth around resources trade.

Over the years 1995–2009, Johnston et al. (2014) identified China to have relatively weak trade and economic policy ties with economies in sub-Saharan Africa with supply and exploitation of weak national resource endowments, against an empirical benchmark derived from gravity modelling. Given the scale of China's African ties, especially with resource exporters, the authors concluded that China's weaker ties with non-resource exporting coastal economies could undermine hope for sustainable long-run regional economic growth and development.

The terms of trade have since shifted in favour of coastal and resource-poor economies. The commodities crash presents a painful shift for established commodities exporters, but is good news for net resource importers in Africa.

This is potentially good news for finding new sources for sustainable long-term economic growth in Africa. The United Nations projects that on current fertility rates by 2050 Africa's population will be double what it is at present. Under the UN assumptions, Nigeria's population will reach some 400 million and Kenya will have a population of almost 100 million. This makes now a good time to construct the tangible and intangible economic infrastructure that will support that future population.

The largest-ever gander or brace of Peking's ducks in Africa?

The depth and breadth of China–Africa ties suggest that slower growth in China will slow growth in Africa. This chapter has, however, traced an underlying good news story in the new normal of China and Africa. That story relates to longer-term potential of the shift towards more diverse African export specialisation combined with excess capacity in China's steel and infrastructure industries. Lessons from other regions' experiences with industrial transformation mean that the pattern of China–Africa ties as a result of the 'new normal' could contribute positively to African development.

China is a continental-sized economy facing tight resource constraints. Home of the world's largest and an ageing population, its slowing economy offers cheap capital and internationally competitive industrial, including infrastructure, capacity. Africa, in contrast, offers a fast-growing and young population, and relatively high natural resource and arable land levels per capita. On the whole, it is in need of massive infrastructure investment, affordable financial capital and investors with an appetite for risk.

Economic historian Angus Maddison identified that it took 1,400 years to double per capita income before the eighteenth century. As the Industrial Revolution spread, however, it took only 70 years to double per capita income from the late eighteenth century to the mid-nineteenth century. In the second half of the twentieth century, it took only 35 years for developed countries to double per capita income (Maddison 2001; World Bank 2008, cited in Lin and Wang 2014). This process of economic transformation has since been even faster in 13 rapidly growing emerging economies. Many of these—including Korea, Taiwan and other East Asian newly industrialised economies, and later China—have followed a pattern of development that can be described by the flying-geese model elaborated on earlier in this chapter.

Economic logic indicates that as African countries continue to accumulate human, physical and financial capital, their export structures will transform and upgrade.

Africa's process will be its own, but this does not preclude lessons from East Asia's experience being valuable reference points for the China–Africa story. The success of the China–Africa partnership, that is, might help to transform not only China's international economic prospects, but also those of Africa.

References

Ademola, O.T., Bankole, A.S. and Adewuyi, A.O. (2009), China–Africa trade relations: Insights from AERC scoping studies, *European Journal of Development Research*, 21(4): 485–505.

Akamatsu, K. (1961), A theory of unbalanced growth in the world economy, *Weltwirtschaftliches Archiv*, 86: 196–217.

Akamatsu, K. (1962), A historical pattern of economic growth in developing countries, *The Developing Economies*, (1): 3–25.

Alden, C. (2007), *China in Africa*, London: Zed Books.

Arbache, J. and Page, J. (2007), *Patterns of long term growth in sub-Saharan region*, Washington, DC: The World Bank.

Baliamoune-Lutz, M. (2011), Growth by destination (where you export matters): Trade with China and growth in African countries, *African Development Review*, 23: 202–18.

Bova, E. (2008), *Exchange rate management for commodity booms: Examining Zambia's copper exports*, Development Viewpoint 19, London: Centre for Development Policy and Research, School of African and Oriental Studies.

Brandt, P. (2013), Chinese aid to Africa: A detective story, *Lowy Interpreter*, Sydney: Lowy Institute. Available from: www.lowyinterpreter.org/post/2013/05/02/Chinese-aid-to-Africa-A-detective-story.aspx. Retrieved 10 January 2014.

Brautigam, D. (2009), *The dragon's gift: The real story of China in Africa*, Oxford: Oxford University Press.

Brautigam, D. (2011), Chinese development aid in Africa: What, where, why, and how much?, in Golley, J. (ed.), *Rising China: Global challenges and opportunities*, Canberra: ANU E Press.

Brautigam, D. and Tang, X. (2011), African Shenzhen: China's special economic zones in Africa, *Journal of Modern African Studies*, 49(1): 27–54.

Broadman, H. (2007), *Africa's silk road: China and India's new economic frontier*, Washington, DC: The World Bank.

Carmody, P. (2009), An Asian-driven economic recovery in Africa? The Zambian case, *World Development*, 27: 1197–207.

Cheung, Y.-W., Haan, J., Qian, X. and Yu, S. (2012), China's outward direct investment in Africa, *Review of International Economics*, 20(2): 201–20.

Collier, P. and O'Connell, S. (2007), Opportunities and choices, in Ndulu, B., O'Connell, S.A., Bates, R.H., Collier, P. and Soludo, C.C. (eds), *Political economy of economic growth in Africa, 1960–2000*, Cambridge: Cambridge University Press.

Corden, W.M. and Neary, J.P. (1982), Booming sector and de-industrialisation in a small open economy, *The Economic Journal*: 825–48.

Cornish, L. (2015), Shandong Iron and Steel acquires Tonkolili mine in Sierra Leone, *Mining Review*, 21 April. Available from: www.miningreview.com/shandong-iron-and-steel-acquires-tonkolili-mine-in-sierra-leone/. Retrieved 30 April 2015.

de Grauwe, P., Houssa, R. and Piccillo, G. (2012), African trade dynamics: Is China a different trading partner?, *Journal of Chinese Economic and Business Studies*, 10(1): 15–45.

Dreher, A., Fuchs, A., Hodler, R., Parks, B., Raschky, P.A. and Tierney, M.J. (2014), *Aid on demand: African leaders and the geography of China's foreign assistance*, AidData Working Paper No. 3, 18 November. Available from: dx.doi.org/10.2139/ssrn.2531966.

Dreyer, E.L. (2007), *Zheng He: China and the oceans in the early Ming Dynasty, 1405–1433*, New York: Pearson Longman.

Drummond, M.P. and Liu, M.E.X. (2013), *Africa's rising exposure to China: How large are spillovers through trade?*, Working Paper No. 13-250, Washington, DC: International Monetary Fund.

Financial Times (2013), Africa must get real about Chinese ties, *Financial Times*, 11 March. Available from: www.ft.com/intl/cms/s/0/562692b0-898c-11e2-ad3f-00144feabdc0.html#axzz2Ww2Horkg. Retrieved 28 January 2015.

Fletcher, R. and Ahmed, K. (2012), Davos 2012: China and Africa to be centre of world trade, *The Telegraph*, 26 January. Available from: www.telegraph.co.uk/finance/financetopics/davos/9042156/Davos-2012-China-and-Africa-to-be-centre-of-world-trade.html. Retrieved 5 March 2012.

Games, D. (2015), Africa: Bust or boom?, *AllAfrica*, 25 January. Available from: allafrica.com/stories/201504031455.html. Retrieved 4 May 2015.

Garnaut, R. (2006), The China resources boom, Presented to Australian Agriculture and Resource Economics Conference, February, Sydney.

Garnaut, R. (2012), The contemporary China resources boom, *Australian Journal of Agricultural and Resource Economics*, 56(2): 222–43.

Garnaut, R. (forthcoming), Indonesia's resources boom in international perspective: Policy dilemmas and options for continued strong growth (the Ninth Sadli Lecture), *Bulletin of Indonesian Economic Studies*.

Giovannetti, G. and Sanfilippo, M. (2009), Do Chinese exports crowd-out African goods? An econometric analysis by country and sector, *European Journal of Development Research*, Special Issue 24: 506–30.

Global Post (2015), Feature: The story, ambition of Chinese auto manufacturer in Africa, *Global Post*, 8 April. Available from: www.globalpost.com/article/6509105/2015/04/08/feature-story-ambition-chinese-auto-manufacturer-africa. Retrieved 17 April 2015.

Gualberti, G., Bazilian, M. and Moss, T. (2014), *Energy investments in Africa by the US, Europe and China*, Cleveland: International Association for Energy Economics.

Heckscher, E.F. and Ohlin, B. (1991), *Heckscher–Ohlin trade theory*, H. Flam and M. June Flanders trans., eds and intro., Cambridge, Mass.: MIT Press.

Hook, L. (2012), Zuma warns on Africa's ties to China, *Financial Times*, 19 July. Available from: www.ft.com/intl/cms/s/0/33686fc4-d171-11e1-bbbc-00144feabdc0. Retrieved 1 July 2014.

Hou, Z., Keane, J., Kennan, J. and te Velde, D.W. (2015), *The oil price shock of 2014*, ODI Working Paper 415, London: Overseas Development Institute. Available from: www.odi.org/sites/odi.org.uk/files/odi-assets/publications-opinion-files/9589.pdf. Retrieved 3 April 2015.

Hurst, L. (2013), West and Central African iron ore development and its impact on world prices, *Australian Journal of Agricultural and Resource Economics*, 57(4): 521–38.

International Monetary Fund (IMF) (2015a), *Direction of trade statistics*, April, Washington, DC: IMF.

International Monetary Fund (IMF) (2015b), Transcript of the African finance ministers press briefing, 18 April, Washington, DC: IMF. Available from: www.imf.org/external/np/tr/2015/tr041815a.htm. Retrieved 8 May 2015.

Jenkins, R. and Edwards, C. (2005), *The effect of China and India's growth and trade liberalization on poverty in Africa*, DCP 70, London: UK Department for International Development.

Johnston, L.A., Morgan, S.L. and Wang, Y. (2014), The gravity of China's African export promise, *The World Economy*. doi: 10.1111/twec.12229.

Johnston, L.A. and Yuan, C. (2014), China's Africa trade and investment policies: Review of a 'noodle bowl', *African East-Asian Affairs*, (4): 6–41.

Kaplinsky, R. (2005), *Globalization, poverty and inequality*, Cambridge: Polity Press.

Kaplinsky, R. and Morris, M. (2008), Do the Asian drivers undermine export-oriented industrialization in SSA?, *World Development*, 36(2): 254–73.

Khan, S.A. and Baye, F.M. (2008), China–Africa economic relations: The case of Cameroon, Mimeo., Nairobi: African Economic Research Consortium.

Kolstad, I. and Wiig, A. (2011), Better the devil you know? Chinese foreign direct investment in Africa, *Journal of African Business*, 12: 31–50.

Krueger, A.O. (1977), *Growth, distortions, and patterns of trade among many countries*, No. 40, Princeton, NJ: International Finance Section, Department of Economics, Princeton University.

Leite, C.A. and Weidmann, J. (1999), *Does mother nature corrupt? Natural resources, corruption, and economic growth*, June, IMF Working Paper No. 99/85, Washington, DC: International Monetary Fund. Available from: ssrn.com/abstract=259928 or http://dx.doi.org/10.2139/ssrn.259928.

Levathes, L. (2014), *When China ruled the seas: The treasure fleet of the dragon throne, 1405–1433*, New York: Open Road Media.

Lin, J. and Wang, Y. (2014), *China–Africa cooperation in structural transformation: Ideas, opportunities, and finances*, WIDER Working Paper 2014/046, Helsinki: United Nations University World Institute for Development Economics Research. Available from: www.nsd.edu.cn/cn/userfiles/Other/2014-03/2014030410441338653249.pdf. Retrieved 20 February 2015.

Macrobusiness (2015), Iron ore shudders as China absorbs Africa, *Macrobusiness*, 21 April. Available from: www.macrobusiness.com.au/2015/04/iron-ore-shudders-china-absorbs-africa/.

Maddison, A. (2001), *The world economy: A millennial perspective*, Paris: OECD Development Centre.

Mao, X. (2011), The path of China's aid to Africa [in Chinese], *Economy*, 10.

Maswana, J. (2010), *Will China's recovery affect Africa's prospects for economic growth?*, JICA Working Papers 19, Tokyo: JICA Research Institute.

Muhoro, M. (2015), China trader Sinosteel clinches Kenya 'steel city' deal, *Kenya Construction Business Review*, 31 March. Available from: www.constructionkenya.com/3243/sinosteel-clinches-kenya-steel-city-deal/. Retrieved 7 April 2015.

Ministry of Industrialisation and Enterprise Development of Kenya (2015), Kenya signs MOU with Sinosteel—Chinese leading steel development company, Nairobi: Government of Kenya. Available from: www.industrialization.go.ke/index.php/media-center/news-updates/176-press-release-kenya-signs-mou-with-sinosteel-chinese-leading-steel-development-company. Retrieved 10 March 2015.

National Bureau of Statistics (NBS) (2013), *2012 Statistical bulletin of China's outbound foreign direct investment*, Beijing: China Statistics Press.

National Bureau of Statistics (NBS) (2014), *2013 Statistical bulletin of China's outbound foreign direct investment*, Beijing: China Statistics Press.

Ochelle, F.O. (2015), How slowdown in China may hurt Africa, *Ventures Africa*. Available from: www.ventures-africa.com/archives/57460.

Out-Law (2014), China signs contract for coastal rail project in Nigeria, *Out-Law*, 24 November. Available from: www.out-law.com/en/articles/2014/november/china-signs-contract-for-coastal-rail-project-in-nigeria/.

Pang, X. (2010), Chinese vice president calls for stronger FOCAC, *People's Daily*, 19 November. Available from: english.people.com.cn/90001/90776/90883/7204133.html. Retrieved 10 September 2011.

Pannell, C. (2013), China's economic and political penetration in Africa, *Eurasian Geography and Economics*, 49: 706–13.

Ministry of Commerce (MOFCOM) (2011), China's foreign aid whitepaper, *China Daily*, 22 April. Available from: english.mofcom.gov.cn/article/newsrelease/press/201309/20130900285772.shtml. Retrieved 4 May 2013.

Ministry of Commerce (MOFCOM) (2013), White paper on China–Africa economic and trade cooperation, *China Daily*, 22 April. Available from www.chinadaily.com.cn/cndy/2011-04/22/content_12373944.htm. Retrieved 5 May 2011.

Ministry of Commerce (MOFCOM) (2014), 2013 Statistical Bulletin of China's Outward Foreign Direct Investment. China Statistics Press.

Ministry of Foreign Affairs, Premier Zhou Enlai's Three Tours of Asian and African countries. Available from: http://www.fmprc.gov.cn/mfa_eng/ziliao_665539/3602_665543/3604_665547/t18001.shtml. Retrieved 20 May 2015.

Publish What You Fund (2014), *2014 Aid transparency index*, Publish What You Fund. Available from: www.publishwhatyoufund.org/index/2014-ati/. Retrieved 24 October 2014.

Radelet, S. (2010), *Emerging Africa: How 17 countries are leading the way*, Washington, DC: Center for Global Development.

Radliki, M. (2015), From Sudan to Senegal, Africa's head-turning new airports … with a helping hand from Chinese friends, *Mail and Guardian*, 6 May. Available from: mgafrica.com/article/2015-03-03-africas-new-airports. Retrieved 11 April 2015.

Rosen, D. and Hanemann, T. (2009), *China's changing outbound foreign direct investment profile: Drivers and policy implications*, Policy Brief 09-14, Washington, DC: Peterson Institute for International Economics. Available from: www.iie.com/publications/pb/pb09-14.pdf. Retrieved 3 February 2014.

Shen, X. (2015), Private Chinese investment in Africa: Myths and realities, *Development Policy Review*, 33(1): 83–106.

Standard Bank (2011), China and the US in Africa: Measuring Washington's response to Beijing's commercial advance, *Economic Strategy, BRIC and Africa*, Johannesburg: Standard Bank.

The Economist (2011), Africa's impressive growth, *The Economist*, 1 June. Available from: www.economist.com/blogs/dailychart/2011/01/daily_chart. Retrieved 10 February 2015.

Thomson, E. and Horii, N. (2009), China's energy security: Challenges and priorities, *Eurasian Geography and Economics*, 50: 643–64.

Tsagas, I. (2013), Chinese PV manufacturers setting up shop in Kenya, *PV Magazine*, 21 June. Available from: www.pv-magazine.com/news/details/beitrag/chinese-pv-manufacturers-setting-up-shop-in-kenya_100011806/#ixzz3VxK7hzwY. Retrieved 1 March 2015.

United Nations Conference on Trade and Development (UNCTAD) (2015), *International investment agreements navigator: China, bilateral investment agreements*, Geneva: UNCTAD. Available from: investmentpolicyhub.unctad.org/IIA/CountryBits/42. Retrieved February 2015.

Wang, J. (2007), *What drives China's growing role in Africa?*, IMF Working Paper 07/211, Washington, DC: International Monetary Fund.

World Bank (2015), *China overview*, Washington, DC: The World Bank. Available from: www.worldbank.org/en/country/china/overview.

World Bank Staff (2008), *The growth report: Strategies for sustained growth and inclusive development*, Washington, DC: World Bank Publications.

Xinhuanet (2013), China's investment in Africa increases 20.5% annually, *Xinhuanet*, 29 August. Available from: news.xinhuanet.com/english/china/2013-08/29/c_132673248.htm. Retrieved 11 September 2012.

Zafar, A. (2007), The growing relationship between China and SSA: Macroeconomic trade, investment and aid links, *World Bank Research Observer*, 22: 103–30.

Zhou, T. (2014), *China's second white paper on foreign aid signals key shift in aid delivery strategy*, San Francisco: The Asia Foundation. Available from: asiafoundation.org/in-asia/2014/07/23/chinas-second-white-paper-on-foreign-aid-signals-key-shift-in-aid-delivery-strategy/.

17. The Trend of China's Foreign Investment Legal System

From the perspective of the China (Shanghai) Pilot Free Trade Zone

Gao Xiang and Huiqin Jiang

Introduction

The China (Shanghai) Pilot Free Trade Zone (SPFTZ) was approved by the State Council in August 2013 and established on 29 September of that year (Central Government of the PRC 2013; Xinhuanet 2013). It is located in the district of Pudong in Shanghai, and is the integration of four existing special customs supervision areas (SCSAs): Shanghai Waigaoqiao Free Trade Zone, Waigaoqiao Free Trade Logistics Park, Yangshan Free Trade Port Area and Pudong Airport Comprehensive Free Trade Zone.[1]

The establishment of the SPFTZ was designed to meet the needs of China's economic and legal development, and is consistent with China's long-time policy of economic reform.[2] China's economic growth has slowed since 2012 (Wang and Liu 2013), which has made it necessary for economic transformation and upgrading to ensure sustained, stable and rapid economic growth. The rapid reconstruction of world trade and investment rules requires China to have new ideas for its opening-up policy (Xu et al. 2013). Moreover, after years in operation, shortcomings in China's foreign investment law have emerged (Gao and Jiang 2014: 549–50), which have made reforms necessary in this area.

The SPFTZ is different from previous SCSAs. It focuses on system innovation, rather than favourable treatment (Xu et al. 2013). The areas involved include not just taxation, but have expanded into investment, trade, finance, law, and so on.[3] The legal and economic reforms tested in the SPFTZ will serve as practical experience, will be mirrored and repeated in other parts of the country, will

---

1 The four SCSAs were established in June 1990, December 2003, June 2005 and July 2009, respectively. See SPFTZ (2013a).
2 'China' refers to mainland China only.
3 Framework Plan for the China (Shanghai) Pilot Free Trade Zone (SPFTZ Framework Plan).

eventually help China to boost the recovery, transformation and upgrading of its economy, as well as furthering its integration into the international foreign investment legal system.[4]

Pilot system reforms in the SPFTZ have been successful and some are now being used beyond the zone. This chapter looks at the direction of China's foreign investment law by examining the legal systems applied in the SPFTZ, comparing them with China's general foreign investment legal system and analysing their application in regions outside the SPFTZ.

The framework of foreign investment laws and policies in China[5]

The basic framework of China's foreign investment law and policy has been developed gradually since it adopted its open-door policy. China's current foreign investment law and policy include laws and regulations, the Guiding Catalogue for Foreign Investment Industries (the Guiding Catalogue), the Catalogue of Priority Industries for Foreign Investment in the Central-Western Region (the Central-Western Catalogue) and a series of policies.

Laws and regulations

China's current foreign investment law comprises three enterprise laws, their implementation rules, the Company Law of the People's Republic of China (the Company Law),[6] and hundreds of administrative regulations and rules. China's first foreign investment law is the Law of the People's Republic of China on Chinese-Foreign Equity Joint Ventures (the Equity Joint Venture Law), made in 1979.[7] Subsequently, the National People's Congress (NPC) promulgated the Law of the People's Republic of China on Foreign-Invested Enterprises (the Foreign-Invested Enterprises Law)[8] and the Law of the People's Republic of China on Chinese—Foreign-Invested Joint Ventures (the Contractual Joint Ventures Law).[9] These laws—generally known as China's 'three investment laws'—are basic laws governing foreign investments in China.

---

4 Notice of the State Council on Issuing the Framework Plan for China (Shanghai) Pilot Free Trade Zone, issued 18 September 2013.
5 See Gao and Jiang (2014: 532–6).
6 Promulgated on 29 December 1993; amended on 25 December 1999 and 28 August 2004; revised on 27 October 2005; and amended again on 28 December 2013.
7 Promulgated on 8 July 1979; amended on 4 April 1990 and 15 March 2001.
8 Promulgated on 12 April 1986; amended on 31 October 2000.
9 Promulgated on 13 April 1988; amended on 31 October 2000.

To ensure the implementation of the three investment laws, the State Council promulgated three regulations or rules: Regulations for the Implementation of the Law of the People's Republic of China on Chinese–Foreign Equity Joint Ventures (Equity Joint Venture Regulations);[10] Rules for the Implementation of the Law of the People's Republic of China on Foreign-Capital Enterprises (Foreign-Capital Enterprise Rules);[11] and Rules for the Implementation of the Law of the People's Republic of China on Chinese–Foreign Contractual Joint Ventures (Contractual Joint Venture Rules),[12] which are collectively referred to as the regulations of the three investment laws. The three investment laws and the regulations of the three investment laws constitute the basic framework of China's foreign investment law.

Since the promulgation of the Company Law in 1993, a basic legal framework has been established by which special laws are to be applied to foreign investment companies, in addition to laws applicable to companies in general.[13] This framework stands after several amendments to the Company Law.[14] In addition, a large number of rules relating to foreign investment have been issued,[15] which, together with the three investment laws, the regulations of the three investment laws and the Company Law, have formed a relatively comprehensive foreign investment legal system in China.

Guiding catalogues

The three investment laws and the regulations of the three investment laws provide guidance on the areas and industries in which foreigners may invest.[16] In 1995, in order to provide further guidance for foreign investment and to ensure foreign investments are consistent with China's national economic and social development plans, the relevant departments of the State Council promulgated the Guiding Catalogue for the review and approval of foreign

---

10 Promulgated on 20 September 1983; revised on 15 January 1986, 21 December 1987, 22 July 2001 and 19 February 2014.
11 Promulgated on 21 December 1990; revised on 12 April 2001 and 19 February 2014.
12 Promulgated on 4 September 1995; revised on 19 February 2014.
13 Article 18 of the Company Law, promulgated in 1993.
14 The amendments of the Company Law in 1999, 2004 and 2013 did not touch the principle. The revision in 2005 broadens the extent of the principle, by including foreign invested corporations owned by shareholders.
15 For example, Measures for Strategic Investment by Foreign Investors upon Listed Companies (promulgated on 31 December 2005); Provisions on Mergers and Acquisitions of Domestic Enterprises by Foreign Investors (promulgated on 8 August 2006); Provisions on the Establishment of Investment Companies with Foreign Investment (promulgated on 10 June 2003; amended on 13 February 2004 and 17 November 2004); and so on.
16 See Article 3 of Equity Joint Ventures Regulations; Article 3 of Foreign-Invested Enterprises Law; Articles 4 and 5 of Foreign-Capital Enterprises Rules; and Article 4 of Contractual Joint Ventures Law.

investment applications.[17] On 11 February 2002, the State Council promulgated the Provisions on Guiding Foreign Investment Direction,[18] providing that both the Guiding Catalogue and the Central-Western Catalogue would serve as a basis for reviewing, evaluating and approving foreign investment projects and enterprises (MOFCOM 2000).

The Guiding Catalogue is a nationwide directory for foreign investments. It sets up three categories of industries: encouraged, restricted and prohibited. Those not included in the catalogue fall into a default fourth category: 'permitted' industries.[19] Since its publication in 1995, the Guiding Catalogue has been revised six times—in 1997, 2002, 2004, 2007, 2011 and 2015. Looking at these amendments, the restricted industries have gradually been reduced and the encouraged industries have increased.

The Central-Western Catalogue was first published in 2000 for the implementation of the Western Region Development Strategy of the State Council, and has been revised three times, in 2004, 2008 and 2013. It was meant to improve the quality of the overall economic development of the central and western regions. The industries listed in this catalogue are those that are seen to have significant advantages in each province in terms of the environment, natural resources, human resources, production, technology and markets, and which may enjoy preferential treatment as industries in which foreign investment is encouraged.[20] The Central-Western Catalogue will not be discussed further in this chapter, as it is not applicable nationally.

Policies

The development of foreign investment laws in China is closely related to and results from changes in Chinese foreign investment policies. The Chinese Government has adopted a progressive opening-up policy since the beginning of the reform period. Two recent policy documents of significant guiding effect are the Twelfth Five-Year Economic and Social Development Plan (Twelfth Five-Year Plan 2011–15)[21] and the Decision of the Central Committee of the Communist Party of China on Some Major Issues Concerning Comprehensively Deepening the Reform (CCCPC Decision 2013).[22] The key points of these two documents are to advance and deepen China's opening-up policy, to reduce limitations

---

17 Article 3.2 of the Interim Provisions on Guiding Foreign Investment Direction (promulgated on 20 June 1995; expired).

18 Article 17 of Provisions on Guiding Foreign Investment Direction (promulgated on 11 February 2002).

19 Article 4 of Provisions on Guiding Foreign Investment Direction.

20 Article 11 of Provisions on Guiding Foreign Investment Direction.

21 Adopted by the fourth meeting of the Eleventh National People's Congress on 14 March 2011.

22 Adopted at the Third Plenary Session of the Eighteenth Central Committee of the Communist Party of China on 12 November 2013.

on foreign investment and to promote the unification of laws and regulations regarding foreign and domestic investors in China.[23] They have sent positive signals to foreign investors aiming to invest in China.

Foreign investment laws and policies in the SPFTZ: Framework and innovations

The economy in the SPFTZ has been performing well since its establishment (SPFTZ 2014b); however, developing the economy is not the ultimate goal of the establishment of the zone. The ultimate goal is to foster China's openness and internationalisation by testing reforms on a small scale before applying them nationally (SPFTZ Framework Plan). This section will focus on law and policy innovations in the SPFTZ after introducing the framework therein.

Framework

A series of laws and policies has been published or modified by authorities such as the National People's Congress Standing Committee (NPCSC), the State Council and the Shanghai Municipal Government to accommodate the operation of the SPFTZ (SPFTZ n.d.). The following are some of the most important examples.

1. The NPCSC adopted the Decision of the Standing Committee of the National People's Congress on Authorising the State Council to Temporarily Adjust the Relevant Administrative Approval Items Prescribed in Laws in China (Shanghai) Pilot Free Trade Zone (Decision of NPCSC on Temporarily Adjusting Administrative Approval Items),[24] authorising the State Council to temporarily adjust the relevant administrative approval items prescribed in the three investment laws.

2. The State Council approved and published the Framework Plan for China (Shanghai) Pilot Free Trade Zone in 2013 (SPFTZ Framework Plan),[25] having identified five critical missions for the SPFTZ: speeding up transformation of government functions; expanding areas for investment; fostering change in trade development modes; deepening the opening-up and innovation in the financial sector; and improving safeguard measures in the legal field.

3. The Shanghai Government issued Measures for the Management of China (Shanghai) Pilot Free Trade Zone (Measures for Management of SPFTZ)

---

23 Twelfth Five-Year Plan 2011–15 and CCCPC Decision 2013.
24 Adopted by the fourth meeting of the Twelfth NPCSC; came into force on 1 October 2013.
25 Issued on 18 September 2013.

in 2013,[26] listing clearly the management institutions and investment management measures.

4. The Shanghai Government issued Special Management Measures for the Access of Foreign Investment in China (Shanghai) Pilot Free Trade Zone in 2013 (the Negative List 2013),[27] and the subsequent amendment in 2014 (Negative List 2014 Amendment),[28] having clearly listed foreign investment projects and enterprises that are not subject to filing management.

5. To implement the filing management system in the SPFTZ Framework Plan, the Shanghai Government issued two sets of administrative rules: Administrative Measures for the Filing of Foreign Investment Projects in China (Shanghai) Pilot Free Trade Zone (Measures for Project Filing in SPFTZ);[29] and the Administrative Measures for the Filing of Foreign-Investment Enterprises in China (Shanghai) Pilot Free Trade Zone (Measures for Enterprise Filing in SPFTZ)[30] on 29 September 2013. The former has provided details for the filing of foreign investment projects outside the negative list in the SPFTZ. The latter has provided details for the filing of foreign investment enterprises outside the negative list in the SPFTZ. For those foreign investment projects and enterprises that are listed in the negative list, approval is needed unless otherwise provided by the State Council (Information Office of the State Council 2014).

6. The State Council published the Decision of the State Council on Temporary Adjustments to the Administrative Approval Items or Special Administrative Measures on Access Prescribed in Relevant Administrative Regulations or State Council's Documents in China (Shanghai) Pilot Free Trade Zone (Decision of the State Council on Temporary Adjustments to Administrative Approval Items),[31] and the Decision of the State Council on Temporary Adjustments to the Administrative Approval Items or Special Administrative Measures on Access Prescribed in Relevant Administrative Regulations or Rules Approved by the State Council in China (Shanghai) Pilot Free Trade Zone (Decision of the State Council on Temporary Adjustments Special Administrative Measures)[32] in 2013 and 2014 respectively, having temporarily adjusted the scope for administrative approvals and special administrative measures with regard to the administrative approval process, qualification requirements, share proportion restrictions and business scope.

---

26 Issued on 29 September 2013.
27 Issued on 29 September 2013.
28 Issued on 30 June 2014.
29 Issued on 29 September 2013; came into force on 1 October 2013.
30 Issued on 29 September 2013; came into force on 1 October 2013.
31 Issued on 21 December 2013.
32 Issued on 4 September 2014.

7. In accordance with the SPFTZ Framework Plan, 18 measures have been taken for further opening-up in six service industries, including finance, shipping, trade, professional services, culture and social services in the SPFTZ. To implement these measures, authorities such as the China Banking Regulatory Commission, the People's Bank of China (PBC) and the Ministry of Transport have subsequently issued a series of rules to trial innovation measures in those areas.[33]

The laws, regulations and policies listed above are essential in at least two aspects: clearly outlining the ultimate goal for the establishment of the SPFTZ and listing details for the implementation of the trial measures.

Innovations

Pre-establishment national treatment plus negative list

One innovation highlight in the SPFTZ is the adoption of the pre-establishment of national treatment plus the negative list, which is a fundamental change to the management of foreign investments in China. This management mode is confirmed by CCCPC Decision 2013, which has provided that a 'uniform market access system will be established. On the basis of the negative list system, all market players can equally enter areas outside the negative list. The mode of pre-establishment national treatment plus negative list for the management of foreign investment will be explored.'

In principle, this gives foreign investors no less favourable treatment than domestic investors at the admission stage in investing in the host country, except as otherwise listed on the negative list. In other words, for areas on the negative list, foreign investors are given not national treatment, but special administrative treatment. In contrast, for those areas not on the negative list, foreign investors are given national treatment.

The Negative List 2013, as the first negative list in China, has attracted great attention at home and abroad since its publication. The filing system used for the management of foreign investment has greatly shortened the time required for approval and improved the degree of investment enhancement (Information Office of the State Council 2014).

---

33 For instance, Announcement of the Ministry of Transport on the Implementation on a Trial Basis in the China (Shanghai) Pilot Free Trade Zone of Implementing Measures for Increasing the Foreign Investment Measures for Increasing the Foreign Investment Percentage in the International Shipping and International Shipping Management Businesses, promulgated on 27 January 2014.

In 2014, the Shanghai Government amended the Negative List 2013 in order to further enhance opening-up, increase transparency and converge with generally accepted international rules (Information Office of the State Council 2014). Compared with the Negative List 2013, the Negative List 2014 Amendment has the following four features. First, it has further eased market access restrictions, through expanding the scope for the items to be filed and reducing restrictions on the entry of foreign investment. For example, it has removed the item that restricts foreign investment in cotton (seed) processing, and removes the requirement of adopting contractual joint ventures or equity joint ventures when investing in the development and application of new or related technologies to improve crude oil extraction efficiency. Second, it has increased transparency by providing more details in the negative list. For example, it has provided that prohibited foreign-invested special teas include 'white tea, yellow tea, oolong tea, dark green tea, compressed tea and others'. In contrast, in the Negative List 2013, special teas referred to the vague 'famous tea and dark green tea and others'. Third, it has further detailed the meaning of national treatment. For instance, since domestic investors are prohibited from investing in areas such as the sex industry and gambling, national treatment logically means the same thing for foreign investors in those areas. Fourth, it has clearly stated that different administrative measures apply to investments within or outside the negative list.[34]

Foreign investment projects and the enterprise filing system

The SPFTZ Framework Plan states that the management mode of foreign investment will be reformed. More specifically:

> [F]or areas outside the negative list, in line with the principle of consistency in policies for both foreign-investment enterprises and domestic enterprises, the approval system for foreign-investment projects will be replaced with the filing system unless the State Council maintains that approval is required also for domestic investment projects, which will be administered by Shanghai Government. The approval of contracts and bylaws of foreign-investment enterprises will be replaced with the filing system and administered by Shanghai Government. The afterwards formalities will be followed according to the relevant national provisions. (SPFTZ Framework Plan)

Therefore, the filing system includes two categories: foreign investment projects and foreign investment enterprises.

---

34 The Negative List 2013 only identifies that the filing system applies in fields outside the list. It does not clarify whether the approval system still applies in fields in the negative list.

The filing system is a breakthrough in China's existing foreign investment laws and regulations. To ensure the legitimacy and effectiveness of the filing system, the NPCSC formulated its Decision to Temporarily Adjust Administrative Approval Items before the establishment of the SPFTZ, authorising the State Council to temporarily adjust relevant administrative approval items prescribed in the three investment laws, which have expanded the legislative power of the State Council. Accordingly, the State Council successively issued its Decision on Temporary Adjustments to Administrative Approval Items in December 2013 and on Temporary Adjustments to Special Administrative Measures in September 2014, which have together temporarily adjusted a series of administrative approval items and special administrative measures on access, in respect to qualification requirements and restrictions on share proportions and business scope in 23 administrative regulations approved by the State Council.

For the establishment of or changes in foreign investment enterprises, the management mode provided in China's foreign investment laws requires approval from relevant commerce departments before registering at relevant industrial and commercial administration departments. The periods for approval are three months, 45 days and 90 days respectively in the three investment laws.[35] In contrast, the SPFTZ has substituted the approval requirement for items outside the negative list with the filing system and greatly shortened the time required. In accordance with Article 7 of the Measures for Enterprise Filing in the SPFTZ, 'the filing management agency shall conduct filing within 1 working day after the investor (or foreign-investment enterprise) having completed the online application'. That is, only one day is needed for such items to be filed.

Reform and innovation in dispute-resolution mechanisms

Judicial system

Since a judicial institution with high-quality professionals is needed to deal with disputes within the SPFTZ, the Free Trade Zone Court (the FTZ Court) under the Shanghai Pudong New District People's Court (the Pudong Court) was established with the approval of the Shanghai Higher People's Court on 5 November 2013 (Wei and Li 2013). The FTZ Court has jurisdiction over commercial, intellectual property and real estate cases that are related to the SPFTZ and is under the jurisdiction of the Pudong Court. Its jurisdiction might be adjusted in accordance with the development and operation of the SPFTZ

---

35 Article 3 of Equity Joint Ventures Law; Article 6 of Foreign-Invested Enterprises Law; and Article 5 of Contractual Joint Ventures Law.

(Tian 2013).[36] In addition to dispute resolution, the FTZ Court is also responsible for researching the application of the law in cases regarding the SPFTZ (Wei and Li 2013).

On 27 May 2014, Pudong Court launched 'a dispute resolution mechanism (DRM) on commercial cases linking litigation with non-litigation DRMs in the SPFTZ' (commercial DRM in SPFTZ) (Wang 2014). This means that for cases under the jurisdiction of the FTZ Court—with the consent and selection of the parties—the Pudong Court may designate a mediation agency before the case is accepted or authorise a mediation agency after the case is accepted to mediate before hearing, and examine and ascertain the enforceability of the mediation agreement. Mediation agencies that can be designated or authorised include commercial mediation organisations, industry associations, chambers of commerce or other organisations with mediation functions (Wang 2014).

The commercial DRM in the SPFTZ has the following special features (Wang 2014): first, the whole process of mediation is based on the full autonomy of the parties—that is, the parties can choose to start or continue the mediation process, to reach a mediation agreement and to apply for judicial confirmation of the mediation agreement. Second, the mediation is authorised by the Pudong Court and performed by specialised commercial mediation organisations with abundant experience and knowledge in areas of investment, trade, finance and intellectual property. Third, the rules applied during the mediation are professional rules of the respective mediation organisations. Fourth, the mediation process is formal, as the Pudong Court and the mediation organisations together have clearly defined a series of procedures such as the implementation period, judicial confirmation, challenges and confidentiality. Fifth, the mediation and trial processes are separate and independent procedures which means the mediation record will not be transferred to the FTZ Court and the compromises reached during the mediation process will not become the basis for the decisions of the FTZ Court. Sixth, it can save time and litigation fees, as the participation of mediation organisations can speed up solutions, and the Pudong Court can provide a discount on litigation fees.

Arbitration system

On 22 October 2013, the Shanghai International Arbitration Centre (SHIAC) established the SPFTZ Court of Arbitration, in order to provide convenient arbitration services, consultation, filing and hearings relating to arbitration (Liu 2013). The first hearing by the SPFTZ Court of Arbitration took place on 26 November 2013 (Yao 2013).

---

36 The FTZ Court has received 380 cases a year since its establishment on 5 November 2013 (SPFTZ 2014a).

In January 2014, SHIAC started the formulation of the SPFTZ Arbitration Rules, which were issued on 8 April 2014 and came into force on 1 May that year. As the first set of arbitration rules in the SPFTZ, they represent another breakthrough in the improvement of the legal environment in the zone (Ye 2014). The SPFTZ Arbitration Rules, made according to generally accepted international practices and the Arbitration Law of the People's Republic of China, consist of 10 chapters and 85 articles (Wen 2014). The innovative points of the SPFTZ Arbitration Rules include the following. They have:

- improved the use of provisional measures and introduced an emergency arbitration mechanism
- established an open roster system, so parties can choose people outside the list
- linked arbitration with mediation by providing mediators before the arbitration tribunal is formed
- added procedures for small claims, which apply to disputes involving no more than RMB100,000
- provided details with regard to consolidation of arbitration, joinder of other parties under the same arbitration agreement and joinder of third parties
- emphasised the system of evidence during arbitration
- included an amiable arbitration system (Ye 2014).

Special taxation policy

The innovation in taxation monitoring policy in the SPFTZ can be summarised as an 'easing [of] control on the first line, effective and efficient control on the second line and full freedom inside the SPFTZ'. The first line refers to the border to entry into the SPFTZ; the second line refers to the border between the SPFTZ and other regions of China (Information Office of Shanghai Government 2013). 'Easing control on the first line' means easing controls on goods imported and exported across the borderline—using the clearance mode called 'entering the SPFTZ before customs declaration' (Information Office of Shanghai Government 2013). 'Effective and efficient control on the second line' means imposing effective and efficient supervision on the border between the SPFTZ and other parts of China, including but not limited to improving inspection and quarantine measures, exploring measures of pre-filing for export and import goods, verification management and follow-up supervision, as well as levying import value-added tax and consumption tax (SPFTZ 2013b). 'Full freedom inside the SPFTZ' refers to a trial 'allowing enterprises to deliver goods in batches and make a centralised customs declaration, and to transport their own goods themselves' (Information Office of Shanghai Government 2013). The aim of the trial of this policy is to transform Shanghai into an international hub port (Information Office of Shanghai Government 2013).

Though the main purpose of the SPFTZ is to trial innovations rather than the implementation of favourable policies, some preferential taxation treatments—such as reductions in customs duty and permission for payment installations for corporate income tax—still exist for those enterprises inside the SPFTZ that meet the requirements.[37]

The breakthrough and impact of foreign investment law in the SPFTZ on China's foreign investment legal system

China has a uniform foreign investment legal system although there exist special rules or policies applicable to the Central-Western and other regions. The foreign investment laws in the SPFTZ, however, are quite different—not only because of their limited geographical application, but also because many new reform measures are being tried.

Breakthroughs

Guiding catalogue versus negative list

Both the Guiding Catalogue and the negative list identify the industries in which foreign investors can invest, but in different ways. There are four categories of industries in the Guiding Catalogue regime: permitted, encouraged, restricted and prohibited. The first three categories allow foreign investors to invest, although investments in restricted industries must be in line with conditions in the Guiding Catalogue. The negative list identifies the industries in a different way—while industries listed therein are either restricted or prohibited to foreign investors, those outside the list are accessible for foreign investment.

Although both the Guiding Catalogue and the negative list have the same function, as outlined above, they have several differences. First, the Guiding Catalogue has a broader scope of application than the negative list. The negative

---

37 See Circular on Relevant Import Tax Policies for the China (Shanghai) Pilot Free Trade Zone (issued on 15 October 2013); Notice of the Ministry of Finance and the State Administration of Taxation on Enterprise Income Tax Policies for External Investment with Non-Monetary Assets and Other Asset Restructuring Activities of Enterprises in China (Shanghai) Pilot Free Trade Zone (issued on 15 November 2013); and so on.

list applies only in the SPFTZ, while the Guiding Catalogue applies nationwide and excludes the SPFTZ. Second, they are different in form. The Guiding Catalogue lists encouraged, restricted and prohibited industries; those that are not included in these three fall into the category of permitted industries. In contrast, the negative list does not outline permitted or encouraged industries, nor does it distinguish restricted industries from prohibited ones. However, a close look at the Negative List 2013 and Guiding Category (2011 version) will find that the Negative List 2013 is almost a duplication of the restricted and prohibited industries listed in the Guiding Catalogue 2011 (Ding 2013). Third, the preconditions for the application of the Guiding Catalogue and negative list are different. While the negative list is based on giving national treatment to foreign investors and their investments before they enter the SPFTZ, the Guiding Catalogue does not have such a precondition.

Approval system versus filing system

A series of approvals is needed during the establishment and operation of foreign investment enterprises. For instance, one category under the approval system is the approval of the articles of association and/or agreement for the foreign investment enterprise from the Ministry of Commerce (MOFCOM), the provincial commerce department and the National Economic and Technological Development Zone (collectively referred to as commerce departments). Another category is the approval of foreign investment projects by the National Development and Reform Commission (NDRC) and its delegated authority (collectively referred to as development and reform departments).

The filing system on trial in the SPFTZ is based on the negative list. In short, while for foreign investment projects or enterprises that are outside the negative list filing is required, for those within the negative list, approval is required (SPFTZ Framework Plan).

There are four major differences between the approval system and the filing system. First, the agencies approving foreign investment enterprises or projects are commerce departments and development and reform departments. In comparison, the agency in charge of filing for foreign investment enterprises or projects is the SPFTZ Administration Committee. Second, the timing and concept of supervision are different. The approval system intends to review whether foreign investors can enter the Chinese market, which is an ex ante approval, demonstrating the idea of control of market supervision. In comparison, the filing system largely eases the ex ante supervision but focuses on ex post supervision, reducing government control of the market. Third, the scope of the approval system is much broader than that of the filing system. For instance, under the approval system, any establishment of or changes in foreign investment enterprises require prior approval.[38] In contrast, only the establishment of or changes in foreign investment enterprises that are within the negative list require approval before investing in the SPFTZ. Fourth, as mentioned above, the filing system in the SPFTZ has greatly shortened the time required to complete the relevant procedures.

Post-establishment national treatment versus pre-establishment national treatment

After years of reform, foreign investment enterprises have gradually been given national treatment under China's foreign investment legal system (Gao and Jiang 2014: 545–6). However, the national treatment mentioned here applies only when foreign investment enterprises have already been established. In contrast, the national treatment on trial in the SPFTZ extends to the phase before investment enterprises are established in China. There are some other key differences. First, the degrees of liberalisation are different. Pre-establishment national treatment implies a further commitment on investment liberalisation, as the discretion of the host country on investment review is reduced and the transparency of investment is increased. Second, the degrees of supervision are different. Post-establishment national treatment supervises foreign investors and their investment before and after they enter China, while pre-establishment national treatment reduces supervision on the entry of foreign investment but focuses more on the operation of foreign investment.

Impact

Expansion of the filing system

The SPFTZ changed the management mode for foreign investment projects from the blanket approval system to a combination of limited approval and a general filing system (Information Office of the State Council 2014). The promotion of this combination is highlighted by the NDRC in the Measures for the Administration of Confirmation and Recording of Foreign Investment Projects (Administration Measures),[39] which have detailed the scope and mode of the approval and filing of foreign investment projects. The NDRC has revised the Administration Measures, but the management mode has been left untouched.[40]

---

38 See Notice of the Ministry of Commerce on Decentralising the Examination and Approval Power for Foreign Investment (issued on 10 June 2010).

39 Issued on 17 May 2014; came into force on 17 June 2014.

40 The Administration Measures are partly modified by the Decision of the National Development and Reform Commission on Amending the Relevant Clauses of the Measures for the Administration of the Confirmation and Recording of Overseas Investment Projects and the Measures for the Administration of the Confirmation and Recording of Foreign-Funded Projects (issued on 27 December 2014).

On 28 December 2014, the NPCSC adopted its Decision on Authorising the State Council to Temporarily Adjust the Relevant Administrative Approval Items Prescribed in Laws and Regulations in China (Guangdong) Pilot Free Trade Zone, China (Tianjin) Pilot Free Trade Zone, China (Fujian) Pilot Free Trade Zone and Expanded Areas of China (Shanghai) Pilot Free Trade Zone (Xinhuanet 2014). The State Council has therefore been authorised to temporarily adjust relevant administrative approval items regarding foreign investment enterprises provided in the three investment laws and the Law of the People's Republic of China on Protection of Investments by Taiwan Compatriots in the regions mentioned above. This decision has replaced the approval system for foreign investment enterprises with the filing system, which has now been expanded in China. On 8 April 2015, the State Council published Special Administrative Measures for the Access of Foreign Investment in China's Pilot Free Trade Zones (the Negative List), which applies to all the pilot free trade zones in Shanghai, Guangdong, Tianjin and Fujian.[41]

Replication of customs monitoring measures

Experience with these reforms has been gained since the establishment of the SPFTZ, and some are now mature enough to be replicated in Shanghai, other regions or even the whole country. In the first half of 2014, Shanghai Customs, with the authorisation of the General Administration of Customs (GAC), announced that 14 customs monitoring measures—including declaration after entering the zone and allowing enterprises to transport their own goods within the zone—could be replicated and used outside the SPFTZ (GAC 2014). In July 2014, customs agencies in Tianjin, Chongqing and Xi'an launched a trial of these measures to identify any problems that may arise from their expansion (China Customs Statistics 2014). On 13 August 2014, GAC announced further expansion of these measures in three stages: replicated in 51 SCSAs in the economic belt along the Yangtze River from 18 August 2014; replicated in all the SCSAs in China from 3 September 2014; and replicated in regions that are not SCSAs from 18 September 2014 (China Customs Statistics 2014).

Implementation of generally accepted international rules

The foreign investment management mode of pre-establishment of national treatment plus the negative list have become a trend in the development of rules for international investment. The trial of this mode in the SPFTZ is in line with this trend, and is also consistent with China's reform of the approval system. In addition to the trial in the SPFTZ, there are many signs that this mode may become the future for China's foreign investment management mode.

---

41 Issued on 8 April 2015; came into force on 8 May 2015.

For instance, during the Fifth China–US Strategic and Economic Dialogue in July 2013, China agreed to negotiate with the United States on the basis of this mode (Sun et al. 2013). MOFCOM signed two free trade agreements, with Hong Kong and Macao special administrative regions, in December 2014, which for the first time adopted this mode on the Chinese mainland (Ma and Li 2014). In January 2015, MOFCOM issued a draft of the Foreign Investment Law of the People's Republic of China, which has also adopted this mode (MOFCOM 2015).

The SPFTZ Arbitration Rules have done more towards adopting advanced systems in international commercial arbitration. For example, they have improved in the area of provisional measures, added an emergency tribunal system and adopted an open roster system of arbitrators.[42]

Conclusion

Responding to challenges arising at home and abroad and in order to improve the foreign investment legal system and deepen reforms of the market economy, the Chinese Government in September 2013 set up a pilot zone in Shanghai. Some generally accepted international rules have been implemented in the SPFTZ, such as the foreign investment management mode of pre-establishment of national treatment plus a negative list, a filing system for foreign investment projects and enterprises, and taxation monitoring policies. In addition, innovative DRMs have also been introduced, such as the launch of the commercial DRM in the SPFTZ, and the formulation of the SPFTZ Arbitration Rules in 2014.

The systems adopted in the SPFTZ for foreign investment differ greatly from those applied previously in China, demonstrating the efforts of the Chinese Government to integrate into the international economic market and adopt generally accepted international rules. The SPFTZ, which has been established for just more than a year now, has achieved a great deal by creating many innovative systems that are to be replicated in other parts of the country. Some of the systems have already been replicated in Shanghai and, in some cases, nationwide. This has demonstrated the value of the SPFTZ in exploring a new economic mode, and in leading reform in China.

---

42 See more in the section regarding the reforms and innovations of the arbitration system; or see Ye (2014).

References

Central Government of the People's Republic of China (Central Government of the PRC) (2013), *The State Council approves the establishment of China (Shanghai) Pilot Free Trade Zone*, Beijing: Central Government of the PRC. Available from: www.gov.cn/jrzg/2013-08/22/content_2472106.htm. Retrieved 9 February 2015.

China (Shanghai) Pilot Free Trade Zone (SPFTZ) (n.d.), *Policies and regulations in China (Shanghai) Pilot Free Trade Zone*. Available from: www.china-shftz.gov.cn/govInfoDir.aspx?GTID=237c0b98-9fdd-4ab3-9f6d-92aba33b9191&MenuType=1&subMenuID=2&tagIndex=2&govMainTagIndex=0&govSubTagIndex=0. Retrieved 9 February 2015.

China (Shanghai) Pilot Free Trade Zone (SPFTZ) (2013a), *Introduction of China (Shanghai) Pilot Free Trade Zone*. Available from: www.china-shftz.gov.cn/PublicInformationConten.aspx?Type=9&subMenuID=0. Retrieved 9 February 2015.

China (Shanghai) Pilot Free Trade Zone (SPFTZ) (2013b), *Record of the seminar on China (Shanghai) Pilot Free Trade Zone*. Available from: www.china-shftz.gov.cn/NewsDetail.aspx?NID=c1c76ce4-f943-4726-92b6-041d533ed91e&CID=16a79677-7b73-4570-a610-761ad7cf52c3&MenuType=1. Retrieved 9 February 2015.

China (Shanghai) Pilot Free Trade Zone (SPFTZ) (2014a), *Free Trade Zone Court: 380 cases filed and characteristics and trends thereof*, Beijing: Free Trade Zone Court. Available from: www.ftzcourt.gov.cn:8080/zmqweb/gweb/content.jsp?pa=aZ2lkPTY0NjE1z. Retrieved 9 February 2015.

China (Shanghai) Pilot Free Trade Zone (SPFTZ) (2014b), *Information session for the first half year by Administrative Commission of China (Shanghai) Pilot Free Trade Zone*. Available from: www.china-shftz.gov.cn/NewsDetail.aspx?NID=bca994d6-18ca-48da-9bd9-d77bdb6296f8&MenuType=3. Retrieved 9 February 2015.

China Customs Statistics (2014), *Replication of the customs supervision innovations in China (Shanghai) Pilot Free Trade Zone*, 15 August 2014, Beijing: China Customs Statistics. Available from: www.chinacustomsstat.com/aspx/1/Information/Infor_Detail.aspx?t=1&Id=10812. Retrieved 9 February 2015.

Ding, Y. (2013), China (Shanghai) Pilot Free Trade Zone: Open or control?, *People*, 15 November. Available from: paper.people.com.cn/mszk/html/2013-11/15/content_1325347.htm. Retrieved 9 February 2015.

Gao, X. and Jiang, H. (2014), Foreign investment laws and policies in China, in Song, L., Garnaut, R. and Fang, C. (eds), *Deepening reform for China's long-term growth and development*, Canberra: ANU Press.

General Administration of Customs (GAC) (2014), *Shanghai Customs announced 14 customs supervision measures to be replicated out of China (Shanghai) Pilot Free Trade Zone*, Beijing: General Administration of Customs of the People's Republic of China. Available from: fangtan.customs.gov.cn/tabid/277/InfoID/948/frtid/266/Default.aspx. Retrieved 9 February 2015.

Information Office of Shanghai Government (2013), *Record of Chinese and foreign reporters' interviews regarding China (Shanghai) Pilot Free Trade Zone*, Shanghai: Information Office of Shanghai Government. Available from: www.shio.gov.cn/shxwb/node185/u1ai10147.html. Retrieved 9 February 2015.

Information Office of the State Council (2014), Seminar on the issuance of Negative List 2014 Amendment in China (Shanghai) Pilot Free Trade Zone, Beijing: State Council. Available from: www.scio.gov.cn/xwfbh/gssxwfbh/fbh/Document/1374308/1374308.htm. Retrieved 9 February 2015.

Liu, J. (2013), China (Shanghai) Pilot Free Trade Zone Court of Arbitration launched, *Legal Daily*, 23 October. Available from: www.legaldaily.com.cn/zt/content/2013-10/23/content_4954240.htm?node=41441. Retrieved 9 February 2015.

Ma, H. and Li, Z. (2014), First time to adopt pre-establishment national treatment in China, *Yangcheng Evening News*, 19 December. Available from: news.ifeng.com/a/20141219/42756362_0.shtml. Retrieved 9 February 2015.

Ministry of Commerce (MOFCOM) (2000), *Catalogue of priority industries for foreign investment in the Central-Western Region*, Beijing: MOFCOM. Available from: www.mofcom.gov.cn/aarticle/subject/swfg/subjectby/200612/20061204135012.html. Retrieved 9 February 2015.

Ministry of Commerce (MOFCOM) (2015), Press agent of Ministry of Commerce Jiwen Sun speaks on the issue of foreign investment law in the People's Republic of China (draft for suggestions), Beijing: MOFCOM. Available from: www.mofcom.gov.cn/article/ae/ag/201501/20150100871007.shtml. Retrieved 9 February 2015.

Sun, S., Zhou, W. and Zhou, W. (2013), A breakthrough in Sino–US negotiation on Negative List: Investment access is as open as joining WTO, *Xinhuanet*, 13 July. Available from: jjckb.xinhuanet.com/2013-07/13/content_455548.htm. Retrieved 9 February 2015.

Tian, X. (2013), Free Trade Zone Court in Shanghai Pudong: Focusing on financial and real estate cases, *Hexun*, 5 November. Available from: news.hexun.com/2013-11-05/159391659.html. Retrieved 9 February 2015.

Wang, X. and Liu, Z. (2013), *Be confident of the Future: Evaluations of the current economic situation*, Beijing: Central Government of the PRC. Available from: www.gov.cn/jrzg/2013-07/16/content_2449157.htm. Retrieved 9 February 2015.

Wang, Z. (2014), *Pudong Court launches a commercial dispute resolution mechanism ('DRM') that combines litigation with non-litigation DRMs*, Shanghai: Shanghai Court. Available from: shfy.chinacourt.org/article/detail/2014/05/id/1305759.shtml. Retrieved 9 February 2015.

Wei, J. and Li, W. (2013), Free Trade Zone Court in China (Shanghai) Pilot Free Trade Zone established, *People's Court Daily*, 6 November. Available from: rmfyb.chinacourt.org/paper/html/2013-11/06/content_72435.htm?div=-1. Retrieved 9 February 2015.

Wen, W. (2014), *Explanation of the promulgation of China (Shanghai) Pilot Free Trade Zone arbitration rules*, Shanghai: SHIAC. Available from: www.cietac-sh.org/NewsDetails.aspx?tid=7&nid=627. Retrieved 9 February 2015.

Xinhuanet (2013), China (Shanghai) Pilot Free Trade Zone established on 29 September 2013, *Xinhuanet*, 29 September. Available from: news.xinhuanet.com/local/2013-09/29/c_125466984.htm. Retrieved 9 February 2015.

Xinhuanet (2014), Authorized to publish: Decision on authorising the State Council to temporarily adjust the relevant administrative approval items prescribed in laws and regulations in China (Guangdong) Pilot Free Trade Zone, China (Tianjin) Pilot Free Trade Zone, China (Fujian) Pilot Free Trade Zone and expanded areas of China (Shanghai) Pilot Free Trade Zone, *Xinhuanet*, 29 December. Available from: news.xinhuanet.com/politics/2014-12/29/c_127341610.htm. Retrieved 9 February 2015.

Xu, S., He, X. and Ye, F. (2013), *Institutional innovations rather than mere favourable treatments: An interview with one of the designers of the framework plan for the China (Shanghai) Pilot Free Trade Zone, Xinkui Wang*, Beijing: Central Government of the PRC. Available from: www.gov.cn/jrzg/2013-09/04/content_2481397.htm. Retrieved 9 February 2015.

Yao, L. (2013), First hearing in China (Shanghai) Pilot Free Trade Zone Court of Arbitration, *Xinmin Evening News Online*, 26 November. Available from: xmwb.xinmin.cn/html/2013-11/26/content_4_2.htm. Retrieved 9 February 2015.

Ye, F. (2014), The first China (Shanghai) Pilot Free Trade Zone arbitration rules issued in Shanghai, *Xinhuanet*, 8 April. Available from: news.xinhuanet.com/finance/2014-04/08/c_1110142614.htm. Retrieved 9 February 2015.

Index

www.ingramcontent.com/pod-product-compliance
Lightning Source LLC
Chambersburg PA
CBHW041427290326

41932CB00055B/3406